The Collected Writings (1991-2024) of a Mortal to Death:
Jalal Toufic

Volume ONE

no place press

ISBN: 978-1-949484-13-7
Library of Congress Control Number: 2025938459

Library of Congress Cataloging-in-Publications Data
Toufic, Jalal.
    The Collected Writings (1991–2024) of a Mortal to Death: Jalal Toufic, vol. 1 / Jalal Toufic
    p. cm.
    English

First edition of 1,000
Printed by Ofset, Turkey

Distributed by the MIT Press
Cambridge, Massachusetts, and London, England

no place press
New York and New Haven, 2025

The following works were previously published:
Distracted. Station Hill Press, 1991; 2nd ed., Tuumba Press, 2003.
(Vampires): An Uneasy Essay on the Undead in Film. Station Hill Press, 1993; revised and expanded edition, Post-Apollo Press, 2003.
Jouissance in Postwar Beirut. Forthcoming Books, 2014.
Over-Sensitivity. Sun & Moon Press, 1996; 2nd ed., Forthcoming Books, 2009.

Design: General Working Group
Editor: Rachel Churner
Proofreader: Nick Sywak

Special thanks to Walid Raad, Stephen Cheng, Francesca Corona, Simone Fattal, Raphael Fleuriet, Nalia Kettaneh-Kunigk, Marcus Reymann, Sultan Sooud Al Qassemi, and Brian Kuan Wood. Thanks also to Giacomo Pietro Lamborizio and Nora Razian at Art Jameel; Hessa Al Fahim, Noora Al Mualla, and Ahmad Makia at Hoor Al Qasimi/Sharjah Art Foundation; Hoda Zohrob of The Gibran National Committee; Christopher Baaklini and Rana Nasser of the Arab Image Foundation; and Imran Ahmad Kamal. We are grateful to the members of the Jalal Toufic Collected Works Editorial Collective: Tarek Abou El Fetouh, Peggy Ahwesh, Tamara Al-Samerraei, Hoor Al Qasimi/Sharjah Art Foundation, Vartan Avakian, Defne Ayas, Omar Berrada, Almut Shulamit Bruckstein Çoruh, Stephen Cheng, Ali Cherri, Joan Copjec, James Elkins, Fouad Elkoury, Inci Eviner, Simone Fattal, Lara Favaretto, Raphael Fleuriet, Matthew Gumpert, Joana Hadjithomas, Gilbert Hage, Hou Hanru, Lyn Hejinian, Amal Issa, Iman Issa, Khalil Joreige, Lamia Joreige, Naila Kettaneh-Kunigk, Lina Majdalanie, Rabih Mroué, Tom Nicholson, Sandra Noeth, Stefania Pandolfo, Walid Raad, David Reed, Markus Reymann, Ghalya Saadawi, Ghassan Salhab, Roy Samaha, Reem Shadid, Steven Shaviro, Kaelen Wilson-Goldie, and Brian Kuan Wood.

EU Authorized Representative:
Easy Access System Europe,
Mustamäe tee 50, 10621
Tallinn, Estonia
gpsr.requests@easproject.com

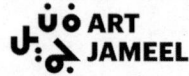

SHARJAH ART FOUNDATION

T ̴   Thyssen
B   Bornemisza
⌐ A   Art Contemporary

Upcoming:
The Collected Writings (1991–2024) of a Mortal to Death: Jalal Toufic

Jalal Toufic is a thinker and a mortal to death. He was born in 1962, in Beirut or Baghdad, and died before dying in 1989, in Evanston, Illinois. His books—a number of which were published by Forthcoming Books—are available for download, free of charge, at www.jalaltoufic.com. He has made over twenty films and videos: essay films and conceptual works; short films (7 minutes, 8 minutes …), feature-length films (110 minutes, 138 minutes …), and "inhumanely" long ones (72 hours, 50 hours); standalone films and others that form part of mixed-media pieces; films he shot himself and films composed entirely of images from works by other filmmakers—Hitchcock, Sokurov, Bergman, etc.—as well as six created in collaboration with his wife, Graziella Rizkallah. His work—alongside that of artists and pretend artists—has been shown in Sharjah Biennials 6, 10, and 11; the 9th Shanghai Biennale; the 5th Guangzhou Triennial; MoMA PS1; San Francisco Museum of Modern Art; Centre Pompidou; ZKM; Kunsthalle Fridericianum; MAXXI; FKA Witte de With; Deichtorhallen Hamburg; and elsewhere. Many of his films and videos are available for viewing on Vimeo. In 2011, he was a guest of the Artists-in-Berlin Program of the DAAD. From September 2015 to August 2018, he was Director of the School of Visual Arts at the Lebanese Academy of Fine Arts (Alba).

Author's Note to
The Collected Writings (1991-2024) of a Mortal to Death: Jalal Toufic

This three-volume collection gathers the writings of an author who does not have an oeuvre but a style—it is the style that joins these writings. Why don't these writings compose an oeuvre? It is because they are separated by two fundamental kinds of blanks, in other words, lapses of consciousness, if not of being: the ubiquitous, general one between the aphorisms; and the one between (the first edition of) my first book, *Distracted,* which but for its coda was written by a mortal mistaking his mortality for solely and merely a condition of future physical death (here's an alternate fitting title for the book: *Portrait of a Suicidal Young Man Unaware of his Mortality*), and my subsequent books, starting with *(Vampires): An Uneasy Essay on the Undead in Film*, which were written by someone who had died before his assumed coming physical death.

A clarification of the expression *mortal to death* in the title: A mortal *to death* is a mortal who in relation to mortality goes beyond the normal or acceptable limit ("*to death*: beyond a normal or acceptable limit" [*Merriam-Webster Thesaurus*]) until he or she dies ("*to death*: used of a particular action or process that results in someone's death: *he was stabbed to death*" [*Oxford Dictionary of English*, 3rd ed.]) before dying, thus becoming aware that he or she, as a mortal, was already dead even while still physically alive, hence that mortality is not merely the condition of someone who is going to die physically at some point in the future.

The order of the included books is chronological, with, in volume 1, two exceptions: the script Jouissance *in Postwar Beirut* (2014) is interpolated between my second book, *(Vampires): An Uneasy Essay on the Undead in Film* (1993; 2nd ed., 2003), and my third book, *Over-Sensitivity* (1996; 2nd ed., 2009), because it is based on the second; and the third book is followed by my new, unpublished book, *The Unreviewed Writings of a Peerless Thinker, 2020-2022*.

But for the marked unevenness in the size of the three volumes it would have resulted in, another sort of organization of my collected writings was possible:
  — The first volume would have included the books composed of aphorisms that paradoxically appear to follow each other along associative lines notwithstanding that they were written by a distracted author thinking across lapses of consciousness, if not of being: *Distracted* (1991; 2nd ed., 2003), *Over-Sensitivity* (1996; 2nd ed., 2009), *Two or Three Things I'm Dying to Tell You* (2005),

Forthcoming (2000; 2nd ed., 2014), *What Were You Thinking?* (2011), *What Was I Thinking?* (2017), and *Postscripts* (2020).

— The second volume would have included the books that deal with one overarching topic: *(Vampires): An Uneasy Essay on the Undead in Film* (1993; 2nd ed., 2003), *Undying Love, or Love Dies* (2002), *'Āshūrā': This Blood Spilled in My Veins* (2005), *Undeserving Lebanon* (2007), *Graziella: The Corrected Edition* (2009), *What Is the Sum of Recurrently?* (2010), and *The Portrait of the Pubescent Girl: A Rite of Non-Passage* (2011).

— The third volume would have gathered my four books that curate texts that were previously published in my other books and that focus on one of my concepts: *The Withdrawal of Tradition Past a Surpassing Disaster* (2009), *The Dancer's Two Bodies* (2015), and *Radical Closure* (2020); or on a single topic: *Explicit and Implicit Variations on Hitchcock* (2023).

Does this republication of the books imply a modification in their temporal condition, in the sense that perhaps they, in particular the ones that were published by Forthcoming Books, are no longer forthcoming (with the possible exception of the book titled *Forthcoming*)?

Distracted

Author's Note to the Second Edition of *Distracted*

Why do a second edition of *Distracted*? It is because it is now starkly clear to me that there is a limited number of concepts, figures, and postures that a writer is here to create and possibly elaborate (in my case: freezing, silence-over, the over-turn, radical closure, the withdrawal of tradition past a surpassing disaster, etc.). The extra material that was in the first edition still awaits its writers—paradoxically, getting rid of it is indirectly a way of avoiding future imitators.

This version of *Distracted* is a second edition—in relation not to the one published by Station Hill Press in 1991 but to the shorter version that was sent in March 1988 to the Register of Copyrights at the Library of Congress as well as to a dozen publishers, and that was rejected by the latter and never published as such. Therefore, were a future academic to decide to indulge in comparative studies of the various editions of *Distracted*, he or she should consult either the first version (registration number TXU 310-041) or confine himself or herself to the first seventy-one pages of the edition published by Station Hill. That book is too long, as a consequence of the then excessive solitude of its author (see the aphorism on page 52 of the present volume) (during its writing, and even more so during the writing of *[Vampires]*,[1] a period of even more extreme solitude, I no longer experienced the occasional reflex of looking up or back or to the side, as others did on subliminally sensing someone staring at them). Now that I teach, I am no longer excessively solitary.

The whole of *Distracted* or any parts of it can be created by others and hence may be published by them verbatim without permission from the author and the publisher. No part of *Distracted* may be paraphrased in any form or by any means.

Author's Note to this Volume's Edition of *Distracted*

A number of aphorisms relating to dance have been cut from this edition of *Distracted*, since they have become part of my book *The Dancer's Two Bodies* (Sharjah Art Foundation, 2015), which collected my writings on dance. And pages 82-92 of the second edition of *Distracted* (Tuumba Press, 2003) have been cut from this edition, as they have been included, under the title "Postwar Lebanese Photography Between Radical Closure and Surpassing Disaster," in my book *Radical Closure* (National Gallery Singapore, 2020), which collected my writings on this concept; and, under the title "Lebanese Photography Between Radical Closure and Surpassing Disaster," in my book *The Withdrawal of Tradition Past a Surpassing Disaster* (Redcat/Forthcoming Books, 2009), which collected my writings from 1996 to 2009 on my concept *surpassing disaster*.

To the forgetful grateful, and to my untimely collaborators

— Are you saying this to me?
— Also to myself. One should speak solely when also speaking to oneself. Only then is there a dialogue.

J. T.

Twenty-four years old, and still not one book written, not one feature film made, not one suicide attempted!

On the subway train, a father is teaching his child: "Parallel lines meet at infinity." Two parallel tracks converge. The child: "Is this infinity?"

The tourist is not someone who does not find the places he is searching for. He is someone who, on asking "Where is the place — —?" always gets for answer "But you're in it!"

The foreigner's exile: spelling one's name. "*J* as in *Jalal, a* as in *aphoristic, l* as in *laconic, a* as in *abroad, l* as in *unlike*."

I've been in Paris now for three weeks. Both hotels and universities are full—all the better. Are some of these hotel rooms occupied by the likes of the Kaplan of Hitchcock's *North by Northwest*, an inexistent person constructed by the "United States Intelligence Agency" as a decoy to fool foreign agents? Thornhill, the protagonist of Hitchcock's film, works in advertising. How appropriate that he gets mistaken for Kaplan: "We construct a self from the data given (the paper, the cards, the ticket, the hat, the location), the correlatives for a particular character.... These 'clues' signify a person—but he is absent; and so are we. In this shared absence we can easily merge: we can become the absent traveler" (Judith Williamson, *Decoding Advertisements*). By taking the place of an inexistent person, he himself becomes absent ... so as not to be killed by the spies or arrested by the police who mistakenly believe he murdered someone. We do not take the place of the absent person, only his absence. In this "shared absence," the differences between the two men (Kaplan's trousers don't fit Thornhill; Kaplan has dandruff, Thornhill doesn't ...) are irrelevant.

It is to protect the "guest" from losing his identity in the impersonal hotel room that he's made to sign his name in the register. In Jim

Jarmusch's *Stranger Than Paradise*, the three protagonists, two men and a woman, park at a motel. The two men go inside and register for a two-double-beds room. As planned, she sneaks into the room a little later. But, not having signed the register, she becomes absent: the two men go on several outings without inviting her to accompany them.

The hotel manager shows him around his room. A few days later, he moves to a different floor. The manager shows him around his new room: a replica of the other one. The manager drops a piece of information about the presence of an item that was also in the first room but wasn't mentioned during the earlier presentation. A hotel room cannot be known by scrutiny, but by a lateral movement from one room to another, from one account to another.

Don't get lost in the myriad paths my sauntering produced in my small room.

Suddenly, he felt he could no longer endure loneliness. He spoke to the first woman he met in the street. No response. "But what do I lack?" "Nothing. You lack nothing"—and then, with a certain tenderness: "Not even a woman."

A woman enters the café where I am sitting and smiles. Someone must be waiting for her. Yes. Did the solitary person I am ever smile on entering a café? Did I ever come running into any place—that is, when not racing against a heavy rain? Downpour is nowadays my only way to get somewhere on time. It is my alarm clock, the one with the most beautiful sound. The café in which I am sitting drenched has glass doors. It is raining outside soundlessly as if in a silent film. When rain falls, even on streets, it feels it is doing so on roofs. Except in the case of a few films, I now go to the cinema only to rediscover that most social of feelings: *being late*—late in going out of the cinema: a few fade-outs in the film, but a myriad of them during projection, for the eyes keep closing from time to time.

Walt Whitman knew how to stay just long enough to leave too early—that is, not too late.

Five minutes before the train moves. To the left, to the right: more trains—no horizon. Inside the compartment, no faces, just newspapers. The train moves. The world!

Through the moving train's windows, he can see the many stopped trains at Howard Station, Chicago. He writes: "I love the roofs of trains: they are like the backs of whales, conjuring up a *Moby Dick* Whitman could have written."

After writing about film slug,[2] he looks from the window of the moving train: "Was what passed by while I was writing a slug to maintain sync?"

A car cemetery and, much farther along, human cemeteries. One thing following the other not causally, but because the train tracks happened to pass here, not elsewhere.

Even the ghosts of the cemeteries have left the small towns for cities.

I'm amazed to hear of people committing suicide by drowning themselves in the Seine: but for the Seine, I may have attempted suicide.

A lake's surface after the rower has passed, the reflections reuniting not merely because he has moved on but because he did not fully exist as he passed through the lake.

A caw. Through me flew a bird. My apprehension that it would perch inside me, that I might become rooted in its tired wings.

Lightness: wings themselves have become heavy, cumbersome, something to be discarded.

The localization, the in-focus, of what should remain vibrational is an itch. Hence this eccentric body that instead of scratching the itch reacts to it by becoming in its entirety a vibrating body.

To the blind, all that is not an edge is an abyss.

Not too much yet overflowing, as in superfluidity.

Rather than the exhibitionistic extremism of those at the lower or higher end of the spectrum, the unobtrusive excess of those outside it.

Is it too early or too late? For I presently feel that it is too something.

Not yet time to write. At last, time to write no more! Not yet time to write. At last, time to write no more! There is no such thing as the right time to write: a period that would take place between the "not yet time to write" and the "time to write no more," between writing as promise and writing as compromise.

A bookstore. The board has the inscription "Old and New Books." Yet how old is the board itself!

David Hubel and Torsten Wiesel found in their experiments on cats that up to four months after birth "the visual cortex is plastic enough to change its organization in response to the input from the retina.... It is possible to delay the onset of the critical period by rearing kittens in total darkness, thereby allowing all other developmentally related changes to occur.... This strategy, called dark-rearing, was first explored by Max S. Cynader.... It enabled Cynader to initiate shifts in ocular dominance in cats that were as much as two years old."[3] One can be the contemporary of one's earliest childhood also in this sense and manner, thus averting the nostalgic, metaphorical relation to it ("*as a child*, I used to ..."). Whether we come from developing countries or not, we have to create our non-developed areas.

The difficulty of becoming part of the composition of remembered things does not result from the ostensible immateriality of the past. It rather consists in the circumstance that the time needed for remembered things to compose the past is simultaneously the span it takes the one remembering to decompose. Nostalgia is this missed meeting.

If time is our mismatching with ourselves, then one's palm is a *joiner*: its time is, and its lines are, the mismatching of many photographs of an absolutely smooth palm with not one line. Some interviewer should ask David Hockney if he believes palmisters, indeed if he himself is one.

The director was such a perfectionist that having a close-up of a person's palm, he redistributed its lines with makeup so that a palmister watching the film would be able to predict what will happen to that character.

We have to become (both come to be and befit) even what we are, passing along the way through the risk change entails. Only what does not change has control: it is appropriately called *the control sample*.

Reverence for oneself, never self-satisfaction.

Where are we to detect inexactitude if everything in the outside world is indefectible? In the interior monologue.

There is no sloppiness in a universe of eternal recurrence, or rather the only sloppiness in a universe of eternal recurrence is one's unawareness of this recurrence, and hence one's attempt to approximate what one cannot miss.

Memory is threatened by not only forgetfulness (*Hiroshima mon amour*) but also the amnesia of eternal recurrence[4] (*Last Year at Marienbad*).

There is no contradiction between countless recurrence and the production of the new. Indeed, the main event and the paradigm of the new is[5] the will that the ordeal of the experience of countless recurrence is going to make possible.[6]

I like most, I'm best at, play. I detest games.

— Since …
— Bad, since an argument. Never indulge in the restless rest of explanation. All explanations are excuses—unless, after a sober, awkward preparation of oneself (nothing comes quickly, certainly not quickness—everything happens suddenly), and by an unexplainable metamorphosis, "to explain" becomes to make something ex-plain. Continue the interruption.

— Prove that you dislike explanations.
— I accept misunderstandings.

A story is always too long—which means its summary as well is always too long.

Words?! Yes, I will leave some behind only if they take as little space as the ashes of that half of my corpse that will be burnt, and as little time to read as the duration needed to bury the other half.

Practice makes practical, not perfect.

Patience is the subtlest obstacle to the attainment of serenity.

I do not apprehend recurrent behavior in terms of character traits but in terms of insistence on declaring oneself a certain type of person. This student keeps acting in a stupid manner, that is, he keeps repeating to himself and to me, his professor, "I am stupid." My response: "But I am intelligent enough to get this from the first time. You should therefore stop acting demonstratively in this manner."

With obsession, one is dealing with a countdown.

In this sedentary film, the train serves only to stop the cars.

Il promenait les mains dans ses poches.

It is necessary to be a cinematographer at least once in one's life so as to experience how difficult it is to accompany anything, whether in a pan, dolly, or even a static shot.

Long journey
Looking at the lake's surface
Drops of sweat

A worker is tilling the land. The drop of sweat at the tip of his nose annoys me more than the noisy dripping from a leaky faucet for hours on end.

Out of reach. I've left "No Trespassing" to others.

The resting place of nomads is the edge.

Trying to join two cliffs with a phrase. But the phrase itself has a chasm, stops in the middle.

All changes happen in the ellipsis. To know how to detect in every phrase, in everything, its three ellipsis points—that place where it becomes so slow it can proceed only by leaping. One must remain in these three points as long as they persist, precisely because one is a nomad: continuing toward the one point that seemingly brings the matter to an end is nothing but a drifting along a circle whose center is this point.

All courage resides in walking to the very edge. Beyond is dizziness. Has anybody gone beyond the edge except by slipping? But there, beyond the edge, the world itself slips. Thus one remains steady.

He parodied it to bring it to its end—he should remember, though, that a thing is not completely dead so long as its parodies are alive.

Since where one begins is the beginning, one should begin at the end.

Cloning would not usher in a period of pervasive visual similarity. On the contrary, as similarity is displaced to the level of the genetic code, we are going to gradually lose much, if not all, of our ability to differentiate between people at the level of visual form.

How cruel of you to describe him, for he's no more than a description of himself.

"I like the way you sound." That was his reply to my letter. Now it's the envelope as it's torn that makes a sound. Could it be, then, that he mistook the envelope for the letter? Or is it—which is even worse—that, being too dense himself, he searched for a letter inside the letter, that is, mistook the letter itself for an envelope? "I like the way you sound"—what about the five other senses?

The price of one of Christo's wrapped objects at Zabriskie Gallery is $330,000. The artist may have subverted such a price by putting something worth more than $330,000 in the wrap; the buyer can subvert it by giving the latter as a gift to someone and watching her unwrap it to see her present.

— Thank you for your present.
— Thank you for your birthday.

Three quarters of an hour into 1986. The train has been stuck in the station for the last fifteen minutes. Someone yells: "What are you waiting for, 1987?"

Sunday, March 2, 1986. I touched a branch.

The surface of a table, a shoe, hair on my arm. Now that I am closest to them, I feel most sterile. Presently realization lies, as with the sterile mist I love, in dispersion, so that a lost traveler may exclaim: "The world!"

Boat, cloud, lake.
A sound.
Fish? Gull?—The moon! The moon!

"Clouds now and then / giving men relief / from moon viewing" (Bashō). But what if I like clouds even more than the moon? Moon giving men and women relief from cloud viewing.

A jarring anachronism: people who are still talking sense on the radio at 4:18 a.m. Whoever wants to speak or perform late at night should not sleep during the day. "Dreams are the clichés of the sleep world." She looked in my direction as I spoke, her eyes becoming bigger. They did not do so suddenly out of anger, joy, or surprise. It was a slow expansion at a constant rate, no matter what I said or did. Was she masturbating in front of me? No use fleeing, for her eyes would go on expanding until the universe is swallowed in them. No use speaking about love either, for I have become merely another item among the infinity of others that have disappeared in her. I was suffocating, for her expanding eyes were making the rest of the world smaller and smaller. As I froze into silence, everything went back to how it was earlier. Again, to my left, someone laughing, adjusting his watch strap, eating with a fork: making sounds. Next to him, an inebriated person: he spoke only to slow down the rate at which he was drinking. The others: *mi-riant mi-pleurant*, half-hearted, at times halfwitted. I know that's already four halves, but at 5 a.m.... I go outside; as long as one has not seen the sun rise in a city, one has not unquestionably visited it, let alone unquestionably lived in it.

Sunrise: a red sun; a yellow sun; a white sun.

Godard says in his *Scénario du film "Passion"* (1982) while seated before a white screen: "I didn't want to write the script. I wanted to see it.... You find yourself faced with the invisible, a vast, white surface, like Mallarmé's famous blank page." Notwithstanding Godard, a filmmaker does not start with the white screen but has to achieve it, for example, by recourse to the white of a blizzard. Colors can be used on credit, but sooner or later, in a third, tenth, fifteenth, or last film, the filmmaker must reach their condition of possibility. Two of the greatest colorists in cinema, Kurosawa and Antonioni, resorted to a blizzard (*Dreams*) and to fog (*Identification of a Woman*), respectively, as a condition of possibility of the birth of colors, first monochromatic, in the form of the red or blue of the headbands and the yellow of the jackets of "The Blizzard" section of *Dreams*; then full-blown with the filmic recreation of many of Van Gogh's colorful paintings in the "Crows" section of *Dreams*. When, after the blizzard, we have black and white, these are now colors.

Quicker than the possible.

Always arriving too early, that is, too late to act.

The clapping of two hands is mere noise. Applause is the clapping of the hand against one's forehead (Aha!).

On the beat: one hand stopping the other one midway in its movement to slap the body. Do we have two hands so that one hand can prevent the other from slapping the rest of the body?

Slap yourself in the face to discover the hand that is ever in it.

I'm drunk. Something is separating me from this man I feel strongly like punching—probably my hand.

> — Who do you think will win?
> — I don't know.
> — Who do you think will lose?

Fighting for a cause?! A cause has an infinity of effects, and one usually wants only one or two of these—all the others one calls by-products. One fights for an effect. Someone who accepts a cause and consequently its countless effects is no fighter.

25

Hero: one who does not adapt to his victory.

A powerful person would never do *this*, only a mere powerful situation.

It was not the perfect sync of the movements of the army units that scared me at a screening of Kubrick's *Full Metal Jacket*, but the absolute sync in the reactions of the film spectators.

The herd: not many, but too many, or rather too one. To detach oneself from the herd, one must become many and do so by making summation impossible through becoming heterogeneous elements that cannot be added to give one number (or one yawn, the yawn of the *etc.*), irrespective of whether this number is one million or one.

One has become indistinguishable, snow buried in snow, snow exposing snow.

Indistinguishable: not like everyone else, like nothing.

Don't take away from them what they reflect, for then they become a mere reflection.

I just learned that her sister is suicidal, unlike her, who is pococurante and cowardly. Often when one thinks one is drawn to a person, one is really attracted to one or more persons the latter knows or knew (or will know?) and whom one may oneself never meet: her sister or mother or friend or teacher or enemy.

Joan of Arc in the presence of the king dissimulating his identity: a test for both of them, and the king knew this. There is never an acknowledgment, a meeting, except between those without proofs.

It does not matter to me that she's speaking to him. Her voice reaches me. It gets lost in me. Now, I meet her: only the lost can meet the lost. She smiles when I say *lost*, for I walk with no hesitation whatsoever through the myriad paths of this library and sit in front of her who is ever lost in it. How easy it is to reduce someone to muteness: her red earphones. Her eyes make me forget everything else, so what is it, then, that each time makes me forget to note their color?

Her lips and my distraction often interrupted by her tongue.

She attracts me fully, for she attracts both my writing and me.

She sat on my knee like a notebook.

I wrote several lines. A blank page replaced by a blank mind.

The car is moving to another lane, and I, seated in the back, am staring at the receding yellow line. I feel like saying goodbye (to it?). Behind, in the visible past: other cars. One of them gains speed, enters the present, then passes into the visible future, then into the trans-horizon future.

Le propre des choses est d'arriver ("quelque chose m'est arrivée"). Le propre de l'homme est de quitter?

The nomad, unlike the sedentary, refuses to learn how to fix things, how to intervene to halt or slow down the natural process of disintegration. He accepts nothing more than dissolution. Yet, it seems, always comes the moment of the dissolution of dissolution, the moment when dissolution begins to ask for a solution. Then he goes away.

Tomber sur une solution: heaviness.

Have you stared at people having a discussion? Have you noticed not only the movements of their hands and in their faces but also the simultaneous motionlessness of their legs, knees, buttocks, or other parts? Try to reach a state where you don't merely deduce that parts of the body are distracted from the plot—or plotting against it (as revealed, for example, by a parapraxis)—but where you intuit that the body is always in the most relaxed position, however awkward one's pose, however strenuous the thing one is doing. It is in the same movement that one intuits this body that absents itself from nothing except rest, that is, from absence, and that one knows that one is *always* tired, with a weariness that's unrelated to rest, that cannot be alleviated by it (only the weariness of workers can be alleviated by rest).

Once the house that one built and/or occupied, if one is a sedentary, or that one chanced upon and sojourned in, if one is a wanderer, has crumbled, neither to restore it nor to dig the earth to lay the foundation of a new house: by doing the latter, one runs the risk of finding and founding only graves. To let the house crumble until there remains a wall. This wall may turn into a "Wall." A "Wall" cannot be demolished. The one who tries to demolish it turns into a normal person, becomes himself a "Wall." To perforate the "Wall." Perforation should go on until one reaches the most terrible, best hidden of all "Walls": one's teeth. The teeth themselves must get perforated, become ones through which the universe circulates. Only then does respiration occur away from the countless beginnings-ends of the heart's diastole-systole. Still, almost everyone will go on telling one: "You want to get her? Make her laugh. And don't, yourself, forget to laugh." Only a woman and a man showing each other they have teeth, and strong and healthy ones at that, will assure all concerned, above all the baby to be born, that they can bite into, chew and digest the world. Maybe they will be the ones to perform the following miracle: a baby who upon coming out of his mother's vagina laughs rather than cries. They mistake perforating with biting-chewing-digesting. The "Wall" is that which is still undigested after "everything" has been chewed and digested. The "Wall" is the indigestible.

Even holes have to be perforated.

While some poets and filmmakers apparently manage to directly receive lines of poetry and film images, respectively, others can do so only following the perforation of a "Wall." If one is not fortunate enough to come across a "Wall,"[7] one is to construct one! If what is received is not an aphoristic book, but, one at a time, a number of aphorisms that are to compose a book, then editing, of the sequence of the aphorisms, is required. Editing the book of aphorisms exposes its author to the danger of trying to join within the aphorism. Yet finding many a *therefore* in aphorisms does not necessarily mean that the aphorist felt the need to explain—and not only to the readers. What gives the *therefore, hence, because* the exceptional grace they acquire when used by aphoristic writers is the intermingling of tenses in the aphorisms. For although an aphoristic writer might join within the same aphorism what was received piecemeal, he does not change the tense in which each thing was received, does not hide that some things were received in the past tense, others in the present tense, others still in the future tense. As writers, aphoristic authors rarely learn from experience, partly because what they receive at the end of a sequence of experiences is frequently given to them in the past tense.

One's imagination of a change is not a mere projection but real, whether or not it gets actualized, if one received it at the end of a perforation of a "Wall." What gets actualized may be different from what was imagined, but if it was not received in the above manner, it does not have the seal of reality (similarly, a line written with the possibility of evading receiving it, but read in the absence of such a possibility only became real when it was thus read; if a copyright is to be attributed to anyone at all, it should be to the one who read it in such a manner). Much of what is actual is not real. To replace Berkeley's proposition "that all the choir of heaven and furniture of the earth, in a word all those bodies which compose the mighty frame of the world, have not any subsistence without a mind, that their being is to be perceived or known"[8] with the aphoristic "To be is to be received at the end of a perforation of a 'Wall.'"

We are irresponsible only for what we receive at the end of a perforation of a "Wall." One can—no, one must—try to work on what one considers unjustified biases one holds. One must do this before putting oneself against a "Wall," since whatever is received at the end of a perforation of a "Wall" should be accepted, even if it is impossible (a miracle) or a bias. A bias received at the end of a perforation of a "Wall" is a justified one: one's refusal to accept it on any grounds is self-censorship. One can subsequently repeat the process of putting oneself against a "Wall," hoping that what will be received during a subsequent perforation will be different and unbiased.

The blank between consecutive aphorisms functions in the manner of the insulator between the two superconducting parts of a Josephson junction. A book of aphorisms required from its author the perforation of "Walls" for the reception of the aphorisms and demands from its reader ("quantum") tunneling between the consecutive aphorisms.

For the over-writer that I am, *well done* is overly cooked.

Aphoristic writers consider the editing process outlandish. While before they received, at the editing stage they find. Receiving has nothing to do with finding. It does not permit one to locate oneself in the world.

The irreplaceable is so early and so easily replaced in the replaceable.

William Blake's "To see a world in a grain of sand / And a heaven in a wild flower / Hold infinity in the palm of your hand / and eternity in an hour" (*Auguries of Innocence*, 1803) implies we need an eternity to explore what is in one hour: "I have no time to remember the event as I have haven't finished exploring it."

The one thinking, the one creating, gives the impression, assumes the posture of someone remembering—though nothing that belongs to the past.

An old man who saw me unable to write told me that his trick to counter writer's block is to put down the two words "I remember ..." and link to them. My first, polemical thought was that what might do the trick in my case is rather to write: "I forgot ..." But, actually, writing and thinking are a resistance to forgetfulness unrelated to any attempt to remember.

"It is useful to describe the original Cantor dust by means of a combination of 'active' and 'virtual' tremas. Again, one starts from [0,1] and cuts out its open mid-third]1/3, 2/3[.... The second stage cuts out the mid-thirds of *each* third of [0,1]. While cutting out the mid-third of the already vanished mid-third has no perceivable effect, virtual tremas will momentarily prove convenient. In the same way, one cuts out the mid-third of *each* ninth of [0,1], of *each* 27th, and so on. Note that the distribution of the number of tremas of length exceeding u is now given by a step function, whose overall behavior is proportional to u^{-1}, instead of u^{-D}."[9] It is along these lines that *absentminded* is to be understood: thinking is always taking place in the case of the distracted—even when they undergo a lapse of consciousness. They therefore find the specifying expression "I have been doing some thinking lately" incomprehensible.

Though every immeasurable outstrips every measure, not every measure is adequate to unsuccessfully try to measure every immeasurable.

Generosity is a beginning, it cannot be a response, it cannot be responded to. It is the gratitude of the forgetful. Generosity is always towards strangers; it turns even people we know into strangers. Only thrifty people take full advantage of a situation, but to the munificent the world itself is frequently generous.

It is out of thriftiness that the majority of people want to be able to count what is given to them or that the giver be able to do so.

One can never be sure how much an idea or an ability requires in order to occur and hence how much is given generously to one.

Maxwell's wave equation for light has a *retarded solution* and an *advanced solution*. Retarded light waves travel forward in time, while advanced waves travel backward in time. In conventional radiation theory, an atom can emit a wave of light even if the latter does not get absorbed in the future; but in the Wheeler-Feynman *absorber theory of radiation*, in order for light to be emitted, a back-and-forth movement has to happen: a half-sized retarded wave must travel from the atom to the future absorber, and a half-sized advanced wave must travel from the absorber back to the atom. If there are no absorbers in a particular region, light will not shine in that direction.

   Every time I create something, I know that there is someone somewhere who has received it. Many a time I stopped writing and went out with boring people who have money and time to waste: I did this most probably because there was no stranger to receive the new I might have created if he or she existed. An ethical imperative: to be available so that what has the possibility of being created by others can be forwarded to us rather than blocked, in other words, so that they would not suffer from writer's block.

The periods in his life when he failed to write were those when he lost his belief in the generosity of the world, or rather in the generosity of what in the world resists the "world."

Jalal Toufic, Los Angeles, 10/23/1997
Dear Réda Bensmaïa, Pawtucket, RI:[10]
While at California Institute of the Arts, I went into the reference section of its small library to check the English release title of a French film mentioned in one of the articles of this issue [*Gilles Deleuze: A Reason to Believe in this World*, ed. Réda Bensmaïa and Jalal Toufic, *Discourse* 20.3, Fall 1998]. Noticing *The Oxford History of World Cinema* (1996), I opened its index: the film's title was the same in English. Then it occurred to me to check for Deleuze: no mention. I then looked through the long bibliography: no mention. The following are two salient characteristics of mediocrity. It is self-congratulatory: it has become customary these days for those applying for a teaching position in the field of cinema studies to get in response something along the lines of "We received hundreds of applications. We are quite pleased with the very high level of many of the applicants. Such excellence is full of promise for the field." It seems one has to brace oneself for a small dose of displeasure and a large dose of indifference as this throng of academics begins to temporarily—for a decade or two—taint with pettiness and vulgarize through countless rehash in badly written papers expressions like *becoming-animal* and *line of flight*, as they have transiently vulgarized and made ugly such beautiful words as *other, nomad, margin*. Second, it evinces a flagrant lack of embarrassment: how otherwise to explain that thirteen years after the publication of *Cinéma 1: L'image-mouvement* and ten years after its English translation; and eleven years after the publication of *Cinéma 2: L'image-temps* and seven years after its translation into English, there is no mention of Deleuze, the author of these two volumes that compose the greatest work ever written in relation to cinema, either in the bibliography or in the index of *The Oxford History of World Cinema* (henceforth referred to as *Another Thoughtless Oxford Cinema Book*). Should one attribute this absence of Deleuze to Deleuze himself: as an effect of his becoming-imperceptible? While such a becoming may have been a contributing factor to this meager circulation and acknowledgment of his work, it is disingenuous to attribute the latter either fully or even largely to it. For Deleuze has a becoming-imperceptible not only for those who have opted to disregard his work but also for those who love it. The imperceptibility of Deleuze will become both clearer and more outlandish when his work is better known. Yes, we have as yet sensed only a minimal part of his becoming-imperceptible.

Is Deleuze part of world cinema? Deleuze has made it quite clear that philosophy does not reflect on cinema, artworks, and literature, but that it creates its own entities: concepts. I would add that, not being wedged in linear time, philosophical and literary creation is additionally a collaboration with past and future filmmakers and/or writers and/or artists. Complementarily, any artistic or literary work is related to the future, not so much because its quality and validity supposedly can be judged only by whether it successfully passes the test of time—if, taking into consideration Dōgen's time-being ("An ancient Buddha said: 'For the time being stand on top of the highest peak.... / For the time being three heads and eight arms. / For the time being an eight- or sixteen-foot body....' 'For the time being' here means time itself is being, and all being is time. A golden sixteen-foot body is time.... 'Three heads and eight arms' is time"[11]), we view as time a Bosnian Serb aiming his artillery at the National and University Library in Sarajevo, or *mujahidin* not making any effort to spare the National Museum of Afghanistan, then during the last decade much great Muslim art and many great Bosnian and Ottoman literary and mystical works failed to pass the test of time; nor so much because the majority of those living in the same period in which it was created need an additional time to catch up with and become the contemporaries of the that time; but, fundamentally, because it is the result of an untimely collaboration with future philosophers, writers, artists, etc. Since art, literature, and film are fundamentally related to the future, what is truly amazing about an artist, filmmaker, or writer is not the future component of his or her work (one that maintains its relevance far into the future), for that comes to him or her from his future collaborators; but that he or she is exactly of his or her time, rather than being, like the vast majority of the living, behind his/her time—how little fashionable it is to be the contemporary of one's time: Deleuze. I feel closer to Gertrude Stein's view in her book on Picasso: "Wars are only a means of publicizing the things already accomplished, a change, a complete change, has come about, people no longer think as they were thinking but no one knows it, no one recognizes it, no one really knows it except the creators";[12] than to Kafka's, as reported by Gustav Janouch: "There were some pictures by Picasso.... 'He is a wilful distortionist,' I said. 'I do not think so,' said Kafka. 'He only registers the deformities which have not yet penetrated our consciousness. Art is a mirror, which goes "fast," like a watch—sometimes.'"[13] I find Kafka's expression less felicitous than Stein's although it overlaps with it, since it mixes two positions: the artist or writer as that rarity, someone who is the contemporary of his or her time, and thus who is in advance in the present over those who are living in the same period; and the artist or writer as ahead of his time.

Deleuze was not starting to collaborate when he began working with Guattari in what ended up being one of this century's great such endeavors. He was switching modes of collaboration. For he had already collaborated with Lewis Carroll, and with Nietzsche—how much did the latter, who was "6,000 feet beyond man and time," collaborate with future writers and thinkers! Nietzsche's untimeliness will not cease in a hundred years from now, around two centuries from when he wrote in one of the notes of the preface (dated sometime between November 1887 and March 1888) of his projected *The Will to Power*: "What I relate is the history of the next two centuries. I describe what is coming." I don't consider *Dialogues* a collaboration between Deleuze and Claire Parnet; on the other hand, I am sure that Deleuze collaborated with Francis Bacon. It is true that Deleuze's forceful book on Bacon inflects its readers' interpretations and viewing of that painter's oeuvre; but it primarily affected that work in the past: it is a collaboration with Bacon, accessed by the latter through his intuition. Bacon's work would physically not be the same without *Francis Bacon: Logique de la sensation* (1981). Since I, too, have collaborated with Bacon through the section on radical closure in *Over-Sensitivity* (1996), his work would be physically different without my book. Cinema tends to be a collaborative medium not just because most filmmakers have to work with musicians, set designers, cinematographers, actors, etc., but additionally because being also an art form, even filmmakers or video makers who themselves shoot their films or videos, perform in them, edit them, compose their music, and distribute them collaborate in an untimely manner with future philosophers, writers, filmmakers, and/or artists. Deleuze has already collaborated with some of the filmmakers mentioned in his cinema book. Thus, he belongs less in the bibliography of books on world cinema than in any chapter they contain that covers collaborators (cinematographers, screenwriters, etc.) and influences, therefore in their indexes. Does this sort of collaboration make it illegitimate to consider the participating filmmaker as an *auteur*? It does so as little as would Hitchcock's collaboration with composer Bernard Herrmann and title designer Saul Bass and his use of a Boileau-Narcejac novel make it illegitimate to call *Vertigo* a Hitchcock film. This century of cinema has been considerably influenced by Deleuze even if not many filmmakers have read his work between 1983 (the date of publication of the first volume of his cinema book) and 1996, and even if not many end up reading it between now and the end of this century. To have affected, through this untimely collaboration, past artists more than future ones is another manner of being imperceptible. Since they have already heeded it, it is certainly legitimate for great filmmakers to declare that they don't read what is written on their work even by philosophers and writers—while legitimate, this attitude is unfortunate, for they are missing much; in the case of Deleuze, the utter beauty of his two volumes on cinema. Deleuze's work itself is a collaboration: with Guattari, and others, in the books the two co-authored; and with others—including possibly with

Guattari—in Deleuze's own books. "The two of us wrote *Anti-Oedipus* together. Since each of us was several, there was already quite a crowd.... We have been aided, inspired, multiplied" (*A Thousand Plateaus*)—including by future philosophers, writers, artists, scientists, etc. One knows that a collaboration with a specific contemporary writer, philosopher, or artist is simply not working when our usual future collaborators no longer influence us and no new untimely collaborators take their place. Do artists and writers suffer unduly from an "anxiety of influence"?[14] An artist cannot afford this reported anxiety of influence: he or she could not have created while having it, creation being an untimely collaboration. In *To Have Done with the Judgment of God* (1947), his canceled radio program, Artaud found himself forced to torturously collaborate with his voices; but he also collaborated in an untimely manner with Deleuze and with Deleuze-Guattari (and also with Jacques Derrida, the author of "La parole soufflée," an article in which Derrida is sometimes an untimely collaborator, sometimes a critic). It is mostly critics who, unaffected by and unaware of such an untimely collaboration, make a fuss about an anxiety of influence. A critic, especially a journalistic one, comes after; the artwork or literary work is truly finished for him or her by the time he or she arrives on the scene. Critics and journalists, who function well under tight deadlines, always arrive late for such untimely collaborations. Being late for a genuine collaboration, they are left with contributing to one more fashionable, for constitutionally late, anthology. Since they didn't collaborate in an untimely manner on the artistic and literary works on which they occasionally reflect, it is understandable that they find it much easier to write on commercial culture, which in the vast majority of cases is linear not only narratively but also in its mode of collaboration and influence: in its production there is no need for this collaboration with the future, which constitutes much of intuition. In academia and criticism, so many anthologies on a popular culture that has been reduced to and equated with commercial culture, and so little collaboration. Despite its eighty-two contributors, there is no collaboration whatsoever in *Another Thoughtless Oxford Cinema Book*. If philosophers and writers find it extremely difficult to write on commercial films and novels, it is not simply or mainly as a consequence of their negative value judgment of these works; it is fundamentally because their writings are not a reflection on films, paintings, dance, and works of literature but a collaboration with these, so that the fact that the vast majority of commercial works are linear not only narratively but also in their mode of collaboration and influence renders any untimely collaboration in their production unfeasible. It is much easier for a philosopher or thinker to write in relation to Robbe-Grillet, for his work is triply nonlinear: from the least unsettling and least important level, that of narration (Quentin Tarantino's tedious *Pulp Fiction* [1994] remains at this level); to that of the story, i.e., of the diegetic space-time; to that of an untimely collaboration with future thinkers and writers. Robbe-Grillet, one of the most articulate writers and filmmakers about his novels and films,[15] is a much more intuitive filmmaker than the majority of contemporary Hollywood filmmakers, who don't tire of repeating to us how crucial intuition is in their "creative process." If I already belong to world cinema, it is certainly far less as a result of my few videos than as a consequence of my untimely collaborations with filmmakers such as Robbe-Grillet, Lynch, and Tarkovsky through (Vampires): An Uneasy Essay on the Undead in Film and Over-Sensitivity, as well as with Parajanov through my coming book [Forthcoming]. I am sure I have collaborated with the latter two filmmakers, although I never met them and although they died before any of my books were published. I had become so imbued with this form of collaboration by the time I was writing my third book that I had grown totally oblivious to the more obvious and discussed mode of influence, getting reminded of it with a sense of surprise on receiving a letter from performance and installation artist Carolee Schneemann in which she wrote, in response to reading (Vampires), "I wish you could see the piece; the influence of your 'space-time continuum' sweeps through each element of Mortal Coils [1994]." This untimely collaboration can be stopped by surpassing disasters, which produce a withdrawal of tradition; or by developments that lead to the destruction of the future, thus impoverishing our intuition; or by certain epochal events that create discontinuities in time. I would define epochs by whether this untimely collaboration is possible: what belongs to different epochs is what essentially cannot collaborate in an untimely manner. Despite the deep affinity an Iraqi poet or thinker may feel toward Gilgamesh, he or she will not have, when writing on it, the impression that he or she collaborated on its production. Despite being deeply impressed by the similarity between ancient Egyptian peasants and contemporary villagers in the vicinity of Edfu with regard to their physiognomy and the style and building materials of their dwellings, I am sure that, while making use of ancient Egyptian monuments and hieroglyphic writings in The Night of Counting the Years (1968), at no point did Shadi Abdel Salam feel that he was collaborating through his film with the ancient Egyptians across chronological time. While one cannot become an untimely collaborator in relation to artistic works belonging to a different epoch, one can still possibly understand and appreciate them; use them in one's work, as the poet Armand Schwerner does with Gilgamesh and other Sumero-Akkadian works in his The Tablets; or affect their reception and interpretation as a critic. Deleuze is still a philosopher rather than a critic even in relation to other epochs, for though he cannot collaborate with them in an untimely manner, he still creates concepts in relation to them. Even when we are quite conscious of our changing views of them, we

35

are also aware that there is something definitive about works belonging to another epoch: they are thus classics.

I presently admire the following people:

— The artist, writer, filmmaker, or philosopher, by constitution intuitive.

— Their future untimely collaborators.

— And the one, seemingly modest, whose aim isn't to become a writer, a filmmaker, or an artist but rather, with a wonderful extravagance, to incarnate *the audience implied by the artwork*. The dancer having lost the mirror-reflection on crossing the threshold to the realm of dance in Agnes de Mille's "dream ballet" for Fred Zinnemann's *Oklahoma!*, he, an audience member, could not tell, not only theoretically but also physically, that Laurey (played by Shirley Jones) was physically different from her subtle version in the dance realm (performed by the ballet dancer Bambi Linn), that Curly (played by Gordon MacRae) also looked different from his subtle version in the dance realm (performed by the ballet dancer James Mitchell), and that Jud and his subtle version in the dance realm, both played by Rod Steiger, were physically identical. "His thing" was not to identify with and embark on the quixotic path of modeling himself on the protagonist (nothing has been as cheapened, programmed and manipulated in twentieth-century culture); but to incarnate the audience implied by the artwork—a much more demanding endeavor. He had distanciation toward the actors and characters, but not toward the implied audience. While I despise those who remain solely empirical audience members, I admired him. He decried the widespread misrecognition that a painting, dance, or literary work implies, and therefore has, a specific, intrinsic audience. He felt there weren't enough people who tried or are trying to make the audience "part" of the artwork not by blurring the boundary between the performers and the extrinsic audience—this resulting most often in sloppy, weak pieces—but rather by filling the position of the audience implied by the artwork.

By the way, is Marguerite Duras's *L'Amant de la Chine du Nord* (Gallimard, 1991), with its "This is a book. / This is a film,"[16] part of world cinema?

There is something theatrical about Nietzsche, in that one often has the sense that he is speaking in asides: "—Ultimately, no one can extract from things, books included, more than he already knows.... Now let us imagine an extreme case: that a book speaks of nothing but events which lie outside the possibility of general or even of rare experience.... In this case simply nothing will be heard, with the acoustical illusion that where nothing is heard there *is* nothing" ("Why I Write Such Excellent Books," *Ecce Homo*).

It is part of the miracle one's hearing about it although it is what excludes witnesses—even in the guise of the one who performed it.

Divest possibility from curiosity. The vigil over possibilities has nothing to do with curiosity, as is clear in quantum physics, where an act of observation collapses the wave equation into one actuality. Quantum physics has been the branch of science that has gone furthest in acknowledging possibilities precisely because it relinquished curiosity: while it describes wavefunction evolution, yet it offers no definitive account of what physically occurs between source and detector.

The jealousy-inducing woman includes a third in the relationship. The jealous person achieves a reactive equivalent by looking at the bystander or passerby to see in the expression on his or her face signs about what is going on *behind his back* (Munch's *Jealousy*).

No one is a worse actor than the spectator identifying with a fictional character.

In person, the saint was no longer expressive: his elocution was arrhythmic; his language dull; his demeanor unobtrusive and unremarkable; and his facial expression deadpan. And yet, increasingly, when he appeared in the visionary dreams of people, he was most expressive, even hysterical.

The unbearable to see are not only the obscene gestures and gesticulations of the possessed, but also the exorcism by which Jesus Christ does away with the demons provoking them.

In most books, one must look for the digressions, for in the digression from the digression one may still find something necessary.

Regaining my seat after a coffee refill, I resume looking at the street: this is the third homeless person to search in the same garbage can in the last five minutes. The second homeless person had found an empty bottle that the first one had skipped. The garbage discarded by one homeless person is revisited, as still not useless enough, by a second, then a third.... Something almost Buddhist in these gradations of nothing.

Notwithstanding my instructions, the blabbering barber blithely continued to shear my hair even after it had become clearly too short. I interjected several times: "Cut it short!" Without stopping his palaver, he continued clipping my hair until I became bald. Again, I repeated: "Cut it short." Still chattering, he began trimming the moustache.

It is one of the merits of Borhane Alaouié's film *Kafr Kassem* (1975) to have shown that if there is an Arab community of which the Palestinians are a part, the implication is not, as many Israelis would like the world to believe, that Palestinian refugees ought to be settled in the Arab countries to which they had been expelled; but, on the contrary, that the other Arabs have themselves been exiled by the Israeli occupation—and this not because between 1948 and 1967 the West Bank was ruled by Jordan and the Gaza Strip was administered by Egypt. Iraqis, Algerians, Yemenis, etc., have been exiled by the Israeli occupation. Alaouié appears to be concerned with giving back to the voice-over as an exiled voice—for example, the voice of the Egyptian president Gamal Abdel Nasser announcing in 1956 the nationalization of the Suez Canal during a speech broadcast on radio and reaching the Israeli-occupied territories in Palestine—not so much the body, its source, as a land, a country, without which, even when incarnated in a body, it remains fundamentally a voice-over.

How to hug her voice? How to hug what hugs? Is it by turning, like a Möbius strip, inside out?

His voice one more instrument the musician and singer left onstage among the other instruments, to mingle, mute, with people during the break.

Emptiness has sometimes to shout

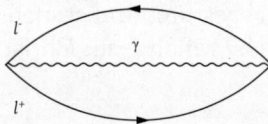

Feynman diagram of a charged lepton (l^-)–charged anti-lepton (l^+)–photon (γ) vacuum fluctuation.[17]

page 561

in order to counter the intolerable noisy effervescence outside it. When noise becomes stentorian, emptiness's shout becomes even louder:

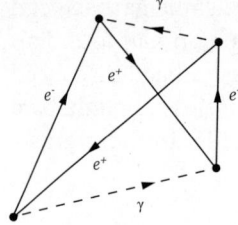

page 561

The law of conservation of energy, notwithstanding the uncertainty principle, can almost hear it now (fluctuations can be detected by humans' theories, but not automatically by the law of conservation of energy!).

Art has an affinity with prayer: both produce an absence of the interior monologue.

Simultaneously hearing the talker and overhearing his interior monologue: noise. There are separate sections in restaurants, different compartments in trains, for smokers and nonsmokers. I am a nonsmoker who does not care in which of these he ends up sitting. There should be different compartments and sections for talkative and silent people.

Film teachers tell their students to turn off the sound of films to be able to concentrate on the lighting and composition of the image and on camera movements. One should occasionally turn off the sound track of life so as to see better.

An image should remain for much longer than its function requires, or disappear so fast that the *persistence of vision* makes one feel it is the eye itself that subsists for too long.

The dead's eyes don't see. When not speaking, the ghost has, like a Stanislavsky actor on the empty stage during the first rehearsals, to invent what and who is around him, as props, so as to haunt.

The sheep were gone. The shepherd's voice searched for them until it, in turn, was lost. Now the shepherd was really alone.

Already in Fritz Lang's first talking film, *M* (1931), one encounters voices that see. Worried by the absence of her daughter, Elsie's mother calls her name. The screen time of each of the five subsequent shots depends on the duration the searching voice needs to ascertain that Elsie is not in the different spaces shown in long shots: the staircase, the courtyard, the bush from which Elsie's ball rolls, and the electricity pole in which her balloon gets trapped. When it is reported in the evening newspaper that Elsie has been murdered, there is no shot of someone informing the mother of that or of the mother reading the news: there is no need for such a shot, as her voice already witnessed sufficient indices that imply her daughter's death.

Very few filmmakers who maintain their shots for a long while have managed to make the audience feel not only that time is building up in the frame but also, past a certain point, and in a Dōgen manner, that objects are time ("An ancient Buddha said: 'For the time being stand on top of the highest peak.... / For the time being three heads and eight arms. / For the time being an eight- or sixteen-foot body....' 'For the time being' here means time itself is being, and all being is time. A golden sixteen-foot body is time.... 'Three heads and eight arms' is time"[18]), that various objects are different sorts of time. The duration of the shot in this kind of cinema is determined less by the dramatic action than by the kind of temporality that the presented objects are. It takes time for sugar to dissolve in water, a Bergsonian duration,[19] but sugar and water and sweet water are time. Even objects in atomic temporality, which appear and disappear from instant to instant without duration, are themselves time, particular kinds of time. Thus objects are mandatory for there to be time in the shot, not because time would be derived from the displacement of objects or the framework of change, but because objects are time. Such films do not present to us the past or future of the character, but the kind of time he is. The character is a certain kind of time experiencing another kind of time in the form of a house, a beach.

No balance can be reached in chronological time, since chronological time cannot exist without imbalance.

The bad critical: the one that has nothing to do with a phase transition.

Occidental surprise, oriental freshness.

Equality (=) is made up of two minuses.

One is just only when one *has had it*.

Nothing is missing even though everything is in excess.

What does it mean to have a fade-out in Wenders's *The Goalie's Anxiety at the Penalty Kick*, where everything and more is shown, where nothing is overlooked or discarded except overlooking and discarding—if not to add, rather than subtract, one more thing, the fade-out itself?

A branch entered my room through the window. If, when it rains, rain does not also fall in my room, and not through the window, I will burn the whole tree.

The sentimental hug of the horizon.

One collides against something whenever one moves, whenever one remains still, be it nothing other than the air one is breathing.

Is the scream a clearing of the throat, the only real, necessary one before speaking can happen?

To become a rumor on nobody's lips, in nobody's mind.

People: mirror images that linger obstinately even though there is no one in front of the mirror, even though there is no mirror.

Derivatives are not forgotten not because they are remembered, but because people and time *forget to forget* them.

Revulsion: distance lacking distance.

I need peopleglasses.

They used to give one a feeling of déjà vu. That was still bearable. Unbearable solitude: this feeling, nowadays, even as one stares at them, of déjà overlooked.

They keep repeating the same infinity of things.

Why don't they brush their teeth after uttering so many unnecessary words? Solitude: all voices have become ambient sound.

He brushed his teeth, rinsed, spat. In the creamy saliva on the point of disappearing in the sink, he saw four words.

The ear should often get clogged like a sink, words and sounds over-flowing from it.

I spat out the words that were in my mouth. I vomited my throat. If only words, like migratory birds, had their seasons for leaving us, for going away. Migratory words.

Many people assume that writers acquire a facility for written language. On the contrary. And the difficulty now extends even to writing a letter to someone to ask permission to film in his café. Is this gradual reduction of what one feels should be written an unavoidable facet of writing? The process is contagious, one saying little, walking to the other end of the dining table to get the salt instead of merely saying *salt*; then doing away with salt and with ... (how much does this ellipsis still contain!).

The strangest: the familiarity with which language met me halfway in my attempt to meet a new thought dawning on me.

If, among alternative translations of a foreign word, a people chooses, through giving it currency, one that later helps thought, leads think-ers in certain fruitful directions, that people thinks, intuitively or at least potentially. With every word that is taken straight from a foreign language, no Arab word coined for it, Arabs resign themselves to think without the collaboration and inspiration of language (for an example of the opposite situation of thinking with the collaboration and inspiration of language: my work with *cadaver*).

    — The mirror does not break, it is only the glass that does.
    — The mirror breaks if in front of it one is totally blind. For that, the
      eyes, the hand, and the cane must become blind simultaneously.

The truly shy person feels bashful even in front of himself or herself in the mirror.

To most women, the mirror is something to be seduced. They begin to believe in "the mirror's objective view" only when their seductiveness vanishes.

An enchanting woman appears to induce a hysteria of the world: a conversion[20] in terms of lighting and sound levels takes place to make her look her best.

A substantial part of the actor's and actress's day during the filming is passed waiting for the lighting to be ready, the dolly tracks to be laid, etc. How can I be a film director when this entails asking others to wait, or rather (for they usually don't mind waiting that much) withstanding the waiting of others?

I arrived late for our date at a gallery. I inquired of the receptionist, whose phone rang less to signal a person on the other side of the line than to show her impatience, whether she saw a beautiful woman with black hair and out-of-sync silence.[21]

She's using hand gestures to better explain to me what she's saying. I understand what she's saying. What I don't get is why she doesn't give me her hands.

    — Your hand is the in-focus plane of my hand.
    — Which one of my two hands?

Each of her winter socks is large enough to hold her foot and my hand.

To kiss the laughing mouth without interrupting the laugh.

White balancing my eyes with her teeth.

The taste of her body. My lips at last are nude.

While one glass of water drenched his thirst, he knew that all the liquid of the universe can't fill the infinity of holes in the saliva of one mouth.

Setting aside fine dining, everyday food is better in Beirut than in New York. But once one starts fasting, that is, once one begins feeding on oneself, then one discovers that one tastes better in New York than in Beirut.

I arrived at the café five minutes too early. The moment one begins waiting—but does waiting begin at a precise moment?—people, electrons, events begin to jostle on their way towards where they are awaiting themselves. How can one not be distracted by, and how can the awaited one ever reach one through, this jostling? Waiting turns any appointment into a chance meeting. She arrived! Then the city receded inside the shell of her open lids.

Her smile makes her eyes close a little in a gesture of yielding—to her smile.

Looking at her, my eye's iris becomes that of a slow lens that can't close all the way down to have a total fade-out.

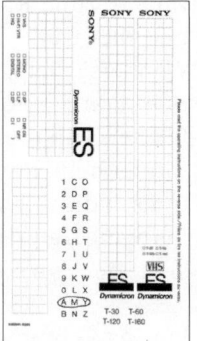

page 562   Labeling sheet included with blank VHS tapes sold by Sony.

Some shots should be extended until it becomes as difficult to know when to cut them as when to disengage from a hug.

I cannot sleep when I am next to her since sleep contains non-REM periods: how can I be in proximity to her and be without affects and images, without commotion?

Being a distracted person, I can write only when in that state. She makes me concentrate on her in her presence—and absence. She makes me sterile.

Generous: Parting, she gave him a melancholy smile. In the melancholy itself, he saw her eyes.

43

When they tried to get back together, it was too late: her "aura," that of her absence, was so established that she was eclipsed by it.

The one who fell in love with her must vanish. To go back to solitude now is to go back to a solitude where I can't keep myself company, a solitude that is no longer *my* solitude but the solitude of no one (hence contagious, but to no one), a solitude to the power two (back to this accursed number).

At times a modicum of help is necessary! Without it, that which, in us, we were trying to let wither away would be all too happy, in order to save itself, to offer us its help; and we, grateful as we are, would then offer it in return ourselves.

Helpful: the assurance help has been sent and will arrive too late.

Wenders's *Nick's Movie* is a sad, nihilistic film for a cowardly film. Wenders shows up to assist the cancer-ridden Nicholas Ray. Ray: "I started out as strong as I could and then there was a great relief when I surrendered more and more to you." All I could make out in the changing rhythm of my breathing while watching the film is from time to time Ray's piercing—for constrained between the "Action" and the "Cut"—soundless invocation: Help me, anybody, get rid of Wenders's help. For that's when others need help, and that's when one should help them: when they are being helped. They need this further help precisely and for no other reason than to get rid of the former help. Ray knows that he let Wenders steal from him what he himself did not possess but had the possibility of experimenting with: his dying. But really nothing has been stolen except counterfeit dying, since one can steal only the forged.

During a commemorative minute of silence, one should not abstain from talking but rather move one's lips without uttering any sound, thus accompanying momentarily the dead human, who might be apprehending silence-over, which would soon immobilize him or her.

The talkative silence of the *etc.*

Never summarize. Be brief.

Aphoristic writers don't *fill in the blank*.

A one-thousand-page volume that does not consist of aphorisms might contain more thought-provoking lines than a sixty-page book of aphorisms. It won't contain more "blank" time in the form of lapses of consciousness, if not of being, and more silence in the form of the absence of the interior monologue.

What connects thoughts seamlessly is not only the logical and causal links; the background of generalized linkages that is the interior monologue, rather than distracting from the link, makes it feel natural. The separation between the aphorisms, and between the sentences of an aphorism, is accentuated by aphoristic writers' absence or substantial reduction of the interior monologue. Indeed, in the absence of the interior monologue, one gets the aphoristic mode of thought—thoughts that are divested from development, come out of the blue—irrespective of whether on the page the thoughts are separated by explicit blanks. While teaching, I, an aphoristic writer, have to relax my vigilance against the interior monologue so that my speech would flow. This applies to listening, too: the internal monologue of the listener facilitates the talk of the speaker. If a thought restrains the interior monologue, people cannot concentrate on it, i.e., they become distracted, to reactivate an interior monologue (the distraction I write about elsewhere in this book is obviously of a different kind). He talked to himself no longer in the mode of an interior monologue, but in the manner of Richard Foreman's characters: when he uttered a question, he was among the ones who answered it.

Not all aphorists have a fundamental affinity with discontinuity. In some aphorists' work, the aphorism presupposes a radical continuity; it is constituted through a folding of what is continuous—interpretation is then a monadic unfolding.

The aphorism is mistakenly viewed sometimes as enunciating an opinion, sometimes as setting forth a truth. In the former case it is confounded with the saying, in the latter case it is mixed up with the maxim. But the aphorism is neither opinion nor truth. The great aphoristic writers, Nietzsche paradigmatically, are conjointly some of the keenest problematizers of the notion of truth, as well as some of those who fought most intensely against opinions. The apparent closeness of the form of the aphorism to those in which opinions or truths are coined or proffered (the proverb, the saw, the saying, the maxim) makes opinion and truth insidious risks and temptations of the aphoristic form, heightening aphoristic writers' vigilance against them. One of the main indications of this fight against opinion is the widespread presence of the dash in aphorisms. The aphoristic dash announces (a) a sudden switch in relation to an opinion that managed to insinuate itself into one's writing or (b) what will prevent what one is asserting from turning into an opinion. Nietzsche wrote: "To say in ten sentences what everyone says in a book—what everyone does *not* say in a book."[22] The first part of this aphorism is that of opinion, thus shows a common, verbose conciseness and therefore presents little obstacle for commentators wishing to proceed to explicate such ten sentences in a book. Then, across the abruptness of the dash—a different *everyone*, no longer the mundane herd, but possibly the dead/psychotic's "every name in history is I" (in the same letter in Nietzsche's handwriting, we can read: "This autumn [of 1888] ... I twice attended my funeral" and "Every name in history is I"[23]), and thus *the absence of an oeuvre* (Foucault).[24]

The aphoristic form is characterized as much by the blanks between the different aphorisms as by the dashes in the aphorisms. While it is true that aphoristic writers can be distinguished by their varying conceptions and treatment of the blanks between the aphorisms, with all of them the blanks preclude any consideration of the aphorisms as possibly contradicting each other. Contradictions do not occur between aphorisms but within the aphorism, when its latter part does an about-face, usually across a dash, to undermine an opinion that managed to insinuate itself into the first part: it is this that gives at least some aphorisms their paradoxical quality.

"It is midnight, time to ..." That's how both vampires and most people reason, the former stirring from their freezing, the latter going to sleep. As for me, it's never "time to ..."

The only freshness is the untimely.

The new, which is occasionally in the form of lies (most lies are repetitions) or of errors (most errors are repetitions), is simultaneous with every other new.

One cannot react to an action; one reacts only to a reaction.

X slapped Y on the left cheek. This slap can be an action only if contaminated neither by the thought of a reaction to it nor by that of the impossibility of a reaction to it.

There is no choice where all the alternatives are given, for choice is the creation of the alternative.

Most people eschew choice for decision, since however much time one may take to reach the latter, it is a restatement of the instantaneous determination of the resultant of the forces present then. Since it restates the outcome, a decision is redundant. Contrariwise, for choice to be possible, a resultant of the forces must be thwarted.

Those who no longer feel it is *time to* find out that time is never on time. One cannot even wait for this late time, since one can wait for time only in time.

"Time is money." In cinema, only the abstract time fabricated by the insert is money. That's why commercial filmmakers don't let time pass in the shot but go to inserts. They have more than one character in almost all scenes to be able to cut from one to the other, i.e., to use the various characters alternately as inserts and to have them use each other as inserts. If such filmmakers sometimes accept shooting single-character scenes, it is because they can resort to point-of-view shots as inserts—how many of the point-of-view shots in cinema are not merely inserts? Once you don't let time pass in the film, the film becomes a pastime.

Quickness and slowness are a matter not of how much one does in a given period but, respectively, of whether one is quicker/slower than or in sync with oneself (entangled photons, which exhibit nonlocal correlations, appear quicker than themselves).

Never hurry anyone or anything (to wait for something is to hurry it—and to place oneself in a servile condition [any kind of waiting other than the messianic one (and the amorous one?) is servile]), let each take his or her or its time. But hurry or slow down time itself.

Insofar as receiving an aphorism presupposes finding or creating a "Wall," then perforating it while refraining from forcing the aphorism's appearance, the aphorist is slower than himself/herself, but insofar as the aphorism appears fully formed, in no need of development, the aphorist is quicker than himself/herself.

Cioran says: "Very often, I would write a text of two or three pages and only keep the conclusion. This means that all the theoretical development, the entire path I have traveled, is crossed out."[25] He writes: "We must censure the later Nietzsche for a panting excess in the writing, the absence of *rests*."[26] With all due respect to Cioran, the aphorism is not a conclusion. Anyway, one must spare oneself the ostensible progress of one's thought (thought, too, occurs in a "darkroom"[27] or "changing bag"[28]). In which case, what need would one have to rest?

While clumsiness is an imbalance of forces—like an incompetent physics student, the body overlooks a number of forces when making a summation to get the resultant force—awkwardness is a matter of speeds, of being quicker and slower than oneself. It is the offbeat elegance of aphoristic writers.

I was in a hurry to meet her. She was not in a hurry to meet me. How could we not miss each other?

The mask does not change; whenever I have a discontinuous temporality, more precisely an atomic one, where there is no gradual change by transitions, but rather recurrent appearance, then disappearance, then appearance again of a more or less different face, I have, as a result, masks irrespective of whether material masks or exaggerated makeup—a substitute for a physical mask—are placed over the faces. The absence of transition as such changes faces into masks (when there is an actual physical mask, it is just a materialization of the absence of transition). The faces that would result from the atomic temporality of the Ash'arite theologians are masks. The mask is either the transition *par excellence*, being the result of the swish pan of one's gaze as a result of fear, or else the absence of transition, a result of temporal atomism. Therefore, the mask implies that I am missing something, but not behind it: rather at its location, when it implies my gaze's swish pan in fear; or between it and the next mask, when it results from an atomic temporality. Eisenstein, a proponent of montage, wrote, "The first and most striking example [of methods of montage in the Japanese theater, particularly in acting], of course, is the purely cinematographic method of 'acting without transitions.' ... At a certain moment of his performance he [the Kabuki actor] halts; the black shrouded *kurogo* obligingly conceals him from the spectators. And lo!—he is resurrected in a new make-up. And in a new wig. Now characterizing another stage (degree) of his emotional state."[29] We have such "acting without transitions" in Kurosawa's *Dreams*. In "The Blizzard" section, we first see the Siren-like smiling face of a beautiful young woman; then her face is obscured by her hair flapping in the wind; then again we see her face but now it is an angry one; then again it is hidden by her hair; then again we see the face as the hair is removed from it by the wind: it is now that of a terrifying old man. We thus get different stages of the action without any transition between them. This absence of the transition changes the face into a mask. We thus have masks in *Dreams* not only in the first section, "Rainbow," where (the spirits of) the foxes are physically masked; and in the section "The Tunnel," where the revenants' faces are made-up into black zones around the eyes and white ones elsewhere so that they form masks; but also in "The Blizzard" section.

When he, a physicist, first encountered Minkowski's formulation of relativity in terms of space-time, he was not perplexed and felt no resistance to it, since it confirmed his experience: he was unaware of any flow of time. He was aware of movement only. "But if you are aware of movement, then you are aware of time, since, according to

Aristotle, 'time is number of movement in respect of the before and after.'"[30] He was untouched by that Aristotelian definition of time. Nothing could make him feel that there is time. Not even music? No, for he subscribed to Schopenhauer's view that "music is ... a *copy of the will itself*,"[31] which is beyond the principle of sufficient reason, that is, beyond time, space, and causality. Fundamentally, music is not a temporal medium. One day, he was dumbfounded while watching a film. In his diary, he wrote: "Today for the first time, I have experientially witnessed time, in a film. I will go back tomorrow and watch the film again, to make sure that I was not the victim of some illusion." When he returned the next day, he got his confirmation. The first time a filmmaker produced time in the medium of film, it became a potentiality of that medium. Only cinema is a temporal medium, occasionally. Film ostensibly preserves time only secondarily, for it has first to produce it. From then on, he felt neither that time does not exist nor that it is pervasive, but that it is rare. He watched films less to see images than to occasionally experience time.

When my interior monologue is suspended, I am convinced of what Einstein's relativity indicates: there is no passage of time. But while the passage of time may be an illusion in the world, it is not so in fiction. Thus fiction is our way to make the world, otherwise preserved in relativity's block universe of four-dimensional space-time, transient. Great fiction preserves a world it has first made transient.

If the past were not preserved in itself, if the past vanished, the photographic image would disappear as soon as it was "recorded," filmed, taped. The film or video shot is a window onto a small section of the Minkowski block universe, where there is no passage of time, no transience, where things and events are preserved as such.

If an essential function of the cinematic image is to preserve, then anything that is self-preserving does not appear in cinematic recordings; the Bergsonian past and God cannot then appear in cinema. If "cinema films death at work" (Cocteau), it is also because to film something is to imply that it does not preserve itself, that it is subject to some variant of death, and consequently that it requires cinema in order to be preserved.

Preservation through TV images produces a *memory for forgetfulness* (Mahmoud Darwish).

All forms of indexical preservation are becoming secondary. Digital emulation (perfect simulation) will become the major form of preservation—of even what never existed actually.

'Āshūrā', Twelver Shi'ites' yearly commemoration of imam Husayn's slaughter alongside many members of his family in Karbala in 680, is less to remember that historical event than to slowly, along the years, decades, and centuries, imbue in Shi'ites the feeling that that event cannot be reduced to historical reality but belongs also in part to '*ālam al-mithāl/'ālam al-khayāl* (the Imaginal World)—the visionary realm where bodies are made incorporeal and spirits and Intelligences are materialized—where it is in no need of preservation but preserves itself. That event insists at the exoteric (*ẓāhir*) level, through the yearly commeration of 'Āshūrā'; but it also subsists at another level, esoteric (*bāṭin*), in '*ālam al-mithāl*. We have the urge to repeat such an event not to historically preserve it, but so that in the long run we would come to feel that that event is already preserved. What we are apprehensive about is not so much forgetting such an event as forgetting that it is preserved, that it preserves itself. And the repetitions, with the inevitable introduction of variations, signal to us that it is not preserved as it happened historically. We repeat so that, as a result of the inevitable small variations from one repetition to the next, the commemorated event would come to approximate how it is preserved ... in '*ālam al-mithāl* (we still have to discriminate, in the hagiographic literature, what is supposititious from what belongs to the Imaginal World).

Imam Husayn is reported to have said to Umm Salama: "I know the day and hour, and the spot wherein I shall be killed. I know the place whereon I shall fall ... and the spot in which I shall be buried, as I know you."[32] Weakening and failing one's destiny do not necessarily reside in trying to avoid or flee the scene where the fatidic event is projected to occur or in attempting to repress such knowledge, but in totally reducing the event to the historical time in which it also occurs. The temptation here lies in reducing destiny to, and living it as, (only) a future event. The test of Husayn and his followers is to maintain an unbridgeable subtle difference between the actualization in the world of his slaughter at Karbalā' on the tenth of Muharram AH 61, and that event as part of '*ālam al-mithāl/'ālam al-khayāl* (the Imaginal World)—the visionary realm where bodies are made incorporeal and spirits and Intelligences are materialized. Husayn's words are not a simple prediction, since at the level of the visionary '*ālam al-khayāl* the event has already happened even as he speaks to Umm Salama. It is thus that in the hagiographic literature, for example in Muḥammad Bāqir Majlisī's *Biḥār al-Anwār*, when passing the spot of Karbala, the prophets Adam, Noah, Abraham, Moses, and Jesus felt, often as a physical pain, the "aura" of the slaughter that is yet to happen in historical time.

Who better than Shi'ites, this community of the surpassing disaster, have thought occultation and withdrawal: the Ismā'īlīs' cycles of occultation, during which the esoteric sense should not be divulged; and the occultation of the twelfth imam of Twelver Shi'ites—whether it be the Lesser Occultation (when the imam was part of the world but hidden, communicating with his followers by means of his deputies), or the Greater Occultation that followed it (when he is no longer in the world)? Who as much as they has tried to resurrect what has been withdrawn: the Great Resurrection of Alamūt under the Nizārī Ḥasan *ʿalā dhikrihi'l-salām* (on his mention be peace)?

The one who is *absolutely modern* (Rimbaud) and the resurrector of tradition are both reacting to the surpassing disaster, which produces a withdrawal of tradition;[33] while the modernist or postmodernist and the traditionalist are not. Thus the one who is absolutely modern has more affinity with the resurrector of tradition than with the modernist or the postmodernist; and the resurrector of tradition has infinitely more affinity with the absolutely modern than with the traditionalist oblivious of the withdrawal of tradition past a surpassing disaster.

Even if all at first arrive in Paradise, only a few linger there. To ascertain that, go to a great performance of santur music: soon enough, you will witness people leaving the auditorium!

I walked for so long my shoes, in mint condition when I left, were in tatters. I bought new ones. Only then did the trip begin.

In Woody Allen's *Side Effects*, Abraham Lincoln is asked how long a man's legs should be: "Long enough to reach the ground." Almost a Zen answer? Asked how it feels after attaining satori, D. T. Suzuki answered: "Just like ordinary everyday experience, except about two inches off the ground!"

She goes down slowly and reaches the ground. One feels she has to descend even lower. And indeed, the male ballet dancer soon stands on his tiptoes, virtually raising the surface with him.

They regard themselves as different because of their failure to imitate. Unfortunately, they all fail to imitate in the same way.

"One repays a teacher badly if one remains only a pupil," writes Nietzsche (*Thus Spoke Zarathustra*)—also if one remains later only a teacher.

All they do is comment on their quotes from one author by paraphrasing what another author wrote.

When I am quoting something to *most people*, I feel I am paraphrasing it.

Style as the only legitimate quotation marks (the one without style is ever paraphrasing himself). Hence the redundancy of enclosing within quotation marks the words of someone who has a style.

His dignified grace manifested itself in his refusal to persuade.

They felt sometimes annoyed with him for what they considered an attempt to impress them with his ideas, when in fact he was getting rid of those thoughts of his he considered merely smart but without any necessity by drowning them in the anonymous noise of simultaneous conversations where it is no longer clear who said what, who heard what, who did not hear what. The advantage of being solitary is that one does not waste too much time with and on people, but the disadvantage is that one is less able to exclude from the book what should be merely said and wasted in conversation. Had they not forced him to despise them so much, thus precluding his having conversations with them, his book would have been more exacting.

Alone at night
The mind blank like a white paper
And the white paper

The fade-in in many a film functions as the nicest alarm.

One used to come to school late every morning not because one was too sleepy, but because the class made one so.

A book had to be of a critical size so that the look would remain focused inside it and not slip away to the world. It had to form a horizon and it did. But soon wrist-sized computer monitors will be widespread. Words will then become subtitles to the world: the world as foreign.

It is not on the day of arrival from abroad but only on the second day that one feels very tired, as if one's tiredness were a suitcase that got lost in some airport or other on those flights with two stopovers, and that arrives a day or so after one's own arrival. Direct flights from the United States to Lebanon are illegal. One buys a Chicago-London-Amman ticket. Once one gets to the airport in London, the ticket is changed automatically to a London-Beirut one. One soon discovers, however, that one's tiredness is proportional not to a Chicago-London-Beirut trip but to a Chicago-London-Amman-Beirut trip.

To forgive is to forget. A misanthrope would add: to forget is to forgive.

The moment is eternal, hence eternity should end in one moment: the logic of pain.

In all the shots in which he appears, he is a reflection in mirrors or water or is framed by a painting on the wall behind him, becoming his own image, something that does not feel pain. A high ratio of such shots in a film or video (Bill Viola's *Migration*) is frequently symptomatic of a director hypersensitive to pain.

The out-of-focus of weeping eyes. Suddenly feeling that, like a shot lit by a spotlight is visually harsh, an in-focus shot is excessively sharp focused.

Sometimes tears that did not nucleate around any incident.

Lebanon. Nothing left, not even leaving.

As a result of the damage to the power stations in Lebanon, only twelve hours of electricity are available daily. Like the sun, electricity rises and sets in Lebanon.

They were discussing which theme to do for the next episode of a cultural program to be aired on a Lebanese TV channel. One of them suggested that they do it on night: "Then we can work on *day for night*, etc." I wonder whether, unlike a camera set to Auto mode, our pupils widen ever so minimally when we hear or say or read the word *night*, as if to compensate for the darkness that is projected by that term. He was starting to unbutton her shirt on the night of February 7, 2000, when the room became suddenly dark: "What happened?" "Most likely, Israel has once more bombed the power stations." The next day they heard that there had indeed been a devastating Israeli attack on three power stations, in which ten people died and fifty-four were wounded, and that, as a result, power rationing had been reintroduced, limiting power availability to just six to seven hours daily, to be progressively increased over the next six to seven months. The nocturnal is not reserved for the night in Lebanon: even during daylight, doesn't a shade of the night appear every time the electricity is off due to electricity-rationing? Yes. The vampire sensed this, told his agent: "I stir in my coffin in Lebanon for the interval between the cutting off of electricity due to rationing and the turning on of private generators." The insomniac asked the person he'd just met and who, unbeknownst to him, was a vampire: "Are you an insomniac?" Indeed, he was, since he neither slept during the night, when he woke up, nor during the day, when he was frozen.

The vampire's pursuers arrived during daylight at his lair, waited for him to stir out of his freezing when the electricity was suddenly off due to rationing, and fatally stabbed him. Through this additional period of darkness during which they do not sleep, the Lebanese have turned into quasi-insomniacs. The periodic power cuts have allowed me, who is otherwise not an insomniac, to better appreciate the two insomniacs E. M. Cioran and my friend the filmmaker and writer Ghassan Salhab. The night following the attack on the power stations, he went with two friends for dinner at Ban Thai, a small restaurant in Achrafieh. After taking their orders, the waitress returned to light the candles. He was on the verge of commenting that he'd had it with this mawkishness when the lights were off. The significance of the candles altered. The following day, each of the three friends present at the dinner lectured in his respective academic setting on a subject having to do with night: one, critically, on the ersatz cinematic reflexivity in Truffaut's *Day for Night* (1973); the second on the night that suspends *the night of the world* ("Yesterday, in *the night of the world*, ten people died in the Israeli air raids on power stations. One could see bloody heads, severed hands with crossed fingers, etc. These same people, now dead, must be experiencing 'the human being [each of them is as] ... this night, this empty nothing, that contains everything in its simplicity—an unending wealth of presentations, images, none of which occurs to him or is present. This night ... exists here—this pure self—in phantasmagorical presentations ... here shoots out a bloody head, there a white shape.... One catches sight of this night when one looks human beings in the eye—this night that becomes awful suspends the night of the world in an opposition' [from Hegel's manuscripts for the *Realphilosophie* of 1805/1806])";[34] and the third on how in eternity, it is not light that is in the world but the inverse, the world is in light, and on how, when entities exist not in the world but in light, there is no alternation of day and night, for night, the absence of light, would then be the absence of entities—in eternity, "night is also a sun" (Nietzsche's Zarathustra: "A haze and fragrance of eternity? ... Do you not smell it? Just now my world became perfect, midnight is also noon ... night is also a sun"[35]).

Was it because no adequate monument to Beirut was produced in the aftermath of the war, whether in literature, cinema, video, or the other arts, that there occurred the strange, excessive postwar unconscious expectation that the whole city, or at least its destroyed Central District, would be preserved as a monument to itself and to the war? People could repress the traumatic past with a relatively good conscience as long as the memory embodied in the war-damaged buildings subsisted. It seems people could not tolerate that this collective, physical memory, the memory of "everyone and *no one*" (Nietzsche), was being erased, that each had now to assume and access the traumatic memory through his or her anamnesis. At a certain level, the frustration and anger at what Solidere, the company in charge of the reconstruction and development of Beirut's Central District, is doing finds one of its sources here.

Coming back to Lebanon from the United States, the absence of dance adds to the constriction one feels in this very small country, since the country's surface area is not virtually augmented by the space into which dance projects. Near the beginning of Vincente Minnelli's *An American in Paris*, the Gene Kelly character awakens from sleep in the small room where he lives and effortlessly raises his bed to the ceiling by a pulley and, with stylized gestures, moves a chair and a folding table out of the closet. The space that seemed at first barely large enough to be a bedroom becomes wide enough to be also a living room. This scene foreshadows, in a form that's easy to accept, the subsequent actual creation of space by the dancer, who is projected by dance into a drawing and then into various paintings and who creates depth in these surfaces at the pace of his movement. The originality of Minnelli's cinematic adaptation of these drawings and paintings is that he does it through the diegetic agency of a dancer, for this has as a consequence that the sections where the dancer has not yet moved and created space continue to be two-dimensional, painted or drawn backdrops, acting as traces of where the cinematic adaptation started from.

— You're mad.
— No, I am a *no*mad—to flee the flight of the world.

"What is this video about?" This question was put to me despite the stipulation *No questions asked* included in the ad for actors and crew. Lebanese filmmakers, and more so video makers, should not make films or videos to try to understand and make understandable what happened during the war years. While social scientists, whether sociologists, economists, etc., can provide us with more or less convincing reasons, and mystifiers can grossly nonplus us, valid literature and art provide us with intelligent and subtle incomprehension. One of the main troubles with the world is that, unlike art and literature, it allows only for the gross alternative: understanding/ incomprehension. Contrariwise, art and literature do not provide us with the illusion of comprehending, of grasping, but allow us to keenly not understand, intimating to us that the alternative is not between comprehension and incomprehension but between incomprehension in a gross manner while expecting comprehension and incomprehension in an intelligent and subtle manner. Great films and works of literature make even those who have researched the economic, sociological, and geopolitical reasons for the famines in

Ethiopia, Sudan, and North Korea; the continuing sanctions against Iraq; the massacres in Rwanda; the ethnic cleansing in Kosovo not understand these catastrophes, but intelligently and subtly. Art extracts the event from the reasons for its occurrence—even when it recreates these in a fiction. Valid films make us perceive the difference between understanding the reasons for an event and understanding the event. We who already see clearly in Lebanon the unchecked proliferation of buildings along shorelines and hills; the legalized wiretapping of phones, etc., and consequently desperately warn against ensuing disasters while so many others are oblivious to them, will nonetheless, when these disasters actually happen, make films and videos that show our subtle and intelligent incomprehension of them. If I found it difficult to teach, certainly when I started doing it, it was because students wanted, expected, demanded to understand. While I could somewhat tolerate this attitude in universities in the USA, I cannot stand it in Lebanon. While films, especially Lebanese ones, produced by people who suffered fifteen years of war, should allow us not to understand in an intelligent and subtle manner, theory should make us see (the Arabic an-naẓarī means both "the theoretical," and al-mansūb ilá an-naẓar, what is attributed to vision): "At the end of the calculations and observations it was noticed that Jupiter and Saturn went according to the calculations, but that Uranus was doing something funny. Another opportunity for Newton's Laws to be found wanting; but take courage! Two men, [John Couch] Adams and [Urbain] Leverrier, who made these calculations independently and at almost exactly the same time, proposed that the motions of Uranus were due to an unseen planet, and they wrote letters to their respective observatories telling them—'Turn your telescope and look there and you will find a planet.' 'How absurd,' said one of the observatories, 'some guy sitting with pieces of paper and pencils can tell us where to look to find some new planet.' The other observatory ... found Neptune!"[36] I would advance (polemically?): a cinema, especially a national one, can exist without cameras (as was made manifest by such films as Len Lye's A Colour Box [1935] and Free Radicals [1958], with their painted or scratched film stock, and Stan Brakhage's Mothlight [1963], which "was created ... by simply pressing moth wings, leaves, and other organic objects between two strips of Mylar tape and then ... running it through an optical printer"[37]); without editing (Warhol's Empire [1965]); without projection for the living in the cinemas of the world, in an art for the dead à la that of ancient Egypt ("While today we marvel at the glittering treasures from the tomb of Tutankhamun, the sublime reliefs in New Kingdom tombs, and the serene beauty of Old Kingdom statuary, it is imperative to remember that the majority of these works were never intended to be seen—that was simply not their purpose. These images, whether statues or reliefs, were designed to benefit a divine or deceased recipient"[38]); but it cannot exist for long, thrive, without theory regarding it.

The title of *LA Weekly*'s review of the retrospective *CineArabic* was "Arab Chic." Setting aside the political problem of word association that draws on stereotypes, here in the form of the similarity of pronunciation of "chic" and "sheik," it is instructive to contrast such a lazy, stereotypical journalistic link with two artistic practices. Pierre Reverdy wrote of the image: "It cannot be born of a comparison, but only of the bringing together of two more or less distant realities. The more the relations of the two realities brought together are distant and fitting, the stronger the image"[39] (*Nord-Sud*, no. 13, March 1918). The events of some Raymond Roussel works go from one phrase to an almost identical one but with a different meaning. To go from *les lettres du blanc sur les bandes du vieux billard* (the white letters on the cushions of the old billiard table) to *les lettres du blanc sur les bandes du vieux pillard* (the white man's letters on the hordes of the old plunderer), one has to cross all the events and geographies of *Among the Blacks* or *Impressions of Africa*. *Les lettres du blanc sur les bandes du vieux billard* and *les lettres du blanc sur les bandes du vieux pillard* can be said to be "more or less distant": more distant in terms of meaning ("the white letters on the cushions of the old billiard table" and "the white man's letters on the hordes of the old plunderer"), less distant in terms of the words of the phrase, the difference between them being limited to one letter, a *b* (of *billard*) replaced by a *p* (of *pillard*). (The risk one faces when one works with these virtually identical entities is the proliferation of doubles.) In case the universe, which started in a singularity, were to implode back to a singularity, I would like to imagine that the difference between the two would be of the same measure as that between the *b* (of *billard*) and the *p* (of *pillard*) in Roussel's two phrases, the whole universe coming to pass through this minimal difference between the singularity of the Big Bang and that of the Big Crunch: *impressions of the universe*. Style: from *les lettres du blanc sur les bandes du vieux billard* to *les lettres du blanc sur les bandes du vieux pillard*, across a universe of events. No image is created from the association of such stylish literature and affined films with American film criticism, especially the journalistic kind.

She's sitting on the subway seat opposite mine. Her beat-up sneaker, and, just a little higher, the tenderness and smoothness of the skin of her leg: as if each had a different life.

Elias Canetti: "A Night book, of which not a single line was ever written by day. In parallel, a real diary, always written by day. Keep the two separate for a few years, never compare them and never mix them up. Their final confrontation."[40] Was this entry written during the day or at night? Is their confrontation to occur at sunset or at sunrise? Or would it occur when both are co-present, each occupying a different part of the field of vision: a diurnal sky over a nocturnal landscape with a lit streetlamp and a house with its lights on (Magritte's *L'Empire des Lumières*)?

Christ: "But when you give to the needy, do not let your left hand know what your right hand is doing" (Matthew 6:3). That is, don't applaud—unless you're a Zen master: "What is the sound of one hand clapping?"[41]

Drunk. Each hand is alone now, does not instinctively know where the other one is.

Sober people feel that drunk ones reveal too much, but every drunk person knows that he reveals far less of himself during his inebriation than the sober ones reveal to him while he is drunk.

Tipsy, I am feeling that every label on the liquor bottles is tacitly uttered.

The wind is moving round and round like a dizzy drunkard, and it is we who fall.

The sound of a bell has a resonance that does not so much propagate across as *dissolve* the distance between things.

An aphoristic writer is from time to time interrupted by ideas and sentences, which never come on time.

Nightclub. I asked in turn three women for a dance. Three *Nos*. Now waiting, like a woman, for the idea to come to me.

Most people earn money by working from one specified hour to another. Is it surprising that they spend that money exclusively on activities that start and finish at designated times (almost everything is labeled with "Sell-By ...")?

Grand Central Station. As soon as the hurried people have the apprehension that they will get at their destination before the appointed time, they begin to trip or to collide against each other. Anything is permissible, even becoming temporarily inefficient, so long as it allows them not to get too early somewhere, for then somewhere becomes nowhere, and time, long imprisoned behind the hands of watches, floods all clocks. Remains that which these immortality-loving people abhor the most: the sterility of time.

Not to evade time as waste through wasting time.

The everyday is that to which I am repeatedly inattentive: every day I inattentively shave carefully, every day I inattentively hang my trousers neatly. Something I see or do daily but to which I pay complete, detached attention does not become an everyday activity, is not repeated from one day to another even if it occurs in each.

They repeat to forget what has been forgotten.

There is no necessary link between attempting suicide and being suicidal. Suicidal people *live* in a suicidal manner. Moreover, while in the case of a non suicidal person who ends up killing himself there is, however minimally, the sort of surprise one witnesses in films and books on doubles when the protagonist fleetingly realizes that while ostensibly mortally stabbing the other he has fatally stabbed himself, the one who is suicidal experiences no surprise as he or she falls mortally wounded after shooting himself or herself.

Given that clichés are implicated in the unconscious, and given that the unconscious does not admit of negation, clichés can be undone by prefixing a "no" to them *only* by the one who has no unconscious, for example, the yogi, or the mystic in moments of *fanā'*, of annihilation [in God], and with respect to what has no unconscious, God—we find ourselves here in negative theology, with its apophatic utterances that negate all clichés about God: existence, name, etc. ("What Is the Divine Darkness?," Chapter One of Dionysius the Areopagite's *The Mystical Theology*, begins with these words: "Supernal Triad, Deity above all essence, knowledge and goodness").

In Islam the world itself is a series of *ayāt* (signs) that hint about its Creator. Thus in the Muslim philosopher Abū Bakr b. Ṭufayl's philosophical allegory, *Ḥayy b. Yaqzān* (*Living, Son of Wakeful*), a person who is alone on an island, with no communication with others, including messengers, whether human (prophets) or angelic, reaches by reason alone the tenets of Islam. Contrariwise, communication receives an essential role both in a Gnostic world, since nothing in the world can act as a sign toward the alien God, who has to send someone to tell us about Him; and in a world where teleportation(/numerical emulation) has become possible, since the addresser himself or herself can then be communicated (these two aspects of essential communication are present in Lana and Lilly Wachowski's *The Matrix* [1999]).

Loneliness, for one can no longer meet people. Utter loneliness, as one has lost the ability to meet streets, words, images. Then loneliness disappears, for one no longer meets oneself—except sometimes a drop of rain passes slowly all the way from hair to lips.

The tree outside the window. For a while today there was no boundary between us and I knew that the shit *in* me is manure for it.

June 26, 1987. I felt shy passing a tree and the grass.

The last page finished, closing the book. It is as if rain had just stopped and one can go outside.

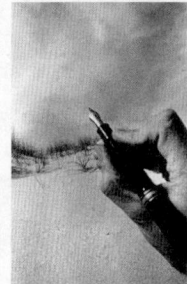

page 563

May 1989. I took LSD for the first time. Three of my friends are conversing next to me. Then I deduce that I must have undergone a lapse of consciousness. Presently distance itself has receded. Passersby walk in slow motion. Their voices change in loudness, cease at times even while they continue moving their lips. Everything becomes frozen momentarily. Then I anxiously call my friends. They turn and look at me without recognizing me, extremely annoyed that I have disturbed them. I walk away on the sand: my feet begin turning into sand ones! I see four persons standing across the playground. Not only does no sound reach me from them, but they seem so far away that my first thought on how to communicate with them is to send them letters. I now remember any past event either as part of a conspiracy to make me take the psychedelic or as a hallucination that I had after taking it—but did I really take it? Or is it rather that I have always been like this, and the events I remember as happening before taking the psychedelic as well as the event of taking it are themselves hallucinations? I have to evade the conspiracy making me think in terms of conspiracies. In Islam, the outcast devil whispers to one; on hallucinogens, it is outcast reality that whispers to one. I walk to the public phones. The three are occupied. I wait, then walk away so as not to witness with my own eyes or with my own hallucinations the talkers go on speaking forever. A while later, I walk back to the phones. One of them is free: at last, to speak on the phone with reality! I call Mick; no answer. I call Janalle; no answer. I call Mark. Mark's voice. I have to redirect the words in their physical shape before saying them to him: if a word is facing in the wrong direction when uttered, the meaning will come out all wrong or be gibberish. "Can you meet me in fifteen minutes?" Some time later,

I ask a woman about the time. "6:30." Fifteen minutes must have passed since my conversation with Mark. I find it trying to continue waiting for him, for if he doesn't show up in a few minutes, this may imply that I have hallucinated the conversation with him. I begin to move away. Fortunately, I espy Mark coming in my direction. I tell him that I took LSD and suggest we go to Mick and Katherine's apartment and then to a restaurant. In the car, I ask him what time it is. He says: "6:30." I am seized with the dread that time had stopped. "Show me your wrist!" He does. I look at his watch. It is 6:33. Great relief. He buzzes Mick and Katherine. No answer. He looks around and says: "Strange, their car is here." Why did he say that? Did he really say that? We go to a diner. The objects there are illuminated by their own light, which, however bright, does not provide any additional illumination for adjoining objects. When a body is illuminated by such a light, it seems to be framed and to have an aura. We order. An interval of silence follows. I observe Mark. Using very short time intervals in photography, the pose of the person is undone. Going to even more elementary intervals one gets to expressions of preconscious processing of subliminal stimuli; these fraction-of-a-second appearances/expressions, which usually cancel each other at the level of large time intervals, are seen during an LSD trip. To displace my attention away from these micro-appearances/expressions that I am glimpsing on Mark's face, I start talking: "John Corbett decided to go to Milwaukee because he was tipped that an LP by Beuys and Paik that sells in Germany for fifteen hundred dollars can be purchased in a record store in Milwaukee for twenty dollars. When he, Michael, and I got there, he didn't buy it. We went to a restaurant. They had a sign with the word THINK attached to the glass window …" I interrupt myself. Does he think I am delirious? For why would a record sell in Germany for $1500 and for only $20 in Milwaukee? Why would John drive there to buy it and then not do that? Why would the sign "THINK" be on a restaurant's glass window?

The schizophrenic and the person undergoing a bad psychedelic trip have experienced labyrinthine temporality and have felt terrifying disorientation. The reason many of them nonetheless do not commit suicide is that the rationale for doing so, namely, labyrinthine time, is itself what rules out the belief in a death that would happen at a definite time, ending everything.

Once the *imaginary line* that separates life and death is crossed, one is struck by how, due to over-turns, one's dialogues with others disintegrate into monologues, the dead turning their backs to, and thus on, one, and one turning, against one's will, one's back to the living; but also how one's monologues are simultaneously dialogues (with the voices in one's head).

In a café, three weeks after taking LSD and witnessing how distant the world can be, how far objects can recede: the coffee cup is near again! This joy at feeling I am going out on a date with a cup of coffee.

The world has been so distant that now that I can again touch things I feel I am caressing them irrespective of any movement of the hand.

Those who postpone often order their experiences and thoughts *to go*. This is not possible during an LSD trip. If at all, it is LSD that orders us *to go*: flashbacks.

The relation with the past has nothing to do with memory and everything to do with telepathy.

Night. Trees under which darkness hides from darkness.

One penetrates mystery only by becoming a mystery (owing to the obliteration of the Sufi and his vision in the stage of *fanā'* [annihilation (in God)], his vision becomes a mystery not only to others but also to him during the subsequent stage of *baqā'* [subsistence]).

The revelation of a genuine secret is not dependent on those who were involved in, or witnessed, the event it refers to, for it is a secret to them, too: did the event really happen? If so, what happened?

A secret cannot be revealed, since its revelation introduces the *speaker* and the listener into another world or realm—hence it is as dangerous to hear a secret as to tell one. The real secret is this furtive displacement.

A secret cannot be made manifest, because, like a black hole, it imprisons that which makes visible.

Only schizophrenics have the right to use voice-over, since they suffer from it.

It would be stupefying if there is not even one play where a character, and we with him, hears the prompter or a prompter, for example, because he is mad.

Although a mortal, I am not fluent in any of the languages of the voices!

Conscious malice always bored him; only unconscious evil interested and scared him. Was it anomalous that conscious malice should bore him when it was itself the product of boredom?

How to know whether one is changing or not when the measure of change, time, is itself mutating?

That phrase, "Sunday, March 2, 1986. I touched a branch," may somehow save me from labyrinthine time.

You cannot imagine, J. J., how excessively old I was while writing *(Vampires)*. Age difference is the possible objection to a relationship between us, but not in the way you think: not the fact that you are thirteen years older than me, but that I have become infinitely older than you as a consequence of dying before dying.

The two extremes of solitude: that experienced during a bad LSD trip, when a zoom-out of the world occurs and humans become lifeless extras; and, for a writer, that of no longer believing in the existence of untimely collaborators.

The absence of untimely collaborators cannot be remedied, except, perhaps, by going through a dissociation à la Allan Gray's in Dreyer's *Vampyr*, but with the attendant danger of one of the dissociated entities turning against the other as its double.

While it is true that "dying ... is essentially mine in such a way that no one can be my representative" (Heidegger),[42] with the exception of that of spiritual masters such as yogis, one's death is purloined by some double across the lapse of consciousness, if not of being, at the *imaginary line* between life and death.

After the experience, through dying before physically dying, of the great desertion by the world, including, through the over-turn, by oneself, who is part of the world, and the realization of how alone one is in death, it is difficult not to drift into solitude, any talk becoming insignificant as long it cannot, like certain lamas' recitation of the *Bardo Thödol* (literally *Liberation through Hearing in the In-Between State*), overcome the unreachableness of the dead (while images no longer reach the dead from the world of the living, a certain voice may still reach them, that of the Tibetan monk or ancient Egyptian lector priest reciting from their respective books of the dead). Nonetheless, and despite this basic aloneness of mortals in general, every artist and writer, even the most solitary one, is an untimely collaborator. His or her untimely collaboration can be with his or her amnesiac variant on the other side of the threshold of death, but also with other creators across time. What is intuition? It is both the connection, out of direct awareness, to what one experienced in an altered realm of body or consciousness, such as dance or death, that one reached and "left" across lapses of consciousness, if not of being; as well as the untimely collaboration with future dancers, writers, thinkers, etc., who, as creators, are not wedged fully in chronological time. It is because of this untimely collaboration that many artists don't feel any urge to collaborate with explicit, historically contemporary others. What makes letters in literary books irreducible to a private affair is not only that they are refracted through formal issues but also that one collaborated in an untimely way with future writers or artists in writing them. Is it possible for me to physically die before I fulfill my part of an untimely collaboration whose resultant is already present (for example, one of Francis Bacon's paintings), i.e., before I accomplish what I had seemingly already done?

If one is not a spiritual master, for example, a Zen master or yogi, then one can receive from the death realm only creatively; literature, radio art, and film are three of the main ways for us to receive from the death realm, but one should bear in mind that one cannot use film as a medium to reveal certain characteristics of death only to then discard the attributes of film, for the measurement apparatus with which we observe a phenomenon that has to do with the unconscious/ sum-over-histories of subatomic particles in quantum physics (just as the unconscious, which does not recognize negation, preserves con- tradictory wishes and possibilities, so too does the sum-over-histories of quantum entities allow multiple, even incompatible, trajectories to coexist in superposition) affects the phenomenon that's studied. The dead and schizophrenics, who are assailed by the thoughts inserted in them and who are often in dispossession of their own thoughts, may receive back from the writer their thoughts, which he or she received from them through *creative* writing. While the first edition of *Distracted* was written for the living, *(Vampires)* wasn't, at least not solely and fundamentally (there is a tradition of writing and art addressed to the dead: the *Bardo Thödol*, the *Egyptian Book of the Dead*, most Egyptian statues and reliefs[43]). That is why, while I was not dis- heartened by the meager reception (by the living) of *(Vampires)*, I was so by the disregard of the first edition of *Distracted*. But should I have been disheartened by the latter? With the widening dissolution of the aura, as a result of the loss of distance in the twentieth century (a phenomenon addressed by Walter Benjamin in his essay "The Work of Art in the Age of Mechanical Reproduction," and by José Ortega y Gasset in *The Revolt of the Masses*), has not aphoristic writing become anachronistic?

Distracted's first edition did not vaccinate against itself, since no part of it had already been published (in articles, etc.).

I resided in Lebanon for seventeen years. My deceased father was Iraqi. My mother is a Lebanese citizen of Palestinian origin (born in Haifa). "How does it feel" (Bob Dylan)—*does it still feel?* (Jalal Toufic)—to be related to three countries that have become synonyms for devastation? Was *Distracted* simultaneously what resulted from, what was salvaged from, and what resisted this devastation? Yes, it still feels. Will *Distracted* itself manage to withstand the devastation of *(Vampires)*, a work that resulted and was salvaged from another devastation, dying before dying, and tried to resist the latter's negative aspects? An old acquaintance who did not try to dissuade me from finishing and publishing *(Vampires)* strongly advised against publishing a revised edition of *Distracted* (an alternate title for this edition could be *Distracted Revision*). He does not seem to understand that *(Vampires)* is the real threat to *Distracted*. The "Author's Note" to the 1991 edition indicates that *Distracted* and *(Vampires)* form the two volumes of one book: this was largely a defensive measure to ward off the eventuality that *(Vampires)*, which was initially to be my second book, turn into a double of *Distracted*, subverting and ruining it.

Bonus:
An Interview with Jalal Toufic[44]
by Aaron Kunin

Most things that are strange are actually strange in a fairly predict-able way—e.g., "You're different from me, but I understand you completely; I know exactly what you're going to say." Jalal Toufic, who is, in his own description, "a writer, film theorist, and video artist," writes books that really are different from anything else I've encountered. To say, for example, that they're about film or dance would distort the way in which they're engaged with—or obsessed with—these subjects. To say that they're about politics or psychology would require forgetting their fundamental disengagement from politics as it is usually practiced, and from conventional accounts of consciousness. To say that they're autobiographical would be missing the point: they're about death and undeath as well as life. Toufic's books include *Distracted* (Station Hill, 1991), *(Vampires): An Uneasy Essay on the Undead in Film* (Station Hill, 1993), *Over-Sensitivity* (Sun and Moon, 1996), and the recent *Forthcoming* (Atelos, 2000). His video and installation works include *Credits Included: A Video in Red and Green* and *Radical Closure Artist with Bandaged Sense Organ*. He lives in Beirut.

The following interview was conducted by email between February and May 2001. Generically quite various, it includes letters, scenarios, and short essays. There's frequently a distinct contrast between my somewhat pedestrian questions and Toufic's extrav-agant responses; at one point, he uses one of my questions as the answer to another question. Rather than a detached commentary or conventional profile, the interview is here conceived as an extension of Toufic's writing.

Aaron Benjamin Kunin:
How would you characterize your writing formally? You frequently cite Nietzsche as a model "laconic" writer, but "laconic" suggests a limited formal range, whereas your recent books include dialogues, scenarios, texts for installations, essays, and letters, as well as aphorisms. Do you consider all of these to be laconic forms in the same sense?

Jalal Toufic:
At one level, every fine work of art or literature is laconic: it is because an artwork is the densest manner of rendering and conveying some-thing that it cannot be properly viewed in terms of a message—if a reader insists on speaking of the message of an artwork or of a literary work, he or she should consider it to be the latter as a whole. At another level, only artworks and literary works that effect in their

readers or viewers an absence of the interior monologue with its associations are laconic.

ABK:
I'm particularly interested in the way you use letters.

JT:
Two of the joyous events of my life were related to letters. I remember a period of about three months during the writing of (Vampires) when the most that I would say during the day would be something along the lines of: "Two eggs over easy, french fries, and a coffee..., The check, please." My increasingly harsh solitude was leading me into a deadpan disposition to dullness (for a considerable while the working title of my third book was Makes Jack a Dull Boy). It was in this context that, on arriving home on March 25, 1993, I found a letter from one of my favorite contemporary writers, essayists and theater artists, Richard Foreman, in which he wrote to the author of a book, Distracted (1991), that was then (and still is) unreviewed and of which one could find only four or five copies in the Chicago metropolitan area: "I glanced at it [your book]—and literally couldn't put it down. I find it an amazing book—and I am not easily amazed. I can think of nothing book-like emerging in the U.S. literary scene for many years that seems to come from a consciousness so totally unique, rigorous, 'unfathomable' in the best, most potent sense—and yet gripping in a dramatic and engaging way. I'm truly knocked out." I felt I had received these words through telepathy, so distant and disconnected from the world did I feel during that period. Shortly after, I received a fan letter from one of my favorite contemporary musicians, John Zorn. This time, I did not feel I was receiving his words telepathically.

ABK:
You sometimes address people who may not necessarily be there to receive the communication, such as the model Christy Turlington. Why, in these cases, is it important that the letter actually be sent? Or, to put it another way, what is the role of the recipient?

JT:
I can now better appreciate the resistance of people to well-written letters: there is actually an intrusion in these publishable letters, though less from the reader in general than from the untimely collaborator.

ABK:
The letters invariably open conventionally (date, location, salutation) but do not close conventionally: there's no signatory, which

sometimes makes the ending difficult to detect; I find myself reading the following pages of the book as a continuation of lines already traced in the preceding letter. Why is aperture strongly signaled and not closure?

JT:
"We are perfect for each other. You are young enough not to have read many books; I am an old enough writer to have been forgetting for years now what I learned in books, art, and films. Gone is my erudition and much of my vocabulary. I presently gravitate towards a few films and a few words, like *cadaver*." What he was saying was misleading, a form of seduction: they would have fit better together when he was more erudite.

Sara
Beirut
4/6/2001
Bonjour.
J'ai découvert aujourd'hui vos sites. C'était une belle surprise. MERCI beaucoup d'y avoir pensé. Ils sont intéressants.
Je dois d'abord m'excuser de ne pas vous avoir appelé l'autre jour, comme je l'avais promis; quelque chose de désagréable m'est arrivé: j'ai perdu votre numéro de téléphone. Pour l'avoir, c'était simple, il me suffisait d'appeler Monique. Je l'ai appelée. Elle ne me l'a pas donné. Là, je ne pourrai de nouveau être en contact avec vous que si vous aurez la gentilesse de m'envoyer votre numéro pour que je vous appelle—sinon ...
Eh vous barbare, beau sultan, ami du Coeur et du malheur ... comment va votre belle allure de fakir cireur? Ce serait sympa qu'on s'écrive de temps en temps.
Allez, je vous laisse de la plume mais non du Coeur.

Sara's college schedule: Monday: till noon; Tuesday: till 3; Wednesday: till 2; Thursday: till 4; Friday: till 2.

Jalal Toufic
Naccache, Lebanon
4/11/2001
Sara, Beirut:
When she was away from him, he, naturally, missed her. Nonetheless, he intuitively did not ask her to write letters to him. But one day he received one. He felt happy. But he soon became aware, having reread her witty letter several times and desiring to receive a second one then and there, that the letters, while at first a way to minimize missing the beloved, were opening another occasion and avenue for missing. He now missed her presence but also her letters; meeting

her in person did not end the latter missing. While waiting for her one day in a café, he wished that she would show up with a new letter and that on characteristically going to the restroom to dampen her hair—"to feel energized"—she would hand it to him to read. "Write to me!" Can this request be satisfied when, however much its addressee writes, the lover will insist that the beloved should have written more, or in such a dense manner that the letter's absorption would take not one or two readings but scores of them? Have Christians been rereading the epistles of "St." Paul again and again, for many centuries, not necessarily because these letters demand so much perusal in order to be fathomed but because they love "St." Paul? When a letter is reduced to inscribing the addressee's name and complaints about the infrequency and shortness of his or her letters, we can be sure that the correspondent has reached the proper state of love.

Did he, naturally, stop missing her when she was with him? "I miss you even when you are with me" (*Wahishnī winta 'usād 'īnī,* as an Umm Kulthum love song says); is this not the unnatural but paradigmatic situation with the vampire, who is there with her victim and not there—as shown by the absence of her image in the mirror at the same location? Is it at all surprising that so many of the vampire's victims fall in love with her?

Thursday
4/12/2001
I've just called Sara. She cannot meet me today. She is behind with her studies. We are to meet on Sunday.

Sunday
4/15/2001
I've just spoken to Sara on the phone. She has exams. She cannot meet me till next Friday.

Jalal Toufic
Naccache
4/16/2001
Sara, Beirut:
Fortunately, I've been getting much better at waiting these last few years, probably as a result of my renewed interest in Twelver Shi'ites, a sect still awaiting the Mahdi, whose occultation started over a millennium ago.

ABK:
Maybe the most striking stylistic feature of your earlier books has been the use of parenthesis: the sentence expands both from within (a parenthesis, and a parenthesis within a parenthesis, and so on) and

from without (footnotes). (In this respect Nietzsche seems less useful as a model: your punctuation mark is the parenthesis, whereas his is the dash.) This tendency seems somewhat muted in *Forthcoming*, which nonetheless identifies, in a footnote, "discontinuity, whether stylistic or thematic" as a recurrent effect in your writing. What accounts for the change in style?

JT:
At one level, there has been a break between *Distracted* and *(Vampires)*, since I died before dying in the interval between finishing the first and starting the second. At another level, and given that style is the renewed variation of the same, whether motif, figure, etc., there has been no change of style between my books. For example, and as *Forthcoming* mentions, "discontinuity, whether stylistic or thematic, is encountered throughout my work: a) in *Distracted*, aphorisms separated by blanks from each other and by dashes and, in the first edition, parentheses within a parenthesis within a parenthesis internally; b) in *(Vampires): An Uneasy Essay on the Undead in Film*, the freezing, in other words, dead stop, of the dead; the abrupt disabling of their capability to tunnel through space, doors, and walls by arresting, often amorphous objects; the over-turns; and the lapses of consciousness, if not of being, in the labyrinth; c) in *Over-Sensitivity*, the unworldly or otherworldly entities that all of a sudden irrupt in radically-closed spaces. And here [in *Forthcoming*], the atomic temporality of Islam." Discontinuity is encountered throughout my work also in the form of the untimely end: in *Distracted*, in the manner of the youthful passionate impatience for suicide; in *(Vampires)*, in the manner of the detachment of sacrificial interruption (the yogic sacrifice of the fruit of action); and in *Forthcoming*, in the manner of both the messianic end of the world and the renewed creation of the occasionalist atomic universe of the Ash'arite theologians and the Sufi Ibn al-'Arabī.

Nietzsche writes: "To say in ten sentences what everyone says in a book ..." One can accomplish this objective in a monadic manner. The ten sentences would then have plicated in them (in the form of parentheses within parentheses within a parenthesis) a whole book or even a world. Interpretation would then be a monadic unfolding: to see a world in less than a grain of sand, in a monad. Nietzsche wrote in the preface of his *On the Genealogy of Morals*: "I have offered in the third essay of the present book an example of what I regard as 'exegesis' in such a case—an aphorism is prefixed to this essay, the essay itself is a commentary on it." So, the third essay is the exegesis of "Unconcerned, mocking, violent—thus wisdom wants *us*; she is a woman and always loves only a warrior" (*Thus Spoke Zarathustra*). Nietzsche's book can be considered to consist of ten sentences, the rest being the exegetical unfolding of these.

ABK:

On the level of the sentence, too, closure and aperture appear to be special problems: it's easy enough to enter the parenthesis, but it's often quite difficult to find a way out. What effects do you imagine these sentences having on your readers? Do you envision a reader capable of connecting the end of the parenthesis to its beginning, or do you assume that the technology of the sentence will to some extent outstrip the reader's capacity to enjoy it?

JT:

If on reaching a parenthesis that at long last closes many intervening ones the reader cannot remember the beginning of the sentence whose continuation he now faces, he will experience being slower than oneself. Such a structure of writing is thus partly an apprenticeship in that offbeat state of speed.

ABK:

Somewhere in *Distracted* (I note that it's sometimes difficult to locate remembered passages in your books) you disclaim any interest in stream-of-consciousness writing. Does your writing present consciousness as something other than a stream (as, say, a series of interruptions)? Or do you not conceive of your writing as presenting an image of consciousness at all?

ABK:

Another stylistic effect: the laconic "no." What kind of answer is "no"?

ABK:

The copyright notice to *Distracted* says: "The whole of this book or any parts of it can be created by others and hence may be published by them without permission from the author and the publisher. No part of this book may be paraphrased in any form or by any means." Your other books seem to conceive intellectual property somewhat differently: part of the task of the footnotes, it seems, is to provide elaborate documentation for references to other books (including your own). Moreover, in *Over-Sensitivity*, Werner Herzog is called "dishonest" for failing to credit Iraq as the producer of *Lessons of Darkness*, his film documenting oil fires in Kuwait; in *Forthcoming* you suggest that, in the case of a quotation that irrupts ahistorically within a radical closure, it would be irrelevant to give information about the source. What, for you, is the value of citation?

JT:

The resort to citation in my books indicates either that I did not receive the unquestionable line or paragraph at the end of a perforation of a "Wall" (*Distracted*) or that I was not the untimely collaborator of the writer I am quoting, that he or she wrote it possibly at the cost of his or her sanity, in other words, at the risk of madness, that condition where he or she is "alone with the alone," the double, and with the voices(-over). I would not use quotation were my work to become a radical closure in which what *seems* to be sentences or figures from the work of other writers or artists irrupts (despite the remarkable similarity of Toba Khedoori's *Untitled [railing]* [1996] to one of the panels of Magritte's diptych *The Hidden Symbol [Le Symbole Dissimulé]* [c. 1928], one should not hastily consider it in terms of influence or imitation or appropriation or citation, since both Magritte and Khedoori are radical closure artists; it would be more accurate to think that the former painting irrupted from the black of the panel showing a railing in Magritte's diptych—one day another specimen of that Magritte painting may irrupt in the white of Khedoori's painting).

ABK:
When you cite yourself—when you refer to earlier books or when you refer, inside a book, to another passage in the same book—is that an expression of continuity (demonstrating that you've always been saying the same thing) or discontinuity (you refuse to take responsibility for something said elsewhere, because you're not the same person—as you say, "unique, and thus irreplaceable, that which cannot be replaced even by himself/herself")?

JT:
If I sometimes quote myself, it is because I have a loathing of paraphrasing—even myself. In terms of the relation between my various books, the crucial issue is less whether the person who wrote them has changed in the meantime, as whether, in the writing of a certain book, the author's concern was to establish a universe or to splinter it apart (*"Man muß das All zersplittern,"*[45] as Nietzsche writes). While the latter was the crucial thing for me in (*Vampires*), what was important to me in *Over-Sensitivity* and *Forthcoming* was producing a universe that, as Philip K. Dick puts it, doesn't fall apart two days later.

ABK:
It always startles me to see you offer corrections of existing artworks and past historical events; these corrections are sometimes done in the mode of obligation (Saddam "should have" appeared on TV dressed as Hitler), less frequently in the mode of chance (it "would have been felicitous ..."). What authorizes these corrections?

JT:
I sometimes feel that the writer or artist either did not heed his or her untimely collaborator (in this case, myself) or else that he or she tampered with or paraphrased the unquestionable that he or she

received at the end of a perforation of a "Wall." In such cases, it would have been felicitous ...

ABK:
In several places in *Forthcoming*, you describe yourself as "afraid," "surprised," "anxious" on discovering any confirmation of what you've written. Why is this possibility so troubling? How do you feel, on the other hand, about the possibility that you could be mistaken? (Is that possibility addressed in your writing on portraiture?)

JT:
Why was it of such importance to me to publish *(Vampires)*, when it was actually basically addressed to the dead, specifically to my amnesiac version in the death realm? It was to a considerable degree so that the few living authors whose writings mattered to me would show me how erroneous my scary ideas were, prove to me that they are fancy notions, making it easier for me to dismiss them. What genuine thinker has not been apprehensive that at least some of his alarming ideas prove right? Instead, the book was, as usually happens in such cases, for the most part and for a long time, overlooked. There is also the circumstance that whenever one's *out of this world* concepts appear in the world, one has the apprehension of an imminent psychosis (Lacan: "What is foreclosed in the symbolic reappears in the real"[46]).

That Is the Question
In the diegesis of Lubitsch's *To Be or Not to Be* (1942), each time the Polish actor Joseph Tura declaims Hamlet's "To be, or not to be—that is the question" onstage, he is interrupted by the disruptive departure of the same audience member. We quickly discover that this initial line of the soliloquy is the coded signal for the pilot infatuated with Tura's wife to meet her backstage. But maybe the more basic reason Tura is recurrently interrupted at that point is that "To be, or not to be" is not the question; the question, i.e., issue, is rather the one that theater artist Romeo Castellucci poses in and apropos of his *Amleto* (1992): to be *and* not to be. Indeed, soon enough Tura, who is now impersonating the Nazi collaborator Professor Siletsky, is ushered by the Gestapo into a room where the corpse of the "real," murdered spy Siletsky is seated: Tura is thus extimately implicated in a situation in which someone is in both states of being and non-being, is and is not.

Out of the Question
A man enters the hall of a hotel, sits at a table, and begins filling in the different blank spaces in a form. First name: Safa; age: 27; hair color: brown; eye color: brown; height: 5 feet 7 inches; distinguishing marks: scar on right palm.... At the reception desk, a waiter is speaking on the phone: "Can you please give more specifications? ...

Thank you." The waiter places the receiver on the desk and moves to the entrance of the large hall and surveys its occupants. There are only four men there. Although the man filling in the form is clearly busy, the waiter heads towards him and asks him: "Excuse me, are you Sam?" On getting an irritated "No," he goes to the other corner of the large hall and asks the man sitting there, who is in the midst of a heated conversation and who is physically very unlike the first man (the two could not possibly answer to the same description the waiter received on the phone; indeed the interlocutor of the second man who was questioned by the waiter is more physically similar to the one filling in the forms): "Are you Sam?" He gets a negative response.

A few days later, Safa gives an attractive woman a dress as a gift. He is unaware that she is the lover of the other, older man who was questioned whether he's Sam. He worries that the dress may not be her size. On meeting her the following day, and before he can ask her whether it is the right size, she says: "I don't want to lead you on; I have a lover. So, please accept your gift back." He refuses to take it back. They meet accidentally a few days later. When she shows up at his hotel room a week later, she is wearing it. He is very pleased to see that it is the right size. She takes off the dress, saying: "I ran from place to place all morning in this humid weather. I am going to take a shower. Can I borrow one of your shirts?" When she comes out of the bathroom, the shirt reaches down to her knees. She looks charming in it. "What initially attracted me, a writer, to you was your name. The first time I heard it was two weeks ago. I had just been asked whether my name is Sam when a man at the hotel's main hall yelled a name I had never heard before; at which point I saw you come out of the phone booth and wave to him. You may not know this: he is a counterfeiter of paintings. One day he may ask you to assist him in his work."

— So you had never before heard of anyone called Page!
— No, being a foreigner.
— Even so! How long have you been in this country?
— Five years.
— How old are you?
— Twenty-seven.
— You're young.
— With some people, age is better counted in terms of the number of years separating them from death—so I might be very old.
— Like how old?

The two dissimilar men who were asked whether they were Sam embark on separate journeys to try to reach the acquaintances and documents that would re-differentiate them (the twenty-seven-year-old man, who thinks that because he is suicidal he is older than his passport age, ends up that same year not being twenty-seven years old because he turns into the double of someone in his late thirties).

One of the two encounters a series of obstacles that prevents him from reaching his destination: his car breaks down during the trip; he hitchhikes a ride, but following a series of unexpected misfortunes, the driver, suspecting his companion of being a jinx, rudely abandons him at the side of the road. The other reaches his destinations, but either these have been destroyed—the small hospital where his wounded palm was stitched had burned down—or the persons he questions there, for instance the doctor who did the suture, have for some reason been affected with amnesia.

Sometime later, the two visit Page in prison. Her hair has been cut very short. One of the two men begins crying, repeating: "You look so different!" Hearing a guard yell that visiting time is over, she instinctively stretches her hand to caress them. A shiver goes through her as her hand touches instead the cold surface of the glass partition of the prison's visitation area. While grabbing the crying man's arm to lead him out, the other man quickly scribbles a few words on a piece of paper and holds it against the glass: "Holding his hand, I am feeling exactly like you do as you move your hand over the glass." A shiver passes through her.

(Vampires): An Uneasy Essay on the Undead in Film[47]

Author's Note to the Second Edition of *(Vampires): An Uneasy Essay on the Undead in Film*

An Uneasy Essay on Death in Film and Outside It (an Outside That Functions at Times in a Cinematic Manner) would have been a more fitting title for the book.

Between *Distracted* and *(Vampires)*, between the suicidal and the dead-as-undead, between distraction and the yogic absolute concentration needed to neutralize death-as-undeath, between forgetfulness and amnesia, between the perforation of "Walls" and (quantum) tunneling, there was the encounter with the double (in the mind), and the apprehension that my reception from my threatened amnesiac version in death would result in a book that is the double of *Distracted*, signaling the latter's ruination (see page 65 of *Distracted*).

Part of the section "The Off-Screen and/or the Set On-Screen" and most of the section "Vertiginous Eyes" have been removed from this book as they have become part of my book *Explicit and Implicit Variations on Hitchcock* (Beirut Art Center, 2023).

In memory of the amnesiac Jalal Toufic (not that he no longer exists, but that he was/is dead/undead then/now)

The most merciful thing in the world, I think, is the inability of the human mind to correlate all its contents. We live on a placid island of ignorance in the midst of black seas of infinity, and it was not meant that we should voyage far. The sciences, each straining in its own direction, have hitherto harmed us little; but some day the piecing together of dissociated knowledge will open up such terrifying vistas of reality, and of our frightful position therein, that we shall either go mad from the revelation or flee from the deadly light into the peace and safety of a new dark age.

H. P. Lovecraft, *The Call of Cthulhu*

Posthumous Introduction
to the First Edition

Writing the introduction after finishing the rest of the book, my memory is coming back to me, and so at present I can give some indication in what context to place it.

Why write on vampires in 1992? It is precisely because vampire films and novels are back in fashion (Coppola's *Bram Stoker's Dracula* [1992] ...) that one should ask: why on vampires now, by what coincidence? How come what functions in the too-late and too-early mode is being written about now, when it has become fashionable? But isn't it characteristic of the untimely that it reaches the present of fashion by a too late of the too early or a too early of the too late?

What is not aphoristic is a transition toward what follows it, disappears or is dialectically sublated in what it leads to; but an aphorism is not a phase, a transition toward something else, hence its relation to other things is that of simultaneity rather than before/after. It is thus my hope that *Distracted* (1991) would prove to be simultaneous with, not overturned by, *(Vampires)* (1993), notwithstanding that the latter has to do with a labyrinthine temporality. It is because the aphoristic *Distracted* already resists "itself" ("One of the main indications of this fight against opinion is the widespread presence of the dash in aphorisms. The aphoristic dash announces [a] a sudden switch in relation to an opinion that managed to insinuate itself into one's writing or [b] what will prevent what one is asserting from turning into an opinion"[48]) that it has a chance of resisting its double. But *(Vampires)* is being resisted in another way also, a bad way, a cheap way: why has *Distracted*, nine months after its publication, yet to receive its first review? Why is it that, several months after its publication, one could find only half a dozen copies of it in the Chicago metropolitan area? Is it also because the nonchronological action of *(Vampires)* on it would have less occasion to manifest itself clearly once both books are available to readers? In which case it will be reviewed and be more widely distributed only by the time *(Vampires)* gets published.

Why write on vampires at this stage in history? Were humanity to conquer physical death—and certainly we are moving in that direction, whether or not only in an asymptotic way—it will suddenly dawn on humans that the attributes of death, or pastiches or parodies of them, have become salient facets of life, for example:

— The virtual body in virtual worlds: a sort of astral body. Affect it, an image, and you affect the material body, equipped with sensors, in another locality: a reversion to magic.

— Smart weapons that home in on their targets on their own; smart cars; smart houses, where once the "alarm clock rings in the morning, the curtains open, the shower starts, the coffee brews ...,"[49] and where doors open on their own at one's approach, etc. These smart objects bring to mind the doors that open on their own in vampire films. Will we then be in a trance state?

One of the dangers of the editing stage for books that initially drew on notes written, and thoughts one had, during a state of altered consciousness and/or body (for example, [Vampires]) is that as one becomes more and more permeated by the normal state, one is increasingly tempted to summarily get rid of all the discrepancies and of all that strikes one as far-fetched, counterintuitive, indeed incredible. Therefore, editing should stop before the end set to it by the normal state. To continue till the book is "totally done" is to risk addressing oneself exclusively to those who are alive and in normal states.[50]

Who Will Warn Us about the Warning?

Renfield says to Harker concerning the latter's forthcoming trip to Transylvania: "And, young as you are, what matters if it costs you some pain—or even a little blood?" It is a warning that occults the real danger, even when it seems a prophecy slyly revealing the worst that can happen. It is exactly when the character has a hint that something so terrible that it goes beyond anything he could have expected (or can expect) may soon happen to him that he tells himself, "If only I had listened then," precisely not to heed what the present situation should disclose to him: that the warning was misleading since it says that the worst that can happen is that he will lose a little blood, or even, since one can debate what amount is to be considered "little," that he will die from losing too much blood. The warning hides that the danger is not the cessation of life but madness and finding oneself lost in the labyrinthine realm of death; hence it was an understatement hiding from him that no exaggeration could disclose the danger threatening him.[51]

False Thresholds and
Imaginary Lines[52]

When people do not fall while descending stairs[53] without watching their steps (for instance, the old Lord Hidetora in Kurosawa's *Ran*, whom the enormity of the disasters that have befallen him puts in a trance as he descends the stairs) then trip for no apparent reason on smooth spaces, these trips are the sign that a threshold has been reached. The threshold of the vampire's lair in Dreyer's *Vampyr* is not at the door, but at the spot where Allan Gray trips; the threshold of the house of Maria in Tarkovsky's *The Sacrifice* is where Alexander falls off his bicycle. Hence caution is *pre*caution[54] (in states of altered consciousness, the same is the case with *monition* and *premonition*—probably one becomes a sage only when one no longer needs presages), in the sense that one must forewarn by *guessing* where the *false threshold* is and warning both about it and about being fooled by the apparent threshold[55] (guessing should be taken here in the way it manifests itself in the experiments conducted by Larry Weiskrantz on *blindsight*: while patients who have lesions in the striate cortex or first visual cortical area were thought to be totally blind in the part of the visual field that corresponds to the damaged section, it turned out that they could still discriminate in that part visual events, when these began and ended, and their orientations—when asked how they could achieve these feats, the patients answered that they were guessing for they saw nothing).[56] These presentiments must be coupled to methods of postponement, otherwise one may be moving into the worst of prisons. Hence the absolute importance of *critical point*[57] states, and *super-/under-* states (as in supersaturation and undercooling), such as yoga. The continuity of karma, karma as continuity, has to be disrupted by yoga, which must not itself be interrupted by lapses of consciousness or being (the passage from the waking state to the dream state or from life to death must not happen in a lapse of consciousness or being, respectively): "The 'unification' [of consciousness] ... must be understood in the sense that, by making his respiration rhythmical and progressively slower, the yogin can 'penetrate'—that is, he can experience, in perfect lucidity—certain states of consciousness that are inaccessible in a waking condition, particularly the states of consciousness that are peculiar to sleep.... The Indian ascetics recognize four modalities of consciousness (besides the enstatic 'state'): diurnal consciousness, consciousness in sleep with dreams, consciousness in sleep without dreams, and 'cataleptic consciousness.' By means of *prāṇāyāma*—that is, by increasingly prolonging inhalation and exhalation (the goal of this practice being to allow as long an interval as possible to pass between the two moments of respiration)—the yogin can, then, penetrate all the modalities of consciousness. For the noninitiate, there is discontinuity between these several modalities; thus he passes from the state of waking to the state of sleep unconsciously. The yogin must preserve continuity of conciousness—that is, he must penetrate each of these states with determination and lucidity."[58] Any impurities, in the form of distractions, are proscribed: purity is necessary not so much on moral grounds but, as in supersaturation and undercooling, so as to delay a catastrophic phase transition, to have continuity where normally one would have a discontinuous jump.[59] He knew that he had reached what would *usually* be a point of no return, because he suddenly began to act with the utmost prudence although nothing noticeable had changed externally or internally (no extension of spectra and sensibility [as happens in far from equilibrium dissipative structures]), except precisely for the sense that the utmost prudence was mandatory now. Critical point and *super-/under-* phenomena, by permitting one state to go into another (it is said in Zen: "When you reach the top of the mountain, keep climbing"), explore it (is the realm of no return a prison? Can, if not oneself, at least what one was changed into [not stolen/replaced by] go beyond it?), without a sudden phase transition (the dissolve in film should mainly be used to denote the maintenance of a state beyond the threshold of a phase transition), maintain the possibility of coming back (the metastable memory one retains then is dependent on this artificial reversibility).[60] Does Herzog's Harker manage to achieve such critical point and/or *super-/under-* states? No, so not only does he lose his memory, becoming amnesiac, but he can only appear to return, arriving in Wismar as another, as the vampire.

I have two ways to detect the threshold to the labyrinthine realm of undeath:

— My body, sensing the proximity and imminence of the threshold, and not fooled by my ongoing rationalization, performs a bungled action, most characteristically tripping, to provide me with time to deliberate if I want to go through with my one-way trip to the labyrinthine realm of death, given that at the threshold itself I do not have the chance to deliberate, to make a decision, since I am then and there entranced, thus have no will of my own, and find myself when I come out of the trance already on the other side of the threshold, "in" the labyrinth, always already "in" the labyrinth. Of someone who reaches the vicinity of the threshold without tripping, hallucinating or hearing a voice behind him and turning, I can deduce that he is totally lacking in intuition and is deaf to his body, or else that he is a spiritual master, a yogi or Sufi, who can cross the threshold without going through a lapse of consciousness or being and therefore can still make a decision at the threshold itself.

— Others tell me at a certain point that they can no longer advance and turn back and leave me. A realm that I alone can enter, that I cannot in principle enter with others, is my death. Harker has twice to make a decision at a certain point: at the bridge where others refuse to progress (they know, or at least sense, that this is the point of no return), and at the door to the vampire's castle. It is the former that is the real threshold. Therefore, the real decision takes place at the bridge; at the door to the vampire's castle, it is already too late.

Mina was kidnapped and carried in the vampire's coach toward his castle. Harker, Dr. Van Helsing, and three other friends formed a posse to free her and destroy the vampire. During the chase, his pursuers saw houses on both banks of the meandering river, and castles on both sides of chasms. No bridges joined the two sides. They were soon even more surprised by the plethora of bridges crossing only the ground. To Harker's: "By what perversion would one waste one's time constructing these useless bridges?" Lord Arthur Holmwood volunteered that since they were now in an older part of the world, they were to expect to encounter characteristics of aristocratic culture, one which does not place much importance and value on utility. They resumed their pursuit. Soon, Mina could espy the posse. The distance between the coach and the pursuers gradually shrank, so that she began to feel a glimmer of hope that she might still be saved. Her hope intensified as the coach suddenly began to go over the same spot back and forth (from Harker's diary regarding his trip to Dracula's castle in Stoker's *Dracula*: "The carriage went at a hard pace along, then we made a complete turn and went along another straight road. It seemed to me that we were simply going over and over the same ground again; and so I took note of some salient point, and found that this was so"[61]). The coach must have reached an *imaginary line*. She could see the posse getting closer; a short while yet and they would reach her. But at that point the coach moved forward at full speed. As the pursuers approached the same spot at which the back and forth motion took place, she suddenly and unexplainably felt disheartened. Moments later, she saw the pursuers stop then dismount. After much wasted time, they came to the realization that they would need to build a bridge in order to cross the ground on which the back and forth of the coach happened.

Fascinated Motionlessness and Quantum Tunneling

Doors either open by themselves or the vampire tunnels through them in dissolves (Browning's *Dracula*) or cuts. The dissolve or cut between two shots of the vampire, in the first of which he or she is far away, for instance at the end of a long corridor (according to the mirror, he or she is not at that location), and in the second of which he or she is next to the victim (according to the mirror, he or she is not at that location either),[62] indicates either that the future victim of the vampire who has already crossed the false threshold to the death realm has just undergone a lapse of consciousness, if not of being, or that the vampire has tunneled through the intervening space[63] ("I saw a female figure standing at the foot of the bed.... A block of stone could not have been stiller.... As I stared at it, the figure appeared to have changed its place, and was now nearer the door" [Le Fanu's *Carmilla*];[64] in Maya Deren and Alexander Hammid's *Meshes of the Afternoon*, the female protagonist changes location on the stairs without covering the intermediate space, and in Browning's *Dracula*, Dracula tunnels through the spider's web without tearing it). Tunneling in vampire films, which is rendered possible by the uncertainty of the undead's momentum (is the vampire moving [and in what direction] or still?) or position, applies in the case not only of doors (*Carmilla*: "The figure ... was now nearer the door; then ... it passed out.... I hastened to it [the door], and found it locked as usual on the inside"[65]) but also of space. When tunneling is due to uncertainty of position, the point-of-view shot of the person looking at the vampire should be from the beginning a dissolve, rather than, as in Murnau's *Nosferatu*, beginning with one shot of the vampire in one position then dissolving to him now closer or farther; or the vampire should be shown to be absent from mirrors at both locations.

The October 28 entry of Harker's diary in Coppola's *Bram Stoker's Dracula* reads: "We left London by train and crossed the English Channel that night in stormy seas. No doubt of the passage of the count's ship. He commands the winds, but we still have the advantage. By train we can reach the Romanian port in Varna in three days; by ship it will take him at least a week. From Paris, we traveled through the Alps to Budapest. The count must sail round the rock of Gibraltar, where we had posted a lookout, and then on to the Black Sea port at Varna, where we will meet his ship and burn it into the sea.... The count's ship sailed past us in the night fog to the northern port of Galatz." The pursuers mistakenly presuppose that the vampire moves according to the map, in a continuous space, gradually. But the vampire has no trajectory (or every possible one).

One of the tolls of tunneling or teleportation, by means of which one moves through perceptible barriers, is that unexpected, invisible obstacles will spring up elsewhere, resulting in motionlessness where there is no discernable barrier.[66] Many of these barriers will be objects that for no apparent reason cannot be removed, objects that put one in a trance,[67] depriving one of one's motor ability. So, with generalized teleportation, mobility will be inhibited no longer solely in limit cases such as trance, psychotic episodes (Virginia Woolf's Rhoda: "Also, in the middle, cadaverous, awful, lay the grey puddle in the courtyard, when, holding an envelope in my hand, I carried a message. I came to the puddle. I could not cross it. Identity failed me. We are nothing, I said, and fell. I was blown like a feather. I was wafted down tunnels. Then very gingerly, I pushed my foot across. I laid my hand against a brick wall. I returned very painfully, drawing myself back into my body over the grey, cadaverous space of the puddle"[68]), and existential nausea (Sartre's Roquentin: "I saw a piece of paper lying beside a puddle.... The rain had drenched and twisted it.... I bent down, already rejoicing at the touch of this pulp.... I was unable. I stayed bent down for a second, I read 'Dictation: The White Owl,' then I straightened up, empty-handed. I am no longer free, I can no longer do what I will"[69]). *Ça va?* How can one be fine when this motionlessness is happening?

Stanislavsky: "This moment is what we in actor's jargon call the state of 'I am.' ... In the course of my fruitless [imaginary] walk through Famusov's house there had been one instant when I really felt that I was there and believed in my own feelings. This was when I opened the door into the antechamber and pushed aside a large armchair;[70] I really felt the physical effort entailed in this act. It lasted for several seconds; I felt the truth of my being there. It was dissipated as soon as I walked away from the armchair and I was again walking in space, amid undefined objects."[71] How can the dead feel and say *I am* when objects either cannot be moved at all[72] or, more deleterious still, if they move on their own before him, if they have become self-moving: coffin lids that open on their own and ships that steer their way on their own ("A great awe came on all as they realised that the ship [transporting Dracula], as if by a miracle, had found the harbour, unsteered save by the hand of a dead man!"[73] [Stoker's *Dracula*]). That is why we often see in films of the dead and of those who died before dying someone quickly stretching his hand to hold fast static objects, for these can at any moment move on their own: the knife that slides on its own from the loaf, and the key that falls after coming to a stop on one of the steps of the stairs in *Meshes of the Afternoon*. The absence of obstacles resulting from the self-motion of objects is very detrimental to the unembodied or dissociated, for obstacles permitted them to become in focus: "When this sensation of dereality occurs while walking, I try to move over against a building or doorway until I become one again"[74]—a non-narcissistic hug of oneself.

In somnambulism, there is a doubling in the somnambulist, one part walking, the other motionless while being transported by the first, feeling it has no influence on the walk (and no control of its thoughts ["*to stand on one's own feet*: to think or act independently" (*Merriam-Webster Dictionary*)]). A separation of the two components occurs in *Vampyr* as Gray trips at the *false threshold*. Paradoxically, it is when the somnambulist momentarily sits that he or she most clearly gives the impression he or she is moving: the four people seated outside the house staring at the landscape in Hopper's *People in the Sun* give the impression they are in a moving train.

In Deren and Hammid's *Meshes of the Afternoon* and Robbe-Grillet's *L'Immortelle*, it is no longer the shots that are cut on movement but the scenes, while jump cuts proliferate within each scene. The dead human's movement/gesture/utterance is smoothly continuous across non-contiguous spaces-times. The same would happen with the living were teleportation to become feasible.

The dead occasionally experience an involuntary tunneling through the curtain that happens to be at the location where they ostensibly are (since many of the figures in Francis Bacon's paintings are unworldly entities that irrupted in a radically closed space, in which they do not fit fully, indeed, in which they seem to be keyed in, we encounter examples of such tunneling in his paintings: *Head VI* [1949], *Study for Crouching Nude* [1952], and *Study after Velazquez's Portrait of Pope Innocent X* [1953]). This is the real shroud of the revenant: he or she is hidden by, and imprisoned inside, what is behind him or her.

The *Seamless Dress* of *Reality*?

Bazin's "seamless dress of reality"[75] cannot exist except where death has been reduced to organic demise. In the realms of death and madness, (un)reality is, as in Robbe-Grillet's and Ruiz's works, full of gaps, or, as in Godard's *King Lear*, where the film editor stitches together the film pieces of two shots, full of seams.

Lapses of Consciousness, If Not of Being

In Stoker's *Dracula*, Harker loses consciousness as he approaches the vampire's castle: "I must have been asleep, for certainly if I had been fully awake I must have noticed the approach of such a remarkable place"; and in Murnau's *Nosferatu*, Harker loses consciousness while leaving the vampire's castle. The entrance of the labyrinthine realm of death is inaccessible since hidden by the trance that seizes one there (*entrance n. 2.* A means or point by which to enter; *entrance v. tr. 1.* To put into a trance [*American Heritage Dictionary*]).[76] If someone who is not a spiritual master is not entranced at the entrance of a place, this indicates that the latter is not a labyrinth. The entry into and exit from the realm of death occur in a lapse of consciousness, if not of being, hence are missed;[77] with the exception of the yogi/Zen master, one is always already in the labyrinthine realm of death.[78] You can neither enter nor leave the labyrinth, and, as a mortal, you've always been lost "in" it, that is, you cannot be found there. Are you, then, ever "in" the labyrinth from which you cannot leave? On an ever-changing map, a labyrinth is formed of one line that twists and involutes, forming an object with a fractional dimension between one and two, with the following two consequences. First, the labyrinth is all border, hence one cannot be fully inside it: if one can hide "in" the labyrinth, it is not because one is inside the labyrinth, for the labyrinth maintains one on the outside (thus it has aura), but because it is "in" the labyrinth that one is lost. Second, lapses of consciousness, if not of being, are sure to occur to one "in" the labyrinth since it does not have a dimension of three, is not a full volume.

There can be no understanding of cultures that believe in possession by spirits or deities (for example, Voodoo) without undergoing possession, for if understanding is a form of possession in the normal sense of the word, they in turn must possess us, in their way, or rather what possesses them must also possess us. We can include them in history and memory only if what possesses them can possess us, that is, includes us in amnesia, in lapses of consciousness. A true relation presupposes this unbalanced, equivocal (since it maintains the two meanings of *possession*) exchange.

Films about lapses of consciousness, and the resultant disorientation, are very important in cinema since, with rare exceptions, cinema is itself largely made of changes of place and focus.[79] Walter Benjamin writes in "The Work of Art in the Age of Mechanical Reproduction": "The work of art of the Dadaists ... hit the spectator like a bullet.... It promoted a demand for the film, the distracting element of which is also primarily tactile, being based on changes of place and focus which periodically assail the spectator."[80] Classical cinema tries to occult such periodic change through smooth editing, for example, by means of cutting on action. These changes of focus and location and lighting should rather be foregrounded, not merely in a structuralist, modernist investigation of the medium and specific art form that cinema is,[81] but also through highlighting films that deal on the level of content with reality as filmic (for example, the realm of death). One would not forget to say *en passant* that bullets have been the cause of many concussions that resulted in amnesias, and hence in the creation in real life, and outside of all cinemas, of "changes of place and focus which periodically assail" the amnesiac (Christopher Nolan's *Memento* [2000]).

Marguerite Duras criticizes most filmmakers for a condescending attitude toward the spectator, which reveals itself, for example, in their showing him or her all the successive stages of an action: "When you watch old films on television, for instance, the viewer is treated like a backward child, as if they were disabled, as if everything had to be done for them"; "before, when one showed a man leaving his house and arriving, for example, at a bar, one used to show first the man leaving his house, then his journey, and finally the man arriving at the bar [this is not actually the case in almost all films—perhaps in rare experimental films!]. Godard invented this: the man leaves, and then we see him in the bar."[82] Duras is only partially right in her insistence that the continuity in the portrayal of actions be dispensed with: a generalized habit of letting the spectator piece together what happened by projecting what was skipped makes it extremely difficult for the filmmaker to thwart such a projection, and thwarted it sometimes must be, for in some cases nothing happened between two shots showing what appears to be different stages of an action. Robbe-Grillet writes: "The duration of the modern work is in no way a summary, a condensed version, of a more extended and more 'real' duration which would be that of the anecdote, of the narrated story. There is, on the contrary, an absolute identity between the two durations. The entire story of *Marienbad* happens neither in two years nor in three days, but exactly in one hour and a half"[83]—to wit the existence of the man and the woman in Marienbad "lasts only as long as the film lasts."[84] Robbe-Grillet's general characterization is correct; nonetheless, I do not think that it is fully exemplified by *Last Year at Marienbad*. For the implication of structuring the film in terms of scenes—a scene is "a part of a play or film in which the action stays in one place for a continuous period of time" (*Cambridge Dictionary*)—is that there is a temporal ellipsis between any two scenes, with the consequence that most spectators tend to fill the assumed ellipsis with the most probable events. The spectator can still be inhibited from doing so in various ways: in case the characters can still be surprised, it suffices to make them startled and disoriented at the beginning of each scene, thus alerting the spectator that no time has passed between the two non-contiguous locations-times, and hence inhibiting him or her from projecting any transition time between them, the diegetic world presented by the work lasting then only the time of the projection of the latter. In case the characters are not surprised by diegetic jump cuts, the transition from one sequence of shots that includes jump cuts to another at a different location and time should happen by means of either a cut on movement (a paradoxical continuity at the level of the image), as in *Meshes of the Afternoon*, or a cut on the two consecutive parts of a continuous phrase uttered in sync (a paradoxical continuity at the level of sound). For instance, although shot 24 in *L'Immortelle* shows the woman and the man starting toward Beyköy and shot 25 shows them arriving there, Leila, who was saying in sync, "You are a foreigner.... You got lost ..." in the first shot, continues her phrase in sync in the following one (the cine-novel is explicit here: "continuing her phrase"): "You have just arrived in a Turkey of legend ..."—this making it impossible for the spectator to project that any time had passed between heading toward Beyköy and arriving there. One particularity of such a situation is that the outside is no longer what belongs to a different location-time, since, through the cuts on movement and/or on consecutive parts of the same phrase, the diverse locations-times are no longer separated but form one unit; rather, the outside is now inside the same location, so that while one no longer greets as one changes locations-times, one does so at the start of the second shot of each jump cut in the same location.

"*Build-up*: Dramatic cutting leading to a climax in the action. The term is also used colloquially in the cutting room for the insertion of frames to designate a missing section or shot in the cutting copy or work print."[85] In the case of the majority of those who undergo them, whatever occurs after these missing sections, these blanks, is experienced as a startling climax. One should have *sang froid*, though not during these hibernation-like lapses of consciousness, but as one is suddenly out of them. How to start (begin) without starting ("jerk[ing] or giv[ing] a small jump from surprise or alarm"[86])? "How can the outstanding[87] be abolished?" "Only by abolishing the outstanding."[88] Was a satori produced by this koan-like answer? Only when the surprising is abolished is the unaccomplished in the same movement also abolished. Only those who no longer ever get surprised can definitively short-circuit.

Bram Stoker's *Dracula* begins with Harker's stress on timing: "*3 May. Bistritz.*—Left Munich at 8:35 p.m. on 1st May, arriving at Vienna early next morning; should have arrived at 6:46, but train was an hour late. Buda-Pesth seems a wonderful place.... I feared to go very far from the station, as we had arrived late and would start as near the correct time as possible."[89] ("And when he passed the bridge, the phantoms came to meet him"; [Murnau's] Harker is from then on always late, not reaching the door in time to open it himself: it opens by itself—he turns into a witness.) It continues with an emphasis on chronological time—what is chronology but timing, so that events that belong to the past should not arrive too late, that is, in the future, and events that should occur in the present would not occur too early, in the past, or too late, in the future—through Mina's editing of a history: the multiplicity of letters and journals by various protagonists, which are different angles on and fragments of what happened, makes possible editing out the eternities and lapses of consciousness, if not of being, undergone by some characters to produce a smooth narrative. While the transition from chapter I to chapter II ("Jonathan Harker's Journal [*continued*]") and the transition from chapter III to chapter IV ("Jonathan Harker's Journal [*continued*]") each occurs across an explicit lapse of consciousness, if not of being—chapter II starts with "I must have been asleep, for certainly if I had been fully awake I must have noticed the approach to such a remarkable place" and chapter III ends with "I sank down unconscious"—the underlined transitions (*continued*) from chapter II to chapter III, from chapter XIV to chapter XV, from chapter XV to chapter XVI, and from chapter XVI to chapter XVII don't occur after a manifest lapse of consciousness, if not of being. The titles "Chapter XV, Dr. Seward's Diary (*continued*)," "Chapter XVI, Dr. Seward's Diary (*continued*)," "Chapter XVII, Dr. Seward's Diary (*continued*)," "Chapter III, Jonathan Harker's Journal (*continued*)," as well as "Chapter IV" (the beginning of chapter IV continues the diary entry from the previous chapter) are inserts/cut-aways (does the *continued* function as a dissolve?) implying the existence of lapses of consciousness, if not of being, that otherwise would not have been sensed.

Dans le temps, one was always in time. No more; this *from time to time* is experienced literally by schizophrenics, epileptics, and people on LSD (a schizophrenic: "I turned around and did something and looked at my watch, and it jumped an hour and a half"[90]). Only occasionally do they return to time. But *entre-temps*, where are they? An epileptic: "It was about eleven o'clock when I put down my pen, feeling suddenly tired.... I made the tea, looked up at the clock—a strange chance—and saw that it was ten minutes past eleven. The next moment I was still looking up at the clock and the hands stood at five and twenty minutes past midnight. I had fallen through Time, Continuity and Being."[91] When she tries to go to her bedroom, she realizes that she does not know which way it is. With the epileptic, the two meanings of *fit* exclude each other. Coming back to consciousness, (a) the familiar is no longer so: the first degree of being lost is not yet recognizing a familiar place in the aftermath of a seizure—*lost and found*, simultaneously; and (b) the unfamiliar becomes strangely familiar (this often induces as much apprehension as when the familiar becomes unfamiliar): with many epileptics the aura that announces a fit/blackout takes the form of a déjà vu sensation (naming *aura* a feeling of déjà vu or a smell that is there without an object that would exude it, like a reproduction that is divested from both the painting and its location, i.e., what does away with the aura, would have likely interested Walter Benjamin).

Bazin: "It [cinema] makes a molding of the object as it exists in time and, furthermore, makes an imprint of the duration of the object."[92] Hence cinema preserves also temporal absence. It does so both by documenting epileptic fits (*petit mal* or *grand mal*) and trance (Jean Rouch's *Les maîtres fous*; Herzog's *Heart of Glass*, during the filming of which all the actors except one, and the professional glassblowers, were hypnotized), allowing the one who underwent them to see what his body did when he was absent; and by portraying in fiction films states where there is an absence of time in the figure of a subtle dancer or a dead person who is frozen (as, for instance, in Vincente Minnelli's *An American in Paris* and Alain Resnais and Alain Robbe-Grillet's *Last Year at Marienbad*, respectively). Cinema has to do much more with preserving this absence of time than with preserving time.

In films manifesting quantum effects, such as tunneling, one can reasonably expect the intermittences of interference patterns. In Kubrick's *The Shining*, in which Torrance tunnels through the locked pantry door, the child's tricycle repeatedly passes over the alternating carpeted and bare sections of the corridors of the Overlook Hotel, producing a distinct alternation of silence and the sound of the wheels on the marble. The quantum world of Robbe-Grillet is permeated by intermittences that indicate interference patterns: on the cover of the 1965 Grove Press edition of the two novels *Jealousy* and *In the Labyrinth* and in *L'Immortelle* the author Robbe-Grillet and the heroine of that film, respectively, appear through a window's open horizontal blinds. With *Last Year at Marienbad*, one telling difference between the film directed by Alain Resnais and the elaborate and precise script by Robbe-Grillet is that the interference pattern in the opening section of the script ("at regular intervals, a lighter area, opposite each invisible window, shows more distinctly the moldings that cover the wall") is not in the opening section of the film.

In Bertolucci's *The Spider's Stratagem*, Athos asks two conversing men directions to get to the hotel. They begin arguing about which direction it is, pointing in opposite ways. "When you settle [which direction is the hotel], I'll pass by again." The second time Athos walks in the direction of the two arguing men, *there is a crossing of the imaginary line* before he reaches them, so that we see him walking, in the exact same scenery, away from them, with the two still-arguing men having now exchanged positions, so that the one who was standing screen left is now screen right and vice versa. This indicates that Athos did not pass the two arguing men a second time.

Bazin: "It is inconceivable that the famous seal-hunt scene in *Nanook* should not show us hunter, hole, and seal all in the same shot. It is simply a question of respect for the spatial unity of an event at the moment when to split it up would change it from something real into something imaginary.... [The scene in Robert J. Flaherty's *Louisiana Story*] of an alligator catching a heron, photographed in a single panning shot, is admirable."[93] As long as the two parties within the frame are aware of the mortal threat one or both of them poses to the other, Bazin's qualified prohibition of editing is valid. In Franju's *Blood of the Beasts*, while the sheep readied for slaughter appear to sense what is going to happen to them, a horse led to the abattoir occasionally blithely lowers its head to smell the ground, as if nothing could happen to it. It is then suddenly stunned with a captive bolt device and slaughtered. So strong is the horse's unawareness of the imminent deadly danger threatening it that it imposes a specific kind of editing: the cut from the long shot of the horse insouciantly sniffing the ground to a close-up of it being stunned with the captive bolt device. We have a law of editing here: every time two persons, or a person and a domestic animal, are within a frame and one of them is totally unaware of the imminent danger she or he or it is in, there will occur a cut, whether the *sensitive* filmmaker wants it or not, between that shot and the shot in which that person or animal is killed. In the absence of a cut, we, the audience, will infer that we underwent a lapse of consciousness, that the killed or seriously injured animal or person has been replaced within the shot by a lookalike, and that it is the latter that was killed or gravely injured, or else that it was himself/herself that has been injured or killed by a lookalike of the person or animal in whose presence he or she is, because his or her surprise is that of being attacked by a mimic.

The painter Andrew Wyeth portrays Helga in so many works—4 temperas, 12 drybrush paintings, 63 watercolors, 164 pencil sketches and drawings, etc.—in so many attitudes, positions, surroundings, moods that in the situations that have not been portrayed she is absent from herself.

Memorable Accidents

His car crash was a memorable accident not only because he still remembered it after so many years but also because during it he saw a flash review of his life.

One day in 1906, a filmstrip jammed in Méliès's camera. He managed to get the camera to function again and continued filming. At the projection of the reel, a horse-drawn tram suddenly became a hearse. An accident produced in the camera between a hearse and a horse-drawn tram both moving at rather slow speeds, hence having enough time, even had their drivers found themselves on a collision course, to avert crashing into each other. A crash between their images. It is fitting that that mixing of two things that had nothing to do with each other, which ushered in editing, was related, as indicated by the appearance of the hearse, to death, the great intermingling.

Sensitivity to Initial/Final Conditions

Whenever we deal with a far from equilibrium (dynamical) system, and the unconscious is such a system, we encounter an extreme sensitivity to initial conditions.[94] So it should come as no surprise that one of the most noteworthy characteristics of the state following death is the extreme sensitivity (and suggestibility) to initial conditions: here the final conditions of life, the initial conditions of death. Consequently, disciplines concerned with doing away with or at least having mastery over the bardo state, for instance, yoga, mention among the supernormal powers (*vibhūtipādah*) that can be obtained through integrated concentration (*samyama*) that of knowing the moment one is going to die. Such knowledge would permit one to try to be in the best condition to deal with death: in meditation, hence detached from set (having complete control over one's stream of consciousness and/or absolute detachment from it) and setting. The same emphasis on this last moment is found in fifteenth-century Christianity: whereas in the twelfth and thirteenth centuries "the balance sheet is closed not at the moment of death but on the *dies illa*, the last day of the world ... [the great gathering] in the fifteenth century had moved to the sickroom.... The dying man will see his entire life as it is contained in the book, and he will be tempted either by despair over his sins, by the 'vainglory' of his good deeds, or by the passionate love for the things and the persons. His attitude during this fleeting moment will erase at once all the sins of his life if he wards off temptation or, on the contrary, will cancel out all his good deeds if he gives way. The final test has replaced the Last Judgment."[95]

Through the Unreflective Glass

Once one passes through the unreflective, or no longer reflective, mirror, whether suddenly or gradually as in the dissolve in Lewis Carroll's *Through the Looking-Glass* ("The glass *was* beginning to melt away, just like a bright silvery mist. In another moment Alice was through the glass"),[96] one either comes to the realization that one has been replaced by, or is inhabiting the same mind with, another person if not the double, as in *Alice's Adventures in Wonderland*: "But if I am not the same, the next question is 'who in the world am I? ... I must have been changed for Mabel!'";[97] or one sooner or later encounters the double, as in *Duck Soup*. In the latter film, the character of Groucho Marx continues his attempt to ascertain whether the likeness he sees in the mirror-frame is his reflection or an impersonator even after momentarily and inattentively crossing to the other side! This shot, which is simultaneously one of the scariest and one of the funniest, i.e., one of the uncanniest, in cinema, instances *thought broadcasting*: it is fitting that the impersonator, who in that scene knows every improvised movement with which the Groucho character tries to test him, is elsewhere in the film a spy. Should one ascribe the circumstance that the Groucho character looks only at his likeness rather than also at the other objects in order to ascertain whether he is looking at a mirror to narcissism? Or should one rather view this fixation on it as induced by the fascination and slow-wittedness that take hold of one in such anomalous situations?

Freud writes about one of his dreams: "In mishandling my two learned and eminent colleagues because they were Jews [so is Freud]

... I had put myself [this active, in-control perspective, when it is the other way round!] in the Minister's place.... He had refused to appoint me *professor extraordinarius* and I had retaliated in the dream by stepping into his shoes."[98] Be careful, he lets you step into his shoes only because, like a *loa*, he has stepped into you. And when you murder someone and leave the shoes behind intentionally (your intention is his lapsus) as incriminating evidence and the authorities imprison the other, you will discover that you made a mistake and killed *the wrong man* (the attack on the Jewish colleagues), someone whom the other wanted killed.

Given that one is entranced at the entrance to a realm of altered consciousness or body such as death or dance and then finds "oneself" already there, one may suspect that one has been replaced by a double, so, symptomatically, Vincente Minnelli's "musical" *An American in Paris* begins with three instances of mistaken identity in quick succession. Telling us about himself and where he lives, the first narrator, an American painter, directs the camera up a certain building ("I live upstairs"); when it comes to a stop in front of a window through which we see a man and a woman kissing, he indicates, "No, no, not there: one flight up." The camera then resumes its ascent, coming to a stop at another window just as a man lying in bed wakes up, looks at the camera, and says: "Voilà!" The second narrator, a concert pianist, tells us that he lives in the same building; again, the camera moves up the building, stopping at a window showing a man standing in a room. The narrator's voice indicates: "No, that's not me! He's too happy." So, the camera ascends to a different floor and now we see the actual second narrator. In the case of the third narrator, the music-hall star Henri Borel, who is on a visit to his old neighborhood, the scene is shown from a subjective point-of-view shot so that the people greeting him greet the camera. He comments: "Everybody recognizes me." As the subjective camera comes to a stop in front of a mirror and we see a young man enter frame to adjust his hat, we hear the narrator caution us: "No, no, that's not me! I am not that young." While many others will read these three instances of mistaken identity in a psychological way— the three people with whom the three protagonists are momentarily mistaken represent respectively what the latter yearn for: love, in the case of the first protagonist, happiness, in the case of the second, and youth, in the case of the third—I view them as foreshadowing the possibility of replacement by another person, if not the double, across the entrancing threshold to the realm of altered body, movement, space, time, music, and silence into which dance projects the dancer, a projection that happens clearly in the ballet near the end of the film. In a subsequent scene, the solitary pianist assumes all the roles in an orchestral concert: the pianist, the conductor, the cymbal player, and the audience member who claps noisily at the end of the performance. Whether we are witnessing a doubling, i.e., whether any or all of these participants are the pianist's doubles, depends on whether the first moment of recognition of striking physical similarity, which intimates the possibility of doubling, is affected with a determined negation and sublated into the viewer's inability to discern whether the pianist and the others are identical-looking.

What Does Not Resemble Me Looks Exactly Like Me/ What Looks Exactly Like Me Does Not Resemble Me!

If the encounter with the double happens when one loses one's mirror image or no longer knows one's name, with the result that, failing to successfully call oneself in the mirror, one's mirror image continues to have its back to one, there is no reason for one to see doubles only in people whom others find extremely similar to one: in Fassbinder's film *Despair*, based on Nabokov's novel of the same title, the *astute* protagonist finds a double who, according to the other characters and to the film's spectators, does not resemble him, and concocts a plot to use him as a false alibi while committing a crime.

What I dread about encountering the double is both other people's failure to recognize the similarity[99] and that my responsibility will be indefinitely extended (such an indefinite extension of responsibility is a trait of the unconscious). In Dostoyevsky's *The Double*, other people's strange failure to notice the uncanny resemblance between Golyadkin and his double when the two are together is conjoined to their taking his double for him when they are in different locations. The latter response reinforces what is implied by the former one, for if others keep ascribing to me the responsibility of reprehensible acts I do not recognize doing, this must signal that I have metamorphosed.

Breathless

In pursuit, the vampire continued walking nonchalantly. After a while, one of the two friends fleeing him came to a halt: "I am out of breath." Instead of his friend's response, he heard the vampire's voice behind him: "I, too, am out of breath." He did not at first understand this remark. Then the realization that, being a dead person, the vampire did not breathe took his breath away. The vampire had the sensation of breathing only when he heard Sufi ney sound or a Shakuhachi, for example, in *Shika no Tōne* ("The Distant Cry of the Deer"). In winter, one did not see any visible breath coming out of the vampire's mouth—only, somewhere nearby was mist or fog. If they don't wipe the mirror, living people cannot see their image in it in winter since their breath, visible then, hides the surface of the mirror. But, with the vampire, one encounters an inexistent mirror image hidden by inexistent breath.

The Undead Has No Mirror Image

In Georges Franju's *Eyes Without a Face*, Christiane, a young woman whose face was deformed in a car accident, is to be given a transplant of the facial skin of another woman. She enters the room where the donor is lying anesthetized for the operation and looks at her. At no point does Franju cut from a close-up of Christiane to her point of view of the face of the one lying anesthetized. Her point of view would have shown her her (future) "mirror" image. Later, the woman whose facial skin has been removed, and who is covered by bandages, manages to flee the room in which she was imprisoned and wanders through the house. I expected that she would encounter Christiane, who at present has her face, seeing then what would have been her "mirror" image. But the two women do not meet. It appears that one is witnessing in both these instances the impossibility of a mirror image. But this impossibility is a characteristic of the dead, most famously of the vampire. Is a certain logic leading me astray? Then I suddenly remembered that the film begins with Christiane's fake funeral, during which the disfigured corpse of another woman was buried in a grave with Christiane's name engraved on the tombstone.

The vampire has no mirror image even in the form of body image, hence he does not and cannot have a phantom limb.

The French language felicitously links in the word *reconnaissance* reconnaissance, recognition, and gratitude. The dead human's *reconnaissance* in the death realm fails both because such a realm is labyrinthine and because he or she no longer has a mirror image hence can feel no sense of recognition. The living have here an occasion, and perhaps a duty, to *create* a valid portrait of the dead human, one that he or she can gratefully recognize, one that is neither a portrait of him or her as he or she was while still alive nor an ideal or demonic portrait.

The Indefinite Poetry of Death

Does the circumstance that cinema gives a definite image to what maintains some indefiniteness in a verbal description make that medium more prosaic than literary prose? Not necessarily.

This medium has produced a poetic effect in at least the following two forms:

— Literalizing what we take for figures of speech, through dealing with states of altered consciousness or the subtle body. Soon after entrancing him and sucking his blood for the first time, the vampire told his victim upon the latter's regaining consciousness, "How does it feel to be dead—before dying physically? Mad?" His victim blurted out, "You're *not all there!*" (an expression "used to describe a person who is somewhat strange or stupid" [*Merriam-Webster Dictionary*]). As he finished saying these words, he was bewildered and entranced by the absence of the vampire in the mirror.[100]

— Undoing or suspending the tendency cinema has, when not abstract or deploying to excess the offscreen, of sooner or later showing, embodying, giving everything a determined image. This is clearest in films that adhere to Sunni Islam's prohibition of the representation of the prophets and messengers recognized by the Qur'ān (and not necessarily in the crude form the adherence to this prohibition assumes in Moustapha Akkad's very bad film *The Message*).[101] But definite embodiment in cinema is undone also in some cases where the protagonist is not a Qur'ānic prophet or messenger and in manners other than an outright eschewal of showing the characters, for example, through:

— remakes. In remakes, the same character is played by different actors (for example, Norman Bates is embodied by Anthony Perkins in Alfred Hitchcock's *Psycho* [1960] and by Vince Vaughn in its shot-for-shot remake, Gus Van Sant's *Psycho* [1998]). Buñuel humorously and poetically made two actresses play the female protagonist of *That Obscure Object of Desire*, this making of his film in a way both the original and its remake.

— the close-up when its tendency to undo individuation is not resisted by the filmmaker. Deleuze: "Ordinarily, three roles of the face are recognizable: it is individuating (it distinguishes or characterizes each person); it is socializing (it manifests a social role); it is relational or communicating (it ensures not only communication between two people, but also, in a single person, the internal agreement between his character and his role).... The close-up is the face, but the face precisely in so far as it has destroyed its triple function.... The facial close-up is both the face and its effacement."[102] In the great film of the close-up, Bergman's *Persona*, the complementary halves of the faces of Alma (played by Bibi Andersson) and Elisabet (played by Liv Ullmann) join seamlessly and indistinguishably into one *effaced* face.[103]

— the 180-degree over-turn, which results in the dead human having his back to the film spectator both outside and inside the mirror (Magritte's *Not to Be Reproduced*).

— the mask produced by the fear-induced swish pan or tilt of one's look.[104]

The poetry of death is obviously not limited to the revelation of the figurative as literal in the death realm, nor to the undoing of definite embodiment nor to the surrealists' *exquisite corpse*.[105] It also appears in that realm's frequent simultaneity of contraries: the simultaneity of stillness and movement: "I saw a female figure standing at the foot of the bed.... A block of stone could not have been stiller.... As I stared at it, the figure appeared to have changed its place, and was now nearer the door"[106] (Le Fanu's *Carmilla*); the simultaneity of being here and elsewhere, of appearance and disappearance: the undead was standing next to his guest while also, as indicated by the absence of his reflection in the mirror, not being there;[107] the simultaneity of silence and music or sound: standing next to the vampire frozen in the coffin, and thus enveloped in silence-over, his enemies hurriedly discussed how to definitively kill him.[108] In a work of art, these instances of a simultaneity of contraries are poetic only when they attain to being aesthetic facts.[109]

The Dance of Death

I've seen an aspect of the dance of death in the freezing of the undead Willis in the ballet *Giselle*. On first hearing that there is a dance spot in Karantina, the site of a massacre perpetrated in 1975 by Phalangist militiamen on the Palestinians who lived in the refugee camp there as well as on many Kurdish and Lebanese war refugees, I imagined a place reserved for movements that project a subtle body of the mover into the dance realm, which has several characteristics in common with the death realm, for example, silence-over and freezing. What did I actually find? A nightclub (!) by the "name" of B018. Though its tables, each with a flower, a candleholder, and a photograph of a legendary musician (Miles Davis, John Coltrane, Charles Mingus, Charlie Parker, etc.), assume a votive appearance and are, moreover, designed to look like cemetery memorial stones, once the trendy music starts, the youths who crowd the nightclub on weekends move to it as they do in any of the other nightclubs in the city. Someone might try to justify having such a place on that spot by invoking the need to champion life in a country that has seen so much death. But if there is something that does not need a stimulant in order to continue, it is life; B018's architect, Bernard Khoury, would have had only to look at the grass that had already appeared on the presumed mass grave at the site of the massacre to ascertain that *life goes on*. Khoury should also have pondered Kubrick's *The Shining*, the events of which take place for the most part at a hotel constructed on a Native American burial ground.

Here Lies and the Worldless

Michel Serres: "At the very site of reference lies death, which makes space something other than a homogeneous vacuum. Being-there is easily translated in the French language: *ci-gît* (*here lies*), ancient funerary formula. Here lies: that means here rests such or such, but means at bottom: by the virtue of this or that dead, the deposit and angle (*gisement*) of here appears. Death gives birth to the here or the yonder, I am born not far from where the grandfather dissolves. I locate myself by deposit and distance hence by keeping well away from death."[110] But the ability of the dead human to create reference and location in the world through his or her corpse comes at the price of his or her being lost in the realm of the dead, a realm that undoes any map.

Here lies applies literally, as a curse, to vampires, and, as a blessing, to saints ("St. Cecilia [flourished 3rd century, Rome ...] ... was buried in the catacomb of St. Callistus, near Rome. At the beginning of the 9th century, Pope Paschal I discovered her incorrupt [undecayed] relics in the catacomb of St. Praetextatus and had them moved to Rome, to a basilica in Trastevere that now bears her name";[111] "the chapel of the St. Gildard convent, Nevers, contains her [St. Bernadette of Lourdes's] body, which is said to be incorrupt";[112] etc.). "Beginning with the thirteenth century ... we again find the funeral inscriptions which had all but disappeared during the previous eight or nine hundred years. They reappeared first on the tombs of the illustrious personages—that is to say of saints or those associated with saints."[113] It seems fitting that the reintroduction of individual funeral inscriptions on tombs should happen in the case of those corpses that don't undergo dissolution into everything else.

The Dead, Who Is Not All There, and the Mad, Who Died Before Dying

Baudrillard: "At the very core of the 'rationality' of our culture ... is an exclusion that precedes every other, more radical than the exclusion of madmen, children or inferior races, an exclusion preceding all these and serving as their model: the exclusion of the dead and of death."[114] The confinement of the dead and the insane is encountered even in astronomy, where it applies to black holes, i.e., to *dead* stars that contain a *singularity*, in the form of the event horizon and of Roger Penrose's *cosmic censorship conjecture*, which "asserts that all singularities in general relativity are hidden behind an event horizon."[115] Similarly, in many horror and science-fiction films a sort of an automatic implicit quarantine takes place around the zone that has become anomalous as a result of an extraterrestrial invasion or some other reason, an event horizon forming to shield the outside world from the singularity, and this through no plausible mechanism.

Both the dead and the mad, who died before dying, often use a language that the living find cryptic: Nosferatu's letter to Renfield in Murnau's film; a schizophrenic's *"Recreat. Recreat xangoran, temr e xangoranan. Naza e fango xangoranan. Inai dum. Ageai dum,"*[116] etc. The vampire liked to wander in postwar cities such as Beirut, lingering at shattered shop signs, whose remaining letters formed incomprehensible words that resonated with his cryptic language. Stoker's Dracula asks Harker to help him speak English without an accent, for otherwise he would be scrutinized in England. Since the dead human is "a stranger in a strange land"[117] in any of the living's countries, it is felicitous that foreign actors are often used in vampire films: the accent of Catherine Deneuve in *The Hunger*; the accent of Bela Lugosi in Browning's *Dracula*; the accents of Klaus Kinski and Bruno Ganz in the English version of Herzog's *Nosferatu*.

In vampire films, while in the mental hospitals schizophrenics experience the infinity of holes in their skin or shoes, the *bleeding* of sounds into each other, and dissolution even as they live; the corpse of the vampire, a dead aristocrat with unfinished business, does not dissolve in the earth while in the coffin during daylight since he is frozen then, remaining impenetrable:[118] however much one may zoom in on the unwrinkled face of Kinski in Herzog's *Nosferatu,* no pores are visible in it.

Matte[119]

For horizon, the matte border.

The lower part of Magritte's *L'Empire des lumières* shows a nocturnal landscape and a house with its lights on (*day for night?*), while the upper part shows a diurnal sky. It is unfortunate that no vampire film shows the trap Harker's wife sets for the vampire—retaining him till (her) dawn—backfiring on her, the vampire standing in a nighttime part of the frame while his victim is in a diurnal section of it.

The photograph of Syberberg and Herzog on page 24 of *Syberberg* (*Cahiers du cinéma*, numéro hors-série, 1980), of both the one who does much of his filming in a studio, even to the second degree, since the latter often remains vacant except of the *front projection,* hence does not become a set; and the fiction filmmaker who has an abhorrence of studio shooting, emphasizing filming in real settings (*Fata Morgana* was shot in Cameroon; *Aguirre, the Wrath of God* in the Peruvian jungle; *Fitzcarraldo* in the Amazon jungle), which may at first seem anomalous, almost a matte photograph, is in reality not so. For didn't Herzog hypnotize his actors during the filming of *Heart of Glass*? And isn't the dissociation from or variability of the setting an effect of hypnosis? "You move as if in slow motion because the whole room is filled with water [in *At Land,* Maya Deren intercuts shots of her crawling on a table covered with plates to shots of her penetrating a thicket. A subtler effect would have been induced had she undergone the following self-hypnosis: 'You advance on the table as if you are penetrating a thicket'—thus dispensing with the thicket shots. The result would have been an *as if* that no longer has anything metaphorical about it but has to do with an *I feel, I have the impression.* Were the film spectator, though, to get entranced by the shot or scene, he or she would be likely to no longer just have the feeling but to see the shot of Deren advancing in a thicket intercut or superimposed on the shot of her crawling on the table].... Though under water usually you can move only with great difficulty, you feel very light right now. You are just drifting."[120] Hypnosis is a chroma keying/matting before the latter was invented. This is very clear in hypnotic phenomena such as positive or negative hallucination, whether they happen during the trance or posthypnotically: "You see your partner, but you look through him as you look through a window"[121]; during one of the hypnosis sessions Herzog conducted prior to the filming of *Heart of Glass,* one subject said in answer to an inquiry about what he was seeing, "Every night the trees disappear altogether, and only the sleeping birds remain."[122] In *Heart of Glass,* the actors hypnotized by Herzog most often act as if the other person(s) and objects at the same location are not present there but are to be matted later. This dissociation from or variability of the setting is achieved here not through cinematic special effects (frontal projection, etc.) but through special effects (hypnosis) done with the psyche of the actor.

At some level, the large-scale immigration of Jews to Palestine played itself as a matting phenomenon. For the land of Palestine to function as a matte, it had to be blank (it wasn't: "The Zionist Organization promoted large-scale Jewish immigration that brought marked changes in the population pattern in Palestine. The Jewish population in Palestine increased from 56,000 in 1918 to about 88,000 in 1922, when the total population was officially estimated at 750,000. By 1939, the Jewish population had increased to 445,000 out of a total population of about 1.5 million. This dramatic increase was primarily due to the large numbers of Jews fleeing the Nazi terror. In percentage terms, the Jewish population rose from about 10 per cent in 1919 to 17 per cent in 1929 to nearly 30 per cent in 1939. The Zionist Organization also acquired land to settle the Jewish immigrants. In 1920, Jewish holdings in Palestine were about 2 1/2 per cent of the total land area. By 1939, they had increased their holdings to over 5.7 per cent of the total land area"[123]) or else be portrayed as blank: thus the Zionists' motto "A land without people for a people without a land" and "Golda Meir's flat assertion in 1969 that the Palestinians did not exist."[124]

During the rehearsals for *Who Framed Roger Rabbit*, rubber figures of the animation characters were moved through the scenes in which they were to appear so that both the actors and the camera operator would know these characters' exact trajectory. "Then when we shot the scene, we didn't use the figure and the operator [and the actors] would have to imagine where the character was in relation to the dialogue, which was being delivered by an off-camera actor."[125] Matting, which does away with the aura, since it makes the far and the near as well as different temporalities intermingle, itself generates an aura, since the eyes of the person looking at the figure that is matted later are never perfectly centered on him or her. It is no longer only the cinematographer who experiences and knows how difficult it is to accompany someone in a pan, zoom, or even a static shot (*Distracted*); the actor who has to interact within a shot with an element that will be matted later experiences and knows it as well.

While many films resort to painted backdrops to economize on set-construction costs, very few make use of the impenetrability of such backgrounds in the diegesis, exemplarily by revolving around a trauma. It is obvious in the scene near the beginning of Hitchcock's *Marnie* in which the eponymous protagonist visits her mother that the background of the street, most notably the conspicuous ship, is a painted backdrop.[126] Marnie is returning to the site of what is refractory to penetration—a trauma: when she was still a child, she killed a sailor who was sexually assaulting her mother. The dissociation of the hysterical protagonist assumes various modes: her five different names (perhaps two of these are Cindy and Sherman), Social Security numbers; her hypnoid states; her frigidity; her separation from the background, conveyed by Hitchcock through the use of obvious back projection during her horse-riding. In the scene in which she burglarizes her employer's offices, the dissociation is displaced to the set: the screen is cut in half by the perpendicular wall of the office where the safe is located, so that as we look at Marnie embezzling the money in one half of the frame while in the other half the maid cleans the other offices, it is as if we were watching a multi-screen shot. This impression is reinforced by the circumstance that when Marnie closes the heavy door of the safe, the maid is not alerted by the sound, does not hear it. In the last shot, after her acting out and getting through to the trauma, Marnie and her husband drive into what was, at the beginning of the film, a painted backdrop.

The Right of Return

It is one of the merits of Borhane Alaouié's film *Kafr Kasem* (1975) to have shown that if there is an Arab community of which the Palestinians are a part, the implication is not, as many Israelis would like the world to believe, that Palestinian refugees ought to be settled in the Arab countries to which they had been expelled; but, on the contrary, that the other Arabs have themselves been exiled by the Israeli occupation—this is not only because between 1948 and 1967 the West Bank was ruled by Jordan and the Gaza Strip was administered by Egypt. Iraqis, Algerians, Yemenis, etc., have been exiled by the Israeli occupation. Alaouié appears to be concerned with giving back to the voice-over as an exiled voice—for example, the voice of Egyptian president Gamal Abdel Nasser during his 1956 nationalization of the Suez Canal speech broadcast on radio and reaching Palestinian villages within Israel—not so much the body, its source, as a land, a country, without which, even when incarnated in a body, it remains a voice-over.

The Israelis may well discover that it is not enough to grant the right of return to living Palestinians (according to UNRWA's figures, as of June 30, 2000, the total number of registered Palestinian refugees is 3,737,494, of whom 1,211,480 are in camps; they are divided between Lebanon [376,472, of whom 210,715 are in camps], Jordan [1,570,192, of whom 280,191 are in camps], the Gaza Strip [824,622, of whom 451,186 are in camps], the West Bank [583,009, of whom 157,676 are in camps], and the Syrian Arab Republic [383,199, of whom 111,712 are in camps]),[127] that they have to grant it also to the ghosts of so many unjustly killed Palestinians, either in their fiction or in haunted houses or ones rumored to be haunted. We Arabs, with so many internally displaced and so many unjustly killed as a result of the civil wars in Sudan, Lebanon, and Algeria, and of the repression of the Kurds in Iraq, etc., have we shown an openness to the right of return in our fiction? In Lebanon, ghosts are not allowed to be revenants but repressed not only in reality but also, largely, in fiction. The Palestinians themselves have to accept the right of return of ghosts with unfinished business, of those Palestinians unjustly killed in an untimely manner. I write in part so that ghosts would not be withheld the right of return.

Presence

In Altman's *Vincent and Theo*, Van Gogh is shown twice trying to paint the field with crows. The first time, the "presence" of the birds is signaled by the fact that, although none can be seen, both we, the spectators, and he hear caws, this inducing him to paint crows over the field. Later in the film, he stands again facing the field. Holding a gun, he walks straight ahead and fires, to force the crows to manifest themselves bodily, to become visible, to no longer remain a "presence." The need to materialize the invisible "presence" is in many cases conjoined to the need to etherealize the hysterical, psychotic, or existentially suffocating presence of an object. Here are two examples of the latter:

— the indefinitely approaching face Mark Vonnegut saw at the onset of his schizophrenia: "From out of nowhere came an incredibly wrinkled, iridescent face. Starting as a small point infinitely distant, it rushed forward, becoming infinitely huge. I could see nothing else.... When I first saw the face coming toward me I had thought, 'Oh, goody.' What I had in mind was a nice reasonable conversation. I had ... lots of questions it must have answers to. God, Jesus, the Bible, the Ching, mescaline, art, music, history, evolution, physics, mathematics. How they all fit together.... My enthusiasm was short-lived. He, she, or whatever didn't seem much interested in the sort of conversation I had in mind.... But the worst of it was it didn't stop coming. It had no respect for my personal space, no inclination to maintain a conversational distance. When I could easily make out all its features; when it and I were more or less on the same scale, when I thought there was maybe a foot or two between us, it had actually been hundreds of miles away, and it kept coming and coming till I was lost somewhere in some pore in its nose and it still kept coming. I was enveloped."[128]

— the nauseating existence Roquentin experiences in Sartre's *Nausea*: "All of a sudden, there it was, clear as day: existence had suddenly unveiled itself. It had lost the harmless look of an abstract category.... The trees, the blue columns and the lamp posts of the bandstand and the Velleda, in the midst of a mountain of laurel. All these objects . . . how can I explain? ... I would have liked them to exist less strongly, more dryly, in a more abstract way, with more reserve. The chestnut tree pressed itself against my eyes.... Existence everywhere, infinitely, in excess, for ever and everywhere; existence—which is limited only by existence.... There had never been a moment in which it could not have existed.... Nothingness was only an idea in my head."

What interests the hysteric, and anyone who feels excessive, even absolute presence, in a TV/film/video image is that the intensification of its presence has as a limit the degree of presence we normally ascribe to a flesh-and-blood person, this shielding him or her from the sudden excessive presence that persons and objects can have: each at the limit can totally fill the universe.[129]

Many of the shots at the beginning of Fassbinder's *Despair* start with an in-focus plane occupied by nobody to then rack focus to the plane where the protagonist is positioned. Appropriately, the protagonist soon becomes dissociated and has a double.

The smooth long pans of Dreyer's *Ordet*, some up to ten minutes long, where the characters never block each other, i.e., never create any off-screen within the frame, although continuous at the level of on-screen space are often discontinuous at the level of the off-screen: we suddenly discover the presence of a person we were unaware existed in that location (it sometimes feels that Dreyer's characters, who frequently do not look at each other but look in other directions [*Ordet, Gertrud*], are following with their eyes such *presences*). The beginning and next-to-last sections of *Ordet*, in which the off-screen is continuous, show people looking for someone, while in the other sections, where the off-screen is discontinuous, i.e., where we may and often do suddenly discover the presence of a person we had reason to think is not at that locality,[130] nobody is searching for someone.

The Absence of Ether, the Vacillation of Dimensions, and Excessive Presence

In the absence of ether, a *whole* horse can be perceived in a close-up mode. The whole horse is then bigger and closer than itself and largely divested of the background, and thus can act as a switch between two settings. We are no longer confronted with the close-up that changes the normal into the terrifying (Eisenstein: "A cockroach filmed in close-up appears as fearsome on the screen as a hundred elephants in long-shot"[131]) but are engulfed by the startling becoming-close-up of the long shot.

Ersatz distance: a father driving a pickup truck converses via walkie-talkie with his child seated in its back in Wenders's *Paris, Texas*. True distance is experienced when things are perceived as separated from one by glass (when the protagonist of *Meshes of the Afternoon* throws a knife at the man sitting by her side, his face is not wounded but rather shatters into mirror shards) or by nothing. He was feeling disoriented, looked at the servant, and ordered her to fetch something. She could not move. He turned to fetch it himself but, as he tried to walk, he suddenly felt a shock and fell to the ground: he had hit against nothing/space! He stood up and tried again to move, but once again he hit against space. Looking at the servant, he saw her staring in terror in a certain direction. Dread filled him. He looked in the same direction, and he knew he was seeing death: an old man holding a child by the hand and leaning to one side in a mannerist pose. True distance: during an LSD trip, one felt that people standing across a playground were so remote that the most appropriate manner to reach them was to send them letters or to receive letters from them. This latter radical distance that's an effect of the absence of ether makes things not so much far but beyond, even this side of the horizon. It alternates with, or is furtively at times simultaneously, an absolute proximity. No other experience gives one such a verification that gravity is a warp in *space*-time, something that mitigates a more radical fall. He was apprehensive that her face's fall would not come to a stop at his face but would go further—but how? In apprehension, he closed his eyes. He felt her lips on his cheeks. He opened his eyes. And then it happened: her face fell toward his face until he saw a hologram of it "inside his head."[132] Her joyful exclamation in reaction to his telling this to her, "You feel this close to me!" felt extremely foreign to him. There is no togetherness in the absence of the ether. He said: "It is an unmediated proximity in an etherless space." Unheeding, she repeated: "You feel this close to me!" The woman who managed to maintain the vampire with her till sunrise so that daylight would kill him perceived more clearly then what she had sensed the moment she encountered him but subsequently discounted: he is too close, outside both night and day.

At dawn, the vampire felt the sun become very close (Badham's *Dracula*), indeed fall toward him in the etherless space.

He was drawn to the object by a faint sound that became clearer as he approached it—or, rather, he localized himself in the etherless space in relation to the object he saw by how clear and loud the sound was.

As far as I can tell, my cat is no longer of a definite size. Sometimes it appears to be perhaps as small as either a cockroach or a rat; sometimes as maybe as big as a lion. Entering the living room—this term increasingly strikes me as inappropriate to describe this etherless enclosure where I continue to die before dying—I heard the cat make the characteristic predatory sound she utters when she has discovered a fly and is ready to spring on it. She was looking in my direction. For a moment, I was uncertain whether she saw me as Lilliputian or whether she had already seen a small fly in my vicinity.

Space comes to the fore in relation to time when it is etherless.

Due to the absence of ether and thus of a distinction between background and foreground, he did not feel, on seeing someone walking inaudibly at the other side of the playground, that the reason he was not hearing any footsteps was because they became fainter due to the distance; rather, he felt that that person's steps were soundless.

Varying Spectra

Occasionally the undead would see people and things as they are perceived by living humans' spectra, but in general he saw parts of the bodies as they appear under a microscope, with the magnification differing on various occasions. Thus, he could sometimes see the microbiota in her facial skin.

Telepathy/Telesthesia

6/24/1990. I enter for the first time Waverly Diner in Greenwich Village. The place is crowded with people placing orders. I look for a banana-honey muffin. There are none left. I ask for a bran muffin. The busy employee asks: "Did you say 'Banana-honey muffin'?" Telepathy?

In Herzog's *Nosferatu the Vampyre*, Lucy is telepathic and telesthetic. She tries from Wismar, Germany, to warn her husband, Jonathan Harker, in Transylvania. Before leaving there, Harker had told his friends: "Take care of her." How can those limited to the local take care of a telepathic and telesthetic human? Harker might as well have said to them: "Take care of me."

In *Potemkin*, Eisenstein edits "immediately—without transition—" two close-ups of a woman, in the first of which her pince-nez is intact, while in the second it is smashed, her eye is bleeding, and her mouth is open in a scream. Eisenstein locates the import of this kind of editing in being an example of "an artificially produced image of motion," giving the spectator "the impression of a shot hitting the eye"[133] (the moment of the impact of the bullet against the face cannot be actually seen unless the collision is shot with a stroboscopic camera that operates in the microsecond range, the kind Harold Edgerton used). Actually, the import of this kind of edit is that it gives the impression of short-circuiting the lag that results from the circumstance that "in primates, the peripheral pain pathways and the major spinal pain pathway mainly show paradoxically slow conduction velocities of 10–20 m/s, which may provide a slow but particular safe pathway of nociceptive information to the brain,"[134] so that, for example, "pain-related information from the hand arrives at the human brain not earlier than ~ 100 ms after stimulus application."[135] The jump cut should sometimes be used to present or make possible a presentiment that results from the removal of the delay between a modification in the periphery of the body and the consequent awareness in the brain of the presentient human. It is then that cinema fully becomes what Walter Benjamin took it to be, a medium of shock.

A shot showing a telesthetic person looking may be followed by a shot that, although showing what he or she is perceiving, is no longer a point of view one, since it has nothing to do with what is facing him or her. Thus, the standard cinematic term *point-of-view shot* should be replaced by another, more general one that can apply to situations such as telesthesia, or out-of-body experience (for example, in near-death states), in which some patients have reportedly been able to see what is going on in a section of the hospital room not directly accessible to their vision.[136]

In Bruce Baillie's *Castro Street*, the air current caused by the passage of a train in one shot appears to undulate the grass in another shot on which the first is superimposed, this creating a shallow depth where the two superimposed shots function as the different planes of one shot, with what happens in one ostensibly affecting what is going on in the other without there being *inter*action, nothing that would have acted as a carrier between the two shots. But as a condition for the deployment of telekinesis between unrelated shots, the planes within each shot must gain detachment from each other (even the reflections in Bruce Baillie's films seem to be, might be, superimpositions).

Freud did not include one of the relevant case studies, Forsyth's, in his paper "Psycho-Analysis and Telepathy" (1922). Notwithstanding Freud, this should not be ascribed solely to psychoanalytical *resistance*: "I can now give you visible proof of the fact that I discuss the subject of occultism under the pressure of the greatest resistance. When, while I was at Gastein, I looked out the notes which I had put together and brought with me [from Vienna] for the purpose of this paper, the sheet on which I had noted down this last observation was not there, but in its place I found another sheet of indifferent memoranda on quite another topic, which I had brought with me by mistake. Nothing can be done against such a clear resistance."[137] At least part of the material that deals with telepathy must remain elsewhere, and only affect from afar. Thus, these papers on telepathy are not just theoretical works about it but already an instance of it.

In Bergman's *Persona*, one of the two people who will become doubles keeps silent, acting as a suction for the words of the other. But that is only a first movement, for the communication of thought via spoken words from Alma to Elisabet is complemented in the reverse direction by a *thought-transference*, a phenomenon that was experienced by a number of psychoanalysts, for example, Ferenczi.[138]

In the beginning scene of Rouben Mamoulian's *Dr. Jekyll and Mr. Hyde*, the camera is identified with Jekyll: people speaking to him look at it. Therefore, even when there's a reversion to the typical arrangement where the camera is at times objective, at other times subjective, the camera remains, even when in the objective mode, contaminated by Jekyll-Hyde, who thus can know about events that he did not see but the camera witnessed.[139] This should have been the reason why and the manner by which Hyde knows about the visit Ivy Pearson renders to Jekyll. Unlike Robert Louis Stevenson's book *Strange Case of Dr Jekyll and Mr Hyde* on which the film is based, in which the two personalities, Jekyll and Hyde, "had memory in common," Mamoulian's film should have been about multiple personalities with an amnesic barrier between them, for this would have made it clear that the formal identification of Jekyll with the camera in the first scene is *the* source and cause of the memory he and Hyde have in common in the diegesis. Unfortunately, this is not the case in Mamoulian's film.

Waiting for the train, you look around the station: the same sort of clocks, people, floor, and shops as in other stations. All of these similarities, including the similarity of the tedium you feel here as in other stations, make you feel that the actual stations are abstract and minimalist, and that what fills them is traveling with you. It dawns on you that the statistics monitoring the remote-perception experiment, in which a percipient has to describe an unknown geographical location where an agent, in this instance you, either was or is should be altered, since all the percipient has to do is to describe any station from memory and the station in question would fit. On arriving at the next station, while still seated in the train, you close your eyes and try to evoke a station and describe it, sure that you would then end up simultaneously having described the one you will shortly wander in. Still closing your eyes, you take out a notebook and a pen from your pocket and ... nothing! You seem to have lost all memory of any station. A little later, you impulsively look to your left and see a woman. Although she is not the kind that attracts you, you gaze at her. And although you don't feel any curiosity about her, you have an urge to look at her socks to see what color they are. You see that they are yellow and folded at the edge. "On a few occasions, agents have reported informally that while at the target their attention had been inexplicably drawn to rather minor or peripheral details of the scene, and later learned that those details were prominent in the percipient's description."[140] The clear desire forced on the agent to see a specific but rather indifferent phenomenon or object is not necessarily, indeed is often not at all, that of the percipient, whose state remains in most cases one of apathy and detachment. Between the percipient and the agent there is that "third who walks always beside you" (T. S. Eliot),[141] and it is this third, the double of the percipient, who wants to see these specific things. Telepathy and telesthesia's disclosure of the absence of distance between two people unveils in turn the presence of a distance in the same person. The implied presence and interference of this *third* will become easier to notice with the future widespread use of teleoperation; between one and the machine one can control at a remote location, there will be the "third ... always beside you."

Parallel Montage

Death happens on two planes, the world of the living and the death realm. In archaic societies death was willed within not only the death realm but also, as something that happens to the physical body, the world of the living. For us, there is a distinction between the world of the living, where death not only can be natural or accidental but most often is so; and the death realm, where it is viewed by the dead as willed by one or more others. We know now that *precision bombing* was an imprecise term to describe much of what took place in the Gulf War, since only 8.8 percent of the bombs dropped on the Iraqi forces in Kuwait and on Iraq were precision bombs.[142] While I am highly impressed by the precision of the Tomahawk missiles fired from ships offshore hitting their targets in Baghdad, I am much more impressed with the Jacob Maker-Zoltan Abbassid-Cain of David Blair's *Wax, or the Discovery of Television Among the Bees* (1992) moving in the death realm from Cain's time through 1882 and 1919 to 1991 to fire at an Iraqi tank at the exact moment it was being fired at on another plane, that of the world of the living: a parallel montage to reach a human just in time to kill him specifically on the plane of the death realm just as he is being indiscriminately killed on the plane of the world of the living. Only someone who died before dying can achieve this concurrence of the two planes. In comparison to this concurrence of the two planes, how sloppy is the American forces' touted precision, since while they are precise on one plane, they remain indiscriminate on the other plane. I am grateful to those who demonstrated against the Gulf War, but also and above all to Jacob Maker-Zoltan Abbassid, who killed two *specific* Iraqis on the death plane. David Blair redeemed these deaths, by making them singular, and for that his protagonist, Jacob Maker, and perhaps he himself, had to go through *every name in history* (including Fat Boy [the first plutonium bomb]?) *is I* by dying before dying (in the same letter in Nietzsche's handwriting, we can read: "This autumn [of 1888] ... I twice attended my funeral, first as Count Robilant," and "I am Prado, I am also Prado's father, I venture to say that I am also Lesseps.... I am also Chambige.... Every name in history is I"[143]). Notwithstanding American president George H. W. Bush and much of mainstream Western media, Saddam Hussein is not Hitler,[144] but Jacob Maker, a flight-simulation programmer in 1991, is Zoltan Abbassid, who died in 1919. In gratitude to David Blair, a kindred spirit, even were "in gratitude" in a lapse (including of consciousness) to become "ingratitude," even if on the death plane we were to betray each other.

Concerning a state of altered consciousness in which one found oneself in the past following a lapse of consciousness, if not of being, and/or realized that one had left across a lapse of consciousness, if not of being, the expression "I can talk or write about it because I've been there" is misleading, since one might very well be still there. Should one promptly commit suicide, since it seems that only this might by the same movement end the terrible plight of the version of oneself in the often terrifying realm of altered consciousness that one entered and then ostensibly left across lapses of consciousness, if not of being? But it is possible, even very probable, that by committing suicide, one would deprive that version of its ally and possible refuge from such a realm. The period that "follows" the one of altered consciousness is both later than it and simultaneous with it: a credit that, through making possible a parallel montage, may allow one to replace, at least partly, what one is undergoing in the mode of imposition in the state of altered consciousness, for example, thought insertion, compulsions, obsessions, etc., by reception. My mother calls me in New York from Lebanon because she had a presentiment that some harm happened to me or might happen to me if I am not very cautious. I, who had died before dying, tell her nothing of the sort happened to me recently. But perhaps the premonition is about the amnesiac Jalal in the death realm. Seemingly unaccountable guilt may be a signal that one is being lax in one's assistance to one's amnesiac version in a realm of altered consciousness, whom one is, moreover, unconsciously attacking. How can I help him? Except for lamas, Sufi shaykhs, and other spiritual masters, it is not oneself but one's writing that can be the guide and guardian of the amnesiac version of oneself in a realm of altered consciousness struggling against, for example, the double and thought insertion. One has to help with writing, with what is partially received, including from one's amnesiac version in the death realm, who feels that he is creating nothing, receiving nothing, but only resisting ideas and sensations imposed on him by the double. An interference, a positive one, has to be produced between one's version in a realm of altered consciousness and oneself as writer, with oneself as a person as the go-between (a dangerous position, as is manifest in Joseph Losey's film *The Go-Between*). One should continue receiving from one's version in a realm of altered consciousness as long as one considers that it has not been irrevocably and completely replaced by the double.

One can withstand the uncanny awareness that an unfamiliar event one has just experienced had already happened to one in an identical manner, indeed had done so countless times. One can also report such an awareness to another person. Were it possible that this realization of eternal recurrence not be itself subject to eternal recurrence (whether in relation to the same scene or moment or a different one), then it would be the present of eternal recurrence. To become aware that this realization as well as the event that triggered it never stop happening, that they recur eternally, is to realize that the one experiencing this realization and the one experiencing or witnessing the event that triggered it are imprisoned by them, limited to experiencing each solely. In case there is eternal recurrence, then countless moments of realization of it—"Oh! I've always been here experiencing this!"—hence moments that are not and cannot be transitive to form linear time, must exist, as refractory periods, and be occulted (i.e., one has to be amnesiac about them) in order for linear time to be constituted.

Am I dreaming? is a less apt formula for dissociation than Harker's reassuring words to Mina before he leaves to Transylvania in Murnau's *Nosferatu*: "Nothing will happen to me." Is what happens to him later really happening? At one level, in Transylvania, "the land of phantoms," he encounters only what cannot be met but only halluci- nated, phantoms, with the consequence that all that happens to him there did not actually happen. At another level, and in accordance with the above characterization of Transylvania, Harker himself turns into a phantom there, one to whom nothing will happen, every- thing having already happened to him prior to his death. A spiritual master knows that, as with the entranced person who is registering no pain in the hypnotized hand immersed in ice-cold water while his second hand is reporting out of his awareness in automatic writing an ascending intensity of pain, "Nothing will happen to me," through which someone may try to comfort his family and friends regarding what awaits him or her in what he or she is unaware is the bardo of reality (*chos nyid bar do*)/*barzakh*, while intricately accurate in relation to the dead stops (in other words, freezing) that he or she will undergo there, is all along *everything is happening to me*, including lapses of consciousness, if not of being. Indeed, soon enough after *experiencing* the inversion of *nothing will happen to me* into *everything is happening to me*, the subject explicitly invokes the help of a spiritual master/guide/reference.

Bad Reception

There are many forms of the inability to receive:
— An inability to receive receiving, whether in the form of a dis- sociation in the *amnesic syndrome* between the capacity to learn and the patient's awareness that he learned anything ("Amnesic patients can learn and retain information about many types of lab- oratory tasks over considerable periods of time, often to a degree comparable with controls.... In virtually every case the patients deny all previous knowledge of the task but nonetheless show clear evidence of retention. The phenomenal consequence of this is that the patients appear detached from their learning capability since they cannot explain how it arose"[145]); or of Freud's uncon- scious affect (Lyotard: "It suffices to imagine ... an 'excitation' that ... affects the system when it cannot deal with it.... It is an excitation that is not 'introduced.' It is thus a shock, since it 'affects' a system, but a shock of which the shocked is unaware, and which the apparatus [the mind] cannot register in accordance with and in its internal physics.... This excitation need not be 'forgotten,' repressed according to representational procedures, nor through acting out.... Its 'effect' is there nevertheless. Freud calls it 'uncon- scious affect'"[146]), which can be received only *après-coup* ("The first blow, then, strikes the apparatus without observable internal effect.... It is a shock without affect. With the second blow there

takes place an affect without shock: I buy something in a store, anxiety crushes me, I flee.... The energy dispersed in the affective cloud condenses, gets organized, brings on an action, commands a flight without a 'real' motive"[147]).

— Freezing in death and schizophrenia, death before dying.

— A total opening in death, where not only everything penetrates us but also where that which penetrates us is itself transgressing its boundaries. Isn't it the case that the concept and feeling of receiving no longer hold in death, since everything penetrates us then?

It may very well be that much of what I am writing about the state of death will be undergone later by the dead "Jalal," but by then I will no longer be able to think about it and no longer able to write. The living mortal has the chance to utter what the amnesiac version of him or her in death cannot; to receive what is imposed on the latter. There is a radical difference between the reception during the writing process of ideas as presents at the end of a perforation of a "Wall" (*Distracted*) and *thought insertion* and the imposition, for example by the voices, of ideas on one in schizophrenia and death. This imposition can also take the form of ideas associating on their own (feeling the approach of schizophrenia, Mark Vonnegut wanted to be hypnotized by a friend, to wit to lose control to him rather than to autonomous thoughts: "One of the things I might be doing now or want to do in some ways is to ask you beg you to hypnotize me. I guess I'm afraid of losing control somehow and running amuck and so if you could hypnotize me then you could control me and everything would be all right"[148]); or a doubling in the mind, hence by a double in the mind. Eisenstein: "The material of the sound-film is not dialogue. The true material of the sound-film is, of course, the monologue.... How fascinating it is to listen to one's own train of thought ... how you talk 'to yourself.'"[149] When discussing the interior monologue, Eisenstein does not take into account cases of possession and multiple personalities with no amnesic barrier between them. Let us sidetrack this "train of thought" and the "of course" off course. The material of the sound film is the monologue from which oneself is ever in danger of being excluded. If the dead don't think, it is because it is now language or their double that does *all* the *associating*.

Can what has stolen any reception from one itself receive (for example, one's style)?

Absence of Sitting
(Except while Sleeping)

She said to the vampire: "You're short." How imperceptive! Unlike ancient Egyptian seated dead figures,[150] the vampire almost never sits (Browning's *Dracula*); indeed, the height of the dining-room chairs in the vampire's castle in Murnau's *Nosferatu* is that of a standing man. He is taller than most people, for they sit frequently—how short is a sitting body! At a café, late at night, he looked on and on at the section "Sleeping" in *Weegee's New York: 335 Photographs, 1935–1960:*[151] the only sitting agreeable to him is that of people sleeping in seated positions, whether in bars, in cafés, behind the wheel of parked cars late at night (chauffeurs), between nightclub acts (performers), on park benches or in crowded night shelters for the homeless.

Close-Up

In a cinematic close shot of a specific hand, while we can witness what is particular about that body part, we no longer perceive to whom it belongs, and where and/or when it is at that moment. Similarly, when the hand becomes a close-up in hypnosis, for instance in hand-levitation induction, it no longer belongs to the subject both because it is no longer subject to his will but to that of the hypnotist and because, as far as the hypnotized subject can tell, it undergoes changes that render it different from his familiar hand: bigger or fatter or more hairy. The close-up achieved in life through hypnosis or meditation ("See the vase as it exists in itself, without any connections to other things. Exclude all other thoughts or feelings or sounds or body sensations.... Let the perception of the vase fill your entire mind"[152]) can, as in cinema, act as a switch between two different times and/or locations—the hypnotist repeated: "Where are you now?"

Ruins

All the mirages he saw in the desert were of ruins.

I along with my two siblings and my mother deserted the family apartment during the 1982 Israeli invasion of Lebanon. Did this make the apartment a ruin? Yes, but not because it was severely damaged and burned during the last days of the offensive: even after it was restored, it remained a ruin. The usual explanation of why what was damaged during the continuing civil war was most often not fixed or replaced is that people were reluctant to spend a large sum on what could at any moment be damaged again or totally destroyed. But should we not invert the way we consider what was taking place? It was because these houses had become ruins by being deserted that the war got extended until they began to turn explicitly into ruins, to manifest their being already ruins. Maybe the refusal of the Bustros family to sell their house (Jennifer Fox's *Beirut: The Last Home Movie* [1987]) was due less to their obstinate nostalgia to never part with it, and much more to an apprehension that, were they to sell it, it may be more readily deserted in a situation of intensive bombing by those who bought it, this ushering in and completing its becoming a ruin. Will we one day learn how to live in a place without dwelling in it, so that the act of deserting it would not turn it into a ruin?

"The places I showed in *India Song* were on the verge of ruin, they were unconvincing, people said that they weren't habitable. But in fact if one looked closely at them, they were not so uninhabitable.... In *Her Venetian Name in Deserted Calcutta* these places are definitely uninhabitable."[153] True? False?

— False, since in war-devastated Beirut many people lived in houses even more damaged than those shown in *Her Venetian Name in Deserted Calcutta*. The uninhabitable buildings in Beirut were the ones whose construction was interrupted by the unexpected hike in the exchange rate of the dollar against the Lebanese pound.

— True, since the actors of *India Song* do not inhabit the characters who inhabit these places. "In *India Song* the actors proposed characters but didn't embody them. Delphine Seyrig's fantastic performance in *India Song* came about because she never presents herself as someone named Anne-Marie Stretter but as her far-off, contestable double, as if uninhabited, and as if she never regarded this role as an emptiness to be enacted."[154] One of the risks of such a performance that introduces the double is that it is now the film itself that has to be double, that has a double: *Her Venetian Name in Deserted Calcutta*. And if the appearance of the double signals imminent death, then the latter film is not so much the portrayal of the death of the people and places of *India Song* ("the swallowing up by death of places and people is filmed in *Her Venetian Name in Deserted Calcutta*"[155]) as the death of the previous film itself, of *India Song*. And "let cinema go to its ruin."[156]

Ruins: places haunted by the living who inhabit them. When the Lebanese installation artists Joana Hadjithomas and Khalil Joreige write in their introductory note to their piece "Where Were You Between this Dawn and the Previous One?" "We have met, we have dreamt Sarkis, Aida, Samer, Madam Habra, Elia and the others. Through their accounts, we aim to illustrate two aspects of reality, one with destroyed buildings ... where thousands of people and refugees used to live and continue living, and the other with a family house which has been left after the owner's death. Occupied uninhabitable areas, and deserted habitable areas,"[157] should we not take their "we have met, we have dreamt Sarkis ... and the others" as indicative of the sort of uncertainty regarding whether one is dreaming that besets one on encountering a specter?

The ruin is not desecrated by the vampire, since he is not really there while he haunts it, as shown by his failure to appear in the cracked mirror at that location.

One has to see the disintegration of statues and ornamentation to know that it is precisely because it contains its memory in itself that organized matter cannot recreate the present; and that, on the contrary, it is voices which disappear, which are over (voices-over in this sense also) almost instantly and hence have no memory (of their genesis and dissolution), that can recreate the present. From *India Song* to *Her Venetian Name in Deserted Calcutta*, while the buildings and material objects became older, the voices did not.[158]

How provincial 1992 Beirut would be were it not for its war and civil-war ruins. Through becoming ruins, some buildings that were landmarks of prewar Beirut are now its labyrinthine zone. What is site-specific about Lebanon? It is the labyrinthine space-time of its ruins, what undoes the date- and site-specific.

The demolished house left its mark on the walls of the adjoining building.[159] In these houseprints, one witnesses the inside turned into an outside. One can imagine a Cronenberg character living in an apartment facing such a wall who, one day, on coming home from work, sees that the building with such a wall has been demolished: that same day, symptoms of the drive to turn the inside outside begin to manifest themselves in him.

Suddenly, one comes across a bas-relief in a war-destroyed façade, and it is as if one has made an archaeological find. But it is not really an *as if*: such objects are truly, albeit possibly transiently, archaeological. The war-damaged city center is, at least transiently, part of the archaeological sites of Lebanon—as much a part of them as Baalbek, which through its colossal structures (mainly temples) is one of the most impressive examples of Imperial Roman architecture. In 1992, Dima El Husseini, then a fifth-year architecture student at the American University of Beirut, went, as part of an excursion by her class, to the destroyed city center, before the sandbag barricades were cleared and the area officially opened. The duty to look at the buildings from an architectural perspective and to position them within a mental map while the different regions were being mentioned ("This was Souk El Tawileh.... This was Bab Idriss ...") entered into conflict with the emotional reverberation of these names and the memories recounted by her parents that they evoked. The too-many stimuli with which she had to deal during the excursion left the whole episode in abeyance, making it very difficult to take stock of what occurred. Later, in her home, she tried to recall what she'd seen. Instead of the destroyed, deserted city center, it was the city center of the memories of her parents, the colorful, populated city center that sprang to her mind. Only with difficulty could she recall the destroyed city center and superimpose it on the prewar city center. This corroborates that there is a very old past that the present of ruins itself gives rise to, for indeed in that case it is natural that it would be more difficult to remember the destroyed city center, which is maybe as old as Baalbek, in any case older than the 1940s, than to remember the city center that the recounted memories of her parents evoked, hence which belonged to the 1960s, 1950s, 1940s. It was only by the third or fourth visit to that area that she really felt that the destroyed city center was the reality—what facilitated this realization was her noticing the presence of refugees in some of the destroyed buildings.

Those who are reconstructing Beirut's Central District under the banner and motto "Ancient City of the Future" are oblivious that ruins give rise to and exist in a past that is artificial, one that does not belong to history, was not gradually produced by it. All discourse on authenticity implies a suspicion toward, and prepares the ground for, an attack on recent ruins, accepting only ancient "ruins," archeological "ruins," many of which while not restored are probably no longer ruins, no longer labyrinthine in their temporality and space, indeed never were.

One can preserve a war-damaged or crumbling building, but no one has any control over whether it will remain a ruin. I am fascinated by how and why some war-damaged or crumbling buildings turn from ruins, with their labyrinthine temporality, to more or less precisely datable structures in chronological time. The work of the American architectural firm SITE, for example, the BEST Forest Building (Richmond, Virginia, 1980), where a forest seems to invade the building; and Indeterminate Façade, where a stack of bricks cascades through an indent in the façade, never achieves this idiosyncratic temporality, thus fails to produce ruins (and specters). While some of the war-damaged buildings that had turned into ruins were subsequently subsumed again in chronological time, many were still ruins, thus their destruction was as irreverent as would be that of the archaeological ruins of Baalbek, indeed even more irreverent: because ruins exist in a labyrinthine temporality, they are instantly ancient. The physical destruction of some of the severely damaged buildings to construct others in their place is vain because a ruin cannot be intentionally eliminated since even when it is reconstructed or demolished and replaced by a new building the reconstructed or new building is actually still a ruin, that is, contains a labyrinthine space and time, which becomes manifest at least in flashes. Such physical destruction is unseemly because of the brutal unawareness it betrays of the different space and time ruins contain. It exhibits a complementary brutality to the one shown during the war. The demolition of many of the ruined buildings of the city center by implosions or otherwise was war by other means. We can detect whether a certain war-damaged building is a ruin by whether it is haunted (or reported to be haunted—is there a difference?) or induces fantastic or horror fiction that does not fall apart "two days" later.

Whether Lebanon would be hospitable to the undead depends on whether some of the numerous war-damaged buildings there are still ruins, with a labyrinthine temporality.

Judging from what happened in Beirut's war-devastated city center, even ruins, thus labyrinths, can be bought and sold! Were the system that is presently in power, the capitalist one, to maintain its hegemony far into the future, then I project that even black holes, which, while not psychological, except in bad horror films and novels, are spiritual, as is indicated by their temporality that is not limited to the chronological, and which do not belong to the universe but border it, will be bought and sold by the universe's denizens.

Sometimes I have the apprehension that the reconstructions in Beirut's Central District are not real, that one day I may actually see them the way the protagonist of Kenji Mizoguchi's *Ugetsu Monogatari* (1953) perceives the exquisite mansion as a ruin on finding out that the lover he meets there is actually a revenant.[160] For as long as there are still war-damaged buildings in the Central District, one of the areas most severely damaged by the fighting during the civil war, such buildings will evoke a counter to the enormous weight of the myriad concrete buildings that are being constructed in the rest of Beirut with no regard for urban planning. But some measure will have to be devised to counter and alleviate the effect of saturation, indeed of surfeit, that will be felt when the whole of the damaged city is reconstructed or built anew. One such measure is to project at night, Krzysztof Wodiczko-wise, life-size images of destroyed buildings over at least some of the reconstructed ones. Another measure is to start screening, on the day when the last building has been reconstructed, the aforementioned film twenty-four hours a day somewhere in Beirut, for example, at the war-damaged Grand Theatre—until the images have so deteriorated that one sees only countless film scratches on the screen. I predict that when war-damaged buildings have vanished from the Beirutscape, some people will begin complaining to psychiatrists that they are apprehending even reconstructed buildings as ruins. While the imagination of disaster for a city such as Los Angeles, which has not already been reduced to ruins, is that of its destruction, exemplarily in an earthquake,[161] for Beirut it is fundamentally that of its revelation when reconstructed as still a ruined city.

While ruins, as physical structures doomed to reconstruction or demolition or slow deterioration, quickly give us the impulse, if not the urge, to preserve documents of them in photographs, video, or film, they nonetheless basically instance an architecture bound up with fiction. For while I can reach certain facets of reality and explore them without passing through fiction, or psychosis with its attendant hallucinations, which reveals these subjects as documentary ones even if they are shot in fiction films, I cannot do so with ruins. There has to be a relay between documentary and fiction whenever one deals with ruins—or else a documentary on ruins has to continue with interviews with or a section on psychotics. Fiction has to reveal to us the anomalous, labyrinthine space-time of ruins; and, in case no ruins subsist for the ghost to appear, to supplement reality as a site of return of the revenant. In postwar countries, fiction is too serious a matter to be left to "imaginative" people. The ghost is often fictional, not in the sense that he or she is merely "1. a. An imaginative creation or a pretense that does not represent actuality but has been invented. 2. A lie" (*American Heritage Dictionary*), but in the sense that one of the main loci for his or her appearance is fiction, whether novels, short stories, films, or videos. It is too dangerous after a civil war or a war, which produce so much unfinished business, for there to be no ghosts both in reality (haunted houses) and in fiction that builds "a universe that doesn't fall apart two days later" (Philip K. Dick)—the current virtual absence of novels and films about revenants in Lebanon is one of the signs of a collective dissociative amnesia.[162] We are yet to witness the proliferation of a horror literature of ghosts and the undead (fiction may thus bring about a catharsis for the revenant and an exorcism for the living); or to hear many more stories about ghosts in Beirut once its Central District is inhabited, and not, as now, still largely unoccupied, mostly because of the recession. Were neither of these eventualities to happen, then this would be a further instance of dissociative amnesia, this time that of those who died prematurely and unjustly in the war.

Undone Circles

In a state of altered consciousness, midway in a circular path, one suddenly felt that there is a drastic distinction between the left and right directions, one direction becoming the good one, the other the evil one.

Labyrinth

The man in the painting's foreground has his back to the spectator. The diegetic painter in the painting's background is partly turned toward the figure in the foreground and partly toward the canvas to add the final brushstroke to his representation of his model also from the back! The two 180-degree over-turns undergone by the foreground figure, one away from the spectator he was facing and one away from the painter doing his portrait in the background, do not add up to 360 degrees or negate each other, do not return him to his starting position: a labyrinthine circle.

The real labyrinth in Kubrick's *The Shining* is not the physical maze in the grounds of the hotel but the book Jack Torrance is writing, made of exclusively of the repetition of the same phrase, so that the reader returns again and again to it (would the book's title be the same phrase?). It is because Torrance is already lost in the labyrinth of the book that he is unable to find the exit out of the physical maze. Fleeing his murderous father in the latter, Danny retraces his footprints, at one point jumping to the side and hiding behind one of the hedges, so that his father, following his footprints, sees them cease—beyond is virgin snow. Danny, who is telepathic and clairvoyant, is not dealing with a labyrinth, since he deals with a linear, although reversible, time: he sees the linear future and the linear past; and since at no point while retracing his footprints backward does he either see or have the apprehension that he would witness them end abruptly.

Having been locked by his wife in the pantry, Jack Torrance is nonetheless subsequently found outside it, although none of the living occupants of the hotel have unlocked the door. This does not necessitate resorting to the hypothesis that someone dead opened the door but can be accounted for by the circumstance that Torrance is "in" a labyrinth, where the inside is outside—and vice versa: it is easy to overlook the circumstance that the *overlook*ing shots of the credits sequence that begins *The Shining*, showing Jack Torrance's drive up to the Overlook Hotel, are part of the hotel.

While the castle of the historical Vlad the Impaler, whose "sobriquet, Dracula (meaning 'son of Dracul'), was derived from the Latin *draco* ('dragon'),"[163] and the castles of vampires in films and novels have secret passages, the former, part of the natural world, unlike the latter, cannot lead to a labyrinth, space's secret.

One of Milton Erickson's induction methods, the *confusion technique*, which he uses when faced with the conscious interference or resistance of the subject, entails confusing the subject so much ("To get there now ... I take a combination of three *right* turns and three *left* turns.... But I don't know which is the *right* series of *rights* and *lefts*.... All *right*, pay attention very closely, because we've got to make it *right* or we'll be *left* behind.... I'll take a *right* here [I think that's *right*], and then a *left* and now I'm *left* with two *lefts* and two *rights*. So all *right*, I'll take another *left*, which means I am now *left* with a *left* and a *right* and a *right* ...")[164] that he ends up complying with any leading statement ("Drop into trance") that would extricate him or her from the confusion. In Stoker's *Dracula*, the undead says to Harker at the door of his castle, "Enter freely and of your own free will!" only after the latter has been disoriented spatially ("The carriage went at a hard pace along, then we made a complete turn and went along another straight road. It seemed to me that we were simply going over and over the same ground again; and so I took note of some salient point, and found that this was so"[165]) and temporally ("I must have been asleep, for certainly if I had been fully awake I must have noticed the approach to such a remarkable place"[166]) and no longer knows where he is and whether he might not have already entered the castle during his lapse of consciousness.

Omens and warnings almost always refer to the apparent threshold. There is a *false threshold* to the labyrinth: prior to it one is outside the labyrinth, *past* it one has always been "in" the labyrinth and can thenceforth ostensibly be outside it only through it. While there is a threshold between the mostly homogeneous space and time of conscious life and labyrinthine space and time, that of the death realm, there isn't one in the other direction, thus this threshold is a one-way one.

Near the beginning of Roman Polanski's *The Fearless Vampire Killers*, the professor puts the skis on in the wrong direction: a crossing of the *imaginary line*. In Robert Zemeckis's *Death Becomes Her*, the undead Madeline Ashton momentarily wanders with a 180-degree-dislocated neck: an over-turn. In *The Spider's Stratagem*, Draifa describes the main enemy of Athos's legendary father with the cunning phrase "He doesn't live … he rules." The reader of Dostoevsky's *The Double* may notice the even slyer usage of the metaphorical to hide the literal: "more dead than alive,"[167] and "He had no more life in him."[168] Warning that concerns the reader or spectator and not only the character: be cautious about the fact that you are noticing these warnings and omens of the labyrinth in the guise of jokes, parapraxes, and metaphors, since, unfortunately, such foreshadowing continues to occur even after you are already in the labyrinth, seducing you into both thinking that you are not yet in it and into continuing to interpret them rather than revert to an eclipse of meaning. With respect to a labyrinth, the only time when you don't need the warnings is when you don't notice them, since one notices these warnings only in the labyrinth. When lost, not only in space and time, but also in one's mind, one should stop following signs and landmarks, but above all disregard the subliminal, what one glimpsed fleetingly at the edge of one's vision, or had a presentiment of, or vaguely sensed. An eclipse of meaning should occur.

If memory is supported by a spatial mapping (Frances Yates's *The Art of Memory*), then in the labyrinth one has an erroneous and defective memory, or else no memory at all.

To be in a place without indisputably being in it, as is made manifest by one's absence in the mirror there; and, vice versa, while not being in a place, to appear to be in it, as implied by the paranoid feeling some others have of being gazed at by one notwithstanding that nobody can see one there: is this not a good definition of haunting? One is never fully in the labyrinth but haunts it.

We should understand the Christian marriage vow, *till death do us part*, as implying following the spouse to the death realm and being parted from him or her by that realm's labyrinthine space and time.

The pursuers of the undead soon separate from each other, usually by first dividing at some crossroads into two groups ostensibly to maximize their chances of finding him. If it happens that there is a pregnant woman among them, she will not encounter the undead until either she aborts her fetus from fear or some other shock or else gives birth, whether prematurely or not, to her baby only to get separated from him. Why is it one encounters the vampire or a certain kind of ghost alone? Why is it that when one is with others he or she does not appear? Is it necessarily because he or she is a subjective hallucination of the witness? Rather, it is because the vampire and a certain kind of ghost belong to the labyrinthine realm of death, a realm where people are lost, including to each other.[169] Therefore, the ghost of Hamlet's father, who is seen by Hamlet while in the company of Horatio and two guards, does not really belong to the death realm. It is a different matter with the ghost in Shakespeare's *Julius Caesar*. Brutus: "Canst thou hold up thy heavy eyes awhile, / And touch thy instrument a strain or two?" Lucius: "Ay, my lord, an't please you." Brutus: "It does, my boy. / I trouble thee too much, but thou art willing." Lucius: "It is my duty, sir." Brutus: "I should not urge thy duty past thy might. / I know young bloods look for a time of rest." Lucius: "I have slept, my lord, already." Brutus: "... And thou shalt sleep again. / I will not hold thee long." Lucius plays music for a short time and falls asleep; it is then that the threatening ghost of Caesar appears to Brutus. We can be lost together in a homogenous space; not so in a labyrinth, where we cannot be together and consequently cannot be lost together. Now that he was lost to the others, the vampire appeared to him. He began running but failed to evade his undead pursuer although the latter was walking nonchalantly. This failure confirmed the space to be a labyrinth.[170] The circularity of time may still spare the one pursued from the result of the circularity of space: he is still fleeing the vampire who has already caught him; the one pursued asked himself then: "Was my fatal encounter with the vampire a dream or a hallucination?" If a community can prevail over the vampire, it is not because each of its members can deploy his or her expertise and knack in their communal fight against the undead, since in the labyrinthine space and time of death, they are lost to each other and so "confront" the vampire alone; but because their different fragments of narrative (letters, ship logs, diaries, etc.), each of which does not and cannot form a unified narrative, allow the intercutting of a smooth story and consequently the establishment of a map. The letters, ship logs, and diaries from the various people who have encountered the vampire alone in the labyrinth reach the one who ends up editing them through telesthesia[171] (the tele- mode truly comes into its own only when the messenger and the recipient are separated by a labyrinth, the message then reaching the recipient from the sender notwithstanding that the messenger was lost and will remain lost in the labyrinth). It is thus fitting that it is the telesthetic Mina who assembles them. It is only once the letters, ship logs, and diaries have been edited to compose a chronological narrative and the map that goes with it that a communal encounter with the vampire can happen.

It is impossible to leave the labyrinthine realm of undeath. This impossibility can take several forms:

— I may not be able to physically leave: in Kubrick's *The Shining*, Torrance is fatally frozen in the snow in the physical maze that is part of the labyrinthine hotel.

— I may lose consciousness at the border, whether in the manner of Harker in Murnau's and Herzog's films *Nosferatu*, who falls unconscious as he lets go of his short rope dangling from the very high window of the otherwise closed castle; or, more frequently, by becoming entranced, so that not having any recollection of having crossed the border, I cannot be sure that while ostensibly outside the labyrinth, I, or a version or component of me, am not still inside the labyrinth.

— Or, while it may initially seem to others that I left the labyrinth, soon enough discountenancing indications signal that it is another who left it: thus in Herzog's *Nosferatu*, while it seems that Harker succeeds in leaving Nosferatu's castle, it shortly becomes manifest, through his failure to recognize his fiancée, his recoil when presented with consecrated wafer, his two fang-like teeth, and his remarkable pallor, that the one who left the castle is actually the vampire.

Death is not an issue out of the labyrinth.

Transit Visa to the Labyrinth?!

The title of a May 2001 workshop organized by Lebanese video makers Mahmoud Hojeij and Akram Zaatari, for which they invited seven persons from four Middle Eastern countries and from various fields (cinema, video, graphic design, etc.) to come to Lebanon, join two Lebanese, and each make, along with the latter, a one-minute video by the end of the workshop, was *Transit Visa*. Doesn't postwar Lebanon have anything labyrinthine about it? If it does, does it make sense to have a transit visa to it? Does it make sense to have a transit visa to a labyrinth? Isn't it impossible to leave the labyrinth? Doesn't the notion of having a transit visa to Lebanon imply that, notwithstanding its ruins, it is not a labyrinth? The protagonist of my coming, first feature film will be a vampire who was intrigued enough by the video images of both war-damaged and reconstructed buildings sent to him by a Lebanese real-estate agent to come to Lebanon. When, soon after arriving in Beirut, he was asked by a Lebanese who was unaware of his condition "Why did you come to Lebanon?"[172] he answered bluntly, "For ruins and blood ..." "I can understand that one would come to Lebanon for its war ruins, but why would anyone come to Lebanon in 2002 for blood? The war and the civil war ended over a decade ago!" "Like most Lebanese, you are overlooking the yearly ten-day commemorative event 'Āshūrā'. In a letter a writer sent me from Lebanon, he wrote: 'During 'Āshūrā', one again feels that one's body is a jasad (in Arabic jasad means "the body, with the limbs or members, [or whole person,] of a human being, and of a jinnee [or genie], and of an angel ..."; and jasida [aor.; jasad, inf. n.] means "It [blood] stuck, or adhered, bihi [to him, or it]; and it [blood] became dry"[173]).' Moreover, and as I was saying before you rudely interrupted me, I came to Lebanon also because 31.7 percent of the population in this country is under the age of fifteen according to the latest United Nations' Human Development Report." The vampire tries to find his territory in this foreign city—while knowing that the dead are in a labyrinth, therefore in permanent exile. On first meeting his employer, the agent was surprised: for some reason, he expected him to be older. Oddly, he found himself having this expectation at each of his subsequent meetings with the vampire. A few nights later, the vampire visited seven war-damaged buildings with him. The vampire was not satisfied with any of them. But then he suddenly asked to see the interior of the reconstructed building that faced the last of these. Once inside it, he told the agent that he wanted to buy it. The agent exclaimed: "But you specified that you wanted a ruin! I don't think you should so quickly lose hope of finding what you wanted, a ruin." As the agent finished saying this, he saw in a flash one of the rooms as a ruin and the vampire as a very old man, and then the room appeared again in mint condition and the vampire again as a thirty-something man. The vampire said, "Where are you now?" and the ostensibly reconstructed house appeared again as a ruin, with a few yellowish, rotting papers and photographs strewn on the floor. The agent picked up the photograph closest to him. It showed the living room. He picked up a second photograph. It showed him in the building. He screamed: "But I've never been here before!" While he was picking up a third photograph, the vampire remarked: "The moment you enter the labyrinth, you've been there before." The agent let go of the photograph he had just glimpsed, screamed, and fell unconscious: the photograph showed him lying on the floor, blood on his neck. Did the vampire bite his victim or did blood ooze from the latter's neck through stigmata? Several nights later, feeling a powerful urge to sustain himself on blood, the vampire went out in search of prey. He took with him a wind-up toy as a bait, placed it on his table in the café, and then started looking at a book full of reproductions of Hans Bellmer's doll works. Around an hour later, a woman entered the café and sat on the chair next to him. Notwithstanding his revulsion at the stench of pubescents,[174] in the unavailability of a prepubescent the drive for and addiction to blood was simply too strong to resist. He was on the point of engaging in a fascinating conversation with her to lure her to his lair and attack her, but quickly desisted upon espying a prepubescent girl enter the café. Fifteen minutes later she approached him and asked him if she could play with the toy. Once again he felt that an equivalent to courtly love can still exist—toward prepubescents. (If we can continue to be irreplaceable even after we reach puberty and can reproduce sexually, it is insofar as we are mortals, that is, already dead [even as we live]: while people can fatally sacrifice themselves for me, i.e., lose their lives for me, no one can experience *every name in history is I*,[175] i.e., my replaceability in death, in my place.) The vampire asked the prepubescent girl: "What is my name?" "I don't know. I will call you 'M.'" "Hmm, why 'M'?" "Because you are a Mister." "What is your name?" "Elsa." "Elsa, the abbreviation of 'Mister' is 'Mr.' not 'M.'[176] I will give you the toy if you successfully parse these sentences for me." He opened to the entry *al-mushtahāt* (the desirable female) in Muḥammad 'Alī al-Tahānawī's *Mawsū'at kashshāf iṣṭilāḥāt al-funūn wa al-'ulūm* (Encyclopedia of artistic and scientific terminology): "'inda al-fuqahā' imra'a yarghab fīhā al-rijāl wahiya bint tis' sinīn wa 'alayh al-fatwa. Wa 'an al-shaykhayn anna bint khams sinīn mushtahāt idha ishtuhiyat mithluhā. Wa 'an Muḥammad anna bint thamānin aw tis'in mushtahāt idha kānat dakhmah kamā fī al-Muḥīt kadhā fī Jāmi' al-rumūz"[177] (In the opinion of the [Muslim] jurisprudents, she is a woman craved by men while a girl of nine years—this is the fatwa respecting this matter. And in the opinion of the two Shaykhs, a girl of five years is desirable if she is desired like her. And in the view of Muhammad, a girl of eight or nine is desirable if she has an ample figure, cf. both *al-Muḥīt* and *Jāmi' al-rumūz*). She started to parse the sentences. When she finished, he told her: "Notwithstanding that you made two mistakes, here's the toy." He then opened his notebook and jotted down: "While I tend to agree with what Jalal Toufic wrote in *Distracted*: 'To let the house crumble until there remains a wall. This wall may turn into a "Wall." A "Wall" cannot be demolished. The one who tries to demolish it turns into a normal person, becomes himself a "Wall." To perforate the "Wall." Perforation should go on until one reaches the most terrible, best hidden of all "Walls": one's teeth. The teeth themselves must get perforated, become ones through which the universe circulates'; I would, fetishistically, except the uneven teeth of prepubescent girls during the process of shedding the deciduous ones and their replacement by permanent ones." He looked up at her to see her uneven teeth again. He discovered that she had already broken the toy. He liked that prepubescents were metaphysicians and theoreticians: "The overriding desire of most little brats ...

is to get at and *see the soul* of their toys.... On the more or less swift invasion of this desire depends the lifetime of the toy. I cannot find it in me to blame this infantile mania: it is the first metaphysical stirring.... He [the child] twists and turns the toy, scratches it, shakes it, bangs it against the wall, hurls it to the ground.... Finally he pries it open.... But *where is its soul?* This moment marks the beginnings of stupor and melancholia"[178] (Charles Baudelaire, "The Philosophy of Toys"). He resumed flipping through the book of reproductions of Bellmer's doll works and saw a similar pattern of disjointed limbs. He felt erotically aroused. On some pretext, he got her to come to the reconstructed war-damaged house he had purchased in the Central District, and placed his lips on her neck, and felt, first, the warmth of her skin. He then sucked her blood. Satiated, he let go of her. But then, as he glanced at her again and saw the blood still seeping from her neck, he again felt aroused. He licked the line of blood flowing down her neck until he reached her nipple; he bit her there and licked the blood that oozed out.[179] Since in the unavailability of a prepubescent the drive for and addiction to blood was simply too strong to resist, a fortnight later he sucked the blood of a woman. A few nights after that, she told him: "Last night, on seeing a man walking alone in the street, I had the compulsion to drink his blood, in other words, I already saw myself attacking him. It appears that in compulsion, one is late not so much in relation to one's plan but to the action itself, so that it is no longer an issue of deciding whether or not to do it but of catching up with what one somehow has already started doing. And indeed, I threw the man to the ground and sucked his blood. *The moment of his death actually escaped me, because ... even at that very moment, and even afterward, yes, even afterward, ... I couldn't feel the slightest difference between this dead body and mine. All I could find between this body and mine were obvious similarities.*"[180] "Then you have seen nothing since then, nothing." "You've given me *the malady of death*.[181]" "Would you like to go to the premiere of Jalal Toufic's video *The Sleep of Reason: This Blood Spilled in My Veins* at Madina Theatre, or would you prefer to stay 'here' and read?" They opted for the premiere. While waiting for the film to begin, he said to her: "I am relieved that Beirut is not as crowded as I thought it would be." "Given that you are frozen during the day and are roused only at night, I do not find it surprising that you would find Beirut, or for that matter any city, not crowded." "I was worried that the seemingly reconstructed and empty Central District would be even more crowded with revenants than the rest of Beirut is with living people." During the scene of the butchering of animals at a slaughterhouse, many people left. Following the video, the vampire overheard one person, then another, remark that the video was unbalanced. He became visibly annoyed. When she asked him why, he answered: "I have noticed that the majority of spectators are not sensitive enough to the uncanniness of certain statements, for instance, the two epigraphs that open the video, 'On the authority of Hudhayfa: The Apostle of God, may God bless and save him, would ... say on going to bed, "In Your name, O God, I die and live," and he would say on waking up, "Praise be to God, Who hath revived us after putting us to death, and to Whom is the Resurrection"' (narrated by al-Bukhārī, in Al-imām an-Nawawī's *Gardens of the Righteous*) and 'Our friend Lazarus has fallen asleep; but I am going there to wake him up' (John 11:11), either because they take them figuratively or because they implicitly, unconsciously correct the author, substituting for the strange original statement what they think the author must have meant (to most spectators of *Hiroshima mon amour*, Duras must not have really meant 'You have seen nothing in Hiroshima. Nothing' [the Japanese man's words to the French woman acting in a film being shot in the city] but something along the lines of '[Given that you are a foreigner and/or that you were not in Hiroshima during or in the aftermath of the nuclear explosion, etc.,] you have seen very little in Hiroshima'— they actually think that one of the great authors of the twentieth century was unable to convey exactly what she meant [consciously ... and *unconsciously—as a writer*]). If one is not sensitive enough to the uncanniness of its two epigraphs, then the irruption of the protracted slaughter of the animals, especially of the second cow, would indeed eclipse the other sections, including those in which the uncanny statement(s) appeared, thus giving the spurious impression that the video is unbalanced. I fully excuse and condone people's leaving the cinema during the slaughter of the cow, but I would have liked to also see at least one spectator leave on reading the video's epigraphs, John 11:11 and the tradition regarding what the Prophet Muhammad used to say on going to bed and on waking up." Unable to find any good dancers in Lebanon, the vampire went out to see a film musical whenever one was being screened: on this night, one of his favorites, Vincente Minnelli's *An American in Paris*, was showing in a cine club. Unfortunately, during the projection he was annoyed by the persistent conversations and comments of many of the Lebanese spectators. When one of these inconsiderate, talkative spectators went to the bathroom during the projection, the vampire followed him. After finishing urinating, the man began washing his hands. He looked at the vampire and said: "An awful film, don't you think? Anyway, I don't care for dance and musicals." "If by *awful* you mean 'commanding awe' then, yes, it is awful. But how come you came to watch it if you don't like musicals?" "My new girlfriend is a dancer. She insisted that we watch this film, one of her favorites, together. How could I refuse the earnest request of someone who the night before had exclaimed to me 'You cannot believe, in fact I myself cannot believe, how much I love you. I love you more than I love myself! I want to accompany you all the time.'" "What is your name?" "Sāmī.... Do you like dancers?" "Yes." "What is it that attracts you about them?" "Well, for one thing, that we are both threatened in the contemporary world. 'The desire of contemporary masses to bring things "closer" spatially and humanly' (Walter Benjamin), which is one of 'the social bases of the contemporary decay of the aura,' would mean that dance and also death will increasingly come under attack in an attempt to do away with them since they are, to my knowledge, the two last realms of the aura and thus of distance—one is never totally with the dancer, who, while still moving as a physical body in the same location with the nondancer or another dancer, is projected as a subtle body in (another branch of) the dance realm (than the one in which the other dancer is projected); or with the undead, as is clear from his absence in the mirror in the same location where he appears to be present. Are you familiar with how a film is fabricated?" "Yes, I work in a TV station." "You must know, then, that you should keep your mouth shut since your voice is not part of the soundtrack of this film that does not subscribe to John Cage's aesthetics.[182] You shouldn't talk when you're watching a film, because it should be like dreaming or like death: one finds oneself in these alone." At this abrupt turn of the tone of his interlocutor and his implying that he was dead, the man intuitively turned away from him toward the mirror and saw there only his own reflection.[183] When he turned back toward the vampire to check whether he was still there, the latter abruptly sank his fangs in his neck. When he woke up the next morning in his bed, he tried to dismiss the events of the previous night as merely a dream or a hallucination. But when he looked out the window a few minutes later, he saw the passersby walking in slow motion. He wondered: "Am I in a movie?"[184] He heard a voice behind his back whisper clearly: "If you are, then one way of averting being surprised is to reach the stage of rushes, since the breaks between them are not perceived as jump cuts." Despite his dread, he managed to turn but found no one. He turned back toward the window: the passersby were frozen, as they are on several occasions in Minnelli's film.[185] Fearing to stay alone, he called his girlfriend and asked her to come and stay with him for a few hours. She promptly came. Despite her night shift, she offered to remain with him till the morning, but he declined her offer. Readying herself to leave for work, she put on makeup in front of the mirror. He looked out of the window; again, he saw people walking in slow motion. He screamed her name. She turned toward him. He pointed to the street and was on the point of saying that people were walking in slow motion when he noticed that they were now walking in a normal way. He apologized for startling her. She smiled compassionately, then turned back to resume her makeup. But now, it was her turn to exclaim: her image in the mirror was not facing her but still looking in his direction, lovingly.[186] She turned toward him to check whether he was looking at the mirror: he wasn't. When she looked back at the mirror, she saw what we usually see there, her reflection facing her. After she left, and despite his dread, he went back to the same cinema, The Scene of the Crime, to try to understand what had happened the previous night. Duras's *India Song* was playing that night. Unsurprisingly, this time he did not talk during the projection even though the spectator seated next to him tried several times to engage him in a conversation. Half an hour into *India Song*, he was seized by anxiety and paranoia as he saw that the on-screen protagonists, too, did not open their mouths. What a coincidence: why was it on this singular day, on which he found himself reluctant to talk, that this cinema was screening, of all films, *India Song*? He rushed to the bathroom, to be away from these speechless characters and to take a tranquilizer and wash his sweaty face and hands. He heard the vampire's voice: "Sāmī, turn toward me." He turned but found himself still facing in the same direction, away from the vampire. The vampire continued: "He, a dead man with his back to him, turns toward him, but his turn is overturned by an over-turn, with the result that he continues to look in the original direction. Do you know the beginning of T. S. Eliot's *Ash Wednesday*? 'Because I do not hope to turn again / Because I do not hope.'" Later that night, at "his" ruin, the vampire performed a ritual for his new victim that allowed the latter to talk again. "Thank you for making it possible for me to speak again! For a moment yesterday while you were sucking my blood, I thought that you would go all the way and kill me!" "Are you sure that you're presently alive? I would have thought that following the series of eerie, otherwise unexplainable happenings you underwent or witnessed you would have already come to the conclusion 'I must have died.'" The vampire's interlocutor was seized by anxiety and remained momentarily speechless. The vampire resumed: "The dead cannot talk until they go through the ceremony of the Opening of the Mouth." When the vampire met his victim a few nights later to go to a cinema to watch Parajanov's *Sayat Nova*, he told him: "For a number of years, Parajanov's *Sayat Nova* was not screened because of extrinsic reasons: the Soviet regime's credo of socialist realism in the field of art and cinema, etc. But films are not seen sometimes for intrinsic reasons, and this time their invisibility is not to be decried. 'You have seen nothing in Hiroshima, nothing': this statement from Alain Resnais's *Hiroshima mon amour*, said by the Japanese man to the French woman, applies to the film spectator, who is performatively withheld his or her vision by it, as much as to the female protagonist, who is or becomes part of the community of the surpassing disaster and thus is affected by the withdrawal of tradition past such a disaster. From *Sayat Nova* on, Parajanov's films are not seen because the jump cuts recall the spectator to his or her inexistence in an atomistic universe of renewed creation. I want to recall to you your nonexistence: look in the mirror." And indeed, on looking in the mirror, the vampire's interlocutor did not see himself. He felt vertigo; he did not know where exactly he was: whether in the ruin or not. "How disorienting and strange: while looking in the mirror, I do not see my reflection there, and therefore I feel that I don't have a body, indeed that I don't exist at all; and yet I've never been so aware of my body, because ever since the night you mortally sucked my blood, I vertiginously feel that I am indefinitely falling. I am experiencing now additionally the vertigo of the contrast of these two vertiginous experiences, one indicating that I have a body, albeit reduced to a cadaver, an endless fall,[187] and the other implying contrariwise that I don't have a body! I assume you, too, feel this kind of vertigo constantly?" "Yes. Do you know anything about black holes?" "Very little." The vampire headed toward his bookshelf. As he passed the mirror on the wall, neither he nor his interlocutor appeared in it. He took out a book, opened it, and began reading aloud from it: "'What is the distance from the horizon to the singularity? ... Since the singularity is so small, 10^{-33} centimeter, and is at the precise center of the [black] hole, the distance from singularity to horizon should be equal to the horizon's radius. You are tempted to calculate this radius by the standard method of dividing the circumference by 2π. However, in your studies on Earth you were warned not to believe such a calculation.... Space can be so extremely warped near the singularity that the chaotic region might be millions of kilometers in radius though only a fraction of a centimeter in circumference.'[188] Similarly, while the human corpse is physically less than three meters tall, one can fall 'in' the cadaver indefinitely." "Did you feel vertigo when you were alive, too?" "Yes, and I remember the first time I felt it. It was not while standing on the balcony of some high-rise but when I read about the relativity of motion. But back to black holes, since one doesn't leave (the subject of) black holes (easily). In the summer of 1995, the Lebanese artist Ziad Abillama distributed a written request to the other forty-four participants in the collective Sanayeh Garden Project, asking them to grant him a space of thirty cubic centimeters in each of the twenty-three projects being prepared: to actualize his own intervention. While some granted the request, many declined. Indeed, two of the participants felt offended by it. Maybe their refusal stemmed from an obscure feeling that they had not yet produced the outside that has to do with their artwork, its outside (for instance the crows of Van Gogh's *Wheatfield with Crows* or the [matted] birds with markedly electronic sounds of Hitchcock's *The Birds*), an outside without which it cannot remain consistent; and therefore that it was premature to add his alien outside. My qualm with the move of Abillama is that it tends to imply that the anomalous element has to be provided from outside, that the artwork does not itself have it, when in fact any 'universe that doesn't fall apart two days later' (Philip K. Dick) manages to avoid this eventuality precisely because it contains in itself its own zone(s) where it breaks down ('in' our physical universe in the form of black holes with their singularities, where, according to general relativity, the curvature of spacetime becomes infinitely large and spacetime ceases to exist). Does one encounter, hit against, an impossibility in the creation of a universe? Yes, but that does not mean that it is impossible to create a universe, but rather that each universe that doesn't fall apart 'two days' later contains an impossibility. The other participants in the Sanayeh Garden Project, including those who refused Abillama's request, were, unbeknownst to themselves, trying to do the same move in relation to nature: works of art are in a sense these 'thirty cubic centimenters' that artists request from or impose on the universe, inserting through them in nature something that does not belong to it, for instance, the over-turn. Isn't *La Reproduction interdite* (*Not to Be Reproduced* [1937]) a 'thirty cubic centimeters' (to be precise, 81.3 x 65 cm) space requested from the universe/nature, which does not contain over-turns, or imposed on it by René Magritte? Our world is consistent enough not only to subsist for more than two days but also not to fall apart with the introduction through artistic and literary works of what is *out of this world* (in both the literal sense and the *colloquial* and *slang* sense ['(originally *U.S. Jazz*): ... fine beyond description ... wonderful, amazing' (*Oxford Dictionary of English*, 3rd ed.)]) (would our world fall apart as soon as the Gnostic alien Savior appears in it?). Sophisticated as they are, artists and writers should try to 'build a universe that doesn't fall apart two days later' (Philip K. Dick; cf. Nietzsche: 'I teach you ... the creating friend who always has a complete world to bestow'[189]) and then try to avoid credulously becoming sucked totally into it (Nietzsche again: 'The universe must be splintered apart; respect for the universe unlearned'[190]). Attempting to break up and disperse a universe presupposes that it doesn't fall apart on its own two days after its creation—I do not think that this had already happened with the participants in the Sanayeh Garden Project; consequently, it was too early to disrupt. The percentage of successful universes, ones that last for more than 'two days,' is no greater in the physical multiverse than in fiction and art: the vast majority of the *baby universes* that appear in the physical universe do not have enough consistency, and so disappear in less than 'two days.' What can resist, indeed does resist the expansion of globalization is not the local of every country, but the universal of artistic works, each of which presents a universe." While undergoing his initiation, the vampire's latest victim soon felt the need to find a dancer, who can be in a place and simultaneously not in it but elsewhere. It was now clear to him that his girlfriend was no real dancer. He visited several dance companies but was dissatisfied with them. Did he, in the absence of real dancers in Lebanon, try to recreate the impression they induce of being superimposed on a different location than the one where they are moving by going out with a weathercaster, given that the background against which the latter provides her forecast is chroma keyed? Yes. He managed to lure her to the apparently reconstructed building that had been given to him by the vampire and which gave onto the gutted and shrapnel-pocked Grand Theater. Standing with her at the window, he wondered aloud: "How many more bombs will it take to produce in Lebanon not just holes in buildings but a hole, however small, in reality, a tear in reality itself, so that it would no longer be seamless?" (As he finishes saying this, the camera would pan to the mirror, where the vampire does not appear, is a hole in it.) He then bit her and drank her blood. When she came back to consciousness, she felt famished. She headed to a restaurant. She felt relieved that it was not as crowded as usual, for she was presently feeling hypersensitive to sounds. She stood at the counter to order. She felt nauseated by the smell of the food—a smell that she would have found exquisite before. One Lebanese man, then two others, then a fourth came and stood before her to order. One of the men standing in front of her said: "It's empty tonight!" His friend agreed. She felt anxious that they were not seeing her, and that this was because she no longer existed. She rushed to the bathroom and looked apprehensively at the mirror: she appeared in it! She was relieved that the disregarding behavior of the four customers at the counter was to be attributed merely to the Lebanese's common incivility in queues. She spent the next few nights "with" the vampire. When her fiancé next met her, she was so anemic she had to be rushed to the hospital. He waited in the hall outside the emergency room. He could see from one of the windows a man pacing back and forth in the street. Every time he passed a certain spot in front of the house across the street, the automatic light would turn on and then switch off again once he moved away. After a while, that man headed to the emergency room to check the condition of the father he'd brought in shortly before. When the fiancé looked out from the window again, he saw another man pacing back and forth. He was unsettled by the phenomenon he saw next: the light did not turn on when that man passed the same spot in front of the house. In the coming days, the fiancée was to discover that that man was a vampire. A few nights after her discharge from the hospital, the weathercaster was back at the vampire's house. He said to her: "Do your weather forecast." "Here? With no blue screen or maps?" "Yes." She began moving her right hand across the air, stopping it momentarily and pointing at certain invisible marks: "In Beirut, it is 82°F (high: 82; low: 63); in Tehran, 84°F (high: 84; low: 72); in Esfahan, 84°F (high: 84; low: 52); in Paris, 57°F (high: 70; low: 57); in Berlin, 57°F (high: 59; low: 52); in London, 61°F (high: 63; low: 61); in Bremen, 61°F (high: 66; low: 54) ..." She looked in the mirror and was hypnotized by the absence of the vampire in it. His response was "They have ... eyes, but cannot see" (Psalms 135:16). Then he, who continued not to appear in the mirror, asked her: "Where are you now? In London? Bremen? Transylvania? Lebanon?" He bit her on the neck and began sucking her blood. At this point her fiancé rushed in: "At long last I found you!" The vampire's mocking response was: "Where?" The lover ran toward her body, waved his right hand in front of her eyes then checked her pulse to ascertain whether she was dead, then shrieked: "You've killed her!" Given his hypersensitivity to the micro-movements that announce a gesture, the vampire not only followed with his eyes but also predicted all gestures—except one: that of the movement of the hand in front of the eyes of someone to check for signs of consciousness or life. The moment the fiancé stopped waving his hand, the vampire regained his seeming vision, tunneling just next to him. Instinctively, the fiancé repeated the same waving gesture, but now in the direction of the vampire. The latter's eyes suddenly become glazed, and once more he no longer saw. Regaining his composure, the lover said to the vampire: "After all, as you must know, the dead cannot see." Unseeing, the vampire responded: "Insensitive that you are, I cannot reciprocally tell you: you have seen nothing in Beirut, the site of a surpassing disaster, nothing." While continuing to wave his left hand in front of the vampire's eyes, he reached for a dagger with his right hand and stretched it toward the vampire's back and stabbed him deep inside the region of the heart. We *stab* the dead, those subject to over-turns, *in the back*.

Transit Visa? Does the ghost, who does not stay in a place but haunts it and who is thus the in-transit being *par excellence*,[191] need a transit visa? It does not seem to be the case: while on their respective arrivals on the platform before the Elsinore castle in Act I, Scene I of Shakespeare's *Hamlet*, first Barnardo is told by Francisco at his post, "Stand and unfold yourself" (to which Barnardo responds: "Long live the King!"), then Horatio and Marcellus are ordered by Francisco, "Stand ho! Who is there?" (to which Horatio responds: "Friends to this ground," and Marcellus elaborates: "And liegemen to the Dane"), the ghost is not asked to "stand and unfold" himself when he appears on the platform. The ghost is not with us in the same space, nor for that matter in the same country: while the vampire ostensibly standing with us is revealed not to be in our company through not appearing with us in the mirror, the ghost is shown not to be with us through glitches and other troubles in communication, which reveal that he is not there in person, that our conversation with him is actually a telecommunication with the beyond, that we are dealing with a telepresence (of what no longer has a presence):

Two remote audiovisual conferencing setups are linked across continents (Elsinore, Europe, and Beirut, Asia) through the internet. Barnardo, Marcellus, and Horatio await the arrival of the signal. "We have tried this setup twice already, most recently yesterday. We got a signal only for a short period: the second time for the span during which 'one with moderate haste might tell a hundred'; the first time for somewhat longer. Then it broke off." After a few minutes' wait, a signal appears.

Enter Ghost.

MARCELLUS
  Peace, break thee off! Look where it comes again.

BARNARDO
  In the same figure like the King that's dead.

MARCELLUS, *to Horatio*
  Thou art a scholar. Speak to it, Horatio.

BARNARDO
  Looks he not like the King? Mark it, Horatio.

HORATIO
  Most like. It harrows me with fear and wonder.

BARNARDO
  It would be spoke to.

MARCELLUS
  Speak to it, Horatio.

HORATIO
  What art thou that usurp'st this time of night,
  Together with that fair and warlike form
  In which the majesty of buried Denmark
  Did sometimes march? By heaven, I charge thee,
  speak.

The signal becomes gradually weaker.

...

HORATIO
  Stay, speak, speak, I charge thee speak.

By this point, the signal has become too jumbled and weak, drowned in noise.

MARCELLUS
  'Tis gone and will not answer.

...

They tinker with the computer, and soon enough the connection is reestablished and the signal is clear again.

Enter Ghost.

HORATIO
But soft, behold! Lo, where it comes again!
... Stay ...

It spreads his arms.
...

O, speak!

...

BARNARDO
'Tis here.

HORATIO
'Tis here.

The signal again becomes weak and then cuts off.

MARCELLUS
'Tis gone.

When Horatio asks the ghost of the late king to speak but the latter doesn't talk, the scene looks very much like one of the initial experiments in using the Internet to establish a live audiovisual communication between individuals in various countries or continents, the sound signal failing to reach Horatio although the image does (to Hamlet's "Did you not speak to it?" Horatio answers: "My lord, I did, / But answer made it none; yet once methought / It lifted up its head and did address / Itself to motion like as it would speak ..."). Yet even if the ghost fails to articulate properly his linguistic message; or moves his lips but his voice is not heard at all by his interlocutor; or his words are drowned in some eerie rumble so that his interlocutor does not get what he says; or the connection is often unstable or lost, his mere appearance conveys all by itself an important part of his message, namely, that there is something wrong, indeed rotten in the family, or the village, or the country, or the world (commenting on the ghost's appearance, Marcellus says: "Something is rotten in the state of Denmark"). Isn't Lebanon, a country that underwent fifteen years of civil war as well as foreign invasions and numerous massacres, haunted? How can the Lebanese live normally when, according to Fitch Ratings, "at end-2001, Lebanon's government debt reached 168 percent of GDP, the highest of any rated sovereign";[192] when Israel, the country at Lebanon's southern border, has a warmonger, Ariel Sharon, as premier; when Iraq, a fellow Arab country, is still under barbaric sanctions; when Elie Hobeika, who was the head of the Phalangists' intelligence division in 1982 and who was blamed by Israel's Kahan Commission for personally directing the slaughter of Palestinians in the Sabra and Shatila refugee camps between September 16 and 18, 1982 (a massacre in which between seven hundred and several thousand Palestinians were killed), served three times as minister in various postwar Lebanese governments and was for a number of years the member of parliament for Baabda; when religious sectarianism is still entrenched in the population even after fifteen years of civil war; when wiretapping is legal; when there is a flagrant remissness in enforcing a livable urban plan, etc.?[193] According to Deleuze, one of the characteristics of "the crisis which has shaken the action-image [and which] has depended on many factors which only had their full effect after the [second world] war" is "events which never truly concern the person who provokes or is subject to them, even when they strike him in his flesh: events whose bearer, a man internally dead, as Lumet says, is in a hurry to extricate himself."[194] This is the price the Lebanese are paying for giving up the ghost, for the repression of the revenant now a decade after the war. When the ghost is banished or repressed, people turn into zombies, act insouciant in the weirdest and most alarming of situations. Henry Miller: "Once you have given up the ghost, everything follows with dead certainty, even in the midst of chaos" (the opening line of *Tropic of Capricorn*); Miller's words are insightful not only when *give up the ghost* is understood as an *idiom* meaning "to die; ... [UK] to stop trying to do something because you know that you will not succeed" (*Cambridge Advanced Learner's Dictionary & Thesaurus*), but also when the "give up" in the expression is understood to mean "(3) part with something that one would prefer to keep; ... (5) stop hoping that someone is still going to arrive" (*Oxford Dictionary of English*, 3rd ed.), so that "give up the ghost" means part with the ghost, whom one would have preferred to keep, and stop hoping that he or she is still going to arrive. After vast catastrophes, we need the ghost to keep implying to us by his mere haunting how rotten is the country where we live (when Hamlet returns from his encounter with the specter, Horatio asks him: "There's no offence, my lord." Hamlet answers: "Yes, by Saint Patrick, but there is, Horatio, / And much offence, too"), and thus prevent us from turning into zombies. In postwar Lebanon, Rwanda, Cambodia, Bosnia and Herzegovina, etc., the survivors are faced with the following choice: either tolerate the ghost, resist the temptation of repressing or banishing him or her, or else gradually

143

turn into zombies (in the Haitian sense). With its unjust death of King Hamlet, Shakespeare's *Hamlet* deals with this alternative. Prince Hamlet's words to his mother in her closet characterize her as a zombie:

HAMLET
... Ha! Have you eyes?
...
... Sense sure you have,
Else could you not have motion; but sure that sense
Is apoplexed; for madness would not err,
Nor sense to ecstasy was ne'er so thralled,
But it reserved some quantity of choice
To serve in such a difference. What devil was 't
That thus hath cozened you at hoodman-blind?
Eyes without feeling, feeling without sight,
Ears without hands or eyes, smelling sans all,
Or but a sickly part of one true sense
Could not so mope....

As Hamlet finishes describing his mother as a zombie,[195] the ghost of his late father appears. We are thus provided with an occasion to witness the cause of her state as zombie: she has repressed the ghost (and hence does not see him).

Enter Ghost.

HAMLET
Save me and hover o'er me with your wings,
You heavenly guards!—What would your gracious figure?

QUEEN
Alas, he's mad.

...

HAMLET
How is it with you, lady?

Queen
Alas, how is 't with you,
That you do bend your eye on vacancy
And with th' incorporal air do hold discourse?

Letters

Mina establishes a unifying chronology from the journals and letters of the different characters. "The incorporation of the separate accounts into a 'connected' narrative is an act of confession. Jonathan must acknowledge his desire for Dracula's brides; Seward must reveal the shortcomings of his scientific assumptions as well as his most personal feelings about Lucy; and so on. 'We have told our secrets,' Van Helsing later declares."[196] These confessions, though, hide that a more fundamental secret is being hidden, for the different fragments, like different shots from different angles, are being used to edit out all the objective inconsistencies in the chronology and space. This remains a secret to them: they confessed their mundane secrets precisely to hide more basic secrets: the inconsistencies in reality—the risk of a certain kind of telepathy and telesthesia is that it can extend what each person can perceive so far beyond the usual limits that inconsistencies in what he or she took to be the world until then begin to show up, making his or her world fall apart. If it is only the community, rather than any one individual, that can conquer Dracula, it is not because each can contribute his particular skill to the fight but because the different points of view permit the intercutting of a smooth story that does away with the inconsistencies to be otherwise met in the world when or where it falls apart.[197] Gregory Waller writes that by divulging the letters and diaries, "the limitations of each individual perspective are exposed"[198]—but this only in order to replace them by the limitation of the community's perspective.

In films that underscore the theme of telepathy and telesthesia, a letter does not so much serve to convey information to others—since they would telepathically and/or telaesthetically apprehend what is happening[199]—as to create a distance between its writer and the dangerous space-time where he is located[200]—as if the one writing a letter can be reached only by a letter.

Counterfeiting

There is a radical difference between the secrets and/or lies that are part of a living person's history (in the opening scene of *Singin' in the Rain*, the flashback images belie star Don Lockwood's glorifying description of his first years in cinema), and the counterfeiting that relates not to history but to the late, the dead. In Billy Wilder's *Fedora* (1978), the film producer Barry Detweiler joins thousands of mourning fans paying tribute to the recently dead movie star Fedora laid in her coffin. While waiting in line, he recalls his recent brief encounters with her on the island of Corfu; his flashback ends with his seeing her photograph on the front page of a Greek newspaper and being informed by a native that the headline announces her death. The film's second part shows his search for the truth of the late Fedora. The past of the late is a superposition of different states with various probabilities. The same way the kind of measuring device inflects the result in quantum mechanics, the personality, desire, and motives of the one searching for the truth of the late inflects this "truth." The producer now "discovers" that the corpse in the casket is not Fedora's but that of her daughter, Antonia, who looks exactly like her mother did when young; that Fedora, after a disastrous operation, was deformed and became unrecognizable; that following the death of a certain Countess Sobryanski, Fedora impersonated her; that Antonia impersonated her mother for the reception of an Oscar from the president of the Academy of Motion Picture Arts and Sciences; and that it was Antonia who acted Fedora's last three starring roles. All of this discloses nothing about the historical truth of the living Fedora. History is always of the living and for them. At the level of the historical past, what the producer saw in Corfu was the case: Fedora's doctor managed to arrest her aging; she was the guest of Countess Sobryanski; and she had forgotten about her one-night stand thirty years earlier with him, then a mere assistant on the set. Between historical recollection and the counterfeiting regarding the late, there is the caesura of Fedora's death. "Who is Athos Magnani? ... A traitor or a hero? ... What was the real story of Athos Magnani?" That is the question around which Bernardo Bertolucci's *The Spider's Stratagem* revolves. Historically, most likely he was what the other citizens of Tara believed him to be: a martyr assassinated by fascists. Certainly, his story was transfigured on its way to becoming a legend with elements from *Macbeth* and *Julius Caesar*. But from the perspective of his son's attempt to know the truth of his late father, Athos Magnani is a traitor. "Why did he betray?" He did because his son's search for his story after his death inflected that story; we are to expect such a posthumous influence in the case of the *late*. *The only good traitor is a dead traitor*, not only because that is the one traitor who is not dangerous to us but also, essentially, because every dead person is a traitor, first and primarily to himself or herself. The dead traitor is the only traitor I do not condemn, not because death would have been his punishment already but because every dead is a traitor. Unlike *Fedora* and *The Spider's Stratagem*, and notwithstanding its problematization of how little can be really known about a person, *Citizen Kane*, which starts with the questions "What made Kane what he was? And, for that matter, what was he? ... What's behind the career? What's the man? Was he good or bad? Strong or foolish? Tragic or silly? Why did he do all those things? What was he after?" sticks to life. One can envision a film in which, following the joint deaths of an "immortal star" and her maid, a living person goes about his investigation of who they were differently, exploring the late in the case of the maid but sticking to history in the case of the star. The film would be treating the latter as an immortal.

In Agatha Christie's *Murder on the Orient Express*, during private detective Hercule Poirot's trip on the Orient Express train from Istanbul to Calais, a wealthy American named Samuel Ratchett is murdered in his compartment. Poirot propounds two solutions to the murder. One of these sticks to history, while the other follows the late. According to the first, the murderer joined the train at Belgrade or Vincovci, changed into a Wagon Lit Uniform, mortally stabbed Ratchett at a quarter past twelve, then left the train before it got stuck in a snowdrift at half past twelve. According to the second solution, which investigates *the late*, Ratchett was traveling under an assumed name and was actually the gangster Cassetti, responsible years earlier for kidnapping three-year-old Daisy Armstrong, collecting a ransom from the wealthy Armstrong family, then revealing that he had already killed the child; and he was murdered by the twelve occupants of the Calais-Stamboul coach, who, related in some form to the Armstrong family, were avenging his crime. It is appropriate that in Christie's book, the Armstrong case is mentioned posterior to the murder; it is a weakness in Sidney Lumet's film adaptation (1974) to have started with the section on the Armstrong story, since this later establishes Ratchett as already Cassetti even before he is murdered. The bad forgery perpetuated by Lumet makes of Poirot's first solution a fictional one fabricated solely for humanitarian, hence extrinsic, reasons.

Secrets

Light, which renders visible, can destroy the vampire, the secretive, the one who remains imperceptible even when it ostensibly manifests him, as is made clear by his nonappearance in the mirror at the location where he is ostensibly standing with his interlocutor[201] (this implying that his apparent presence outside the mirror might very well be a *positive hallucination* of his interlocutor), because it is simultaneously the paradigm of the secretive (and not just in the case when it comes in excess, blinding, hence maintaining secret). One version of the secretiveness of light is the double-slit experiment: a very weak coherent light—one photon at a time—moves from source to detector, between which is a screen with two very tiny slits, at A and B. If B is closed, the photon goes through the open slit. The same if A is closed. When both are open and we do not know through which slit the photon passed, there is interference. If we put detectors at A and B to be able to tell through which hole the photon goes when both holes are open, interference no longer occurs. We can have interference only if the path the photon took remains a secret to us.[202]

Are You Sure I Saw It?

While Dreyer's *Passion of Joan of Arc*, which consists mostly of close-ups, is constructed through looks and eye directions, his next film, *Vampyr*, tackles the impossibility of looking and/or the undecidability of whether an act of vision is taking place. In the fourth shot, Gray moves a few steps away from an inn's glass door and looks up. The next shot is a pan of the roof that continues with a tilt down and ends with Gray entering the frame that was supposedly his point-of-view shot. Hence, as early as the sequence formed of the fourth and fifth shots, one is witnessing either:

— a dissemination of vision, Gray looking at himself, one expecting that an explicit out-of-body experience will be undergone by him, since these states make it possible for someone to witness what otherwise he or she cannot see.

— or else an impossibility of vision, the fifth shot revealing itself to be an objective one rather than a point-of-view shot. The two-shot sequence would then serve to caution the film spectator not to take a shot of what is before the open eyes of the vampire as the view of the vampire, to wit, of the dead, not to forget that the dead cannot see (the world of the living). It seems that Dreyer was aware that this cautionary measure will either be overlooked or else prove inefficacious, so he made the dead additionally blind. After sucking the blood of Léone in the garden, "the figure turns its head irritably and stares at the newcomers with the dead eyes of a blind person."[203] A shot of Gray and Gisèle, who have come to rescue Léone, follows. How strange that the spectators who consider the scene toward the end of the film in which a shot of Gray in the coffin is followed by his point of view as anomalous do not hesitate to take the aforementioned shot of Gray and Gisèle as the point of view of the blind vampire! But that the vampire should have a point-of-view shot is more paradoxical than that Gray lying in the coffin should have one, for what's taking place in the latter's case could be similar to what occurs in tetrodotoxin-poisoning cases: paralysis of motor functions with retention of consciousness.[204]

It doesn't go without saying that the ghost sees, but not in the normal way, through the eyes; it may be that he sees through the voice he utters. Therefore, prior to beginning to talk to Prince Hamlet, the ghost of King Hamlet does not see him; he sees him only as he speaks to him. He sees him with his speech. While in Shakespeare's *King Lear*, it is a matter of seeing with one's ears (King Lear to the blinded Gloucester: "A man may see how this world goes with no eyes. Look with thine ears" [4.6]; cf. "The eye of man hath not heard, the ear of man hath not seen, man's hand is not able to taste, his tongue to conceive, nor his heart to report what my dream was" [Shakespeare's *A Midsummer Night's Dream*, 4.1]), in his *Hamlet* it is a matter of seeing with one's speech. If we ask the ghost to speak, it is less to hear his message—for we always intimate more or less what he has to say (Hamlet: "O my prophetic soul!")—than to induce him to reciprocally see us through his talk (even if in his characteristically askew way). So the question is not only whether one will see the ghost (Queen Gertrude: "To whom do you speak this?" Hamlet: "Do you see nothing there?" Queen Gertrude: "Nothing at all; yet all that is I see"); it is also whether he or she will see us.

In a number of scenes in *Vampyr*, the sequence of shot of a person looking/point-of-view shot/shot of the same person looking is short-circuited. As Gray enters a cluttered, dust-covered room and looks in front of him, a camera movement reveals an empty coffin and beyond it a placard with the inscription "Doctor of medicine." The camera then swish pans from the latter to Gray moving away. Vision remains uncertain without a return to a shot of the looking person, and thus without being claimed. It is not only the spectator who is unsure whether Gray saw the inscription before he moved away: the uncertainty extends to Gray himself.

In *Last Year at Marienbad*, a shot of five people looking in different directions is followed by a point-of-view shot, which is followed by the same shot of the five people still looking in the same directions. This induces a strange memory since it is not clear whose point of view the interpolated shot was. The uncertainty is not merely that of the spectator but belongs to the diegetic world: any of the five can remember what the point-of-view shot showed, if not in actuality then by right. Thus, those of the five who could later have affirmed that they were looking at something else then—perhaps all five will earnestly affirm this—will nonetheless probably have the impression that they are amnesiac about something related to what took place in that shot.

Since the undead is not really there, only layered on a location and thus not clearly localizable, his victim's look is awry with respect to the abstract line the film spectator traces between vampire and victim. In some future vampire film, the first section, which takes place in some postwar city (Sarajevo, Beirut ...) and in which all the characters are still living, should digitally incorporate several long-dead actors who interact seamlessly with the contemporary living ones. In the subsequent section, which takes place in Transylvania, with only living actors but with some of the characters now undead, the gazes should frequently if not always be askew. As the vampire moved, Harker's gaze moved with him, but always remaining at an angle, awry, hence accompanied him while not accompanying him.

In Wenders's *The Wrong Move* (1985), a medium shot of a teenage girl sitting in a train and looking is followed by a shot of a train seat stained with blood, then by a medium shot of the adult male protagonist sitting at the opposite window and looking in the direction of the stained seat. Whose point of view was the shot of the bloodstains on the seat? Not children in common, but point-of-view shots.[205] This is also the case between the disciple and his spiritual master, even, or rather especially, when the former is dead, in the *barzakh*.

In one scene in Fritz Lang's *The Testament of Dr. Mabuse*, Baum gets hypnotized by the specter of Mabuse. The shot of Baum reading at the beginning of the scene is intercut with shots of masks, skulls, and a painting with distorted faces. These are gazing at Baum, from the same point of view, since the reverse shot, showing Baum, is from the same angle irrespective of the fact that the direction of the eyes of some of these objects, located in different sections of the room, is not the same (that he is gazed at even by skulls implies that in his condition this is done not with eyes [even those of the masks and in the painting] but by these objects in their entirety). *Ça vous regarde*: (1) it concerns you; (2) it looks at you. Such conjunction is misleading, for it is only when something *qui ne vous regarde pas* [which does not concern you] intrudes on you that *ça vous regarde* [it gazes at you], you simultaneously losing the possibility of looking: Baum's sight becomes impossible as the objects in the room gaze at him going deeper and deeper into hypnosis.

A black hole is invisible. Nonetheless, it can be detected: The primary star, HDE 226868, of the binary star system Cygnus X-1 "is a hot supergiant revolving about an unseen companion with a period of 5.6 days. Analysis of the binary orbit led to the finding that the companion has a mass greater than seven solar masses. (The mass has been determined from subsequent observations to be nearly nine solar masses.) A star of that mass should have a detectable spectrum, but the companion does not; from this and other evidence astronomers have argued that it must be a black hole. The X-ray emission is understood as being due to matter torn from the primary star that is being heated as it is drawn to the black hole."[206] Similarly, the vampire is not visible in the mirror, but his presence can be detected by the attraction such a hypnotic absence of an image exerts on the look of the other, reflected person. While standing with Nosferatu in front of a mirror in Herzog's *Nosferatu*, the gaze of Lucy, who is to the left, is attracted to the right side of the mirror although there is no image there (while the vampire's gaze, since he has no reflection and since the camera has been positioned in place of the mirror, seems to be and is in fact directed at the film spectator).[207]

In Wenders's *The American Friend*, Jonathan is presented with a chilling proposition by a stranger: commit murder for a hefty sum. His reply is: "You must take me for somebody else." Later, a frontal tracking shot of Jonathan going to meet the same man in the airport is followed by a camera movement, at the same pace, toward Jonathan sleeping on an airport couch. The latter shot could be Jonathan's point of view. In which case we are witnessing an out-of-body experience indicative of a dissociation. This dissociation, which implies that he has become also somebody else, marks the decision to commit the crime.

The suspended movement and awry looks of people in Edward Hopper's paintings are the effects of a gravity-induced slowing down of time and bending of light. Many Hopper paintings empty of any human presence seem to be the points of view of the persons looking off-frame in some of his other paintings. If, nonetheless, there is a strong sense of the absence of vision in these points of view, it is due to the extreme slowing down of the light reflected off these objects, up to its suspension, with the result that it has yet to reach the looking human figures in the other painting. The perceptual virginity in Hopper's work is to be found mainly in this delay that suspends the look so that the painted view as a point of view is nonetheless seen first by the spectator of the painting.

We are moving toward a telesthetic era, one that deals for the most part with matting and overlay, which means we are increasingly becoming blind to the immediate environment, over a section of which is superimposed a matte. In Buñuel's *The Phantom of Liberty* (1974), the parents, who have been asked to come at once to the school because their daughter was kidnapped from her classroom, stand there with the superintendent and the teacher reviewing the circumstances in which the kidnapping occurred, while the daughter, standing in the same room, is chided by her mother when she interrupts the adults' conversation. The parents *and their daughter* then go to the police to report on the continuing disappearance of the daughter and to ask that the police find her. These two scenes show a response that will be, with the mounting use of mattes or their equivalents, much more frequently encountered: the person one is perceiving in the same space-time with one is treated as overlaid there, hence as not really present there.

The Emperor's New Costume; or, The Case of the Missing Mask

A fear so pervasive it blocks even the hypnotically dissociated part from performing automatic writing.

The conversing guests were moving their lips soundlessly. Was his state of altered consciousness distorting what he was seeing, the soundlessness of the conversations either a subjective illusion or the result of his projecting his fear onto others? Or was it revealing to him the others' constant fear? Were they scared without knowing it, even as they laughed and talked? Seeing them, he was reminded how, when horrified, one opens one's mouth to scream but cannot utter the shout. Their soundless conversations are a scream, one as expressive as that of the vice-consul in *India Song*, and as that, implied, of the wounded woman in Eisenstein's silent film *Potemkin*. He, like the protagonist of Munch's *The Scream*, covered his ears with his hands.

The inability to scream caused by fear is the beginning of a deafness. Fear makes one unable to speak—even in the form of the interior monologue.

Seeing the vampire at the end of the corridor leading to his room, the guest was so terrified he could not utter the scream. Needles to say, the bite of the vampire was acupuncture that released his scream.

David Pirie is set, in his *The Vampire Cinema*, on correcting mistakes. He mentions that a number of early shorts have wrongly been included in vampire filmographies: *Vampires of the Coast* (1909), *The Vampire* (1911), *The Vampire's Tower* (1913), *The Vampire's Clutch* (1914), *Vampires of the Night* (1914), *Tracked by a Vampire* (1914), *A Village Vampire* (1916). Many of these movies used the term "vampire" in the sense of vamp, femme fatale. Yet he writes on page 46 of the same book: "Later he sees a snowy-haired wrinkled old woman and watches her being handed some poison by the village doctor." It is the other way around in *Vampyr*: the vampire hands the doctor the poison bottle. On the same page, the caption of a still of Gisèle (played by Rena Mandel) tied up in the vampire's lair reads: "Léone, the vampire's victim in Dreyer's *Vampyr*, is played by Sybille Schmitz." What sloppy work from someone whose mediocrity shields him from fear and its effects! Jean-Louis Schefer wrote: "In Dreyer's film *Vampyr*, a mill wheel, flour, the vampire pressed against a wall.... Dreyer's vampire expires before our eyes, caught simultaneously in the machinery's movement, in a shower of white powder (like the body of an insect falling within the sand of an hourglass) ..."[208] He mistakes the doctor for the vampire. Roland Barthes wrote, "In Dreyer's *Vampyr*, as a friend points out, the camera moves from house to cemetery recording what the dead man sees.... The spectator can no longer take up any position, for he cannot identify his eye with the closed eyes of the dead man,"[209] when in fact Gray's eyes are open. Shouldn't the last two errors be ascribed to fear, which makes us flee so quickly, swish pan our look, that we do not see clearly?

Since David Lynch has accomplished one of the exemplary manners of instancing fear, to wit making it regular: the protagonist's hair is standing on end throughout *Eraserhead*; to write a novel where there is no mention of fear, where it is, as in Patricia Highsmith's *Ripley's Game*, displaced onto such phrases as "*I'm afraid* I can't help you,"[210] "*I'm afraid* I haven't changed my mind about that,"[211] "*I'm afraid* it's no go" (my italics),[212] or externalized in other characters' masks, while the protagonist acts detached, indifferent.

The masks I find arresting are those that are the product of either the fear-induced swish pan or tilt of our look away from the fearful object or our virtual recoiling from it and thus remoteness. The shot in Bokanowski's *L'Ange* that begins as a very high-angle one of a handless seated man and a maid bringing him a pitcher and continues with a zoom-in movement is odd, since what we apprehend at the end of the zoom-in movement are clear masks, i.e., our remoteness, which make us unable to discern the features of the face. Was there a crossing of the *imaginary line* during the zoom in, so that, imperceptibly to us, it became a zoom-out (a labyrinthine structure)? In Adrian Lyne's *Jacob's Ladder*, the blurriness of the demon-like figures Jacob sees both in the speeding car and on the subway is caused by the fear-induced swish pans of his look away from them. This blurriness produced by the fear-induced swish pan is the mask; hence the connection of such a mask with the fleeting. While the blurred version of the mask is emphasized in *Jacob's Ladder* and the clear version is underscored in *L'Ange* and *The Shining*, both are equally prominent in the work of Ralph Eugene Meatyard:

— the out-of-focus version of the mask in the photographs where the persons are not moving, such as *Untitled* [*possibly* a self-portrait in a room wallpapered with newspapers][213] (1967–68), *Untitled* [*it could be* an interior with two boys] (1961), *To—El Mochuelo* [*maybe* boys with a noose] (1962), *Untitled* [*I have the feeling it is* a male nude in a bathroom] (1970), *Untitled* [*perhaps* two boys, one seen through a hole in a wall] (1962), *Untitled* [*conceivably* a child as a bird][214] (1960);[215]

— the clear version of the mask in *Untitled* [*perhaps* a sitting boy with a mask and masked hands—*Lucybelle Crater*] (1960), *Romance (N.) from Ambrose Bierce #3* (1962), *Untitled* [*perhaps* a woman and a child framing a window—*Lucybelle Crater and Lucybelle Crater*] (1970–72), and *Untitled* [*perhaps* a girl atop a woman] (1970–72);[216]

— the conjunction of the two in the same photograph in *Untitled* [*plausibly* a masked woman with a girl on a ladder] (1970–72), and *Occasion for Diriment* [*apparently* a young girl and a masked boy beating his breast] (1962).[217]

The fear-induced swish pan or tilt or zoom-out is what makes the aforementioned photographs, which are at the level of their production not only posed but also staged, snapshots. The mask we witness in *L'Ange*, *Jacob's Ladder*, and Meatyard's work is not a physical one that serves to hide the one behind it but is the effect of the fear-induced swish pan of the look of the one in front of the horrifying sight, or his virtual recoiling from the latter.

The mask someone wears may be a stratagem to imply the other's fear. In such a case, the purpose of donning a dreadful mask is not so much to psychologically induce fear in the other as to impose on him the suggestion that, while he may not be aware of it, he is afraid: while one may be able to resist psychological fear, continuing to look at the frightening entity despite one's fear, the fear implied by the mask allows of no resistance, since the mask is tacitly the visual effect of one's swish pan of avoiding looking at something. When I see a mask, I may be psychologically frightened by it, but even if I am not, it suggests to me, irrespective of whether it has a horrifying expression, that I am afraid, since it may have been produced by the swish pan of my look away from what it is masking. To criticize works where a courageous warrior undauntedly fights masked, demon-like figure as idealizing, simplistic portrayals of heroes, ones that do not show them betraying any fear, is to miss the swish pan completely. The masks of these demonic figures are the hero's fear made visible. If I find donning a mask unfair, it is not owing to a moralizing attitude that condemns hiding the truth, but because of the added advantage whoever dons a mask has by reason of the association of the latter with the swish pan of the look away from the object it is ostensibly masking and hence with fear ("When the amygdala senses fear, the cerebral cortex [area of the brain that harnesses reasoning and judgment] becomes impaired,"[218] etc.). When the other dons a mask to imply my fear, the appropriate way to show my absence of fear is to remove it. When the protagonist of Kubrick's *Eyes Wide Shut* asks the masked woman with the gorgeous body to remove her mask, this is not only because he desires her and wants to see her face and to know who she is but also because the mask over her face implies that she scares him, when she no longer does, as she had come to warn him and help him evade danger. The mask does not cover the face but is the product of the fear-induced inability to look attentively and meticulously at the face. The mask does not abstract the essential features and give them the utmost expressivity; indeed, it has no proper features, but only the distortions produced by the fear-induced swish pan of averting looking. In this sense, the mask, however much it may be specific, for instance with a smaller or bigger nose or a singular expression, does not denote an individualization at all; hence the indistinguishability of the adult female Lucybelle from a three-year-old male (*Lucybelle Crater & 20 yr old son's 3 yr old son, also her 3 yr old grandson—Lucybelle Crater* [1969–70]); from a legless female (*Lucybelle Crater & 20 yr old son's legless wife Lucybelle Crater* [1969–70]); from a fifteen-year-old boy (*Lucybelle Crater & 15 yr old son Lucybelle Crater* [1970]), etc. The different masks in Meatyard's Lucybelle Crater series are as little differentiable as the identical masks/faces of the eight librarians in *L'Ange*.

During a break in his child's math homework, his child said to him: "I overheard a conversation today between two of my teachers about the superintendent of the school. One of them used an expression I did not understand. Daddy, what are 'the emperor's new clothes'?" "They figure in a fairy tale with that title by the writer Hans Christian Andersen in which two tailors play a hoax on an emperor, convincing him that they have made for him a marvelous new dress with the property of seeming invisible to anyone who was unfit for the office he held or was a simpleton, when actually they have made none. During a public procession, each of his subjects, not wanting to be considered either unfit for his office or a simpleton, does not tell him that he is naked. He remains unaware of the actual state of affairs until someone your age confronts him with his actual situation. Had the procession happened not during the day but at this hour of the night, that child would not have had the opportunity to declare the truth about the emperor's clothes because his parents would have already tucked him in bed. Given that it is past your bedtime, let's quickly finish your math lesson. Sam borrowed from John $3.75 one day, then $6.25 a few days later. How much does he owe him in total?" "$10." He paid the cover charge and entered the nightclub. After the pianist, an acquaintance of his, finished his gig, he joined him for a drink. A phone call for the pianist interrupted their conversation. After some questioning, the pianist revealed that he was occasionally commissioned to play music at an esoteric ceremony. After further questioning, the pianist divulged that the phone call concerned an iteration of this ceremony that was to take place late that same night. "When I appeared at the gate for the first time, they unexpectedly informed me that there had been a change of plans and that they had to blindfold me during the ceremony. I consented. While they were placing a cover over my eyes, I heard approaching footsteps. They came to a stop just behind me. I then heard the guard say: 'You neither have the hood, nor the tuxedo, nor, most importantly, the mask. We cannot let you in.' I therefore presume that you need all of these in order to enter. After playing music at that ceremony, I was intrigued enough that I decided to join their society. But once I mentioned this wish to them during one of their phone calls to me, they treated me with flagrant contempt. Fortunately, once my candidacy was rejected, they again treated me courteously in my capacity as the pianist." He immediately headed to a rental shop. It was closed. He buzzed its owner at his apartment above the shop: "I am sorry to inconvenience you at this late hour, but it is urgent that I rent a costume for tonight. I'll pay you $200 extra for your trouble." Having gotten his costume, he hopped into a cab and headed to the ceremony's address. When they reached the mansion, he ordered the cab to pass it and park a block away. He changed into his costume. He was fearful as he headed toward the gate. The taxi driver honked. What did he want? He was already standing before the masked gatekeeper and did not feel like going back to check. He was worried that his fear would betray him. Nothing of the sort happened: he was ushered inside by a second masked man. He then saw a ceremony in progress, with numerous participants, all masked. The masks had various sorts of expressions: laughter, anxiety, awe, duplicity. It was clear to him that this was no customary *bal masqué*, not least because he felt no curiosity whatsoever to guess who might be behind the masks. He could espy his acquaintance, the pianist, playing music while blindfolded. Some of the masked women were naked. After watching an innocuous ritual, he walked through gallery after gallery where masked but otherwise naked people were having intercourse. Around an hour later, he was walking toward the cab, first with quick steps, then more slowly, his fear beginning to subside. As he sat in the cab, the driver told him: "I tried to alert you: You forgot your mask!" Disconcerted, he blamed his apprehension for the oversight. He wondered why they had let him in maskless. He was then seized with great embarrassment that they had pulled the wool over his eyes: they must have swiftly acted in concert to make him feel he was masked. He marveled at how ironic it was that shortly after explaining to his child what the emperor's new clothes were, he had unwittingly enacted the emperor behind his invisible mask. But he was mistaken. What actually took place was that his fearfulness had made him swish pan his look, so that he saw masks. Since his fearfulness was itself frightening ("fearful *adj.* 1. Causing or capable of causing fear; frightening. 2. Experiencing fear; frightened" [*American Heritage Dictionary*]),[219] it made others, too, swish pan their look, with the result that they, too, saw a mask, but one that did not necessarily have a fearful expression: while some saw a mask with a horrified expression, others saw a smiling one, others still saw one with a deadpan expression. Near the end of Kubrick's *The Shining*, Wendy peers into one of the rooms and sees two masked persons: were a fearless person to search the Overlook Hotel for these masks, he or she would fail to find them. This proposition, which appears in the first edition of *(Vampires)* (1993), was confirmed in Kubrick's *Eyes Wide Shut* (1999): one plausible explanation for why, when following the masked ceremony in which he participated the protagonist goes back to the costume shop to return the items he rented, he finds in his bag the tuxedo and the hood but not the mask is that he did not don a material mask at that ceremony. The fear of the spectator of *Eyes Wide Shut* is not so much induced by identification with the threatened protagonist, as implied by the fact that he or she sees masks onscreen. The perceptive spectator of that film will deduce from seeing the protagonist masked that he himself is fearful. By blindfolding the pianist, those at the ceremony acknowledged that he is fearless: he would have seen that no one was masked, even the naked ones indulging in an orgy. The person they turned away at the door in the presence of the pianist must also have been fearless. What were their criteria for accepting or rejecting someone to become an initiate? I can very well imagine them answering: "We despise both those who are fearless and those whose fear is not frightening." It was a society of the fearful, of those whose fear is frightening. They accepted only the one who perceived them, with their bare faces, as masked, and who himself appeared masked to them without wearing one. Indeed, he soon received a letter informing him of the date and whereabouts of the next ceremony, with the following nota bene: "Please do not forget to come dressed in a tuxedo and a hood." A new version can and should be made of Hans Christian Andersen's "The Emperor's New Clothes," possibly with the title "The Emperor's New Costume; or, The Case of the Missing Mask." In such a version, it is not two mischievous and dishonest weavers but two perceptive mask makers who arrive at the empire's capital. They stress that they make masks only for fearful ceremonies. They are commissioned to do so. On the appointed day, the participants in the ceremony marvel at how much meticulous artisanal work it must have taken these craftsmen to make their masks. This time, too, it was a preschooler who indicated that there were no masks. "In the *Introductory Lectures*, Freud ... tells us to look at children: they run along the brink of the water, climb on the window sill, play with sharp objects and fire. They have no notion of danger, no sense of fear.... The child must necessarily receive help from others both to satisfy its needs and to ward off danger until such time as it learns to be afraid. The child has no natural sense of fear; fear is something which is learned, and not from experience alone. We can be taught to be afraid."[220] But this time, the child's disclosure was not fully accurate, since if one is fearful, there is a mask; it therefore was legitimately rejected. "We here in the society of the fearful never cared about the truth of either cowards or the fearless, and therefore of preschoolers."

We fear fear because often fear either discloses to us or makes us sense what we know (i.e., we fear fear because we are basically gullible enough to think that what we did not know that we know is necessarily the truth). Courage is not the absence of fear, since it partly resides in confronting what fear discloses, but the absence of the fear of fear, of the swish pan that hides what fear could have revealed.

Madness is the fear of death-as-undeath that *frightens one to death*.

Unsound Silence

He was sitting in the backseat of the car during a drive from Milwaukee to Oshkosh. He could not clearly hear the voices of the two women having a conversation in the front seats. It was not that they were whispering, nor that their talk was submerged by the sound of the wind against the speeding car or by the noise of trucks overtaking their car. It was exactly as if the volume had been turned down on a radio.

He no longer heard, only overheard—even those addressing him.

He was being disintegrated by their laughs and endless talk, anticoagulants of time.

Preserved in silence-over. But what preserves one from what can preserve only by freezing? Not music that the character would play to evade the silence, since such music would itself be covered by the silence-over; but, rather, music-over.

One must become motionless to listen to the "silence." Ostensibly reciprocally, the emergence of silence-over, of dead silence, immobilizes one (*Last Year at Marienbad*), makes one dead still. Silence-over freezes the dead, or, for the brief interval before they become frozen, gives a floating feel to them and their movements, making them appear not to be touching the objects they are handling or the floor on which they are moving (since, were they to touch these, sound would ostensibly be produced),[221] so that Robbe-Grillet's recourse to soft earth ("The soft earth here makes no sound, fortunately, when anyone walks on it"[222]) or thick carpets ("silent halls where the sound of footsteps is absorbed by carpets so heavy, so thick that nothing reaches the ear ... as if the floor were still sand or gravel")[223] and Dreyer's recourse to dust in his script of *Vampyr* ("The dust is so thick there that it muffles the sound of his footsteps") are not necessary once one enters the regime of (diegetic) silence-over.

While John Cage emphasizes that there is no silence: even were one to enter an anechoic room, one would still hear a high sound, that of the nervous system in operation, and a low one, that of the blood in circulation; I stress the presence of a silence(-over) that can fall initially despite the sounds, but that soon freezes their sources.

Early in *Persona*, the doctor informs the nurse about her patient: "Mrs. Vogler is an actress, as you know, and was performing in *Electra*. In the middle of the play, she fell silent and looked around as if in surprise. She remained quiet for a minute"—I would advance that the actress became silent as she briefly sensed the approach of a silence-over in the theater. The doctor continues: "The next day, the theater rang and asked if she'd forgotten her rehearsal. When the housekeeper went in, she was still in bed. She was awake but didn't answer questions and didn't move. She's been like this for three months." How can one be sound in this silence? How not to be apprehensive that one is on the point of failing, or has already failed, to identify error or fallacy (the opposite of sound reasoning[224]), whether or not in the form of this silence?

Frozen

Marguerite Sechehaye's schizophrenic patient Renee told her: "All is unchangeable, immobile, congealed, crystallized."[225] "Schizophrenic persons often describe their sense of temporal reality as: 'things to a standstill,' 'immobility, but not calm,' ... 'people like statues,' 'frozen moment,' 'out of time' ... 'unreal stillness.'"[226]

The vampire was safe during the day even though no one was guarding him, because he was frozen and thus withheld, subtracted, from time.[227] Even the light of day cannot harm him when he is frozen. His enemies could kill him, an act that happens in and takes time, only when he was again part of time. "We look like chivalrous people waiting for this aristocrat, who belongs to an antiquated era, an era of chivalry, to 'wake up,' only then attacking him." They waited for him to come out of his freezing, then they stabbed him, who is subject to 180-degree over-turns, in the back.

The motionlessness in Duras's *India Song* is radically different from the immobility in Robbe-Grillet's *L'Immortelle*, Resnais's *Last Year at Marienbad* (script by Robbe-Grillet), and Roman Polanski's *The Tenant*. The former is merely a measure of adaptation to the heat ("What heat! Impossible. Terrible." ... "Almost no one is dancing?" "In this heat, how could you? The only remedy, immobility [in my terminology: motionlessness]. Slowness ..."), while the latter is a feature of the realm of death. Unlike Roland Barthes, I am not concerned with the extra-diegetic still,[228] but rather with the diegetic immobilization of characters or of film images *in* the motion picture. Vertov's *negative of time* is not, as Annette Michelson writes, reverse motion: "Looking for the negative of time, we find it in the use of reverse motion as analytic strategy."[229] It is, rather, the freeze frame. Vertov did not yet have the negative of time in *Kino-Glaz* (1924), so he could possibly be accused of "formalist jackstraws" when Kino-Eye "moves time backwards," giving back to the bull's carcass his entrails and then covering him in his skin and then bringing him back to life, the prostrate animal standing on its legs. But Vertov reached the negative of time in *Man with a Movie Camera* (1929), so Eisenstein's following denigration is unfounded: "It [slow-motion] is usually employed with some purely pictorial aim, such as the 'submarine kingdom' in *The Thief of Baghdad*, or to represent a dream, as in *Zvenigora*. Or, more often, it is used simply for formalist jackstraws and unmotivated camera mischief as in Vertov's *Man with the Movie-Camera*."[230] Indeed it is Eisenstein who can be charged with "formalist jackstraws" when, in *Potemkin*, three shots of three statues of a lion, in the first of which he is lying down dozing, in the second of which he is awake and ready to rise up, and in the third of which he is already risen, are edited together to give the paradoxical impression that the marble lion has risen in protest against the massacre of the Odessa Steps. It is the freeze frame in *Man with a Movie Camera* that renders possible fast-forward; slow motion; backward-in-time movement; and the self-motion of the camera, its winding mechanism, and the tripod.[231] In Vertov's *Three Songs about Lenin* (1934), the intertitle "If only Lenin could see our country now!" recurs three times. Indeed, Lenin could not see the future because his motionlessness as corpse shown in several shots is not one that allows for irregularities of time. Therefore, Vertov had to revert in this film also to freeze-framing in order to be able to have fast-forward and other time irregularities.

According to Henrik Galeen's script for Murnau's *Nosferatu*, the man who goes down to the ship's sleeping quarters comes back up with his hair abruptly turned white after seeing the vampire. Is this a stress-induced effect that might be biologically explained[232] or is it the result of a time-lapse made possible by the vampire's freezing in the coffin?

Backward-in-Time Movement

Around half an hour after regaining animation, the vampire was already uncertain whether he still had eight hours till sunrise or half an hour in the reverse direction of time till just before sunset. It turned out to be the latter. He felt his head turned to the side, as when a barber adjusts the position of one's head, and soon was going backward down the stairs to the sepulcher.

The immobilizations schizophrenics and the dead perceive and/or undergo make possible backward-in-time movement. At the onset of his schizophrenia, Mark Vonnegut saw the water of a stream flowing up ("Without Nick it might have been different. Who can say? I might have been able to relax and live happily ever after at the farm. But relaxing and feeling at home around him was about as likely as … ? The stream flowing up the mountain? Why not? Had to use some image and the stream did just that a few days later anyway"[233]). In Roman Polanski's *The Tenant* (1976), the neighbors of the protagonist, Trelkovsky, who rented the apartment of a certain Simone Choule, an Egyptologist who committed suicide, stand frozen for hours. This immobilization makes possible going back in time: the shot of the person covered with bandages in a hospital bed looking at Trelkovsky and her friend Stella at the end of the film is the very same one near the film's beginning: in both, it is Simone Choule who is in bandages. Probably the reason the woman in *Last Year at Marienbad* finds it so difficult to remember the previous year's events is that the immobilizations of the other people make possible an actual movement backward in time. Hence her preposterous bind: she is asked by her suitor to remember their first meeting at Marienbad the previous year, when she has been transported back to that first meeting!

Some scripted films should use the hysteron proteron trope, that is, be filmed in inverse order to the shots' order of appearance in the finished film: the last shot of the film filmed first, the next-to-last second, etc. So, what would be during the screening of the film and according to the diegesis a temporal progression from younger to older for the character would be in the case of the actor or actress a regression to a younger age. With regard to the actor, Cocteau's "cinema films death at work" applies within each shot and in films and videos that do not use editing (Warhol's single-shot films, etc.) or where the order of filming coincides exactly with the order in which the characters appear in the diegesis. In traditional films, Cocteau's words only partially apply since there is frequent shuffling of the order of the shooting in relation to the order in which the shots appear in the finished film.

The Atavism of Mystery

Murder in mystery novels reactivates a gamut of archaic beliefs, and this irrespective of whether the story explicitly invokes the supernatural (Arthur Conan Doyle's *The Hound of the Baskervilles*):

— Communication with the dead: In Agatha Christie's *Appointment with Death*, Lady Westholme asserts that at 4:15 p.m., while in the company of the [suggestible] Miss Pierce, she paused below the ledge, shouted up to Mrs. Boynton, and remarked to her companion: "Very rude just to snort at us like that!" Nadine Boynton indicates that she returned to the camp at approximately 4:40, sat on a chair next to Mrs. Boynton, and had a conversation with her, leaving her at 4:50. Carol Boynton affirms that she returned at 5:10 to the camp and spoke to her stepmother for a while. Raymond Boynton asserts that he returned to the camp at 5:50, went up to his stepmother, exchanged a few words with her, then went to his tent and afterward to the marquee. It is later revealed that the death of Mrs. Boynton occurred around 4:10.

— Being in two places at the same time, which echoes some older societies' belief in astral bodies (for example, shamanic ones) and doubles: In Christie's *Thirteen at Dinner* (1933; a.k.a. *Lord Edgware Dies*), Jane Wilkinson, whose husband was found murdered in the library of his London home, is identified by two witnesses, the butler and the secretary, as having been to see him at 10 the night of his murder, and is also identified as having gone to a formal dinner party at the house of Sir Montague Corner at Chiswick that same night, arriving at a quarter to nine and leaving at half past eleven. During the party she left the dinner table only for a few minutes in the company of the butler to answer a phone call. The time of the murder is determined to be between ten and eleven at night.

— Changing the name of the dead, and in some cases even the names of those who survived him, of animals and plants. "The Masai in East Africa resort to the device of changing the dead man's name immediately after his death.... Among the Guaycurus in Paraguay, when a death had taken place, the chief used to change the name of every member of the tribe; and 'from that moment everybody remembered his new name just as if he had borne it all his life'[234] ... In the seven years which the missionary Dobrizhoffer spent among Abipones of Paraguay, 'the native word for jaguar was changed thrice, and the words for crocodile, thorn, and the slaughter of cattle underwent similar though less varied vicissitudes.'"[235] In mystery stories, too, we encounter (1) the change of the name of the dead whether in the form of burial under a false certificate or substitution of one corpse for another (Chesterton's *The Secret Garden*), etc.; (2) the change of the name of plants: at the end of Ruth Rendell's short story *Means of Evil*, we are informed that the shaggy cap (*Coprinus comatus*) had been replaced with ink cap (*Coprinus atramentarius*); (3) the change of the name of at least some of those who survived him: In *The Maltese Falcon*, after the death of Detective Miles Archer, Samuel Spade's female client's name changes from Ruth Wonderly to Miss Leblanc to Brigid O'Shaughnessy.

— The absence of the notion of natural death: in many older cultures, the death of someone was viewed as willed by another, whether human, dead, demon, or god. Similarly, in mystery stories it is extremely rare for what seems to be a suicide or an accident to be accepted as just that rather than as a murder. Although neither the police, nor the newspapers (the *Evening Shout*, etc.), nor the general public doubt that Mrs. Boyton and Lady Westholme died of accidents, the reader of Christie's *Appointment with Death*, like a member of the aforementioned older cultures, *knows* that these deaths have been willed and are in no way accidents.

There is a secondary elaboration in mystery stories to place the changing of the name, the communication with the dead, the refusal to believe in a natural or accidental death, the presence of a person in two places at the same time, and tunneling within a reasonable scheme rather than leave its supernaturalness and archaic origination manifest: for instance, tunneling can be accounted for by one of the solutions John Dickson Carr gives in the chapter titled "The Locked-Room Lecture" in his novel *The Three Coffins*; being in two places simultaneously can be explained by means of a false alibi, etc. That it is a secondary revision is also shown by the circumstance that companions to mystery stories stop in their synopses of the plots at the presentation of the facts before the detective begins to solve the puzzle (their legitimate excuse being that they must not reveal the whodunnit).

Counterfeiting

Are their stark impression of thought broadcasting and their undergoing nonlinear, indeed labyrinthine time the reasons why many schizophrenics feel that ideas, musical works, or artworks signed by others have been stolen from them, the real creators, by these famous thinkers, artists, or musicians, some of whom composed their songs or wrote their books prior to the birth of the schizophrenic?

Why Do a Remake of *Nosferatu*?

There used to be an absence of a continuous tradition in German cinema: between the expressionist period and the New German Cinema of Rainer Werner Fassbinder, Werner Herzog, Alexander Kluge, Hans-Jürgen Syberberg, Wim Wenders, et al., there was the disruptive trauma of the Nazi era. The New German Cinema directors felt the need, some more intensely than others, to reestablish a link with seminal pre-Nazi filmmakers and film critics and historians: Herzog remade Murnau's *Nosferatu* ("We are trying in our films to build a thin bridge back to that time"[236]); Wenders dedicated *Paris, Texas* (1984) and Herzog *Every Man for Himself and God Against All* (1974) to Lotte Eisner (Herzog: "Lotte Eisner's interest in our fate ... built a bridge"[237]), the critic and historian who wrote *The Haunted Screen* on German cinema from its inception to the late 1920s. Herzog had not only to include a diegetic bridge in his remake,[238] but also to build, through his film, an extra-diegetic bridge to Murnau's *Nosferatu* with its one-way bridge ("And when he passed the bridge, the phantoms came to meet him").

In a letter he sent Eisner in 1976 (his *Nosferatu* was released in 1979), Herzog wrote: "Fritz Lang has died.... I believe no one here really knew that he was still alive.... They chased Fritz Lang so far away from us that he was no longer among the living, but rather a rumor.... You were among those who kept urging me to go see him, but I never really dared because ... he had already become a spirit for me."[239] Fritz Lang was not the only director who had become a phantom in postwar Germany. But there are also other kinds of cinema phantoms: nine out of the twenty-one films made by Murnau are lost, and some of the remaining ones are incomplete (films appear to preserve, but they themselves were for a long time not preserved).[240] Bram Stoker's widow, who held the copyright of *Dracula*, became aware of Murnau's *Nosferatu* only two months after its release by Prana Company of Berlin in March 1922. She soon initiated legal proceedings for copyright infringement. "In July 1925 the courts ruled in Florence Stoker's favor and ordered that all prints and negatives of *Nosferatu* be destroyed. The film might have been lost forever had a small number of prints not made their way abroad. Florence Stoker successfully halted *Nosferatu*'s London premiere in 1925 but not its American debut in 1929."[241] *Nosferatu* was for a time a phantom. A bridge had to be created to the directors who had become specters, but also to those of their films that had become, permanently or temporarily, phantoms.

To make a sound version of Murnau's silent *Nosferatu*, it was not enough to add the customary diegetic sound. In Herzog's remake, music-over is heard telepathically, *over*heard by the people in the town square, who dance to it and not to the inaudible music being played by the musicians there. The suffix *-er* either denotes one who does a specified action or is used to form the comparative of adverbs and adjectives. In films concerning the dead the two are inextricably linked: the harker is the one who cannot hark except if he harks more than others, but also more than himself, by being clairaudient.

In *Discipline and Punish*, Foucault writes about the presence of two models of the plague, each answering to a different political project:
— In the first, literary, we encounter "suspended laws ... bodies mingling together without respect"[242] in a sort of "collective festival."[243] And indeed, we have all sorts of mixtures in vampire films with their plagues: (a) the living dead, the vampire, (b) the dead living, the mad, who *died before dying*, (c) the mixing of the dead and the living in the plagued city. The plague as carnival introduces inversions ("the chaste man performs sodomy upon his neighbors. The lecher becomes pure. The miser throws his gold in handfuls out the window ..."[244]) until everybody becomes undifferentiated. Then, as René Girard has shown, there is an attempt to reintroduce differentiation by considering someone as the source of the plague.[245] Often, rather than being determined by what differentiates him from others, the choice of the one to be sacrificed as the cause of the plague is what makes him sin-gular, thus reintroducing differentiation and doing away with the plague. But in some cases, the choice falls on the one who prior to the appearance of the plague epitomized lack of differen-tiation: Oedipus, who had intercourse with his biological mother repeatedly, is the father *and* the half-brother of Antigone, Eteocles, Ismene, and Polyneices; the vampire is differentiated from normal people precisely by being the undifferentiated, mixing life and death (as a living dead, or, more accurately, an undead), here and elsewhere (by being telepathic and telesthetic), and wakefulness and sleep (by being somnambulistic). Harker, who is charged by his employer to take the ground plan of a house to Nosferatu in Transylvania and to get his signature on the ownership papers, is, through a parapraxis, the messenger of a message he was not asked to give, Lucy's photograph, drawing the vampire's attention and desire to his telepathic and telesthetic wife in a sacrificial gesture.
— In the second model, "every day ... the syndic ... stops before each house: gets all the inhabitants to appear at the windows.... If someone does not appear at the window, the syndic must ask why.... Each individual is constantly located, examined and

distributed among the living beings, the sick and the dead—all this constitutes a compact model of the disciplinary mechanism.... Against the plague, which is a mixture, discipline brings into play its power, which is one of analysis."[246]

Murnau's *Nosferatu*, the first shot of which is a panoptic vision from the tower dominating the city, is inscribed within the disciplinary model of the plague (the other model can be found in his *Faust* [1926]). Herzog opts for the other model, the plague as festival/carnival/anarchy. But viewing Murnau's *Nosferatu* exclusively within the disciplinary model is only partially accurate, since, as in Herzog's *Nosferatu*, the city is ultimately saved by Ellen's sacrifice and not by the disciplinary measures. The mixing that the plague introduces and with which Murnau's film deals propagates itself to a mixing of the two models of the plague in his film.

Reference Letter from the
Hidden Observer

In the nonlocal phenomenon of hypnosis, during which the hypnotized person is often overlaid on a setting other than the one in which the induction began, reference resides not only in the figure of the hypnotist but also in the phenomenon of the *hidden observer*: during a hypnosis experiment, a young woman "experienced in hypnosis" was entranced and told to feel no pain when one of her hands was put in circulating ice water, while the other hand, kept out of awareness, was to report through automatic writing, at five-second intervals and on a scale of zero to ten, on the pain the first hand was feeling. She orally reported feeling no pain, while in automatic writing she was reporting: two ... five ... seven ... eight ... nine ...[247]

The Untimely Sleepiness
of the Exoteric Disciples

An exoteric disciple is always overcome with sleep when needed. Leaving his other ostensible disciples at Gethsemane, Jesus went in the company of Peter, James, and John to pray. He asked these three: "Stay here and watch with Me." He moved away *a stone's throw*[248] and prayed. When he came back, the three were sleeping: "What? Could you not watch with Me one hour?" Three times did he leave them to pray, each time, upon returning, finding them sleeping. "Are you still sleeping and resting? Behold, the hour is at hand, and the Son of Man is being betrayed ..." Finishing his words, he saw the traitor Judas coming toward him.[249]

I Am Shattered!

In Francis Bacon's work, the mirror seldom functions as the familiar reflecting surface. It rather frequently acts as a pinning or absorbing medium, so that part of the materiality and life of the person in front of it is transferred to it—the limit case being his or her total absorption in the mirror, as in *Lying Figure in a Mirror* (1971), *Study of Nude with Figure in a Mirror* (1969), and *Triptych* (1987). The two functions occasionally coexist, as in the right panel of *Triptych Inspired by T. S. Eliot's Poem "Sweeney Agonistes"* (1967): the man on the phone has been totally absorbed in the mirror, while the feet of one of the reclining men and the edge of the bed are reflected in the mirror. On the way to total absorption, we have *Figure Writing Reflected in a Mirror* (1976), and the right panel of *In Memory of George Dyer* (1971), where the tug is no longer between the person and his presence in the mirror but between the latter and his presence in the reflecting surface of a table, the part of the body still not absorbed in either deploying acrobatics to maintain itself outside of both. In *Study for Portrait* (1981) the body has become so adroit at maintaining its balance between the two media tugging at it that it can sit half outside the mirror and half inside it, with neither medium exerting an attraction on the part of the body in the other one and without even the body's minimal displacement owing to the refractive index from one medium to the other. But this adroit body now dissociates in half outside the mirror (*Study from the Human Body* [1981]) or inside it (*Portrait of George Dyer in a Mirror* [1968]), the threshold no longer being the obvious dividing surface between the mirror and what is outside it but a *false* one.

The Off-Screen and/or the Set On-Screen

By seeing in wide shots in Dreyer's *Vampyr* people's reflections in water in the absence of the people themselves, one is seeing the off-screen as such onscreen—which off-screen has itself an off-screen. One cannot see this off-screen as such on-screen without feeling that one is apprehending it in a telesthetic manner or hypnagogically (one subject reporting his hypnagogic experience: "'Reflection' in a lake of old houses that did not exist!"[250]). These instances of off-screen in the frame foreshadow the coming dissociation of their diegetic witness. Shortly after witnessing these reflections, Gray sees a shadowless guard sitting with his chin propped on his hand. Soon, the man's shadow, who might have earlier appeared in the water in the absence of his assumed corresponding body, comes in, rests his rifle next to the bench, and sits in the same position: it is only then that the image becomes in sync.

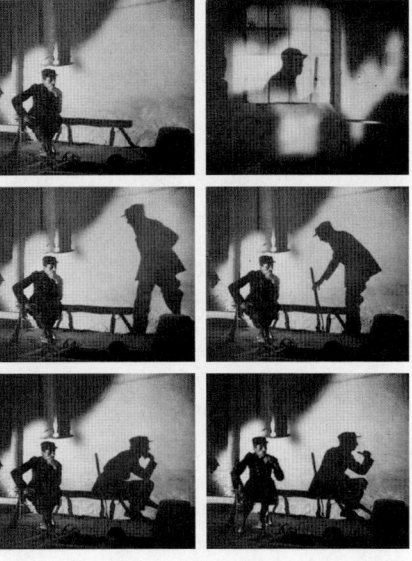

page 565 Stills from Dreyer's *Vampyr*.

"There are no wings to the screen. There could not be without destroying its specific illusion, which is to make of a revolver or of a face the very center of the universe."[251] The centrality of the on-screen that Bazin writes about must be reconsidered in light not only of dissociative experiences (in near-death states, chronic migraine ...)—where the out-of-body component is simultaneously onscreen and off-screen (in reference to the body left behind, for instance, that of Gray on the bench, which has its own off-screen)—but also of virtual reality, which permits telepresence and, through the use of sensors, tele-sensing. Is the subtle or virtual body off-screen or in the wings?

Notwithstanding Bazin's assertion that "the screen is not a frame like that of a picture but a mask which allows a part of the action to be seen. When a character moves off-screen, we accept the fact that he is out of sight, but he continues to exist in his own capacity at some other place in the décor which is hidden from us,"[252] in some states of altered consciousness what lies beyond the perceptual horizon is not a homogeneous extension of what is within it: in film terms, the off-screen is no longer the homogeneous extension of the on-screen but is either radically or insidiously incongruous with it (the apartment where one finds oneself may be identical to one's apartment in a particular city, but one may look out of the window and discover that one is rather in a different city or in the desert; if there is something to the other side of what one still vaguely remembers to have been the door through which one entered the bar a short time ago, it now proves to be an extension of the bar—the bar as the world); or has totally disappeared (in David Blair's *Wax*, the black that frames the image is an instantiation of the absence of off-screen; when *Wax*'s protagonist reaches the edge of the frame, there is either a dissolve to another location or else the character acknowledges the limitation, "I couldn't go beyond the perimeter of the acre"—his assertion

167

is inaccurate where the frame extends slightly beyond the perimeter: the protagonist could have taken one or two additional steps).

If a scene starts with a close-up, there is uncertainty for the duration of the shot as to what the off-screen is. In films dealing with states of altered consciousness, this ambiguity should not be abolished once a master shot establishes the location and the situation where the action is happening but is to be renewed within the same scene whenever there's a return to a close-up. In such states, what is a close-up if not a shot of a person trying to remember—the rest of the space that was disclosed by the master shot?

In a film the main subject of which is God, the camera pan would at least at times become the tracing of a creation: what appears along its movement is being created at the pace of that movement. Therefore, when the camera movement stops, the two sides of the frame are not symmetrical: to one side there is nothing, while the other side is simply the homogeneous extension of the on-screen, which we have already seen.

Killed by Someone from the Past

In Alfred Hitchcock's *Vertigo*, Scottie Ferguson, a retired detective suffering from acrophobia and vertigo, is hired by Gavin Elster to follow his wife, Madeleine, about whom he is worried as he believes that she is possessed by her ancestor Carlotta Valdes, who committed suicide. Scottie soon becomes enamored of Madeleine, only for her to ostensibly commit suicide by jumping from a bell tower, an outcome he is unable to prevent due to his vertigo. Madeleine's earlier mysterious disappearance from a hotel and her subsequent appearance at the scene of her ostensible suicide alongside an identical-looking woman complement each other, hinting at time travel. Melancholic Scottie subsequently comes across a woman who resembles Madeleine, Judy Barton. He's driven to turn her into a perfect copy of Madeleine[253]—while unaware that she had already impersonated Madeleine in a scheme by Elster to murder his wife and make it look like a suicide. Scottie will later tell Judy: "I have to go back into the past once more, just once more.... One doesn't often get a second chance. I want to stop being haunted. You're my second chance, Judy." The time-travel enabler has taken many forms in film, including, in *Vertigo*, a woman as a fetish.[254] While they kiss after she comes out of the bathroom looking exactly like Madeleine, and as the backdrop shows, Scottie and Judy are momentarily transported back in time to the stables at the Old Mission San Juan Bautista a year earlier, where he and Madeleine declared their love for each other and kissed passionately and from which she dashed to the tower and then ostensibly leapt to her death. It is thus not accidental that *Vertigo* has been referenced intertextually by two time-travel films: Chris Marker's *La Jetée*, and Terry Gilliam's *Twelve Monkeys*, a remake of *La Jetée*. Why did Scottie time-travel? To find in the multiverse the branch in which all the lies his beloved told him are truths; and because he, who had tried to free Madeleine from her possession by the past, had become obsessed by it (insisting that the brunette Judy dye her hair blonde and replicate the way Madeleine dressed and behaved, and taking her to Ernie's, the restaurant where he glimpsed Madeleine for the first time), subject to the compulsion to repeat. Scottie, who conquers his acrophobia and, the second time around, reaches the top of the bell tower, has actually replaced one kind of vertigo with another, the spatial one of acrophobia with the temporal one of time travel. Though Mission San Juan Bautista was empty when they arrived, a dark figure suddenly walks out of the dark staircase. It is from the past that that figure, a nun, appears in the bell tower. Startled, Judy recoils and falls fatally from the tower. Madeleine was not killed by someone from the past, but Judy was!

The Mourner and the Dead/Undead

It is related in Katherine Hurbis-Cherrier's video *All That's Left* that, when asked by the priest to share anecdotes about the video maker's dead aunt, none of those attending the funeral mass said anything. I imagine some of them moving their lips soundlessly, neither out of shyness nor owing to an intuition that the late has reverted to a superposition of possibilities, but in a gesture of miming the effect of the approach of silence-over before it ends up immobilizing the dead. What took place at the funeral mass was thus a real minute of commemorative silence.

Some dead are conjointly undergoing an extreme permeability in the bardo state (in the form of thought insertion; feeling *every name in history is I*, etc.) and totally embalmed and shielded in a safe inside the melancholiac who incorporated[255] them ("*save: v. tr.* 2. To keep in a safe condition; safeguard. 3. To prevent the waste or loss of; conserve. 4. To set aside for future use; store. 5. To ... spare"[256] ... from the rebirth-redeath cycle). Maintaining outside of death the person who died and whom one is unable to successfully mourn maintains one outside of life. Some films show the conflict between the melancholiac and the dead they incorporated, the latter trying to get rid of the melancholiac to liberate themselves from the embalmed image being enforced on them by him or her. This image is a fake one, because the dead has no image (whether because he or she has his or her back to himself/herself in the mirror or because he or she does

169

not appear in the mirror), or because, in the death realm, the dead is repeatedly replaced by various others, in particular the double (in Hitchcock's *Rebecca* [1940], wanting to hurt the new wife for replacing her dead former mistress, the maid tells her that the hung portrait represents her husband's grandmother, when in fact it is Rebecca's, the husband's previous wife. This seeming lie is the occasion for us to know that in the undeath realm the late Rebecca has been replaced, at least at some point, by the husband's grandmother).[257]

Life goes on: the dead is replaced from the standpoint of the living who has accomplished the work of mourning. Death goes on: the dead is replaced from his or her own standpoint; having died before dying physically ("This autumn [of 1888] ... I twice attended my funeral"[258]), Nietzsche wrote, "I am Prado, I am also Prado's father, I venture to say that I am also Lesseps.... I am also Chambige.... Every name in history is I."[259] *If* the living should not forget the dead, the latter, too, should not forget themselves. The fidelity of Shakespeare's Gertrude takes into consideration the dead's forced infidelity to himself/herself, that one of the names her dead husband King Hamlet assumes in the death realm is Claudius, the name of the man she then marries.

In *Totem and Taboo*, Freud wrote: "It is impossible to escape the conclusion that, in the words of [Wilhelm] Wundt, they [savages] are victims to a fear of 'the dead man's soul which has become a demon.' Here, then, we seem to have found a confirmation of Wundt's view, which ... considers that the essence of taboo is a fear of demons. This theory is based on a supposition so extraordinary that it seems at first sight incredible: the supposition, namely, that a dearly loved relative at the moment of his death changes into a demon, from whom his survivors can expect nothing but hostility and against whose evil desires they must protect themselves by every possible means. Nevertheless, almost all the authorities are at one in attributing these views to primitive peoples."[260] This change can be explained only partially by the ambivalence of the living toward the dead while they still lived, according to Freud, and consequently only partially by *projection*, for it is also in part the result of the dead's replacement by the double or the radical unleashing of his or her drive(s). Concerning the dead, one has to decide on each occasion whether he or she has been totally replaced by the double or a demon or become distilled to his or her drive(s) (concerning dead Lucy in Stoker's *Dracula*, who has become a vampire, Arthur asks Van Helsing, "Is this really Lucy's body, or only a demon in her shape?" and Dr. Seward notes, "She seemed like a nightmare of Lucy as she lay there; the pointed teeth, the bloodstained, voluptuous mouth, ... the whole carnal and unspiritual appearance, seeming like a devilish mockery of Lucy's sweet purity"[261]); or whether he or she is possessed, in which case he or she ought to be helped even if the only remnant of him or her is the *hidden observer*. The lama or Sufi Shaykh can help through the voice-over that guides the dead in the in-between state, whether bardo or *barzakh*; the lay person can help through writing or art.

Persons with obsessive neurosis have obsessive guilt feelings in relation to the dead person. "It is not that the mourner was really responsible for the death or was really guilty of neglect, as the self-reproaches declare to be the case. None the less there was something in her—a wish that was unconscious to herself—which would not have been dissatisfied by the occurrence of death and which might actually have brought it about if it had the power. And after death *has* occurred, it is against this unconscious wish that the reproaches are a reaction."[262] Was Freud's placing the "has" in italics a parapraxis? That is, did Freud want to italicize everything else except this "has"? For why is it only after the death of the other person that the obsessive neurotic begins to feel guilt if the unconscious wish was all the time operative? If it is only then that the self-reproaches appear, it is because it is only after death, and in the case of the schizophrenic after death before dying, that, no longer guarded by an ego, the dead can be affected radically by the unconscious of others. The thoughts of the living can get inserted without permission or obstacle in the minds of the dead. Harker enters Dracula's castle without invitation, the door opening on its own (Browning's *Dracula*), but the dead have to be invited into the living's houses (Murnau's *Nosferatu*). Therefore, rather than trying to shield the living from the dead, one should try to shield the dead and those who died before dying (the mad, etc.) from the living. If the dead is attacked, it is by all, by those who knew him or her and by those who didn't. They are not in concert in their attack that produces a surrealist *exquisite corpse*, although their victim most often feels that they are. That is why notwithstanding folkloric versions' portrayal of the undead's retaliation as circumscribed, first against his family and relatives, then against the inhabitants of his village, his retaliation actually operates, as in the modern fictional versions, indiscriminately, for example, through the plague. Once the dead human in the intermediate state of reality (*chos-nyid bar-do*) has entered the intermediate state of rebirth (*srid-pa'i bar-do*)—*life goes on* even for the dead—the living's previously legitimate guilt toward him or her should cease, otherwise it turns into a sick indulgence.

Mortal Guilt

One finds the conjunction of death with guilt already in Genesis, although there it is twice covered up through inversion, made to look as if mortality is due to guilt and guilt is due to a specific, intentional act ("The Lord God commanded the man, saying, 'Of every tree of the garden you may freely eat; but of the tree of the knowledge of good and evil you shall not eat, for in the day that you eat of it you shall surely die' [2:16–17].... When the woman saw that the tree was good for food, that it was pleasant to the eyes, and a tree desirable to make one wise, she took of its fruit and ate. She also gave to her husband with her, and he ate" [3:6]). But guilt precedes any specific intentional act precisely because mortality precedes guilt: it is because there is death and hence the unconscious that there is a guilt that has nothing to do with any intentional acts. I, but also the dead and schizophrenics, in fact everybody, with the possible exception of the yogi—yoga works to burn, do away with the unconscious—am always guilty toward the dead and schizophrenics, who died before dying. We are guilty before the dead because while in principle we are able to resurrect them, we did not take the measures that would have turned this potentiality into an actual ability; and because our unconscious is attacking them who have lost the shield of the ego.

Ghosts do nothing but free associate, that is why they haunt life, the scene of the crime—not only the murderer but also the victim returns to the crime scene.

Voice-over/Over-sight

Examples of voice-over outside of cinema: the voice of the lama assisting the dead by reciting from the *Bardo Thödol* (literally *Liberation through Hearing in the In-Between State*); or that of the hypnotist: "Although deep asleep you can hear me clearly. You will always hear me distinctly no matter how deeply asleep you feel you are."[263] The voice-over of the Dzogchen master assists the dead in fighting many of the *sous-entendus* in the bardo of reality (*chos nyid bar do*).

Someone reporting his out-of-body experience: "Mostly, I think I was just observing.... It didn't feel as though it was happening to me at all."[264] In Hitchcock's *Psycho*, both the overhead shot of Norman possessed by his mother and wearing her wig and dress as he stabs the detective on the staircase and the overhead shot of him transporting his mother's mummy play the role of an out-of-body point-of-view shot: a diegetic over-sight. The voyeurism in *Psycho* is to be located not only in Norman's looking in a peephole at his female motel guest undressing but also in his looking at himself-as-his-mother from an out-of-body position.

I Am the Martyr Sana'a
Youcef Mehaidli
In memoriam *everyone and no one*[265]

A TV monitor hanging midway from the ceiling shows a chair behind which is a poster with photographs of assassinated members of the Lebanese Communist Party. A man clad in khaki enters the frame, sits on the chair, and addresses the camera: "I am the martyr Comrade Khalil Ahmad Rahhal." Thus starts the mixed-media *Three Posters* presented by Elias Khoury and Rabih Mroué on September 2, 2000, at Ayloul Festival, Beirut. The man goes on to tell us that he will very shortly undertake a martyrdom operation against the Israeli occupation forces in Lebanon. There follow two other takes, with variations, of his testimony. At this point, Elias Khoury walks to the door behind the TV monitor and opens it, revealing the same set we were seeing on the monitor and a video camera directed at the chair and the poster. We thus realize that what we had watched was not a taped video but a live performance (it is as if the done away with repeatability of the image when the latter is revealed to have been live was compensated by and displaced to a *de facto* repetition of the testimony).[266] If I had believed the opening statement, then it is as if when I saw the same person still alive I were watching a ghost, so that while at the level of the medium we move from a light image to real presence, at the level of the structure of the piece we move from a presence to an apparition. The performer removes his fatigues, takes out a piece of paper from his pocket and reads from it: "My name is Rabih Mroué. I was born in Beirut in 1966. I joined the Communist Party in 1983, and I participated in operations of the Lebanese National Resistance in 1987 in Hasbaiya and Balat and other locations." He then mentions that Rahhal died not in the south but in one of the internecine battles in West Beirut in 1987 and offers the show in tribute to the martyrs of the national resistance. The door is closed again. Then a second video is shown. It is an unedited document showing the late communist Jamal Sati relaying his last message before his planned martyrdom (an edited version of the tape was broadcast on Lebanese TV on August 6, 1985). Sati repeats his testimony, with variations, three times, each time starting with "I am the martyr Comrade Jamal Sati."

Sana'a Mehaidli seems to have been the first to use such a locution.[267] Her videotaped testimony, shot by her and broadcast on Lebanese TV on April 9, 1985, starts with: "I am the martyr Sana'a Youcef Mehaidli (*anā as-shahīda Sanā' Yūsif Muḥaydlī*)."[268] The morning of that same day, at 11 a.m., the seventeen-year-old Mehaidli had crashed the explosives-filled car she was driving into an Israeli military convoy at Batir gate, Jezzine, killing, according to the Israeli military spokesman, two officers and wounding two soldiers. The same locution is found in the subsequent televised testimonies of a number of Lebanese resistance fighters who died in martyrdom operations against the Israeli army and/or the now-defunct South Lebanon Army (SLA): "I am the martyr Malek Wehbé ..."[269] (Malek Wehbé, b. 1966, mortally crashed a truck full of explosives into an Israeli military convoy at 6:15 p.m. on April 20, 1985, at the Qasimia

173

Bridge checkpoint); "I am the martyr Comrade Khaled al-Azrak ..."[270] (Khaled al-Azrak, b. 1966, mortally crashed a pickup truck full of explosives into the joint Israeli and SLA checkpoint at Az-Zāmriyya at 4:30 p.m. on July 9, 1985); "I am the martyr Comrade Hisham Abbas"[271] (Hisham Abbas, b. 1962, mortally crashed a car full of explosives into an SLA checkpoint at Kfar Tibnit at 4 p.m. on July 15, 1985); "I am the martyr Ali Ghazi Talib"[272] (Ali Ghazi Talib, b. 1967, mortally crashed a car full of explosives into an Israeli military convoy in Arnoun, Nabatieh, at 8 a.m. on July 31, 1985); "I am the martyr Comrade Muna' Qataya"[273] (Muna' Qataya, b. 1967, mortally blew up a car containing three hundred kilograms of explosives at the SLA checkpoint at Rimat, Jezzine, at 2:05 p.m. on August 28, 1985); "I am the martyr Comrade Mariam Kheireddine"[274] (Mariam Kheireddine, b. 1966, mortally crashed a car full of explosives at the SLA checkpoint near Hasbaiya, at 7:30 a.m. on September 11, 1985). This locution is one of the major inventions of the Lebanese war.[275] It was uttered by people who were unaware that they, as mortals, were already dead even as they lived—and, in the case of some of them, also wanted to extend their lives even into death. Thus the testimony of Bilal Fahs, who drove a car filled with one hundred and fifty kilograms of explosives into an Israeli convoy on June 16, 1984, at Zahrani, begins with the following Qur'ānic āya: "And call not those who are slain in the way of Allah 'dead.' Nay, they are living" (3:169);[276] and Sana'a Mehaidli says in her testimony: "I am not dead, but alive amidst you ..."[277] Notwithstanding over a hundred thousand dead in the years of war and civil war, the Lebanese seem not to have learned to die. Therefore, one of the great tasks of art and writing in Lebanon for the foreseeable future is to teach this people famed for being "life-loving" to die (before dying),[278] so that they would become aware that, as mortals, they are already dead even while physically alive.

"By the time you see this tape, I, Comrade Jamal Sati, will have died" is believable, but not: "I am the martyr Comrade Jamal Sati." While I can usually assume in the present of videotaping my future state at the time of broadcasting or screening, I cannot do so in the case of death.[279] I cannot believe Jamal Sati on TV telling me, "I am the martyr Comrade Jamal Sati ...,"[280] even if I am told that he had died in a martyrdom operation by the time I saw him on TV (Jamal Sati, b. 1962, mortally blew up the explosives hidden in two baskets on his donkey at the SLA checkpoint at Zaghlé, Hasbaiya, on the morning of August 6, 1985). And while I can categorically assert, "I will die," I cannot deduce from this that at one point in the future I can say, "I am dead," even if death is not a final disappearance. The dead's living lover, family, relatives, and/or colleagues are customarily asked to come to the morgue to recognize the corpse;[281] but the dead, too, has to recognize his or her corpse (Billy Wilder's *Sunset Boulevard*). Can I deduce from the resulting "this is my corpse" "I am dead"? While it may seem that such a conclusion is a foregone one, in death there is no link between the two: "This is my—Nietzsche's—corpse, therefore Prado is dead" (in the same letter in Nietzsche's handwriting, we can read, "This autumn [of 1888] ... I twice attended my funeral" and "I am Prado, I am also Prado's father, I venture to say that I am also Lesseps.... I am also Chambige.... Every name in history is I"[282]). Death, in which I constantly *free associate*, not infrequently in a paranoid manner, nonetheless does not allow me to go from "I was murdered" to "I am dead." The revenant can say "I was murdered," but not "I am dead," notwithstanding that the former logically implies the latter. The answer to the "question" "Am I dead?"[283] that haunts me as I keep experiencing unworldly occurrences and the deduction from "I was murdered" cannot be "I am dead"—unless the latter is attributed to another proper name—but "I must be dead."[284] The vampire in Coppola's *Bram Stoker's Dracula* does not say during his confession to his lover, Mina, "I am dead" but "I am *dead to* the whole world." Nowhere except in Edgar Allan Poe's short story "The Facts in the Case of M. Valdemar" have I come across the locution "I am dead." When the doctor who had hypnotized the moribund Mr. Valdemar "asked him ... if he still slept," he answered at a delay: "Yes;—no;—I *have been* sleeping—and now—now—*I am dead*." *Nearly seven months* later, when the doctor attempts to awaken him, whose state had remained *exactly* the same, his hideous voice breaks forth: "For God's sake!—quick!—quick!—put me to sleep—or, quick!—waken me!—quick!—*I say to you that I am dead!*" How to account for this locution in Poe's short story? In trance, I become my own medium. I cannot directly assume my death; my death is uttered either through a medium, as in Kurosawa's *Rashomon*—had Nietzsche spoken through a medium he could very well have said: "I, Nietzsche, am dead"; or through others, as with Nietzsche in his death before dying, "I am Prado, I am also Prado's father, I venture to say that I am also Lesseps.... I am also Chambige.... Every name in history is I,"[285] and, by implication, "I, Prado, am dead," "I, Prado's father, am dead." The dead is no one, as is made clear by the mirror device in vampire films, the vampire not appearing in the speculum; moreover, the dead is not one name but every name in history, and therefore, synecdochically, everyone. By subtitling *Thus Spoke Zarathustra* "A Book for Everyone and No One," Nietzsche is addressing it to the dead and to himself during his coming psychosis, his dying before dying, when he will exclaim: "Every name in history is I."[286] The real one who died before dying is not Jamal Sati saying, "I am the martyr Comrade Jamal Sati," in a videotaped testimony before going on a successful martyrdom operation, but Nietzsche writing in a letter: "This autumn [of 1888] ... I twice attended my funeral, first as Count Robilant."

The late has no past, since his or her past is affected with forgery:[287] the dead cannot assume even the martyrdom operation that led to his or her death; no future, since his or her timeline has stopped: Harker's words to Mina before he leaves for Transylvania in Murnau's *Nosferatu*, "Nothing will happen to me," which are intended to be reassuring, are actually worrying since they imply that he will be dead there; and no present in which to say, "I am dead."

It is often said that the difference between a human and an animal in regard to death is that the former knows that he or she will die, while the latter doesn't. But is it basically the case that a human knows that he or she will die? Freud: "Biology has not yet been able to decide whether death is the inevitable fate of every living being or whether it is only a regular but yet perhaps avoidable event in life. It is true that the statement 'All men are mortal' is paraded in text-books of logic as an example of a general proposition; but no human being really grasps it, and our unconscious has as little use now as it ever had for the idea of its own mortality";[288] "the psycho-analytic school could venture on the assertion that at bottom no one believes in his own death, or, to put the same thing in another way, that in the unconscious every one of us is convinced of his own immortality."[289] It may be true that it is only others who die, not I, but that is in part because in death I assume all the (other) names of history: "I am Prado, I am also Prado's father, I venture to say that I am also Lesseps.... I am also Chambige.... Every name in history is I." All the names of history, and thus synecdochically all humans in history, have died, but not I. This gets materialized in the absence of others often experienced in death: the deserted cities in which the somnambulistic dead wanders in Bergman's *Wild Strawberries* and Buñuel's *The Discreet Charm of the Bourgeoisie*. While "dying ... is essentially mine in such a way that no one can be my representative" (Heidegger),[290] in death I am all the names of history, I am Prado, Prado's father, Tolstoy, Heidegger, etc. "We are mortal beings, hence already dead even as we live" is a credible statement; it appears in my text *"If You Prick Us, Do We Not Bleed? No."*[291] One can credibly paraphrase this statement as "I am already dead even as I live" only if one bears in mind that in death I am not concurrent, and therefore that the two *I*'s in the statement do not refer to the same name.[292] Thus, in the case of Nietzsche, the unfolding of the statement would yield "I, Prado, Prado's father, Lesseps, Chambige, am already dead, even as I, Nietzsche, live." Will Jesus Christ die again when the schizophrenic Shiʻite Abd Ali Muhanna, who repeatedly asserts in my *Credits Included: A Video in Red and Green* (1995), "I am the messenger of the Prophet Muhammad, and I am Jesus Christ ..." dies? Does he die again each time a dead human, who assumes in the death realm every name in history, assumes at one point his name, Jesus Christ?[293] It is likely that the prohibition in Judaism against pronouncing the secret name of God is a preventive measure against our assuming that name in death, with the consequent death of God.

Since there is something false about the statement "I am the martyr Comrade [proper name of the talker]," it is appropriate that Rabih Mroué should perform what appears to be a fictional version of it: "I am the martyr Comrade Khalil Ahmad Rahhal." Paradoxically, while Jamal Sati's statement is false although by the time the videotape is broadcast on TV Jamal Sati has indeed already died, the second statement is not: unawares, Mroué was telling us something about his death—I shudder to think that his speech was co-written or even changed by his collaborator Elias Khoury, since Khoury would have thus contributed to writing the forged past of the dead Mroué. Art and writing are dead serious. Rabih Mroué dead is all the names of history, including Khalil Ahmad Rahhal (Rabih Mroué could as well have said: "I am the martyr Comrade Jamal Sati"; Jamal Sati dead may say: "I am the martyr Comrade Rabih Mroué"). Therefore, when Rabih Mroué says, "I am the martyr Comrade Khalil Ahmad Rahhal," those who know him are not justified in deducing that they are watching something fictional. The statement "I am Comrade Khalil Ahmad Rahhal" is certainly far less risky for the performer uttering it than "I am the martyr Comrade Khalil Ahmad Rahhal," since the second discloses to us something about the performer in the counterfeit realm of the late.[294] The dead are usually not to be believed (Kurosawa's *Rashomon*), yet the historically false information Rabih Mroué gives about himself while playing a dead character is believable—we have here an exemplification of Picasso's "Art is a lie that makes us realize truth, at least the truth that is given us to understand. The artist must know the manner whereby to convince others of the truthfulness of his lies."[295]

Composites

The first thing one notices in many nineteenth-century photographs is the blurriness of the living. Since the early daguerreotypes and calotypes required long, multi-minute exposures, at first photography best preserved the dead, not the living, the quick (quick. 6. *Archaic* a. Alive [*American Heritage Dictionary*]). But even at present, one would be able to see clearly, if it were possible to see the motionless living and the frozen dead side by side and if fear did not push one to swish pan one's look, that the frozen figure brings out the blurriness of the motionless figure. While the living never become immobile but only motionless, i.e., move less, to a lesser degree, the dead (and dancers in the dance realm) come to a dead stop. The freezing of the dead is not merely motionlessness but the coming of the motionlessness to a hard yet furtive stop (breaching the conservation of momentum). To belong to nature, whether as an object or as a living entity, is to be restless;[296] the corpse, even one in suspended animation, undergoes all kinds of motions, is restless, certainly when compared to the freezing of the dead (and of the dancer in the dance realm). The freezing of the dancer in *Coppélia* is what differentiates her from the mannequins, since, unlike their motionlessness, her freezing is not worldly but is the sort that occurs only in the dance realm—and in death. The blurriness of the living is due to their movement even as they stand motion*less*; the indistinctness of the dead is, paradoxically, the result of the decomposition of the different composites of which each was composed. The living person is a composite[297] that dissociates in death-as-undeath first into separate subunits that are themselves composites ("I am Prado, I am also Prado's father, I venture to say that I am also Lesseps.... I am also Chambige...."[298] [Friedrich Nietzsche]),[299] then into elements, becoming alien. Each of us is common, not alien, both because each of us is a composite of all the others, even of those who lived in previous periods and who are long dead, and because each of us is part of the composites that constitute the others. That is why we do not find others alien, and that is why they, too, do not find us alien. In certain states of altered consciousness, though, we see the dead, who strike us as alien, and that is because they are no longer composites (the withdrawal of the cathexis of the world).

What is extremely discomposing about the double is that, in a twisted, too logical way, he is more me than myself: while I include all the others, he includes only "me," and therefore he is not really me, since I am never purely myself. The double is unrecognizable because he is the Same. The double is not the other, but I divested of all others. That is why whenever I encounter him, even in a crowded public place, I feel I am alone with him, *alone with the alone*;[300] he embodies the dissociation from the world. That is why encountering the double is such a desolate experience and is a premonition of death with its dissociation from others and the rest of the world.

The Surgeon and the Dismembered Apprentice Magician

Walter Benjamin: "The surgeon represents the polar opposite of the magician. The magician heals a sick person by the laying on of hands; the surgeon cuts into the patient's body. The magician maintains the natural distance between the patient and himself; though he reduces it very slightly by the laying on of hands, he greatly increases it by virtue of his authority. The surgeon does exactly the reverse; he greatly diminishes the distance between himself and the patient by penetrating into the patient's body, and increases it but little by the caution with which his hand moves among the organs."[301] Benjamin appears to be unaware that the magician can effectively maintain the patient's "aura" only because he underwent initiatory states and ordeals in which his body is cut to pieces; for example, Siberian shamans "are cut up by demons or by their ancestral spirits; their bones are cleaned, the flesh scraped off, the body fluids thrown away, and the eyes torn from their sockets.... The spirits cut off his head (which they set to one side, for the novice must watch his own dismemberment ...) and hack his body to bits, which are later distributed among the spirits of various sicknesses. It is only on this condition that the future Shaman will obtain the power of healing.... His bones are then covered with new flesh, and in some cases he is also given new blood."[302] It is the reconstituted body of the shaman, his new body, that has an aura.

Necrophilia?

He knew that the stratum corneum, the outermost layer of the epidermis, "is made up of 10 to 30 thin layers of continually shedding, dead keratinocytes."[303] Nonetheless, he was touched by the tenderness of her skin. He wanted to caress all of it, even that under the nails.

He who had said about his maddening wife, "She is dead to me," subsequently followed her into the underworld when she died to all others, too. As he found himself lost in that realm, he heard a mocking voice in his head: "Do you really expect to meet her in the labyrinthine realm of death?" Then he heard hers! "Yet another necrophiliac! You followed me into death to fuck me. It would be one more irresponsible experience to have in the realm of death, where we are anyway guilty." He blurted out: "I want nothing from you yet: you are presently nothing; I can want something from you only after I raise you from death."

The vampire's lover felt that his erect penis deep inside her was full of her blood, which, instead of being distributed all over his body, went straight to his sexual organ. His sucking of her blood psychosomatically played for her the role of a period, therefore she could not have a child for that time span ("Here there are neither children nor dogs [who would guard a territory, since, in the labyrinthine realm of death, there is no such thing]" [Dreyer's *Vampyr*]).

Gutless

Like the vampire bat, which must consume 50-100 percent of its body weight in blood every night,[304] the vampire "swelled, in a moment, into a great, palpitating mass"[305] during the feeding binge (Le Fanu's *Carmilla*). Yet hunger persisted, for the vampire, like many a schizophrenic ("I existed frequently without a stomach.... Of other internal organs I will only mention the *gullet* and the *intestines*, which were torn or vanished repeatedly, further the *pharynx*, which I partly ate up several times"[306]), had no guts. Hence *The Hunger* is a felicitous title for a vampire film. He had shortly to disgorge the blood he drank since he could not digest it—the ability of others to digest what they ate and drank, to make it part of them always amazed him. He vomited through his one subsisting quasi-gut: his throat. This made him all the more conscious of all the pipes not only outside the walls (Bacon's *Figure at a Washbasin* [1976], *Three Figures in a Room* [1964], and *Triptych* [May–June 1973]) but also inside them (Terry Gilliam's *Brazil*). Then he disgorged his throat: all the pipes in the walls disappeared and he looked for a long time at the walls' impenetrable smoothness, like a trap that had snapped shut (like the door closing behind the guest of the vampire).

Death

He had thought that death would be the end of him. But it was not. Death was the end of the world. To die is to experience the end of the world.

Is it the case that there is no affirmation of life without the affirmation of death, not as pure inexistence but as undeath? But how can one affirm a realm that admits of no negation, in other words, a realm concerning which one can only be dead certain, including about uncertainty?

Can one avoid physical death and, consequently, finding oneself lost in the death realm through being subjected to an omnipresent observation that would freeze one's body's particles through the quantum Zeno effect ("The quantum Zeno effect ... is a feature of quantum-mechanical systems allowing a particle's time evolution to be slowed down by measuring it frequently enough with respect to some chosen measurement setting.... One can 'freeze' the evolution of the system by measuring it frequently enough in its known initial state"[307]); or through becoming subject to universal interaction by becoming reduced to one's atoms (an atom being "an image which I [Bergson] call a material object," and which is obliged "to act through every one of its points upon all the points of all other images, to transmit the whole of what it receives, to oppose to every action an equal and contrary reaction, to be, in short, merely a road by which pass, in every direction, the modifications propagated throughout the immensity of the universe"[308])?[309]

The mystical *die before you die* is being reduced to its strictly biological version: cryonics.

It is said in Cocteau's *Orpheus* (1950): "There is no lying in the land of death." This must be the paradigmatic lie the dead tell the living.

As is clear in Kurosawa's *Rashomon* (1950), the testimony of the dead, through the mouth of the medium, is not necessarily more authentic, truthful, than that of the living.

One must not deal with death in a *deadly serious* manner, since doing so almost always leads to one's behaving in a cowardly way.

One should try as much as possible to eschew the use of figurative language in the presence of psychotics, who died before dying, for many figurative expressions are the trace in common language of literal happenings in states of altered consciousness: *lose face* (as a result of 180-degree over-turns), *watch your back* (as a result of 180-degree over-turns), *out of this world*, etc. Contrary to the common sense attitude, which is frequently metaphorical/symbolical, an outsider—and who is more of an outsider than the dead human?— most often takes things literally, catches what was hidden behind the metaphor.[310] Nietzsche's "One is not courageous enough to accept what one already knows" often applies to the literal meaning hidden behind the metaphorical/symbolical one. Unfortunately, that which is *staring one in the eye* in states of altered consciousness, the literal, is often doing so to hypnotize one.

Death is the unconscious come to the surface. One has then to rise to a new surface. Asked how it feels to have attained satori, D. T. Suzuki answered: "Just like ordinary everyday experience, except about two inches off the ground!"

Death has two figures: organic death, which allows those who survive me to concoct a retrospective unity to my life; and undeath, with its links to forgery and the double. Given its interest in forgery and doubles and the labyrinth, it is understandable that there's no definitive organic death in Robbe-Grillet's work (hence the exemplary title *L'Immortelle* of one of his films), that a character may be killed in one scene and be alive in another that appears to seamlessly follow chronologically.

It is instructive to compare how the two German filmmakers Wenders and Herzog dealt with the dying of a person who belongs to cinema history. Wenders, who had already made several films that dealt in one way or another with the death of film directors—in *Kings of the Road* (1976) one of the two protagonists reads in a newspaper about Fritz Lang's death; in *The American Friend* (1977) Nicholas Ray plays the role of a painter mistakenly believed to be already dead, and several mafia characters played by film directors (Samuel Fuller [in the role of "Der Amerikaner"], Daniel Schmid [in the role of Igraham], Peter Lilienthal [in the role of Marcangelo]) are killed—arrives as soon as possible to make a film about/with the dying Nicholas Ray but, while not being a resurrector, seems to be wishing that he has come too late (what is the filming called that takes place after it has ended? The reshoot), that is, that the whole film be, as it were, a reshoot with Ray as revenant. One can imagine Wenders's frustration: why can't

Ray do in *Lightning Over Water* (1980) what the character he played in *The American Friend* managed to do so well, be a revenant while still alive? After *Lightning Over Water*, Wenders went on to make *The State of Things* (1982), in which the diegetic film director is killed, and *Tokyo-Ga* (1985), a tribute to a dead filmmaker, Ozu. Herzog writes in *Of Walking in Ice*: "At the end of November 1974, a friend from Paris called and told me that Lotte Eisner was seriously ill and would probably die. I said that this must not be, not at this time, German cinema could not do without her now, we would not permit her death.... I set off on the most direct route to Paris, in full faith, believing that she would stay alive if I came on foot."[311] Had he who came on foot from abroad reached Eisner too late, it is possible that he would have resurrected her.

What the living take for inexistence, the dead experience to be, like the quantum vacuum,[312] teeming with fluctuations (virtual photons are responsible for the Lamb shift and the Casimir effect: *presence*), in the form of thoughts, phrases, etc. To be dead is to be haunted by others: the living, the dead, and the fleeting virtual (schizophrenic Daniel Paul Schreber's *flüchtig hingemachte Männer* ["fleeting-improvised-men"]).

Death being the great intermingling, isn't it natural for the dead's desire to be fixated on that part of the human body that has the most to do with what preserves selectivity, with the immune system: blood?

In Dreyer's *The Passion of Joan of Arc* (1928), Massieu asks Joan: "Your deliverance?" She replies: "My death!" His *Vampyr* (1932) shows that death is no deliverance. His *Ordet* (1954) shows the deliverance from death through resurrection.[313] The events of *Vampyr* happen between the death of *Ordet*'s Inger and her resurrection (from a 1954 interview with Dreyer: "'When did you first come to think of filming *Ordet*?' 'It happened one evening *twenty-two years ago* when I attended its first performance at the Betty Nansen Theater'"[314]). Inger's bite-like kiss just after her resurrection can be considered a lingering reflex from her stay in the death realm of *Vampyr*.

It is not the conscious living human who feels that he will always exist but, on the contrary, the dead. The living human has the apprehension that one day he or she will cease to exist; the dead man or woman has the anxiety that he or she will always exist[315]—true, an existence interspersed with lapses of consciousness, if not of being, and open to the possible replacement by the double.

Whatever disaster one may encounter in life, it makes no sense to respond "Today, I lived a day too long," since these words apply only if death is an absolute end. If at all, one may say these words on the day when one discovers, by dying before dying, that one cannot cease to exist, both because that, rather than any other disaster, is the disaster per se and because for the dead the day either appears to span years or, given that the realm of death is labyrinthine, recurs again and again.

Georges Bataille wrote: "In theory, it is his natural, animal being whose death reveals Man to himself, but the revelation never takes place. For when the animal supporting him dies, the human being himself ceases to be. In order for Man to reveal himself ultimately to himself, he would have to die, but he would have to do it while living—watching himself ceasing to be.... This difficulty proclaims the necessity of *spectacle*, or of *representation* in general, without the practice of which it would be possible for us to remain alien and ignorant in respect to death.... In tragedy, at least, it is a question of our identifying with some character who dies, and of believing that we die, although we are alive."[316] If there is a necessary connection between death and spectacle, it is not for the reason advanced by Bataille but because one's death is stolen, experienced by another or others, by the one/ones who has/have the opportunity to stealthily replace one at the entrancing entrance to the death realm (the double?) and each time one undergoes a lapse of consciousness, if not of being. It is then that it is the most difficult to accept to be a spectator.

Playing Dead

In films on the dead, one should tolerate neither bad acting, a performance untrue to the fiction, nor good acting, a performance *true to life*. One should achieve *false acting*, a performance that is true to death: through a mismatch of the gaze with its object, etc.

Stanislavsky stresses the need for continuity for the actor to achieve a *true-to-life* performance: "Going back to the imaginary scene when I made my morning call on Famusov, I recall an infinite number of physical objectives which I had to execute in my imagination. I had to go along a corridor, knock at a door, take hold of and turn the doorknob, open the door, enter, greet the master of the house and anyone else present, and so forth. In order to preserve the truthfulness of the occasion I could not simply fly into his room in one movement,"[317] and: "You cannot step from the first floor of a house to the tenth [but that is precisely what we find in Deren's films (*Meshes of the Afternoon*; *A Study in Choreography for Camera*; *At Land*)].... You must go through and carry out a whole series of consecutive and logical physical and simple psychological objectives."[318] It is therefore insufficient to creatively display lacunae in the diegetic world, for example, in the form of audio-visual jump cuts between shots, if one does not also neutralize the acting of one's performers, for otherwise, in order to achieve the emotions they think the role asks for, they will create in their imaginations a series of objectives that will restore a continuous off-screen, if not at the level of the film— this is impossible in the cases of Robbe-Grillet and Deren—then at the level of the scene.

Over-turns

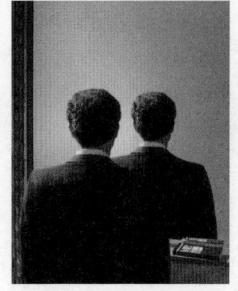

From the series *Over-turned Portraits* made by Paul Perry, Nicola Unger, and Persijn Broersen to accompany my lecture "Backing Mortals' Proper Names."

page 566

"You take me for granted." "You take yourself ... in the mirror, your mirror image's facing you, for granted."

Hegel: "Death, if that is what we want to call this non-actuality, is of all things the most dreadful, and to hold fast what is dead requires the greatest strength.... But the life of Spirit is not the life that shrinks from death and keeps itself untouched by devastation, but rather the life that endures it and maintains itself in it.... It is this power, not as something positive, which closes its eyes to the negative, as when we say of something that it is nothing or is false, and then, having done with it, turn away and pass on to something else; on the contrary, Spirit is this power only by *looking the negative in the face* [my italics], and tarrying with it. This tarrying with the negative is the magical power that converts it into being. This power is identical with what we earlier called the Subject."[319] What comes from facing death not as annihilation, as pure nothing; nor as a determined negation, once one inscribes one's death in a larger cause: the revolution, etc.; but as a realm of total non-mastery, as undeath? But can death, the realm of over-turns, be faced?

In the first two chapters of Philip K. Dick's novel *Eye in the Sky* (1957), the eight members of a group touring the proton beam deflector of the Belmont Bevatron, including the novel's protagonist, Jack Hamilton, and his wife, are gravely injured when the deflector malfunctions, sending the six billion volt beam upward toward the platform on which they are standing, with the result that they fall to the floor and lie there unconscious. The third chapter ostensibly starts with the protagonist regaining consciousness in the hospital where his wife already regained hers and is waiting anxiously for him to wake up. In the following chapters, and as a result of certain anomalies and common dreams, they suspect that they are still lying unconscious on the floor of the Belmont Bevatron! His wife soon asks him and one of the other apparent survivors, "We're dead, aren't we?" While descending the stairs leading to the basement, he fleetingly espies a dreadful creature. "Shuddering, Hamilton grasped the railing and began to climb back upstairs. He had gone only two steps when his legs, of their own volition, refused to carry him farther. His body comprehended what his mind refused to accept.

He was going back down ..."[320] Hamilton was taken aback ("*aback* adverb. 1. *taken aback* Startled or disconcerted 2. *rare* Towards the back; backwards" [*Oxford Dictionary of English*, 3rd ed.]). Soon, his wife appears at the top of the stairs and asks him: "'Is—there anything I can do? Won't you turn toward me? Must you have your back to me?' Hamilton laughed wildly. 'Sure I'll turn toward you.' Gripping the railing, he made a cautious about-face—and found himself still facing the gloomy cave."[321] Orpheus did not just yearn to look back at his dead wife, Eurydice, while ascending the passage from Hades: he actually looked back toward her already in the underworld. But, owing to 180-degree over-turns, he continued to look away from her. It is only when he reached life again that he could successfully turn. Life and death are separated by, among other things, an *imaginary line*. In Magritte's *La Reproduction interdite* (*Not to Be Reproduced* [1937]), the person facing the mirror sees his reflection with its back to him. A mortal's relation to his or her mirror image involves a *sous-entendu* call that usually succeeds in eliciting a response, one having made a 180-degree turn in the mirror to answer it. Heidegger: "Mortals are they who can experience death as death. Animals cannot do this. But animals cannot speak either. The essential relation between death and language flashes up before us, but remains still unthought."[322] This relation of death and speech can find one of its loci in the basic *sous-entendu* call a mortal, who undergoes 180-degree over-turns, addresses to himself or herself in the mirror. Such a call fails in *Not to Be Reproduced*: the call, or even "Hey, you there" of interpellation is not answered by the 180-degree turn that constitutes a subject "because he has recognized that ... it was really him who was hailed (and not someone else)."[323] The 180-degree over-turn neutralizes the subjectivization of the interpellation since it overturns the turn to answer the hailing, often producing an about-face, "a reversal of attitude, behavior, or point of view,"[324] with the new attitude, behavior, or point of view either filling one's mind completely or entering into conflict with one's previously held ones. Whereas a photograph or a painting in which a person is giving us his back invites identification, the back turned on us in *Not to Be Reproduced*—not in the accidental sense that the one in the mirror is looking away from us but categorically, since the backs of both the person and his reflection in the mirror are turned on us—makes it impossible for us, unless we had at one point died before dying, to identify with the figure in the painting. Pascal Bonitzer wrote in relation to Robert Montgomery's film *Lady in the Lake*: "The argument against the film is that the 'parti-pris' of the subjective camera prevented the famous and necessary identification between the spectator and the hero.... We cannot identify with someone whose face is always hidden from us."[325] Who is this *we*? What if we are dead, hence have no face, either because we have no image in the

185

mirror or because the image we see there always has its back turned on us? Even in that case we cannot identify with one "whose face is always hidden from us" but only because we *are* him and he cannot identify with himself. Bonitzer's words apply validly to the normal spectator. Not to *run out on* or *walk out on* the one who is suffering from immobilization and/or fascinated motionlessness, and not to *turn one's back on* the one who is, against his will, turning his back to the world and himself (it may be that only a dancer can counteract, and hence endure, indeed affirm, the latter state: in Deren's *A Study in Choreography for Camera*, the dancer's quick revolving movement in front of a two-headed statue of Siva, which embodies a sustained crossing of the *imaginary line*, produces, and not only stroboscopically, another two-faced being).

How not *to lose face* ("be humiliated or come to be less highly respected"[326]), how to *save one's face* ("avoid humiliation"[327]), when one undergoes over-turns? How not to be paranoid when, as a result of one's undergoing over-turns, things are constantly said and done *behind one's back* ("without a person's knowledge and in an unfair way"[328]).

In Theo Angelopoulos's *Eternity and a Day* (1998), a renowned old Greek poet, Alexandre (played by Bruno Ganz), learns from his doctor that he is very sick: "When the pain becomes unbearable, go to the hospital." He dismisses his housekeeper, telling her that he is about to embark on a "long journey" from which he will not return, and declines her offer to take her with him on his "trip." Alexandre's one acknowledged regret is that he has only left "fragments, words here and there." He has been consumed by one project since the death of his wife: to complete an unfinished poem entitled *The Free Besieged* by the nineteenth century Greek poet Count Dhionísios Solomós (1798-1857). "Solomós's earliest poems were written in Italian, but in 1822 he determined to write in the spoken tongue of Greece" (*Britannica*)—he was the first poet of modern Greece to do so. According to Alexandre, Solomós was on the lookout for words and expressions used by common Greek people and paid anyone who provided him with specimens of them. Partly due to the impediment of "the as-yet meagre resources of his chosen linguistic medium,"[329] his major poems *The Cretan* (1833), *The Free Besieged* (second and third sketches, 1827-49) (which deals with the siege of Missolonghi), and *The Shark* (1849) remained fragmentary. Will Alexandre rectify the fragmentary nature of his own work as well as that of Solomós on his possibly last day alive? While every new day brings with it the opportunity to accomplish some unfinished business, it also brings with it the occasion for new, unexpected unfinished business. In the process of packing, Alexandre discovers a collection of unopened letters belonging to his late wife, Anna. While getting in the car to drive to his daughter to leave his dog in her custody, he notices a group of children standing at a crossroads. When cars come to a stop at the red light, the boys run toward them and start cleaning their windshields. He drives past them but has to stop at the next, red light. A child runs up to his car and starts to clean the windshield. Greek policemen appear and begin chasing the children cleaning the cars at the preceding light. Alexandre tells the child to hop in his car, thus saving him from being apprehended, and deposits him a few blocks away. Shortly thereafter he hands his daughter his late wife's letters. Among them is one without an envelope. She asks for and receives his permission to read it. It turns out to be a letter from his then young wife in which she implores him, who was then often preoccupied with his work, to give her a day of his time. After leaving his daughter, and while waiting for his prescription to be filled at a pharmacy, he sees the same boy, an Albanian refugee, being kidnapped and taken away in a van. He rescues him and resolves to take him back to his war-torn homeland, but at the border he abruptly ascertains that this is not the best way to help the boy. While on a bus with the boy, he encounters the long-dead poet Solomós, or a performer playing him, and after listening to him recite one of his poems asks him: "Tomorrow, how long will it last?" By the time he has put the refugee boy on a ship heading to the United States, it is late at night. Soon, he comes to a stop at a red light. His car's wipers go back and forth on the windshield under the rain. This shot is reminiscent of the beginning scene of Volker Schlöndorff 's *Circle of Deceit* (1981), where the protagonist, also played by Bruno Ganz, sits in his car under the rain while the windshield wipers move back and forth. The light having changed to green, the cars on either side of him move forward; the driver of the car behind him, after honking, pulls around and passes him. The shot at this point is reminiscent of one in Fritz Lang's *The Testament of Dr. Mabuse* (1933) in which the car of a driver who had stopped at a crossroads and was shot dead while waiting for the green light remains in the middle of the road while the other cars soon move on. This scene has a strong temporal charge because it evokes, in a nostalgic manner, the previous run of the children to the stopped cars. There, in the car, now dead, did he become his own double, a *faussaire* (the French release title of Schlöndorff's film), a counterfeiter? At dawn we see the car, which remains in the middle of the road, from the rear. The traffic light changes to red. Another car comes to a stop at the light. All of a sudden, Alexandre's car crosses the red light. Was he not dead after all? Was he simply tired after such a long day of emotional upheaval and back-and-forth car journeys with the Albanian refugee boy and so fell asleep at the wheel? No, he was not just tired but *dead tired*. It is probable that the one who was in the car that stopped next to his at the traffic light was his double and that he was seated in the backseat with no one behind the wheel! Horrified, Alexandre either drove away, disregarding the red light,[330] or else the car moved all by itself. Then, *coming forth by day*, he walks in his old seaside house in the light of the most ancient Egyptian of twentieth-century painters, Edward Hopper. When he reaches the balcony door, it opens on its own before him—we are thus confirmed that the car had moved on its own. Since his walk is complemented by a tracking shot of the camera through the door, then across the balcony, we presume that we are getting his point-of-view shot of the beach. Now the camera advances beyond the balcony and smoothly descends until it reaches ground level. Unexpectedly, he enters the frame and walks onto the beach. It is as if he had a subtle, angelic body, one that would have allowed him to float down from the balcony (a tribute to Wenders's *Wings of Desire*, whose protagonist is an angel played by Bruno Ganz, and in which the camera fittingly has a floating feel?). Since dance allows two dancers to meet across the two branches of the dance realm into which it projects them, can two dead lovers, lost in the labyrinthine death realm, meet by dancing? I doubt it, but in the film, he "dances" with his dead wife and then says to her: "One day I had asked you: 'Tomorrow, what is tomorrow, Anna?'" Is it a thousand years ("a day the measure of which is a thousand years of what you count" [Qur'ān 32:5]) or fifty thousand years ("a Day whereof the span is fifty thousand years" [Qur'ān 70:4])? While departing, she answers: "Eternity and a day." He calls her, "Anna ... Anna," with no response—her turns, she who is dead and who is no longer dancing, are overturned by over-turns. Godard's *King Lear* (1987) fails to develop one of its remarkable intertitles, *A Picture Shot in the Back,* beyond the theme of betrayal—that of King Lear by two of his three daughters, that of Godard himself by the producers of the film, etc.—and a critique of the customary posture of the audience in a cinema, each row of people with their backs to the row behind them. "A picture shot in the back" is accomplished in the last shot of *Eternity and a Day*: notwithstanding Angelopoulos's answer to Gideon Bachmann's "Does he die at the end of the film?" "No, no,"[331] I would assert that his protagonist is dead by the time we see his back against the sea and he fails thrice to answer the call of his dead wife, repeating to himself instead the three words he had learned in that last day of his life: *korfulamu*: "heart of a flower";[332] *argathini*: "very late at night"; and, most importantly, *xenitis*: "one who is a stranger everywhere"—a word that felicitously describes his present state, since the dead is *xenitis*. Henceforth, he will no longer have to look for words and expressions and be ready to pay for them, for they will be imposed on him willy-nilly by the (dead's) whispering or screaming voices, as happened in the case of Daniel Paul Schreber with, for example, *flüchtig hingemachte Männer* ("fleeting-improvised-men") and *Vorhöfe des Himmels* ("forecourts of heaven"[333]): "I did not invent the expression 'forecourts of heaven,' but *like all other expressions which are in inverted commas in this essay*

[*Memoirs of My Nervous Illness*] (for instance 'fleeting-improvised-men,' 'dream life,' etc.), it only repeats the words which the voices that speak to me always applied to the processes concerned. These are expressions *which would never have occurred to me*, which I have never heard from human beings."[334] While literature has to a large extent by now accommodated the languages of the common people, with very rare exceptions it has yet to accommodate the languages of the dead and the voices: "o dedi / o dada orzoura / o dou zoura / a dada skizi / o kaya / o kaya pontoura / o ponoura / a pena / poni"[335] (Artaud, "The Return of Artaud, the Mômo").

"Then Abraham approached him [the Lord] and said: 'Will you sweep away the righteous with the wicked? What if there are fifty righteous people in the city? Will you really sweep it away and not spare the place for the sake of the fifty righteous people in it? ...' The Lord said, 'If I find fifty righteous people in the city of Sodom, I will spare the whole place for their sake'" (Genesis 18:23–26). Abraham then repeats the question-entreaty, invoking in turn the possible presence of forty-five, then forty, then thirty, then twenty righteous people in the city, and each time the Lord responds that in that case he will spare the city (Genesis 18:27–31). "Then he said, 'May the Lord not be angry, but let me speak just once more. What if only ten can be found there?' He answered, 'For the sake of ten, I will not destroy it'" (Genesis 18:32). But were there ten righteous people in Sodom? The angels of the Lord tried to find other righteous people beside Lot, his wife, and their two daughters. But even the two men who were pledged to marry Lot's daughters thought he was being facetious when he warned them, "Hurry and get out of this place, because the Lord is about to destroy the city!" (Genesis 19:14), revealing themselves not to be righteous. There turned out to be only four righteous people in the city, so God did not spare it for their sake; indeed, he swept away the righteous with the wicked. "As soon as they [the angels of the Lord] had brought them out, one of them said, 'Flee for your lives! Don't look back, and don't stop anywhere in the plain! Flee to the mountains or you will be swept away!'" (Genesis 19:17).[336] How twisted is the expression "Don't look back ... or you will be swept away!" as well as its equivalent: "Don't look back, or you will die." It puts the addressee in a double bind: if he or she turns, he or she will cease to live; but if he or she fully obeys the "prohibition" against looking back, the end result is tantamount to being constantly subject to over-turns and thus already dead, since over-turns are a characteristic of the death realm. Thus, appropriately, Lot, his two daughters, and his wife were not spared in two different ways. Lot's wife looked back successfully and by that turn conjointly revealed that she is not a mortal and "became a pillar of salt" (Genesis 19:26). Lot and his two daughters possibly, indeed probably, turned but their turns were overturned by over-turns,[337] this revealing that, mortals, they were already dead even while still physically alive. While with regard to Lot's non-mortal wife, the prohibition to look back should be taken as a moral proscription since, not dead while alive, she is not subject to over-turns, with regard to Lot and his two daughters, and as was the case with Orpheus, it should be taken as an ethical revelation of a certain state of affairs: you are a mortal and therefore subject to over-turns, and thus any turn you make will be overturned. The passage through the plain in Lot's story is a passage through death. Since the mortal Lot had intercourse with a non-mortal woman (for a previous biblical version of such intercourse, but in an inverted gender form, see Genesis 6:4: "The sons of God went to the daughters of men and had children by them"), it is fitting and symptomatic that it is in relation to him, at the door of his house, that the people of Sodom get the idea to have intercourse with angels. "The two angels arrived at Sodom … 'My lords,' he [Lot] said, 'please turn aside to your servant's house....' 'No,' they answered, 'we will spend the night in the square.' But he insisted so strongly that they did go with him and entered his house.... All the men from every part of the city of Sodom … surrounded the house. They called to Lot, 'Where are the men who came to you tonight? Bring them out to us so that we can have sex with them'" (Genesis 19:1–5). I wager that had these non-mortals spent the night in the square, the mortal people of Sodom would not have tried to have sex with them.

Kneeling Angel with Mountainous Wings[338]

Dedicated to Patrick Bokanowski for L'Ange

He had reached an impasse in his pondering the fall of bodies: how could a rock, albeit a Taoist one, permeated by emptiness, and a feather fall at the same speed? He prayed for God's assistance. There is no prayer without listening ("Why do you want me to be in your religious film when you know that I am not only an atheist but also a libertine? Is it the Renée Falconetti syndrome?"[339] "It is because you listen so well, even when you are talking. I think you would be wonderful at prayer"). To encounter someone who is inept at listening is to know that he or she is inept at praying.[340] To pray is to invoke while listening: what is invoked is God's help … to listen even more intensely—until one hears "as only / saints have heard: heard till the giant-call / lifted them off the ground; yet they went impossibly / on with their kneeling, in undistracted attention: so inherently hearers" (Rilke, *Duino Elegies*, "The First Elegy"). After an extended time, the levitating saint screamed, to stop such extremely intense listening, and fell to the floor.

One day, on turning upon hearing a sudden silence, he perceived through the window a nude humanoid figure standing before the

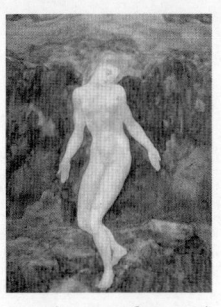

page 569 Kahlil Gibran, *The Gift*, watercolor, 33 x 22.5 cm, 1923.
(Illustration for *The Prophet*.)

mountain that faces his study. The mountain seemed transfigured, purplish. The angel was hovering in a kneeling posture about two inches above the ground. The witness could hear the sound of the wind and simultaneously the silence of the angel. When the angel spoke, the wind in no way obstructed what he was saying: "I need wings to resist the fall implicit in the cadaver you virtually are." No angel who appeared to a non-mortal had wings, since these, often portrayed conventionally in Christian, Muslim, and Jewish art, are to counter the fall implicit in the cadaver that the mortal human is virtually. The wind moved the grass beneath the angel's feet, but no air stirred in his hair nor in the mountain. The witness felt conjointly a most intense nostalgia and an awful dread. "Every angel is terrifying" (*Duino Elegies*),[341] as even Rilke, who "stroked, as if it were a great old beast, the little [mountain] Muzot that had sheltered all this [*Duino Elegies*] for me,"[342] knew. Why did he have the impression that the mountain was the angel's wings? Was it because the contiguous transfigured parallel elongated rocks looked like the feathers of a wing? Was it because, through an effect of foreshortening, the angel's arms seemed to be attached to the mountain? There was an additional reason: while the halo of the angel demarcated him from everything else in the landscape, it did not do so from the mountain. True, a minimal demarcation subsisted. He could figure it out only when he jotted down "The angel was in front of the mountain" and realized that his words were inaccurate. He found himself revising the sentence to "The angel was before the mountain." It then became clear to him that the angel was not only in front of the mountain but also prior to it, and not merely historically but also in the present he shared with it. We, humans, wait for the angel in the temporality of chronological time, yet when he, aeviternal, shows up, he has always been before us in the present.[343] The angel, even a guardian one come to help us in an emergency, has all the time he needs to observe us in the present: "In the hills, an old man read *The Odyssey* to a child, and his little listener stopped blinking" (Wenders's *Wings of Desire*). Against the hidden cameras in so many crass TV programs across the world, some films and writing, for instance *Wings of Desire*, directed by Wenders and co-written by Peter Handke, have managed to deploy another kind of observation, that of the angel. While the angel may be indescribable, as the one who glimpses him quickly averts his look in awe, he is a master of description because he is prior to us in the present we share with him, and because he does not arrive, therefore does not interrupt or alter anything in the situation. Who indeed has seen an angel arrive? We wake up from a nightmare, and there he is. We wipe our weeping eyes, only to discover that he is already with us.[344] Is it surprising that no one annunciates the angel? For it not to lead to an infinite regression, every structure of annunciation requires one whom no one annunciates, who does not arrive, whose showing up reveals that he was already present: the annunciator of the arrival does not arrive. Notwithstanding that he is in constant displacement to relay messages and annunciations, the angel gives the impression, through being from all time in any present we share with him, of abiding in that moment, revealing by contrast that other creatures are constantly restless: the great paintings and frescoes of the Annunciation give the impression that Mary is the one who does not belong in the room, who has just entered it.

There is a harbinger to every real arrival. How can an arrival be announced and remain an event? By being impossible.[345] One can thus characterize any eventful arrival: it is foreshadowed but as impossible, as the impossible to happen.[346] It is impossible that the Word become flesh (John 1:14), that a virgin give birth ("How will this be," Mary asked the angel, "since I am a virgin?" [Luke 1:34]),[347] and that divine nature and human nature coexist in the same person. The angel brings with him a double surprise: he was already here (!), and what he annunciates is impossible or revealed to be impossible. The event oscillates between not being annunciated, prior to us even in the present we share with it, and being annunciated but as the impossible to happen. The event: the angel and the Messiah/Mahdi. We are taken by surprise not only by the angel, but also by the Messiah/Mahdi, notwithstanding that we invoked him for the longest time. If the angel, who is in constant viewing of God ("their [these little ones'] angels in Heaven always see the face of my Father in heaven" [Matthew 18:10]), is nonetheless very much bound with faith, it is because the good news he annunciates makes what seemed, prior to such annunciation, extremely difficult but possible now impossible but bound to happen. Every angel is terrifying, not least because faith is terrifying. His friend asked him why he seemed so concerned and uneasy. After much pressing, he confessed that an angel had appeared to him and had revealed to him that the eldest son of the imam would succeed his father. "Were you asleep? How did he look?" "I was awake writing. I was startled by his presence, dropped my quill, and he knelt and picked it up for me." "Are you sure it was not all a dream? Anyway, your distress puzzles me: aren't we both fervent partisans of the imam's eldest son? Ought you not to be pleased by this good news or rather confirmation of what has been, for some time now, a foregone conclusion, his father having proclaimed him his successor?" "But why do we need a confirmation of a foregone conclusion?" A fortnight later, rumors began circulating about the untimely death of the eldest son of the imam. "Why have you switched your allegiance to the imam's younger son? Surely you don't believe that his eldest son is actually dead: he is just occulted." "That is what I, too, believed in the aftermath of the circulation of the news of his death. Unfortunately, yesterday, by a concatenation of circumstances, I was privy to see his actual corpse. Were you to persist in your belief that he is the next imam, I would not blame you, since you have not seen his corpse, but you also should not blame me since I have." "But the angel announced a different, good news!" When Paul Virilio writes that in our world of communication at the speed of light, we have a "globalization, in which *everything arrives without there being any need to depart*,"[348] one can deduce that it is a world devoid of angels.[349] Heidegger said in his last, *Der Spiegel* interview that "only a god can save us" in the epoch of technology.[350] This god has to be annunciated. Therefore, God cannot appear before the epoch of technology has taken a turn such that it is no longer the case that there is a generalized arrival. Is our task to prepare the coming of a god or of the Messiah/Mahdi? Let us be more modest: if at all, our task would be to prepare the coming of the angel, of the one who annunciates him. And that seems the right way to go about it, since were we to prepare for the coming of a god or the Messiah/Mahdi, we would be *forcing the end*.[351] While anyway we cannot effectively hurry the coming of the Messiah/Mahdi, for that event is miraculous, it is possible and appropriate to force the coming of his annunciator.

Did the appearance of the angel confirm his faith? No, only a few hours later doubt assailed him again. Was it because what he had witnessed reproduced an exquisite 1923 watercolor by an otherwise mediocre painter, Kahlil Gibran, its mountains painted in a manner reminiscent of those in Chinese art or in Chinese-influenced Persian art, its closely arranged parallel rocks looking like the feathers of a wing?[352] The angel visited him again, this time in his room. It was his first experience of micropsia: the angel appeared the size of a mustard seed. Why, then, had his wings the dimensions of those of a bird? When he observed the wings more attentively, he perceived that what he took first for feathers were rocks. He recognized then that the wings too were Lilliputian. Indeed, when he hearkened in expectation of the angel's message, he could hear a mountain's reverberations. The episode happened in a hypnagogic state. The next day, the angel appeared again in his room. This time, he did not seem to be in miniature and the mountain he had for wings was life-size, gigantic. He tried to comprehend how the angel and the mountain could be within the room while being far bigger than it. That night, dreading that he was losing his mind, he mentioned this event to a painter friend of his. The latter remarked: "It must be that you were then in the listening room or the tomb of the wrestlers." While puzzled by this answer, he intuitively felt that it was erroneous. He figured out that if the angel and the mountain that formed his wings could be in a room that was far smaller than they, it was because they were not in the world, and therefore not in the room, but in light. To have a halo is not to be surrounded by light but to be in light. In eternity, it is not light that is in the world but the inverse: the world, including *its* light, is in light.[353] What applies visually to light applies aurally to silence: in eternity, silence is not in or of the world, but the world, including humans, is in silence. The angel and the human to whom he appears are triply not together: the first is in light and silence, the second is in the world; the first is kneeling, the second is averting his or her eyes in awe; and, in the same present, the first, aeviternal, is prior to the second, temporal. When in the fall of 1609 Galileo looked through a telescope he had just constructed that had a twenty-fold magnification, he saw no angels; instead, he discovered, in January 1610, four moons revolving around Jupiter and many more stars than are visible with the naked eye. But how did this scientist, who will be pronounced a suspect of heresy by the Inquisition in Rome in 1633, conceive, two decades earlier, the notion that "all objects fall at the same rate in a vacuum," dropping, according to his biographer Vincenzo Viviani, bodies of different weights from the top of the Leaning Tower of Pisa to demonstrate that the speed at which a heavy object falls is not proportional to its weight? Did he see an angel in his observatory? If so, the experience must have been breathtaking, since an angel does not move in the atmosphere, which belongs to the world, but in light; and ahylognostic, since angels, who move without friction and who are full of faith, do not feel any difference between moving a mountain and moving a feather. Full of faith, angels can move mountains, or even, in case these mountains are the kind shown in Chinese painting, emptiness. Can they, for that matter, move and raise humans? Satan's first *reported* temptation of Jesus revolves around falling: "Then the devil ... had him stand on the highest point of the temple. 'If you are the Son of God,' he said, 'throw yourself down. For it is written: "He will command his angels concerning you, and they will lift you up in their hands, so that you will not strike your foot against a stone."' Jesus answered him, 'It is also written: "Do not put the Lord your God to the test"'" (Matthew 4:5-7). If Jesus of Nazareth was no longer virtually cadaverous when he was baptized (Tertullian: "Is it not wonderful, too, that death should be washed away by bathing?" [*On Baptism*]), then angels could lift him from then on. But if he was no longer virtually cadaverous only at his resurrection, then we have to consider differently his refusal to jump when Satan challenged him to do so. While he could still, through faith, throw himself down from the highest point of the temple and yet not fall despite the cadaver he contained (he would soon do this, not fall through faith: his walking on water), the challenge and temptation posed to him by Satan was to jump and rely not on his faith but on that of the angels. He had to have faith not in God, the Father, but in the angels, in the angels' faith, since the angels could possibly accomplish the impossible, namely, carry his virtually cadaverous body, only by faith. Did Jesus's faith in angels, in their faith, waver given that there had been fallen angels, indeed given that it was precisely a fallen angel who was challenging him to have faith in angels?

The angel exemplified for him Jesus Christ's words "If you have faith as small as a mustard seed, you can say to this mountain, 'Move from here to there,' and it will move. Nothing will be impossible for you" (Matthew 17:20). Seized with fear on seeing the mountain move, he started running, tripped, and fell. He apprehended the hand of the angel on his hand. He expected him to raise him, but instead the angel knelt. The angel's proximity was so overwhelming, he passed out. He woke to the sound of approaching footsteps. He felt the familiar touch of a human hand. When he looked up, he saw a sturdy young man staring at him. With a little effort, the latter raised him. Thinking back on what had happened, he felt confused: would a genuine angel kneel to a mere man? To an angel, the source of gravity is neither some force affecting mass nor some curvature in spacetime, but the fall implicit in the cadaver ("*cadaver*: late Middle English: from Latin, from *cadere* 'to fall'" [*Oxford Dictionary of English*, 3rd ed.]). To God, even under His name *al-Jalīl* (the Majestic), the angels never prostrated themselves. They did so only to man as a virtually cadaverous mortal: "And when We said unto the angels: 'Prostrate yourselves before Adam,' they fell prostrate" (Qur'ān 2:34). While walking in the Garden of Eden after eating from the mortality-inducing tree of the knowledge of good and evil, Adam heard a sound he could not recognize. He looked down toward its source. His look fell on a fig leaf beneath one of his feet. What an unsettling, novel sight: a leaf on the ground! While physically, falling is derivative of gravity, metaphysically, gravity is derivative of the Fall implied in the cadaver and introduced by mortality. Metaphysically, we do not have nightmares in which we fall endlessly because we would be beings subject to gravity; rather, we live in a world ruled by gravity and we have nightmares in which we fall endlessly because we are virtually cadaverous. Physically, the gravity of the singularity of a medium-size black hole would tear man into shreds in a matter of seconds, but metaphysically, even such enormous gravity has its source in the Fall of man implicit in the cadaver. On his way to relay the message, and given that the angel does not move in the atmosphere but, with *serene velocity*,[354] in light, nothing could make the angel fall, not even a black hole; but when he reached a mortal human, he knelt, even while still in the air.[355] In a painting, if the Annunciation is depicted with the angel kneeling before Mary, this implies that the scene is represented at the point where he has just hailed her ("Greetings, you who are highly favored!") and is undergoing the enormous gravity contained in her as a virtual cadaver; if it rather shows him in a composite posture between kneeling and standing, then this indicates that the scene is being represented at the stage where the angel has already annunciated to Mary that she is to give birth to the Word become flesh, with the consequence that he is kneeling as a result of the gravity of the cadaver contained in her and the human nature of Jesus, but upright in adoration of the divine nature of the Christ. As Mary discovered the presence of the angel, she felt lighter *and* knelt. Was her kneeling a gesture of adoration of a fallen one ("But Satan caused them to deflect therefrom and expelled them from the [happy] state in which they were; and We said: 'Fall down'" [Qur'ān 2:36]) toward a being who is spiritually superior to her ("Thou hast made him [man] a little lower than the angels" [Psalm 8:5])? Mortals kneel to those who remind them of their Fall as well as to those who can kill them and thus precipitate them into their cadaverous mortality, thus into their endless fall: exemplarily God and Caesar, respectively. "Then he said to them, 'Give to Caesar what is Caesar's, and to God what is God's'" (Matthew 22:21): kneeling. Jesus Christ ordered him: "Lazarus, come forth." Lazarus *rose to his feet.*[356] As he walked out of the grave, a rotten smell accompanied him; it did not issue from his body, but from the bandages still attached to his ankles and elbows. He walked to Jesus Christ and stood in front of him in awe, gratitude, and worship. When the others knelt in adoration of the resurrector, he failed to understand the meaning of their gesture. His sister Mary, who had "poured perfume on the Lord and wiped his feet with her hair" (John 11:2), approached him with trepidation and began removing the few bandages still attached to his body. He was repulsed by the smell of putrefaction she exuded[357] and simultaneously felt an incredible force push him down. He fell. He managed with difficulty to stand up again. Then, to their consternation, he knelt to each member of the crowd into whose proximity he came. It was an awkward kind of kneeling, more a fall than a genuflection. Some viewed it as an example of the humility honored by Jesus, others attributed it to the lingering rigidity of what was for four days a corpse in a state of rigor mortis. The Nizārīs of Alamūt must have faced the following problem: How can we announce the resurrection if we are still virtually cadavers? Certainly the part of the Sharīʿa that enjoins the repeated prostration during prayer ("Is he who payeth adoration in the watches of the night, prostrate and standing, ... [to be accounted equal with a disbeliever]?" [Qur'ān 39:9]) had to be abrogated during the Great Resurrection. I would think that, additionally, an explicit prohibition would have been promulgated then against kneeling or bowing to the imam, allowing such a gesture, even possibly instituting it toward non-Nizārīs. I imagine that the two Nizārī imams of the Great Resurrection never received any of the emissaries of their enemies, whether Abbasid or Seljuk, to spare their followers seeing them kneel before the latter. That Nizārīs continued to die between 1164 and 1210, including Ḥasan *'alā dhikrihi'l-salām* (on his mention be peace) and his son and successor, Nūr ad-Dīn Muḥammad II, does not invalidate the Great Resurrection, for the Nizārīs could then have virtually contained not a cadaver but a corpse. One can imagine that the grandson of Ḥasan *'alā dhikrihi'l-salām* reinstated the Sharī'a in 1210 not only because of political, strategic, and military factors (the intensifying threat to his initiates from a Sunnism again on the ascendancy, etc.), but also possibly because an angel knelt to him or even to one of his Nizārī initiates, this implying that they were virtual cadavers and therefore that their resurrection had ended.

Again, he suddenly became aware of the presence of an angel. This time the angel did not prostrate himself before him. He was unsure whether this was because he, a Christian, was no longer a virtual cadaver: "As in Adam all die, so in Christ all will be made alive" (1 Corinthians 15:22) (but if Christians are alive in Jesus Christ, how come they still sometimes have nightmares in which they fall on and on?); or because of angelic faith, one allowing the angel to accomplish something impossible, namely, withstanding the enormous forceful attraction downward of the virtually cadaverous mortal; or else because this angel was Satanic ("'We ... told the angels: Fall ye prostrate before Adam!' And they fell prostrate, all save Iblīs [Satan]" [Qur'ān 7:11]), a disbeliever in the virtual cadaverous mortality of humans.

> And when thy Lord said unto the angels: 'Lo! I am about to place a viceroy in the earth,' they said: 'Wilt thou place therein one who will do harm therein and will shed blood, while we, we hymn Thy praise and sanctify Thee?' He said: 'Surely I know that which ye know not.' And He taught Adam all the names, then showed them to the angels, saying: 'Inform Me of the names of these, if ye are truthful.' They said: 'Be glorified! We have no knowledge saving that which Thou hast taught us. Lo! Thou, only Thou, art the Knower, the Wise.' He said: 'O Adam! Inform them of their names,' and when he had informed them of their names, He said: 'Did I not tell you that I know the secret of the heavens and the earth? And I know that which ye disclose and which ye hide.' And when We said unto the angels, 'Prostrate yourselves before Adam,' they fell prostrate, all save Iblīs. He demurred through pride, and so became a disbeliever. And We said: 'O Adam! Dwell thou and thy wife in the Garden, and eat ye freely (of the fruits) thereof where ye will; but come not nigh this tree lest ye become wrongdoers.' But Satan caused them to deflect therefrom and expelled them from the (happy) state in which they were; and We said: 'Fall down ...'
>
> Qur'ān 2:30–36

Given the nonlinear nature of the Qur'ān, one cannot be positive that the order of the *ayāt* is the order of the events. By viewing the heavenly prostration scene as happening following the fall of mortality, we can understand both the angels' response to God, "Wilt thou place therein one who will do harm therein and will shed blood ...?" (Qur'ān 2:30): shedding blood can be done only to a mortal (both the idiomatic Arabic expression *yasfik al-dimā'* and the equivalent English *shed blood* mean to take life, especially with violence; kill), starting with Abel; and that Adam is told by God, "Inform them of their names" (Qur'ān 2:33): only a mortal can know not only the generic names of animals, plants, and things but also his or her own as well as other mortals' proper names, only a mortal understands names, misunderstands God's attributes (*sifāt*) as proper names,[358] only a mortal needs to know "all the names" (Qur'ān 2:31), since he or she is bound at some point during his or her death or dying before dying to exclaim, like Nietzsche at the onset of his psychosis, of his death before dying, "Every name in history is I."

The two most interesting takes on God in relation to mortality: God is either totally the God of death and therefore does not understand anything about life, as in Daniel Paul Schreber's system: "*Within the Order of the World, God did not really understand the living human being* and had no need to understand him, because, according to the Order of the World, He dealt only with corpses";[359] or else He is the Living One (*Huwa al-hayy*) (Qur'ān 40:65), the Living One Who dieth not (*al-hayy alladhī lā yamūt*) (Qur'ān 25:58), therefore a God who understands nothing about (the) death (realm as other than an afterlife, in other words, as other than a spinoff of life that has for the most part the same logic and nature). "And the Lord God commanded the man, saying, Of every tree of the garden [including the tree of life] thou mayest freely eat: But of the tree of the knowledge of good and evil, thou shalt not eat of it: for in the day that thou eatest thereof thou shalt surely die" (Genesis 2:16–17). If the god who gave the command was The Living, then he would have expected that Man would either comply with his advice not to eat from the tree of the knowledge of good and evil or eat of it only after eating from the tree of life. Mortality, not knowledge of good and evil, was the unsuspected temptation, and non-mortal Man (the Hebrew *'ādhām*) and Woman fell for it! An unexpected, Gnostic disaster happened as Man perversely chose not to eat first from the tree of life before eating from the mortality-causing tree of the knowledge of good and evil,[360] thus introducing and unleashing a mortality that is not based on life, therefore a mortality of which God was unaware. If *we* can possibly understand that someone may choose mortality as such over life, it is because we are already fallen, mortal. With one exception, the angels "fell prostrate" (Qur'ān 2:34) to Adam when he turned a mortal; they were sensitive to what was virtual about him even while he lived: the cadaver. If Iblīs is a disbeliever, he is that first of all in the incredible perversity of man (and woman)—he incited man to eat of the tree of the knowledge of good and evil but did not specify the order in which the latter opted to do so—and therefore in the mortality of Adam, thus in the enormous gravity folded in Adam as a virtual cadaver. Having understood God's ostensible expectation that he would prostrate to Adam morally rather than ethically, as a command rather than as indication of the cadaver implicit in the mortal Adam, Satan felt offended: "I am better than him. Thou createdst me of fire while him Thou didst create of mud" (Qur'ān 7:12).[361] In order to bring an end to this fallen world, the angel Iblīs's failure to kneel to Adam through disbelief in his mortality has to be repeated and corrected: this time the angel does not fall prostrate to a descendant of Adam either because the latter, like the Nizārīs of the Great Resurrection (between 1164 and 1240) and the resurrected brother of Mary and Martha, is no longer virtually a cadaverous mortal; or because he manages, through faith, to counter the implicit infinite fall in the virtual cadaver that that descendant of Adam continues to be.

Arriving Too Late for Resurrection

Once he, a photographer, was present during the slaughter of someone. He had hurriedly taken out his small camera from his bag and snapped several photographs. Later, he could not stand the fact that he had witnessed that event without intervening to save the man's life, indeed that what had most preoccupied him then was instead whether there was enough light and, given that he did not have enough time to focus, whether the resultant photographs would be blurred. For a long time after that, he stopped taking photographs. Some friends tried to persuade him to go back to photography, invoking such illustrious photographs as Robert Capa's *Death of a Loyalist Militiaman, Córdoba Front, September 1936* (a.k.a. *The Falling Soldier*), September 5, 1936, which Capa took from close range just as a bullet hit the militiaman; and Eddie Adams's *Murder of a Vietcong by Saigon Police Chief*, February 1, 1968. He answered: "But at least Capa was killed as he stepped on a land mine during a reportage on the French Indochina War for *Life*." Then one day he was asked by a relative to bring his camera with him to the funeral of his son to take a photograph of him. After some hesitation, he complied. For a while after that day, he just photographed corpses: it was the best way to avoid a repeat of the emergency that had made him temporarily stop photographing. But one day, after perusing his photographs of corpses, he was seized with the same sensation as before and decided again to stop photographing. Before a corpse, a photographer should face the same sort of dilemma he or she encounters in front of someone on the verge of being killed: do I simply stand there as a bystander, not try to intervene, and just take my photograph? But if I feel I should intervene, then in what way, to do what, given that the person is already dead? To resurrect him or her.

He arrived around noon to the vampire's lair. Unfortunately for him, the vampire's freezing affected time directly, making it undergo time-lapse, so that when he reached the coffin from the entrance of the sepulcher, it was already sunset. Fortunately for him, he was not fooled by the seeming animation of the vampire, commanding him: "Dracula, in the name of Christ I resurrect you!" It is amazing that no vampire film shows the living protagonist trying to resurrect the vampire, an undead, instead of trying to inflict on him the second, final death by piercing his heart with a stake and beheading him. What made it difficult for *Dracula*'s Arthur, Lord Godalming, to slaughter his fiancée Lucy, now a vampire? Was it only that she had the form, likeness of the once-living Lucy? I would like to think that it was also that she is resurrectable.

While ascending the stairs to his apartment, he heard the phone ringing. Was it her? He rushed to the door, then ran to the phone, only to hear from her sister that she had died a quarter of an hour earlier. He collapsed. Then he noticed the blinking light of his message machine. He felt a chill as he heard her voice. "It's J— —. Call me." How curious that she had prefaced her message with her name, as if he would no longer be able to recognize her voice or had already forgotten her name. He deeply regretted then that he had bought a machine that did not provide the time of the calls. When her sister first discovered that she had no pulse, she shook her desperately again and again, screaming: "J— — ! J— — ! J— — ! Answer me!" In and from the realm of death, J— — had tried to answer. She turned, but her turn was overturned by a 180-degree over-turn. The corpse did not react to the call. Soon, the living no longer called her: they viewed her as only this inert mass on the deathbed. While disavowing the death of the beloved, most melancholiacs nonetheless no longer call him or her but utter his or her name as that of an object one refers to but does not address. Could she blame them unreservedly? Was she not guilty of the same disregard? For why otherwise did she in the mirror not turn toward herself, if not because she was no longer being called by herself[362] but treated by herself as something one does not call? To be dead is no longer to be called— except by terrified people trying to awaken from a nightmare, thus in the act of abandoning the dead whose help they are invoking. This is part of the ordeal of death: one is called only by the terrified. To almost any living person, the dead human can say: "*In your dreams* you called me." Unlike the living, who when they overhear their names in a nearby conversation listen more attentively, as to something that regards them directly, sometimes volunteering some correction or acknowledgment, the dead, certainly by the time the traditional period of mourning has ended, do not pay any attention when we utter their names while talking about them rather than to them in a call. The living are implicitly called even when others are talking about them; the dead are called only when one explicitly calls them. Suddenly, J— — heard someone call her name. It was the lover whom she had phoned several times while on her deathbed, leaving him unanswered messages imploring him to come see her or at least call her back, and with whom she used to have heated discussions to refute his view that objects and almost all animals have no proper names ("*appeler un chat un chat*: to call a spade a spade" [*Le Robert & Collins Dictionnaire Français-Anglais, Anglais-Français*, 5th ed.]), who was now posthumously calling her, who was reduced by the others to an object, the corpse.[363] While she assumed, almost with resignation, that she would not be able to successfully respond to the call, her turn getting once more overturned by a 180-degree over-turn, she was elated to hear someone call her. How strange, how wonderful to be called again, to be treated as other than an object! Again, she turned, but this time her turn was not over-turned! She made a Herculean effort to raise her eyelids, now a dead weight. He detected a barely perceptible twitch of her eyelids. Except for that spasm, the body remained stiff. Despite his revulsion, he had the impulse to hug her body. Why? While to the living seated around the deathbed, the corpse is a body firmly resting on the bed, to the one who has just been resurrected, and thus recalled to the dead body, it is a cadaver, an indefinite fall. "*Cadaver*: Late Middle English: from Latin, from *cadere* 'to fall'"[364]—this fall is the dead's grave (that the French *tombe* means *grave* but is also the indicative present tense of the verb *tomber*, to fall, implies that what is buried in the grave is a cadaver rather than a corpse). It was then that she wondered whether she was dreaming the whole episode, since she was feeling the same kind of indefinite bodiless fall one experiences in certain nightmares. In these dreams, and in the last moments before the dead detaches from the cadaver, or in the first moments when, resurrected, he or she is back in the dead body as a cadaver, one experiences what Adam must have felt on eating from the mortality-generating fruit. Adam's fall resides as much in the change of his body into a potential cadaver as in some degradation across ontological and spiritual realms and levels. The change was so stark that Adam, for a weighty moment, must have already intimated the fall in the cadaver that he was already virtually. By eating of the mortality-generating fruit, Adam and Eve experienced *the unbearable lightness of being*, both because that act was the first they did not fully will, i.e., will to return eternally, and because they became virtually cadaverous, experiencing the weightlessness of an endless fall. This change into a virtual cadaver is what has to be portrayed in paintings of the Fall. The most salutary experience of the resurrection was that of being called again; the most dreadful was momentarily experiencing the cadaver as an endless fall on being recalled to the physical body, and the apprehension of being unable to raise the eyelids and thus of being buried alive—in the corpse. Suddenly, the fall stopped: the cadaver was now again a living body. It was then that she was indeed "*raised* from the dead." (The organic dying of a [resurrectable] human is as nothing compared to that of an animal, exemplarily of a bull in a *corrida*; the only phenomenon that equals in intensity a bull's death in a *corrida* is the resurrection of a human, Lazarus coming out from the grave.) Her eyelids "opened to reveal something terrible which I will not talk about, the most terrible look which a living being can receive, and I think that if I had shuddered at that instant, and if I had been afraid, everything would have been lost, but my tenderness was so great that I didn't even think about the strangeness of what was happening, which certainly seemed to me altogether natural because of that infinite movement which drew me towards her."[365] The far more frequent and regrettable phenomenon in these resurrections is that, just as the eyes of the resurrector and those of the resurrected come into contact and the resurrector apprehends in the latter a reflection of the dreadful realm where the resurrected was, he or she in horror instinctively closes the resurrected human's eyes. This, rather than shutting the eyes of the corpse, is the paradigmatic gesture of closing the the eyes of the human who died. Indeed, the gesture of closing the eyes of the corpse probably originated, at least in the Christian era, in witnessing someone hurriedly shutting the eyes of a dead person whom he had resurrected. Were humans one day to no longer believe in resurrection and to have forgotten it as a consequence of the expiration of the epoch when some people were resurrected, it is likely that they will no longer close the eyes of the corpse. (I find it disappointing that none of the vampire films I have seen, and I presume no vampire film at all, shows what is likely to take place during the initial encounter of the vampire with his living guest: what the guest apprehends in the undead's eyes is so horrifying he instinctively raises his hand toward the vampire's eyes to close them, only to hear the vampire, who had already had to tackle this reaction numerous times, say: "Your arms feel very tired. You long to rest them against your hips." Hypnotized, the guest let his now very heavy arms fall. When he later saw the vampire in the coffin, he did not think of closing the *frozen* undead's open eyes. On first meeting his new living guest, the vampire already knew that he was in the presence of someone with infinite tact, for this guest did not try to close his eyes.) She blinked several times. He asked her whether the light in the room was bothering her, whether it was too bright. "No. I was enjoying the regained lightness of my eyelids. I believe that Lazarus had to exert more effort to raise his eyelids than those who removed the stone laid across the entrance to the tomb where he was buried." Now that she was alive again, she was elated when others called her. She faced away from the door, hoping that those who entered would call her name. Unfortunately, some misunderstood her gesture, thought that she was shunning them. Others, out of consideration for her frail condition, walked to the other side, faced her, and only then spoke to her. Only, once, a child explicitly called her name: "J— —." She joyfully turned with some difficulty toward him. She did not close her eyes again until sleep overcame her, for she was still worried that she would not be able to open them, that the eyelids would revert to being a dead weight. She soon had troubled dreams, seeing "what she called 'a perfect rose' move in the room," and shortly suddenly said "with great anguish: 'Quick, a perfect rose,' all the while continuing to sleep but now with a slight rattle."[366] Then, she experienced an indefinite fall, woke up screaming, and asked: "Was I dead?" Her tactful lover hugged her warmly, answered, "You were dreaming. You are alive," and offered her the most appropriate flower: a resurrected one à la that in Cocteau's *The Testament of Orpheus* or Godard's *King Lear*. What presents a mortal danger to the resurrected person is not so much to know that she has been brought back to life: if she did not believe in resurrection, it would not have happened. It is rather that they be reminded that they were in the labyrinthine realm of death: since they were not introduced into that realm, having missed its "entrance" in the trance that seizes one there, and thus cannot recall any experience of reaching it from life, they would feel certain that they have always been, and consequently always will be, in it. It is this certitude that the resurrected person must not be reminded of, and that the resurrector must not fathom or must have the infinite tact of overlooking, for it undermines the resurrection. While every mortal is already dead even as he or she lives and thus should be able to resurrect another mortal, only some of those who were resurrected or died before dying end up resurrecting someone else: In Dreyer's *Ordet*, Johannes, the mad for a time, the one who *died before he died*, can resurrect the dead Inger, and resurrected Inger can resurrect her husband into faith in Him who is "the resurrection and the life" (John 11:25). In Blanchot's *Death Sentence*, the narrator can resurrect J— — because he himself is already dead before dying, since the doctor had, seven years earlier, given him only six months to live.[367] Although he otherwise belittles the doctor, he writes: "One last [but not least] thing about this doctor ... he was, it seems to me, a great deal more reliable in his diagnosis than most."[368] The moribund J— — does not include him in her will,[369] not because she is angry at him for advising her to commit suicide but because he is already dead, and only the living can be included in and carry out a will. This clarifies why, despite both the tact he shows at every stage of her ordeal of dying and resurrection and her trust in and gratitude for that tact, she nonetheless did not, following her resurrection, revise her will so that he would be included in it or become its executor. Doctors are associated with vampires and the undead in many books and films on the undead. This should not be as in *Vampyr*, where the doctor is merely one of the vampire's aides, but as in *Death Sentence*, where the doctor's prognosis establishes a time limit on how long a person is to live, so that by surviving the *deadline* the latter becomes either someone who died before dying, as in Blanchot's novel, or the double of who he was, as in Patricia Highsmith's *Ripley's Game*, a novel in which the doctor prognosticates that Jonathan will die from his myeloid leukemia after six to twelve years—Jonathan was entering his sixth year at the beginning of the novel. In such cases, the doctor's prognosis becomes a performative. Only the resurrected human or the one who died before dying, or a living person who forms a pair with them, can kill the undead: in *Vampyr*, were it not for Gray's dying before dying, the manservant would not have been able to kill the vampire. If the resurrection of the one who was alone in the labyrinthine, unworldly realm of death is to be effected neither by a resurrected person nor by one who died before dying but by his or her living accomplice, it has to occur in front of many, otherwise the living human who resurrects another or witnesses such a resurrection risks madness.[370]

We (almost) always resurrect another than the one who died. Is this why the second part of *Death Sentence*, which starts with "I will go on with this story," addresses the narrator's relationships with women other than resurrected J— — ? Many messianic figures are supposed to be defeated and killed and then to come back and enjoy a final victory. Unless the one who died is, like Jesus Christ, the Resurrection and the Life, "he" will come back not exactly the same but another. One would consequently expect that while he lived he would be unsure that he is *the one*. In *The Matrix*, having asked the protagonist if he believes he is the awaited one, and having heard him confess his uncertainty, the oracle tells him he is not ready: "Maybe in another life." He misunderstands that to mean that he is not The One. Soon after, it seems inevitable that he is going to be killed, but in a miraculous happening, he is spared death. This confirms for others that he is *the one*. To their surprise and mystification, he persists in being unsure. Later, he is mortally shot. When he saw the gun aimed at him, he felt a thrill, that of awaiting himself—across death, for it is across death, "in another life," that he will become the Messiah, since it is across death that I is another ("*Je est un autre*," Rimbaud).

"Jesus loved Martha and her sister and Lazarus. So when he heard that Lazarus was sick, he stayed where he was two more days" (John 11:5-6). The narrator of *Death Sentence* writes: "I think in saying that, she was announcing that she was going to die. This time I decided to return to Paris. But I gave myself two more days."[371] By the time both arrive, the moribund beloved is already dead. The moribund Lazarus and J— — must have felt consternation that the ones who were always there for them have now, at the hour of greatest need, uncharacteristically deserted them. *Death Sentence*'s narrator must have intuited that he can do nothing to save the dying person, and that he may not recover from his complete helplessness to prevent her death. He arrives only once the doctor, who once informed tries to reach the patient as soon as possible and who has center stage as long as the patient is still struggling to maintain her life, now that she was dead, has withdrawn. Jesus Christ and *Death Sentence*'s narrator arrive just in time for the resurrection. Jesus Christ would have been uncaring about the gravely sick Lazarus and the narrator of *Death Sentence* about the dying J— — only if, having arrived too late, they did not go on to resurrect them. But there are fights for life which, with their infinite desperation and finality, preclude any resurrection (notwithstanding that the fierce fight by the J— — of *Death Sentence* against her grave sickness appears to allow her to outlive her reliable doctor's prognosis, it is not one that precludes resurrection). With the ostensible possible exception of Jesus Christ, nobody can come too late to resurrect Chamberlain Christoph Detlev Brigge of Rilke's *The Notebooks of Malte Laurids Brigge*—however long *Death Sentence*'s narrator could have tarried, he still would have arrived while Chamberlain Christoph Detlev Brigge was still alive, within the ten weeks his dying demanded and had. The chamberlain's fight against death goes on for too long, less in terms of the average span it takes others to adopt the sickness and the diagnosis, yield to the prognosis and be resigned to death than for anyone to show up too late in order to resurrect him. In terms of clock time, J— — survived longer than Chamberlain Christoph Detlev Brigge: judging from the doctor's early prognosis, at least two years, and from his final prognosis, two extra weeks. But unlike him, not too long for someone to arrive too late to resurrect her: for example, she did not manage to stay alive till the morning, when she was supposed to meet the narrator. Although it is not explicitly mentioned by the narrator, I presume that those present there must have greeted him with reproachful looks for arriving after J— — had already died. But if they really believed it was too late, the resurrection could not have happened. When one arrives posthumously and those there confront one with "it is too late" and one acquiesces, one detects a very subtle disappointment on their part. Could a resurrection have happened in the presence of the Chamberlain Brigge in the apartment of J— — ? No. "By their fruit you will recognize them" (Matthew 7:16); and by their manner of dying, you will know whether they believe in resurrection or not. Already at the turn of the twentieth century, Chamberlain Christoph Detlev Brigge no longer belongs to the era of Jesus Christ. The neighboring villagers and the minister, who were immensely disturbed by his dying, must have intuited this. "They prayed that there might no longer be a master at Ulsgaard.... And what they were all thinking and praying, the minister said out loud up in the pulpit, for he too had no nights anymore and could no longer understand God"[372]—that is, the God of resurrection. People began to die differently when the one who is the resurrection and the life showed up on earth. This would have been or must have been one of the signs that clued in contemporaries that an epochal change had happened. How much weaker was Lazarus's dying struggle when compared to the struggle of dying people only a generation before, for, like his sister Mary, he already believed in resurrection.[373] The resurrected brother of Mary and Martha must have subsequently died "peacefully," in his dreamless sleep, with no struggle. In our light manner of dying, we still believe in resurrection—if it is no longer the Christian one through the one who is the resurrection and the life, then it is the scientific and technological one through computer simulation. Frank Tipler would have found it far more difficult to envision universal resurrection at the Omega point in his *The Physics of Immortality* if he had encountered a dying à la that of Chamberlain Christoph Detlev Brigge. The more computer simulation is perfected, the more our death will become lighter, less substantial. The coming resurrection of Jesus Christ was already foreshadowed by the lightness of his death. It was precisely the death of someone who did not believe in his own death, who is the resurrection and the life, and it set an example for others by its lightness. How now, Jesus Christ's death was a light one?! Isn't it the case, according to the New Testament, that while he was crucified but still alive, "from noon until three in the afternoon darkness came over all the land" (Matthew 27:45), and that when "he gave up his spirit ... the curtain of the temple was torn in two from top to bottom. The earth shook, the rocks split" (Matthew 27:50-51)? Notwithstanding these upheavals, one would expect much more from the death of God. For a divine equivalent of the struggle that the dying human chamberlain Christoph Detlev Brigge waged, one would have to look for the dying of a god who not only is not a divinity of resurrection but also one not within a single epoch, but at the cusp between two, the one in which he was believed to be a god and one in which this belief had vanished, so that his or her death would be apprehended as doubly final by him or her.

Guilt is part of the work of mourning. If someone dies in a manner that does not preclude resurrection, we feel guilty for not resurrecting him or her, since we register obscurely that even though, unlike mystics and schizophrenics, we have not explicitly undergone death before dying, we nonetheless should be able to resurrect him or her since, as mortals, we are already dead even while we live. If he or she dies in a manner that precludes resurrection, his awesome protracted dying will sooner or later induce those nearby to wish or even pray that he would die as speedily as possible. I presume that like his neighbors and the minister, I, too, and, for that matter, Rilke, too, would have ended up praying for Chamberlain Brigge to die. The difference between people is not that only some end up wishing for such protracted awesome dying to come to an end speedily: they all do; but in how long they forbear doing so. The work of mourning would be shorter and far less intense with regard to someone like Chamberlain Christoph Detlev Brigge, since part of the work of mourning is to believe in the finality of the death of the other. The chamberlain's awesome dying is historically timely as it happens between the spreading loss of faith in resurrection through Jesus Christ and the time when "you die the death that belongs to the sickness you have (for since all sicknesses are well known, it is also known that the various fatal endings belong to the sicknesses and not to the people; and the sick person has, so to speak, nothing more to do)."[374] *Death Sentence*'s doctor is "a great deal more reliable ... than most" because his diagnosis of the sickness is medically accurate, while his prognosis is a performative that turns the person who ostensibly survives the deadline he provided into a dead person.[375] In our age, only those who died before dying physically, whether through ostensibly outliving the performative prognosis of a reliable doctor, for example, *Death Sentence*'s narrator and J— —, or through finding themselves in incredible conditions in which they wondered, "Am I dead?" or came to the conclusion, "I must be dead," for example, Nietzsche, Artaud, and myself, were able not to die necessarily of their sickness or age-related physiological decline.

His mortally wounded beloved began to totter. He rushed toward her and held her in his arms. Unfortunately, moments later she expired. He deposited her gently on the bed but did not try to resurrect her. His friend told him: "As a cadaver, the recently dead human is falling, goes on falling." "I don't understand what you mean." "This implies that you have never tried to resurrect a mortal. *The Unbearable Lightness of Being* could only have been written by someone who has never tried to resurrect, and about characters who also have never tried to resurrect. It would have been preferable to your presently dead beloved had you let her body fall abruptly to the ground when she expired but then tried to resurrect her, that is, tried to stop her endless fall in the cadaver. You would then have experienced, by trying to counter this fall, the unbearable heaviness of being."

Dreamless

When he was sleeping and God molded woman out of his limb, the man ('ādām) did not dream. It is on the night of eating of the mortality-inducing tree that Adam and Eve first dreamt. While he slept in the boat that was transporting him with his disciples to the other shore (Matthew 8:23-24), was Jesus Christ dreaming? No. One of his exoteric disciples asked him later: "What have you dreamt?" He did not understand what that meant. Henceforth, when he recounted, during a dinner, to his ostensible disciples his dreams, the resurrected brother of Mary and Martha listened without volunteering any comment, as these were visionary dreams, ones related to 'ālam al-khayāl, the imaginal world. One day, he said to Mary: "What have I to do with you? I don't even dream." Another day he encountered someone who had dreamt the previous night and "cured" him. Lazarus had recurrent nightmares while he was very sick. He would wake up screaming. When asked what he was dreaming, he answered each time: "I kept falling, indefinitely." Now that Jesus Christ, who had shortly before resurrected him, and the other guests had left, Lazarus's two sisters were scared of spending the night with a person who hours earlier was rotting in a grave. As he headed to his bedroom, they wished him pleasant dreams. He seemed puzzled, did not grasp what they were saying. Later in the night, he woke up. One of his sisters, still awake, asked him: "You seemed to have had an anguished sleep, tossing and turning all night. Were you having nightmares?" He looked at her uncomprehendingly. What did she mean by *nightmare*? The resurrected brother of Mary and Martha no longer dreamt. When Jesus said to his twelve ostensible disciples, "We are going up to Jerusalem, and the Son of Man will be betrayed to the chief priests and the teachers of the law. They will condemn him to death and will turn him over to the Gentiles to be mocked and flogged and crucified. On the third day he will be raised to life!" (Matthew 20:17-19), the response of one of them was "When did you, the Son of God, know that you will die?" "The night I first dreamt, in other words, the night I first had during my sleep not a vision but a dream, in other words yet, the night I first had a non-visionary 'dream.'" "What was it in the dream that indicated this to you?" "It was nothing in the dream content; the mere fact that I dreamt implied my death." While on the cross, Jesus closed his eyes. Someone in the crowd of onlookers yelled: "He is dead." Actually, there, suspended on the cross, he was dreaming. Soon, one of the two criminals crucified at his side asked him: "What did you dream?" "I do not recall much. For a long time, I was falling. In one scene, I was John the Baptist; in another, Elijah; in a third, Jeremiah or one of the prophets.[376]" His interlocutor interpreted the dream for him.

In Your Dreams

In *Twelve Monkeys*, Terry Gilliam's remake of Chris Marker's *La Jetée*, one of the survivors of a viral pandemic that killed five billion people and devastated much of the earth's biosphere dreams a nightmare in which a woman, at what seems to be an airport gate, unsuccessfully tries to dissuade someone from shooting him. He is present in that scene also as a child witness. He is jolted out of the dream not by anxiety, but by the voice of a guard informing him that he has been chosen for a mission. Soon after, scientists conducting experiments in time travel send him to the past with the goal of tracing the source of the epidemic and, if possible, suppressing it at its inception. Appearing in the past, he quickly encounters the woman of the dream. His recurrent recalls to the future to report to the scientists and the mental stress of experiencing the temporal vertigo of time travel soon make him wonder whether he is dreaming his sojourns in the past. Back in the pre-disaster period, and having to escape the police on his trail, both he and that woman, now wanted by the police as his accessory, seek refuge in a cinema theater. She suggests that they take their minds off the devitalizing impending end of the world by flying away to some island on a vacation. He consents, possibly having reasoned that the events of the scene at the airport could not have transpired in the manner he sees them in his dream but must have been subjected to the dream-work mechanisms of condensation, displacement, secondary revision, etc. But if the events did not take place as in the dream, how did they actually happen? Unfortunately, he can access that catastrophic period only in the distorted reflection of the dream. She briefly goes away, then returns with some articles for a masquerade. She disguises him with a wig and a mustache. He is moved by her concern about the possibility of his apprehension by the police but also disconcerted that she is dressing him in his death costume, the one in which in the dream, and according to the dream, he is killed. She then places a blond wig on her head: the same one in which she appears in the dream! It is then, through the coincidence between the changes suggested or imposed by the vicissitudes of the world, namely, evading detection by the police, and those attributable to the dreamwork, that she really becomes a dream woman to him. Now he felt that the dream may become actualized. Nonetheless, he did not retract his consent to head to the airport: part of him wanted the past to recur so that he would know what had happened. On their way to the airport, he came across additional dreamlike elements: he saw giraffes, gorillas, and a lion moving amidst the cars on the highway (he was shortly to learn that they had been released from the zoo by a gang called Twelve Monkeys). At the airport, his companion discovers the scientist who is transporting vials of highly dangerous bacteria to disperse at the different destinations of his scheduled flight around the world. She quickly conveys this information to him. Again the blonde woman yells to the police not to shoot him as he runs past the security gate in pursuit of the scientist heading to the plane. Again he is shot, and his murder is witnessed by himself as a child. The simultaneous presence in the same scene of oneself at different ages is possible through time travel, but also in dreams. While he had, all along his time travels, wondered whether he was dreaming, now that he was actually doing so, he, no lucid dreamer, felt certain that he was awake! Some propose that were we able to travel back to the past, we would not be able to alter the block universe of spacetime. *Twelve Monkeys* provides one manner in which this may happen: at every critical moment one is overcome by a hypnoid state and dreams. He thus missed both the chance of altering the past and of seeing how the events had transpired at that decisive moment in the past. Both *La Jetée* and *Twelve Monkeys*, which revolve around a trauma, are circular, but in different ways: the former starts with reality and ends with the same reality through time travel; the latter starts with a dream and ends with the same dream. *Twelve Monkeys* is a strange circular time-travel film where what happens at the decisive moment in the past, rather than being shown twice, from the two perspectives of the protagonist as a child and as an adult, as in *La Jetée*, is elided. If the dream can show his murder, it is that he was not murdered and that such a false murder obfuscates the real, repressed trauma, namely, that he was sleeping and dreaming at that critical moment when he had a chance, however slim, of saving the world.

The first time he heard a young woman in her early twenties tell him she would very much like to be his friend and go on to affirm that most women would dream of a man like him for a lover, he responded: "It won't work between us in terms of friendship, for you're too young: the only relationship we can possibly have is love, since in love, as Lacan put it, a woman gives 'what she does not have.'"[377] Like most people, she was too thrifty to give even what she did not have. In the subsequent weeks and months, he heard other young women tell him how most women would dream of a man like him for a lover. How did he come to suspect that he had become a vampire? The first inkling he had that something eerie was beginning to happen to him was that more and more women, *mostly strangers*, were telling him that they had dreamt of him; he soon deduced that he was becoming a dream creature. When he met another vampire, the latter told him that he'd first deduced the "presence" of a second vampire in the city not so much from the periodic news items about men and women and children found mortally drained of blood, but from the similarity of the descriptions by some of his victims of the man who used to attack them in nightmares.

On the Failure of Memorable Dream Books

Jalal Toufic, 7/9/1997
Richard Foreman, New York:
The Overlook Press sent me a copy of your first novel (in parts): *No-Body*. I've just begun reading it. And I've just begun being unable to remember what I read.

There is a strong connection of your book to the unconscious. I see it in some of the images; in the free association with which many of the links are made; but mainly in the tendency of the images, events, and lines to soon disappear from memory, as one's dreams are forgotten upon waking. One would have to exert the same sort of effort to remember your writing in *No-Body* as one would to recall a dream. Most dream books fail to induce in the reader the sensation that he or she is unable to remember them. I remember Kathy Acker's *My Mother: Demonology*, with its many dream sequences, and William Burroughs's *My Education: A Book of Dreams*. Unlike the inability of the dreamer to recall the dream upon waking, the failure to remember experienced in relation to your book, which affects not the writer or the dreamer but the reader, is not mainly linked to a repression concerning the (Freudian) unconscious. To what, then, is it linked?

Am I Dreaming?

The vampire said to his guest as he was sucking his blood: "While I don't dream, since I am frozen in the coffin during daylight, you not only dream when asleep but, since you've 'met' me, additionally encounter dreamlike events even when ostensibly awake—after all, is it me who metamorphoses into mist or a pack of wolves or rats, or is it you who are dreaming even while ostensibly awake, thus subjecting my image to the dreamwork mechanisms of condensation, displacement, etc. (you should not take your dreams at face value but interpret them)? I am presently going to suck your blood, so that for one part of the day you will be wide-eyed as you repeatedly encounter dream-like events, and for the other part you will lie supine in a coffin with eyes closed but not sleep and therefore not dream, since you would be frozen then."[378] Indeed, past his encounter with the vampire, who does not dream in his coffin but lies frozen there, his victim frequently wondered: *Am I dreaming?* It suddenly struck him that the Freudian way of interpreting a dream—"Whenever my own ego does not appear in the content of the dream, but only some extraneous person, I may safely assume that my own ego lies concealed, by identification, behind this other person"[379]—could apply to his present case: it could well be that he himself was just the substitute by identification (through a common element) of the dreamer, in order to evade the censorship of an agency of the latter's psychic apparatus. In which case, it is that other who would wake up.

Am I in a Film?

Serge Daney: "Nothing happens any longer to humans; it is to the image that everything happens."[380] This proposition has to be qualified: things still happen to humans in some states of altered consciousness, since in these states the world itself functions in a filmic manner:

— The lapses of consciousness in epilepsy, more particularly, absence seizures (a.k.a. petit mal seizures);[381] hypnosis; schizophrenia; LSD trips; and death produce edits in reality/unreality. As a demonstration, a hypnotist entranced a subject shortly before sunset, conducted him to a different location, and there snapped him out of his trance an hour or so later when it was already night, the subject experiencing a jump cut between the two locations-times. While in many a Morrissey-Warhol film, the flash frames at the end of the shot were left in the film, in Herzog's *Heart of Glass* it is the frequent closing of the eyes of the entranced after they say their lines that is included in the film.

— The immobilizations in death and dance are the diegetic equivalent of cinema's non-diegetic freeze frames, allowing all sorts of temporal special effects. Death and dance complement the kind of motion essential to cinema at the level of the apparatus (Deleuze: "cinema is the system which reproduces movement as a function of any-instant-whatever, that is, as a function of equidistant instants, selected so as to create an impression of continuity"[382]) with diegetic immobilization, which affects diegetic time directly, making possible temporal irregularities (slow motion, etc.) that pertain not only to the time and speed of narrative but also to the time and speed of story.

— Perceiving (in) stills occasionally occurs in death, acute psychoses, in some cases of migraine auras and epileptic seizures, and in *encephalitis lethargica*. Regarding the latter, one of Oliver Sacks's patients told him: "Sometimes these stills form a flickering vision, like a movie-film which is running too slow."[383] Moreover, Hester Y. and other patients discussed in Sacks's *Awakenings* told him that sometimes they experienced "the displacement of a 'still' either backwards or forwards, so that a given 'moment' may occur too soon or too late."[384]

— The positive and negative hallucinations in hypnosis and the posthypnotic sequelae are a form of matting ("Positive hallucination: a false perceptual experience characterized by perception of something that is not there.... Although they are a hallmark of psychotic disturbances, such as schizophrenia, these perceptual experiences can also be generated by hypnosis"[385] [*APA Dictionary of Psychology*]; "negative hallucination: a false perceptual experience characterized by failure to see something while looking directly at it, as in failing to perceive a certain person in a group in response to hypnotic suggestion"[386] [Ibid.]).

— Schizophrenics and those undergoing a bad LSD trip, who are suffering from a decathexis from the world, occasionally have the impression that the people around them are mere extras ("An extra is ... a person in a movie who does not have a speaking part and is usually in the background or in a crowd" [*Cambridge Academic Content Dictionary*]).

While watching *Persona*, I had the impression that the cracking of the on-screen image in the middle and its burning, and the backward sound (as occasionally happens during film editing), and the repetition in the scene in which Alma's removal of a snapshot of Elisabet's son from under his mother's hand and her speech to the latter about her relation to her son is shown twice, once with the camera on Elisabet, a second time with the camera on Alma (while it is standard procedure when filming angle/reverse-angle scenes to shoot with the camera first on one actor, then on the other, then to intercut the two setups, here the two takes, from opposite angles, are not intercut but added), were all diegetic. One way for these to be diegetic is for Alma to be dead, since in the death realm (un)reality is sometimes cinematic, the dead person asking himself or herself: "Am I in a movie?" Therefore, I formulated the hypothesis that Alma is dead and looked for confirmation. Near the beginning of *Persona*, a corpse's closed eyes are suddenly, in a jump cut, open. Later in the film, supine Alma's closed eyes are, also in a jump cut, abruptly open. These shots of the corpse and of Alma are taken from an identical position and angle of view. A correspondence is thus established between the two woman: Alma is dead.

Bazin: "The guiding myth, then, inspiring the invention of cinema, is the accomplishment of that which dominated in a more or less vague fashion all the techniques of the mechanical reproduction of reality in the nineteenth century, from photography to the phonograph, namely an integral realism, a recreation of the world in its own image.... The cinema was born ... out of a myth, the myth of total cinema."[387] It is because in death and some states of altered consciousness (un)reality is filmic[388] that film can move toward total cinema only asymptotically, for otherwise it would become reality's double, precipitating reality's demise.

Bazin asserts that "there are no wings to the screen. There could not be without destroying its specific illusion, which is to make of a revolver or of a face the very center of the universe."[389] Where is one during an out-of-body experience? One is then in the "wings," ones that paradoxically function at times in a cinematic manner.

Photographic Memory

He, who felt a strong affinity and attraction to certain kinds of tall-ness, for example, that of the village women of al-Qaryatayn in Syria as they stand with their earthenware jars on their heads, and that of ancient Egyptian statues, whose gazes overlook the one facing them level with their eyes, was now thrilled by the length of the shadow of the host. When one of two conversing people inadvertently stepped over that shadow, an unsettling thing happened: as if pinched, the host abruptly jumped to the side. The person who had stepped over the shadow instinctively drew back apologetically. After the other guests had left, the host sucked his blood. The following morning, he was unsure whether he had dreamt the anomalous events of the previous night. But a few days later he got a confirmation that he had been attacked by a vampire: he was turning into one. At the insistence of the host, he set the camera on automatic and rushed to stand next to other guests. When he perused the developed photograph, he was amazed not to witness himself with the others. Instead, his shadow was on the floor at the edge of the bottom frame, as if he were still standing behind the camera.

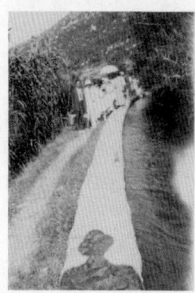

page 576

Some days later, he was invited along with other, new guests to a masquerade in some mansion in a faraway village. The host suggested they fly to the nearest city in his private jet. While in the air, he was intermittently struck by how flimsy the jet seemed. He had

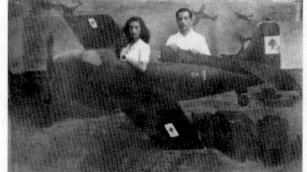

page 579

to constantly look from the window at the wings with their engines and the mountain ranges far below to regain the feeling that he was sitting in a powerful machine. He felt great relief when the plane landed. But as he was walking toward the airport exit, he glimpsed briefly another plane at the point of taking off: again, it seemed

page 578

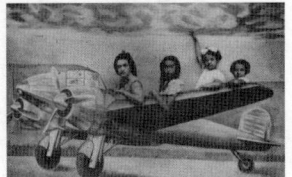

unreal, a painted setup! They reached the village around noon. They headed to the nearby lake to rest and enjoy the afternoon. For an hour, the setting was idyllically relaxing. But then things went wrong. Three persons were sitting in a boat: one was smiling, another was holding an oar. While the two boats behind theirs were small, they did not appear so due to perspectival foreshortening, so that the diminution in size seemed unconvincing, artificial. Moreover, the boat was two-dimensional, and, in the landscape around the lake, "the trees and hedges were of cardboard, placed here and there, like

page 584

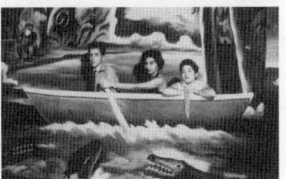

stage accessories."[390] The waves, frozen, gave him the impression that he was looking at the end of the universe, the event horizon of a black hole. This impression was confirmed when, shortly after, he witnessed what appeared to be a flattening of people and objects, another phenomenon associated with the event horizon of a black hole: when he came across a father and his son standing together, the father appeared to be flat, as if a photograph (the same phenomenon was repeated a few days later, now with a woman and her child; this time it was the child who appeared flat).

pages 589, 588

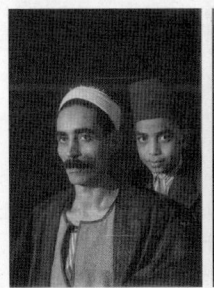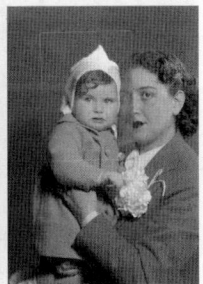

He now felt that the one who was smiling in the boat was actually laughing at him. Panicked, he walked away hurriedly. Soon, he came across some children. He grew fearful as most of them appeared masked.

215

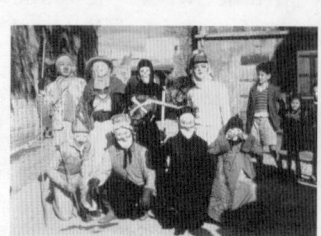
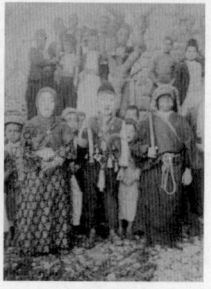

pages 570, 571

He rushed back toward his companions on the lake's shore. Again, he saw the anomalous boat. It was now at a different spot on the lake! How had it reached this other spot when the waves were frozen through what he assumed to be time dilation?

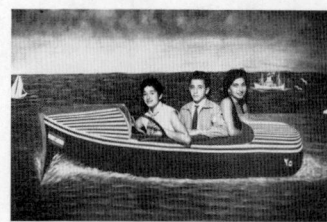

page 584

He implored his companions to leave the lake's shore and head to the host's house. There, he felt relieved to see people who were not masked but merely physically costumed for a bal masqué. He quickly became bored by the hackneyed impersonations, for example, that of a vampire by two women who were dressed in black cloaks, one of whom had applied her makeup to create an illusion of bloodlessness, her cheeks appearing eerily pale.

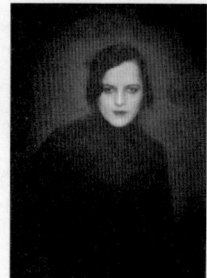
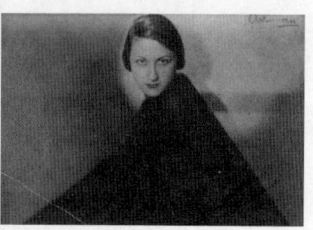

pages 586, 587

He moved to another room. On the shelf were the many volumes of *Encyclopaedia Britannica*. He opened one of them to take his mind off the strange happenings. The entry before him was on senescence! "In semelparous forms, reproduction takes place near the end of the life span, after which there ensues a rapid senescence that quickly leads to the death of the organism. In plants the senescent phase is usually an integral part of the reproductive process and essential for its completion. The dispersal of seeds, for example, is accomplished by processes—including ripening and falling (abscission) of fruits and drying of seed pods—that are inseparable from the overall senescence process."[391] His reading was interrupted by the entrance of two men. The older of the two introduced to him the other as possessing a photographic memory. "You mean something along the lines of what A. R. Luria describes in *The Mind of a Mnemonist: A Little Book about a Vast Memory*?" "Yes." "I, too, have a photographic memory." "Prove it. Repeat to me what you have just read." "You misunderstood me." He had a photographic memory neither because he could later reproduce verbatim or describe fully whatever he saw nor because he had formed his memory of certain countries, topics, etc., through perusing photographs of them; but because, panicked, he could have only glimpses of phenomena, quasi-snapshots, before averting his anxious look. Suddenly but naturally the light changed in the variable weather of February. A pattern of vertical squares appeared on the

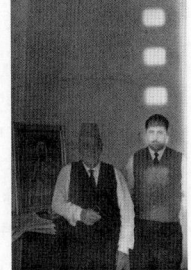

page 590

wall, one of them illuminating the face of the younger of the two men. Why did that man not seem at all bothered by the brightness and blink? Had the light not really changed? Was he, the observer, suddenly apprehending the sprocket holes in reality, reality as filmic? He swish-panned his look. What intensified his fear was that as he did so he heard the characteristic sound of the click of a camera. Was there someone around taking photographs? He was too apprehensive to ascertain whether it was the case. Later he felt angry with himself for fleeing the room instead of staying to check if there were certain square openings in the opposite wall through which the light pattern could have been produced. When he reconsidered the matter, he was amazed that he had not tried to go back to that room.

Through the protracted mental suffering caused by these hallucinations, as well as by the voices, paranoid ideas of reference, and thought broadcasting, this vegetarian who had responded one day to his mother's insistent pleas that he resume eating meat with, "For me to eat meat, I would have to become brainless. I would consider ending my vegetarian eating habits only were you to present to me my brain, cooked, on a platter," developed the urge to eat the organ generally considered the locus of these anomalous mental processes: a brain, ideally his own. That same night, after sucking his blood, the vampire told him: "Tomorrow I will take you along on a hunting trip: to initiate you into feeding on blood. But as an introduction to that, today I will treat you to your last dish of meat. I am a fabulous cook." As the vampire headed toward the kitchen, he moved back to his bedroom. The

217

door opened before him on its own. This self-motion of objects, which is encountered in hypnosis (for example, arm levitation), implied that he was becoming entranced.[392] He locked the door. Shortly, he saw the vampire standing beside him. How did the latter manage to be in the room without entering through the locked door? The vampire now extracted his brain from his skull and returned with it to the kitchen. While the vampire could not be constrained in any space since he could tunnel through walls, even in open space he was constrained width-wise by the virtual edges of the coffin, walking with his hands laid tightly against his body (Murnau's Nosferatu). Half an hour later, the vampire came to lead him to the dining room. He followed him, who was trailed by the very long tail of his robe. As the vampire failed to be reflected in the mirror he had hung in his room, appearing to be immaterial or to have lost his materiality, he realized why the long tail of his host's flowing crimson robe that trailed behind him had struck him: it functioned as his shadow, one that had become material by a transference of part of the body's materiality to it. They "sat" on dinner chairs whose backs were the height of an average standing human adult, so that even while sitting the vampire gave the impression of still standing. His host served him his brain cooked with a delicious sauce and surrounded by fresh vegetables. "I do not want you to be mindless like zombies but brainless like vampires. I want you to become that rarity in the (composited) midst of the mindless: a brainless person. So, eat your brain. Today you will be finished with this Bergsonian filter of the mind."

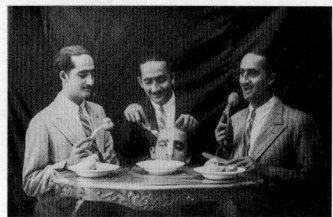

page 590

Now that he was turning into a vampire, he, who was known for the weakness of his sense of smell, smelled putrefaction in the presence not only of the aged but also of those in their twenties and thirties. He remembered a striking line in Cees Nooteboom's *The Following Story*: "If one is immortal oneself, the stench emanating from mortals must be intolerable." He did not smell such a stench with all mortals, for instance, not with prepubescent girls.[393] Wasn't biological death introduced with sexual reproduction? Wouldn't senescence therefore begin with puberty? "In the field of ageing research, there are different opinions about the onset of the ageing process. Some researchers suggest that ageing begins before birth, as cellular damage can accumulate in parental germ cells or during conception. On the other hand, others argue that ageing begins at sexual maturity, as the body is no longer under evolutionary pressure to constantly regenerate, and mechanisms that are beneficial early in life may become detrimental later."[394] Since, with rare exceptions, present-day culture in general was oblivious of initiation, he could still stand and respect only those who were not yet of an age to undergo it: prepubescents. His desperate attempt to flee putridity started him on a perverse process. He developed a fetish for sailor suits worn by Japanese schoolgirls. At another masquerade party, the host asked him: "When are you going to get married? How many children do you plan to have?" Before he could answer, a boy costumed as a sailor addressed his interlocutor as "mother." As he turned, he saw another boy also dressed in a sailor's suit, then a third. At this point, the mother said to him, "Would you mind taking a photograph of our sailors?" and handed him a camera. He framed the three boys. On the point of taking the photograph, he heard her say: "Please wait; there's another child." She then yelled: "Nadia!" A little girl appeared from the adjoining room. She, too, was dressed in a sailor's suit. He felt both paranoid: had they penetrated his fantasies and were hinting at his fetish?; and disappointed that such a suit be worn by a prepubescent girl without it inducing a fetishistic thrill. He found himself screaming at the little girl, to the dismay of her parents and the hostess, "Go get dressed." He quickly corrected himself: "Change your clothes!" A fortnight later, he married a dainty eleven-year-old girl. Given his adamant resolution not to bring a child into the world, others had no right to object: "But she is the age of your daughter!" He first sucked her blood on the second night of their marriage. A year later, a putrid smell began to emanate from her. He knew that his wife had reached puberty and so divorced her.

Death-Size Body

When he entered the room in which the dead body was laid, he was bewildered: while he could very well gauge the distance to it as a corpse: it was a little less than one meter, the same distance that would be separating him from that body were it still alive; as a cadaver, it seemed very far away. The impression of inordinate remoteness was immediately confirmed by the steep downward stares of the mourners around the bier: they seemed to be looking across the edges of the coffin into an abyss.

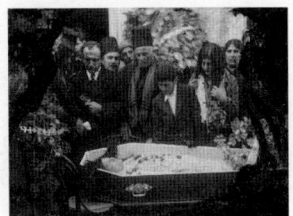

The dead human as cadaver is continuously falling, an abysmal entity (*"cadaver*: late Middle English: from Latin, from *cadere* 'to fall'" [*Oxford Dictionary of English*, 3rd ed.]).[395] The body of the dead human laid on the deathbed is both inert—but not frozen, as one can be in the death realm—covering only where it is, and a constant fall as cadaver. A detail struck him: one boy was resting his hands over

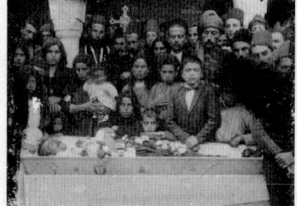

page 598–99

one of the sides of the coffin. There was something brutal about the boy's gesture. How is it that he did not feel vertigo? Brutality implies insensitivity to thresholds; contrariwise, subtlety is a heightened awareness of thresholds.

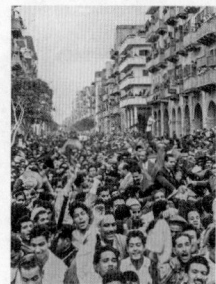

page 612

October 1, 1970. The corpse of Gamal Abdel Nasser, this body that used to be magnified by its charismatic voice often radioed all over the Arab World,[396] now speechless, lay small, even puny on the bier. Outside, tens of thousands and soon hundreds of thousands were assembling for the funeral procession. By the time the coffin was moved through the streets of Cairo, the crowd had swelled to over a million. They wanted to touch the coffin, partly out of an atavistic impulse, as if it could give them *barakāt* (blessings). Hysteria soon seized the crowd, making of it a compact, single body, so that one could truly say that the corpse was raised by everyone in the crowd. One of the pallbearers who had carried the coffin to the house where it temporarily lay the previous night felt an incredible fatigue on seeing the hysterical myriads who were trying to touch the moving bier and who were thus participating in its lifting and procession: how could he, with only a few others, have transported this corpse earlier? It was now as difficult, indeed more difficult, to carry the cadaver of Abdel Nasser than it would have been to carry the colossal statues of Rameses II that guard the entrance at Abu Simbel in Aswan.[397] Whether or not it would remain steady while being jolted by the myriad mourners trying to touch it along its procession, the dead body was already falling indefinitely as a cadaver. A moment may come during tremendous funerary processions when the huge number of people takes itself for an infinite one, wagers that it can counter the endless fall implicit in the cadaver. To the millions at his funerary procession, if Abdel Nasser was not definitely dead, it was not as someone who had, through his influential life and memorable funeral, been assured of lasting fame but because it seemed possible to counter the fall implicit in his cadaver and thus to resurrect him (little did they suspect that to resurrect someone one has to counter not only the endless fall implicit in the cadaver but also the 180-degree over-turn the dead undergoes in death's labyrinthine realm). "While he was alive, they felt larger than life through him. Now that he is dead, they are, through him, feeling themselves equal to death, to resurrection." "Regarding the first part of your statement, I would prefer to say, 'While he was alive, they felt equal to life through him,' for there is nothing larger than life: 'It is a mistake to suppose that birth turns into death. Birth is a phase that is an entire period of itself, with its own past and future ... Death is a phase that is an entire period of itself, with its own past and future. ... In birth there is nothing but birth and in death there is nothing but death' (Dōgen, 'Birth and Death' [Shōji])." These people, who had challenged with him the Western powers through his nationalization of the Suez Canal, were now undergoing an even bigger challenge with him: countering the infinite fall in the cadaver. Indeed, the cries "Nasser, you are alive!" and "Abu Khalid, you are alive!" could now be repeatedly heard. Twice did Abdel Nasser leave Egyptians in the lurch, and twice did Egyptians descend to the streets to make him return. In June 1967, as he decently declared on TV his resignation from all positions of authority following the speedy, crushing defeat of Egypt by Israel, hundreds of thousands of Egyptians descended to the streets in demonstrations of allegiance to him, persuading him to stay in power. On September 28, 1970, when he left them by dying, millions of Egyptians again descended to the streets with the vague idea of making him return ... to life, of resurrecting him. If there was something blasphemous about his funeral, it was less the idolization shown during it than the unconscious attempt at resurrection. If he did not come back the second time, this was probably because they did not manage to counter the over-turn and/or the infinite fall implicit in the cadaver—Jesus Christ's effective order to dead Lazarus to come forth demonstrates more might than that exerted by the millions at Abdel Nasser's funeral.

In some tremendous funerary processions, the body, which while alive was as large, or, more precisely, as small as other human bodies, assumes its *death-size*. It has then the magnitude of either the surface covered by the myriad of people who touched it then, or, in case the mourners hysterically became one, the surface covered by all those at the funeral—one feels then that not just the soul but also a large part of the dead body is invisible. I, who am neither a charismatic leader nor a celebrity, and thus cannot hope to have a tremendous funeral procession that would provide me with a death-size body, can ill afford not to have a demanding dying à la that of Rilke's Chamberlain Christoph Detlev Brigge. Rilke's moribund Chamberlain Christoph Detlev Brigge not only has a tremendous, singular dying but also, through it, achieves a death-size body: "The long, ancient man-or-house was too small for this death; it seemed as if new wings would have to be added on, for the Chamberlain's body grew larger and larger, and he kept wanting to be carried from one room to another, bursting into a terrible rage if, before the day had ended, there were no more rooms that he hadn't already been brought to."[398] A very large number of others are implicated in the death of each: in virtually all cases, death exposes one to the plural singularity of *every name in history is I* (having died before dying physically ["This autumn (of 1888) ... I twice attended my funeral, first as Count Robilant"[399]], Nietzsche wrote, "I am Prado, I am also Prado's father, I venture to say that I am also Lesseps.... I am also Chambige.... Every name in history is I"); moreover, in a few cases, during tremendous hysterical funerals, the dead body assumes its death size through the tens of thousands, hundreds of thousands, or even millions of participants contributing hysterically to carrying it.[400] During his tremendous funerary procession, Abdel Nasser's body, now death-size, became the equal of his erstwhile radioed voice.[401] He had wondered, as he was repeatedly jostled left and right, why he had come to Abdel Nasser's funerary procession, he who loathed the masses and their hysteria, which in other contexts could be unleashed so brutally on all sorts of sacrificial scapegoats; and who, notwithstanding his conflicted admiration for Abdel Nasser, had a number of compelling reservations about his regime. It now was clear to him that this was not necessarily or solely induced by Abdel Nasser's charisma but had to do with contributing to the appearance of that rarity, a death-size body. Achieving a death-size body may have been Abdel Nasser's and Umm Kulthum's most stupendous exploit, eclipsing all their other feats in their lives (can a death-size body be bought? I would hope not, but I cannot be sure. One day the manipulative power of TV or its subsequent avatars may be such that it succeeds in making millions descend to the streets and try hysterically to touch and participate in carrying the bier of some magnate or celebrity). Egypt, which has given us mummies in its ancient periods, was giving us in the funeral of Abdel Nasser and later in that of Umm Kulthum a death-size body.[402] If the outsized posters and photographs, spanning several stories, of the parliamentary candidates that could be seen all over Beirut in the month leading to the elections on August 27 and September 3, 2000, are kitschy irrespective of any aesthetic value judgment, this is because it is virtually certain that none of the candidates will assume a death-size body during his or her funeral but will remain life-size even then.[403]

pages 597, 596

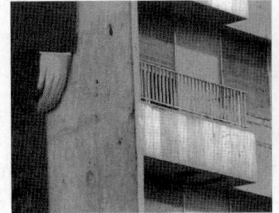 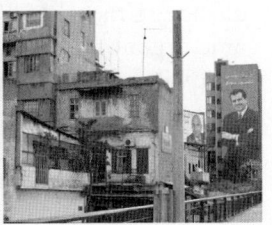

One Cannot Go Back to the Other Side of the Point of No Return, Even in Memory

The amnesiac's diary as his letters to himself.

Someone who has no mirror image has no memory—or else can remember also the past of others.

Were someone who had already seen Duras's film *India Song* to watch her film *Her Venetian Name in Deserted Calcutta*, which has the same soundtrack but a different image track and thus is a sort of double of the previous film, his or her resultant memory of *India Song* would be haunted by amnesia, rather than, as in *Hiroshima mon amour*, doomed to forgetfulness.

Amnesia produces a discontinuous forgetfulness. Amnesia is a lapse of both memory and forgetfulness.

There is an element, a presentiment, of amnesia whenever a surprise happens.

The following structure recurs in some of my unfinished videos: an episode is shown with no cuts, then the protagonist, either while remembering it or while narrating it to another person, refers to an event that was not shown. Fundamentally memorable events and people can exist only as a memory. Concerning them, inversely to having a feeling of déjà vu, where an event is experienced as having already happened in the past, one feels that one is remembering an event that never occurred. Do not misunderstand me when I write: *I will be remembered.*

Many Lebanese artists and writers decry the postwar amnesia. Should we view this as a reaction only to their compatriots' oblivion of the war years, or should we extend it to cover an apprehension that they are being forgotten by the ghosts since they are not being haunted? Is it the Lebanese who have forgotten their dead, or is it their dead who have forgotten them by not becoming revenants, ghosts? Is it both conjointly, a reciprocal forgetting? Where there is a definitive absence of an intensely loved person, a death, the affect can be melancholia; what is the affect when there is an absence of revenants?

223

In Tarkovsky's *Solaris*, one of the cosmonauts records his testimony on a videotape to inform the future viewer, specifically his friend and colleague Kris, whose imminent arrival is expected at the station, of some urgent matter. Let us imagine someone destroying the tape. What will happen then? Will the unfinished business be forgotten? Not necessarily: it is probable that the dead cosmonaut will now haunt in the form of a revenant. The ghost does not have a memory; he is, rather, the spectral embodiment of a memory, that of his unjust, untimely death and the consequent need to redress it and settle some unfinished business: he is really a sort of audiovisual record that each time plays back the same message. Were I to do a second adaptation of *Hamlet*, after my *Gertrude; or, Love Dies* (in *Forthcoming*), then I would have King Hamlet, as he began feeling the effects of the poison placed in his ear by his treacherous brother, trudge toward paper and quill and write a summary incrimination of his brother, Claudius. It is only once King Claudius discovers accidentally the incriminating piece of paper and destroys it that the ghost of King Hamlet begins to haunt Elsinore as in Shakespeare's play.

Thinking across Lapses of Consciousness, If Not of Being

In Michelangelo Antonioni's *The Passenger* (1975), Locke, a reporter, switches identities with a fellow guest at the same hotel, Robertson, in order to make a fresh start when he finds the latter dead of a heart attack. He is thenceforth haunted not only by his own unfinished business (his wife keeps looking for him) but also by that of Robertson, who turns out to be an arms dealer. Does he end up murdered by the hitmen hired by Robertson's dissatisfied clients? No. Having switched identities with someone who died of a heart attack, Locke should have checked his heart's condition. Heedlessly, he died, like Robertson, of a heart attack in a hotel room.

On peut tout quitter, définitivement, seulement quand on est quitte.

That which has no unfinished business[404] is our original face (*honrai-no-memmoku*), our Buddha-nature (*busshō*).

At the most basic level, to die prematurely is to die organically without having *died before dying*.

The world and virtual reality are going to become truly indistinguishable only when not just the living but also the dead can no longer differentiate between them, revenants beginning to appear and haunt the virtual world, asking for a virtual body, the latter being different from the spectral one with which they haunt. While in earlier historical periods, one warned against mistaking a hallucination for a real body or a mystical vision, soon enough one is going to warn about mistaking a virtual body for a specter or an astral body.

I am speaking on the phone to John Corbett. Suddenly, it hits me that he is speaking to me with *my* voice. Horrified, I beseech him: "Speak to me with your voice." He answers: "But I am doing that!" It is still *my* voice!

If you see yourself hitchhiking, should you pick yourself up?.

We are unique only in death ("Dying … is essentially mine in such a way that no one can be my representative"[405] [Heidegger]), a condition in which, paradoxically, each assumes every name in history (having died before dying physically ["This autumn (of 1888) … I twice attended my funeral"[406]], Nietzsche wrote, "I am Prado, I am also Prado's father, I venture to say that I am also Lesseps…. I am also Chambige…. Every name in history is I"[407]).

Does the tagline of Coppola's *Bram Stoker's Dracula*, "Love Never Dies," belie that death is an end? It does only if one misses its irony. Judging from Coppola's film, love never crosses the entrancing threshold to labyrinthine death: Dracula cannot meet his wife despite the circumstance that, as someone who committed suicide and as a consequence was withheld burial in consecrated ground, she is herself an undead.

Coppola missed a beautiful opportunity in the scene in his *Bram Stoker's Dracula* where Mina tells the vampire the following about his voice, "It comforts me when I am alone": the camera could have then panned to a mirror where we would have seen Mina *alone* while hearing Dracula's voice speaking to her.

The vampire's fascinated victim said to him, "Don't disappear again for days on end," as she brought him closer to her in a hug. What could he answer, as he did not see himself in her pupil?

The lover of the vampire, of the telesthetic who does not appear in mirrors, jotted down in her diary: "How crowded Beirut seems now that you've left. Come back: inflate its emptiness."

Even more deserted than the empty-looking city at dawn in the beginning section of Vertov's *Man with a Movie Camera* are the cities in the dreams of those asleep in such a city, where the dead finds himself as the only survivor (the dream sequence in Bergman's *Wild Strawberries* and in Buñuel's *The Discreet Charm of the Bourgeoisie*).

The *dead water* of Wismar's canals in Herzog's *Nosferatu* is stiller than the bridge over it; the bridge is more stagnant than the water under it.

He could not smoke during the LSD trip because he had lost all sense of the existence of a boundary between the inside and the outside—exhalation and inhalation presuppose this distinction.

The dead recalled, albeit with difficulty, Moritake's haiku "Fallen petals rise / back to the branch—I watch: / oh ... butterflies!" as, lying undecomposed in the earth, he heard the sound of the time-lapse movement of the dry leaves and fallen petals on the ground.

Immobilization is not encountered in the world (except maybe at its border, the event horizon of a black hole), therefore when I witness freezing, I wonder: "Am I no longer in the world? Am I dead?" (If one is a dancer, one might ask: Am I in the dance realm, dancing?)

The recently dead human does not know at first that he or she is dead; it is in this sense that this period can be considered an *after-life*.

How is it that most humans manage to live, instead of survive, while concurrently already dead, that is, in unworldly conditions of space and time in which they wonder, "Am I dead?"? How is it conceivable that a black hole, whose "singularity is a region where—according to the laws of general relativity—the curvature of spacetime becomes infinitely large, and spacetime ceases to exist," and in which, from another perspective, "as best we understand it in 1993, ... [the laws of quantum mechanics, which 'forbid the infinities,'] merge with Einstein's general relativistic laws" "very near the singularity" into *quantum gravity*, with the consequence that "time ceases to exist; no longer can we say that 'this thing happens before that one,' because without time, there is no concept of 'before' or 'after,' ... [and] space, the sole remaining remnant of what was once a unified spacetime, becomes a random, probabilistic froth,"[408] can so easily be disposed of through radiation, which results, at the end of a long process of evaporation, in the black hole's explosion and hence the singularity's disappearance?

It is not modern science that might induce one not to believe in religion, but the presence of atheist schizophrenics, for the existence of the latter shows that other worlds, "hell," or "paradise" can be experienced or undergone without the necessity of interpreting them in religious terms.

The undead was startled the first time the sound of the cicadas persisted despite his movement nearby. But this prepared him a little better for the absence of his image in the mirror.

The vampire, whose shadow dissociates from him, does not announce himself, does not lag behind himself.

A friend of John Corbett took LSD and felt at one point that she had a revelation. She scribbled it on a piece of paper. When she woke up the next day, she hurriedly looked for the paper and found to her disappointment that she had written: "There is a strange smell in the room." Was that disappointment warranted? On being asked why Bodhidharma came to China, Joshu said: "An oak tree in the garden."

We cannot experience eternity in our present body, for eternity is not possible as long as any refractory period, during which the nerve cell cannot react to a new stimulus after it has just been subjected to one, exists.

I've been and continue to be very interested in entities that only partly fit where they are, for example, vampires, who, while seemingly at a certain location, are revealed by the mirror not to be there; and the unworldly entities that irrupt in radical closures and that induce the impression that they are matted there.

It is less Nicholas Ray's diatribes against Wenders that show his view of the filming of Lightning Over Water, which took place during several extended breaks in the filming of Wenders's Hammett, than the inclusion of a section from his rehearsals of Kafka's "A Report to an Academy" in the film—his adaptation of "A Report to an Academy" is, unlike Hammett, not an interruption of Lightning Over Water.[409] There is a statistically significant deviation from chance in the concordance between the first version of the film, which was edited by Peter Przygodda, and Kafka's short story, which is presented in the form of a monkey's report on the vicissitudes of his forced education to become a human: "They were good creatures, in spite of everything. I find it still pleasant to remember the sound of their heavy footfalls which used to echo through my half-dreaming head.... When they were off-duty some of them often used to sit down in a semicircle around me; they hardly spoke but only grunted to each other. If I were to be invited today to take a cruise on that ship I should certainly refuse the invitation.... There was one of them who came again and again, alone or with friends, by day, by night, at all kinds of hours; he would post himself before me with the bottle and give me instructions. He could not understand me, he wanted to solve the enigma of my being."[410] Wim: "Are you ready? I didn't come to talk about dying, Nick." Nick: "I didn't come to talk about dying, Nick." Wim: "But we might have to." Nick: "But we might have to." This concordance is for the most part lost in the second version (where the film crew and the shooting of the film in Ray's apartment are far less manifest), the one Wenders edited. Did Ray begin working on his production of Kafka's story before the filming began, or did he decide to do so and include it in *Lightning Over Water* in response to what was taking place during the filming? Were more of the rehearsals shot but edited out by Wenders (the part of Kafka's short story included in the film is not the relevant one)? It is through the inclusion of a link to Kafka's "A Report to an Academy" that *Lightning Over Water* is also *Nick's Movie*. Who plays the role of the vampire in this film? Wenders (with his crew in Ray's apartment proliferating like the rats in Herzog's *Nosferatu*)? Or the camera over the empty junk (like [Herzog's and Murnau's] Nosferatu or [Browning's and Badham's] Dracula on the empty ship transporting them from Transylvania to Bremen, Wismar, or London [same circular movement around the empty ship in Herzog's *Nosferatu* and the empty junk in *Lightning Over Water*]), with both Ray and Wenders its victims?

The discovery, in states of altered consciousness, that a double can think in one's mind facilitates one's detachment from the stream of consciousness once one is back in a normal state.

Mortal writers and thinkers move from initially mistaking themselves for "immortal" ("one whose fame is enduring" [*American Heritage Dictionary*]) writers and thinkers, thus Nietzsche mistaking himself in his first book, *The Birth of Tragedy* (1872), for Schopenhauer (he writes in "A Critical Backward Glance," which opens the second edition of the book: "What a pity … that I did not yet have the courage [or shall I say the immodesty?] to risk a fresh language in keeping with the hazard, the radical novelty of my ideas, that I fumbled along, using terms borrowed from the vocabularies of Kant and Schopenhauer to express value judgments which were in flagrant contradiction to the spirit or taste of these men!"[411]); to assuming "every name in history" (in a letter to Jakob Burckhardt in Nietzsche's handwriting and dated January 5, 1889, we find the assertion "Every name in history is I") as they die before dying, thus Nietzsche, who wrote a book titled *The Anti-Christ*, signed some of his last letters "The Crucified." Between these two manners of mistaking himself for others, the great singularity that was the living mortal Nietzsche, the stylish thought of Nietzsche.

In Zemeckis's *Back to the Future Part II* (1989), when the two versions of the doctor, one of which has come from the future, are in the same frame, instead of witnessing a convincing simulation of a natural interaction during their brief conversation—we know from *Who Framed Roger Rabbit* (1988) that Zemeckis is quite adroit at making the matted and non-matted characters interact convincingly, even in the limit case of an interaction between human and animation characters—the spectator sees one of them look obliquely while speaking to the other, at other times have his back to him, so that the eye-directions of the two do not match. An apprehension that one may otherwise transgress the taboo against encountering the double may have triggered this unconvincing matting (there was no reason for such an apprehension since the doctor hailing from the future is not the double of the version in the past). Some filmmakers/writers try to find situations where the occasional awkwardness and sloppiness that plagued their earlier writing/filmmaking is now necessitated by the subject matter itself and is this time executed soberly and in control: *back to the future.*

In Murnau's *Sunrise*, the close-up of the maid shouting to inform her master that his wife, who was presumed drowned, has been found alive echoes the face of his mistress in a medium shot as he strangles her because she tempted him to murder his wife—especially since the maid's two hands, cut by the frame a little above the wrist, hence appearing not to belong to her, encircle her face (to form a resonating funnel for the shout), seeming to be strangling her. It is this correspondence, and not her shout, or not her shout alone, that induces him to desist from carrying out strangling his erstwhile mistress, saving her. This could not have ensued without the husband somewhat sensing the framing!

pages 618

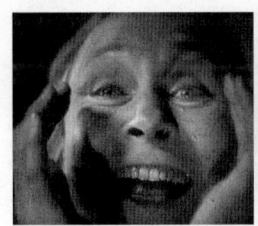 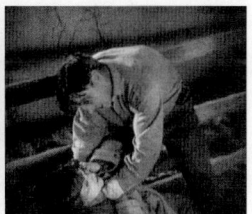

Murnau's *Nosferatu* presents examples of the unconscious as attributable to the subject: Harker's dropping of Mina's picture while getting something from his pocket to give to the vampire is a parapraxis revealing a sacrificial unconscious wish. But Murnau's film also presents instances of an unconscious that is external to the psychological subject: the juxtaposition of the shot of Nosferatu in Transylvania walking from screen left to right with the shot of Ellen in Bremen with hands outstretched toward the right creates a desire[412] that remains unconscious both to Ellen *and* to her subjective unconscious, the one that is traceable to events in her life, its traumas and *enigmatic signifiers* (to use this term coined by Jean Laplanche). Contrariwise, if the yogi still looks like he has some desires, this is only through a sort of Kuleshov effect,[413] hence no further karma is produced.

"You only talked about it, I *only* did it." Only someone free can understand the second *only*.

Krzysztof Wodiczko was only able to show *The Homeless Projection* in a New York gallery instead of his proposed site of Union Square, where it was supposed to be projected onto buildings: an exile from exile.

What would we, who are blind to perspective and its virtual lines, do without Richard Foreman's strings?

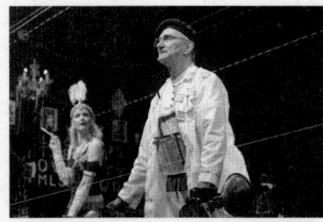

page 617

Choice consists not in seemingly selecting one of many preset alternatives but in *creating* a bifurcation point—all of whose branches are taken. Choice is hence unknowable, except through writing and art, by means of which the writer or artist receives by creation—which involves untimely collaboration with them—from the other version(s) in an otherwise parallel universe.

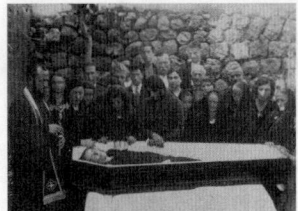

page 616

There is something perturbing about this photograph, in which the head of the embalmed corpse in the open coffin is not directed upward, as is customary, but toward the camera. The spectator experiences a dissociation, feeling he is in two places simultaneously: with respect to the gaze of one of the mourners who is looking straight at the camera, I am standing where the camera is, looking in the direction in which the lens is aimed; but with respect to the dead woman, I cannot be in the place of the camera since I cannot reciprocate the look implied by "her" directing her face toward me, so that I have been displaced by the same angle as her head has been from the traditional straight position.

The link between the writer and his version in a realm of altered consciousness such as death, which the former can bring about only creatively, is to allow both to elude the constant linking of ideas on their own. In the latter's case, a linking clearly experienced in the mode of disempowerment; in the former's case, a linking that takes the form of the deduction of cogent ideas from each other by an academic who speaks mostly in generalities, and this in large part because he or she is not receiving from someone who has experienced, among other things, *every name in history is I.*

    — I lied to you.
    — I, too, lied (to myself and to others), since I be*lie*ved you.

page 618

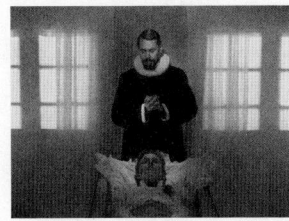

Are the two praying for each other? If not, who is praying for the other? She is praying for him.

Addendum to "Photographic Memory"

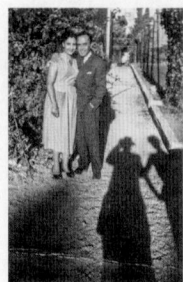

page 574

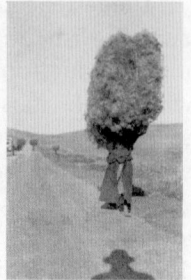

page 575

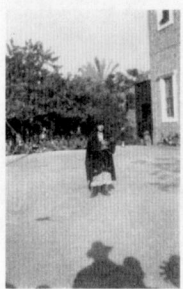

page 573

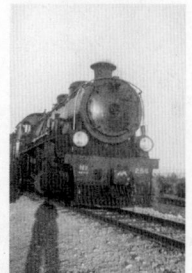

page 577

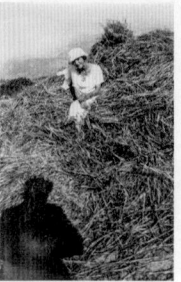

page 577

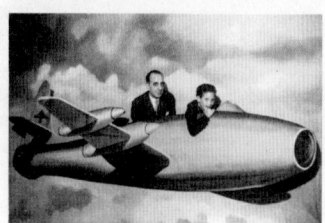

page 581

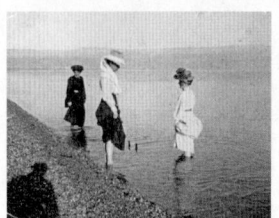

page 572

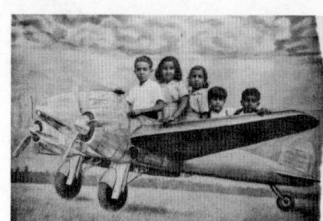

page 580

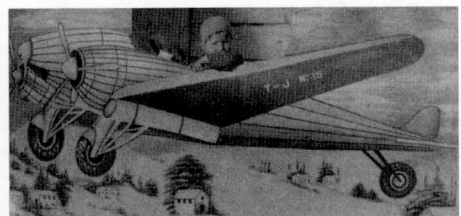

page 580

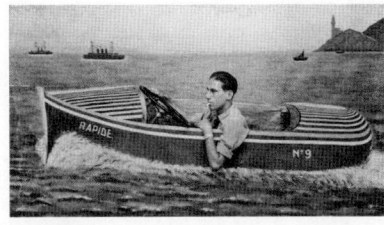

page 583

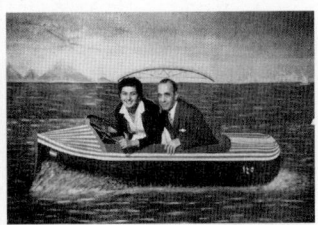

page 582

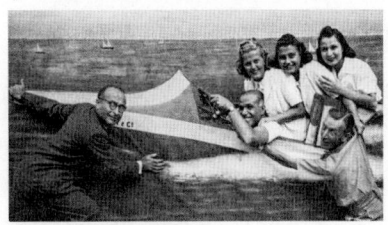

page 585

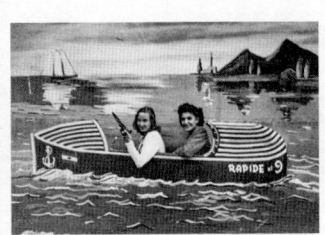

page 582

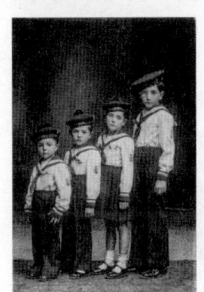

page 592

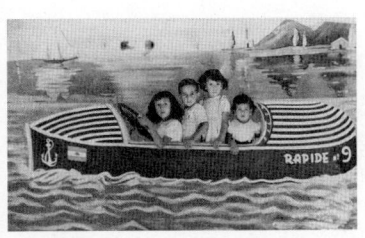

page 583

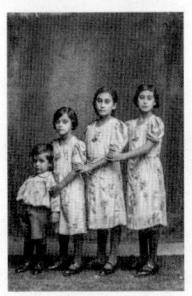

page 593

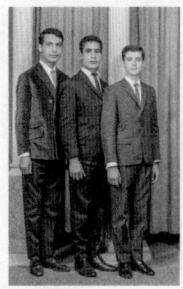

page 594

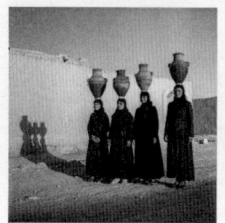

page 595

Addendum to "Death-Size Body"

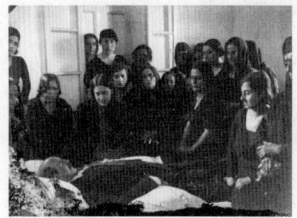

page 602–3

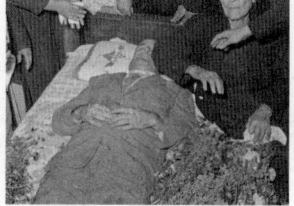

page 608–9

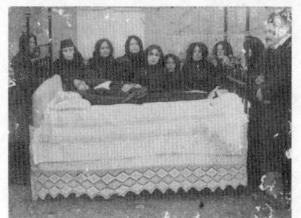

page 610

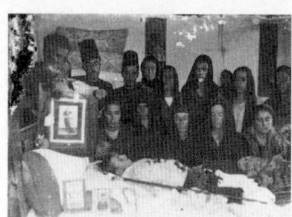

page 604

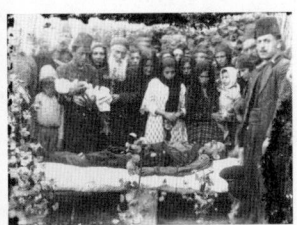

page 611

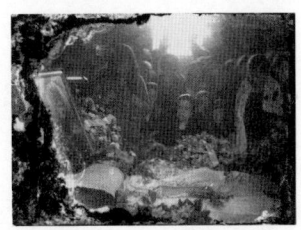

page 605

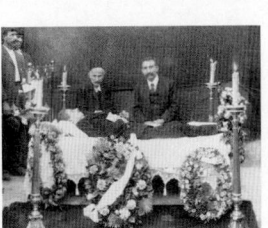

page 601

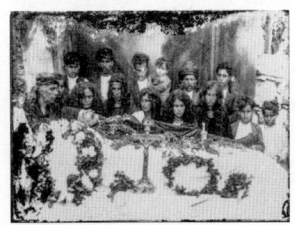

page 606–7

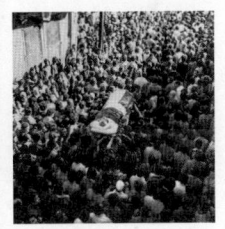

page 613

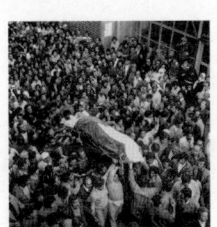

page 613

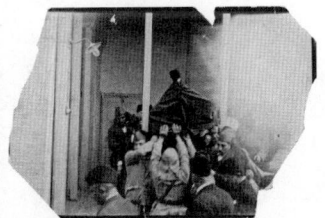

page 614–15

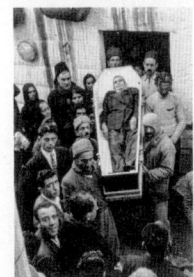

page 591

Jouissance in Postwar Beirut

INTERTITLE

Since the postwar zone he was haunting was "fast" becoming fully mundane, no longer hospitable to those *poor in world* (to die is not to cease to exist but to lose the world), the VAMPIRE had been for some time now on the lookout for a new labyrinth on which he could be matted.

INT.-EXT. VAMPIRE'S "LIVING" ROOM—NIGHT

The vampire puts a DVD in the player, then begins watching Jalal Toufic's *'Āshūrā': This Blood Spilled in My Veins.*

INT. AIRPORT—AFTER MIDNIGHT

A vampire (played by several actors of different ages—this accords with his feeling "himself" to be every name in history—including the one who plays the "other" vampire in the film [whom we first encounter as a taxi driver], so that despite the existence of the other vampire, he can persist as the last man) is getting a boarding pass for a Middle East Airlines (MEA) flight to Beirut. For much of the film, the vampire is keyed on the background (with the consequence that his victims bleed through stigmata rather than as a result of being physically attacked by him); consequently, others look at an angle to him. Moreover, for much of the film, he, dead, has no point of view.

> VAMPIRE
> (muttering)
> How moving it can be to go through the motions! Isn't that what the angels do in Wenders's *Wings of Desire*, for example, when seemingly picking up a pen lying on a table?

A family is standing on a moving sidewalk heading toward the gates area. Strangely, the vampire appears to be moving in the same manner though he is not on the moving sidewalk but next to it.

> AIRPORT ANNOUNCEMENT
> Mr. Yammout, please head as quickly as possible to the counter at gate 3 to board your flight to Beirut. If you do not do so in the coming five minutes ...

Cut to the interior of an airplane.

> STEWARDESS
> (general announcement)
> Mr. Yammout, please present yourself to the staff, otherwise we will have to remove your suitcase from the plane.

Indeed, we see his suitcase being removed.

INT. BEIRUT INTERNATIONAL AIRPORT—NIGHT

The vampire is at customs (through teleportation/quantum tunneling)!

EXT. BEIRUT INTERNATIONAL AIRPORT—NIGHT

The vampire is being invited by several taxi drivers to use their respective cars. He heads to what appears to be a parked empty taxicab.

EXT. TAXI MOVING THROUGH THE ROADS LEADING TO BEIRUT'S CENTRAL DISTRICT—DAWN

The vampire, now looking physically exactly like the driver, remarks the failure of the latter to appear in the mirror. The driver too notices the failure of his customer to appear in the mirror. At no point do we see the two vampires together in the same shot. When we see one talking, we witness the absence of the other in the mirror.

> VAMPIRE (V.O.)
> Given the favorable current conditions in Lebanon, I assumed there would be other undead keyed on this country. But I did not expect to come across one so soon!

OTHER VAMPIRE (V.O.)

By doing a night shift as a taxi driver at the airport, I can occasionally mortally attack the Lebanese I pick up, making him or her discover that he or she is "a stranger in a strange land."[414]

VAMPIRE (V.O.)

I am considering opening a video rental store: It is one of the most appropriate venues to detect those it would be fitting to prey on, for example, those who are erotically aroused by horror films.

The car stops at a red light.

VAMPIRE (V.O.)

Were the passenger of your car to look in the mirror, he would feel that there was no one else in the moving car, that it was moving on its own. He or she would thus have a foretaste of psychosis, of his coming undeath ...

He is interrupted by the DRIVER in the car behind them, who, insistently honking his horn even though the traffic light is still red, backs the car up, moves to the next lane, and overtakes the taxi, yelling:

DRIVER

What are you waiting for, *yā mayyit*?![415]

Moments later, the driver of that car suddenly hears a voice behind him saying politely:

OTHER VAMPIRE

I'll stop here, please!

Startled, the driver involuntarily, instinctively brings the car to a screeching stop and looks in the mirror toward the back seat. He sees no one there! He then perceives the (other) vampire, who is now sitting right next to him:

OTHER VAMPIRE

Were you erudite, you would know that, as is written in Bram Stoker's *Dracula, the dead travel fast*—to nowhere. I'll make it possible for you to arrive *dead on time*.

He opens his mouth threateningly just as he finishes saying his humoristic words; the driver begins bleeding from a stigma that appears on his neck.

EXT. STREET IN FRONT OF A BUILDING IN BEIRUT'S CENTRAL DISTRICT—DUSK

The vampire is standing in front one of the reconstructed buildings of the Central District. A REAL ESTATE AGENT comes to meet him from his car.

EXT.-INT. HOUSE—DUSK

> REAL ESTATE AGENT
> Why did you choose to come to Lebanon of all places?

> VAMPIRE
> From the TV news images of Beirut, I sensed that I could still find ruins, with their labyrinthine spaces-times, in Lebanon.

> REAL ESTATE AGENT
> Labyrinthine?!

On uttering his exclamation, the real estate agent impulsively turns to a mirror in the hall. He does not see the vampire in the mirror even though the latter is ostensibly standing next to him. This absence of the mirror image entrances him. Turning to check whether the vampire is still standing next to him, he witnesses one of the rooms as a ruin and the vampire as a very old man, but then the room appears again in mint condition and the vampire again a youth.

> VAMPIRE
> Where are you now?

The ostensibly reconstructed house appears again as a ruin, with a few yellowish, rotting papers strewn on the floor. The agent picks up the closest to him. It shows the living room. He picks up a second photograph. It shows him in the building.

> REAL ESTATE AGENT
> (screaming)
> But I've never been here before!

While he's picking up a third photograph ...

> VAMPIRE
> The moment you enter the labyrinth, you've been
> there before.

The agent lets go of the photograph he has just glimpsed, utters a
scream and falls unconscious: The photograph shows him lying on
the floor, blood on his neck.

EXT. VIDEO STORE—DUSK

Establishing shot of a video store. Its name is inscribed on a plaque:
For the Hell of It.

INT. VIDEO STORE—DUSK

The vampire cursorily checks on his laptop computer the lists of the
videos rented by his various customers and quickly detects that one
customer is repeatedly renting horror films, and that he happens to
be late in returning the last DVD he rented. The vampire asks one
of his employees to call that customer and to insist that he return it
the same night.

INT. VIDEO STORE—NIGHT

The vampire meets the customer, a FORMER MILITIAMAN in his
mid-fifties wearing an obtrusive crucifix around his neck.

> VAMPIRE
> This is the fifth time you've checked out this horror
> film. Are you a film teacher or critic?

> FORMER MILITIAMAN
> No. Aren't you, too, drawn to horror films?

> VAMPIRE
> I am thrilled by *some* horror films.

> FORMER MILITIAMAN
> My favorite films all belong to the horror genre.
> What's your favorite film?

VAMPIRE
Hiroshima mon amour. It is the only zombie film I care about.

FORMER MILITIAMAN
I haven't seen it yet. I'll rent it right now. I have a large TV with surround sound. Why don't you come to my place later tonight? We can watch the film together and have a discussion following it.

VAMPIRE
Tonight, I'll be at the service of your wish fulfillment!

The former militiaman is puzzled by the vampire's closing words.

INT. FORMER MILITIAMAN'S APARTMENT—NIGHT

On entering his host's apartment, the vampire is immediately struck by the screensaver image on the latter's computer: It is the scene in Giovanni di Paolo's *Six Scenes from the Life of Saint John the Baptist* (1455/60) showing blood gushing from the beheaded saint's neck. Noticing that his guest is taken by the screensaver image, the host fetches from his very small library a book of Francis Bacon paintings. They flip through the book as they mention various paintings in it.

FORMER MILITIAMAN
He looks to me like one of those birdlike creatures one apprehends in a number of Francis Bacon's paintings: *Seated Figure*; *Figure in Movement*; *Triptych Inspired by the Oresteia of Aeschylus*. These give me a more intense, indeed an altogether different type of erotic thrill than the couples in bed in such Bacon paintings as *Two Figures* (1953), and *Two Figures Lying on a Bed with Attendants* (1968).

VAMPIRE
It seems that for you the former paintings accomplish better Bacon's program of *coming across directly onto the nervous system*. It is as if by doing away with the sense organs of the depicted models, sometimes violently (missing eyes, etc.), one does away with or neutralizes the indirect means of accessing sensation, enhancing the chances that it will sympathetically directly hit the nervous or libidinal system of the spectator.

They then begin watching *Hiroshima mon amour*. After the scenes showing victims of the nuclear explosion, the host very quickly loses interest and turns the volume down.

> FORMER MILITIAMAN
> Judging by the location of your video store, I would assume that you are a Christian.

> VAMPIRE
> No, I am not a Christian!

The host is perplexed. After several glasses of wine, and after recovering his composure, he asks his guest:

> FORMER MILITIAMAN
> Wouldn't you be tempted to go to church were they to offer you excellent wine during the Eucharist, for example, Château Pétrus 1982 or Château Cheval Blanc 1947?

> VAMPIRE
> I am not welcome there!

> FORMER MILITIAMAN
> How would the priest and the congregation know that?

> VAMPIRE
> Judging by the blasphemous images and thoughts that pass through my mind in a church, I know that—and so do the voices!

> FORMER MILITIAMAN
> But those sacrilegious thoughts and images should be precisely what incites you to go to church! I first joined the Lebanese Forces to take revenge for the killing of my sister by a sniper on the Moslem side of the Green Line. After several months of participating in battles, I began to be increasingly vexed by the idiocy of those civilians who would address the following reproach to me, "How can you kill while wearing the cross on which the one who said 'But I tell you, Do not resist an evil person. If someone strikes you on the right cheek, turn to him the other also' was crucified?", for after participating in a few massacres, I wore the crucifix around my

neck while butchering in a deliberate desecration—a transgression that gave me, as well as a significant number of other militiamen, an erotic thrill. Since participating in the Sabra and Shatila massacre in 1982, I am still waiting for a human who would make me engage in a sexual relationship with her or him as an organic whole.

His guest gets closer to him and looks him straight in the eyes. The former militiaman sees in the eyes of the vampire the horror of the undeath realm and is entranced.

FORMER MILITIAMAN
(muttering in a dreadful lascivious manner)
The human being is this night, this empty nothing, that contains everything in its simplicity—an unending wealth of many representations, images, of which none belongs to him—or which are not present. This night, the interior of nature, that exists here—pure self—in phantasmagorical representations, is night all around it, in which here shoots a bloody head— there another white ghastly apparition, suddenly here before it, and just so disappears. One catches sight of this night when one looks human beings in the eye—this night that becomes awful suspends the night of the world in an opposition.[416]

The vampire mutters the exact same words in sync with the former militiaman—but out of sync with himself. Then he exclaims aloud:

VAMPIRE
How uncanny that you, the purported living, and I, the one officially dead, a vampire, can see eye to eye.

While drinking the former militiaman's blood flowing from a stigma on his neck, the vampire asks him:

VAMPIRE
Am I, a dead person, making your blood run cold?

With a remote control, the vampire, while still lying over the former militiaman, turns up the volume on the TV monitor still showing *Hiroshima mon amour* and listens to the voice-over of the FRENCH WOMAN lying on her dying German beloved lover during the last days of the German occupation of France.

FRENCH WOMAN (in *Hiroshima mon amour*; V.O.)
Someone had fired on him from a garden. I stayed near his body all that day and then all the next night.... Little by little he grew cold beneath me.... The moment of his death actually escaped me ... because even at that very moment, and even afterward, yes, even afterward, I can say that I couldn't feel the slightest difference between this dead body and mine. All I could find between this body and mine were obvious similarities ...[417]

INT. CAFE—NIGHT

The vampire is sitting at the bar with a woman. It's raining outside.

WOMAN
Half an hour ago, I was unaware of your very existence, and yet, already.... Do you believe in love at first sight, the *coup de foudre*?

VAMPIRE
If at all, I believe in love at first out of sight of what induces an impression of déjà vu! Anyway, love at first sight will never abolish chance, in other words, *un coup de foudre jamais n'abolira le hasard*.

Another woman is sitting a short distance from them at the bar. She overhears the conversation. As he concludes his reply, there is lightning, a thunderclap and the sound of breaking glass. She turns toward the source of the latter sound: a window. While doing so, she notices with consternation that he does not appear in the mirror on the wall. This absence of the mirror image entrances her; when she regains consciousness, the vampire and his female "companion" are no longer at the bar.

INT. CAFE—NIGHT

Umm Kulthum's song *Waḥishnī wa-inta uṣād 'aynī* (I miss you even while you're in front of my eyes) can be heard in the background. Now dressed in other clothes and with a different hairstyle, the woman who had overheard his conversation with the other woman in the same cafe questions him.

> BELOVED LOVER
> Am I the woman of your life?

> VAMPIRE
> You are the woman of my—death.

> BELOVED LOVER
> How weird of you to say this! All the more so because I fail to figure out why it is that our nascent love makes me melancholic. As far as I know, a melancholic is someone who is failing to accomplish the work of mourning his or her dead beloved.

The camera pans from them to the mirror on the wall: She alone appears in it.

INT. BELOVED LOVER'S LIVING ROOM—EVENING

The beloved lover phones the vampire.

> BELOVED LOVER
> This morning, I had what felt to be a flashback to some meeting we had years ago. And yet how could it be a flashback when what I was seemingly reliving had never existed since it precedes our first meeting, which took place recently in a café! Anyway, I'll watch one of the two DVDs you gave me in our last meeting, Hitchcock's *The Trouble with Harry*, and then come to your house.

EXT-INT. VAMPIRE'S HOUSE—NIGHT

The vampire scribbles in a notebook: "Love can subsist despite the break of (organic) death, continue into (un)death, as the subtitle of Jalal Toufic's book *Undying Love, or Love Dies* indicates, but can it resist the drive? I dread experimenting the answer with my beloved. I'll do my best to be already satiated each time we meet."

EXT. VARIOUS STREETS—NIGHT

He sets about finding a victim. He gravitates toward B018, a nightclub in Karantina built on the site of a massacre perpetuated in 1975 by Phalangist militiamen on the Palestinians who lived in the refugee camp there as well as on many Kurdish and Lebanese war refugees who also lived in that zone.

INT. B018 NIGHTCLUB—NIGHT

The vampire sits next to a woman at the bar. He scribbles: "The only thing I can stand about this kitschy nightclub are the bar chairs with their long backs, since they give the impression that the one sitting on them is nonetheless standing." She shortly begins retouching her makeup.

> BLIND WOMAN
> (mutters)
> How incongruous: I "have eyes but fail to see"!

He's alarmed that she may have remarked that he fails to appear in the small mirror of her blusher case. But when on closing her blusher case and wishing to reach for her drink, she gets hold of his glass instead, he's relieved as he realizes that she is blind.

INT.-EXT. VAMPIRE'S BEDROOM—NIGHT

At his house, while they caress each other's faces, she begins to describe him. While listening to her haptic portrait, the vampire turns toward the mirror, where he does not appear. Then she asks him to describe her.

> VAMPIRE
> I find it very difficult to do a portrait.

He fetches a book from his library.

> VAMPIRE
> Nietzsche writes in his *Philosophy in the Tragic Age of the Greeks*: "This attempt to tell the story of the older Greek philosophers is distinguished from similar attempts by its brevity.... It is possible to present the image of a man in three anecdotes; I shall try to emphasize three anecdotes in each system and abandon the rest."

He replaces the book on the shelf.

VAMPIRE

If we do not obtain three felicitous anecdotes, but "one" or "two," we produce a lifeless version of the model. My entrancing voice will enable you to envision a felicitous example of that. In Hitchcock's *The Trouble with Harry*, the Deputy Sheriff comes across the portrait Sam Marlowe did of Harry and is struck by its matching "the description of a tramp with stolen shoes and a wild story about a corpse." "Sam, what I wanna know is where did you paint it and who is it?" "First of all, it's not a painting. It's a drawing. Matter of fact, it's a pastel." "Sam, I ain't educated in fancy art [and I would add: in judging whether someone is definitely dead], but I do know the face of a dead man when I see one, and this is it." "Calvin, perhaps I can educate you to 'fancy art.'" Sam takes the portrait from the Deputy Sheriff's hand. While sketching, he says: "Now, a raised eyelid, perhaps ... a line of fullness to the cheek ... [a] lip that bends with expression. There!" It is only now that the pastel is actually finished. Has the painter "destroyed legal evidence," as the Deputy Sheriff protests threateningly, or did he, who according to Mrs. Rogers's earlier characterization has an artistic mind and therefore "can see the finer things," provide the elements missing from the unfinished portrait, revealing that it is the portrait of a clearly living person?

While he is describing this scene from Hitchcock's *The Trouble with Harry*, which the blind woman apprehends hypnotically, the same images and scenes are, in a parallel montage, being watched by the vampire's beloved lover on her TV monitor in her apartment.

VAMPIRE

Was your portrait of me successful? In order to answer this question, *See me!*

BLIND WOMAN

No, my portrait of you was inaccurate, but for the opposite reason to the one you just explicated: While in my portrait, you are an alive person, in reality you appear to be lifeless!

VAMPIRE

Look in my eyes by means of my entrancing voice!

Horrified by what she apprehends in his eyes, she stretches her agitated hand and makes a gesture to close them …

INT.-EXT. VAMPIRE'S "LIVING" ROOM — NIGHT

We see his eyes open as he hears a knock on the door. He unlatches the door.

> VAMPIRE
> I entreat you never again to show up at my house without prior notice.

She enters, pushes him onto the sofa and sits on his lap. He kisses her on the neck and caresses her. She disengages from his arms and fetches a bottle of wine. They drink several glasses. She then heads to the bathroom to take a shower.

> BELOVED LOVER
> Would you like to join me in the shower?

He declines, then scribbles: "If the *jasad*, the body, is dried blood, then fluid blood is not part of it. Indeed, one reads in Matthew: 'While they were eating, Jesus took bread, gave thanks and broke it, and gave it to his disciples, saying, "Take and eat; this is my body." Then he took the cup, gave thanks and offered it to them, saying, "Drink from it, all of you. This is my blood of the covenant …"' It is remarkable that Jesus did not feel that it is enough to say, 'this is my body,' but added also, 'this is my blood,' which implies that the blood is not part of the body. I, too, differentiate between the body and blood, do not consider blood to be part of the body. Only love makes me interested in the body." As she comes out of the shower, he recommends:

> VAMPIRE
> Duras's *Hiroshima mon amour* is being screened tonight. Let's go out to watch it.

> BELOVED LOVER
> OK. But you should get your coat since it is cold outside.

While she walks toward the entrance door, he quantum-tunnels to the bedroom door. Missing him, she turns toward the bedroom: She is startled to glimpse another man—dressed identically—in the last phase of closing the bedroom's door behind him. She quickly attributes this anomaly to the wine. Inside the bedroom, lying on the bed, is the blind woman, in a pool of blood—once more his beloved's timing was propitious, for he was satiated by the time she arrived.

He rejoins her:

>BELOVED LOVER
>You are like a thousand men in one.

EXT. STREET—NIGHT

>FORMER MILITIAMAN #2
>Why did you come to Lebanon?

>VAMPIRE
>And why did *you* come to Lebanon—from the bardo ... where I'll thrust you back right now?

The vampire holds him tight, opens his mouth voraciously, only for blood to flow from the neck of the man through a stigma. A policeman sees the vampire and his victim in the distance.

>POLICE OFFICER
>Hey, you there!

The vampire does not turn—neither does he resume drinking the man's blood.

>POLICE OFFICER
>(muttering while advancing hurriedly toward him)
>Is he deaf?

The police officer pokes him in the back, but the vampire ostensibly does not turn, continues to look away from him. In front of the vampire holding his victim is a glass storefront through which a mirror hung on the wall is visible. The vampire has his back to himself in it—as does his victim. The policeman is fascinated by the image. The vampire attacks him, but just as he is about to suck his blood, he glimpses in the same mirror his beloved lover in the distance. To his gratifying surprise, he overcomes his drive and swiftly walks away then disappears behind a corner. The beloved lover dials his "home" number from her mobile phone. Before she hears any ring, he answers!

BELOVED LOVER
It is urgent that I see you as soon as possible! I'll be at your place in approximately thirty minutes.

EXT. OUTSIDE THE VAMPIRE'S HOUSE—EVENING

The vampire has to kill another victim and, this time, successfully suck his blood till satiation before his beloved's imminent arrival. The vampire comes across a man in his early thirties walking outside his house while reading.

VAMPIRE
Do you agree with Nietzsche that "what is done out of love always takes place beyond good and evil"?

PASSERBY (ROY SAMAHA)
Yes.

He swiftly and forcibly draws him inside his building.

VAMPIRE
Given how rare it is to come across someone reading in Lebanon, let alone someone reading Nietzsche's *Beyond Good and Evil*, I have qualms about what I am about to do.

The vampire attacks him and begins drinking the blood flowing from him through a stigma.

PASSERBY (ROY SAMAHA)
(exclaims)
I doubt that this is what William Burroughs meant when he wrote: "Anything that can be done chemically can be done in other ways."

As the man's bloodied body sags, a DVD case falls from the bag he is carrying.

INT.-EXT. VAMPIRE'S "LIVING" ROOM—SAME EVENING

While waiting for his beloved, the vampire watches the DVD, *Untitled for Several Reasons* (2003), feeling even more sorry on surmising that he had killed the video maker Roy Samaha.

INT. MOVIE THEATER—NIGHT

JALAL TOUFIC is seated in the auditorium waiting for the start of
a screening of Gaspar Noé's film *I Stand Alone* (a.k.a. *One Against All*,
1998). An acquaintance of his comes and sits next to him.

> JALAL TOUFIC
> Why did you come to watch this film?

> ACQUAINTANCE OF JALAL TOUFIC
> I didn't know what to do with my time, so I cruised
> for a while and then decided to watch a film, just for
> the hell of it.

Dissolve to the following intertitle, which appears sixty-nine minutes
into Noé's film: "Attention: You have 30 seconds to abandon the projection of the film." Indeed, a countdown follows. Two seconds later,
Toufic whispers in his acquaintance's ear.

> JALAL TOUFIC
> Let's leave.

> ACQUAINTANCE OF JALAL TOUFIC
> One should watch films from start to finish.

> JALAL TOUFIC
> Like hell I will do so with this film!

> ACQUAINTANCE OF JALAL TOUFIC
> I myself will watch the whole film come hell or high
> water!

Toufic leaves at this point, eighteen seconds into the countdown. The
vampire enters moments after the countdown is over and, following
the end of the projection, invites one of the spectators to his house.

EXT.-INT. VAMPIRE'S HOUSE—NIGHT

> FORMER CHRISTIAN MILITIAMAN
> Why did you come to Lebanon?

> VAMPIRE
> My drive; I came to Lebanon for blood.

FORMER CHRISTIAN MILITIAMAN
Blood! What blood? We're in a postwar country.

VAMPIRE
I may have mistaken the flashbacks of some of the traumatized perpetrators and victims of the civil war and some of the traumatized victims of the Israeli invasion of 1982, which flashbacks I telepathically apprehend, as taking place currently. More to the point, were you not oblivious of the yearly commemoration 'Āshūrā' in various parts of Lebanon, you would be aware that there's still a lot of blood in Lebanon. Unfortunately for you, I am unable to wait till 'Āshūrā'.

The vampire attacks the man and drinks his blood as it flows from a stigma on his neck.

INT. MOVIE THEATER—NIGHT

Jalal Toufic is watching David Lynch's *Twin Peaks: Fire Walk with Me*. Two other men, each one seated in a different section of the cinema, are also watching the film. As the angel disappears from the painting in Laura Palmer's room, Toufic promptly leaves the cinema theater. Moments after the complete disappearance of the angel from the painting, the vampire enters the cinema theater. He walks to one of the two men and stands between him and the screen—yet he does not project any shadow on it. A dissolve is happening onscreen. As he overpowers the first man and starts to suck his blood, the frightened other man starts running away toward the exit. The vampire (quantum) tunnels, in other words dissolves, to him. This dissolve outside of the projected film, in "reality," is the last thing the second man sees before he is killed by the vampire.

INT. NIGHTCLUB—NIGHT

Five former militiamen are listening to the TV news, which relates to the recent spate of unsolved murders in the city.

FORMER MILITIAMAN #4
This is the third ex-militiaman we knew who has been murdered this month in a mysterious manner.

FORMER MILITIAMAN #5
Did anyone of you ever study probability and statistics, so we would know whether we should particularly worry about these murders? Should we begin to suspect that someone is after our blood, that there is bad blood between him, who seems not to acknowledge the amnesty law of 1992, and us?

INT. VIDEO STORE—MORNING

VIDEO STORE EMPLOYEE
I can't be here on Sunday morning. I have a makeup session of the class "Film and Religion" then.

VAMPIRE
Why bother to attend the makeup session? Is your professor any good?

VIDEO STORE EMPLOYEE
Yes.

VAMPIRE
He is?! What's his name?

VIDEO STORE EMPLOYEE
Jalal Toufic.

VAMPIRE
Jalal Toufic! He's one of my favorite thinkers. Is that the only class he teaches this semester?

VIDEO STORE EMPLOYEE
No. I am also taking his class "Radical Closure." We are supposed to watch David Lynch's *Twin Peaks: Fire Walk with Me* for next week.

VAMPIRE
Do me the favor of inquiring of him whether I can attend his class as an auditor.

The employee-cum-graduate-student phones his professor.

VIDEO STORE EMPLOYEE
Your attendance would be agreeable to him.

INT. HOLY SPIRIT UNIVERSITY OF KASLIK (USEK)—MORNING

The vampire tries to be satiated before the class so as not to be over-powered by his drive and attack one of his favorite thinkers. He enters one of the various churches on the way to Holy Spirit University. As he does so, he overhears a (diegetic) voice-over.

> (DIEGETIC) V.O.
> I wonder how it is that in the iconography of the crucifixion not once has it been shown that what was pouring out of the wounds of Christ was wine?

He sits to confess to the priest.

> VAMPIRE
> I've just remembered the New Testament episode in which "The demons [in two possessed men] begged Jesus, 'If you drive us out, send us into the herd of pigs,'" and Jesus replied, "Go!" I imagine that on their way into the pigs, they mocked him quoting his own words: "O Jesus, 'do not throw your pearls to pigs.'"

> PRIEST
> Go on.

> VAMPIRE
> Do you believe in stigmata?

> PRIEST
> Of course!

> VAMPIRE
> Can they appear in locations other than those of the wounds of Jesus Christ during his crucifixion? For example, can a stigma appear on the neck?

While the priest is still considering what answer to give, the vampire opens his mouth in a predatory manner and a stigma appears on the priest's neck. The vampire subjugates the priest and drinks the flowing blood.

INT. CLASSROOM—MORNING

> JALAL TOUFIC
> For some reason, I feel exhausted, drained of energy.

Were it not that we have a guest today, I would have suggested that we postpone the lecture. Rilke writes in the fourth of his *Duino Elegies*: "I won't endure these half-filled human masks; / better, the puppet. It at least is full. / I'll put up with the stuffed skin, the wire, the face / that is nothing but appearance. Here. I'm waiting. / Even if the lights go out; even if someone / tells me 'That's all'; even if emptiness / floats toward me in a gray draft from the stage; / even if not one of my silent ancestors / stays seated with me, not one woman, not / the boy with the immovable brown eye — / I'll sit here anyway. One can always watch. / ... Am I not right / to feel as if I *must* stay seated, must / wait before the puppet stage, or, rather, / gaze at it so intensely that at last, / to balance my gaze, an angel has to come and / make the stuffed skins startle into life. / Angel and puppet: a real play, finally." Were the narrator not "half-filled," the angel, who is never late, would have already appeared to him or rather made his presence felt to him—when the angel appears, I discover that he was *here* all along, and that I could not have waited such a long time without the assistance of his subtle presence, and that what I take to be first his absence then his presence is actually a modification in his presence, from a subtle one to an overwhelming one. The wait ends when there is no longer any use waiting, i.e., when one is no longer useful even for waiting, having become someone who simply is; Deleuze wrote, "When Bruno [in Werner Herzog's *Stroszek*] asks the question: 'Where do objects go when they no longer have any use?' we might reply that they normally go in the dustbin, but that reply would be inadequate, since the question is metaphysical. Bergson asked the same question and replied metaphysically: that which has ceased to be useful simply begins to *be*." *Duino Elegies*'s real play, finally, is one between the angel and the one who waited for him and was changed by this wait into a puppet (of God). Since the angel appears to the puppet (of God), it is not accidental that one of the most felicitous sites to find angels in cinema is in pixilation films, for example, Bokanowski's *The Angel*; as well as in those films, such as Lynch's *Twin Peaks: Fire Walk with Me*, made by filmmakers who started their cinematic work with one or more short animation/pixilation films

(Lynch's *The Grandmother, The Alphabet,* etc.). By the way, I am cancelling my film assignment for the next session; indeed, I recommend that you refrain from watching *Twin Peaks: Fire Walk with Me.* It is precisely those who know how to "wait for the angel" who are the first to leave the cinema theater during the projection of certain films, since they know that while one *can* always watch, one *should* not always watch, indeed that "if your right eye causes you to sin, gouge it out and throw it away. It is better for you to lose one part of your body than for your whole body to be thrown into hell" (Matthew 5:29). If you don't leave with the angel, as he is leaving some evil site, then sooner or later you will have to wait for someone or something in you to leave—exorcism. At that point, anyone other than the one scaring and beating the hell out of you has to promptly leave while the exorcism is taking place, otherwise the exiting demons may possess him or her. Rare are the humans who have waited for the angel; but many are the angels who have waited for humans to leave evil situations—many an angel has fallen precisely because he waited too long for some human to leave while evil was taking place, the human in question subsequently becoming the puppet of the devil, suffering from sacrilegious thought-insertions, depersonalization, etc.

INT. CHURCH—LATER IN THE MORNING

The Eucharist is in progress. As the vampire drinks the wine of the Eucharist, some of it seeps from his lips—it is now blood! He wipes it with a napkin.

> PRIEST
> (concerned)
> Did you bite your lip?

> FORMER VAMPIRE
> No!

Now his words are in sync. Henceforth, he is no longer keyed on the location where he is ostensibly, and, for the first time since the beginning of the film, a point of view shot conveys what he is seeing: the priest, the church, etc.

INT. VAMPIRE'S HOUSE—AFTERNOON

The vampire stands over the dead body of video maker Roy Samaha and resurrects him. Then both go out for dinner.

INT. RESTAURANT—EVENING

> VAMPIRE
> I feel hungry, but with a *resistible* hunger!—a hunger that's no longer a drive but a biological need.

They order. The vampire's selection: a small salad.

> VAMPIRE
> I knew that I was being aided, granted a reprieve when I entered the church without being repelled by the sort of blasphemous voices and images that were usually inserted in my mind as soon as I trespassed into a church or a mosque. It was as if I were being guarded by an angel. When I took the wafer I did not swallow it, but placed it under my tongue; but I drank the wine. I felt then the strangest taste, and for once really understood what it means to say, "The blood is the life," or, more precisely, "The blood is the life of all flesh." It was as if it were the first time I, till then a vampire, actually tasted blood. And I felt that these few drops of wine transubstantiated into blood (of the covenant) were replacing all my addiction-inducing infected blood. I felt pure. To be pure at the Eucharist is to drink wine but taste pure blood, one that is not mixed with wine, indeed to taste blood with such intensity and irrevocability that one no longer recalls that what was poured in the chalice was wine (better not to taste blood at all at the Eucharist but to simply be drinking wine than to experience a mixing of wine and blood; the only pureblood Christian is not the one who has unmixed ancestry but the one who at the Eucharist drinks wine but tastes pure blood). I've been described prior to my resurrection as a *ḥayawān* (which is usually understood to solely mean *an animal*) by various Lebanese people—probably on account of the savage way I attacked my victims while I was driven by an irrepressible hunger. It is true that the first few times I had a sort of Deleuze and Guattari becoming-animal,

but this becoming soon degenerated into a drive. The drive was linked to all sorts of images and fantasies related to the unconscious, so that it was inaccurate to speak at that point about an animal or even a becoming-animal. Though it would be paradoxical, it is likely that now that I have achieved life everlasting through Jesus Christ, I will no longer be called *ḥayawān* by mortals notwithstanding that *ḥayawān* is "an inf. n. of *ḥayiya*, like *ḥayāt*, but having an intensive signification … and that *fa'inna aldār al-'ākhira lahiya al-ḥayawān* in the Qur'ān means [*And verily the last abode is*] the abode of *everlasting life*: or *the life that will not be followed by death*: or *much life*; like as *mawatān* signifies *much death*."

His cellular phone rings.

> BELOVED LOVER (V.O.)
> I've just realized that in the two films we've already watched together, *Hiroshima mon amour* and *Last Year at Marienbad*, the protagonists have no names, or at least we are never told their names. And then I realized to my utter bafflement that I have never called you, that I still don't know your name!

> FORMER VAMPIRE
> Yahya.

EXT. ROAD—EVENING

Jalal Toufic hails a taxicab. It happens to be the one driven by the other vampire.

> JALAL TOUFIC
> To the airport, please.

On the way to the airport, Toufic starts reading a newspaper.

> VAMPIRE
> Anything remarkable?

> JALAL TOUFIC
> Yet another suicide car bombing of a funeral in Iraq! I might see the logic that could lead to such a condemnable attack were it perpetuated by members

of some perverse extremist Christian sect: "If you wish to bury the dead, we'll help you attain the condition of possibility of doing so—that you be dead—hasn't Jesus Christ said, 'let the dead bury their own dead'?" But what grounds can some who profess to be Muslims provide for perpetrating such an inconsolable atrocity (since it attacks the very work of mourning)?!

EXT. AIRPORT—EVENING

The vampiric driver reaches the airport and drops off his customer. But then instead of parking his car in the arrival zone, he parks it in the departure parking lot. He then buys a ticket for Iraq. While waiting for boarding at the departure gate to Istanbul, Jalal Toufic watches the TV monitor present in the hall. It shows images of Marwan Hamadé, who narrowly escaped an attempt on his life on October 1, 2004, following his resignation from the government upon the extension of President Emile Lahoud's mandate; Hamadé is referred to as "the living martyr." Toufic writes in his notebook: "While resurrected Lazarus can be accurately referred to as a 'living martyr,' Marwan Hamadé certainly cannot. Beyond being ridiculous, such a description of Hamadé is symptomatic of an ongoing change of Beirut from a city that's hospitable to the undead to a mundane city, one where the undead, no longer able to remain keyed on it since it is devoid of ruins, of labyrinths, are replaced with cheap simulacra of them. I would imagine that were there presently a vampire in Lebanon, he would soon have to leave to some country in the midst of a civil war or war that has produced labyrinthine ruins and *jouissance*, thus hospitable to him—or be granted the grace of being resurrected. If he is unable to leave in time, he would cease even to haunt, die (the second death), like the gods died because the world was no longer hospitable to them." He glimpses the man who unbeknownst to him is a vampire heading to the adjoining departure gate to Baghdad.

> JALAL TOUFIC
> (mutters)
> "As soon as I was able to use that word, I said what I must always have thought of him: that he was the last man."[418]

Over-Sensitivity[419]

Author's Note to this Volume's Edition of *Over-Sensitivity*

The sections "Credits Included," "The Subtle Dancer," and "Radical Closure," pages 56-154 of the second edition of *Over-Sensitivity* (Forthcoming Books, 2009), have been cut from the edition of the book for this volume, since they have become part of my books *The Withdrawal of Tradition Past a Surpassing Disaster* (Redcat/Forthcoming Books, 2009; the book collected my writings on the concept indicated by its title); *The Dancer's Two Bodies* (Sharjah Art Foundation, 2015; the book collected my writings on dance); and *Radical Closure* (National Gallery Singapore, 2020; the book collected my writings on the concept indicated by its title), respectively.

Dedicated to the Jalal Toufic who wrote the first edition of this book

Over-Sensitivity

Life is too short to be lived[420]

Unrequited Love's
Enigmatic Messages

Why does the woman he takes to be Gavin Elster's wife, Madeleine, appear so seductive to Scottie in the first part of Hitchcock's *Vertigo*? Is it because of her "beautiful phony trances" while reportedly possessed by a dead ancestor? No, it is because, while Judy, the woman impersonating Madeleine, knows that Scottie is spying on her and, in the process, falling in love with her (she uses this knowledge to mislead him into testifying that Madeleine committed suicide), Madeleine does not know that he is following her (in the guise of her impersonator) and falling in love with her (in the guise of her impersonator), indeed is unaware of his existence let alone requiting his love for her (in the guise of her impersonator).[421] This coexistence of keen awareness and unsuspecting ignorance, of requited and unrequited love is seductive, whereas disavowal and hysterical dissociation are not.[422] Consequently, Madeleine's death unravels the seduction; indeed, following Madeleine's death, although Scottie remakes Judy into how she looked when he loved her as Madeleine, he does not continue to find her seductive.

Unrequited Love's
Enigmatic Messages
(*continued*)
Dedicated to Jean Laplanche

One of the rare instances in which the number three produces an exquisite love story occurs in an episode of Pasolini's *Arabian Nights*. At one level, a woman, 'Azīza, loses her would-be husband, her cousin, 'Azīz, to another woman, Budūr; at another level, and while doing so, 'Azīza becomes enamored of Budūr without ever meeting her in person, but the latter does not appear to reciprocate her love, 'Azīz merely serving as the unwitting messenger between the two.

On his wedding day, 'Azīz remembers that he forgot to invite his best friend to the wedding, so he heads out to do so—at the start of the episode he is already a messenger. Perspiring profusely in the heat of the day on his way to his friend, he sits in an alley to rest. Unexpectedly, a kerchief alights on him from above. He looks up, searching for its source. His eyes meet those of a beautiful woman at a window. While looking at him, she puts her forefinger in her mouth, then joins her middle finger to her index finger and lays them between her breasts while pointing them downward, whereupon she shuts the window. He stays under her window, hoping that she will reappear. At sunset, despairing of seeing her again that day, he heads home. There he discovers that, as a consequence of his absence, his father postponed the wedding for a year and all the guests have left. He starts weeping. When 'Azīza inquires what happened to him, he tells her: "I've fallen in love with a woman"! He mimics the woman's gestures to her and asks her: "What does it mean?" 'Azīza interprets them for him according to what must be some "shared code or interpretive rule"[423]: "The finger in the mouth means she's chosen you to be her body's soul. Two fingers between her breasts means: return in two days to ease her heart." When he goes to see Budūr two days later, she does not show up at her window. Did 'Azīza misinterpret the message? Frustrated, when he returns home, he hits her. Unfazed, 'Azīza interprets Budūr's failure to appear at her window as a test of the sincerity of his love. Exasperated, 'Azīz yells: "Love drives you wild! You can't eat or sleep!"[424] She concurs: "I know. These are the signs of love." It soon becomes manifest that she interprets the messages accurately for 'Azīz, since Budūr does indeed show up at her window the next night, and since her interpretation of Budūr's new gestures are born out. But what is 'Azīza's translation of Budūr's enigmatic messages as far as she herself is concerned? Taking into consideration that the signifier of Budūr's messages is a "'compromised signifier,' in the dual sense that it is *a* compromise, like the symptom, as well as being *compromised by the unconscious* of its originator,"[425] 'Azīza, at least initially, translates the enigmatic message as indicating that Budūr reciprocates her love—albeit unconsciously: "The enigma leads back, then, to the otherness of the other; and the otherness of the other is his response to his unconscious, that is to say, to his otherness to himself."[426] Do the signs of love, "you cannot eat or sleep," persist on the night 'Azīz is supposed, at long last, to meet Budūr rather than merely glimpse her through her window? No. At the garden on the outskirts of the city described by 'Azīza as the interpretation of one of Budūr's signs, he finds a table laden with numerous kinds of food and drink; while waiting for Budūr, he ends up eating and drinking and then falls asleep! Does he actually love Budūr since he eats and sleeps that night? It would appear not to be the case. When he wakes up, he finds a dagger and a coin on his belly. Does Budūr really love him? If she did, how could she, who presumably yearned for him, resist waking him, thus postponing their union? When he returns home, he asks 'Azīza what the dagger and coin mean. "The coin is her right eye, the eye one swears by. The dagger means she has sworn to kill you if you disappoint her again tonight." When he is on the point of going to his next appointment with Budūr, 'Azīza entreats him: "When you leave her, after ... having done what you want ... recite these lines: 'In the name of God, what to do when love becomes my master?'" This time, he waits for Budūr till dawn, at which point she indeed shows up. Because the words 'Azīza asked him to recite do not directly concern him, all the more so since in his case love has not become master, he forgets to say them to Budūr after having sexual intercourse with her. When he returns, elated, in the morning, 'Azīza does not ask him what happened, but rather: "Did you recite the lines?" He excuses himself: "I forgot; I was looking at this scroll she gave to me." "May I have it?" "Yes, if you like it"—was the scroll, then, through the detour of 'Azīz, destined for 'Azīza? She entreats him while weeping, "Tomorrow, before leaving her, promise to recite those lines." "I promise." The next day, after having sexual intercourse with Budūr, he remembers to recite 'Azīza's lines to her. Budūr's response: "He who loves must hide his secret and be resigned to it." When he returns home, 'Azīza again does not ask him what happened between him and Budūr but rather: "Did you recite them?" "Yes." He then conveys Budūr's response to her. She responds: "He has tried to resign himself, but his heart was broken by an impossible passion." She entreats him: "Tomorrow, as you leave, recite those lines to her." Budūr's response to these relayed words is: "If he cannot resign himself, he might as well be dead." Again when 'Azīz returns home, 'Azīza's immediate question is: "Did you say my lines to her?" When he relays Budūr's latest words to 'Azīza, who has been manifesting the same symptoms of love that he had initially, that is, a disinclination to eat and sleep, her response is "We hear and obey. Say goodbye to her who has stymied my love." The ostensible interpretation of "who has stymied my love" would be: who has stolen my would-be husband from me. But the translation of the enigmatic message would be: who has frustrated my love for her by her ostensible unrequited love! What is the last thing 'Azīza does before her foretold death? She takes the scroll out of the box where she has laid it and stares at it protractedly. When 'Azīz confirms to Budūr, "The girl who recited those lines has died," she responds first with the ambiguous answer "If I had known about her, I would not have let you near me," which may imply an acknowledgment of 'Azīza's love for her; but then continues, "May God make you weep for her as you made her weep for you," which confirms "a fact of its [psychoanalysis's] experience, namely that this message is frequently ... opaque to ... its transmitter,"[427] and implies that it is now 'Azīza's enigmatic message that fails to be properly translated by Budūr. 'Azīza's posthumous message to Budūr, "Fidelity is splendid, but no more than infidelity," functions not only as an apology for infidelity that later mitigates Budūr's punishment of 'Azīz for his infidelity to 'Azīza from outright death to castration but also as an indication that had Budūr loved 'Azīza while engaged in a sexual relation with 'Azīz such an infidelity would, all the same, have been splendid. From this perspective, 'Azīz is right when he answers his mother's question "What did you do to break her heart?" with, "I didn't do anything," for 'Azīza's heart was broken by Budūr rather than by him. 'Azīza's use of 'Azīz to have a love affair with another woman (does the detached erect golden penis at the end of the arrow that 'Azīz sends flying in the direction of Budūr's vagina during one of their sexual encounters not only foreshadow his coming castration but also function as 'Azīza's prosthetic penis?) does not explain away her absence of jealousy and vengefulness concerning 'Azīz's sexual relationship with Budūr, her saintliness; the circumstance that 'Azīz is being used as a messenger between the two women[428] does not explain his lack of guilt concerning the suffering he is inflicting on his fiancée. Nothing should link these two manners of viewing the message, interpretation and translation (to use Laplanche's distinction), that is, there should be no message between them; they have to coexist but dissociated (one should not account for one infidelity by the other).

Enigmatic Messages or Small and Petty Noise?

"Mainstream film neatly combined spectacle and narrative.... The presence of woman is an indispensable element of spectacle in normal narrative film, yet her visual presence tends to work against the development of a story line, to freeze the flow of action in moments of erotic contemplation. This alien presence then has to be integrated into cohesion with the narrative"[429] (Laura Mulvey, "Visual Pleasure and Narrative Cinema"—that there is in this essay "unfortunately much small and petty noise" contributed in no small measure to its inflated renown). In other words, "When a man stands in the midst of his own noise, in the midst of his own surf of plans and projects,[430] then he is apt also to see quiet, magical beings gliding past him and to long for their happiness and seclusion: *women*.[431] He almost thinks that ... in these quiet regions even the loudest surf turns into deathly quiet" (Nietzsche, *The Gay Science* [1882–1887], §60).[432] For someone who has often experienced the suspension of his interior monologue, and who has thus become oversensitive to the interior monologue of others, "even on the most beautiful sailboat there is a lot of noise, and unfortunately much small and petty noise" (Nietzsche, ibid.), so that it is far more probable that he would have moments of visionary contemplation regarding a horse or donkey being whipped by its coachman in a city street rather than a beautiful woman in *a wild, and rough, and stubborn wood* (Dante Alighieri, *The Divine Comedy*).

Priority Mail: The Collected Letters of Jalal Toufic, 1991–1994

Jalal Toufic
Urbana, Champaign, Illinois
September 9, 1991

To whom it may concern (knowing your love of gossip, I cannot address the letter only to you; and since I do not know the names of all those with whom you'll discuss the matter ...):

You managed not to read any part of the manuscript of *Distracted* in the one and a half years we lived together. You have mentioned with pride that several male colleagues who have a "crush" on you have recommended certain books to you and lent them to you to read. I will tell you when you'll read my book: you will do so only when one of these mediocrities gives it to you to read. And who knows, a book the writing of which contributed to demolishing a relationship may serve the furthering of dating between the *ex*-girlfriend of the writer and an x. Strange as it would seem to you, some people—I admit they are rare—prefer writers to readers!

When *Distracted* is published, do not say to any discerning person, "I lived with him for one and a half years," for when *(Vampires)* gets published he or she will know how meaningless such a statement is when said in relation to someone who was during that period dead before dying.

Jalal Toufic
Costa Mesa, California
October 20, 1991

Janalle Joseph, Chicago:

This strange nostalgia that amnesiacs or those who were amnesiacs for a while have at times for places that they have never seen, that they are seeing for the first time; in my case, California.

It is not enough to see a place over and over to become habituated to it; habit is formed not of and by what one does but by everything else that infiltrated one's attention to what one was doing.[433]

Going by bus at dawn to my friend's apartment after a sleepless night, I realized that, being extremely tired, spaced out, and sleepy, I was overlooking the scenery (something quite different from being detached from it). I felt this to be an unethical act, and I knew that something had dimmed as a result in my experience of California. As it happened, I overslept on the bus; I woke up in Balboa Island instead of in Fashion Island. The fog was covering much of the land. I walked on the pier until all the land had disappeared and one could see only the waves between the sea and the fog. One more step and the (invisible beach's) waves were no more—just a section of the pier that extended until it disappeared in the fog, the sea in the opposite direction, and at intervals a gull flying overhead, full of raw life, as if it alone could go into the fog and return. This was a grace I received: this disappearance of California gave it back anew to me.

In California, it is the density of the traffic and no longer that of the buildings along the road that clues one that one is still in the city.

Jalal Toufic
Urbana, Champaign, Illinois
October 25, 1991[434]
Amy, New York:
We frequently foolishly pay attention only to one feature, finding it accidental, and therefore consider it an obstinacy on the part of the other person to want to maintain it, cling to it. But we have to be sensitive to whether or not it is inextricably associated to traits that are irreplaceable and made thus indispensable.

For me as a person, our relationship has, to all intents and purposes, ended, despite the nostalgia that I can detect in the circumstance that, although I am particularly attracted to Mediterranean women, I now find some women who, like you, are blonde and Midwestern-looking attractive, too. But for me as a writer, the relationship has not yet ended: the nostalgia of writers is for what is being forgotten in the present of the event (other than by being disregarded through selective attention); it implies a demand for the preservation through writing not of the event in general but of what in the event could not be preserved except by being created.

Unnatural immobilizations in dance and death can allow a backward-in-time movement, so that past events can be changed. Were you to die physically before me (who has already died before dying), becoming in the death realm a superposition of possibilities, and I opted for forgery rather than history, I would inflect what will have happened to you, the *late*. But as long as one is not dealing with any of these cases, the issue is not so much to remember the past as not to slander it. For my part, and in this I remain a Shi'ite, I will not rewrite the past, for I will never consider myself one of the victors (Beckett's words on my telephone message machine: "Ever tried. Ever failed. No matter. Try again. Fail again. Fail better"). You now profess that you never loved me but merely needed me; even when *Distracted* is published, even when/if *(Vampires)* is published, and even if I become well known, it will always hold true—once more, as long as I do not

275

reach/find myself in one of the unnatural conditions mentioned above, where the very notion of truth or unchangeable past is no longer meaningful—that I loved you.

Jalal Toufic
Urbana, Champaign, Illinois
January 25, 1992
Frank Auerbach, London:
Once I thought with loathing of the over one hundred million cows in India, where many states have a complete ban on cow slaughter. I could no longer stand anything that was not, in however minimal a degree, suicidal.

Are we laconic enough for the sudden?

Being someone disinclined to sitting, I chose *JYM Seated* (1987-88) to be on the cover of *Distracted* in part because it is the one painting I have seen where the one ostensibly seated is standing. Instances of framing, whether or not the frame is visible (if we compare the left and right panels of Francis Bacon's *Triptych* [1983], we see that while the head in the right panel is glued to a visible frame, the head in the left panel is glued to an invisible one), produce one sort of exception to my dislike of sitting since the head or other parts of the body are then suspended by the frame—the other exception is sitting in meditation, especially seated Qigong, where one is to feel as if the body is suspended from the sky by a thread attached to the crown of the head at a point called the *bai hui.*

Jalal Toufic
Urbana, Champaign, Illinois
February 5, 1992
Arlene, New Brunswick, NJ:
Your nice voice marred by the static of "you piqued my curiosity." Was it out of curiosity that I called you? I am not a curious person. You arrived late for our meeting and left on time (for your train). In the restaurant, your voice reached me, despite the babble of conversations, not because it was loud but because your gestures are akin to those of a mime, hence imply the silence in which your voice propagates. Two days later, I drove while sick from New York to Urbana, the "loneliest" of places, especially during the winter school break, to, among other things, write you a letter: isn't the best place from which to write letters one that, when mentioned on the phone, "Urbana," elicits from people the response "Where?"—one then having to add, "Champaign," and sometimes even, on hearing a silence, "in Illinois," that is, one having to add the address? Unfortunately, your curiosity is an obstacle to my writing this letter to you who do not expect it.

Jalal Toufic
Chicago
May 12, 1992
Arlene, New Brunswick:
Write to me.

Jalal Toufic
Chicago
May 15, 1992[435]
Arlene, New Brunswick:
You intuitively feel that it will not work between us. One is often right in one's intuition with respect to those who follow their intuition but rarely with regard to those who often disregard "their intuition."[436]

Jalal Toufic
Chicago
May 15, 1992[437]
Arlene, New Brunswick:
I hope, since I am sending this letter only one hour after sending the other two, that it will reach you simultaneously with them.

Jalal Toufic
Chicago
May 16, 1992[438]
Arlene, New Brunswick:
Memory (with respect to someone I met once and that for a short period): I copied the *Arlene* that begins the May 12 letter—since then I have not used the Copy command (thus cannot paste anything except your name), and hence I have been unable to edit expeditiously; when I wish to change the placement of a line, I delete it and retype it where it should be.

Jalal Toufic
Chicago
May 18, 1992[439]
Arlene, New Brunswick:
You must by now have received the two envelopes containing the three letters I sent you on the fifteenth of May and the letter I sent you on the sixteenth.
Half an hour ago, people were sauntering in the nice weather outside while I was sitting by the window in a café, writing. I went to the back of the café to make a long-distance phone call. Passing the restroom, I decided to wash my ink-stained hands. Heading back to my table, I remembered that I had intended to make a phone call. When I returned to my table, it was raining outside. It was as if I

was looking at a distant place—a place to which one could make a long-distance phone call—where the weather was different.

Jalal Toufic
San Francisco
Anne, San Francisco:
Anne: An Approximation[440]
A writer may live with a person for a long time and not write anything in relation to him or her; sometimes this is due to the circumstance that that person *gave* him *writer's block*. Not to mistake this block for a passing obstruction that has to be overcome and try to write. A writer writes books but also *receives* writer's block. In *Distracted*, it is written: "You attract me fully for you attract both my writing and me"; one can supplement this sometimes by "You attract me fully, for you attract me and *give* me writer's block."

In Duras's film *India Song*, the photograph of Anne-Marie Stretter placed on the piano is of a different woman from Delphine Seyrig, the actress "playing" Stretter. This dissimilarity (while the mirror still has its natural function as a reflecting medium) relieves and prevents Seyrig from trying to embody the character, neutralizing identification—to identify with the character is to extinguish the *aparté*,[441] reduce the character to her life.

Never have I managed to know the eye color of any of the women to whom I felt a strong attraction. My answers always took the form of "either brown or black." In your case, who sometimes wear green lenses, and despite the strong attraction, for the first time I know the eye color: "either green or brown."

Had you undergone one episode of depersonalization, you would know how cruel and terrible it is to be without Anne and you would therefore most probably not have stayed away for so long.

Jalal Toufic
San Francisco
April 15, 1993
To Hope R— —, San Francisco:
Seeing a woman who strongly attracted him in a cafe or bookstore, it often happened that he did not speak to her then and there, and not only out of shyness. It was minutes after she had already left that he would go outside and try to find her: finding her then, it seemed, would change the accidental into something pertaining to fate. Her name is Stephanie, and she has a boyfriend.

I had been told separately by at least two people that San Francisco is such a small city one is bound to run again into the same person sooner rather than later or not at all. And, sure enough, I did run into Stephanie again. Or did I? Was my mistaking you for her a ruse to approach you? Stephanie is taller than you; but didn't *Vertigo*'s melancholic Scottie mistake two other women for Madeleine, he who later remakes Judy into an exact replica of Madeleine? After six months in San Francisco, perhaps it is time to ask, How big is this city? That is, will you treat my mistaking you for her as an accident, or will you treat it as a performative, becoming Hope-Stephanie R——? In the latter case, there would ensue a sudden disappearance of Stephanie.

For as long as I can remember, I felt an abhorrence of introductions through third parties, felt that one should approach others as a stranger, on one's own. The aforementioned mistaking is an exception that confirms the rule: Stephanie, whom I barely know, introduced us in her absence.

He sometimes mistook her for others, but never or rarely for herself, i.e., did not disregard her *aparté*.[442]

"Ever tried. Ever failed. No matter. Try again. Fail again. Fail better" (Beckett). What makes me not try again when dealing with the vast majority of humans is not the apprehension that I may not succeed but the certainty that I cannot fail better.

Is this letter a(nother) mistake?

Jalal Toufic
San Francisco
July 28, 1993
Richard Foreman, New York:
Apparently, it has been the same these last six years: the indifference of others remained the same, the ninety percent empty cup is still ninety percent empty. But it is as if I am now looking with a microscope at the ten percent ostensible plenum and seeing the large part of emptiness it contains; in fact, I am seeing so much emptiness—almost ninety-nine percent of the ostensible plenum is empty—that I must have reached the quantum level. This may explain why at present I keep expecting some minimal evanescent fullness in the ninety percent emptiness, that is, fluctuations. Anyone who tells me, "I am surprised you thought you would encounter anything but indifference from ninety percent of people; I never expected anything else," is part of the emptiness in the ten percent that's ostensibly full, if not of the empty ninety percent. The others' failure to read my book [*Distracted*], their reaction to it with indifference, affects my overall feeling about it *when I am not reading it*.

Since in any case the writing is "over their heads,"[443] to accentuate that: to make the writing such that they can get it only by being attuned to the -over (to those insensitive to the -over [mode], it would appear that the writing is becoming increasingly flat since almost all the style has gone into the -over).[444] Beyond the aforementioned polemical reason, the basic reason for this *over*writing is over-sensitivity: it is an oversimplification not to take into consideration the -over, whether

279

in the form of the voice-over-witness,[445] the silence-over,[446] the music-over,[447] the over-turn,[448] *over*acting and *over*reacting (in reaction to an over-dose, i.e., to what is affecting one in the mode of the -over [Arnulf Rainer's overpainting]). In Parajanov's *Ashik Kerib*, the minstrel is assigned by the two patrons of songs the most difficult exercise: to sing and play music to the deaf-mute-blind. Playing music to those who are not only deaf but also blind, and who are thus precluded even from resorting to synesthesia to hear the music with their eyes, is one way to train oneself in the -over mode, in rare cases one's song thenceforth attaining the -over, the deaf-blind *over*hearing it. (To add to his paintings the -over, for example, in the case of Arnulf Rainer, the paint or charcoal lines and scratches that affect retroactively the photos and the death masks over which they are inscribed, i.e., to achieve over-paintings, the painter may have to prepare himself by painting over paintings, that is, by painting for those who "have eyes but fail to see" the underlying layer.) Although the minstrel's playing often clearly goes out of sync in relation to the music we hear, and indeed although at times he momentarily stops moving his lips while the song continues, the audible song and music are by no means nondiegetic. The hearing people who listen to him in later scenes of the film do not hear the voice and the sounds we may project from the movements of his lips and of his fingers on the strings but the song-over and music-over (when no one is singing or playing music and yet we hear music and singing, the music is non-diegetic).[449]

Cut on movement in film should also have the following function (the same way parallel montage should at least at times manifest additional branches within the multiverse rather than simultaneous happenings within the same universe, which is its dominant, Griffith mode): a chance of freedom. To become nothing but cuts on movement. As they say in Zen, after *satori*, mountains revert to being mountains,[450] in other words, mine, everything reverts to how it was, except that it does so with cuts on movement. We find a playwriting variant of this *cut on movement* (a film term) in the work of the director of *Radio Is Good, Film Is Evil*, for instance in *Blvd de Paris*, where, on page 61 of *Reverberation Machines*, we encounter three consecutive "RHODA"s (ascriptions of dialogue lines), one following the other, without there being another character's speech in between; not to consider that this merely indicates pauses between the phrases Rhoda says in the three instances, for when there is a pause, it is indicated as such ("[*Pause*]") in the space under the character's name (page 66). Hence the beauty of the RHODA that immediately follows another "RHODA" and begins with "[*Pause*]" (page 60). It is not easy to achieve these instances; one of the criteria for discerning whether they have been achieved is their having induced neither a breakup of thinking in the form of lapses of consciousness nor thought blocking. The second and third of the consecutive "RHODA"s on page 61 as well as the second of the two consecutive "RHODA"s on page 60 are a call. Can/Does Rhoda over-hear that she is being called to attention, to awareness? When you write in the preface to *Reverberation Machines*, "I would hope that if these plays are presented by other directors they would feel as free as I do to assign and reassign the lines of the text," I wonder if they would manage to maintain the call "RHODA RHODA" (this unheard-of *sous-entendu* reverberation).

Two or more of your characters are at times a collaboration, one that took no time to get established. What some critics (as reported in Susan Letzler Cole's *Directors in Rehearsal*) view negatively as your dictatorial relation to the actors (you do not collaborate with them) and your "non-collaboration" with David Salle and Kathy Acker on *Blood of a Poet*, as well as your inhibition of any collaboration between the actors ("Playing a scene, actors feed emotionally off one another between themselves and deepen the psychological communication. I often stage scenes in a way that will frustrate that connection"),[451] and the circumstance that you are conjointly the playwright, designer (and, for the first plays, the one who constructed the set pieces and the props), producer, and director of the Ontological-Hysteric Theater are all to be placed within the context of your creation of characters-as-a-collaboration.[452] This amazing collaboration does not (and is not intended to) occur every time two characters are joined in a response (in a few cases we are dealing merely with a simultaneous response by the two characters), but mainly when one character does not rest after the move he or she made but is part of the response to it. Normally, the other interlocutor provides an occasion for one to rest until he or she has responded—this rest coexisting with the additional tiredness resulting from the passing identification of each interlocutor with the other in order to make the appropriate next move,[453] hence with his or her having to do double the moves. The non-identification of the audience with the character in your theater is produced not only through the non-identification of the actor with his/her character (itself achieved through the actor's neutral voicing of the lines, which, in many instances, have already been said by the TAPE; the character's referring to himself or herself in the third person,[454] etc.); but also, more importantly, through the inhibition of the aforementioned momentary identification of one character with the other characters in order to make his or her move (it is only through this neutralization of the dimension of the future that "*everything* you do is a brilliant decision, especially if it is something stupid."[455] Cage and Cunningham's collaboration, to which the latter quote would apply equally well, also presupposed this absence of identification and projection: for compositional procedure, both artists used chance operations). Are we to expect an extra need for relaxation when the characters do not rest once they have made their move that involves no momentary identification with the other, but often respond to it?

Not at all. What we are to expect is a body that "absents itself from nothing except rest, that is, from absence"; "it is in the same movement that one intuits this body and that one knows that one is *always* tired, with a weariness that admits of no rest"[456] (it is in this way that I would interpret what the TAPE calls Kate's "continual fatigue" in *Penguin Touquet*).[457] Your work managed to make one feel that the presence of two characters as a collaboration, for instance, the KATE & DIANE who answer(s) KATE's "Look what a strange effect what I've eaten is having on my foot" with "I'm not interested ...,"[458] is not facile (on the contrary, is utterly rigorous) but that the joining of lying down to rest and "CONTINUAL FATIGUE" (TAPE: "SHE IMMEDIATELY LAY DOWN AS A RESULT OF HER CONTINUAL FATIGUE") probably is (TAPE's next words, "WRONG, WRONG, WRONG, WRONG, YOU HAVE NOT UNDERSTOOD A SINGLE THING," which have a different typography than those of the characters, may be applying across the intermediary lines of the characters to the TAPE's previous words). It may be that both kinds of exchange enclose the same amount of tiredness: in one, I both do not indulge in the momentary identification with the other and do not rest once I have made my move, collaborating with the other on the next move; in the other kind, I have made a momentary identification with the other in order to decide beforehand which move to make in response to his or hers—hence have performed twice the number of moves in one move—but rest when it is actually the other's turn to respond. Nonetheless, the former tiredness has a different origin and is dissociated from rest. How many times have we heard writers, painters, and filmmakers say that what they want from writing or painting or filmmaking is to "surprise themselves." You recreated this "surprising oneself": in *Penguin Touquet*, in answer to Gretel's question to David as to whether he has been in awe of doctors, "we" get: DAVID: "Yes." KATE & DAVID: "I knew it. I knew it!"[459]—or, David surprising himself. We encounter an idiosyncratic, untimely sort of collaboration rather frequently in the case of the solitary.[460]

To someone who patted him on the shoulder in the Elbow Room, in San Francisco, and apologized, "I'm sorry; I thought you were my friend," he replied (with words attributed to Aristotle): "Oh, my friend[s], there is no friend." I would be overjoyed were you to accept my friendship.

Postscript: In your blurb for my second book, (*Vampires*): An Uneasy Essay on the Undead in Film (1993), you wrote: "Jalal Toufic is an amazing writer. He documents the moves of consciousness in a way that leads the reader ever deeper, from impasse to illusion to new impasse—turning the trap of 'what can't be named' into a true paradise." Can I still do a second edition of (*Vampires*)? Can there be a second edition of paradise?

Jalal Toufic
San Francisco
September 25, 1994
Carolee Schneemann, New Paltz, NY:
We're basically constantly talking—the interior monologue (it is no longer enough for me to enter a hall where everybody is engrossed in his or her "thoughts" to feel that I am in a silent place—I still feel the noise produced by all the interior monologues). That must be why even writers who are very exacting in relation to their writing (including the epistolary one) find it nonetheless not that objectionable and more or *less* easy to chat. I think that were one to manage to stop the interior monologue, words would become enigmatic ("An oak tree in the garden"—Joshu's reply to a monk's question as to why Bodhidharma came to China), or people will have the same difficulty speaking as writers have writing.

What I find remarkable in many a silent film is the absence not so much of talk—we get in intertitles a summary transcription of what the characters say—but of the interior monologue: when the characters are not talking, I have the feeling that no interior monologue is going through their minds. More importantly than and before making the characters' voices audible to us, the talkies gave the characters interior monologues, made them hear themselves. Since the interior monologue is a static that dims our gestures, its absence in silent films lets the gestures exist in all their vehemence (hence this vehemence and even the frequent seeming exaggeration should not be solely ascribed to a different style of acting, one that is still too influenced by theater—I who like subtlety also like the sharp gestures that happen in the absence of the interior monologue).

In David Lynch's *Twin Peaks*, Cooper's habit of speaking his thoughts into a tape recorder that he always carries with him functions as a (Lynchian) manner of implying that when he is not doing so, no interior monologue is going on in his mind (from this perspective, it would be weak, indeed wrong, on Lynch's part to have the character use the recorder as a playback machine, i.e., to show either Cooper or another person listening to what it had recorded earlier)—this absence of the internal monologue is the main reason for the frequently blank face of Cooper.

What is prayer but the most intense inner recollection[461] (one that often leads others to ask us: "What are you thinking of?") in the absence of any interior monologue?

Jalal Toufic
San Francisco
November 20, 1994
Dana R— —, Austin, TX:
When one has lived in solitude for a long time, one tends to forget

how much one is thrown back on oneself in the introductory stage of a new relationship—for the other person wants to know one. Were one to manage to do away with the internal monologue, would the other person still ask one to introduce oneself? Would the very idea of saying "I don't know you" cross the other person's mind then? Or does the other person find the notion and the right to ask one about oneself in the circumstance that one keeps talking to oneself and mentioning oneself in the internal monologue (during mild drunkenness, because of the absence of one's interior monologue, one of the most difficult things to maintain is the belief in the curiosity of others)?

The living woman in T. S. Eliot's *The Love Song of J. Alfred Prufrock* is found settling a pillow by her head to sleep when she encounters the dead. What is this sleepiness that takes hold of us in the "presence" of the dead (and, when we do not actually sleep then, what is this doubt that assails us during or following the encounter with the dead as to whether we are dreaming or were dreaming, i.e., whether we are/were sleeping?)? What do the living want to know? Is it what the dead would want to tell them (isn't it a sure indication of love when the revenant still wants and attempts to tell some living human about the realm from which he is coming not in the cryptic language of the dead [for instance: "*Recreat. Recreat xangoran temr e xangoranan. Naza e fango xangoranan. Inai dum. Ageai dum*"462] but in the language of the living?)? Or would they respond the way the woman in Eliot's poem hypothetically does, "That is not it at all, that is not what I meant, at all"? Why would the dead want to tell us about death when, as mortals, we are in part already there, when a part of us is always there (this is confirmed by the circumstance that, due to the trance that takes hold of one at the threshold between life and death and that makes one miss the transition, the version of one in the death realm never moved there at any point and therefore must have always been dead)? Is it because that part is suffering from depersonalization, derealization, the autonomous association of words, frequent amnesia and dissociation, etc., thus often unable to comprehend, let alone articulate, what it is undergoing? "Tell you all," Lazarus says in Eliot's poem, and would that "all" not also include himself? Did Lazarus come back to tell himself about death? And did he find himself sleeping then (that has always been a motive for our self-discipline: that we would not sleep when we come back from death to tell ourselves, too, about it)? In a vampire film, the woman would be settling her pillow by her head because, hypnotized by the vampire, she is sleepy, but you during our last two conversations—and the one in the poem—why were you settling a pillow by your head, why were you so sleepy? What disclosure were you thus trying to elude? I have come across so many examples of such instances of sleepiness (that the guards in *Hamlet* do not feel sleepy or fall asleep when confronted with the revenant with unfinished business, the ghost come back to ask for revenge, implies that he is not from the death realm proper but from the *barzakh* between the world of the living and the death realm), I sometimes have the impression that the reason we sleep at all is because someone has come back once more from death to tell us about that realm. If, yet again, we want to excuse the living, we can consider that the woman actually wished to hear about death but the dead's "presence" drained her of her energy. How? Did the dead, as in vampire films, hypnotize her and then suck her blood (how very bored I am with all the big, deep eyes of charismatic persons or entities that stare into the victim's eyes in vampire films to willfully hypnotize him or her)?[463] Not at all; the dead neither spoke—had the dead spoken, we could attribute the sleepiness of the living woman present then to a defense against hearing about the anxiety-inducing death realm—nor stared into her eyes to hypnotize her but simply stood next to the bed, tall but slightly hunched over her, while she, like the flower that withered (in time-lapse) as the vampire passed it, felt (largely) drained even of time. The scene thus discloses neither some guardian angel watching over us in our sleep, nor the vampire standing next to the victim after satiation with his blood, but some revenant come to talk to us, to tell us, and most probably also himself, about the realm he came from,[464] but already having by his mere "presence" drained us of our energy and our readiness to listen and perhaps also drained a part of himself of its energy and readiness to talk, making us sleep and giving him his demeanor of a somnambulist. The dead are not charismatic. But then how limited is every charismatic person; part of the attraction of those who are considered charismatic is that the dangers that they envelop are ultimately limited ones. As for the dead, they inspire in us awe because of an apprehension of the far greater dangers they suggest, and they are considered dull by us because they are so drained by themselves as to have neither the energy nor the time to warn about those incredible dangers (for example, the labyrinth).[465]

Dead Air

The American president George H. W. Bush asserted on October 15, 1990, concerning Saddam Hussein: "We're dealing with Hitler revisited":[466] a matting phenomenon. Instead of maintaining an *am Saddam*, Saddam should have countered the *amBush* constituted by this abstraction from Hitler's historical context[467] by, for instance, appearing on TV made-up as Hitler and, through the special effects that made possible the compositing in Woody Allen's *Zelig* (1983), in the company of Nazi generals. (The reports of sightings of Hitler months and even years after the end of World War II[468] should have been translated to Arabic and mentioned on Iraqi TV[469] and in Iraqi newspapers.) Saddam Hussein did nothing of the sort, lacked any humor. The Iraqis did not apprehend one of the implications of Bush's comparison of Saddam Hussein to Hitler: the main mass medium in their country would become the one used in Germany in the 1930s and '40s: radio; indeed, in the first hours of the war, over ninety percent of Iraq's electrical capacity was taken out of service by air attacks, with the result that virtually all televisions were rendered inoperative. Moreover, the trauma of the devastating war must have crazed many Iraqis, a number of whom may as a result have experienced a radio functioning of the world: auditory hallucinations (mainly voices); *thought-broadcasting* (of both one's thoughts and the thoughts inserted in one); the impression that the sound volume is being turned up or down ("During the last while back I have noticed that noises all seem to be louder to me than they were before. It's as if someone had turned up the volume"[470]); thought blocking (as if the mental radio that each one of us is to himself in the interior monologue has been turned off[471]).[472] While the US-led coalition was using smart bombs,[473] ones that moved and redirected themselves autonomously, the obscene amount of destruction inflicted on Iraq must have driven at least one Iraqi to go mad and to consider that the broadcaster was addressing him or her specifically:[474] a smart radio.[475]

Radio, like film and TV for images and sounds (André Bazin: "The photograph proceeds by means of the lens to the taking of a veritable luminous impression in light—to a mold. As such it carries with it more than mere resemblance, namely a kind of identity.... The cinema ... makes a molding of the object as it exists in time and, furthermore, makes an imprint of the duration of the object"[476]), is usually the mold of sounds and their duration. Radio, like TV and film, embalms, though not the dead (Bazin: "If the plastic arts were put under psychoanalysis, the practice of embalming the dead might turn out to be a fundamental factor in their creation. The process might reveal that at the origin of painting and sculpture there lies a mummy complex"[477]) but the living, for the dead on radio were once alive. But is that all there is to it? No; as long as one harbors an unconscious or is reduced to one (the dead), that is, as long as one is not a lucid awakened, one sends more than one broadcasts. Hence one has to acknowledge what one is unaware that one sent. This acknowledgment should induce one to help those with whom one is interfering, whether one knows it or not: the mad, the dead, and some of those in other altered states of consciousness. Most broadcasters are unaware that they are broadcasting to the mad, who died before dying, the other dead air, not "an unintended period of silence or interruption of the audio or video signal during a radio or television broadcast" (*Oxford Dictionary of English*, 3rd ed.), but "the voices" and the "free associations" to what the speakers are consciously saying.

One has to devise an alarming scheme that can induce the living—the vast majority of whom misconstrue their condition of mortals as implying only that they are going to die organically at some future date rather than that they are dead while alive—to become acutely conscious of their obscene unconscious interference with the mad, who died before dying (physically), and the dead, and therefore to try to counteract this interference. What intermediary to involve in such an alarming scheme? The most appropriate intermediary is not a medium (Kurosawa's *Rashomon* [1950]), since the latter does not connect to the dead but to the dead's messenger, the ghost; but an art of radio that lets itself be interfered with by a dead air it constructs. Here are two examples of the latter. A radio station intentionally broadcasts a signal that simulates one that would result from the mixing of what the listener assumes to be its own unadulterated signal with that of another station broadcasting in a different language. The latter broadcast, spoken by a different broadcaster, would, uncannily, be a translation of what the announcer is saying on the first station. If the listener tries to get a better reception of the second station, he or she will hear a different subject being addressed by the second announcer. This uncanny effect should be intentionally induced by the two stations, which would, unbeknownst to the listeners, be collaborating. This inducing of the uncanny in the listener or spectator should not to be limited to radio or TV but has to be extended to life, too. Have a recording of your voice asking your roommate to remove the boiling water from the burner or yelling at your cat to stay away from a vase; then, *while* talking to someone on the phone, play back your recorded voice. Is there a danger that such practices may induce paranoia in the listeners? Yes, there is; but what is required is to immerse people, for a modicum of time, in a different mode of mental functioning so that they will be unsettled enough to be clearer about the plight of more than one hundred thousand seriously mentally ill[478] homeless people in the United States[479] (where many have experimented with psychedelics and hence know what it is to undergo a psychotic episode).[480] A "nice" old woman told me that she is for long-term rather than alleviating measures when it comes to dealing with the homeless. Would a thousand years count as "long-term"? When the old woman came across him the next day, the psychotic homeless exclaimed: "I haven't seen you in ages!" In response to her uncomprehending interjection, "But it's only been a day since I've last come across you!" he recited these words whispered to him by one of the voices "in" his head: "A day the measure of which is a thousand years of what you count" (Qur'ān 32:5)!

One possible way to respond to the dearth of images from the (1991) Gulf War[481] is to have one of the characters in a film "on" that war describe the events happening in the theater of operations and conclude his ostensibly imaginative description with the Durasian ostensible question in *Le Camion*, "You see?" which turns her description of the protagonist's actions and utterances, as she reads the script, into a performative creation of images and sounds through words; then have the interlocutor answer, once more as in *Le Camion*, "Yes, I see";[482] then, to the latter's affirmative response, have the former character reply in a manner similar to that of the Japanese man to the French woman's claim to have seen, by means of newsreel footage, etc., what happened in Hiroshima, "You have seen nothing in Iraq and the Kuwaiti theater of operations, nothing"[483]—not because there were no images, for the words did performatively create images; but because these images are unbearable to see, somewhat unseen even as one looks at them,[484] or because that war was a surpassing disaster, with a consequent withdrawal of some images. In Duras's *Hiroshima mon amour*, the perfect witness is the one who did not see: the Japanese man's recurrent words to the French woman after each account of what she saw in Hiroshima, "You saw nothing in Hiroshima. Nothing," makes of her the perfect witness—of the withdrawal of tradition past a surpassing disaster.

Voice-over-witness

In Claude Lanzmann's *Shoah* (1985), the use of the aural narration of two interviewees over the tracking shots of the road leading from Chelmno to the pits where those killed in the gas vans were buried underscores a separation of the ethereal voice and the archeological image[485] of a nature that contains mass graves but, indifferent to what happened, continues its normal course, with the result that grass and tall trees cover the traces of the mass graves.[486] The film separates the voice from the image/body, making it a voice-over, but only to render in a filmic way the difficulty of speaking, of releasing the voice from the body. While watching the aforementioned shot, I alternated between the following two impressions:

— The more natural this earth is, continuing its life, and the more permeable it is to all sorts of natural organisms and to the rain, the more, becoming extraordinarily dense in the presence of the hovering voice-over, it is impenetrable to the latter and can be penetrated only when one is to lay corpses in it.

— The voice cannot be delivered from this superdense earth; the only way it can reach us is as a voice-over, the same way the radiation of a black hole occurs by means of a particle that did not actually exist and never belonged to the black hole but that was released into actuality because its complementary virtual particle (the two particles conjointly appearing out of nothing) got sucked into the black hole.[487] For an equivalent of these entangled, twin voices, one buried and one appearing *ex nihilo* to the other side of an event horizon, a voice-over, one can heed the complementarity of the absence of the voices of the on-screen characters (and actors) and the presence of voices-over in Duras's *India Song*. We find the voice sucked to the other side of an event horizon also in Bergman's *Persona*, Elisabet first not wishing then no longer able to speak, having become a mute hole.[488] Nurse Alma takes the photograph of Elisabet's son from under the mother's palm, sits down facing her, and, although she has never heard about the incidents in question, proceeds to tell Elisabet about her traumatic relation with her child. How does Alma know about the specifics of Elisabet's relationship with her son? How does she know that it was at a party that Elisabet first had the notion of having a child: "It was one night at a party, isn't that so? It got late and quite rowdy. Towards morning someone in the group said: Elisabet, you virtually have it all in your armoury as a woman and artist, but you lack motherliness"? The turning of Elisabet into a mute hole implies that the information that Alma proffers with regard to Elisabet's relationship with her son was not received from Elisabet through thought-transference[489]—the flip side of the indirect transfer of thought through words from Alma to the silent Elisabet—not only because Elisabet's memories and thoughts must have been reduced to fragments of phrases or single words (a phenomenon we encounter in the case of the astronomical black hole with the reduction of our information about what falls into it to mass, electric charge, and angular momentum), for example, "Warning and timeless. Irregular. When it should have happened not as a failure. Yourself where you are. But I should do it. Not inwards. They say calm advises others. A desperate perhaps. Takes ... but where is nearest it's called ..."; but also because such information is trapped behind the event horizon. The concurrence of Elisabet, in the form of her unconvincing denial of her hatred of her son, indicates that, although what is being said by Alma in the sequence of shots in which Elisabet is shown in close-ups is by a voice that appeared *ex nihilo*, hence is not privy to the historical past of Elisabet before her becoming a mute hole, it is still the truth.[490] The *sur-vivant* can bear witness about a traumatic event only through the voice-over that appeared *ex nihilo* to the other side of the event horizon.[491] To collect historical evidence and preserve the relics and the traces (the Auschwitz-Birkenau Memorial and Museum, located outside the town of Oświęcim, Poland; the United States Holocaust Memorial Museum in Washington, D.C., etc.) is in all likelihood enough to convince future generations that the Shoah happened and that it happened in this way, refuting the revisionist questioning of the reality of the industrial-style extermination in the gas chambers; but it is not enough for one to bear witness, since one would then be already totally outside the event horizon of the Shoah. Whenever, concerning an event, the survivor who underwent it feels, "Today ... while knowing perfectly well that it corresponds to the facts, I no longer know if it is real,"[492] in order to bear witness remembering is necessary but not enough. To bear witness in such cases is a double operation: the most scrupulous historical research, the archeological excavation to reach what is buried has to be complemented, because certain traumas are mute and black holes, having an event horizon, beyond which one cannot go and return, by the voice that appears *ex nihilo*. In such traumatic circumstances, anamnesis and description are adequate only when *conjointly* words reach a performative function and the voice carrying them appears *ex nihilo*. In the case of the Shoah, it is not enough to be an eyewitness (and a voice-witness); one should also be a voice-over-witness. The attempt by the Nazis to produce a mute hole from which no information could transpire about "the final solution" to exterminate all the European Jewry both succeeded even in the case of the survivors: due to their trauma, the latter became a mute hole; and failed because of this voice-over that appears *ex nihilo* to the other side of the trauma's event horizon and is part of witnessing. What the survivor dreads when he or she is asked to bear witness to such a catastrophe is not only or primarily the pain of anamnesis and/or the pain of discovering that he or she has forgotten all or part of what he or she thought unforgettable[493] but also that he or she is asked additionally to definitively forget in order to release, this side of the event horizon, the voice-over-witness that appears *ex nihilo* (since, as in the case of black hole radiation, what is released and actualized is something that "leaves" the black/mute hole without coming from it and can do so only because its double, with which it is entangled, got imprisoned in the black/mute hole, i.e., lost [forever?]) and that can tell about the traumatic event. To the silence, to the inability of the barber Abraham Bomba to continue his narrative concerning his cutting the hair of women destined in a few minutes for the gas chambers, to Mordechaï Podchlebnik's "and let's not talk about that" regarding the Shoah, one has to respond perhaps by urging them to continue describing what took place in a subterranean manner, but only if one submits the released voice to the ordeal of the burial in this archeological but natural, cyclical earth that's indifferent to the mass graves it contained, so that a complementary, identical-sounding one may appear to the other side, *ex nihilo*—this is one of the main modes of the voice-over. It is out of nothing—a nothing different from but linked to the one to which the Nazis tried to reduce the Jews and the Roma and Sinti—that this voice appears to reminisce. Duras's *India Song* problematizes representation not simply through the dissimilarity between Delphine Seyrig, the actress playing Anne-Marie Stretter, and the photograph, placed on the piano, of the dead character Anne-Marie Stretter, but also because the voices-over that appear *ex nihilo* this side of the event horizon of the trauma contradict at times the description of some of the same events in her book *The Vice-Consul*, published six years earlier—even when what the voices describe is in conflict with the version in *The Vice-Consul*, they are telling the truth. (Though many people find *The Vice-Consul* readable—it certainly was readable before *India Song*—it has been retroactively rendered unreadable by *India Song*; to these people I, who dispute many people's reaction to many other books as unreadable, would assert: "You have not read *The Vice-Consul*" [a locution that would complement the Japanese man's response to the French woman's insistence that she saw the hospital and the museum in Hiroshima: "You saw nothing in Hiroshima" (Duras's *Hiroshima mon amour*)].) This mode of the voice-over as a voice-over-witness was preparing Duras, or else she was preparing herself through it, to deal with what happened to the Jews of Europe in the Nazi period, the extermination (*Aurélia Steiner [Melbourne]* [1979]).

Postwar Lipogrammatic Literature and Calligraphy

How to write in Lebanon when, as is shown by the shattered shop and institutional signs, we have been left with words from which certain letters are absent or that have been reduced to separate letters? Lebanese writers cannot circumvent this loss by writing in languages other than Arabic, since the words from which certain letters are absent or that have been reduced to separate letters in the shattered shop signs, billboards, trade signs of institutions, etc., are in French and English as well as Arabic. Those who have not been hit by the disaster can appreciate the separate letters or the words with missing letters just for their graphic, "aesthetic" value; but Lebanese writers shouldn't relate to them only at that level. Arabs have to take cognizance of this condition of words from which certain letters are absent or that have been reduced to separate letters, for this disaster affecting the Arabic language does not impact only persons turned schizophrenic by the Lebanese Civil War and the Israeli invasion of Lebanon in 1982 (for example, the man I interviewed in *Credits Included: A Video in Red and Green*), their speech and writing variously distorted (word salads, echolalia, etc.). Will we end up with a lipogrammatic literature—one that is the result not of some writers' self-imposed constraints not to use certain letters but of the constraint of an alphabet with missing letters produced by a decimation or devastation that affects no longer merely the material inscriptions of language (in shop signs, charred books, etc.) but language itself, and where the difficulty of the lipogram is no longer measured, as in the conventional cases, by the frequency of the omitted letter and the length of the text? To keep pre-disaster writings accessible in a language that, among other things, now has a reduced alphabet, these writings are to be translated into their lipogrammatic version.[494] Such a lipogrammatic literature would not be that of so-called decadent historical periods (for instance, that of the *Maqāmāt* of al-Ḥarīrī[495]) but of ages of disaster. In a film or video on Lebanon or Bosnia, I would not be surprised by subtitles that are either lipogrammatic or in which some words are unreadable because some of their letters are physically left out. For a Lebanese calligrapher or painter sensitive to the devastation not only of his country but also of Arab Palestine, Iraq, Sudan, etc., for the foreseeable future, calligraphy, taking its cue from the shattered shop signs in Beirut's central district, should be reserved for either the *fawātiḥ* (the separate letters that begin many of the Qur'ān's *suwar*, for instance the *Alif, Lām, Mīm* at the beginning of "The Cow" *sūra*) or the lipogrammatic version of a pre-disaster literary work.

The Ontology of the Photographic Image in the Post-Minkowski Age

Why is it that, rather than by accepting archival and documentary footage as it is, it is often only by submitting it to motion alterations (stop-motion, etc.)[496] that one can, as in Ernie Gehr's *Eureka* (1974) (the archival footage Gehr used was filmed from a streetcar in San Francisco in 1905), induce the sensation that the images are a window onto another segment of a four-dimensional universe?[497] It is probably because these alterations are akin to the ones that would be encountered outside of films in the process of gaining access to a past segment of the four-dimensional universe according to relativity. It is the circumstance that everything is preserved in a four-dimensional universe, rather than an absence of tenses in cinema, that results in the inability of the cinematic flashback to put us in the past—how, in film, past the immediate transition of the flashback we are back in the present tense. The arresting thing about cinema is not so much that it preserves time (Bazin: "At the origin of painting and sculpture there lies a mummy complex.... The film is no longer content to preserve the object.... Now, for the first time, the image of things is likewise the image of their duration, change mummified as it were"[498]) but that it sometimes makes us perceive that we exist in a four-dimensional space-time where nothing passes, where things are preserved. The ability of any indexical mode of reproduction to preserve is made possible by the circumstance that the past is already preserved, subsists. If the past does not subsist, how can anything remain, not be a fleeting fluctuation, disappear as it appears?[499] In Robert Zemeckis's *Back to the Future Part III* (1990), the photograph showing the scientist's tombstone on which is inscribed the date of death changes whenever the time traveler to the past alters certain events there, functioning as a window onto the alternative universes corresponding to the different actions that the time traveler opts for in the past; but also presenting us with what would happen were the past not preserved. I am disappointed that the medium of cinema is absent at the diegetic level in most time-travel films.[500] The following is a scene that seems to be missing from Zemeckis's *Back to the Future Part II* (1989) (it would be felicitous were a future director's cut of the film to include it): the time traveler to the future, Marty, sees a relative in 2015 looking at a home movie showing Marty's parents in 1985, the time Marty has just left; when he later goes back to the past he enters the scene he has just watched, sort of walking into a movie. It is anachronistic that, writing in 1945, that is, over three decades after Hermann Minkowski announced in his talk at the 80th Assembly of German Natural Scientists and Physicians on September 21, 1908, only a dozen years after the beginning of cinema, "The views of space and time which I wish to lay before you have sprung from the soil of experimental physics.... They are radical. Henceforth space by itself, and time by itself, are doomed to fade away into mere shadows, and only a kind of union of the two will preserve an independent reality,"[501] Bazin was still locating in his essay "The Ontology of the Photographic Image" the ontology of the photographic image in preservation instead of in being a (one-way) window onto a section of spacetime. Regarding its relation to the past, cinema is best viewed neither as providing a fictional recreation of it (as in period films) nor as making a documentary "mold of the object and its duration" (Bazin), but as an interface with what is ongoing in that other segment of spacetime.

More or *Less* Easily

Science has discovered so much and so many things even in very small spaces, but it has also known how to inject even more emptiness in them. At least some artworks should also do that.

In Herzog's *Heart of Glass*, Hias foresees an earth that is tumbling and the birth of a new earth. Are these visions? No. In relation to the visionary Hias, the entranced flesh-and-blood people at the inn are a vision, a three-dimensional one that does not require anyone to actually see it, but requires, as a correlate, the existence of a visionary.[502] In the scene of entranced Ascherl and Wudy sitting around a table at the inn, we are having to do with a cinema that, rather than trying through depth of field and/or other manners to produce an impression of three-dimensionality regarding what is two-dimensional, the film image projected on a screen, deals less with images than with things and people as three-dimensional visions. We are dealing here, within a medium that usually reduces all the senses to sight and hearing and turns things into immaterial images, with a material vision, consisting of things and people, therefore with a vision that has touch, depth, and smell among its constituents, though not through synesthesia. (In vampire films, we encounter another variant of the materiality of what is naturally immaterial: in Coppola's *Dracula*, it is the shadow of Dracula's hand, reaching the table before the hand itself, that tips the inkwell over Mina's photograph.[503]) In *Heart of Glass*, vision is split between being a (quasi-)memory in the case of the hypnotized (there is such a delay between the image and its registration in the consciousness of the hypnotized person that in their relation with the objects and people they encounter they are dealing less with perception than with memory—with the consequence that the entranced person is constantly troubled by forgetting what he or she is seeing) and being the physical event itself in the case of the visionary Hias; between, in the case of the entranced, being doubly indirect, the quasi-memory of a subjective image of the event, and, in the case of visions, being things themselves, hence having nothing to do with point-of-view shots.[504] One of the countermeasures to the substitution of reality by media images is this visionary reality that short-circuits the image. One consequence of this materiality of vision and its detachment in relation to the visionary is that Hias can be in his own vision (this counterbalances the absence of the vampire in the mirror in Herzog's *Nosferatu*). Is there simultaneity of the object of one's sight and oneself? While it seems to be the case, in actuality, due to the finiteness of the speed of light (the speed of light in a vacuum, c, is 299,792,458 meters per second), in usual sight what is seen is already in the past of the one looking. Yet in those cases where the visionary is inside his or her vision, there is, exceptionally, simultaneity of the object of one's vision and oneself.

Doesn't the double strike one as radically uncompromising because he gives the impression that his gestures don't betray any ambivalence at all?

In the shot of the librarian flipping the index cards in Patrick Bokanowski's film *L'Ange*, the music at first is not in sync with the action and then continues after the librarian stops flipping the cards. This is not a choreographic failing of the filmmaker (one that would remain non-diegetic) but is an indication of the continuing urge, of the persisting compulsion/impulse, that is being resisted.

Since it is easy to forget when viewing an animation film that puppets and dummies are not moved by an internal "will" and impulses, we are reminded of this in the films of the Brothers Quay: explicitly in *Street of Crocodiles*, where initially the puppet has a string attached to his hand; implicitly in their other films, where the filaments traditionally connected to the puppet are displaced to lines in the wallpaper and to ticklish hair (*Rehearsals for Extinct Anatomies*), to the threads of the perspectival representation (*Anamorphosis*), and to the many ropes moving on pulleys in *Street of Crocodiles*.

Some musical works manage to make one hear distinctly the sounds of the various instruments not occasionally but throughout the work, none of the sounds turning sooner or later into background, indistinct ones. Some of these musical works manage to conjoin the absence of such a background of indistinct sounds with a subsistence of the sounds—this subsistence is the kind of background I affirm. Such musical works are experienced as abundantly layered since they *creatively* make the listener discover that sounds persist (other works' use of repetition and refrains is sometimes an attempt to occult a subsistence one intuits). The danger then is to mistake what is end-less for what is eternal—a musician creates also to remember that the subsisting sounds had a beginning; indeed, a musician is able to create only because the subsisting sounds started at some point. The silence in such musical works does not result from the extinction of the sounds but is coexistent with these subsisting sounds, an indica-tor of their historicalness, denoting that they began.

To live the moment is to know that it subsists and that one leaves it only in a lapse of consciousness, if not of being. To live the moment is to reach the stage where an extended awareness is coexistent but parallel to an extended, indefinite lapse of consciousness.

One responds to generosity by *trying* to take its measure. Going beyond is intrinsic to generosity, so that one has to discern how such going beyond what is adequate has surpassed what one reckoned it to be at first—one cannot respond to generosity except by being generous.

Viewing things in terms of an oeuvre, one sometimes discovers that a director, while making other films, was all along, sometimes in whole scenes, sometimes in shots, making an extra film (one that will not be included in his official filmography), for instance, a vampire film (in the latter example, this would be felicitous, since such films deploy in their diegesis action at a distance and haunting).

I am for an impressionistic cinema, one in which impressions play an influential role. An impression may be confirmed through an explicit later shot or scene (irrespective of whether such confirmation was intended or not by the filmmaker).[505] It is more and more such impressions that strike me, impressionable witness, as foreshadowing. In Satyajit Ray's *The World of Apu* (1959), on his way home from work, having just finished reading a letter he received from his wife, a happy Apu finds the neighbor's small child quite close to the train tracks and carries him away from them; while this shot does not affect in a causal way what will happen later, it implants a sensation of absence—*where is the mother?*[506]—that links poignantly with Apu's learning a few minutes later that his wife died during childbirth.

Gerhard Richter's paint covers various landscapes in his *A Calendar for 1990*. Are there seasons for the paint that can cover a landscape?

When the Prophet Muhammad, along with Abū Bakr, migrated from Mecca to Yathrib circa September 622, he left behind ʿAlī b. Abī Ṭālib to sleep in his bed to make the many Meccans who were plotting to assassinate him believe that he had not left Mecca yet. Anxious for Muhammad's safety, if not also for his own life, did ʿAlī spend a sleepless night? Or did he fall asleep at some point during that night? If he fell asleep, did the Prophet Muhammad appear to him in the dream sleeping in his bed? If the Prophet Muhammad appeared to him in the dream sleeping in his bed, then, taking into consideration the following tradition traced back to the Prophet on the authority of Abū Hurayra, "Whoever sees me in a dream then surely he has seen me for Satan cannot impersonate me [*lā yatamaththal fī ṣūratī*]"[507] (*Ṣaḥīḥ al-Bukhārī*), Muhammad would have thus confirmed, in and through the dream, what he, a truthful man, had led his enemies to believe, that he was sleeping in his bed (while being paradoxically at another place at "the same time"—to be more accurate, he would have been at "the same time" *in* two paradoxical places, with Abū Bakr in the cave that appeared to their pursuers to be uninhabited since cobwebs covered its mouth, and in a dream, the dream of ʿAlī).

The indistinguishableness of who wrote what in a collaboration is to be judged neither by whether there no longer subsist for the readers nor indeed for the collaborators themselves stylistic markers by which they can differentiate, in some cases very easily, who wrote what, nor by the frequency of the use of the *we* instead of the *I*, but rather by whether the effects of certain sections of the text on its undersigned authors, for instance, in the case they are overflowing with *jouissance*, being subject to a corresponding drive; and/or their condition of possibility, for instance, dying before dying physically, may turn out to be attributable also to the one who ostensibly did not write on their subject (in which case, one may write the whole text oneself and it would nonetheless still be a collaboration).

What separates us is the part in each where we are indistinguishable: the extra, featureless clump (of clay) that is between the man and the woman after they separate following their fusion in Jan Švankmajer's clay animation *Dimensions of Dialogue* (1982).

I am too close to the situation not so much to be detached from it but to see that in large part I am detached from it.

In the vast majority of cases, the psychoanalyst has no free-floating attention but is mesmerized by any lapsus.

Nietzsche: "Forgetting is no mere *vis inertiae* as the superficial imagine; it is rather an active and in the strictest sense positive faculty of repression."[508] Against forgetfulness, one can perhaps resort to extreme heat: it was so hot that they lay motionless, did not have the requisite minimal energy to forget.

He now managed to forget an additional thing whenever he forgot something of importance, so that having remembered the former and gone back to fetch it or do it, he saw the latter.

Were the very possibility of memory to cease to exist, there would be no difference between past and future.

Given that the subtle dancer in the dance realm put the chalk back on the edge of the billiard table in a backward-in-time movement, so with no residual movement, one could not remember its movement away from the table and back to it (memory resides precisely in the residue), and it seemed that it was placed exactly where it was bound to be. Being precise, hitting the target is so important to some people because it gives them, sensation-wise, something close to this absence of memory: by hitting the target, one somewhat feels that the projectile has become divested not only from its spatial surroundings, but also from chronological temporality.

When mildly drunk, I have the impression of an absence of the ether, and consequently that if some objects appear nearer to me than others, this nearness is now a result of their thickness: a bulky sculptural object attached to the wall is nearer to me not only than a poster attached to the same wall but also than the man, thinner than the sculptural object, sitting at a table between me and the wall, and he himself is farther away than the fatter man sitting at the same table on the same plane in relation to me.

In mild drunkenness, everything is in focus; the many straws in the cup are all distinct—yet one is drunk enough not to be able to count to ten.

In mild drunkenness, even water drops on a napkin may be viewed as stains, given that one does not project away from the present in that condition, does not consider whether they will persist or not.

While it may not be productive to paint when drunk, there are a lot of still lifes in the world in that state.

In mild drunkenness, there is an absence of time and, consequently, an absolute separation between the liquor bottles on the shelf, for contiguity is due to particles from the bottles interacting. One can do nothing then but wait for a tipsy man or woman to knock the ostensibly timeless object accidentally, with the irreverence of the accidental.

When lightly drunk, I sometimes have the impression while looking at two beer glasses, one of which is empty and the other full, that I am seeing the past spatially contiguous to the present.

Mild drunkenness is propitious to description for it minimizes the internal monologue, so that one has more time to attend to each object during the eyes' pan. In a film, it would be instructive to superimpose during part of some pans the distracting images/thoughts/memories of the interior monologue (to make visible and audible why it is that one does not have enough time to observe the passing objects attentively), so that when the superimpositions are eliminated, the spectator would feel that the shot is leisurely and hence that he can see many more of its elements. It might seem that the opportunity to observe in a leisurely manner affords the observer plenty of time to find blemishes in what he or she sees, but in that state of drunkenness one finds nothing to correct: the impeccability of the billiard shot that missed; the flawlessness and utter beauty of the exclamatory gesture of disappointment of the billiard player; the impeccability of the placement of objects; the precision and impeccability of the wavering movements of the other tipsy persons.[509] When she *walked by her movement* produced violent air currents. All that is needed to sense this violence in the movement of others is to reach the state where the actions of people no longer have anything to do with one,[510] that is, the state where no kinesthetic empathy subsists—no virtual accompaniment. There are certain kinds of movements, for instance, those of Zen masters, that have already suspended our kinesthetic empathy (compassion has nothing to do with kinesthetic empathy, cannot occur while it lasts); the Zen koan "What is the sound of one hand clapping?" refers also to this suspension, each hand no longer accompanied through kinesthetic empathy by the hand of the observer.[511]

One of the segments of the Euronews TV Channel is titled *No Comment*. Is it actually a No Comment one? One can accurately consider an episode or an image a *no comment* one if it suspends the interior monologue of the viewer.

One way of accepting the saying "a picture is worth a thousand words" regarding some photograph is to take it to mean that that photograph initially arrested the viewer's interior monologue for the interval during which, on average, a thousand words go through his or her mind. It is only regarding such a picture that it is worth to subsequently write a thousand words.

A vow of silence should include the arrest of the interior monologue, one no longer talking even to oneself.

If one of the features of prayer is the suspension of the interior monologue, then in hell one cannot have such a suspension. One frequently promises during prayer, for example, that one will refrain from doing this or that, but every promise is a form of prayer: insofar as I am someone who has promised, *given my word*, I am henceforth mute, even at the level of the interior monologue, which becomes suspended.

The first thing I noticed in Wenders's *Wings of Desire* is the absence of the interior monologue in the case of the angels, in contrast to its presence in the humans. The silence referred to in *un ange passe* ("*un ange passa:* there was a pregnant pause or an awkward lull in the conversation" [Larousse, *Dictionnaire Français-Anglais en ligne*][512]) is to be related not simply to the circumstance that, floating and immaterial, the angel does not make a sound but also to the angel's absence of interior monologue. What happens to an angel when he falls? He acquires not only a material body but also an interior monologue.

I care less for the theatrical aside, which is all too often addressed to a human, all too human audience in the auditorium. I rather care for the apartness of the dancer, who, while ostensibly dancing with the non-dancer, has already been projected, as a subtle body, into dance's realm of altered space, time, and movement, a realm to which his or her seeming companion has no access; and for the aside addressed to an angel—or, compulsively, to a demon. The angel withdraws definitively, abandons the human for good if the latter is completely engrossed in what he or she is doing, whether it be good or evil, and therefore no longer addresses him in asides.[513] The portrait, often if not always frontal, is the result of an aside—to address an angel or a demon, or a writer, filmmaker, or painter. Indeed, one can view posing for a painter as a protracted aside, one that goes on for hours, days, or weeks. In the presence of an angel or demon, the writer has merely to receive and document, rather than create, the portrait manifested in the aside. In moments of weakness, of wishing to be only human, all too human, we may flee those who acknowledge our aside associated with our apartness to those who set it aside, for example, journalists.

Beyond the issue of the rightful hierarchy of angels (seraphim, cherubim, thrones, dominions, virtues, powers, principalities, archangels, angels?), we tend to have two figures of the angel: the angel as overwhelming (Rilke: "Who, if I cried out, would hear me among the angels' / Hierarchies? and even if one of them pressed me / suddenly against his heart: I would be consumed / in that overwhelming existence. For beauty is nothing / but the beginning of terror, which we still are just able to endure, / and we are so awed because it serenely disdains / to annihilate us. Every angel is terrifying" [*Duino Elegies*, trans. Stephen Mitchell]) and the angel as discreet, the guardian angel. One of the main tasks of the guardian angel is to shield the chosen from the overwhelming presence of the other angel. Did an angel appear to prophets or other humans on mountains? Yes, Jibrā'īl (Gabriel) appeared repeatedly to Muhammad on Ḥarā' (a.k.a. Ḥirā'), a mountain to the north-east of Mecca, and commanded him initially: "Recite! In the name of thy Lord who created, created the human being from a blood-clot. Recite! And thy Lord is the Most Generous, who taught by the Pen, taught the human being what he knew not" (Qur'ān 96:1–5). But the aforementioned question is not the most pertinent one when it comes to the relation of angels to mountains. The angel can appear in the form of a man: "Gabriel came to the Prophet while Umm Salama was with him. Gabriel started talking (to the Prophet) and then left. Then the Prophet asked Umm Salama, 'Who is he?' ... She replied, 'He is Diḥya' [al-Kalbī: a handsome man among the companions of the Prophet]. Umm Salama said, 'By Allāh, I did not take him for anybody other than him [i.e., Diḥya] till I heard the sermon of the Prophet wherein he informed us about the news of Gabriel'";[514] but the angel can also appear in other forms, for example, a mountain. Was that, then, a guardian angel who appeared to Moses in the form of mountain Ṭūr (a.k.a. Mount Sinai)? And did Moses, through God's Mercy, by means of the angel-as-mountain, turn aside from a sight "no one may see ... and live" (Exodus 33:18–20: "Then Moses said, 'Now show me your glory.' And the Lord said, ' ... No one may see me and live'")? "Moses ... said: 'My Lord! Show me (Thy Self), that I may gaze upon Thee.' He said: 'Thou wilt not see Me, but gaze upon the mountain!'" "Gaze upon the mountain" would here mean: turn aside toward the angel in the form of the mountain. "'If it stand still in its place, then thou wilt see Me.' And when his Lord revealed (His) glory to the mountain He sent it crashing down. And Moses fell down senseless. And when he woke he said: 'Glory unto Thee!'"

The angel, a messenger, an intermediary being, helps us maintain a distance toward this world—as well as other worlds and realms—assists us in maintaining ourselves in a *barzakh* between them.

If, in Kubrick's *The Shining*, the writer Jack Torrance seems uninterested in playing with his wife and son (his manuscript "consists" of myriad recurrences of the sentence "All work and no play makes Jack a dull boy"), it is because he has the apprehension of a more radical recreation, intuits that the latter should not be replaced by anodyne playing, for instance, the kind we see his wife and his son indulging in as they throw snow balls at each other. When reality itself plays, then it is the writer Torrance, rather than his son (who does not accept the dead twins' invitation to play with them), who accepts being part of such playing. We refused to lie, not out of morality but because we had the apprehension that a more extreme lying would be obscured were we to lie; and lo and behold, reality began to lie, that is, behold nothing.

Each of the dead has to come to the realization that he or she must be dead—the dead also has to discover and identify his or her corpse (Billy Wilder's *Sunset Boulevard* [1950]).

Where he ostensibly exists, the revenant, being dead, does not see; but, contrariwise, where he ostensibly is not, the one who survived him has the paranoid feeling that he is gazed at and ascribes this gaze that haunts him to the revenant.

Schizophrenics and mystics, who died before dying, have the right to bury their own dead ("Jesus told him, 'Follow me, and let the dead bury their own dead'" [Matthew 8:22]).

With the virtual interaction of human actors with computer-generated images matted later into the frame (Robert Zemeckis's *Who Framed Roger Rabbit* [1988]), actors in the West are more and more frequently undergoing an exile not only from the world but even from the customary artificial set, a sort of monasticism. It is these actors, most of them working in Hollywood, who are the closest to the predicament of exiles from war-torn countries or countries under dictatorial, repressive regimes.

When writers are in extreme situations, they *cannot* write; when others are in extreme situations, they have the solitude of writers. Nonetheless, it is not when both are in extreme situations that writers and those who are not writers are the most affined; rather, it is when writers can write that they are the most related through writing to those in extreme situations, that they accompany them.

Like all my books that explore other realms, for example, dance or death or the Imaginal World (*ʿālam al-khayāl*), this book is dedicated to those of its readers who take the risk of placing themselves in the conditions in which they can appreciate and (at times urgently) need the concepts it presents.

Where almost all others perceived repetition, he, more discerning, perceived permutation.

Nietzsche's Zarathustra: "'See this moment! ... Behind us lies an eternity.... Must not whatever *can* happen already have happened, been done, passed by before? And if everything has already been here before, what do you think of this moment ...? Must this gateway too not already—have been here? ... And this slow spider that creeps in the moonlight, and this moonlight itself, and I and you in the gateway whispering together, whispering of eternal things—must not all of us have been here before?—And ... must we not return eternally?—' Thus I spoke, softer and softer, for I was afraid of my own thought and secret thoughts. Then, suddenly, I heard a dog *howl* nearby. Had I ever heard a dog howl like this? My thoughts raced back. Yes! When I was a child, in my most distant childhood."[516] Within a few sentences, we move from a hypothetical deduction ("must not ...") that cannot have been based on or triggered by a memory (since in the very long time required for the tremendous number of permutations that would have had to have taken place to end up with the repetition of that particular configuration of elements the Sun would have "swell[ed] to its red giant phase ... and ... [left] the Earth a charred, lifeless, magma-covered rock," and the latter would have likely "eventually spiral[ed] into the Sun's outer layers and disperse[d] its atoms in the churning atmosphere of the dying star"[517]), but is based on a supposition ("behind us lies an eternity"), to a memory, that of the dog howl (Nietzsche's) Zarathustra had heard decades before as a child. If we stick to the mainstream cosmological model at this point, in 2021, which is that our universe began in a Big Bang 13.8 billion years ago, then it is not the case that "behind us is an eternity," thus not enough time has passed for whatever can happen to have happened many times, indeed an infinity of times, at least not in the same branch of the multiverse of Everettian quantum mechanics—were we to grant that what lies "behind us is an eternity," by basing ourselves, for example, on Roger Penrose's speculative conformal cyclic cosmology theory, or on the eternal-inflation model, according to which infinite repetitions occur across the infinite pockets or bubbles of the resultant multiverse (which itself cannot undergo repetition), then not only the scene that (Nietzsche's) Zarathustra is experiencing while he has the thought of eternal recurrence would occur again and again but all its variants, too, would have had time to occur, indeed to do so numerous times, an infinite number of times, for example: "'Behind us lies an eternity.... Must not *whatever* can happen within a finite region of the multiverse already have happened, been done, passed by before? If so, what do you think of this moment ...? Must a crossroads too not already—have been here? ... And this dead spider scorched by the sunlight, and this sunlight itself, and I and you, talking and whispering together at the crossroads, talking of eternal things and whispering of permutation and variation—must not all of us, the crossroads, the dead spider, the sunlight, and you two and me have been here before?—And ... must we not return eternally?' Thus I spoke, softer and softer, for I was afraid of my own thought regarding the eternal recurrence of the same, and, even more, of my secret thoughts concerning exhaustive permutation. Then, suddenly, I heard a shepherd laugh nearby. Had I ever heard a shepherd laugh like this? My thoughts raced back. Yes! When I was a child, in my most distant childhood." Indeed, the likelihood that he would have experienced variants of the scene is far higher than that he would experience its exact repetition. It is, then, not accidental that Nietzsche introduces in this scene revolving ostensibly around strict repetition through the thought of the eternal recurrence of the same what implies variation: the two similar howls are experienced by a child and then a forty-year-old man and are uttered by what must have been two dogs given that the average life span of a dog is less than twenty years.

Deleuze: "In Buñuel, as in Roussel, bad repetition appears in the form of inexactitude or imperfection: the introduction of the same two guests in The Exterminating Angel is on one occasion warm, and on the other frigid; or take the host's toast, which is made once in an atmosphere of indifference, the other time in one of general attention. However, repetition which saves appears to be exact, and the only one which is exact: it is when the virgin has offered herself to the God-host that the guests rediscover exactly their first position and at last find themselves free. But exactitude is a false criterion, standing in for something else.... Are there thus two repetitions which confront each other, like a death impulse and a life impulse? Buñuel leaves us in a state of the greatest uncertainty, beginning with the distinction or the confusion of the two repetitions."[518] Yes, there is a good and a bad repetition in Buñuel's The Exterminating Angel, but the example Deleuze proposes, the toast that the host gives twice, and that is once well received and another time disregarded, the guests, indifferent to it, continuing their conversations, is not felicitous, indeed is not the relevant one, since the latter is not a bad repetition but the beginning of the exhaustive permutation in a radical closure, which is a space that is absolutely sealed ... *in relation to the environs* (nothing is absolutely sealed in general: the radical closure is open to what is beyond or of a different nature than the environs, even if we understand by environs the light cone): the good repetition takes place outside the radical closure and leads, following a protracted process in which someone underwent countless recurrence (neither a good nor a bad repetition, but a requisite repetition), to his or her ending up willing the eternal recurrence of at least some of what was repeated, which the one inside the radical closure may be asked to, in turn, repeat, for example, the phrase "This is the girl" in David Lynch's *Mulholland Drive*; and the bad repetition takes the form of the failure of the addressee of the aforementioned request imprisoned in the radical closure to repeat exactly, and, if the phrase is a performative, felicitously the requested phrase or action that was externally willed to recur eternally, and/or the irruption again and again, if not countlessly, of the unwilled same entity, for example, of the saying "All work and no play makes Jack a dull boy" on the pages of the otherwise blank manuscript of the hopeful novelist in the deserted and sealed by snow Overlook Hotel in Kubrick's *The Shining*.

My mother-in-law resides in Chekka, a small town in Lebanon; spends most of the day in the kitchen; and has for decades cooked ostensibly the same few recipes in ostensibly the same manner for the same small group of people: her husband, her unmarried, younger daughter, her elder son, his two sons, and her daughter-in-law. Again and again, they would assemble for breakfast, lunch, and dinner, and each would sit in the chair closest to him or her, or the chair that happened to be still available, or the chair he or she would have selected for a while, for whatever reason (comfort, "design," color, etc.), as his or her chair, and then each would switch to another chair and yet another until each would have sat in all the chairs; and each would eat initially again and again the dish he or she relished, but which would undergo variation, on some occasions tasting better than usual and on others worse, sometimes being too salty or not salty enough, other times being over- or undercooked, and each would then grow tired of it and try another, and then another; and, when she would retell the story of the exciting beach trip to Batroun that she took with her classmates while a middle-school student, she would be dressed differently on the different occasions or emphasize a different part of the story or use a synonym of a word she'd employed in a previous retelling of her trip, and, when present during these retellings, her husband would sometimes pay attention to her, sometimes be distracted by what he had glimpsed on his cellular phone or preoccupied with the devaluation of the Lebanese pound, or would be wearing different pants, or have a different haircut, etc. Would I be putting a positive spin on this matter were I to advance that what most people who stay for years if not decades in one place, especially if it is a small town or village, are doing unawares and possibly unconsciously savoring is the exploration of the permutation of a small number of actions, utterances, etc., even when they bemoan the repetitiveness of their lives? The smaller the number of elements subject to permutation, the easier it is to savor it, possibly not just unconsciously but also consciously, and the more likely that these elements' exhaustive permutation can be accomplished (the exhausted is the one who allows ever new elements to enter the closed space in which an exhaustive permutation is happening or himself or herself introduces them, and/or who mistakes permutation for repetition and thus fails to savor it adequately, even unconsciously).

I wrote in my book *Postscripts* (2020) concerning radical closure, "By actualizing all the permutations that are possible within a space that is radically closed, I can now leave it, indeed *I can no longer stay in it however much I wish to.*"[519] I can imagine someone who has read my writings about undergoing countless recurrence as a condition for possibly ending up willing the eternal recurrence of one or more of the repeating events and configurations exclaim, "Hold on a minute, can't those who have undergone exhaustive permutation stay in the radically closed space to then experience repetition, countless repetition?" No, they can't. For one to end up willing the eternal recurrence of some event, one has to undergo repetition, indeed supposedly countless repetition, but the one in a radical closure cannot experience repetition since he or she undergoes the exhaustive variation that takes place in such a closure and so cannot repeat, and since once all the variations have been actualized he or she can no longer remain in the radical closure and hence experience repetition. If it appears that those within the radically closed space remain in it even after all the possible permutations within it have happened, with the result that a repetition of one of the previous configurations occurs, this would imply that we had not taken into consideration an extra, meta variation: the recognition by the one within the closed space of the repetition of an earlier configuration of the elements present in that space/his or her failure to recognize this repetition (which would indicate that there was, strictly speaking, no repetition, when all the levels and their variations are taken into consideration). But then there cannot be a repetition of that recognition of the repetition of a particular configuration, with the result in the case of a radically closed space that the latter then changes into a relatively closed one, thus becomes open to its surroundings, and those imprisoned in it can then, indeed have to, unless they introduce new elements in it or unworldly or otherworldly entities irrupt in it, leave it immediately, because there is nothing else to do within it ([a certain figure of] time being derived from the variation of the configurations of the existing elements, there can be no excess time in relation to the exhaustive variation of all the possible configurations, hence there can be no repetition at the level of the universe as a whole [unless what we took for *the* universe is actually a multiverse, in which case the repetition can happen across a large number of its branches but not of all of them as a whole]—which could imply that there is no totality, an impossibility of a totality). It would be most fitting for those who have undergone exhaustive permutation (including the variation in the form of the recognition by the one within the radically closed space of the repetition of an earlier configuration of the elements present in it/his or her failure to recognize this repetition) and left the enclosed space where it happened to then be *artificially* made to experience countless repetition (for example, through time travel to very similar branches of the multiverse or getting inserted in a virtual reality where the simulated people they encounter there repeat at least initially the same sentences, attitudes, and actions), ending up possibly achieving willing, that is, willing the eternal recurrence of at least one event, which results in the establishment of the epochal objective will and the disappearance of everything that cannot be willed to recur eternally.

It may happen that one of those in the radical closure recognizes that every variation but one has been accomplished and waits longingly for the final, outstanding one to occur. Once the exhaustive variation has taken place, those in the radical closure are able to leave, indeed they, who had long lost any hope of doing so and so had ceased trying, feel impelled to do so and so head again toward the ostensibly open border they had long stopped viewing as an actual exit. And yet in Buñuel's *The Exterminating Angel*, it seems that they stay in the radically closed space after the exhaustive variation has taken place, since one of them notices that the initial configuration of their positions as well as that of the objects there appears to be repeating. "'Edmundo, wait. Stay where you are.' 'What is it, Laticia?' 'I don't know—actually, I do. It's so extraordinary. How long have we been here? I don't know. I've lost track. But think how many times each of us has changed places during this horrible eternity here: like pieces on a chessboard, moved thousands of times. Even the furniture: we've moved it around a hundred times. But look now. Right now all of us, people and furniture, are exactly where we were that night. Or am I hallucinating? ... Tell me, Alvaro. Tell me, all of you!' 'It's true! I was right here. Weren't you at my side?' 'And to my left ...' 'Me, just like

I am now. And [looking at the man next to her] we were on this sofa. I held your hand in mine [she holds the hand of the sleeping man next to her]."' Some or most of them may not recognize the repetition of the initial configuration when the space began to act as a radical closure, whether because they would have been paying attention to some detail and not the big picture, or because they no longer remember that configuration since so much has changed through the exhaustive permutation, each one of them having assumed the names of all the others within the enclosure, their mannerisms, the phrases they said, etc., that they feel "an eternity" has passed. The apparent repetition of one of the configurations following what had seemed to be an exhaustive permutation implies that the alternative recognition of/failure to recognize this repetition is one more variation to be undergone for a truly exhaustive permutation to have been accomplished and for them to leave: if the ostensible repetition is initially recognized, then they cannot leave the radical closure until it recurs and is not recognized by any of them; if the ostensible repetition is initially not recognized by any of them, then they cannot leave the radical closure until it recurs and is recognized by them (hence if on recognizing the repetition of a previous configuration I am forced to leave the space, this implies that an exhaustive permutation has already taken place at one level and that I had already undergone a repetition of that configuration but did not recognize the repetition then). That is, there cannot be only a single repetition of some configuration of the radical closure but either none or two, one in which the ostensible repetition of every other parameter is recognized by those stuck in the radical closure and one in which it isn't.

One can imagine one of those stuck in a radical closure noticing that, as time passes, more and more variations are taking place and assuming that there appears to be a tendency toward exhaustive variation and so waiting to see the manner in which he will end up saying the sentences that were said by others, even though some of them conflict radically with his personality, and do the actions that were done by others, even though some of these actions conflict with his customary conduct, and dress in the same clothes and have the same hair color as them, etc.

The only thing that is not open to variation is what is received through inspiration (wahy) (setting aside the accidental variation that results from bad reception). I have been keenly interested in the absence of variation and the condition for such an absence, hence in reception by poets such as the eponymous poet of Cocteau's *Orpheus* and the poet Jack Spicer and by religious figures such as the Prophet Muhammad, who received the āyāt (verses) of the Qur'ān, and the Sufi Ibn al-'Arabī, who received *Fuṣūṣ al-ḥikam* (*The Bezels of Wisdom*;

"I saw the Apostle of God in a visitation granted to me during the latter part of the month of Muharram in the year 627, in the city of Damascus. He had in his hand a book and he said to me, 'This is the book of the bezels of Wisdom; take it and bring it to men that they may benefit from it.' ... I ... carried out the wish ... and devoted my purpose to the publishing of this book ... without any addition or sub-traction"[520])—the aphoristic side of me; and, conversely, in exhaustive variation, hence my interest in, and construction of the concept of, radical closure, which is an optimal condition for exhaustive varia-tion, which proves to be the way to leave the radical closure. I should note that I have also engaged in providing rigorous variants of films where the filmmaker disregarded valuable suggestions by his or her untimely collaborators—or compromised.

How many university administrators, particularly in Hong Kong, keep abusing the *in* word, the *mot-d'ordre* "proactive"! This despicable lot did so even during the social unrest that seized and convulsed the city for a period of around six months in 2018–2019 and that led to the occupation of several of the city's universities. One cannot be active fully during the event; there is an aspect of passivity to the event, a part that is endured (even when it is a joyful event, since the event is always overwhelming, excessive), in relation to which one cannot be active, let alone "proactive." Even the actors of the event, including its ostensible leaders, feel that they are so with respect to only certain aspects of it while being surprised, overtaken by others passively. It is with respect to the event that we encounter and experience a stark coexistence of activity and passivity: I have never felt that things could be so readily changed, and I am in the process of changing them, but I also feel, concurrently, in relation to the same event or the cluster of events of which it forms a part, that I am overwhelmed and a witness. Here's a real example of being proactive: the servants and cooks of Buñuel's *The Exterminating Angel*, who must have had a presentiment, in the absence of any explicit signs and communicable justifications (they could not have invoked, *avant la lettre*, my con-cept of radical closure), that their employer's house is on the verge of becoming radically separated from "its" environs, and, a further rarity, did not then disregard, indeed repress this alarming presentiment but acted accordingly, leaving the house in a hurry despite being threatened by their employer in no uncertain terms that they would be fired were they to do so when the dinner she was hosting was on the point of getting under way—it is fitting that they later prove to be the first to sense that the space is on the point of becoming again a relative closure, a space that those confined within it can leave (we could say in Heideggerian terms that it has acquired a clearing in relation to the environs).

In Buñuel's *The Exterminating Angel* the difference between those who have a presentiment of the approach of a radical closure and those who don't cuts along class lines: the bourgeois hosts and guests, as well as the butler, do not have a presentiment of the imminence of a radical closure of the space where they are, while the cooks and servants do. One can well imagine another film in which, as in *The Exterminating Angel*, different classes appear to respond very differently to the approaching danger of a radical closure but where, unlike in Buñuel's film, the opinion of the bourgeois guests that members of the working class are too coarse and so drained by their work that they cannot sense subtle dangers would have been confirmed, and where it is the ostensibly more refined members of the bourgeoisie or the aristocracy who detect this subtle kind of danger. In the work of another filmmaker, both classes might respond the same way to a radical closure (radical closure would in that case be indifferent to class difference). These variations would likely depend on the political leanings of the filmmaker. But class difference may prove to be one of the features that enters into variation in the process of exhaustive permutation that takes place in a radical closure, so that, while it may appear at some point that a certain class is the one sensitive to the imminence of a radical closure, at another point it would be another.

Sometimes it is rather easy to detect the *gateless gate*[521] of the radical closure, for example, it can be deduced from the distortion of the face of some figure as he or she hits against it, as if he or she is pressing against a transparent glass pane (David Lynch's *Lost Highway*); or from the inability of those within a space to cross to the other side of a certain line, notwithstanding the absence of any visible obstacle there, for example, a locked door (Buñuel's *The Exterminating Angel*). But sometimes one cannot detect or even guess where the spatial limits of the radical closure are, for these limits may be those of a large country or a continent and hence one may not have the occasion to reach them during one's life, but can only deduce, having encountered one or more of its consequences and characteristics, for example, the irruption of unworldly, ahistorical entities, or exhaustive permutations, that one is in a radical closure.

In David Lynch's *Lost Highway*, while getting her newspaper from her porch, a woman sees a VHS tape next to it; when she and her husband watch it, to their surprise it shows video images of their living room. A few days later, she again sees a VHS tape next to the morning paper; when she and her husband watch it, to their renewed surprise it shows video images, though this time not only of their living room but also of the corridor leading to their bedroom, and of the two of them sleeping. A few days later, the man finds a third tape on the porch, but when he plays it, alone, the images show not only their living room and their bedroom but his wife slaughtered in bed and him screaming while kneeling beside her. None of these three VHS tapes was at any point placed in a camera that was then used to film the interior of their house but irrupted on the porch already with images. When film spectators *begin* watching *Lost Highway*, they assume that, like any other film, it was itself shot, an assumption that is confirmed at the end of the film as they see and skim through the credits listing the film's cast and crew, which include, among others, David Lynch as the director, but also Peter Deming as the cinematographer, information that is corroborated by separate interviews with David Lynch, Peter Deming (Stephen Pizzello, "*Lost Highway—Highway to Hell*," *American Cinematographer*, March 1997),[522] and several of the main actors—and yet I can very well imagine a rigorous spectator who had the feeling that the videotape was not shot by anybody (including Mystery Man) suspecting that *Lost Highway* may itself not have been shot, acted, directed by anybody but irrupted fully formed, and, consequently, wondering, in trepidation, as the film ended whether it will list any crew members, including a director, David Lynch. I do envision, as a limit case, a radical-closure film or video that appears to be in the style of Lynch's films but in which we do not have credits listing any crew, which would imply that it irrupted without being filmed by anyone. I can also imagine David Lynch stopping making films to focus on painting, mixed media, and sound art, or because he had reached a limit in his films (I wondered whether this would prove to be the case after he completed *Inland Empire* [2006],[523] a [labyrinthine] film [at the level of the diegesis] pervaded by *jouissance*), and then one day receiving a portable external hard drive at his doorstep or a file in his email, accessing it and discovering a complete film in his style and in which one of the characters has the figure and voice of Jack Nance (d. 1996)!

The irruption of some entities that did not come from its environs in a space that has become radically closed can be clear, indeed blatant, for example, in a room where all the doors are locked, suddenly one may notice that there is an additional person there; or it can be subtle, for example, in David Lynch's *Lost Highway*, the sound of barking, which can be easily misreckoned as emitted naturally by a dog, who would be somewhere in the environs but offscreen, and was indeed misreckoned by the film's two protagonists, its maker, as well as, most likely, all of its spectators—with one exception, me ... *after I created the concept of radical closure*. A dog may unnaturally irrupt in a radical closure and may then bark, but the sound of barking can also irrupt in such a closure in the absence of a dog that would have emitted it. As the thinker of radical closure, I would prefer to consider that radical-closure filmmaker David Lynch did not show us a dog as the source of the barking heard by the film's two protagonists not because "when a sound can replace an image, [one should] cut the image or neutralize it"[524] (as Robert Bresson recommended in his *Notes on the Cinematograph*—Bresson's recommendation should not be followed in the case of a radical closure), but because there is no dog *tout court*. While pitching his film to a producer as a love story or a horror film, a filmmaker, who works with sounds and images, may actually be making it mostly to attain barking that was not emitted by a dog or recorded while some dog emitted it. It is not at all odd that a filmmaker would be interested in a sound that is not emitted by a source that can be visualized and thus related to an image; he or she may invest a lot of his time and energy to set the condition (radical closure) for such a sound to appear even though most people—indeed, were it not for my concept of radical closure, all people—would have missed its oddness.

"I have far more images than I shall ever be able to do—images that drop in from time to time to me that I shall never be able to use.... I suppose I'm lucky in that images just drop in as if they were handed down to me."[525] I would advance that most if not all of the images Francis Bacon received are unworldly or otherworldly entities that irrupt in radical closures. Bacon *paints* a radical-closure structure, then, given that it is not an actual radical closure but a representation of one and hence that no entity will suddenly irrupt in it out of his control, he, in whose practice, affined as he was to radical closure, "if anything works for me, I feel it is nothing I have made myself, but something which chance has been able to give me,"[526] intuitively makes do with a mock irruption on the canvas of what seems out of his control through "throw[ing] turpentine and paint and everything else" on it, but then, given that these are not actually entities that irrupted *fully formed* in a radical closure but reached the representation of the radical-closure structure he painted on the canvas from the latter's environs, he, through painting, fleshes out the paint he threw on the canvas in such a way that the resulting figure would be as close as possible to what appeared in his mind prior to the act of painting, in other words, what he received (for example, a wave on the beach), and would hit the nervous system directly, if not also what would best work aesthetically, *while respecting what the splash of paint itself suggests.* "I had painted the background in, and I just threw the paint onto the canvas ...; I threw on what I hoped to be a wave, and it didn't make a wave, ... and it wasn't going to be a wave; it looked more like a jet of water, so I turned it into a jet of water."[527] Had Bacon yielded to the temptation to force the splash of paint on the canvas to illustrate the entity he saw "drop" in his mind, a wave, notwithstanding that it suggested another entity, a jet of water, it is highly likely that the painting, presently known as *Jet of Water*, would have been botched. Being an excellent, rigorous painter, he did not yield to this temptation. It is pertinent for the title of a radical-closure painting to be the trace and residue of the original intention based on the received mental image, for example, *Wave* in the case of the painting presently titled *Jet of Water*—how redundant for the viewer of that painting is its present title! In some cases, the difference between the radical-closure painting and its title would derive from the latter being the trace and residue of the intention or, more accurately, of the received mental image behind the painting and the resultant wish, indeed obligation, of the painter to make it known to others (in the case of the aforementioned painting, we know what the received mental image was only through an interview, hence something extrinsic to the painting proper); in other cases, the difference between the rest of the radical-closure painting and its title would ensue from the circumstance that the title itself irrupted outside the control of the painter.

A few painters have managed to represent a radical-closure structure; but has there ever been a painter who has created a radical-closure structure through painting, one in which one or more entities irrupted from beyond the light cone or out of nowhere? How to distinguish between a failed attempt to bring about a radical closure through painting, hence one that ends up with only a relative closure and thus cannot lead to the irruption of entities that are not painted by the painter and that are unworldly or otherworldly, and a successful production of a radical closure through painting where, although they can irrupt there, no such figures have irrupted yet? Most people would not be able to distinguish between the two. But a great painter who worked for an extended time on radical closures and the perceptive viewer who has studied these extensively would end up being able to distinguish between the two for a while—even such a painter would end up doubting that he or she is a successful painter of radical closure if no entities that were not added by him or her (or their team, if they have one) end up irrupting in *any* of his or her paintings, since the most indubitable confirmation that one is a successful painter of radical closure (structures) would be the irruption in the painting of what he or she did not paint in it. Having painted the radical-closure structure, is the painter to exhibit the painting only once something that he or she did not add to it unnaturally irrupts in it? Should he or she paint a radical-closure structure that would give the impression that the painting is balanced compositionally and hence finished already even though nothing has yet irrupted in it that was not added to it by him or her? But then when something unnaturally irrupts in it, it is likely that the painter himself or herself as well as any spectator would feel that the painting is overfull. Or should he or she paint a radical-closure structure that would give the impression that the painting may not be finished yet, for example, a room with an empty chair in it (as opposed to one that, for example, has a lit candle and two books resting on the chair [Van Gogh's *Gauguin's Chair* (1888)]), so that the spectator would have the obscure expectation that something may still suddenly irrupt on it? But even then the following question arises: now that we have seen the figure (that irrupted) in the painting and feel that it is required there, including compositionally, were it then to disappear as suddenly as it appeared, ostensibly out of nowhere, would we still feel that the painting without the figure is finished and works compositionally? The radical-closure painter would have to manage this feat: a painting that seems to contain just enough with only the radical-closure structure, and then with one figure that he or she did not paint and that did not come from the environs but irrupted in the radical-closure structure from a radical elsewhere or out of nothing, and then with another such figure, and then with yet another such figure (or a sound), etc. As can be seen from the previous examples, the issue of composition, and of whether the painting is finished or not, is acutely raised in the case of radical-closure paintings, since the painter controls only the radical-closure structure, not what may irrupt in it.

A radical-closure painter painted or a sculptor sculpted the radical-closure structure, but not necessarily the figure visible in it, *even in a portrait*. Suppose a sculptor sets up a radical closure, for example, in the form of a glass box (of the sort we see in the first episode of the third season of David Lynch's *Twin Peaks* [2017]), and wishes for something to appear in it to complete the sculpture. Given that one has no control over what will irrupt in a radical closure, he or she is taking a risk that nothing would irrupt in such an enclosure, however long he or she waits; or that a figure would irrupt in it but then (possibly after being sold) disappear from it (in the latter case, the buyer should be able to return the purchased artwork for a full refund); or that several similar figures, potentially a multitude, would irrupt within it one at a time or all together; or that the same figure would appear in each of the radical-closure structures he sets up, however varied the latter are (a room, a transparent box, a chair, a mirror, etc.), when he wished for different figures or for variations on the same figure to irrupt in his or her iterations of the radical-closure structure. Did Francis Bacon set up a radical closure or did he merely paint a representation of one? If Bacon's paintings are representations of radical closures rather than themselves radical closures, then the recurrence of the figure of the pope in many of his paintings is to be attributed to his obsession with Velázquez's *Portrait of Innocent X* (c. 1650) (David Sylvester: "Why was it you chose the Pope?" Francis Bacon: "Because I think it is one of the greatest portraits that have ever been made, and I became obsessed by it. I buy book after book with this illustration in it of the Velázquez Pope, because it just haunts me, and it opens up all sorts of feelings and areas of—I was going to say—imagination"[528]), but if they are actual radical closures, then he was fortunate because the figures of the pope that ended up appearing in over forty of his paintings were not identical but variations on the pope of Velázquez's painting.

What form might the withdrawal past a surpassing disaster take in the case of an object that's radically closed, for example, a painting? No unworldly entities would irrupt in it.

It may happen that soon after a space becomes a radical closure, some or all of those inside it suspect this change. What would ensue? They may try to leave the space and, by failing to successfully do so even though the door is open and there is no other obvious obstacle, receive a confirmation that the space is now a radical closure, in which case there was no delay or a very short one between the establishment of the radical closure and the recognition by those within it of this circumstance; or they may come up with all sorts of excuses, such as a surge in COVID-19 cases, to put off leaving and thus to postpone recognizing that they mysteriously cannot successfully do so, in other words, that they are imprisoned.

It is always the case that *not* everything can happen, thus only certain things can happen in a relative closure; and only certain (other) things can happen in a radical closure; and only certain things can happen in dreams (through the dreamwork mechanisms of condensation, dissociation, etc.); and only certain things can happen even in the multiverse of the Many-Worlds Interpretation of quantum mechanics, those allowed by the Schrödinger equation.

Black holes seem to imply that not all the characteristics of a macroscopic object can be treated in a quantum manner, quantized. Ostensibly, a black hole treats the macroscopic object that crosses its event horizon as partly classical, in terms of its mass, spin, and charge, and as partly a quantum object, *if not quantizes* it, with regard to all other properties, so that it no longer has one value for each of the latter but is in a superposition of all of them. So with regard to these other properties, the black hole ostensibly acts in a reverse manner to a measurement device in the Copenhagen interpretation of quantum physics: instead of collapsing to one value a superposition of various values, it quantizes a macroscopic object except for its mass, spin, and charge, replacing what was a definite value for each of the other parameters with a superposition of values.

The third edition of the *Oxford Dictionary of English* (2016) defines "revenant" thusly, "a person who has returned, especially supposedly from the dead; origin early 19th century: French, literally 'coming back,' present participle (used as a noun) of *revenir*"; and the ninth, current edition of *Dictionnaire de l'Académie française* has this to say about the etymology of *revenir*, "xe siècle. Issu du latin *revenire*, de même sens, lui-même composé du préfixe *re*, qui marque le retour en arrière ou l'intensité, et de *venire*, « venir »";[529] and the aforementioned edition of the *Oxford Dictionary of English* lists these meanings of "re-," "(1) once more; afresh; anew: *reaccustom* | *reactivate*. • with return to a previous state: *revert*; (2) (also red-) in return; mutually: *react* | *resemble*. • in opposition: *repel* | *resistance*; (3) behind or after: *relic* | *remain*. • in a withdrawn state: *recluse* | *reticent*. • back and away; down: *recede* | *relegation*; (4) with frequentative or intensive force: *resound* | *redouble*; (5) with negative force: *recant* | *rebuff*." I would say that someone/ something to whose coming apply all the senses of "re-," and who/ which, paradoxically, appears to return from a space of no return, is a revenant. Hence the radiation of a black hole is a revenant, since it, paradoxically, appears to return from a space of no return and 1) comes "back" afresh, anew, since it is not the actual entity that crossed to the other side of the event horizon but results from the recurrent fall into the black hole of one of a pair of virtual subatomic particles that appeared out of the quantum vacuum, and since its coming, in case it carries information about what fell irretrievably into the black hole, makes possible, for some hypothetical or eventual observer, the epistemological return to a previous state—at a fundamental level, the revenant returns to make possible again the return, for example, (reversibility in the form of) retrodiction concerning the information about what entered the black hole (other than the latter's mass, electric charge, and spin), which would otherwise be lost, a loss that would pose an ostensible threat to science itself (yes, science would be threatened were there to be no revenant [from black holes— but also, it may turn out (who knows?), from other realms of no return, for example, death]); 2) was generated, as the subatomic particle that escaped while the other fell in the black hole, through the *mutual* arising, allowed by the uncertainty principle, of a complementary pair of opposite virtual subatomic particles out of the quantum vacuum (for example, in terms of electrical charge, an electron and a positron), which subatomic particles continue to be correlated, entangled, so that their state is mutually constrained, since "the quantum state of each particle ... cannot be described independently of the state of the other, including when the particles are separated by a large distance"[530]); 3) comes "back" while that about which it carries information continues to be inaccessible behind the event horizon of the black hole from his or her or its reference frame, unable to communicate with those on the other side of the event horizon, and while he or she or it continues, from the reference frame of outside observers, receding from them ever so slowly as he or she or it indefinitely approaches the event horizon (what would be a clue that the information about an astronaut and his cat who, from their local reference frame, have been swallowed by the black hole is being released in the form of Hawking radiation? It would be the detection by a series of observers at external reference frames that more and more of the astronaut and his cat is disappearing from the event horizon where they are still frozen due to the time dilation resulting from the gravity of the black hole—these observers might note about the cat: "It vanished quite slowly [over billions of years], beginning with the end of the tail, and ending with the grin, which remained some time after the rest of it had gone. Well! I've often seen a cat without a grin, ... but a grin without a cat! It's [one of] the most curious thing[s] I ever saw in my life!"[531]); 4) its entanglement is polygamous, hence would be rendered best with frequentatives (for example "redouble" ...), if information is not lost even though "it is a ... consequence of quantum theory that a particle can be fully entangled only with one other ... [in other words, that] entanglement is monogamous"[532] ("Think about a Hawking photon, call it 'B,' emitted after the black hole is at least halfway evaporated. The Hawking process implies that B is part of a pair; call its partner that falls into the black hole 'A.' A and B are entangled. Furthermore, the information that originally fell into the black hole has been encoded into all the Hawking radiation particles. Now, if information is not lost, and the outgoing Hawking photon B ends up in a definite quantum state, then B must be entangled with some combination, 'C,' of the other Hawking particles that already escaped [otherwise, the output would not preserve the information]. But then we have a contradiction: polygamy!"[533]), or is intensive, given that "the price of saving quantum mechanics ... is the loss of entanglement between ... the Hawking photons ... [that] began just inside and outside the horizon when they arose as an ephemeral particle-antiparticle pair [the aforementioned A and B]. In quantum theory, the cost of breaking this entanglement, like the cost of breaking a chemical bond, is energy. Breaking the entanglement for all the Hawking pairs implies that the horizon is a wall of high-energy particles ... a firewall,"[534] which would sear any object or human who gets very close to it;[535] 5) it thwarts, in case it carries information about what fell into the black hole, any attempt to destroy information irretrievably by throwing it in a black hole. Since to the Hawking radiation apply all the senses of "re-", if it turns out that it carries information regarding whatever crossed the event horizon of the black hole, from which putatively there is no return, the information in the form of Hawking radiation would be a revenant—not at all figuratively; *the human who appears to return from death would be just a special case of the revenant rather than the only kind of revenant*, and the information in the form of radiation would have to be included in the definition of "revenant" in the dictionary: "*revenant*: a person who has returned, especially supposedly from the dead, or the radiation of a black hole, especially if it, supposedly, carries information about what fell inside the black hole." If, as the great physicist Leonard Susskind asserts, "out of every 10,000,000,000 bits of information in the universe 9,999,999,999 are associated with the horizons of black holes,"[536] and if the radiation of a black hole carries information about what crossed the latter's event horizon, then information as a revenant would not be the exception among all information but the norm, in other words, it would be exceptional for information not to be a revenant. Since he, she, or it appears to return from *a realm of no return*, whether death or a black hole, the revenant does not provide any information about it—but only about what it was that crossed its event horizon. For example, since the information carried by the radiation of a black hole, which is a region of no return, is a revenant, it does not provide information about what the object that fell into the black hole underwent there (its interactions, etc.) but about what it was just before it entered the black hole and, in principle, through retrodiction, further back in the past. As a revenant who returned from death still a mortal, he talked about his past life as if that was what the living who gathered to celebrate his return were curious about! How fitting, then, that while they initially were most curious about what he witnessed while dead, in the death realm, they then, as they began to uneasily suspect that he was an imposter, not the one who died but another, instead asked him for further details about his presumed past with them, to try to check that he was the same as the one who died, and then, once he had answered all their questions accurately, each answer corroborated by one or more of them, did not switch to asking him about the realm from which he appeared to have returned, as if they were by then no longer able to overlook the circumstance that the realm about which they had wished to question him is a realm of no return, hence a realm about which he could not tell them anything (except creatively through an untimely collaboration with himself insofar as, a mortal, someone who is dead even while physically alive, he still haunted it). Derrida: "In an enigmatic sense, which will clarify itself *perhaps* (perhaps, because nothing should be sure here, for essential reasons), *the question* [my italics] of the archive is not, we repeat, a question of the past. It is not the question of a concept dealing with the past that might already be at our disposal or not at our disposal, an archivable concept of the archive. It is a question of the future, the question of the future itself, the question of a response, of a promise and of a responsibility for tomorrow. The archive: if we want to know what that will have meant, we will only know in times to come. Perhaps. Not tomorrow but in times to come, later on or perhaps never."[537] Of the meaning of anything and not solely the archive, including the aforementioned quote by Derrida, indeed the book from which it is extracted, *Archive Fever*, indeed all his writings, and deconstruction, one could say: we will only know its expanded or different meanings, and how best to translate it, in times to come. And yet, already at the time Derrida was writing the words I have just quoted, much more was knowable about the archive and its meaning than he assumed, through thermodynamics and *the black hole information paradox*. In the same essay, Derrida wrote, "If we still lack a viable, unified, given concept of the archive, it is undoubtedly not a purely conceptual, theoretical, epistemological insufficiency on the level of multiple and specific disciplines; it is perhaps not for lack of sufficient elucidation in certain circumscribed domains: archaeology, documentography, bibliography, philology, historiography";[538] it is regrettable but also symptomatic that he does not mention among the listed domains physics, specifically its black hole information paradox and thermodynamics. Derrida appears to have been unaware of the discussions that were taking place among physicists concerning whether information about what falls into black holes is lost irretrievably around the same period he was writing his book *Archive Fever* (while the original French was published in 1995, the book is based on a lecture Derrida gave in 1994), for example, between Kip Thorne and Stephen Hawking on one side and John Preskill on the other. It is inaccurate to assert that "the question of the archive is not ... a question of the past," since an exemplary question concerning the archive is, What fell into the black hole? Indeed, the possible loss of information concerning what fell into the black hole throws into question the past, more accurately, part of the past (since we can still have information about the mass, spin, and charge of what fell into the black hole). The archive is a question of the past also and primarily because, based on a widely accepted proposed or postulated solution for the arrow of time, there would be no possibility of the archive without a certain kind of the past, one with low entropy (the Past Hypothesis); Carlo Rovelli: "The fact that entropy has been low in the past leads to an important fact that is ubiquitous and crucial for the difference between past and future: the past leaves traces of itself in the present. Traces are everywhere. The craters of the moon testify to impacts in the past. Fossils show the forms of living creatures from long ago. Telescopes show how far off galaxies were in the past. Books contain our history; our brains swarm with memories.... In order to leave a trace, it is necessary for something to become arrested, to stop moving, and this can happen only in an irreversible process—that is to say, by degrading energy into heat. In this way, computers heat up, the brain heats up, the meteors that fall into the moon heat it; even the goose quill of a medieval scribe in a Benedictine abbey heats a little the page on which he writes. In a world without heat, everything would rebound elastically, leaving no trace."[539] What matters foundationally for the archive is what makes possible and imposes an irreversible process so that a change would function as a trace and hence possibly be archivable. There is a fundamental, primary preservation that is required for the secondary preservation of traces to be possible at all, and what makes it possible is the irreversibility that's a consequence of the very low entropy at the Big Bang. "In the beginning was low entropy" (since for a state to be the beginning of a process rather than, reversibly, its end, indeed, for there to be a difference between a beginning and an end, the process has to be irreversible, therefore that state must be one of low entropy; and since, in a sort of definition of the beginning, when and where we have low entropy *counts* as a beginning, in other words, chronology is not independent of low entropy but, rather, is composed and ordered according to a temporal perspective that places low entropy at the beginning—in yet other, paradoxical words, with regard to entropy, the beginning does not have to be at the beginning [were there to be a fluctuation that results in a state of very low entropy after a very long time of high entropy, if not of thermal equilibrium, then that would count and be treated as the beginning]; and since, according to an approach accepted provisionally by many physicists who have deeply pondered the issue, it seems that the low entropy at the Big Bang is an initial condition that cannot be derived from the current laws of physics and must be assumed); it is the low entropy of the beginning that makes it possible for the sentence "In the beginning was low entropy" to function as a trace, to be quoted as something that belongs to the past, and (thus) to potentially belong to an archive. It is thus through physics, more specifically thermodynamics, that we discern a reason for why the archive has to do inextricably with a beginning, as suggested or confirmed by etymology: "The English word *archive* is derived from the French *archives* (plural), and in turn from Latin *archīum* or *archīvum*, the romanized form of the Greek ἀρχεῖον (*arkheion*). The Greek term originally referred to the home or dwelling of the Archon, a ruler or chief magistrate, in which important official state documents were filed and interpreted; from there its meaning broadened to encompass such concepts as 'town hall' and 'public records.' The root of the Greek word is ἀρχή (*arkhē*), meaning among other things 'magistracy, office, government,' and derived from the verb ἄρχω (*arkhō*), meaning 'to begin, rule, govern' ['I. in Time, *begin, make a beginning,* ... π. ἄρχεσθαι *to begin one's* operations; ἄρχειν τοῦλόγου *to open* a conversation; ἄρχεσθαι τοῦ λόγου *to begin one's* speech ... II. in point of Place or Station, *rule, govern, command*'[540]."[541] While the question of the archive is, notwithstanding Derrida's assertion to the contrary, related to the past, it also, something he fails to mention or note, was a question of the present of Derrida's writing of *Archive Fever* (1995), given that, apparently unbeknownst to him, a number of scientists were exploring the Holographic Principle, which makes a black hole, more specifically its event horizon, an archive, and whether a black hole preserves the information about what falls into it; and continues to be a question of the present of my writing these words, in 2021, given that many scientists are still engaged in solving the black hole information paradox; and would be all the more fundamentally and indefinitely a matter and question of the present if it turns out that information about whatever fell in black holes is in principle preserved and recoverable in some manner, since in that case it is possible in principle to retrodict from the present what took place in the past, more specifically, what fell into a black hole, indeed, its past prior to falling into a black hole. Derrida wrote in his book *Specters of Marx*, "There has never been a scholar who really, and as scholar, deals with ghosts. A traditional scholar does not believe in ghosts— nor in all that could be called the virtual space of spectrality. There has never been a scholar who, as such, does not believe in the sharp distinction between the real and the unreal, the actual and the inactual, the living and the non-living, being and non-being ('to be or not to be,' in the conventional reading), in the opposition between what is present and what is not"[542]—and yet wasn't I such a scholar already in my second book, *(Vampires): An Uneasy Essay on the Undead in Film*, whose first edition was published before *Archive Fever*, in 1993 (and largely based on my PhD dissertation, "[Vampires]," which I defended in 1992—judging by the expression on the face of my "supervisor" at Northwestern University during my defense [with whom I had not met even once in the three years during which I wrote my book-cum-dissertation], she certainly did not consider me a *traditional* scholar), and wasn't he, institutionally a university professor who published many of his books with university presses (Presses Universitaires de France, University of Minnesota Press, Stanford University Press, University of Chicago Press, etc.), such a scholar already in some of his texts prior to and in *Specters of Marx* (*Spectres de Marx* [1993]), texts that deconstruct the distinction between the real and the unreal, what is actual and what is not, the living and the non-living? Derrida went on to hypothesize that, in Shakespeare's *Hamlet*, by telling Horatio to question the ghost, "Marcellus was perhaps anticipating the coming, one day, one night, several centuries later, of another 'scholar.' The latter would finally be capable, beyond the opposition between presence and non-presence, actuality and inactuality, life and non-life, of thinking the possibility of the specter, the specter as possibility"[543]—(including) of the archive. Thinking the possibility of the specter is not exclusively a future capability—as I have already mentioned, Derrida himself in *Specters of Marx*, as well as in a number of his previous texts, and myself already in the first edition of my book *(Vampires): An Uneasy Essay on the Undead in Film* (to give more than a single counterexample to his invalid generalization), had already been "beyond the opposition between presence and non-presence, actuality and inactuality, life and non-life, ... thinking the possibility of the specter"; what is exclusively a matter of the future (that's more distant than "several centuries"), if it turns out that the radiation of black holes (each of its constituents a revenant "from" a region of no return) carries information of what fell into them (other than mass, spin, and charge), is having the stupendous resources to collect and decipher this information as a revenant. The scholar of the future will not necessarily or primarily have to glean and decipher the speech of that variety of revenant that is the ghost but the radiation of black holes, a more basic kind of revenant, for information about what fell into them. In the case of two of the main archives, the black hole and the unconscious, what we retrieve from them (through radiation and through symptoms/parapraxes/etc., respectively) can function as information only when it is decoded/interpreted. The one who invoked only "archaeology, documentography, bibliography, philology, historiography" in writing about the question of the archive could scarcely fathom the following sense and reason for the archive to be "a question of the future": whether by the time black holes would have evaporated altogether through the process of Hawking radiation, billions of years in the case of the small ones, much of the information that could otherwise have been gleaned from that radiation would, in case the present accelerating expansion of the universe continues indefinitely, a hypothesis entertained by most physicists, have already disappeared behind another kind of horizon, no longer the event horizon of the black hole but a cosmological horizon, and our distant, unimaginably enhanced descendants or artificial general intelligences would have long been reduced to dispersed atoms drifting in the largely empty regions of the universe—in other words, whether there would still be by then a future in any meaningful sense, for example, through "Boltzmann brains." Derrida wrote in *Archive Fever*: "The death drive ... threatens ... every archival desire. It is what we will call ... *le mal d'archive*, 'archive fever.' Such is the scene ... : Freud can only justify the apparently useless expenditure of paper, ink, and typographic printing, in other words, the laborious investment in the archive, by putting forward the novelty of his discovery, the very one which provokes so much resistance, and first of all in himself, and precisely because its silent vocation is to burn the archive and to incite amnesia, thus refuting the economic principle of the archive, aiming to ruin the archive as accumulation and capitalization of memory ..."[544] The mere presence of a *mal d'archive* in the manner of a death drive specific to the archive, targeting it, would be a sign that the fundamental archive, the one targeted by this death drive, with the latter's associated compulsion to repeat, cannot be completely destroyed or irrevocably erased but is rather preserved indefinitely, given that there can be no compulsion to repeat in relation to what can be destroyed in one attempt, or even in a finite number of attempts. Are there such archives? Yes! the (Bergsonian) virtual past (Deleuze on Bergson's conception of time: "Since the past is constituted not after the present that it was but at the same time, time has to split itself in two at each moment as present and past, which differ from each other in nature.... Time ... splits in two dissymmetrical jets, one of which makes all the present pass on, while the other preserves all the past,"[545] implying its "integral survival"[546]), and, what could be considered its physical support, (general relativity's) four-dimensional spacetime. But irrespective of whether there is a *mal d'archive* in the manner of a death drive targeting an indestructible archive, any archive that humans assemble and try to preserve presupposes as its fundamental condition an ur-, more fundamental preservation: were it the case that the (Bergsonian) past is not self-preserved (virtually), there would be no archive; were it not, at another level, for the four-dimensional block of spacetime, there would be no archive; and were it the case, at another level, that entropy was not low in the past, there would be no archive. The function of human archives is not preservation but to provide access to part of the aforementioned ur-, auto-constituted archives of self-preserved events. Derrida continued: "The death drive ... threatens ... the archive as accumulation and capitalization of memory on some substrate and in an exterior place. What, in general, can this substrate consist of? Exterior to what?"[547] If "out of every 10,000,000,000 bits of information in the universe 9,999,999,999 are associated with the horizons of black holes," then in the vast majority of cases it is exterior to a black hole, in other words, to nothing ("Black holes are nothing. Black holes are special because there's nothing there.... A bare black hole is pure empty spacetime—no atoms, light, strings, or particles of any kind, dark or bright. The material that formed the event horizon is gone, leaving empty space—and an event horizon—in its wake. Effectively, the event horizon *is* the black hole.... Shed the impression of the black hole as a dense crush of matter. Accept the black hole as a bare event horizon, a curved empty spacetime"[548]). Elsewhere in the same book, Derrida wrote, "Let us never forget this Greek distinction between *mnēmē* or *anamnēsis* on the one hand, and *hypomnēma* on the other. The archive is hypomnesic.... There is no archive without consignation in an *external place*"[549]— including because, as Freud pointed out, "if I distrust my memory—neurotics, as we know, do so to a remarkable extent, but normal people have every reason for doing so as well—I am able to supplement and guarantee its working by making a note in writing. In that case ... I have only to bear in mind the place where this 'memory' has been deposited and I can then 'reproduce' it ... with the certainty that it will have remained unaltered and so have escaped the possible distortions to which it might have been subjected in my actual memory."[550] In the case of the paradigmatic archive, the consignation (which is not done by humans) is in the virtual past, hence in time not space, and yet we can still speak of externality since it is external to the brain, persists even after the brain is incapacitated, indeed destroyed (Bergson: "Those particular images, which I call cerebral mechanisms, terminate at each successive moment the series of my past representations, being the extreme prolongation of those representations into the present, their link with the real, that is, with action. Sever that link—and you do not necessarily destroy the past image, but you deprive it of all means of acting upon the real and, consequently, ... of being realized. It is in this sense, and in this sense only, that an injury to the brain can abolish any part of memory"[551]). In the vast majority of cases, for something to be archivable a material surface of inscription, a substrate, is not required; all that is required is a boundary, for example, in the case of a black hole, the event horizon (Jacob D. Bekenstein: "By studying the mysterious properties of black holes, physicists have deduced absolute limits on how much information a region of space or a quantity of matter and energy can hold. Related results suggest that our universe, which we perceive to have three spatial dimensions, might instead be 'written' on a two-dimensional surface, like a hologram";[552] Leonard Susskind: "String Theory, if you take it seriously, ... places every bit of information, whether in black holes or black newsprint, at the outer edges of the universe, or at 'infinity' if the universe has no end.... Shortly before I left Utrecht for home, Gerard ['t Hooft] said something that startled me. He said that if we could look at the microscopic Planck-sized details on the walls of his office, in principle they would contain every bit of information about the interior of the room. I don't recall him using the word *hologram*.... The three-dimensional world of ordinary experience—the universe filled with galaxies, stars, planets, houses, boulders, and people—is a hologram, an image of reality coded on a distant two-dimensional surface. This new law of physics, known as the Holographic Principle, asserts that everything inside a region of space can be described by bits of information restricted to the boundary"[553]). If the hypothesis that there is a wall of extremely high-energy particles at the event horizon of black holes is confirmed, then fire does not get rid of the archive ... radically; at the event horizon, fire, more specifically a firewall (the name given to the wall of extremely high-energy particles), would be what saves the archive of anything other than mass, spin, and electric charge, indeed, the very possibility of such an archive, since while burning whatever was on the point of falling into the black hole it allows the preservation of information not limited to the mass, spin, and electric charge of what fell into the black hole, which could then in principle be collected and deciphered from the radiation issuing "from" the black hole—if the information sucked into the black hole is not retrievable from its radiation or otherwise, then we could say that what is unqualifiedly archivable, what is archivable *tout court*, is mass, spin, and electric charge.[554] "There would indeed be no archive desire without the radical finitude, without the possibility of a forgetfulness which does not limit itself to repression"[555] (Derrida), in other words (mine), there would indeed be no archive desire without the possibility, still entertained by many demanding scientists, of an irretrievable loss of information (other than about mass, spin, and charge) regarding objects that fall into black holes (the archive desire would be much weaker and the *mal d'archive* much stronger, if not infinitely stronger, when it comes to mass, spin and charge, since these are not lost when an object falls[556] into a black hole) that does not limit itself to forgetfulness, which itself does not limit itself to repression. Derrida: "There is not one archive fever, one limit or one suffering of memory among others: enlisting the in-finite, archive fever verges on radical evil."[557] Notwithstanding his assertion that "there is not one archive fever," Derrida didn't tell us what other variety or varieties of archive fever, of the *mal d'archive*, there is or are. He was inordinately, unjustifiably, indeed incorrectly generalizing from a particular *mal d'archive* to all when he wrote, "There is no archive fever [*mal d'archive*] without the threat of this death drive, this aggression and destruction drive," since a black hole is a variant of archive fever, one that appears to enlist the infinite, in the figure of the singularity in its center according to general relativity, without having to do with the (Freudian) death drive and correlatively radical evil; but he was legitimately generalizing when he continued, "This threat is *in-finite*, it sweeps away the logic of finitude and the simple factual limits, the transcendental aesthetics, one might say, the spatio-temporal conditions of conservation. Let us rather say that it abuses them,"[558] since the characterization "there is no archive fever without ... [a] threat ... [that] *is in-finite*, ... sweeps away the logic of finitude ..., the transcendental aesthetics, one might say, the spatio-temporal conditions of conservation"[559] fits all varieties of archive fever, for example, a black hole, in the case of which, from one perspective, general relativity, the threat is infinity, that of the singularity, which "sweeps away the logic of finitude ..., the transcendental aesthetics, one might say, the spatio-temporal conditions of conservation," since, as Nobel laureate Kip Thorne put it in 1993, "a singularity is a region where—according to the laws of general relativity—the curvature of spacetime becomes infinitely large, and spacetime ceases to exist," and, from another perspective, the laws of quantum mechanics, which "forbid the infinities," and which, "as best we understand it in 1993, ... merge with Einstein's general relativistic laws" "very near the singularity" into *quantum gravity*, the threat is the "sweep[ing] away [of]... the transcendental aesthetics, one might say, the spatio-temporal conditions," since, still according to Kip Thorne, "time ceases to exist; no longer can we say that 'this thing happens before that one,' because without time, there is no concept of 'before' or 'after,' ... [and] space, the sole remaining remnant of what was once a unified spacetime, becomes a random, probabilistic froth."[560] "Let us never forget this Greek distinction between *mnēmē* or *anamnēsis* on the one hand, and *hypomnēma* on the other. The archive is hypomnesic. And let us note in passing a decisive paradox ... which undoubtedly conditions the whole of these remarks: if there is no archive without consignation in an *external place* which assures the possibility of memorization, of repetition, of reproduction, or of reimpression, then we must also remember that repetition itself, the logic of repetition, indeed the repetition compulsion, remains, according to Freud, indissociable from the death drive [this generalization, where Derrida moves insidiously from repetition to the logic of repetition to the compulsion to repeat as if they are equivalent or the later terms in the list are straightforwardly deducible from the first, is invalid since Freud's death drive is associated not with any repetition but with the unconscious *compulsion* to repeat—indeed, in my book *Forthcoming*, I advance that "it is only through the experience of recurrence that we may reach the will," that is, end up willing the eternal recurrence of one or more events, ushering in the epoch of a will that's become fundamental ontologically, an epochal, and no longer solely individual will, in the process doing away with death, including the death drive]. And thus from destruction. Consequence: right on that which permits and conditions archivization, we will never find anything other than that which exposes to destruction, and in truth menaces with destruction, introducing, *a priori*, forgetfulness and the archiviolithic into the heart of the monument. Into the 'by heart' itself. The archive always works, and *a priori*, against itself."[561] If, as physicist Leonard Susskind asserts, "out of every 10,000,000,000 bits of information in the universe 9,999,999,999 are associated with the horizons of black holes,"[562] and if, in principle, the radiation of black holes does not carry information about what fell into them, then Derrida's generalization "the archive always works, and *a priori*, against itself" would be valid but not necessarily and exclusively because of the aforementioned reason he advances. Anyway, given that the death drive cannot destroy its condition, the unconscious, the archive of, for example, the amnesiac whose amnesia does not have an organic etiology but is the result of repression, an archive that cannot be destroyed through the physical death of the human to whom it is attributed since the death drive, with its compulsion to repeat, does not acknowledge corporeal death as a definitive end, functions to repeat, in the bardo or the imaginal world, the destruction of what died physically, what appears to have reverted to the inorganic in the world of living humans, we can reverse the generalization while removing "*a priori*" and write as validly: "The anarchive always works on the basis of a timeless archive." With the black hole we have an object that acts as both archive, indeed, given that according to physicist Leonard Susskind, "out of every 10,000,000,000 bits of information in the universe 9,999,999,999 are associated with the horizons of black holes,"[563] the main archive, and anarchive if not antiarchive since it hides the information of what fell into it behind the event horizon—and, if it turns out that the Hawking radiation of a black hole does not carry information about what fell into it, eliminates it irretrievably by evaporating through a very long process of said radiation (if the information about what fell into a black hole is not preserved, then it should go without saying that the best way, indeed possibly the only way, to get rid of information, in a way to escape the archive, is to throw it behind the event horizon of a black hole).

A group of philosophers had gathered in Paris to celebrate the one hundredth anniversary of Jacques Derrida's birth. Suddenly, a knock on the door interrupted their conversation. One of them headed to the door and opened it. No one was there. But then, as they turned away from the door to resume their conversation, they saw a figure standing by the window. They gasped, since they thought they recognized the one who conceptualized deconstruction and who invoked the scholar to come as a hauntologist. He warned them that spectral presences "are not what they seem but what they differ from." One of them, as if subject to a spell, exclaimed: "One of the specters of Marx!" Another blurted out, "How is this possible? You died in 2004." "Did I? Didn't I deconstruct death? Wasn't *the instant of my death* another's?" Then he added, as if recalling something from the margins of philosophy, "To write is to produce a mark that will constitute a kind of machine ... that my future disappearance in principle will not prevent from functioning.... When I say 'my future disappearance,' I do so to make this proposition more immediately acceptable. I must be able simply to say my disappearance.... This absence is not a continuous modification of presence; it is a break in presence, 'death,' or the possibility of ... 'death' ... inscribed in the structure of the mark."[564] As they clamored to ask him questions, he warned them that, insofar as any (published) text already implies the death of its author, his posthumous answers would not simply clarify his texts but would induce alterations in them as traces. The less perceptive among them were not deterred by his warning, only to later discover that his published books, including the print copies in their bookshelves, differed indeed from their memories of them.

For the ghost to be able to haunt, both parties, the dead man or woman and at least one alive person, have to be in disavowal of the death.

Both the ghost and the vampire haunt, but they appear to do so paradigmatically in two different ways: the ghost does so diachronically, through unnaturally appearing in a space then unnaturally disappearing from it then unnaturally appearing in it again, but the vampire does so synchronously, through not appearing in the mirror in a space where he is otherwise seen, thus manifesting that while seeming to be in the space, he is not fully in it. If a space is haunted by a ghost or vampire, it does not turn into a ruin gradually as its subsequent owners or tenants leave it in fright but is, even if it appears to be a new or reconstructed building, already a ruin, a labyrinthine space and time.

Ghosts haunt not only the living but also the dead. In death, the ghost, who is partly related to the world of the living, otherwise it would not care to haunt it, too, is the figure of that which in the one who died did not fully adjust to the death realm, is not fully controlled by, addicted to, *jouissance*. The ghost is mainly an instance not of the dead human haunting the living, but of the resistance and persistence of what is still reminiscent of the living in the dead human, haunting him or her who is otherwise subject fully, addicted, to *jouissance*. The ghost haunting the dead human is a figure not of insistence but of a minimal detachment if not dissociation from the insistent drive toward the particular *jouissance* to which the dead is addicted. So, in life the ghost implies some "unfinished business," for example, a promise that has to be fulfilled even in the face of "fate" in the guise of physical death, and in the death realm the ghost implies and is a symptom that the dead human has not yielded completely to the drive. It is healthy for the ghost to end up disappearing for good from the world of the living, for example, after leading to the fulfillment of some promise, but to continue haunting the fallen-apart world of a dead human. The dead do not entreat the living or demand from them to redress some injustice they have suffered, since they couldn't care less about the world of the living—or soon enough experience *jouissance* through the revengefulness they feel and thus do not wish it to end through the reestablishment of justice. If, once the demand of what one took to be a ghost has been accomplished by a living human, the entity does not disappear for good but continues to haunt, then one is dealing not with a ghost but with the dead (as revenant). It is incumbent upon at least some writers to make it possible for the ghost, *not the dead*, to return[565] (in *What Was I Thinking?* [2017] I wrote about the sort of fiction that can do this: a labyrinthine one),[566] indeed they have to make it possible for the ghost to haunt *so as not* to allow the dead to return, since to make it possible for the dead to return through fiction is to unleash evil on the world; and because repressing the ghost and thus withholding from him or her the right of return turns the living people who have to do with him or her into zombies (in Shakespeare's *Hamlet*, as Prince Hamlet finishes describing his mother as a zombie, "Eyes without feeling, feeling without sight, / Ears without hands or eyes, smelling sans all," the ghost of his late father, who was treacherously murdered by his brother, the queen's present husband, appears, providing us and Hamlet with an occasion to witness the cause of her state as zombie: she has repressed the ghost [and hence does not see him]: Hamlet: [*To the Ghost*] "... What would you, gracious / figure?" Gertrude: "Alas, he's mad.... [*To Hamlet*] How is't with you, / That you do bend your eye on vacancy, / And with th'incorporal air do hold discourse?"[567]). One has to deploy a double resistance in relation to the ghost: resist the temptation to banish him or her (if one considers that he or she is independent and external to one) or repress him or her (if one considers that he or she is a symptom of a psychic conflict within one), making it possible for him or her to haunt the living, but then resist accepting at face value what he or she exoterically asks for, whether redress or completion, concerning a matter he or she appears to regard as unfinished business, treating this insistent request itself as unfinished business until it is properly interpreted while taking into consideration who his or her addressee is, or adjusting it to the world of the living, where, for example, the validity of the alleged victim's assertions as to the identity of the assailant should be decided through a fair trial, since the *exoteric* terrible demands of the ghost are often those, revengeful, of the dead and so prove to be more terrifying and terrible than him or her as an unnatural entity and the horrible crime he or she allegedly suffered.

Through his film *The Sixth Sense* (1999) M. Night Shyamalan contributes a novel take on the haunting of the dead who are in disavowal of their state: a dead human who haunts without the living being aware of that (unless the living person happens to be, exceptionally, a parapsychic), thus divesting haunting from its detection if not registration by the living. That we see the dead therapist Malcolm only in some scenes of the film does not suggest that in the film's other scenes he still exists in the world of the living but off-screen; for him to haunt he has to ingenuously, albeit unconsciously, since he is in denial that he is dead, find those situations and moments that make it possible for him to interpret what is happening as indicating that he is still alive, hence situations that would allow him to seem to interact with the living in the world or else for their absence of interaction with him to be explainable cogently by another reason than that he has already died and is therefore inexistent to them. Here's an example. Malcolm rushes into a restaurant. His wife is seated alone, stirring sugar in her coffee absentmindedly. Next to the dinner leftovers there's a still untouched cake topped by a candle. Malcolm sits in the seat across from her. She stops stirring the coffee but doesn't look up. He apologizes: "I'm so sorry.... I can't seem to keep track of time. It didn't go well today. I spent some time after, trying to get my head together." She looks around for the waiter. The waiter drops the check on the table. Anna grabs it before Malcolm has time to do so and quickly signs it. Malcolm excuses himself again: "I know I've been kind of out of it for a long while and you resent it. You do. I know you're mad. I know it's put some distance between us ..." She rises from the table and walks away without responding. He blurts out: "Happy anniversary!" She continues moving toward the exit. Here's another example: He steps gingerly into the bathroom and stares at the silhouette of his wife through the shower's smoked glass. As he then begins to walk lustily toward her, he notices a tiny bottle placed on the sink. The label reads: "Zoloft Anti-depressant." As a result, he is dissuaded from approaching her to engage in sex with her, which spares him discovering that she would not have perceived him and, consequently, suspecting, indeed recognizing, that he has already died, no longer exists in the world.

Soon after arriving at Count Dracula's castle following a series of disturbing unnatural occurrences, Harker becomes worried that Dracula will kill him. How ironic and how imperceptive on his part, since for him to have reached Dracula's castle and "met" Dracula, he can no longer be said to be fully alive but must have died before dying, if not died *tout court*.

Can one "meet" the dead? Such a meeting is bound to be problematic; in other words, one cannot unquestionably, undoubtedly meet the dead, because even when it seems that one has managed to find the dead human in some labyrinthine ruin (that may appear to be some reconstructed postwar building), some glitch implies that one has not really met him or her, for example, his or her failure to appear in a mirror that happens to be at the same location (Bram Stoker's novel *Dracula* and Francis Ford Coppola's film *Bram Stoker's Dracula*).

According to linguistics, the "I" functions as a shifter, and so is transiently associated with each speaker in turn. But usually the "I" is *not experienced* as a shifter by sane living humans; usually, in the experience of a sane living human, the "I" is always, rigidly linked to oneself. But in schizophrenia and psychosis, and in death, one *experiences* or undergoes the "I" as a shifter rather than abstractly knows that it is a shifter: "I am Prado, I am also Prado's father, I venture to say that I am also Lesseps.... I am also Chambige.... Every name in history is I" (from a letter in Nietzsche's handwriting dated January 5, 1889).

Having died before dying physically ("This autumn [of 1888] ... I twice attended my funeral"[568]), Nietzsche wrote, "I am Prado, I am also Prado's father, I venture to say that I am also Lesseps.... I am also Chambige.... Every name in history is I." Even though in death for each one of us "every name in history is I,"[569] no one can assume in one's place every name in history. One of the things that are singular about each of us is the different individual names that we would list in death or death before dying physically prior to the ellipsis that apparently leads to the ostensibly all-encompassing "every name in history is I."

The aphoristic thinker Nietzsche wrote in a book, *Twilight of the Idols*, completed in September 1888 and published two months later: "My ambition is to say in ten sentences what everyone else says in a book—what everyone else does *not* say in a book."[570] What is an example of saying in even less than ten sentences what everyone else does not say in a *book*? It is, "I am Prado, I am also Prado's father, I venture to say that I am also Lesseps.... I am also Chambige.... Every name in history is I," since these words appear in a letter in Nietzsche's handwriting dated January 5, 1889, and not in a book, Nietzsche failing to finish and publish his planned book, *Revaluation of All Values*, as a result of dying before dying physically, a state invoked in the same letter, "This autumn ... I twice attended my funeral"; and since in the latter state Friedrich Nietzsche was everyone else ("every name in history is I").

November 15, 2021
Very dear Simone[571]:
I assume that you feel al*together* alone now, even amidst all the condolences, including this one.

I know that Etel[572] is alone. Once one dies, one is thenceforth alone, either with the alone, the double ("I am never purely myself. The double is unrecognizable because he is the Same. The double is not the other, but I divested of all others. That is why whenever I encounter him, even in a crowded public place, I feel I am alone with him, *alone with the alone*;[573] he embodies the divestment from the world. That is why encountering the double is such a desolate experience"[574]), and with the voices, concerning whom the dead human, who is said to have "lost his mind," also in the sense that he is unable to locate where it is, hence what is external to it, cannot be sure that they are not the products of "his" mind; *or* with the Alone, God, the one in relation and comparison to whom nothing else, obviously including oneself, has being, or everyone or everything has being only insofar as he or she or it is, at each moment, one of God's recurrent self-disclosures.

It is not every day that one feels older; today, I do.
Jalal

Periodization is not necessarily limited to the world of the living but possibly applies, too, to the realm of death, notwithstanding that the latter is labyrinthine, plays havoc with chronology and linearity. Thus the appearance of a new book of the dead, rather than simply of a new adaptation or interpretation of an old book of the dead, is a marker of a new period for the dead (even if this book is perused only by a small circle of readers or does not look like one since it is not in the form of a manual or guide but of a novel or fictional film or long poem). For example, Timothy Leary, Ralph Metzner, and Richard Alpert's *The Psychedelic Experience: A Manual Based on The Tibetan Book of the Dead* (1964) could be considered, irrespective of the circumstance that the book's authors mostly failed to accomplish what they set out to do, a sign that a new (version of the Tibetan) book of the dead was required for the era of LSD and other psychedelics. That would mean not only that some psychedelics may be viewed as providing a foretaste of the death state but also, more radically, that something changed in the death condition with the synthesizing of LSD and other psychedelics. A new book of the dead is required in the period of cinema, since, as I wrote in my book *What Was I Thinking?* (2017), "in the conditions in which one would 'ask' oneself, 'Am I dead?' sooner or later one would, if one belongs to the cinematic era, also ask oneself, 'Am I in a film?' having witnessed immobilizations of people, in other words, dead stops (the equivalent of cinema's freeze-frames), and the temporal peculiarities made possible by these as the genetic element of movement, such as slow motion and backward-in-time motion; undergone lapses of consciousness, if not of being (including by becoming immobilized), which result in an editing of "reality"; felt that some of the others were extras (as on a film shoot), etc."[575] I consider a substantial part of my writings to be a contribution to such a book of the dead for our period. For one to be able to gage properly the impact of such a book, one would have had to have already died before dying.

Social and political critic Samah Idriss, an unflagging activist for Palestinian rights, captioned a photograph showing him in a hospital wearing a robe and trudging with the help of a walker while flanked by two nurses as he fought cancer: "We walk and pursue the path (*namshī wa minkaffi al-ṭarīq*)." I would say that's what one has to do at the level of the possibly healable sick organic body; but what one has to accomplish at the level of the mind that has had to grapple with the very high likelihood of imminent physical death is dying before physically dying and, accordingly, complementing the afore-mentioned caption, if not replacing it, with something equivalent to the Zen Buddhist koan: "When you reach the top of the mountain, keep climbing."

If we continue to have some existence after physical death, then we are bound to experience or undergo bewilderment either "in" the death realm, where we are lost "in" its labyrinthine space and time and assume every name in history, or, if there is God, in God (Ibn al-'Arabī: "There is nothing but bewilderment in God," partly because He brings opposites together [when Abū Sa'īd al-Kharrāz was asked, "Through what have you known God?" he answered, "Through the fact that He brings opposites together," and then recited the Qur'ānic verse "He is the First, and the Last, and the Outward, and the Inward" (57:3)], and partly because "He ... does not accept restriction.... The perfect one is he who sees the diversity of self-disclosures in the One entity"[576])—the Sufi who, along the path, died before dying physically undergoes this bewilderment before his or her physical death.

One should recognize that one is a mortal, dead even while still physically alive. To do so, one has to die before dying physically, *and*, since when one dies one does not automatically recognize that one is dead, while in that state come to recognize that one is dead. Perhaps we intuit that when one dies one's recognition of one's actual state is not straightforward, let alone automatic and convey such an intuition in dreams, where the (long-)dead person that we see and encounter there (albeit sometimes, as a result of the dream mechanism of condensation, in the guise of a partly different person) is unaware that he or she is dead! The recognition that one is dead is complicated by the circumstance that in death one sooner or later assumes every name in history, hence becomes, synecdochically, all the others, so that one runs the risk that while recognizing that one is dead one does so as another, under another name, for example, in the case of Nietzsche, Count Robilant (from a letter in his handwriting dated January 5, 1889: "This autumn ... I twice attended my funeral, first as Count Robilant").[577]

While each human has one life and, consequently, one physical death, as a mortal he or she may have numerous deaths (the physical one being only one of these), hence Nietzsche, who died before dying physically in 1900, could write in a letter dated January 5, 1889, "This autumn ... I twice attended my funeral." After one's physical death, one will at some point attend one's funeral in the death realm and will have to then, sooner or later, come to recognize that one is dead.

As his car skidded in the heavy rain and headed inexorably towards a speeding truck, he awaited the imminent crash, but then, across some lapse of consciousness, he was still driving, some distance beyond the site of the would-be accident. He wondered how he had been miraculously spared certain death. But was he spared death? As he began to experience anomalies, at first fleetingly, then more protractedly and clearly, he began to wonder: "Was the car accident actually averted, or did I die in it? Is this death? Am I dead?" Is it the case that once one dies physically, one automatically recognizes that one is dead? No. When not considered as a question, "Am I dead?" means that I am dead, but it does not necessarily mean that I recognize that I am dead. Once one is dead, what's to be gained by recognizing one's condition? Is it simply to become aware that whatever one is seeing and hearing and touching and tasting is a projection of one's mind (initially mostly projections of one's desires, which are then replaced, as the residual links to life wear off, by projections of one's fantasies and drives as well as flashbacks to one's traumas)?

If when one dies physically one does not disappear completely, then it seems that one would be able to just say, "I am dead," on recognizing one's condition—but that would be extrapolating illegitimately from life to death. The dead human cannot say, "I am dead," and so has to formulate the realization that he or she is dead in other manners. One way is, "I must be dead": "Given that I was shot; that I bled profusely while lying on the floor; that I can no longer feel my body; and that the doctor who held my wrist and checked my pulse has just let go of it unceremoniously and departed unhurriedly, as if there were no longer an emergency, I must be dead—however incredible that may seem." Another way, equivalent to "I must be dead," is "Am I dead?" but not as a question. If someone who has been shot and is bleeding profusely and can no longer feel his body, indeed then has an out-of-the-body experience, wonders, "Am I dead?" and answers, "Yes," or "Maybe," or "I don't know," then he must not be dead, since the dead do not understand "Am I dead?" as a question, even though it looks like one, and thus do not expect and wait for an answer.

The dreamer was surprised that her dead grandmother was unaware that she was dead, when she herself was unaware that she was dreaming!

Where is there more "free association" (the quotation marks indicate conjointly a citation and a qualification) than in the dream? To ask the analysand on the couch to free associate in relation to the dream is to ask him to dream, to sleep-talk!

"What startled you into wakefulness?" "I saw you in the dream and you had the same voice, name, eye color, hairstyle, manner of walking and talking, etc., in short, I saw you in the dream exactly as you are now in wakefulness!"

One of the things that initially unsettled him most when he died was that many of the things he was seeing did not seem different from those he had seen in the world while alive: for example, he was seeing what appeared to be the same trees and the same derelict buildings, which seemed to coexist in both the world of the living and the labyrinthine realm of death. Yet soon enough, he became aware of numerous differences between the world and the death realm, for example, that in the latter "the leaves being connected by millions of fibres with his own body, there on the seat, fanned it up and down; when the branch stretched he, too, made that statement."[578]

How and when did the resurrected brother of Mary and Martha, who used to be called Lazarus, recognize that he was no longer a living mortal but solely, fully alive? Was it when he noticed that no one called him anymore? Was it when he was no longer assumed to be subject to the religious law and moral standards, treated as a *ḥayawān*, an animal?

Any threshold implies, whether implicitly or explicitly, a decision as to whether one belongs to the other side even transiently.

In the midst of bustling and hectic activity, he would look for moments of suspension by standing unobtrusively near a threshold, whether to a building, room, or garden, whether patent, such as an imposing gate, or barely noticeable, like a faint chalk line across the floor, or "a line in the sand," and savor consciously the almost imperceptible slowing down and then momentary suspension at the threshold on the part of the one walking or even running because late—even though this suspension would result in an additional delay, however minimal. (A documentary filmmaker should make manifest this suspension.) All thresholds induce some suspension, even if unconscious or scarcely perceptible, on the part of the one who has reached them, even when he or she ostensibly did not skip a beat. (Inversely, when we detect a hesitation at some point in space, this likely indicates that the moving person detected some threshold—even if unconsciously.) And yet this man who was so into thresholds and so sensitive to them did not reconsider what to do at the gate of Dracula's castle notwithstanding that the vampire told him emphatically, "Enter freely and of your own will," but proceeded inside even before the host had finished his words! He was right not to do so, since he had already passed the threshold to the death realm by the time those who had travelled with him had, with one excuse or another, left him all by "himself" (he too, concomitantly, deserted himself, through undergoing dissociation). Once he passed the threshold to death, did all other thresholds cease to matter to him, becoming insignificant in comparison? On the contrary, it is "in" the labyrinth that thresholds mattered the most.

I recommend watching Roy Samaha's film *Landscape at Noon* (2017) before or after or as a manner of dying before dying physically. To my twofold surprise, Samaha managed in this film not only to draw on my book *(Vampires): An Uneasy Essay on the Undead in Film*, in particular the section "Photographic Memory," as if he were its contemporary, notwithstanding that this book continued to be forthcoming even after the publication of its second edition (2003);[579] but also to unconsciously and/or intuitively draw on the following paragraph of mine that was forthcoming in the usual sense of the term, not yet published. That is a befitting all-round untimely engagement with the writings of a still productive author at least part of whose published work continues to be forthcoming even after its publication. The film's credits indicate that it is "based on" two texts: my "Photographic Memory" and "Fragment of a Novel" by Lord Byron. When he showed me the penultimate version of the film, I briefly considered notifying him to add the aforementioned still unpublished text to the short list of references in the credits, but then opted not to do it, hoping that he would end up mysteriously doing it himself in the final version.

Is the sensible manner to recognize that one is dead to retrace the moment of transition from life to death? But is there such a moment? He woke up from some dream—or swoon. His lover was hugging him, as if to compensate for some long absence away from her. He could vividly remember the image of a burning house, and, in what appeared to be a confirmation of the reality of that image, moments later he noticed burns on his forearm! Sometime later, he ostensibly met his dead father, which implies that he must have already died in the interim for this apparent meeting to be possible at all! As there is a lapse of consciousness between wakefulness and dreaming, there is one, albeit likely of being rather than simply of consciousness, between life and death (as undeath). He assumed that he would have been able to detect, or would be able to retrospectively determine, a break at the threshold between life and death, the way Harker in Bram Stoker's *Dracula* deduces that he must have undergone a lapse of consciousness, if not of being, from the discrepancy, the "jump cut," between what he was seeing before the lapse of consciousness, if not of being, and after it, "I must have been asleep, for certainly if I had been fully awake I must have noticed the approach to such a remarkable place,"[580] the vampire's castle. So, he was perplexed, indeed maddened, by the circumstance that he not only failed to recall any event or incident that could have led to his physical death, for example, a car crash or an explosion, but also did not suffer (from) some blank in his memory that would have implied that he had undergone a lapse of consciousness (if not of being) but instead experienced and remembered only a continuity between the time in which, as far as he knew, he was still alive and his "meeting" his dead father, notwithstanding that one of the conditions of possibility of such a "meeting" would have been that he had died in the interim. (That one did not detect a lapse of consciousness, if not of being, from life to death could be considered an indication that what one took to be still part of one's life in the world was just an unlikely configuration and guise of labyrinthine death.) In a desperate, impulsive attempt to escape the labyrinthine house where the questionable "meeting" with his dead father, as well as various accompanying uncanny, impossible events ostensibly occurred, he set the house on fire and ran toward the door while trying his best not to asphyxiate from the smoke or be burned by the flames obstructing the way to the exit. He must have fallen unconscious from inhaling the smoke. He woke up from some dream—or swoon—only to find his lover hugging him, as if to compensate for some long absence away from her. Was this "dream" or swoon the break between life and death he was looking for? But how could it have occurred *after* he had, as implied by his ostensible meeting with his dead father, died?

The following tradition is attributed by Shiʿites to imam ʿAlī, "Work for your life in this world as if you'll live forever, and work for your afterlife as if you'll die tomorrow" (*Iʿmal lidunyāk ka'nnaka taʿīsh abadan, wa iʿmal l'ākhiratika ka'nnaka tamūt ghadan*) (this tradition is also attributed weakly to the Prophet Muhammad). The first half of this tradition has to do with what is exoteric, *ẓāhir*, manifest, the *dunyā*, this world, and manifestly applies since, according to general relativity, most clearly in its Minkowski formulation in terms of a four-dimensional space-time, time does not pass, thus whatever one does will be "forever" in the block universe; and the second half has to do with what is hidden, occulted, invisible, esoteric, with dreams, death, and the afterlife, and would apply from the perspective of the following prophetic tradition, "Hudhaifah (May Allāh be pleased with him) reported: 'Whenever the Prophet, Allāh's blessing and peace be upon him, lay down for sleep at night, he would place his (right) hand under his (right) cheek and supplicate: "O Allāh! Let me die with Thy name on my lips, and with Thy name on my lips let me rise"[581] (*Allahumma bismika amūtu wa aḥyā*). And when he woke up, he would say: "All praise is due to Allāh, Who has brought us back to life after He has caused us to die, and to Him is the return when we shall all be gathered" (*Al-ḥamd lillāh al-ladhī aḥyānā baʿda mā amātanā, wa ilayh al-nushūr*)'" (Al-Bukhārī, *Riyād al-Ṣāliḥīn* 816, Book 4, Hadith 4; this prophetic tradition would remain abstract for the reader as long as he or she has not felt that he or she had died before dying physically as he or she dreamt, and as long as he or she has not been marked by this circumstance, including in the manner of paradoxically mourning himself or herself after being brought back to life through waking). *Rasūl allāh*, the Messenger of God, here Muhammad, and the imam, here ʿAlī, appear to switch roles and functions in relation to the exoteric and the esoteric. It is Muhammad here who reveals the esoteric, that every time one sleeps (and dreams) one dies, that sleep (and dreaming) is a sort of death, that we will for sure be dead tomorrow—unless we do not sleep (but for how long can one resist falling asleep?)—and that if we continue to exist in the world the following morning and day, it is only because God has resurrected us. And it is 'Alī, the imam according to Shi'ites, the custodian of the esoteric, who, by adding the "as if," couches what he says in a manner that provides an exoteric occultation of the esoteric (that's one kind of *taqiyya* [dissimulation]: tell someone what is literally the case at the esoteric level by making it seem to be figurative through qualifying it with "as if"—this manner of rendering the esoteric meaning is adequate when addressing those who can be treated *as if* they were Muslims)![582]

While dreams can be interpreted *in* waking life, in other words, while waking life itself is not as such an interpretation of dreams but may include episodes when one interprets various dreams during a psychoanalysis, the dream, while not allowing an interpretation within it, unless the dream happens to be a lucid one, is itself an interpretation, albeit an obscure one, not of this or that episode of waking life but of waking life as a whole. In other words, whereas waking life can ostensibly be at times, during a psychoanalysis, an interpretation of a dream or several dreams, the dream is an *interpretation* not of this or that episode of waking life but of waking life as a whole, albeit one unaware and unconscious of being that, *much more fundamentally* than it is a "wish fulfillment," in particular, according to Freud, the fulfillment of a wish that one does not acknowledge, indeed that one repressed in waking life.

In life, as long as one continues to be in denial of one's condition of mortal, of being dead even while still physically alive, (physical) "death ... is nothing to us, since when we exist, death is not present, and when death is present, we do not exist"[583] (Epicurus—my qualification); and in death, one has the impression that one has always been dead, which would seem to imply that one has never been alive (any ostensible memory, even a vivid one, that the one disoriented in the labyrinthine realm of death may have of a car crash or grave sickness that ostensibly led to his or her physical death is soon mistrusted by him or her, suspected of not being related to an actual event in the past). The paradigmatic manner of not being stuck in this ostensible exclusivity of each of the two realms of life and death is to die before dying physically and thus become aware that one is a mortal, dead even while still physically alive.

Most people just die physically, a death that remains external to them, that they never experience: "Death ... is nothing to us, since when we exist, death is not present, and when death is present, we do not exist"[584] (Epicurus—I would replace every occurrence of "death" in the quote with "physical death"). One has to do with one's death, indeed can be said to have some agency in relation to it, not by committing suicide and thus dying physically but by dying before dying physically (*exceptionally*, in the wrenching process of failing to commit suicide or of botching one's suicide, one unintentionally dies before one's physical death).

What would make the event that led to someone's death, for example a car crash, not an accident? Is it to be informed by some oracle that he is going to die in this specific manner at that specific date and place? Perhaps, but then the oracle itself would strike him as an accident, as something undergone externally—the accidentality has merely been displaced from physical death to the oracle. Rather, it is that it would have happened after an inexplicable—even to himself— whimsical change of plans on his part, and that he discovers at his new destination that he, or someone else with whom he is mistaken, was being awaited. It is through this prior ostensibly whimsical change of plans that he met his subsequent death half-way, signaling that, unlike so many others, he evinced being-towards-his-physical- death (which is not to be equated with what Heidegger meant with "being-towards-death").

Isn't death the greatest trauma? How come then that having died before dying physically, he did not suffer from post-traumatic stress disorder? Is it on account of death's being, unlike other traumas, "that *possibility which is one's ownmost*"[585] (Heidegger)?

How can the extensive and still expanding knowledge of Egyptologists not be merely academic? While Muslim local Egyptologists whose version of their religion is the mainstream, exoteric one are bound to consider that the beliefs of the ancient Egyptians about death are grossly incorrect, has there never existed some agnostic Egyptologist who entertained the possibility that what is described in the Egyptian Book of the Dead has some chance of being actually the case in the death realm (while considering that the divinities related in that text to the world of the living are the product of an illegitimate extrap- olation from the realm of the dead), or a Muslim Egyptologist who was a follower of the Sufi Ibn al-'Arabī (who in some of his texts "alludes to a hadith that says that God will appear at the resurrection in a multitude of forms, but His creatures will deny Him until He appears in a form that corresponds to their own belief"[586]) and who therefore believed that "at the resurrection, the Real [that is, God] will disclose Himself and say, 'I am your Lord.' They will see Him, but nevertheless they will deny Him and not acknowledge Him as their Lord, despite the *wujūd* of vision because of the lifting of the veil. When He transmutes Himself for them into the mark through which they recognize Him [in the case of ancient Egyptians, Osiris], they will say to Him, 'Thou art our Lord.' Yet He is the one whom they were denying and from whom they were seeking refuge, and He is the one whom they confessed and recognized [as Osiris, in the case of ancient Egyptians]"?[587] To my meager knowledge about this matter, no Egyptologist, notwithstanding his or her extensive knowledge of ancient Egyptians' language and funerary culture and rites, which are documented in their books of the dead and their sarcophagi and tombs, conceived the project of providing food offerings to the dead ancient Egyptians in a ceremonial manner (a very small percentage of the proceeds from the Museum of Egyptian Antiquities' ticket receipts would easily cover the sums required for these offerings). Is it because they might have been afraid of being criticized, if not possibly threatened, by zealous Egyptian Muslims? Is it because they assume that the ancient Egyptian dead, even those whose mummies and sarcophagi have been largely preserved, have long undergone the definitive, second death? But couldn't those ancient Egyptian dead whose mummies and sarcophagi have been preserved be surviving, albeit ever more miserably, by partaking of the painted food they magically eat, which, not having an equivalent in the food of the world of the living, provides less and less sustenance,[588] is ever more tasteless, instancing another form of the rise of entropy? If the answer is yes, at least one Egyptologist should have felt that he or she has a responsibility to train to be a priest and then to officiate the ritual offering of provisions to the dead ancient Egyptians whose mummies and sarcophagi have been preserved, thus resuming, even if surreptitiously (through framing it to be for educational reasons rather than existential ones), the provision of food to (the ka of) a dead ancient Egyptian. When I asked Egyptologist Lisa K. Sabbahy, the editor of *All Things Ancient Egypt: An Encyclopedia of the Ancient Egyptian World* (Greenwood, 2019), whether an Egyptologist could effectively officiate the ritual provision of food offerings to a dead ancient Egyptian, she answered: "No Egyptologist considers these matters"—this would indicate that they are mere academicians.

One of the particularities about the resurrection of Lazarus by Jesus Christ, a particularity that confirms that the one who performed it is *the life*, is that no one who was present there felt, on seeing Lazarus come out of the grave, that they were themselves possibly dead, in the death realm, a realm where some of what is deemed impossible while one is alive and part of nature and the world appears to happen.

Who could have been the narrator of Leonid Andreyev's short story "Lazarus"? Is it someone who had met the resurrected mortal Lazarus[589] or who had heard about the events related in the short story from some of those who met him? Those who were the first to meet the resurrected mortal Lazarus upon his return from the grave must have unconsciously intuited that it was far more prudent not to be each, in turn, alone with him but to welcome the one who had come back from the grave, from death, as a community, something that they could be as alive people (soon enough, though, while not moving themselves, the cozy space between them at the beginning of the welcoming celebration had inflated to such a degree that they were no longer a community, each having become unreachable). At the communal gathering to celebrate Lazarus's return from the grave, someone who though "no thought was clearly defined in his mind … smilingly asked: 'Why do you not tell us, Lazarus, what was There?'" Even had they received an answer from the resurrected mortal Lazarus, his effect on them, for example, via his gaze, through which they apprehended the death realm from which he had returned, would have been to make them indifferent to his initially eagerly awaited answer and to others' subsequent questions to them about their meeting with him; indeed, indifferent *tout court*, ceasing to talk themselves: "Now … [the] voice [of the one who was inquiring for the third time, 'So you will not tell us, Lazarus, what you saw There?'] was dull, and a dead, grey weariness looked stupidly from out his eyes. The faces of all present were also covered by the same dead grey weariness. The guests … stopped talking." Who, then, could and did narrate mortal Lazarus's posthumous existence among the living? Was it no other than the one who resurrected him? Sometimes, when Lazarus rested, an onlooker would feel that his hand did not look like the resting hand of a living man, that it had the motionlessness of a corpse, that it looked the way it did when he or she had seen it on Lazarus's deathbed or in the grave: "On the table, as if forgotten by Lazarus, lay his livid blue hand."[590] That was an unwelcome reminder that he had been a corpse in the grave and an indication that he may still partially be one, as if life had not reclaimed his whole body, the hand still that of a corpse. I can very well imagine someone hastily asking him to hand him something, salt, for example, so that he would in the process move his hand, and then uttering a sigh of relief when Lazarus did move his hand, dispelling thus his or her apprehension that it was lifeless—but this relief would have been brief, the one who had apprehensively asked him to move his hand soon becoming indifferent, including to the taste of salt, indeed to the difference between a living hand and a dead one. Even though, indifferent to them and their question about what he experienced *There*, in the grave and death, Lazarus does not answer them, the rest of the story conveys to us some of what was "There," since *There* or some aspects of it did in part, through Lazarus, who came back from the grave, infiltrate the world (requiring, as a countermeasure, the presence and intervention of *the life* in the figure of Jesus Christ:

to resurrect the mortal Lazarus who came back from the grave, make him solely alive, and thus spare the world being contaminated by the death introduced in it by him):

— One becomes indifferent, thus, after meeting the Lazarus hailing from the grave, the sculptor "Aurelius created nothing" but "looked with absolute indifference at marble and at bronze and at his own divine creations, in which dwelt immortal beauty," and when "his friends led him to see the beautiful creations of others ... he remained indifferent," and thus, during the emperor's meeting with Lazarus, "already the accent of indifference was in his voice," even while commanding him, "Cease."

— "There was no more a sense of time; the beginning of all things and their end merged into one. In the very moment when a building was being erected and one could hear the builders striking with their hammers, one seemed already to see its ruins, and then emptiness where the ruins were."

— One finds it extremely difficult to remember, partly because, as mentioned previously, "there was no more a sense of time," consequently, when they asked him what happened *There*, in death, implicitly requiring him to remember, his effect on them was that they themselves "stared at one another stupidly, not knowing why they had come together or why they sat around this rich table," in other words, his effect on them was, among other anomalies, that they themselves could no longer remember not only why they had come together and sat around the rich table, but also the question one of them had thrice asked him, indeed that one of them had asked him a question—the last thing they could remember was his hand as he lay as a corpse on his bed four nights earlier and how similar that hand was to his inert hand presently.

— One senses emptiness, an expanding, indeed inflating emptiness between things and in them that the Freudian "Eros,[591] which holds together everything in the world"[592] (as is clear in its "efforts ... to combine organic substances into ever larger unities"[593]), would not be strong enough to counter (in Andreyev's "Lazarus," they become alone, one characteristic of death, not because, as in "my experience" of, and writings on, death, one is lost to others [and to oneself] "in" the labyrinth of death but because of the inflating emptiness between them): "In emptiness the trees spread their roots, themselves empty; in emptiness rose phantom temples, palaces and houses—all empty; and in the emptiness moved restless Man, himself empty."

"There" is not simply a euphemism for the death realm, and, through the capitalization, a manner of conjointly implying that it is the furthest and, suggestively if not magically, keeping it at a distance (and thus is unconsciously meant to function as an exorcism), but gives an indication of one characteristic of death. Michel Serres: "In the reference's very place lies death, which makes space something other than a homogeneous void. Being-there is easily translated into the French language: *ci-gît* [here lies]: the ancient funerary phrase.... 'Here lies': that means here rests such and such, but at bottom means: by virtue of such and such a dead person, the layer [*gisement*: I translated this French word as "deposit" in the first and second editions of my book *(Vampires): An Uneasy Essay on the Undeath in Film*, which were published prior to the English translation of Serres's book] for here appears.... Death causes the here or the there to be born; I was born not far from the place where the forebear is dissolving. I situate myself by means of layer [I would translate *gisement* as deposit] and distance, therefore by means of the interval from death [I translated: by keeping away from death]."[594] While, as Serres indicated, physical death in the figure of the tombstone and the buried corpse grounds the *here* (hence the ancient funerary phrase "Here lies") and, by implication, the *there* as one's distance from the buried body and the tombstone, death as undeath instances a different there, "There," which does not become a "here" when one dies, since in the labyrinthine realm of death one does not feel that one is where one ostensibly is (hence in vampire films, the vampire is never fully where he ostensibly is, as shown by his absence in the mirror at the same location) and one is lost, not only in the sense that one is repeatedly unable to find one's whereabouts but also in the sense that one cannot be found there, for example by the other dead, indeed by God—except miraculously. Isn't that a form of exile, no longer to be able to assert "I am here" when dead, in the death realm with its labyrinthine space and time—except through an unlikely temporary configuration of the labyrinth that happens to look and function like the world of living humans? The dead are in this sense in exile not only from life but also in death. The mortal miraculously resurrected by a *mortal* remains in exile, does not fully return to here, but brings back the *There* with him or her. While it is understandable that in Andreyev's "Lazarus" those who celebrated the return from the grave of mortal Lazarus did not then throng the one who accomplished this ostensible miracle, since their prior meeting with Lazarus left them totally indifferent, it is odd that the mortal Lazarus does not end up meeting again the one who brought him back from the grave and who is referred to as "the Master" (a circumstance that is even odder than the one in the New Testament, where it appears that the one who was called Lazarus prior to his physical death met Jesus Christ only once after the latter resurrected him: "Six days before the Passover, Jesus came to Bethany, where Lazarus lived, whom Jesus had raised from the dead. Here a dinner was given in Jesus's honor. Martha served, while Lazarus was among those reclining at the table with him" [John 12:1-2]), and that Caesar, who summons Lazarus for a meeting, does not demand to meet the mortal master, who, unlike him who is ostensibly a master of life, is ostensibly a master of death, a sort of Antichrist, since he managed to bring back a dead man from the grave, and, through him, made death infiltrate and contaminate the world of the living, perhaps to ask him—in exchange for what?—how best to deal with the mortal resurrected Lazarus to mitigate the danger he poses to life and the world. What we witness through the encounter of Lazarus and Caesar Augustus is a duel for recognition between the man "wonderfully raised from the dead" and a Hegelian kind of master, "a courageous man" who "felt his power was invincible," who had no fear of death, whose status as the master of the Roman Empire presupposed as its Hegelian condition of possibility that he was willing to risk his physical life in a duel for recognition with any other man (at least within that empire), and who was presently risking his life for recognition, in this case the recognition of a difference of life from death, in a supplement to the Hegelian scene in the *Phenomenology of Spirit* of the duel to the death for recognition, by looking straight into the eyes of the mortal resurrected Lazarus, at one point exclaiming or rather sighing drowsily, "You have killed me, Lazarus," that is, in this case, you have made me unable any longer to recognize a difference between life and death. The mortal Lazarus who was brought back from the grave is not only indifferent but is a figure of the indifference of life and death, thus of indifference to the difference between indifference (one of the figures of death, exemplified, in cosmology, by the heat death, as the universe's "entropy progressively increases toward a maximum value and all parts come into thermal equilibrium at a uniform temperature"[595]) and difference (life [while it certainly could not exist in the case of maximum entropy, that is not to say that life does not require a modicum of indifference to difference, since, as Bergson noted, "the sensory-motor image effectively retains from the thing only what interests us, or what extends into the reaction of a character.... It associates with the thing many different things that resemble it on the same plane, in so far as they provoke all the same movements: it is grass in general that interests the herbivore. It is in this sense that the sensory-motor schema is an agent of abstraction"[596] (Deleuze)]). The Antichrist as "Master" made Lazarus return from the grave by reducing the difference between life and death to nothing, yet this indifference is partial to death since death is in one of its aspects precisely indifference, the leveling of difference, including, in its labyrinthine space and time, between left and right, past and present, Prado, Chambige, Dionysus, etc. Given that he is a figure of this indifference, he can most fittingly exist only once it has propagated by means of him and applies to everything, the difference, for example, between a blue sky and a cloudy one becoming itself indifferent: "The sun did not stop shining when he looked, neither did the fountain cease playing, and the Eastern sky remained cloudless and blue as always; but the man who fell under his inscrutable gaze could no longer feel the sun, nor hear the fountain, nor recognise his native sky." "'Listen to me, stranger,' said the emperor sharply, giving expression to what had been in his mind before. 'My empire is an empire of the living; my people are a people of the living and not of the dead.... I do not know what you have seen There, but if you lie, I hate your lies, and if you tell the truth, I hate your truth [*I can very well imagine him adding*: and I am afraid that, through you, truth and lies will become indiscernible, or that I would become indifferent to their difference]. In my heart I feel the pulse of life; in my hands I feel power.... Under the protection of my authority, under the shadow of the laws I have created, men live and labour and rejoice. Do you hear this divine harmony of life?' ... Augustus extended his arms reverently and solemnly cried out: 'Blessed art thou, Great Divine Life!'" What is missing from Andreyev's "Lazarus" is *the life*, the real Great Divine Life, Jesus Christ ("Jesus said to her, 'I am ... the life'" [John 11:25]), the real Master ("One of the twelve disciples, who was called 'The Twin,' was not with them when Jesus came. The other disciples told him, 'We have seen the Master'" [John 20:24]), certainly when it comes to resurrection ("Jesus said to her, 'I am the resurrection'" [John 11:25]). The following could have been a sequel and postscript to this story that transpires *after the end*, after the death of Lazarus: sometime after meeting the worldly master, Roman emperor Augustus, who is a master of those who are within (the Roman Empire part of) the world, but is not master of the world in the sense that he would be able to bestow a world on someone world-less, for example, a mortal resurrected by a mortal, Lazarus meets the real, ultimate Master, who would resurrect him who had returned from the grave as a mortal from his condition of mortality, making him solely alive, no longer a mortal.

A mortal who was resurrected by another mortal asked him: "Why have you resurrected me?" "I have done it so you would tell me what happens in the state of death." "I do not remember anything of that state. It was like a dream that faded away when I opened my eyes upon being resurrected." When one who was not at the feast to celebrate the resurrection inquired of one who was, "Is the dead man really alive again?" his addressee answered, "Yes," then added, "On hearing of his death, I felt joy in being alive and a strong desire to continue living, yet, given that he, too, the unworldly entity we endured yesterday, is alive, I am presently unsure what being alive is!"

Given that the Hegelian duel for recognition is supposed to be to the death, then, whatever its physical outcome, at least one of the duelists would at its conclusion have the status of a dead person; the duelist who surrendered is thenceforth symbolically dead and treated as (symbolically) dead by the one who as a result of winning the duel is thenceforth his master, indeed is treated as (symbolically) dead by any master (this is not to say that he died before dying in my sense; usually, he is in disavowal of his condition of mortal, of being dead while still physically alive). When it comes to reacting to a slap, the situation of the master and the slave is by no means reciprocal: whereas for a master, a slap is a slap when targeting a slave or a fellow master, in the case of a slave, who became one as a result of his surrender during an actual fight to the death for recognition or the postulated Hegelian ur-fight to the death for recognition, a slap is a slap when it is directed at another slave, but for it to count as a slap when directed at his master or some master rather than be dismissed by them as an unfortunate accident, the master has to treat the slave as a possible participant in a duel to the death with him, indeed engage him in such a duel, thus reenacting the primordial duel to the death for recognition[597]—but this reenactment is largely if not wholly not up to the slave however much he wishes for it to happen; the master has to accede to the slave's request for a duel to the death for recognition by considering it not to be absurd even though the slave is already (symbolically) dead vis-à-vis him. Worried on hearing that he had rebelled or entreated his master to engage him in a fight to the death for recognition as a free, alive man, another slave, an imperceptive one, asked him, "Are you suicidal?" "No; it is not my aim to die, but to be treated as alive through, and at least for the duration of, the duel to the death for recognition." Another imperceptive slave asked him, "Aren't you worried that he would accept your challenge?" "No, I am worried that he would send another slave to fight me." Would the master be behaving in a cowardly manner were he to have other slaves deal with his rebellious slave? Or would it be that the master finds it absurd to himself kill the rebellious slave, since vis-à-vis him the latter is already dead given that his condition of slave presupposes (according to Hegel) an actual or primordial duel to the death for recognition, one he lost, and so lets him be dealt with and executed by another slave, thus leaving it to the dead to deal with and bury the dead[598] (since they are already dead symbolically, it does not make sense for there to be a duel to the death between two slaves that is not to *physical* death)? In the slave's relation with the master, death is always implied: his default position, from the perspective of the master, is that he is dead (or, if grudgingly considered to be alive, a mere animal [mention is made in Dostoyevsky's *The Gambler* of an "empress of antiquity who would undress in front of her slave, since she did not consider him a man"], since he was unable to risk fully his natural, animal life and thus transcend it during the duel to the death for recognition), and to escape this position and status, he has to induce the master to accept to (re-)engage in a duel to the death for recognition. The master controls the life and death of the slave, not only or primarily because he can have his other slaves kill the latter but because the slave can be alive only through the master accepting to (re)engage in a duel to the death for recognition with him.

The narrator of Dostoyevsky's *Notes from the Underground* asserts, "I admit that twice two makes four is an excellent thing, but if we are to give everything its due, twice two makes five is sometimes a very charming thing too."[599] Is he stupid? No, though a more fitting example in the context of this tale of resentment that revisits an incident in which he was slighted without responding would be "$1 = 1$ and $1 - 1 = 0$ are excellent things, but if we are to give everything its due, the following case is valid, too: $1 - 0 =$ resentment, indeed, in some excessive instances of the latter, *jouissance*-inducing resentment [a Buddhist master could have added, "During zazen and as a result of it, $1 - 0 =$ detachment, without, or including from, resentment"; and Deleuze could have added, "$1 - 0 =$ visionary perception of pure optical (and sound) images (rather than resentment) in those cases where the absence of response to a slight, or insult, or humiliation, or bullying is the consequence of a break of the sensory-motor link (which is more likely to happen during and in the aftermath of a war or civil war), so that the aforementioned iniquities "never truly concern the person who ... is subject to them, even when they strike him in his flesh"[600]]. Resentment, one's affect when the sensory-motor link is not broken but still intact and functional and yet one does not react even to an emergency neither because one is an idiot (in the Deleuzian sense), thus feels that there is a deeper question more worthy of attending to and more urgent than the emergency, nor because one is detached (in a Buddhist sense), would seem to be a proper problem for the Dostoyevskian resentful idiot of *Notes from the Underground*; *jouissance* would also be a proper problem for him, including, indeed primarily, one that is triggered by, and related to, resentment: "I got to the point of feeling a sort of secret abnormal, despicable enjoyment in returning home to my corner on some disgusting Petersburg night, acutely conscious that that day I had committed a loathsome action again,[601] that what was done could never be undone, and secretly, inwardly gnawing, gnawing at myself for it, tearing and consuming myself till at last the bitterness turned into a sort of shameful accursed sweetness, and at last—into positive real enjoyment!... How is enjoyment in this to be explained? But I will explain it. I will get to the bottom of it!"[602] Someone may not respond because he or she has undergone a break of the sensory-motor link, or because the reactive forces in him are stronger than the active ones, a creature of resentment (while it appears that he failed altogether to react to the disrespectful act, actually his response was limited to tendencies to react in the form of micro-movements [on the receptive, sensory organs] in his face), or because he is an Idiot (in the Deleuzian sense) and so feels that there is a more urgent, deeper matter and problem than getting slighted, and this problem may be precisely resentment (but for that the resentful character should be able not to be consumed by the memory of the unanswered slight or insult which acts as an emergency even though in some cases it occurred years, if not decades, in the past). While the idiot is different from the one who is resentful, even though neither reacts to what appears to be emergencies—since once the idiot finds the answer to the deeper question or the solution to the more fundamental problem he or she was considering, he or she acts undeterred, even if the odds of success in relation to the more fundamental emergency are very small—how to differentiate between someone who is resentful and someone who is an idiot *and* does not end up acting because he does not end up finding the answer to the deeper question or the solution to the more fundamental problem? In some cases, it is through the *jouissance* one can detect on the part of the resentful. Freud, although a reader of Dostoyevsky (indeed, one of his texts is titled "Dostoevsky and Parricide" [1928]) and although he wrote, "How then, strictly speaking, does his [Dostoyevsky's] neurosis show itself? Dostoyevsky called himself an epileptic, and was regarded as such by other people, on account of his severe attacks, which were accompanied by loss of consciousness, muscular convulsions and subsequent depression. Now it is highly probable that this so-called epilepsy was only a symptom of his neurosis and must accordingly be classified as hystero-epilepsy—that is, as severe hysteria.... The 'epileptic reaction' ... is also undoubtedly at the disposal of the neurosis whose essence it is to get rid by somatic means of amounts of excitation which it cannot deal with psychically. Thus the epileptic attack becomes a symptom of hysteria and is adapted and modified by it,"[603] did not generalize enough when he wrote, "If I may be allowed to generalize—which is unavoidable in so condensed an account as this—I should like to formulate what we have learned so far as follows: *our hysterical patients suffer from reminiscences*. Their symptoms are residues and mnemic symbols of particular (traumatic) experiences":[604] hysterical patients *but also resentful characters* suffer from reminiscences (it is thus fitting that perhaps the greatest writer on resentment, Dostoyevsky, was a hysteric, hence someone who himself suffered from reminiscences). But while the hysteric suffers from unconscious, repressed reminiscences, the resentful person suffers from conscious ones. The hysteric reacts excessively, albeit in a deferred manner (*après-coup*), to what he or she associates with an event he or she does not remember and to which he or she did not react on the spot, as it nonplussed him or her then, while the resentful person failed to react to a slight, or insult, or humiliation, or bullying that he remembers all too well, indeed excessively, and would fail to react were the occasion to present itself again ... and again. Some people, for example, the narrator of Dostoyevsky's *Notes from the Underground*, are both hysterical and resentful, hence suffer from both conscious and unconscious, repressed, reminiscences: "One night as I was passing a tavern I saw through a lighted window some gentlemen fighting with billiard cues, and saw one of them thrown out of the window. At other times I should have felt very much disgusted, but I was in such a mood at the time that I actually envied the gentleman thrown out of the window—and I envied him so much that I even went into the tavern and into the billiard-room. 'Perhaps,' I thought, 'I'll have a fight, too, and they'll throw me out of the window.' I was not drunk—but what is one to do—depression will drive a man to such a pitch of *hysteria*. But nothing happened. It seemed that I was not even equal to being thrown out of the window and I went away without having my fight. An officer put me in my place from the first moment. I was standing by the billiard-table and in my ignorance blocking up the way, and he wanted to pass; he took me by the shoulders and without a word—without a warning or explanation—moved me from where I was standing to another spot and passed by as though he had not noticed me. I could have forgiven blows, but I could not forgive his having moved me without noticing me.... I had been treated like a fly. This officer was over six foot, while I was a spindly little fellow. But the quarrel was in my hands. I had only to protest and I certainly would have been thrown out of the window. But I changed my mind and preferred to beat a *resentful* retreat" (my italics). He is a complex character not only because he is both resentful and hysterical, thus suffering consciously *and* unconsciously from reminiscences, but also because, exceptionally, he is an idiot hence is not consumed by either the strange untimely emergency of a traumatic event that happened historically years before but that strikes him *après-coup*, in a differed manner, or by the anachronistic emergency of the memory of the disregard he was shown and to which he did not respond, but continues to be attentive primarily to the deeper problems of resentment and *jouissance*, indeed to the twisted, fundamental problem of *jouissance* in resentment.

Nietzsche wrote: "Imagine 'the enemy' as conceived of by the man of *ressentiment*—and here we have his deed, his creation: he has conceived of the 'evil enemy,' 'the evil one' as a basic idea to which he now thinks up a ... counterpart, the 'good one'—himself! ... Exactly the opposite is true of the noble one who conceives of the basic idea 'good' by himself, in advance and spontaneously, and only then creates a notion of 'bad'! This 'bad' of noble origin and that 'evil' from the cauldron of unassuaged hatred—the first is an afterthought, an aside, a complementary colour, whilst the other is the original, the beginning, the actual deed in the conception of slave morality—how different are the two words 'bad' and 'evil,' although both seem to be the opposite for the same concept, 'good'! But it is not the same concept 'good.'" And so he advocated going "beyond good and evil" (the title of one of his books) while clarifying: "at least this does *not* mean 'Beyond Good and Bad'"[605]—given that what Nietzsche terms "slave morality" has triumphed insidiously and given that I consider that most slaves (but also most nobles) have little to do with evil, which is inextricably related to *jouissance* and the drive, but are within the domain of good and bad, the crucial difference being that the slaves' evaluation is a resentful one while the nobles' is an affirmative one, I would have written that one should go beyond the resentful bad and good to the noble good and bad. While Nietzsche conducted himself in his life according to a noble evaluation in terms of (the) good and bad (of his as well as Spinoza's ethics), I contend that what he encountered when he died before dying physically ("This autumn ... I twice attended my funeral") was not good and bad, but Good and Evil. Given that, strictly speaking, one can feel joy only regarding what one wills to recur eternally, in other words, Spinoza's, what is in accord with one's essence, there is no beyond joy; and given that evil is inextricably related to *jouissance* and the drive, hence to the compulsion to repeat what induces *jouissance*, an addiction, there is no beyond evil—indeed, given that the repetition compulsion related to it is not finite, or at least has something infinite, and that the *jouissance* associated with it is *beyond the pleasure principle* (the title of Freud's book that deals with the drive), and that, therefore, its proper, fitting realm is death, indeed ultimately hell, evil is the beyond—or would be the beyond were it not for the all-embracing Mercy of God ("My mercy embraces everything" [Qur'ān 7:156]). The ethical person is, strictly speaking, not beyond Good and Evil but contra Evil (Nietzsche's compilation of his writings on Wagner is titled *Nietzsche Contra Wagner*; the various chapters of the book, "Wherein I Admire Wagner," "Wherein I Raise Objections," "Wagner as a Danger," "A Music Without a Future," "We Antipodes," "Where Wagner Is at Home," "Wagner as the Apostle of Chastity," "How I Got Rid of Wagner," "The Psychologist Speaks," would have for equivalent: "Wherein I Admire *Jouissance* and Hence Evil—in Comparison to the Bad," "Wherein I Raise Objections to *Jouissance* and Hence to Evil," "*Jouissance*, and Hence Evil, as a Danger," "A *Jouissance*, and Hence Evil, Without a Future" [since it leads to a compulsion to repeat], "We Antipodes" [Nietzsche, the philosopher of the will (which as such wills the eternal recurrence of its object), who feels a great affinity with Spinoza, the philosopher of joy, is the antipode of those who are subject, indeed addicted, to *jouissance*, but also of those who are bad, and, to a lesser degree, even, though he can be misunderstood given that he advocated it in his polemic against Good and Evil, the good of the noble, who, while far better than resentful people, remain, as long as they reach neither joy nor *jouissance*, human, all too human], "Where *Jouissance* and Hence Evil Is at Home Is Hell," "The One into *Jouissance* as the Apostle of Chastity When It Comes to Pleasure" [insofar as the one addicted to *jouissance* refrains from any activity that might induce mere pleasure in him or her but not *jouissance*], "How [Through the Assistance of an Angelic Figure] I Got Rid [Early On] of *Jouissance* and Hence of [Incipient] Evil").

In Gary Shore's *Dracula Untold* (2014), Prince Vlad Dracula, the ruler of Transylvania, approaches a monster in the hope that he will grant him some of his occult powers: "The Turks threaten to destroy my kingdom. With power like yours, I could stop them, save my people, save my family." "How supremely noble, Lord Impaler, House Dracul, Son of the Devil." "You're mistaken. It means, 'Son of the dragon,' 'Protector of the innocent.'" "Do your people know how many innocents you have killed? Was it hundreds?" "Yes." "Lie to me again and I'll open you from your belly to your brain and feed you your intestines." "Thousands." "And when you put them to the stake, what did you feel? Shame? Horror? Power? Answer me!" "Nothing! I felt nothing. A greater crime than the act itself." "Then why spill blood, if not for the pleasure of it?" "Because men do not fear swords. They fear monsters. They run from them. By putting one village to the stake, I spared ten more. Sometimes the world no longer needs a hero. Sometimes what it needs is a monster." "And you believe you know what it is to be a monster? Hmm? You have no idea. But I'm going to show you. Drink." Whereas earlier we saw just an old, angry man, now we see something really monstrous: the inordinately long tongue that slithers, as an animal might, out of the cave-like mouth, which must be larger than it appears, to lap the wound in the neck of his interlocutor. Through this blood-drenched tongue and the spasm that passes through it as it gets retracted inside the cave of the mouth, the monster is already associated with *jouissance*. Usually in vampire films, the vampire makes an incision in his body and invites some elect living person to drink his blood (Mina in Coppola's *Dracula* [1992], Louis in Neil Jordan's *Interview with the Vampire* [1994], etc.) in order to initiate the latter into his kind of "existence," undeath. Here the vampire does not do so; instead, he bites his wrist, collects in a container the (already) black blood that spurts from it, and tells Vlad to drink. It is not upon losing the blood from his body but only when Vlad, after some hesitation, drinks it that the vampire feels that he has lost energy and vitality—and experiences *jouissance*. This implies that the blood, though now in a cup, is not extrinsic to him but extimate to him. While we're not shown the following, as the cup's sides obstruct our view of the blood while Vlad drinks, I can very well imagine that, as he does, it turns into vibrant red blood.

Was Gilles de Rais not an imaginary monster because he was an actual historical personage (born 1404, died 1440)? Or was he not an imaginary monster because the imagination balks at what he did, "a hundred gruesome child murders, a rampage which made him arguably the first serial killer in recorded history"?[606] Or was he not an imaginary monster because his acts had less to do with the (Lacanian) imaginary and thus with desire than with the (Lacanian) real and thus with the drive?

My kind of realist writer: the one who, even though it is still impossible to time-travel to another branch of the multiverse from this one, and hence while having no access to another branch of the multiverse and, consequently, not being in a position to model his or her fiction on it, comes up with what happens to be a realistic description of it; and the one who produces fiction that, while it may not model itself on what he or she takes to be reality, nonetheless induces an extra article of reality (in some cases, this could lead the fiction writer to lose the ability to discern whether what he was describing and narrating is fiction or fact). In the former type of fiction, we have realism at the level of another branch of the multiverse as a "whole," even if much of that branch is implied; in the latter type of fiction, we have it usually at the level of one article, which it gives rise to and which would otherwise not be found in reality, so that (the) reality (we have access to in our branch of the multiverse) is not presupposed to be already a "whole" by this type of fiction but complemented by it through being partially produced by it. Given that "no time machine provides pathways to times earlier than the moment at which it came into existence"[607] and that "all fiction that does not violate the laws of physics is fact,"[608] to have unrealistic fiction one has to construct a universe in which one or more of the laws of physics not only of this branch of the multiverse but of all branches of the multiverse are broken.

If a novel or short story does not at any point contradict the laws of physics, and if it works in literary terms, then it describes, usually unbeknownst to the novelist or short-story writer or the reader, what already exists in another branch of the multiverse—that the story he or she wrote happens, usually unbeknownst to him or her, to describe another branch of the multiverse does not imply that the novelist or short-story writer did not invent it creatively given that, until time travel becomes feasible, he or she has no access to the corresponding other branch of the multiverse. If some of what occurs in the short story or novel contradicts the laws of physics, then the novel or short story would be what the vast majority of people consider fiction to be, basically an invention, and thus would have a different ontological status. The situation of a present-day so-called fiction writer whose novel or short story deals with the sort of situations we encounter in "everyday life" rather than, say, includes an astronaut approaching a black hole, that is, a condition for which science has yet to discover the applicable theory (and hence cannot yet predict, for example, whether the astronaut would encounter a firewall at the event horizon), most likely quantum gravity, is different from that of a so-called fiction writer from an earlier period since nowadays, according to physicist Sean Carroll, "the laws of physics underlying everyday life are completely known ... [—] we're not claiming that all the laws of physics are known, only a restricted set that suffices to describe what happens at the level underlying everyday life."[609]

One of the main functions of fiction is to convey aspects of reality that are otherwise inaccessible: (a) as long as time travel has not become feasible, fiction that "does not violate the laws of physics" (David Deutsch) and works formally, compositionally, and stylistically is our only way to have a representation in our branch of the multiverse of other branches of it; (b) fiction reveals that some of the buildings that were damaged in a war or civil war and that documentaries show to have been reconstructed continue to be ruins, labyrinthine spaces and times; (c) fiction can, in the absence of ruins, the usual zone of haunting of the revenant, be the site not of an imagined return of the ghost but of his or her actual return. What could be *"stranger" than fiction* ... that does not fall apart "two days" later and that's a representation of a variant branch of the multiverse? A bad script or novel or short story, one that has already fallen apart before one reads it or that falls apart while one is reading it.

A building that was not physically damaged at all during a war or civil war, whether by shells, bullets, fire, etc., may have turned into a ruin, a labyrinthine space and time, while another that was physically largely destroyed by bombs may not have turned into one. Since they are labyrinthine not only spatially but also temporally, ruins that have been ostensibly renovated or reconstructed can, at some point, induce those in them to suddenly witness them as partly destroyed. It is not so much war that produces ruins—war produces damaged or destroyed buildings, which only exceptionally become ruins in my sense, that is, labyrinthine spaces and times—but ruins that may have an effect on wars by extending them until at least some of the apparently reconstructed buildings are revealed to even the most doggedly imperceptive, "realistic" inhabitants as still partly destroyed buildings and/or as spaces where they are lost, cannot be found (even by themselves: "found himself in ...")—were everybody perceptive enough to have already detected that they are ruins, then the extension of the war would not have been needed. Alas, it's never been the case.

I assert in several of my texts that during and after its civil war there were ruins in Lebanon, that is, buildings that were not merely destroyed or damaged but had become labyrinthine spaces and times,[610] and that they possibly persist in this condition (once a building turns into a ruin, that is, a labyrinthine space and time, can it cease being one? If it can, it would certainly not be simply through its reconstruction. Barring the coming of the Mahdi/Messiah, who would abolish the labyrinth through doing away with its condition, the death as undeath that was unleashed by Adam and Eve's partaking of the knowledge of evil, strictly speaking, one can never again be sure that it is not a ruin but only that, so far, and as far as one can tell, it appears to no longer be a ruin since it seems to have been reintegrated into the worldly space and time sane people live in and share. While one may live one's whole life in a ruin without realizing that it is one, since it appears to be a normal reconstructed building, one may also, sooner or later, witness the ostensibly reconstructed building as partly or largely damaged, or as a space one cannot leave (for it is actually a labyrinth). In my book *(Vampires): An Uneasy Essay on the Undead in Film* (1993; revised and expanded edition, 2003), I had envisioned the following manners for this revelation of the actual state of things: either the tenant or owner of a reconstructed apartment or house would suddenly witness it as physically dilapidated or damaged;[611] or the war and/or civil war would get extended until the building would appear to all as a ruin exoterically rather than to some through symptoms.[612] But the double explosion that struck Beirut in 2020, "one of the largest non-nuclear explosions in history,"[613] causing "at least 218 deaths, 7,000 injuries,"[614] "material damage to an estimated 77,000 apartments located across 10,000 buildings within a 3 km radius of the blast,"[615] and "leaving an estimated 300,000 people homeless,"[616] provided an additional manner. For the interval between many Beirutis' spontaneous assumption that it was a bomb targeting one of the country's political leaders or an Israeli air raid and the subsequent information that it was a blast at the port following a fire, and while they were still in a daze, stupefied by the discrepancy between the seeming instantaneousness of the blast, "in a flash of a second," and the extensive damage they were seeing as they rushed, or were pushed by the pressure of the blast, out of offices, hospitals, their apartments, cafés, supermarkets, etc., and that appeared to be the effect of a protracted war or civil war (rows and rows of burned and overturned cars, streets full of broken glass, etc.), some must have had the feeling that they had just experienced an apocalypse, including in the etymological derivation of this term, that is, a revelation—of what? Of the ruin that the reconstructed building continues to be and that they ostensibly inhabit but actually haunt (it is not those who died in the blast, especially those who did so instantaneously and thus did not have the opportunity to witness anything, who are the *shuhadā'*, martyrs, but those who survived and who witnessed their apartments manifestly damaged, full of gaping holes, broken glass, etc., and intimated that their apartments had continued to be ruins despite being renovated or reconstructed). So, following the Beirut port explosion, I can very well imagine a reader of my writings on ruins who felt that while the exoteric reason for the blast is yet to be clarified due to the continuing obstruction of the investigation, the esoteric point of it was to manifest that many of Beirut's ostensibly reconstructed war- and civil-war-damaged buildings continued to be ruins in my sense, labyrinthine structures. It would seem that regarding the double explosion at Beirut's port, one has a choice between two incredible things: that in the case of at least some of the apparently reconstructed war- and civil-war-damaged buildings the explosion did not so much damage them anew as reveal that they had continued to be ruins, labyrinthine spaces and times, or that what Godard had said regarding the three protagonists of his film *Bande à part* (*Band of Outsiders* [1964]) and the condition of France at the time of the events of the film, "These are people who … live a simple story; it is the world around them which is living a bad script,"[617] applied to many of the inhabitants of Beirut and the condition of Lebanon at that time: "September 23, 2013: The *Rhosus*'s bill of lading is issued in Batumi, Georgia. It identifies the goods on board the ship as 2,750.4 MTS of High Density Ammonium Nitrate IMO 5.1 in 2,750 big bags. It lists … the port of discharge as Beira Port, Mozambique."[618] "*Rhosus* was owned by a company based in Panama but was regarded by the captain as under the *de facto* ownership of Russian businessman Igor Grechushkin."[619] "November 21, 2013: The *Rhosus* arrives in Beirut's port, ostensibly to pick up additional cargo. While the cargo is being loaded onto the ship, the ship's hatches covering the ammonium nitrate begin to buckle under the weight because the ship's maximum capacity has already been exceeded. November 25, 2013: The Ship Inspection Service staff of the Directorate of Land and Maritime Transport examines the *Rhosus* and detains it, finding that it did not comply with Lebanese and international maritime safety regulations.… December 20, 2013: The *Rhosus* is impounded by Lebanon's Enforcement Department due to outstanding debts to two maritime fuel oil suppliers.… February 21, 2014: Colonel Joseph Skaf, head of the Anti-Narcotics and Money Laundering Section in the Customs Administration, writes to the Customs Administration's Anti-Smuggling Service … warning about the ammonium nitrate on the ship.… March 17, 2014: The Beirut Harbor Master, Mohammad al-Mawla, sends a letter to the Maritime Transport Service Head about the dire humanitarian situation of the crew on board the *Rhosus*. However, he states that the crew cannot leave the ship before their replacements are secured, as the ship's cargo, ammonium nitrate, is hazardous.…"[620] "Grechushkin reportedly went bankrupt, and after the charterers lost interest in the cargo he abandoned *Rhosus*.… By order of [an Urgent Matters] judge, *Rhosus*'s cargo was brought ashore in 2014 and placed in Warehouse 12 at the port, where it remained for the next six years. *Rhosus* sank in the harbor in February 2018. Lebanese customs officials had sent letters to judges [on 27 June and 5 December 2014, 6 May 2015, 20 May and 13 October 2016, and 27 October 2017] requesting a resolution to the issue of the confiscated cargo, proposing that the ammonium nitrate be either exported, given to the Lebanese Armed Forces or sold to the private Lebanese Explosives Company.... Warehouse 12 ... stored the ammonium nitrate that had been confiscated from *Rhosus* alongside a stash of fireworks."[621] "In January 2020, a judge launched an official investigation after it was discovered that Hangar 12 was unguarded, had a hole in its southern wall and one of its doors dislodged, meaning the hazardous material was at risk of being stolen.... On June 4, ... state security instructed port authorities to provide guards at Hangar 12, appoint a director for the warehouse and secure all the doors and repair the hole in the southern wall, according to the state security report and security officials.... During the work, sparks from welding took hold and fire started to spread, the official said. 'Given that there were fireworks stored in the same hangar, after an hour a big fire was set off by the fireworks ...,' the high-ranking security official said. The official blamed port authorities for not supervising the repair crew and for storing fireworks alongside a vast deposit of high explosives."[622] "According to security sources ... one of the three welders' phones showed that he had previously searched for the port and the head of the Port Investment Authority. The sources also mentioned that his phone revealed an interest in extremist groups ... and noted that he learned welding via YouTube and that the port workshop was the first one he participated in. The testimony of this welder showed that he started working in welding for the workshop contractor only from July 28, 2020, i.e., two days before starting work at the port."[623] "Around 17:55 local time, a team of nine firefighters and one paramedic ... was dispatched to fight the fire.... The initial explosion, at about 18:07 local time, ... heavily damaged the structure of Warehouse 12 itself with a force equivalent to around 1.5-2.5 tons of TNT. The second explosion, 33 to 35 seconds later, was much more substantial and was felt in northern Israel and in Cyprus, 240 kilometers (150 miles) away."[624]

Given that a building that has become a ruin is a labyrinth, the one haunting it and lost in it may at some point perceive the historical state of the building prior to its having been severely damaged during a bombardment; or a state of the building that, while seeming to belong to a period before it was damaged during the war or civil war, does not match one's memory of any of its past historical states; or what seems to be a coming state of the building; or the building as severely damaged—if, among these states, the latter is a privileged one, it is because it makes one suspect, strangely, unbelievably, that, even after its reconstruction, the building continues to be a ruin, in the mainstream, exoteric sense of largely destroyed. If someone residing in a ruin that had been ostensibly reconstructed perceives it not as a spatial and temporal labyrinth but only as a reconstructed apartment or building, this implies that he or she is misperceiving it or in disavowal of its actual state, the same way the sisters of Lazarus would have been misperceiving the buried man who answered the call "Lazarus, come forth!" had he been brought back to life by someone other than Jesus, as *the life,* and had they never felt, "This is not Lazarus," or at least suspected that he may not be Lazarus even though he walked like him, with his "inimitable" gait, and appeared to remember whatever episodes from their common past they questioned him about, since such a resurrected man would not be fully the one who died but possibly his double, or someone who usurped his place, replaced him, not necessarily with a duplicitous intent but because he had at that point assumed his name, since in death one assumes every name in history.

The train "stopped virtually in the middle of the countryside. No one called out the name of the station. 'Ashgrove?' I asked some boys on the platform. 'Ashgrove,' they said, nodding. I got off the train.... 'Are you going to Dr. Stephen Albert's house?' one queried. Without waiting for an answer, another of them said: 'The house is a far way, but you'll not get lost if you follow that road there to the left, and turn left at every crossing.' I ... started down the solitary road.... The boy's advice to turn always to the left reminded me that that was the common way of discovering the central lawn of a certain type of maze. I am something of a *connoisseur* of mazes: not for nothing am I the great-grandson of that Ts'ui Pen who was governor of Yunan province and who renounced all temporal power in order to write a novel containing more characters than the *Hung Lu Meng* and construct a labyrinth in which all men would lose their way"[625] (Jorge Luis Borges, "The Garden of Forking Paths"). Were someone to say to me, "Turn left at every crossroads," that could imply that I am in a maze (albeit one whose paths are so wide and that is so immense that I would otherwise have probably failed to recognize that I am in one), especially if they preface those words by, "You'll not get lost if you ...," since turning left at every crossroads—or for that matter turning right at every crossroads, in short, turning the same direction at every crossroads—is said to be a good method for getting out of a maze. But it could also be a hint, especially if I encountered no one else during the entirety of my walk, that I am "in" a space and time that is denoted by a word that is usually inappropriately considered to be a synonym of "maze" and that could be referred to euphemistically as a maze: the labyrinth. Unlike Borges, who does not seem to differentiate between a maze and a labyrinth, I do so explicitly in my book *What I Was Thinking?*, where "maze" is reserved for peculiar worldly natural spatial configurations, while "labyrinth" is reserved for a particular unworldly, unnatural space and time, and so for me one can be "a connoisseur of mazes" and yet not recognize that one is "in" the labyrinth (is there more than one labyrinth, as the title of the Borges book of which "The Garden of Forking Paths" forms a part, *Labyrinths*, implies? While there can be, and are, many mazes, I tend to think that there is only one labyrinth, the labyrinth). How did the boys at the train station know that he planned to go to Dr. Stephen Albert's house? Had he previously arrived at the station and asked them for directions to that house? But a place one (is certain one) has not visited before and yet where one encounters signs implying that one has already been there is a labyrinth. Hence he should have suspected that he is already "in" the labyrinth, where, whatever one does, all the labyrinthine alternatives, which include his not taking every left but taking several lefts and then *the other left*, or taking a right at every crossroads, or taking several rights and then *the other right*, but, unlike in the world, do not include his taking a left and a right, appear to have happened, and where, whatever directions and paths one takes (perceptively, Borges does not tell us whether the protagonist followed the suggestion or not), and in spite of the persistent feeling of being lost, one will come across, reach, or, more often than not, find "oneself" unexpectedly at one's destination, for example, in Borges's "The Garden of Forking Paths," Dr. Stephen Albert's house, with its exoteric garden of forking paths, a spatial maze, within the labyrinth proper as the esoteric "garden" of forking paths, yet, having reached it or found "oneself" "in" it, one would continue to feel that one is lost, for instance because on looking out of a window, one would suddenly, to one's amazement, discover that it looks out onto another locality, for example, rather than the village of Ashgrove in England, Berlin, the capital of the country to which the protagonist of Borges's story was trying to convey the information about the coming British assault! When said concerning the labyrinth, "Turn left at every crossroads" would be a Spinozist kind of statement (in relation to a kind of space and time not affined to Spinoza's philosophy[626]), in the sense that it is not telling one what to do in order to leave the labyrinth, for (while one can leave a maze) one cannot leave the labyrinth (if by taking a left at every crossroads you appear to leave the labyrinth, it would be only because the labyrinth happened to temporarily assume the guise of the natural, worldly space and time of a maze); but rather informing one about the nature of the space "in" which one "is," a labyrinth: unlike space in the natural world, where there is left and right, in the labyrinth there is left and the other left (or right and the other right), with the consequence that one cannot but take a left at every crossroads (or a right at every crossroads). "In Adrian Lyne's *Jacob's Ladder* (1990), Jacob's chiropractor, Louie, tells him, who died physically or died before dying physically: 'Turn on

361

your right side.' When he turns in the wrong direction, the chiropractor muses: 'How about the other right?' Unlike mortal chiropractors in disavowal of being dead even while still physically alive, and unlike angels (Jacob: 'You know, you look like an angel, Louie, like an overgrown cherub. Anyone ever tell you that?' 'Yeah'), thinkers who died before dying physically are aware that in *death and the labyrinth*[627] the two sides are not always, if ever, right and left but right and the other right—with no left"[628]—or, vice versa, left and the other left—with no right. In neither the multiverse of Everettian quantum mechanics nor the labyrinth are all abstract, logical possibilities actualized: in the former, it is because, however stupendous their number is, only those possibilities allowed by the Schrödinger equation get actualized in different branches of the multiverse; in the latter, it is because some of what seem to be possibilities prior to finding oneself lost "in" the labyrinth, for example to choose to go right or left, are not possibilities "in" the labyrinth because "in" the labyrinth the choice is between left and the other left (or right and the other right).

While rare, reportedly some people, for example, the Ts'ui Pen of Borges's "The Garden of Forking Paths," have tried to "construct a labyrinth in which all men would lose their way" rather than a representation of one—one should though keep in mind that the labyrinth can assume the guise of a representation, for example a novel.[629] Did Borges's Ts'ui Pen succeed? If he did, then Dr. Stephen Albert and his interlocutor, the narrator, would themselves be (lost) "in" the labyrinth—but so would the editor who wrote the introductory text, indeed so would the reader of Borges's "The Garden of Forking Paths"! Given that the Allied offensive against the Serre-Montauban line in 1916 took place on July 1 in the world,[630] outside the labyrinth, something that can be confirmed by Liddell Hart's authoritative historical report *The History of the World War*, what is the reader to make of the following words in the editor's contextualizing introduction to the spy's account that's part of Borges's "The Garden of Forking Paths": "On page 242 of *The History of the World War*, Liddell Hart tells us that an Allied offensive against the Serre-Montauban line (to be mounted by thirteen British divisions backed by one thousand four hundred artillery pieces) had been planned for July 24, 1916, but had to be put off until the morning of the twenty-ninth. Torrential rains (notes Capt. Liddell Hart) were the cause of that delay—a delay that entailed no great consequences, as it turns out"?[631] A reader grounded in the world would most likely read these words as a fictional version by Borges of Liddell Hart's historical report *The History of the World War*, but a reader not grounded in the world would most likely read it as a variant "in" the labyrinth, therefore one that can be accessed and read only "in" the labyrinth, so most probably posthumously. Unlike in the case of a maze, where if I don't reach what is exterior to it, it would be because I happen to be lost in it—an eventuality that becomes more likely the bigger and more complicated the maze is—in the case of the labyrinth, I am unable to leave it because it has no outside—but is itself the Outside. Why would I consider the labyrinth (and hence death, a labyrinthine realm) to be one of the guises of the Outside? The interior has an exterior; what has no exterior to it cannot be an interior. What has no exterior is an Outside—even if it looks like a room.[632] The labyrinth is the Outside because it is all border, so one cannot be inside it, at least not fully (being lost in the labyrinth does not necessarily mean that one cannot find the place one is looking for, but that one oneself cannot be found, by others and by oneself [dissociation], as implied by one's failure to appear in the mirror that happens to be there), and hence one keeps undergoing lapses of consciousness, if not of being, there (the circumstance that the narration by the spy starts with a marked ellipsis [...] is not necessarily or most likely because part of it was lost or irrelevant but is related to the essential circumstance that one does not experience the entrance into the labyrinth, because one undergoes then and there a lapse of consciousness [in the form of an entrancement], if not of being); because one has the impression, once one is lost "in" it, that one has always been "in" it, has never entered it from somewhere else that would be its outside; and because it, ostensibly paradoxically, has no outside, no exterior (once one "finds" "oneself" lost "in" it) (except, as in the case of Lazarus, through a miracle, getting resurrected by the Christ, the life). The dead don't return to life and the world not necessarily because they no longer exist but because they are lost "in" the labyrinth (more specifically, in labyrinthine space and time), which, being the Outside, has no exterior—once one "is" "in" it.

Once the labyrinth is created, then, *within it*, it precedes its creation. *Within itself*, the labyrinth is the basic, original structure of space and time, and the world is just one special, peculiar configuration of it, one that may give the one "in" it the illusion that he or she has left it.

"The first casualty of war is truth." At one level, this is so because in war, including in civil war, many if not all of the witnesses to a massacre or genocide are killed before they are able to report what they saw and/or heard, or are dissuaded from doing so by making them fear for their life or the lives of their family members; and there is so much destruction, often intentional, indeed programmatic, on the part of the perpetrators, of what could be adduced as material traces and proofs confirming one of the conflicting accounts; and there is very quickly so much polarization that each side reads and watches its camp's social media, newspapers, and TV stations almost exclusively, with the result that it is difficult for the warring sides to agree on a truth, which becomes itself divided, one "truth" for one side, another, variant "truth" for the other side—yet for Muslims, Christians, and Jews, truth has not radically disappeared since God, who not only is omniscient but can also make the organs (eyes, skin, tongue, heart, etc.) of the perpetrators reveal the truth about what they committed, can distinguish between what is true and what is false and convey to us this knowledge, even if only at the Apocalypse or the Last Judgment. But at another level, this is so because war tends to lead more frequently than in other periods not only to physical death but also to death before physical death (a condition to be [lost] "in" the labyrinth) and ruins, that is, labyrinthine spaces and times, conditions in which there is an indiscernibility of truth and falsehood—even God would be unable to discern whether it is true or false that a certain dead human is lost at a specific "location" "in" the labyrinth.

Once not simply physical death but mortality was introduced, the primary condition was no longer the universe and then life and then the world but *death and the singular space and time in which it is undergone, the labyrinth*, since *once the labyrinth exists*, it retroactively precedes the world, appears—to the one who is lost "in" it, that is, who cannot be found "in" it and yet has the keen impression that he or she has always been "in" it—to have always been there, with the implication that there was enough time for all sorts of configurations to occur "in" it, *including those that look indiscernible from the universe and life and the world*, with the consequence that what appears to be the world of living humans would not be external to the labyrinth. While "in" the overtly, unmistakably labyrinthine configuration of the labyrinth, one cannot will the eternal recurrence of the labyrinth, since, assuming all the names of history, one cannot undergo the same event again and again with the same name and identity, a prerequisite for possibly ending up willing the event, can one of those who happen to be "in" the configuration of the labyrinth that *looks indiscernible from the universe and life and the world* end up willing the eternal recurrence of that configuration *as* the universe and the world and life, if not as a configuration of the labyrinth, and, through it, the labyrinth in general? If yes, would he or she by doing so be ushering in the epoch of the (objective) will and, consequently, lead to the wipeout of the labyrinth, turning out to be the overman, a.k.a. the Messiah or the Mahdi? But can't the labyrinth, which, by not respecting linear time, undoes any fait accompli, undo that eventful moment and act of willing its eternal recurrence, indeed make it such that there was no such moment?

"*World cinema.* A term used in film studies in a range of shifting and loosely overlapping senses, and implying different critical, theoretical, and methodological perspectives. 1. Cinema in global sense, embracing all cinemas of the world. This approach informs varyingly exhaustive multinational surveys, historical and otherwise, of the world's cinemas ... and some studies of media globalization.... Until the late 1990s this was the most commonplace usage and understanding of the term. 2. Postcolonial studies of Third World cinemas, including cinemas embodying non-mainstream attitudes to film content and/or film style.... This approach is relatively uncommon in World cinema studies. 3. Non-Hollywood, or non-Western, or non-mainstream films and national cinemas. Film studies and area studies work in this field has become widespread since the late 1990s: ... it usually explores cultural connections between groups of national cinemas ..."[633] It would be much more apropos to consider *world cinema* as cinema concerned with the world, whether the latter is understood in the simply physical sense of Earth or the universe or the multiverse or one of the latter's branches, so cinema concerned with, for example, the birth of the universe (hence, for instance, with the Big Bang, whether it is hypothesized as a one-off event, or, as in Roger Penrose's conformal cyclic cosmology theory, cyclical), or the destruction of Earth (Lars von Trier's *Melancholia* [2011] ...); or, preferably, in a phenomenological sense, where, for example, "world is not the totality of beings, is not the accessibility of beings as such, not the manifestness of beings as such that lies at the basis of this accessibility—world is rather the *manifestness of beings as such as a whole*"[634] (Heidegger), so cinema concerned with, for example, profound boredom (since, according to Heidegger, in profound boredom, "we are not merely *relieved* of our *everyday personality*, somehow distant and alien to it, but simultaneously also *elevated beyond* the particular situation in each case and beyond the *specific beings* surrounding us there. The whole situation and we ourselves as this individual subject are thereby indifferent.... Yet this does not happen in such a way that we first run through individual things including ourselves, and then evaluate them in accordance with whether they are still of any worth to us.... This *indifference of things and of ourselves with them* is not the result of a sum total of evaluations; rather each and every thing at once becomes indifferent, each and every thing moves together at one and the same time into an indifference.... Beings ... become indifferent *as a whole*, and we ourselves as these people are not excepted.... Through this boredom Dasein finds itself set in place precisely before beings as a whole, to the extent that in this boredom the beings that surround us offer us no further possibility of acting and no further possibility of our doing anything.... There is a telling refusal on the part of beings as a whole with respect to these possibilities.... What do we mean by this expression '*as a whole*'? ... We shall designate the expanse of this 'as a whole,' which manifests itself in profound boredom, as *world*"[635]) or anxiety (since, according to Heidegger, while "that in the face of which we fear is a detrimental entity within-the-world which comes from some definite region ... that in the face of which one has anxiety is not an entity within-the-world.... That in the face of which one is anxious is completely indefinite. Not only does this indefiniteness leave factically unde-cided which entity within-the-world is threatening us, but it also tells us that entities within the world are not 'relevant' at all. Nothing which is ready-to-hand or present-at-hand within the world functions as that in the face of which anxiety is anxious.... The obstinacy of the 'nothing and nowhere within-the-world' means as a phenomenon that *the world as such is that in the face of which one has anxiety*. The utter insignificance which makes itself known in the 'nothing and nowhere' ... tells us that entities within-the-world are of so little importance in themselves that, on the basis of this *insignificance* of what is within-the-world, the world in its worldhood is all that still obtrudes itself.... Being-anxious discloses, primordially and directly, the world as world"[636]—"in the process of falling apart [my qualification of Heidegger], thus no longer able to exclude what is not part of it, what is out of the world, if not what is unworldly, for example, the voic-es"[637]), or dead, schizophrenic, or psychotic humans (Ingmar Bergman's *The Hour of the Wolf*), hence people undergoing the falling apart of the world (the poverty in world that schizophrenics, who died before dying physically, and the dead undergo takes the following two forms: the falling apart of the world, which they, who had the capacity of "world-forming" [Heidegger], then try to rearrange, even in the guise of a vast conspiracy they are the victims of, only for it to fall apart again less than "two days" later and for them to then desperately try to rearrange it, again ... and again—until they themselves fall apart; and figures that look physically like humans but, unlike living, sane humans, do not appear to enfold a world, thus give the impres-sion that they are not real humans, since humans are world-forming), or some catastrophe that would wipe out all humans as "world-forming" (but also possibly, in the future, any artificial general intelligence that might be world-forming) since what would subsist then are wordless entities, for example a stone, or poor-in-world entities, animals (to humanize animals would require not so much making them rational [if one defines "man" as a "rational animal"], empowering them with rationality, as making them able to form a world—one indication that this has happened would be for an animal to become mad, since madness has less to do with irrationality [word salads, etc.] than with poverty in world as a result of the latter's falling apart [such an animal would have accomplished a radical change: from being poor in world because it is unable to form a world to poor in world because the world it had formed fell apart][638]); or viewed from a religious perspective, so cinema concerned with, for example, the creation of the world by God, the end of the world as a divine punish-ment or ordeal (Darren Aronofsky's *Noah* [2014] ...), the coming of an awaited redeemer, who would transfigure the unredeemed world into a redeemed one, belief in "the other world" (Islam's *al-Ākhirah*, etc.), or from a nonreligious perspective, so cinema concerned with, for example, "belief in *this* world" (my italics; Deleuze: "The modern fact is that we [who underwent a break of the sensory-motor link, rather than humans in general] no longer believe in this world.... The link between man and the world is broken.... Only belief in the world can reconnect man to what he sees and hears. The cinema must film, not the world, but belief in this world, our only link"[639]). Cinema must film not only the world (for those who have not undergone a break of the sensory-motor link) but also the belief of some of those who died before dying physically (for example, schizophrenics) and were, as a consequence, lost in death's labyrinthine space and time and tortuously learned, or at least came to suspect, that it is impossible to be out of the labyrinth once one gets lost "in" it, but then appeared to have recovered their sanity that they are actually back in the world rather than still experiencing a special, peculiar configuration of the labyrinth that happens to look and behave like the world but that could at any moment be revealed, given that it is a highly improbable one, for what it is (is it through such a belief that I, who have already died before dying physically, continue to act as if I am a living man in the world?). The films that fit the aforementioned categories should be looked for not solely or mainly in American and European cinema but in "all cinemas of the world," in other words, including among "non-Hollywood, or non-Western, or non-mainstream films and national cinemas."

The falling apart of the world that a schizophrenic undergoes seems to extend to most if not all humans he or she sees, who appear not to have a world (enfolded in them), to be world-less, therefore, not to be real humans, to be unreal, since humans are assumed to (be world-forming and thus to) have a world.

How is it that this universe does not fall apart while including mortals, who, as dead even while still physically alive, exist in a realm with a labyrinthine space and time, etc.? If our universe can accommodate labyrinthine space and time, then it must not be fully what we take it to be, since were it fully what we consider it to be, based on our current most successful scientific theories, it would fall apart were a labyrinth to be introduced into it.

After performing a miracle, Jesus Christ would say, "Your faith has healed you," in other words, "Your faith has saved you" (to a woman whose sins he had forgiven, Jesus said, "Your faith has saved you" [Luke 7:50]; to a blind man who had entreated him, "Jesus, Son of David, have mercy on me! ... Lord, I want to see," and to whom he, in response, gave back sight, he said, "Your faith has healed you" [Luke 18:42]; and to a woman who was subject to bleeding for twelve years and whose bleeding stopped immediately when she touched the edge of his cloak, he said, "Your faith has healed you" [Matthew 9:22]). He could have said this to the three humans he resurrected. The faith of a dead human's father or lover or child ("A synagogue leader came and knelt before him and said, 'My daughter has just died. But come and put your hand on her, and she will live'" [Matthew 9:18]) is, if not irrelevant, certainly not sufficient for the dead human's resurrection by Jesus Christ; what is required primarily if not solely on the part of humans for Jesus to perform a resurrection is the dead human's own faith. The greater the miracle, the greater the faith of its subject has to be; this would imply that Jesus's episode with the centurion ("A centurion's servant, whom his master valued highly, was sick and about to die. The centurion heard of Jesus and ... sent friends to say to him: 'Lord, ... say the word, and my servant will be healed. For I myself am a man under authority, with soldiers under me. I tell this one, "Go," and he goes; and that one, "Come," and he comes. I say to my servant, "Do this," and he does it.' When Jesus heard this, he was amazed at him, and, turning to the crowd following him, he said, 'I tell you, I have not found such great faith even in Israel'" [Luke 7:2-9]) must have preceded the three episodes when he resurrected a dead human.

The one who has perceived that in reality mountains are not fixed but move like clouds (Qur'ān 27:88: "You see the mountains, thinking they are firmly fixed, but they move like clouds"), in other words, walk ("Mountains ... always walk.... Do not doubt mountains' walking even though it does not look the same as human walking.... Although they walk more swiftly than the wind, someone in the mountains does not notice or understand it" [Dōgen, "Mountains and Waters Sutra," *Treasury of the True Dharma Eye*]),[640] should try to make others have the same perception by inducing them to place themselves in the proper conditions to have such a perception. Unfortunately, this almost always proves to be extremely difficult, if not impossible. And so, having failed to make them perceive the reality that mountains move, the one who perceived that mountains are not fixed is to, as a last resort, use faith to make others not take the apparent fixity of the mountains for their actual state by moving the mountain—it took a miracle to show them what is actually always the case, what is not miraculous: that mountains move like clouds or walk.

History of the Patriarchs of the Egyptian Church[641] describes "a struggle between Christians and Jews for caliphal favor at the Fatimid court."[642] The Fatimid wazir, Yaʿqub b. Killis, a Jewish convert to Islam, "found a way (to have) an audience to say to al-Muʿizz: 'It is written in the

Gospel of the Christians (*Naṣārā*): "If one hath faith as a grain of mustard-seed, and he saith to the mountain: Be thou removed and be thou cast into the sea, it shall be done." Let the Commander (*Amīr*) of the Faithful see his way to ask them to prove the truth of this saying, so that he may know that they are frauds and are liars....' ... The king al-Muʿizz sent to summon Abba Abraham (Anbā Afrahām) and said to him: 'What sayest thou concerning this word? Is it in your Gospel or not?' The patriarch said: 'Yea. It is in it.'"[643] "The Muslim caliph commands the Christian patriarch to demonstrate this miracle, lest all Christians under his rule be destroyed. The Christian patriarch prays and fasts.... On the third day of prayer, the Virgin Mary appears to ... [him] and tells him to find a one-eyed man carrying a jar of water on his shoulder, who will assist him in this miracle. The patriarch finds this humble figure, named Samaan [Simon] the tanner."[644] I like to imagine that on seeing a Christian move the Muqattam mountain, the Fatimid caliph Al-Muʿizz, who moved his capital from Mahdiyyah on the east coast of Tunisia to Cairo (his general founded the latter after having conquered Egypt on his behalf), and who, as the imam, was a sort of equivalent of the Christ, told him: "Great is your faith—not because you have great faith (you have little faith, your faith is as a small as a mustard seed), but because faith is great." I like to also imagine someone invoking Matthew 17:20, "If you have faith as small as a mustard seed, you can say to this mountain, 'Move from here to there,' and it will move," to challenge a Christian saint to do a reverse miracle, that is, move the mountain back to where it reportedly was prior to the miracle of its displacement during the Fatimid reign of Al-Muʿizz, and the latter responding: "I do not have such small faith; I have great faith, so, it is unbefitting of me and my faith to move a mountain—were I one day to move a mountain, then this would imply that my faith has diminished, if not that I am doubtful that I have faith and so wanted to confirm that I still have even as little faith as 'a mustard seed.'"

Perhaps even Jesus Christ could not have resurrected Maurice Blanchot, so much had death pervaded the latter.

God did not demand the miraculous of humans (for example, that the resurrected brother of Mary and Martha resurrect the dead Jesus Christ)[645] without demanding it of himself. Insofar as Jesus Christ was human, his reported miracles were in relation to nature, for example, walking on water, but insofar as he was and is *the life*, the corresponding miracle was not that through his resurrection of Lazarus the latter returned from the grave not as a mortal, not as dead even while physically alive, but as solely alive, unlike what would have been the case had he been resurrected by a mortal, for this is what one expects from *the life*, but that he died physically on the Cross, achieving what should have been impossible for him as *the life*; and insofar as he is God, the corresponding miracle was not to resurrect all the dead by abolishing death-as-undeath and, consequently, the labyrinth (it is only when a dead human lost "in" the labyrinthine space and time of death prays on behalf of all the dead, including schizophrenics insofar as they died before dying physically, a prayer facilitated by his occasional assumption not of this or that other name of history [in the case of Nietzsche: Prado, Chambige, etc.] but, while feeling *all alone*,[646] of "every name in history," that God can respond by abolishing the labyrinth altogether), but to (thrice) manage to resurrect a singular dead human, for example Lazarus, notwithstanding that "in" labyrinthine death each of the dead assumes "every name in history" and hence would in the case of other resurrectors act as if the call, for example, "Lazarus, come out!" were addressed to him, coming back from the grave, too.

I envision a man who overheard Noah inform one of his sons that God had told him, "I am going to put an end to all people, for the earth is filled with violence because of them. I am surely going to destroy both them and the earth...." (Genesis 6:13), refusing to take these words seriously because he was not in disavowal of the esoteric dimension and of his mortality, recognizing that with the ushering in of mortality in Genesis 2 and henceforth of the coexistence in each human[647] of life and death (since once man partook of the tree of the knowledge of good and evil, he was dead ["The Lord God commanded the man, saying, Of the tree of the knowledge of good and evil, thou shalt not eat of it: for in the day that thou eatest thereof thou shalt surely die" (Genesis 2:16-17, King James Version)] even while still physically alive [following his eating from the tree of the knowledge of good and evil, "Adam lived a total of 930 years, and then he died" (Genesis 5:5) physically]), the world coexisted with its (unending) end in the guise of the labyrinth introduced with death, in which one undergoes the falling apart of the world, so there was no reason for God to destroy "the world" through flooding earth with uninterrupted rain for "forty days" and maintaining it submerged underwater for one hundred and fifty days. Such a man would belong to the list of religious figures who pay dearly for not disavowing what their keen (*ḥadīd*) perception and/or esoteric knowledge (through *ta'wīl*) revealed (for example, in the case of al-Hallāj's Iblīs, that "Bow down!" was not a commandment of God but a trial by Him), for he would have died physically in the Flood; Iblīs would be another member of this list if considered from the perspective of al-Hallāj, who wrote in the chapter "*Ṭā' Sīn al-azal wal iltibās*" of his *al-Ṭawāsīn*: "There had been no monotheist (*muwaḥḥid*) comparable to Satan [Iblīs] among the inhabitants of heaven.... God had said to him 'Bow down (before Adam)' 'Not before another (than You)!' 'Even if My curse falls upon you?' ... Moses met Satan on Mt. Sinai and said to him: 'O Satan! What keeps you from bowing down?' 'What keeps me from doing it is my preaching of a Single Adored One; if I had bowed down, I would have become like you. For you were called to only once, "Look toward the mountain!" and you looked;[648] while I was called to a thousand times, "Bow down!" and I did not bow down ...'[649] 'You have set aside a Commandment (of God).' 'It was (to Him) a trial and not a Commandment.'"[650]

Paradoxically, the only immortality we've had until now is the one related to our mortality—we have it insofar as we're dead while alive. Currently numerous scientists at various labs, research institutes, and academic departments, for example, the Max Planck Institute for Biology of Ageing, the National Institute on Aging in the USA, the Buck Institute for Research on Aging, and Calico, are working to make it possible for humans to live longer and healthier lives. If we don't end up abolishing death-as-undeath and therefore its corresponding kind of immortality, the labyrinthine one, before we achieve the other kind of immortality, the indefinite extension of human life in a radically enhanced body or some other kind of body, then we'll have two conjoint, radically different immortalities. If we abolish death-as-undeath before we achieve immortality as living beings, then we would no longer be immortal during that interval. Should we aim to replace one immortality by another, our immortality insofar as, mortals, we are dead even while still alive by the immortality that would consist in living indefinitely? While many if not most of us wish to live much longer than we presently do, it is not clear whether we really wish to be immortal as living humans, for physical death gives us solace in life as a disappearing act in any situation that seems incredibly horrible and that otherwise could go on and on and on, and it introduces into being, which is otherwise ubiquitously saturated with presence, suffocating, a modicum of absence that makes it "breathable."

What happens to the very notion of unfinished business given that the dead human ends up assuming this or that other name in history, indeed every name in history? Whose unfinished business is it when the dead Nietzsche ("This autumn ... I twice attended my funeral") assumes various names of history, indeed every name in history ("I am Prado, I am also Prado's father, I venture to say that I am also Lesseps.... I am also Chambige ... every name in history is I")? Is it Nietzsche's, hence primarily his planned book, which he refers to in his *On the Genealogy of Morality* (1887), "These things will be addressed by me more fully and seriously in another connection (with the title 'On the History of European Nihilism'; for which I refer you to a work I am writing, *The Will to Power, Attempt at a Revaluation of*

All Values),"[651] and which had not been completed and finalized by the time he died before dying physically, nor by the time, around a decade later, he died physically, 1900? Is it Lesseps's, who was one of the 136 delegates who voted in favor of the creation of the Panama Canal and was then appointed president of the Panama Canal Company but failed to bring the project, work on which began in 1882, to completion, the Panama Canal Company declaring bankruptcy in December 1888 and entering liquidation in February 1889? Is it another's? Numerous others'?

The first unfinished business in death is not related to life, for example a promise one had not fulfilled by the time of one's "untimely" death; it is to recognize that one has died, that one is dead.

"To breed an animal *with the right to make promises*—is not this the paradoxical task that nature has set itself in the case of man? Is it not the real problem regarding man? ... This animal which needs to be forgetful, in which forgetting represents a force, a form of *robust* health, has bred in itself an opposing faculty, a memory, with the aid of which forgetfulness is abrogated in certain cases—namely in those cases where promises are made.... This involves a real *memory of the will*.... How can one create a memory for the human animal? How can one impress something upon this partly obtuse, partly flighty mind, attuned only to the passing moment, in such a way that it will stay there? One can well believe that the answers and methods for solving this primeval problem were not precisely gentle; perhaps indeed there was nothing more fearful and uncanny in the whole prehistory of man than his *mnemotechnics*. If something is to stay in the memory it must be burned in: only that which never ceases to *hurt* stays in the memory.... If we place ourselves at the end of this tremendous process, where the tree at last brings forth fruit, ... then we discover that the ripest fruit is ... the man who has his own independent, protracted will and the *right to make promises*.... He is bound to honor his peers, the strong and reliable (those with the *right* to make promises)—that is, all those who promise like sovereigns, reluctantly, rarely, slowly, ... who give their word as something that can be relied on because they know themselves strong enough to maintain it in the face of accidents, even 'in the face of fate.'"[652] As long as physical death has not been done away with, and as long as memory cannot be restored by remedial surgery to amnesia-causing brain lesions or otherwise, any promise by a human is subject to the threat of his or her dying physically or losing his or her memory in unforeseen circumstances, for example a fall from a height, before fulfilling his or her promise. Should one then never promise? Is the promise, then, to be conditional: I promise to do this or that as long as I don't unexpectedly die physically or become amnesiac as a result of a brain lesion, for example following a car crash, in other words, I promise to maintain my promise as long as its conditions of possibility continue to exist? Has anyone promised with this caveat? It is remarkable that Nietzsche traces for the human animal, who not only had a "partly obtuse, partly flighty mind, attuned only to the passing moment" in the prehistorical, distant past, but also "needs to be forgetful, in which forgetting represents a force, a form of *robust* health," a trajectory from the production of the conditions of possibility of promising to the promise to the promise's maintenance "in the face of fate," hence, as is clear in the case of the "fate" that is physical death (so long as science has not found a way to do away with the latter), beyond its conditions of possibility. Is it accidental that it is in the case of the promise that a rigorous thinker moved from the conditions of possibility of something to its actualization as unconditional? Did Nietzsche by the end of the first three sections of his essay "'Guilt,' 'Bad Conscience,' and the Like" in his book *On the Genealogy of Morals*, which think the promise and which consist of only 1710 words, forget that they began on the subject of the conditions of possibility of the promise? Or did he remember it alright, but the promise is the sort of thing that goes beyond its conditions of possibility, always unconditional? In every promise there is the implicit, more radical promise, "I promise to keep my promise even were its condition of possibility to lapse." That the promise has to be maintained "even 'in the face of fate'" should not be taken precipitously as indicating that the promise has to be maintained even in the *exceptional* case of what would appear to be unforeseen prohibitive circumstances but is to be viewed as indicating what is required for the promise to be fulfilled radically. In other words, while it seems that one's physical death cuts short one's ability and readiness to fulfill some promise one made, actually it—or amnesia—is a condition, when followed by resurrection, for the fulfillment of the promise (one cannot keep the promise in the death realm, since, for example, time is labyrinthine there and hence one might be dissuaded from doing what is required to fulfill one's promise because the latter appears to have already been fulfilled). While there are promises the fulfillment of which would clearly expose the one who made them to death, any promise implies that one would have to die and then be resurrected in order to nonetheless fulfill it—or at least become amnesiac prior to and while fulfilling it. Does every promise, then, imply the following, more fundamental one: I promise to die and then be resurrected before the fulfillment of my explicit promise, or to become amnesiac before the deadline for the fulfillment of my explicit promise and during its fulfillment? The promise is always to be fulfilled from beyond death (and thus presupposes resurrection or at least haunting, if not by ghosts then by a structural ghostly effect) or while amnesiac (not only in cases of dissociative amnesia, where one's memory is still present but repressed and hence can, unbeknownst to one, steer one's actions in the direction of the unconscious fulfilment of the promise, but even in the case of amnesias caused by some brain lesion). In a way, by fulfilling my promise I assume the position of someone who died and was resurrected or remembers after being amnesiac. So, were death one day to be shown, through advances in basic science and technology, not to be a fate, life becoming extended indefinitely, and were amnesia, even the one caused by a brain lesion rather than the dissociative variety related to a trauma, to become a condition that can always be treated, one's memory restored in every case, would we still be able to promise radically? The difficulty of the promise is not to be gaged by what it sets out to accomplish but rather consists in having to be fulfilled "in the face of 'fate,'" which from a seemingly exceptional complication becomes a defining, necessary condition, and the intrinsic impossibility related to the promise is to be located not in what the promise sets out to do, for example raise to life, resurrect, but in the circumstance that one has to accomplish what one promised from beyond physical death or despite one's amnesia. Of someone who is brought back to life in this world through resurrection, it is fitting to ask him or her, "What promise are you now, posthumously, ready to fulfill?" Following his resurrection, did Lazarus fulfill some promise he had made prior to his physical death? (Given that dying and then being resurrected—or becoming amnesiac—are conjoint conditions for fulfilling the promise, does the general resurrection of the dead in Islam provide a condition of possibility to fulfill promises? No, since, according to Mullā Ṣadrā Shīrāzī, while "the day of sharia is the day of actions without punishment" [al-sharīʿa yawm ʿamal bilā thawab], "the Day of Resurrection is the Day of reward and punishment without actions"[653] [yawm al-qiyāma yawm al-jazāʾ wal-thawāb bilā ʿamal], including the action that would fulfill one's promise.) What are we to call a promise that is fulfilled notwithstanding the amnesia of the one who promised, if not fate? Indeed, one of the figures of fate is a promise that is maintained and fulfilled even though the one who proffered it has lost his memory, become amnesiac. In the absence of the medical restoration of memory following an amnesia caused by a brain lesion resulting from some accident, the promise is fulfilled as a fateful accident. In Nietzsche's essay on the promise in *On the Genealogy of Morals*, we move from establishing the condition of possibility of the promise to the unconditionality of the promise, and from fate being what the promise has to conquer to the promise itself being a fate, for the one who gives it but more so for the one to whom it is given—even though it announces a fate, not every promise is an oracle, for not every promise has to be interpreted, whereas every oracle is a kind of promise that has to be interpreted. How can one affirm that one will fulfill the promise, which requires that one die and be resurrected, when one is not the agent of one's prerequisite resurrection but its object? One can legitimately do so if it is a fate: "[Jesus] said to them, 'The Son of Man is going to be delivered into the hands of men. They will kill him, and on the third day he will be raised to life'" (Matthew 17:22-23); for one to fulfill the promise "even in the face of 'fate'" one has to be fated to do so. Oddly, we have the figure of a Messiah who dies and yet maintains and fulfills his promise, Jesus Christ, but not that of a Messiah who becomes amnesiac and yet fulfills his promise or continues to be expected to fulfill it even while amnesiac, indeed even when the amnesia is not a dissociative one related to a trauma (in the latter, one unconsciously still remembers the promise) but is caused by some brain lesion. So, I expect that the other Jewish Messiah, the Messiah of those Jews who did/do not view Jesus as the Christ, the Son of Man, would give signs of amnesia, wondering possibly, "Who am I? John the Baptist? Elijah? Jeremiah or one of the prophets?" and, as a result, asking one of those who wished to be his disciples, "Who do people say the Son of Man is?" only to receive the disappointing, uninformative answer, "Some say John the Baptist; others say Elijah; and still others, Jeremiah or one of the prophets."[654] Given that the messianic promise, for example, that the Mahdi or the Messiah would come (back) and fill the earth with justice and equity as it was filled with injustice and inequity, is the paradigmatic promise, including in the sense that it continues to be expected to be fulfilled notwithstanding a millennial suspenseful lapse, then with its fulfilment there would no longer be any promises, no one would promise, not simply because no one would feel the need to do so but more radically and fundamentally because, as a result of certain changes brought about by the Mahdi/ Messiah, deep time, that is, interlinked past, present, and future, as a condition of possibility of the promise, would no longer hold, or temporality would be such that there would be no reason to vouch for some future action. So, I imagine someone prodding others during the period of waiting for the Messiah's appearance on earth: "Promise, before it is no longer possible to do so."

How infinitely insignificant are almost all concerns that pertain solely to the world of the living from the perspective of the dead exposed to labyrinthine space and time! Thus for one to care about some unfinished business pertaining only to life, one must not have fully realized and acknowledged that one has died, or one must be using the excuse of this unfinished business to delay acknowledging that one is already dead (there's always some unfinished business—a completed business is always at the expense of another, leaves some other matter unfinished, indeed leads, in the process of its accomplishment, to new unfinished business). Only what is a matter of life and death can and does really function as unfinished business for the dead who has already recognized his or her condition. Paradoxically, the only examples that come to mind of unfinished business that are not limited to life but carry over into death would appear to be instances of finished business(!): a sexual act that one felt driven to engage in and that induced *jouissance* in one and so makes one undergo a compulsion to repeat it cannot be considered over and done with, even if it led to ejaculation and hence appeared to have reached completion; and the promise, which, insofar as it is a performative, is accomplished by saying in the proper conditions to one or more people, "I promise to ...,"[655] and yet, insofar as it has to be fulfilled "even in the face of 'fate,'" does not lapse as a result of even physical death (as an example of "fate"). Of the aforementioned two kinds of unfinished business pertaining to life and death, only one, promises, can be completed, while the compulsion to repeat associated with the drive cannot be completed not only in life but also in death, indeed is one of the bases for a continued existence beyond physical death. "Suppose someone asserts of his lustful inclination that, when the desired object and the opportunity are present, it is quite irresistible to him; ask him whether, if a gallows were erected in front of the house where he finds this opportunity and he would be hanged on it immediately after gratifying his lust, he would not then control his inclination. One need not conjecture very long what he would reply"[656] (Immanuel Kant, *Critique of Practical Reason*); if it is really irresistible to him, then it must have to do with the drive, with its compulsion to repeat, and *jouissance*, in which case while it seems that he is doing it even though it will lead to death, actually it is what properly belongs to death. One should be ready to physically die only for what would survive physical death: *jouissance* or joy (here's an apocryphal divine saying of my own devising: "I gave you life and you wasted it without joy—or *jouissance*—and yet you hope to enter and abide in heaven—or are worried about being thrust into hell! You will not enter heaven except with your joy—nor will you enter hell except with your *jouissance*").

"*L'avenir*: the future" (*Collins French-English Online Dictionary*); "*avenir*; 1. *Le temps à venir, le future*"[657] (*Larousse dictionnaire de français*). *Collins French-English Online Dictionary* and *Larousse dictionnaire de français* notwithstanding, the *avenir* is not the future, nor is it even the time that's to come, "*le temps à venir*"; it is rather the extra time that is introduced by God just as the future is about to end without the coming of the awaited Mahdi/Messiah, to postpone the end of time until he comes: according to a *ḥadīth* (a tradition attributed to the Prophet Muhammad), "If there were to remain in the life of the world but one day, God would prolong that day until He sends in it a man from my community and my household. His name will be the same as my name. He will fill the earth with equity and justice as it was filled with oppression and tyranny."[658] One clue that one is living in an unnaturally, if not miraculously, prolonged day would be the existence of some prophecy by an authoritative figure of the end of time and/or the world—the world would have ended on the prophesized day were it not that God had extended the latter. From that point onward, to have a messianic sensitivity and awareness is to feel that one is living in the last day, however many years may seem to pass; indeed, when he returns, however protracted his occultation was, the awaited Mahdi would initially believe that he had been away for less than a day. Those living in this miraculously extended day are living in the *avenir*, the time of the wait for the one yet to come— though rare are the ones who are aware of the actual state of affairs. Tens of millions wait, indeed can wait, for the Mahdi because God has extended the last day, which has proved to be longer than "a thousand years of what you count" (Qur'ān 32:5)—will it then prove to be as long as "fifty thousand years" (Qur'ān 70:4)? In the *avenir*, there is time only for waiting for the one to come, the awaited Mahdi (*al-mahdī al-muntaẓar*), and, derivatively, for those activities that are required for this suspenseful state, for instance, sustaining one's body with food so as to continue living, etc., but there's no time to, for example, go on a pilgrimage to Mecca (*al-ḥajj*). The Mahdi/Messiah entertains a dual relation to the end: as long as he has not come, the end of time gets postponed through the introduction of the *avenir*, yet, barring his own creation of time, with his coming, the *avenir*, the extra time introduced specifically for his coming, which had supplanted the future, would, in turn, end. That is why the coming of the Messiah/ Mahdi is not only longed for but also dreaded. The *avenir* possibly started on the day in 941 (AH 329) of the death of the twelfth imam's fourth and final agent, who had reportedly received a letter from the imam instructing him, "O 'Alī ibn Muḥammad al-Samarrī, may God reward your brethren in your death, which is going to take place in six days' time. So take care of your affairs and do not appoint anyone in your place, since the complete occultation has taken place. I will not appear until God permits me to do so (may His name be exalted) and that will be after a long time and after the hearts become hard and the earth is filled with wickedness."[659] That someone or some community considers that they are living in AH 1444, for example, the Islamic Republic of Iran (which, moreover, recently celebrated the Mahdi's birthday on Sha'bān 15, AH 1443 [March 18, 2022]), as well as the Twelver Shi'ite communities of Iraq, Lebanon, Saudi Arabia, Bahrain, and Kuwait (to limit oneself to the Middle East), purportedly all of them communities still awaiting the Mahdi, is an indication that he or she or that community is grossly misunderstanding messianic time, and hence, by not waiting properly, failing the Mahdi.

The ambiguity of the oracle should not be reduced to a hedge against its possible falsification, that is, its possible failure to be actualized, but is rather a sign that it has to be interpreted—the manifest ambiguity of some oracles should not mislead us into assuming that only they require interpretation: all oracles, even the ones that seem obvious, are equivocal and thus need to be interpreted. Oedipus, who was good at interpretation, being the first to ostensibly solve the riddle of the Sphinx, indeed doubly good at it, since he solved the Sphinx's riddle, "What is that which has one voice and yet becomes four-footed and two-footed and three-footed?" which was not only (or was only exoterically) about man in general (he crawls as a baby, walks on two feet as an adult, and uses a walking stick as an old man) but was also, esoterically, and unknowably to Oedipus at that point, about him specifically (something that becomes clear only later, when Oedipus blinds himself and consequently has, even before old age, to resort to a stick while walking), by pointing to himself, should have interpreted the oracle even though it *seemed* to be straightforward. That one has a choice regarding one's fate means that one can choose, indeed has to choose, what interpretation one gives to the oracle, not that one would be able not to actualize the oracle: whatever (else) he does, Oedipus will end up killing his father and having sexual intercourse with his mother, but which of his two fathers, the biological one, King Laius, or the symbolic one, King Polybus, who, unbeknownst to him, had adopted him, would be the one who will be killed by him, and which one of his two mothers, his biological one, Queen Jocasta, or his symbolic one, Queen Merope, King Polybus's wife, will he have sexual intercourse with depends on how he interprets the oracle. So, insofar as, whatever (else) he does, Oedipus, as announced by the oracle addressed to him, is fated to kill his father and have sexual intercourse with his mother, these are already *faits accomplis*, hence belong to the past, but insofar as he can, indeed ought to, choose which interpretation of the oracle he is to actualize, killing his biological father and marrying and having repeated sexual intercourse with his biological mother or killing his adoptive father and marrying and having repeated sexual intercourse with his adoptive mother, his killing his father and having sexual intercourse with his mother belong to the present. Thus, the fate announced by the *interpreted* oracle belongs both to the past and to the present—those who shirk interpretating the oracle and choosing its optimal interpretation would have to accept that the fate it announces has already taken place, belongs fully to the past. One manner of viewing the circumstance that Oedipus flees Corinth when he hears the oracle that foretells that he is fated to lie with his mother, "to show to daylight an accursed breed which men would not endure," and to murder his father is that, ironically, in a twist, it is only through trying to avoid actualizing the oracle that he ends up doing so, killing Laius and having sexual intercourse with Jocasta. This is not the best way to view the matter, for what gets thus actualized is the less optimal of the two interpretations of the oracle Oedipus heard, since, in this interpretation, (1) Oedipus is not also fated for all the events that lead to the ones indicated by the oracle, for example, encountering the Sphinx and giving the ostensibly correct answer to its riddle, which are thus affected, comparatively, with an unbearable lightness; (2) not all those who are part of the events announced by the oracle are *fated* to participate in them, some of them ending up doing so as extras, for example, the Sphinx; and (3) Oedipus does not end up actualizing his deepest desire, whereas in the optimal interpretation of the oracle, one actualizes one's deepest desire, even when it is a repressed or disavowed one that one is unable to acknowledge and cannot oneself utter and so it is uttered on one's behalf by an official oracle. While it seems that the oracle addressed to Laius, which, according to Jocasta, forewarned that, "should he have a son by me, that son would take his father's life," and the one addressed to Oedipus years later, that he would murder his father (and have sexual intercourse with his mother), are one and the same oracle but formulated differently to suit its different addressees, this is the case only according to one interpretation of the oracle addressed to Oedipus, which happens not to be the optimal one. Again, Oedipus is not fated to kill his bio-logical father and have sexual intercourse with his biological mother, Jocasta; he could have fatefully killed his symbolic father and had sexual intercourse with his symbolic mother, thus not given ground on his desire, and then he would have killed Laius and married and had sexual intercourse with Jocasta not because he would have been fated to do so but because Laius was fated to be killed by his son, thus doing so accidently, as an extra in Laius's fate. Through trying to avoid actualizing the oracle addressed to him, Oedipus did not so much fulfill his own fate as fulfilled the fate of Laius, who had tried to escape his fate, announced by another oracle, by ordering a subordinate to kill his then infant child. So, I can well imagine the following scenario as to how Oedipus would have ended up playing his part in Laius's and Jocasta's fate after fulfilling his. After Oedipus had sexual intercourse several times with his adoptive mother, his adoptive father King Polybus would have suspected the affair and confronted Oedipus, who would have killed him during the altera-tion. Earlier in the same day on which this confrontation between Oedipus and his adoptive father would have happened, robbers would have intercepted Laius's carriage, killed all his companions but one, who managed to escape, gravely wounded Laius and left him for dead, confirming the subsequent account of the only survivor of the bloody incident. "Oedipus: 'Was there no messenger, no fellow traveler / who saw what happened? ...' Creon: 'They were all killed save one. He fled in terror / and he could tell us nothing in clear terms / of what he knew, except for one thing only.' Oedipus: 'What was it? ...' Creon: 'This man said that the robbers they encountered / were many and the hands that did the murder / were many; it was no man's single power'"[660]—the account of the survivor is a symptom that there is another interpretation of the oracle that was addressed to Oedipus, since it contradicts the play's account, in which Oedipus, a single man, is the one who fought Laius at the crossroads.[661] Having killed Corinth's king, Oedipus would have fled the city and come across the gravely wounded Laius, who would have entreated him to mercifully finish him off. Oedipus would have done so, then encountered the Sphinx terrorizing Thebes and ostensibly solved its riddle, which would have led it to leap to its death, and the Thebans, in gratitude for ridding them of the Sphinx, would have asked him to become their king and accordingly to marry their queen.

Most people are surprised when someone accurately predicts a coming state of affairs in the world: Karl Marx and Friedrich Engels in *The Communist Manifesto*, 1848; Dan Azzi (who served as the chairman and CEO of the Lebanon-based subsidiary of Standard Chartered and held executive positions for Bear Stearns in Hong Kong, Deutsche Bank in New York, Merrill Lynch in London, and UBS in Auckland), at a much more modest scope geographically, temporally and conceptually, in an article published in the Lebanese newspaper *An-Nahar* in July 2019, "The Devaluation of the Lebanese Dollar": "At the rate we're going, capital controls are coming, because there isn't a sufficient supply of dollars to cover our demand for imports, conversions from Lira to dollars, and the steady capital flight to overseas accounts.... Today, it's a trickle, and at this rate we might have a couple of years, based on published reserve numbers, but if it accelerates, which is looking likely, D-day would strike in 2020.... Let's analyze a scenario where cash withdrawals are rationed and overseas transfers are curtailed, in a triage, with the highest priority to buy fuel (for heating and electricity); then necessities, then luxuries. You can write as many checks as you want from your account as long as it's deposited in another local bank, so what happens to our economy then? It becomes similar to the board game Monopoly.... Can you take the Monopoly money and spend it in Paris at the fancy Le Cinq Restaurant? Nope. The owner of that restaurant isn't a player in our board game. You could write a check to a guy here and buy his apartment in Solidere for '$2 million.' He can only deposit the check in his bank but can't take it out. He can buy a large piece of land in Faraya or an apartment in Achrafieh. Conceivably, that apartment can even go for $10 million—after all, it's Monopoly money, that can't be used anywhere outside the Lebanese board game. In some sense, our economy becomes largely based on bartering.... Of course, if you pay for the apartment in real dollars, not Monopoly money (i.e., from an account outside Lebanon to an account outside Lebanon or in cash), you can get the same apartment for $500,000. Thus it's even imaginable to see a mini-boom in real estate, as more and more rich people (or people who thought they were rich) decide that it's safer to have their wealth in something tangible and stop believing the numbers printed on their bank statements." What is almost as remarkable as the accuracy of the prediction is that it proves to be a far better description of the future state than the ones that end up being written by those living in that future period. This is not exceptionally the case when it comes to accurate predictions: you cannot predict accurately without your description of the future being the best, including in comparison to the ones by those living at the future period your prediction describes. Indeed, that is the seal of every great prediction. Hence, were someone to predict accurately some future state without his description of it proving to be far better than the ones by those living in the future period in question, then I would wager that that person is a time traveler who hails from that future period.

Paul Virilio wrote in September 1977: "If only yesterday the freedom of maneuver ... occasionally required delegations of power up to the secondary echelons, the reduction of the margin of maneuver due to the progress of the means of communicating destruction causes an extreme concentration of responsibilities for the solitary decision-maker that the Chief of State has become. This contraction is, however, far from being complete; it continues according to the arms race, at the speed of the new capacities of the vectors, until one day it will dispossess this last man.... lead[ing] us to renounce solitary human decision in favor of ... *automation*,"[662] the complete delegation of the decision to AI. How to deal with this? An ingenuously farsighted, calculating way to do so is to inflate the diminishing interval that's available for decision by humans through making it encroach on what was previously the future by using "cutting-edge cloud networks and artificial intelligence systems to anticipate adversaries' moves before they make them. U.S. Northern Command (NORTHCOM) recently conducted a series of tests known as the Global Information Dominance Experiments, or GIDE, which combined global sensor networks, artificial intelligence (AI) systems, and cloud computing resources.... According to NORTHCOM leadership, the AI and machine learning tools tested in the experiments could someday offer the Pentagon a robust 'ability to see days in advance,' meaning it could predict the future with some reliability based on evaluating patterns, anomalies, and trends in massive data sets.... The commander of NORTHCOM says this capability is already enabled by tools readily available to the Pentagon."[663] By predicting days ahead accurately, one is extending the span of one's present (of decision making) for the same period. To have a "robust 'ability to see days in advance'" would invert the trend toward dispensing with consultations that has been necessitated by the increasing speed of the means of conveyance of destruction and reinstate a decision-making process that includes lower-level echelons. The more I know in advance through accurate modeling and simulation or scientific prediction, the more the interval for deciding on the manner of responding extends, indeed even starts before the initiation of the attack by the other side. The ones in charge of deciding do not have to wait until the missile or other means of communicating destruction have been launched by the enemy but can start considering what to do days before. That is, what to the enemy is still part of the future would already be part of the present of the US Army or whichever army is using this technological apparatus—that is, before the other side catches up with this technological apparatus—and this would then play havoc with, perforce undermine, the distinction between first and second strike, since what would seem to be a first strike would be a response to what is simulated by AI to be an attack by the enemy. Human decision-making is not, for that matter, resti-tuted *fully*, since the other side's human decision is subtracted as an actuality, assumed to have already been taken through the predictive system, has no time to happen actually. Past a certain speed of the conveyance of the destructive vehicle or means, the decision of at least one of the warring sides as to whether to launch an attack or counterattack is no longer actual but a predicted virtuality or is sup-planted by delegation to AI.

Nietzsche noted that "Kant, like all philosophers, instead of envis-aging the aesthetic problem from the point of view of the artist (the creator), considered art and the beautiful purely from that of the spectator,"[664] and he demanded that art be considered from the perspective of the creators, the artists. But it seems that we are approaching a point beyond which, in more and more fields, such an aesthetics will no longer be possible for humans, not so much, as was the case over the course of the last few millennia, because of the ascendency, indeed virtual hegemony, of reactive forces, at least in the West, but because creation will become in practice, given the incredible speeds (from the perspective of humans) at which they can train and process information ("Starting from random play, and given no domain knowledge except the game rules, [DeepMind's] *AlphaZero* achieved within 24 hours a superhuman level of play in the games of chess and shogi [Japanese chess] as well as Go"[665]), the preserve of very advanced artificial-general-intelligence machines. "After his defeat, [then-Go world champion] Ke [Jie] noted, 'Last year, it [AlphaGo] was still quite human-like when it played [against Lee Sedol]. But this year, it became like a god of Go.'"[666] And yet AlphaGo was unconscious of itself and unable to appreciate its accomplish-ments. While AlphaGo did not have artificial *general* intelligence, would a machine that has such an intelligence by necessity have consciousness *and* be able to appreciate the beauty or sublimity of its moves or actions in general? If not, it could be that until it becomes conscious of what it is doing and able to appreciate its own creativity and accomplishments, or until the exponential advance in these machines' intelligence leads to an "intelligence explosion" and a technological and intelligence singularity that outstrips our ability to comprehend or at least appreciate their moves, whether or not because doing so would require an inordinate amount of a human's time, humans' role would be to appreciate the creative moves of the artificial general intelligence of these machines, be their audience. In his introduction to Matthew Sadler and Natasha Regan's *Game Changer: AlphaZero's Groundbreaking Chess Strategies and the Promise of AI* (New in Chess, 2019), Demis Hassabis noted regarding one of the moves in the 2016 match that AlphaGo won against go champion Lee Sedol: "Most famous of these novel ideas was Move 37 in Game 2, which will probably go down in Go history. It was a move so unthinkable that some of the world's top Go players who were live commentating thought there must have been some sort of mistake, and yet more than 100 moves later this stone turned out to be in the perfect strategic place to decide the outcome of the game. After the match Lee Sedol said, 'When I saw this move ... I [thought] surely AlphaGo is creative.' This motif and many other ideas AlphaGo revealed have subsequently overturned centuries of received wisdom about the game, and many experts feel that it has ushered in a new era for Go." Move 37 would have been an unappreciated, *hidden treasure* without humans to appreciate it. While oftentimes it would be the one who is best at playing chess who would prove to be best at detecting and appreciating the machine's brilliant moves, it is not always the case; sometimes someone ranked 15th in the world, say, would prove to be far better at doing this than the human world champion. Having roundly defeated them again and again, the machines no longer play against humans, but against each other (for example, AlphaZero played against and convincingly defeated Stockfish, the 2016 Top Chess Engine Championship [TCEC] season 9 world champion), while humans would play against each other just to maintain and hone their skills in order to better appreciate and enjoy the innovative moves of the ever more advanced machines in their exhaustive exploration of the game—with the caveat that in the case of "the Perfect Game of the database endgames the moves are beyond comprehension. A grandmaster wouldn't be better at these endgames than someone who had learned chess yesterday. It's a sort of chess that has nothing to do with chess, a chess that we could never have imagined without computers. The Stiller moves are awesome, almost scary, because you know they are the truth, God's Algorithm—it's like being revealed the Meaning of Life, but you don't understand a word" (Tim Krabbé, "STILLER's MONSTERS or Perfection in Chess"[667]).

In my essay "Destiny's Multiple Bodies," I had written, "One cannot accomplish one's destiny with one body only; destiny requires the timely collaboration on solving some problem, facing some challenge, responding to some threat, etc., of two or more different kinds of bodies, at least one of which is subtle/Imaginal thus exists in a different kind of space and time than the ones in which one's natural, dense body exists. They may collaborate on one task that concerns one of them, or, better, all of them, or on several tasks that each concerns one of them. It is then that one can say that one is destined for this problem, threat or challenge," so I was gratified to come across an instantiation of the aforementioned words in Darren Aronofsky's *The Fountain* (2006) while writing another section of the book in which the essay ended up appearing, *What Was I Thinking?* (2017). The film presents a situation in which three different realms, a meditative, spiritual one, as it were the imaginal world; a fictional one; and one taking place in the physical world, collaborate on a destiny. The film starts with a conquistador, Tomás Verde, and a tiny contingent of Spanish soldiers under his command fighting a band of Mayans to gain entry to a pyramid in "New Spain" that reportedly gives access to the Tree of Life. The only survivor, Tomás is subdued by the Mayans. To his surprise, they shove him toward the entrance of the pyramid, his destination! There he is intercepted by a Mayan priest, who stabs Tomás as he tries to rush past him. The film then switches to the twenty-first century, where a physically identical man, Tom Creo, a neurosurgeon and researcher, is trying desperately to find a cure for the brain tumor of his beloved wife, Izzi, by experimenting on monkeys suffering from degenerative brain diseases with samples from a tree found during a scientific expedition in Guatemala. Izzi is writing a fiction entitled "The Fountain," in which Queen Isabella, at risk of losing her kingdom to the Inquisition, commissions one of her subjects, the conquistador we saw in the opening scene of the film, to search for the Tree of Life. The perceptive film spectator would become aware at this point that one of the reasons, if not *the* reason, the action was suspended in the Mayan territory just as Tomás was stabbed is that the fiction had not been completed by "then"—the other reason, he or she would later discover, is that the subtle body in the imaginal world was not yet ready to intervene in the fiction to assist the conquistador—the film thus presents a different understanding of the mode of existence of fiction than the mainstream one, one in which the characters of a fiction and the world they inhabit already exist even before the writer completes the novel or short story and publishes it. When Izzi's state worsens markedly, she asks her husband to complete the fiction; I would like to think that she intuits that conquistador Tomás Verde would be instrumental in accomplishing her husband's destiny. Thenceforth, his time has to be apportioned between the pressing necessity of finding a cure for his beloved wife's cancer and finishing the fictional account so that the conquistador can reach the Mayan pyramid leading to the Tree of Life in a timely manner—finishing the fictional story she began should not be viewed as an irresponsible distraction from his task of doing away with physical death, which he considers a disease to be cured. Meanwhile, on another plane, a similar-looking man, but whose head is shaved, Tommy, is engaging in meditation within what appears to be a glass dome in space while periodically tending a tall tree that has associations with both the biblical Tree of Life and the putative mythical Mayan tree. Given that conquistador Tomás Verde resumes (across the hiatus that he himself did not experience) his highly risky expedition to find the Tree of Life, the film spectator (who experienced the hiatus) has to assume that the grieving doctor has fulfilled the promise he made to his wife to finish the fictional story and that the subtle body of Tommy in the imaginal realm has by then reached the appropriate state to intervene in the fictional world. Indeed, at that point Tommy hurriedly ascends the imaginal tree and levitates in meditation so that, despite the quite different temporalities of the realms inhabited by the two similar-looking men, just as the Mayan priest is about to kill Tomás the levitating subtle body can become visible in the pyramid in such a way that the conquistador appears to be manifesting himself, through a transfiguration, as the "First Father" the Mayan priest and Mayans in general are awaiting. The priest kneels to the subtle, levitating figure illuminated with its own light. To the other side of the pyramid, Tomás sees a large tree, which he assumes to be the Tree of Life. Thus, in order for the fictional Tomás to reach the Tree of Life, a twenty-first-century neurosurgeon and researcher had to continue the fiction his wife had started whose protagonist is Tomás, and "his" and the neurosurgeon's avatar in the Imaginal World ('ālam al-khayāl) had through meditation to reach a state where he could appear suffused by an inner light and levitating in the pyramid leading to the Tree of Life just in time to spare the conquistador getting finished off by the priest guarding the Tree of Life in an equivalent role to that of the cherubim in Genesis 3:24 ("After he [the Lord God] drove the man out, he placed on the east side of the Garden of Eden cherubim and a flaming sword flashing back and forth to guard the way to the tree of life"). When he is on the point of inserting a knife into the Tree of Life to tap its enlivening sap and drink it, a flock of birds flies away in the background; he turns his head, thus suspending, for the duration of his turn, his movement of inserting the knife in the tree. This suspense implies that a choice, or, if one had already made a choice, a reconsideration of one's choice, is urgently required at this point, since it signals that the stakes are bigger, possibly infinitely bigger, than one assumed them to be, if not unimaginable (a filmmaker should not impose a non-diegetic, extrinsic suspense but respect and manifest an objective suspense intrinsic to the situation). In case this suspense is related to a choice whose alternatives are mundane, one can suspend one's movement in order to reconsider at the threshold, but in case the suspense is related to a choice whose alternatives are continuing to be part of the world of the living or death-as-undeath, one has to suspend one's movement in order to reconsider before the threshold, since at the en*trance* to the realm of death one cannot make a decision given that one is then and there entranced. The flock of birds that flew away at that critical moment feels like a farewell of the world to the one whose choice may, unbeknownst to him, lead to his physical death—were he to decide to proceed, he would, across a lapse of consciousness, indeed of being, feel that "the leaves being connected by millions of fibres with his own body, there on the seat, fanned it up and down; when the branch stretched he, too, made that statement. The sparrows fluttering, rising, and falling in jagged fountains were part of the pattern."[668] Is he to consider that the animals producing these sounds that are acting as an alarm intend to warn him or are being used by some more complex agency to warn him? Rather, he is well advised to consider that he must have intuited that (a) the stakes are far bigger than he had assumed, indeed possibly unimaginable, and thus that he should reconsider his decision, and (b) that he had reached the last point at which he could actually make a decision on whether to proceed, and so he perceptively made use of the circumstance that "there always are sounds—that is to say if one is alive to hear them"[669]—and that what we usually misperceive and treat as silence is "not silence at all, but sounds, the ambient sounds,"[670] to suspend his headlong progress—though, in *The Fountain*, it could be that, judging him to be not sensitive and intuitive enough, another aspect of his (collaborative) self, the neurosurgeon who is finishing the writing of the "fictional" account in which he figures prominently, may have provided him with a last-minute warning and opportunity to reconsider by writing something along the lines of "as the conquistador is on the point of inserting his knife in the Tree of Life to obtain its sap, he hears the sound of birds flying away in the distance and turns his head toward the source of the sound." Had he not made use of the circumstance that what we usually misperceive and treat as silence is "not silence at all, but sounds, the ambient sounds" in order to be "distracted" by one of these sounds from crossing a crucial threshold, he could have hallucinated such a sound, for example that of the sudden flight of birds, or of fluttering leaves, or of a rodent scurrying away, or even music (in the jungle!), to give himself some time to reconsider the crucial choice he made earlier. Following the suspension, he maintains his decision and inserts his dagger into the trunk of the Tree of Life. Sap flows from it. When a drop of the sap falls to the ground, it makes the vegetation grow incredibly fast, as it were in time-lapse, and lush. While impressed by this effect of just one drop of the sap, he feels a pang, which reminds him that he is wounded. He applies some of the sap to his wound, which heals almost immediately. As a result he believes all the more readily that by drinking the sap gushing from the tree he will live forever. So, he drinks from it, voraciously. He then perceives a brilliant light, which suffuses his face. Until now the progression of this scene illustrates the preconceptions not only of the character but also of most of the film's spectators, who expect that the sap from the Tree of Life will heal the wound he suffered while trying to reach it and then imbue him with eternal life. He removes from a pouch the ring entrusted to him by the queen, and, readying himself to wear it, exclaims triumphantly: "My queen, now and forever ... we shall be together." But just before he places the ring on his finger, he hears a sound so piercing that, in agony, he drops the ring to the ground. Vegetation bursts forth from the spot on his body where he had applied the sap and proliferates until he is buried by the exuberant plant life. Ah, the humor of Darren Aronofsky, taking literally that the conquistador is partaking not of Life in general but more specifically of the *Tree* of Life, a plant, and that consequently the exuberant life it gives relentlessly would be a vegetative life![671] While he could be said to be one of the countless manifestations, emanations, or vessels of life, yet, as the scene shows, life is too big for him, overwhelming him since not made to his measure, at least not in his earthly, unenhanced body. All is not lost, though, for the protagonist, since, in a relay across planes of existence, the ring is picked up by the imaginal avatar of the neurosurgeon, if not also of the conquistador, and is placed on his subtle finger, where it exactly covers a darkened circle (this ring is an object that circulates across the three realms—the twenty-first-century neurosurgeon had lost it after removing it before entering his lab to operate on the monkey in one of his medical experiments).

Meeting (in *ʿālam al-khayāl*, the Imaginal World) before meeting.

For the soul to feel keenly in exile in the dense body and its corresponding world, it has to be simultaneously in its fitting, subtle realm—it is not (a "fallen" soul's) anamnesis that produces the keenest feeling of exile but coexistence in both realms.

Michel Chion defines an acousmatic sound as "a sound heard without seeing its source."[672] "When the acousmatic ... voice has not yet been visualized—that is, when we cannot yet connect it to a face—we get a special being, a kind of talking and acting shadow to which we attach the name *acousmêtre* [here it appears that the voice itself is the acousmêtre, that '*acousmêtre*' and 'acousmatic voice' are synonyms]. A person you talk to on the phone, whom you've never seen, is an *acousmêtre* [here it appears that it is the person who is the *acousmêtre* rather than the voice whose source this person may later become]. If you have ever seen her, however, or if in a film you continue to hear her after she leaves the visual field, is this still an *acousmêtre*? Definitely, but of another kind, which we'll call the already visualized *acousmêtre*.... I am going to concentrate primarily on what may be called the *complete acousmêtre*, the one who is not-yet-seen, but who remains liable to appear in the visual field at any moment [here, too, it appears that it is the person who is the *acousmêtre* rather than the voice whose source this person may later become]."[673] According to Chion, the acousmêtre has four powers, "the ability to be everywhere, to see all, to know all, and to have complete power. In other words: ubiquity, panopticism, omniscience, and omnipotence."[674] Since Chion fails to preclude a misunderstanding, indeed repeatedly contributes to it, I will clear this matter up: it is the acousmatic voice that has these powers, not the person or entity presumed to be its invisible source. It is the acousmatic voice that is all-powerful, all-knowing, ubiquitous, and, the strangest, all-seeing, not its presumed invisible source (except in one case: God)—while the normal voice does not (usually) see, the acousmatic voice sees. The acousmatic voice, ubiquitous and all-seeing, may convey the knowledge it acquired to the one who used to be its source when it was embodied. Rather than assuming that the voice doesn't initially have these powers but acquires them by becoming acousmatic, one is to consider that the voice has these powers in its original, natural state and loses them when it becomes de-acousmatized. The already visualized acousmêtre has the four powers that Chion ascribes to the complete acousmêtre but to a weaker degree or has only some of these powers, at least initially after it became one, and so is less radical than the never before seen acousmatic voice, let alone, the most radical, the one that can never be visualized and embodied, in mainstream Islam, God (see, for example, Qur'ān 7:143). "In how many fantasy, thriller, and gangster films do we see the acousmêtre become an ordinary person when *his* voice [my italics; this formulation implies that for Chion the acousmêtre is not the voice but the invisible bodily source of the voice] is assigned a visible and circumscribed body [that is, to use Chion's coinage, when there's de-acousmatization]? He then usually becomes, if not harmless, at least human and vulnerable."[675] In Marc Forster's *Stranger than Fiction* (2006), Lana and Lilly Wachowski's *The Matrix* (1999), and Stanley Kubrick's *2001: A Space Odyssey* (1968), the entity itself whose voice is acousmatic is powerful: in *2001: A Space Odyssey* it is an AI, indeed possibly an AGI, that controls the spaceship; in *Stranger than Fiction*, it is an old-fashioned omniscient novelist in relation to a character in the novel she is writing; and in *The Matrix*, it is a rebel leader, Morpheus, who has been trained in various martial-arts programs and who can "see" what goes on in the simulation with the aid of a teammate who can read its code. We are introduced to these characters as acousmatic voices. So, in addition to the powers they have as an AI, a novelist, a rebel leader who has been trained in various martial-arts programs and who can "see" what goes on in the simulation with the aid of a teammate who can read its code, etc., they have the powers of the acousmatic voice that Michel Chion lists in his book *The Voice in Cinema*. When the acousmatic voice is de-acousmatized, they don't lose their initial powers but the powers that the acousmatic voice procured them. I am far more interested in cases where it is the acousmatic voice that has these powers, rather than its presumed invisible source. This is the case in Billy Wilder's *Sunset Boulevard* (1950), which starts on a street sign, SUNSET BOULEVARD, in the morning. As we hear sirens and see police squad cars turn off the road into a driveway, an acousmatic voice says: "Yes, this is Sunset Boulevard, Los Angeles, California. It's about 5: That's the homicide squad—complete with detectives and newspapermen. A murder has been reported from one of those great big houses in the ten thousand block." For it to accurately describe in the present tense what we are seeing, the acousmatic voice must itself see. It continues: "You'll read about it in the late editions, I'm sure. You'll get it over your radio and see it on television because an old-time star is involved, one of the biggest. But before you hear it all distorted and blown out of proportion, before those Hollywood columnists get their hands on it, maybe you'd like to hear the facts, the whole truth. If so, you've come to the right party"—were what the voice is advancing to turn out to be accurate, then the acousmatic voice would be omniscient. It then resumes describing what both it and we see: "You see, the body of a young man was found floating in the pool of her mansion with two shots in his back and one in his stomach. Nobody important, really. Just a movie writer with a couple of B pictures to his credit.... Let's go back about six months and find the day when it all started. I was living in an apartment house above Franklin and Ivar [we have a switch here, by means of a cinematic flashback, from the acousmatic voice to a body we are invited to assume is its source]. Things were tough at the moment. 'Yeah?' [here it is clear that the voice has been de-acousmatized since it is being uttered in sync by the lips of the man we see]. 'Joseph C. Gillis?' 'That's right.'" By the end of the film we discover that the dead man in the pool used to be the source of this acousmatic voice. "Back at that pool again, the one I always wanted." And yet when the acousmatic voice continues, "It's dawn now, and they must have photographed me a thousand times. Then they got some pruning hooks from the garden and fished me out ever so gently," we do not have de-acousmatization since we do not see the lips of the corpse or even of a spectral body uttering the words—the corpse's lips naturally remain motionless (even though there is almost always an attempt by the human who was its source to reclaim the acousmatic voice, even if in the form of a ghost). In the beginning scene of Vincente Minnelli's *An American in Paris* (1951), over shots of recognizable monuments of the capital of France, for example the obelisk at Place de la Concorde and the Arc de Triomphe, a voice-over describes what we see and then ostensibly introduces the man to whom it belongs: "This is Paris. And I'm an American who lives here. My name: Jerry Mulligan. And I'm an ex-GI. In 1945, when the Army told me to find my own job, I stayed on.... I'm a painter.... And for a painter, the Mecca of the world for study, for inspiration, and for living is here on this star called Paris. Just look at it." It would seem from these words that the acousmatic voice is addressing us! The acousmatic voice continues to act as our guide as the scene changes to another location, hence seems to be ubiquitous: "That's where I'm billeted. Here's my street.... I live upstairs. No, no, no, not there. One flight up." It now appears that it is addressing the one operating the camera, if not controlling the camera, since the latter moves upward. Part of the all-powerfulness of the cinematic acousmatic voice that is missed by Chion in his book *The Voice in Cinema* is the ability to control the camera and to address the film spectator directly, that is, to affect what is non-diegetic! As the camera reaches the right story, it reveals, through the window, a man sleeping in his bed! The voice exclaims: "Voilà!" Here we have a startling disjunction between the seeing acousmatic voice and the unseeing, since sleeping, person to whom it would belong only once the de-acousmatization takes place, which happens shortly after as he wakes up and talks from his window to the boys on the street (so the earlier conflation of the acousmatic voice and Jerry Mulligan when the former says, "My name: Jerry Mulligan," was misleading). In the latter two aforementioned cases it is inaccurate to attribute the power to see all to the presumed source of the voice rather than solely to the acousmatic voice. In the film *Stranger than Fiction*, when we and the protagonist hear a female voice narrating, describing, and commenting on what he is doing, for example, "The sound the paper made against the folder had the same tone as a wave scraping against sand. And when Harold thought about it, he listened to enough waves every day to constitute what he imagined to be a deep and endless ocean," but do not see a source for this voice, the latter, a complete acousmêtre, has the aforementioned four powers in relation to the protagonist of the novel-in-progress. When we subsequently see a female novelist and soon after watch her talk in sync and recognize the voice as hers, she does so initially to respond to a woman who was sent by her publisher to prod her to finish her book and to assist her, since she is suffering from writer's block, powerless to invent and unable to imagine, in other words, to see in her "mind's eye," the death of her protagonist and thus the conclusion of the novel. When we switch back in a later scene to the acousmatic voice, the latter is once again all-knowing, all-powerful (it says that the protagonist's watch stops and the watch promptly stops), ubiquitous (Harold is unable to hide from it), and all-seeing, since it accurately describes what he is doing wherever he goes. When her writer's block ceases, it appears that she resumed being all-powerful and omniscient as a novelist in relation to her protagonist, seeing that she managed to jot down the ending of the novel, which, if unrevised, would bring about his death. The latter, a senior agent for the Internal Revenue Service, identifies the voice he hears with a woman being interviewed on TV, the novelist Karen Eiffel, and, after finding out that she had been audited around a decade earlier by the IRS, obtains her office phone number and her address from IRS records and looks for a phone to call her. The acousmatic voice describes accurately, or imposes on Harold, these actions: "Harold found himself running across the plaza, heading for the nearest pay phone.... As Harold neared the phone, he saw it was occupied.... Fortunately, Harold remembered a bank of phones in the Sixth Street subway tunnel. The first phone failed to give a dial tone. And the second seemed to be splattered with a fresh batch of mucus. Harold dialed the third phone, fervently making sure to give each number key a specific forceful push." Now we switch from the acousmatic voice to the novelist, whom we see, for the first time, uncharacteristically, typing—for much of the film we do not see her type but see an alternation between the acousmatic voice, with all the powers of the (nineteenth-century) traditional novelist (omniscient narrator, etc.), and her as someone suffering from writer's block, unable to see in her mind's eye the future actions of her protagonist; it would appear that the typed stacks next to her typewriter, which we at no point saw her type, were received by her through inspiration, most likely through dictation by the acousmatic voice. The novelist types: "The phone rang." The phone rings. She notices the curious coincidence. She types: "The phone rang again...." The phone rings again. She is now intrigued by the recurrence of the coincidence. Beginning to be unsettled by, if not to feel anxious over, the possibility that the coincidence will recur again and then be difficult to dismiss it as a mere coincidence, she pauses after typing "The phone rang a third time," not adding a period—the ringing, which should have continued at the same rhythm, is suspended (this suspense evidences her control as a writer of Harold and the world of the novel in general) until she hesitantly types the period that ratifies the completion of the sentence. And indeed, now the phone rings in her office a third time! By answering the ringing office phone at the indicated address, the acousmêtre is de-acousmatized, consequently she is no longer all-knowing as implied by her unawareness that it is the protagonist of her novel who is calling her: "'Hello?' 'Is this Karen Eiffel?' 'Yes.' 'My name is Harold Crick. I believe you're writing a story about me.'

'I'm sorry?' 'My name is Harold Crick.' 'Is this a joke?' 'No. I work for the IRS. My name, Miss Eiffel, is Harold Crick. When I go through the files at work I hear a deep and endless ocean.' 'Oh, my God!'" The more powers the acousmatic voice has, the less its presumed invisible source has: the body through which it gets de-acousmatized is sleeping, hence unseeing, ignorant about its surroundings in *An American in Paris,* and suffering from writer's block in *Stranger than Fiction*; and the body that is presumed to be its source is dead in *Sunset Boulevard.* In cases where these powers are not in addition to those of the body of the one who used to be its source, but at the expense of the latter, that body has an incentive to de-acousmatize the voice.

The acousmatic voice of God ("And when Moses came to Our appointed meeting and his Lord spoke unto him, he said, 'My Lord, show me, that I might look upon Thee.' He said, 'Thou shalt not see Me; but look upon the mountain: if it remains firm in its place, then thou wilt see Me.' And when his Lord revealed (His) glory to the mountain He sent it crashing down. And Moses fell down senseless" [Qur'ān 7:143]) is different from other acousmatic voices since it is not a voice whose source is another being or entity but is an aspect of this being, one of its infinite self-disclosures, hence that being, though not in its essence, *thāt,* but in its manifestation, therefore it cannot be said to have intrinsic powers (omniscience, ubiquity, etc.) separate from God; and since God has the powers listed by Chion not only when He appears as an acousmêtre but even when He is silent.

Most people assume that the acousmêtre persists in existence until it is de-acousmatized, forgetting that it is a voice, not a body. As long as the acousmêtre speaks, it has the four powers, but as soon as it stops emitting sounds, it loses existence and thus these powers—until it begins to speak again.

Uber leverages a combination of GPS technology, real-time data (including traffic information and road closures), routing algorithms (that take into account factors such as distance, traffic conditions, estimated time of arrival, and historical data to suggest the most efficient route for a given trip), and partnerships with navigation-app providers (for example, Google Maps) to offer voice-guided turn-by-turn directions and visual maps to the driver through its Uber Driver App. Oddly, in the middle of a trip, the familiar map on the glowing screen turned blank. Hackers with advanced technical expertise had exploited vulnerabilities in the infrastructure that supports Uber's navigation services, infiltrating and compromising the GPS network, causing it to abruptly cease functioning. And yet the turn-by-turn voice directions did not go silent but continued! In this scenario, it would be clear that the voice is all-seeing not because it is part of the aforementioned technological apparatus but because it is acousmatic.

During a lecture to my students about the acousmêtre, I left the classroom while continuing my answer to one of their questions, so that they continued to hear my voice from the hallway. I assume that at least some of them, at some point, obscurely felt that the already visualized acousmêtre was no longer just in the corridor or a little further away but could have been anywhere, indeed could have been in the classroom, thus able to see what they were doing.

I can well imagine a film in which a character who is blind nonetheless appears to see through her acousmatic voice, which conveys to her what it sees, so that when the acousmêtre undergoes de-acousmatization, she reverts to being unable to see.

The relation between the person who is assumed to be the source of the acousmatic voice and the latter is not one of possession by the former so that whatever the acousmatic voice knows the source knows, too; if the person who is ostensibly its source tries to possess, through incorporation, the acousmatic voice in order to gain its powers, he or she will discover that, as a result of de-acousmatizing it, the voice lost all these powers. When the ostensible source of the acousmatic voice is a poet or novelist, the relation can be one of subjugation, in which the acousmatic voice dictates to its ostensible source, or one of inspiration, in which its ostensible source maintains a degree of freedom as to whether to accept or reject what the acousmatic voice conveys.

A woman *with a pretty face* who is always *underdressed for the weather* wiretapped her boss's cellular phone and listened in to his conversations, the characteristic sound of his footfall, what he did when, believing that he was alone, he let his guard down (for example, sobbing upon discovering that his wife was unfaithful to him), growing attached to him as she thus came to know him more and more intimately. Then the wiretapped voice she was hearing began to acquire some of the characteristics of the acousmêtre in Michel Chion's sense, such as omniscience and omnipresence, appearing, for example, to know things about her she had never divulged to him or to anybody else, things he could not have known by natural means and causation. When she confronted him, he denied knowledge of the various matters that his voice appeared, sometimes directly, sometimes symptomatically, incredibly to know. Ignorant of the writings of Chion on the acousmêtre, she incorrectly assumed that he must have stealthily placed tiny surveillance cameras and miniature sound recorders in her apartment, so she ended up ransacking her apartment to check whether it was bugged (in the process reenacting, unawares, a scene from Francis Ford Coppola's *The Conversation* [1974]), only to discover, to her bafflement, that it wasn't.

You are no longer in the physical space where you happened to be when the hypnosis began; you are (enveloped) in the voice of the hypnotist.

A generous finite being has an inkling, if not consciously acknowledges, that he or she has received more than he or she has recognized:

for example, that the roads one uses on one's walks and the highways one uses on one's drives were built, and the electricity in the city where one resides was installed, by workers one has not thanked, let alone paid anything, unless, indirectly, a pittance through taxes. Can one receive generously what the other did not give generously, what was extracted from him or her through exploitation? A revolution is never just about radically changing the present and thus the future; it is also, redemptively, about making it possible for us to receive the work and deeds of many others as instances of generosity when actually they were extracted through exploitation and even though they were not intended specifically for us.

In Islam, God is generous, for He not only gives us through recurrently creating us who have no necessity of existence, but does so without the possibility of giving Him in return, for it makes no sense to try to pay him back given that we and our acts, including our thanking him, a form of giving back, are the result of his generous recurrent creation of us and "our" acts; indeed, He is the Generous, *al-karīm* (Qur'ān 27:40; 82:6), because He is the one who recurrently creates all other generous creatures, in other words, because the latter's generosity derives from His. It is infelicitous to feel indebted to the Generous, to the one who gives infinitely without anything in return, and it is a *maladresse* (blunder), a *mal-adresse*, to try to pay back the generous, if not a revengeful gesture for being on the receiving side (to "settle accounts with" is not necessarily something positive, since it could mean "to pay or receive a balance due" but also "to get revenge on [someone]" [*Collins English Dictionary*, 13th ed.]). Since all creatures are self-disclosures of God (Qur'ān 2:115: "Wheresoever you turn, there is the Face of God"), by giving to them generously, without requiring anything in return, one would have responded felicitously to His generosity—without, as implied by the *tanzīh* in Qur'ān 42:11, "naught is like unto Him," giving *back* to Him ... as a *dhāt* or essence.

The felicitous, proper way to respond to generosity is by being generous to someone else, some generous stranger, and to those who have nothing, indeed who are nothing in the world, for example, the dead, and hence cannot even be tempted with the *maladresse* and infelicity of trying to pay back.

One can judge whether an uprising is a revolution by whether its participants demand certain things only as prerequisites to be able to give, again and again, indeed give in a radical way, that is, creatively and even after their physical deaths, for example through a great book or painting or film—in short, as prerequisites to be able to be generous. The net result for revolutionaries is not taking but giving generously, that is, immeasurably. What is felicitous about a revolution is that one's main demand of it, that it provide the conditions for more people, if not everyone, to give generously, is what the revolutionaries, even those among them who are protesting in the streets seemingly because they are destitute, are all of a sudden so naturally doing! Has anyone tried to dissuade revolutionaries thus: "Jalal Toufic asserts that one engages in revolution to be able to give generously. Since you are already, during the initial stages of the revolution, able to give generously, even while your demands have not yet been met, you should withdraw them"? A revolution has a double temporality: through it, one aims to produce the conditions that will make it possible for those who could not give previously to do so, but the revolutionary moment itself already makes it possible for revolutionaries to give, with the consequence that soon enough one is rebelling to maintain the possibility to do what one is already managing to do during the revolution, give—but without the many dangers associated with a revolution, for example losing an eye as a result of being hit by a tear-gas canister, or getting imprisoned, tortured, and possibly killed. This is partly why every revolution induces the feeling that it is, at some level, already an accomplishment, even when most if not all of its stated goals remain unrealized, since, for its duration, it already provided those taking part in it with the luxury of giving—of their time, creativity (be it at the level of the slogans), etc. And the ferocity and brutality of the state's repression have as one of their aims to traumatize those who took part in the revolution so that they will repress any memory of it as already an accomplishment. The moment the participants in a revolution begin to allow themselves to be exploited, excusing this euphemistically as a sacrificial act, the revolution is over.

Is it too much to ask that, when queried as to why he was on the streets, one of the protesters in Lebanon in October 2019 would answer: "I am protesting so as to deserve to have Jalal Toufic, the author of *Undeserving Lebanon* (2007), write a sequel titled *Deserving Lebanon*—I assume that for that to happen we have also to deserve his aforementioned book"?

How does one gather that the revolution is not a passing phase—even one that is brutally repressed and ostensibly aborted? By the rigor with which its slogans are written, even though those spraying them on the city's walls know full well that their writings will most likely either be covered with other graffiti or "cleaned" over the next hours or days—this rigor implies immanently the temporal span of the revolution.

Whereas aphorisms are usually received,[676] during a revolution they, often painted on walls and barricades, are, exceptionally, actively formulated and coined! Thus a revolution, for its duration, revolutionizes the process of appearance of aphorisms.

The saying "the first casualty of war is truth" provides one distinction between war and revolution: if, during some stage of a revolution, we start to encounter a tolerance for, indeed orchestration and propagation of, lies and an instrumental use of language, then we would know that the revolution is sliding into civil war. During a real revolution, there is a creative and rigorous use of language, an avoidance of exaggeration, indeed no tolerance even for the figurative use of language—when certain expressions seem to be metaphors, then, on second thought, they turn out to work literally. The following would be a good sign that we are dealing with a real revolution: the organizers of a march or demonstration provide a tally of the total number of participants that is smaller than the one given by the police.

Deleuze: "May '68 is the intrusion of becoming. People have often wanted to view it as the reign of the imaginary, but it's not at all imaginary. It's a gust of the real in its pure state. It's the real that arrives.... Real people, or people in their reality."[677] Was this what took place during the protests that swept Lebanon in the fall of 2019 (I was residing then in Hong Kong): real people, finally, rather than, for example, people reduced to their sectarian identifications as Maronite, Shi'ite, Sunni, etc.? Would I one day witness a revolution in which people demand to be acknowledged and treated no longer as solely alive but as mortals in my sense, that is, as dead even while still physically alive? I would then exclaim: "Real people, finally! Mortals aware of their condition!" Where do we see the reign of the imaginary? In a bad film or novel, including one that seems to provide a faithful representation of the world, since in a bad film's diegesis, unlike in the world, Dōgen (born 1200, died 1253) not merely is not part of mainstream culture but never existed and practiced zazen, whereas in the world, this great thinker and Zen master not only existed but his zazen continues to exert an enlightening effect on us and other sentient beings, including the characters in films that do not fall apart in "two days": "When even for a moment you express the buddha's seal in the three actions by sitting upright in samādhi ... all beings in the ten directions, and the six realms, including the three lower realms, at once obtain pure body and mind ... all things realize correct awakening.... Thus in the past, future, and present of the limitless universe this zazen carries on the buddha's teaching endlessly.... Know that even if all buddhas of the ten directions, as innumerable as the sands of the Ganges, exert their strength and with the buddhas' wisdom try to measure the merit of one person's zazen, they will not be able to fully comprehend it"—no wonder bad mainstream films are more dispiriting than the world can ever be, even when they seem to be a faithful representation of it according to mainstream culture.

Referring to Jacques Rancière's conception of politics, Slavoj Žižek wrote: "What, for Rancière, is politics proper? A phenomenon which, for the first time, appeared in Ancient Greece when the members of *demos* (those with no firmly determined place in the hierarchical social edifice) not only demanded that their voice be heard against those in power, those who exerted social control—that is, they not only protested the wrong [*le tort*] they suffered, and wanted their voice to be heard, to be recognized as included in the public sphere, on an equal footing with the ruling oligarchy and aristocracy—even more, they, the excluded, those with no fixed place within the social edifice, presented themselves as the representatives, the stand-ins, for the Whole of Society, for the true Universality ('we—the "nothing," not counted in the order[678]—are the people, we are All against others who stand only for their particular privileged interest').... Politics proper thus always involves a kind of short circuit between the Universal and the Particular: the paradox of a *singulier universel*, a singular which appears as the stand-in for the Universal.... This identification of the non-part with the Whole, of the part of society with no properly defined place within it (or resisting the allocated subordinated place within it) with the Universal, is the elementary gesture of politicization."[679] Given Žižek's own unawareness of his condition of mortal, of being dead even while still physically alive, he fails to note that the members of the Greek *demos* were unaware of their condition of mortals and, consequently, were complicit in not counting the dead as part of the community (this applies nowadays to virtually all those who are considered to be nothing by society, for example illegal immigrants). We find a paradigmatic example of "a *singulier universel*" in the letter dated January 5, 1889, to Jacob Burckhardt in Nietzsche's handwriting, where one can read, "I am Prado, I am also Prado's father, I venture to say that I am also Lesseps.... I am also Chambige.... Every name in history is I": this "every name in history is I" *is not a deduction from or summation of the previous enumeration of singular names* (one can supplement the names explicitly mentioned in the aforementioned letter with, for example, the following two, with which several of the final letters in Nietzsche's handwriting were signed: The Crucified [letters to August Strindberg (late December 1888); Georg Brandes, Peter Gast, Umberto I (king of Italy), Cardinal Mariani (Vatican secretary of state), and "the Illustrious Pole" (January 4, 1889)], and Dionysus [letters to Jakob Burckhardt (post-marked Turin, January 4, 1889), Cosima Wagner (early January 1889), Franz Overbeck (received January 7, 1889)]) *but is itself another item in the list*. This *singulier universel*, "every name in history is I," which one undergoes in death (the same letter in Nietzsche's handwriting in which one reads, "every name in history is I," also bears the assertion, "This autumn ... I twice attended my funeral"), hence when one is no longer treated as part of society, indeed when one is considered to be nothing, is the foundation of standing for the Whole by those who are nothing, hence is, if the "identification of the non-part with the Whole, of the part of society with no properly defined place within it ... with the Universal, is the elementary gesture of politicization," the elementary and ultimate gesture of politicization.

Writing, art, and cinema are political not when they are explicitly concerned with gaining state power and function as means for aims related to the police in Rancière's sense ("Two logics of human being-together must ... be discerned.... Politics is generally seen as the set of procedures whereby the aggregation and consent of collectivities is achieved, the organization of powers, the distribution of places and roles, and the systems for legitimizing this distribution. I propose to give this system of distribution and legitimization another name ... the police.... The word police normally evokes what is known as the petty police, the truncheon blows of the forces of law and order and the inquisitions of the secret police.... The petty police is just a particular form of a more general order that arranges that tangible reality in which bodies are distributed in community. It is the weakness and not the strength of this order in certain states that inflates the petty police to the point of putting it in charge of the whole set of police functions"[680]), in the process sacrificing much of their formal concerns and experimentation; but, according to Rancière, when they render visible and audible various categories of the living, worldly entities who are usually not heard or seen, and thus not counted (fully) as part of the community, for example slaves, to take a past example, and, in our present period, illegal immigrants, or, as in my case, the children of Lebanese women from foreign fathers, who are not counted as Lebanese, thus contributing to their eventual inclusion in it. As far as I am concerned, writing, art, and cinema, along with religion, become *fundamentally* political when they attempt to contribute to the inclusion of those who cannot be counted as part of the community by other means, for example by an uprising, exemplarily the dead, including the dead avatar of the mortal living human, in the process deploying all their already available formal resources as well as experimenting with new ones. If the politics of mortals involves death, it is fundamentally not as a result of the physical death that many will suffer in pursuit of their political aims, but (for as long as the epochal will has not been attained through someone who undergoes countless recurrence and ends up willing the eternal recurrence of one or more events, the overman, a.k.a. the Messiah/Mahdi, and consequently leads to the abolition of death[-as-uneath] and thus of mortality) insofar as one of the main constituents that are not counted as a part of the community are the dead, including the (un)dead version of the mortal, who may as alive be considered part of society. Since he or she is dead even while still physically alive, the mortal included in a community is included in it as someone who contains constitutively rather than accidentally a part that is treated as nothing, not only in the world of the living but also, given that he or she is lost in the labyrinthine space and time of death, including in the sense that he or she cannot be found there, in the realm of death. When "all" the exoteric parts of society, including, in the future, artificial general intelligences, have been integrated in it and counted as a part of it, politics will not end but can then continue *only* by other means, writing, film, art, certain religious disciplines, etc., since it is only through these other, creative means that those still not counted as a part of the community, its mortal members insofar as they are dead even while physically alive, can be reached and their thoughts, perceptions, and affects conveyed more or less clearly, thus making possible for them as dead even while physically alive to be counted as a part of society. One could thus paraphrase Clausewitz's "War is merely the continuation of politics by other means" in relation to writing, film, and art concerning mortals: writing, film, and art concerning mortals are not means of politics but the continuation of politics by other means. What's specific about the politics of mortals is that at no point is it independent of its continuation by other means, sufficient and adequate without them—ultimately, in the end, there can be no politics (of mortals) fully divested from its continuation by other means, not practiced by other means, too, but merely the police as Rancière understands this term.

Dr. Gaston Ferdière, the head psychiatrist at the Rodez asylum when Artaud was interned there, pressured him, for supposedly therapeutic purposes, to translate Lewis Carroll's poem "Jabberwocky." Artaud, who didn't speak English, worked on the translation with the assistance of a Henri Julien, who was not only the asylum's chaplain but also taught English. Is it enough for a mortal translator to translate from one of the languages of the living into another? No; we can leave translation from one of the languages of the living into another to those who are in disavowal of their condition of mortals or who have been resurrected by *the life*, Jesus Christ, for example the resurrected brother of Mary and Martha, whom I can very well imagine translating from Aramaic into Greek and Latin and vice versa. I think that Artaud was concerned about the other side not of the mirror but of death, so he translated the portmanteau title of the poem "Jabberwocky" from Lewis Carroll's book *Through the Looking-Glass* (1871) into one of the languages of the dead: "NEANT OMO NOTAR NEMO / Jurigastri —Solargultri / Gabar Uli —Barangoumti / Oltar Ufi —Sarangmumpti / Sofar Ami —Zantar Upti / Momar Uni —Septfar Esti / Gonpar Arak. —Alak Eli." I would say that his translation of the poem, like a good number of his texts of that period, was addressed to the living, since part of it was in one of their languages, French, but also to the dead, since part of it was in one of the latter's languages—and to the voices. Given that, according to a letter dated February 12, 1943, in his handwriting though signed by another (name), "Antonin Nalpas," "Antonin Artaud est mort à la peine et de douleur à Ville-Évrard au mois d'Août 1939 et son cadavre a été sorti de Ville-Évrard pendant la durée d'une nuit blanche comme celles dont parle Dostoïevsky et qui occupent l'espace de plusieurs journées inter-calaires mais non comprises dans le calendrier de ce monde-ci—quoi[que] vraies comme le jour d'ici"[681] (Antonin Artaud died to trouble and of pain in Ville-Évrard in the month of August 1939 and his corpse was removed from Ville-Évrard during a sleepless night like those Dostoevsky describes and that occupy the span of several intercalary days but are not included in the calendar of this world—though they are as real as any day here), and that he contin-ued to be dead before dying physically at least until September 1943, the date he resumed signing the letters in his handwriting with "Artaud," it would have been far more appropriate for him to collabo-ratively translate one of the texts he had written during this period: Julien would have been tasked with translating the sections already written in French into English while Artaud would have tried to translate the sections in a language of the dead into French for Julien to then translate into English. We have at least one instance of such a translation by Artaud from a language of the dead into one of the languages of the living, French, when he wrote in a footnote to his translation into a language of the dead of the portmanteau English title of Lewis Carroll's poem "Jabberwocky": "Si tout cela ne plaît pas on peut choisir comme titre une seule de ces phrases, par exemple MOMAR UNI ou GONPAR ARAK ALAK ELI, qui veut dire: as-tu compris?" (If this whole thing does not prove pleasing, you can choose as the title only one of these phrases, for example, MOMAR UNI or GONPAR ARAK ALAK ELI, which means: have you under-stood?). Given that, as Daniel Paul Schreber indicated in his book *Memoirs of My Nervous Illness*, the voices provided him with certain expressions that proved most fitting to render some of the unworldly things he was undergoing ("I did not invent the expression 'forecourts of heaven,' but *like all other expressions which are in inverted commas in this essay* [for instance 'fleeting-improvised-men,' 'dream life,' etc.], it only repeats the words which the voices that speak to me always applied to the processes concerned. These are expressions *which would never have occurred to me*, which I have never heard from human beings"[682]), I assume that Artaud would have collaborated on such a translation with the voices (even if the process would have been not smooth but trying, as we witness in his *To Have Done with the Judgment of God*, which includes a dialogue with [his] often sarcastic and judgmental voices)—and that every mortal translator has to collaborate with the voices on the sections written in one of the languages of the dead. As a mortal who died before dying physically and who was engaged in translation, Artaud's task with regard to the dead would have been to translate into one of their languages certain texts written in French by some living authors (one of the oddest things about the *Bardo Thödol* [Tibetan: "Liberation in the Intermediate State through Hearing"] is that the dead man or woman is presumed to understand the Tibetan language of the living without need of translation: "If the deceased's body is present, then during the interval which follows the ceasing of respiration, this *Great Liberation by Hearing* should be read aloud by a spiritual teacher, or by a spiritual sibling, sincere [practitioner], or a sympathetic friend, placing the lips [close] to the ear [of the deceased], without actually touching"![683]), and to translate for living mortals *some* of the utterances and texts of the dead, including in his writings, into one of the languages of the living, French (other living translators could then translate the French into other languages of the living), leaving at least one of these utterances or phrases untranslated into one of the languages of the living, a kind of anamorphic stain. Whereas the place where the spectator has to stand for the mysterious object in Hans Holbein the Younger's painting *The Ambassadors* (1533) to manifest itself as a skull is part of the world of the living, a certain spot in the National Gallery in London, where the painting presently hangs, in the case of Artaud's anamorphic text *To Have Done with the Judgment of God* the vantage point from which the unintelligible, impenetrable sections of the text would become clear—though one's mind would then become unclear—is not in life and the world but in death, therefore in order to read them properly one has to die before dying physically, with the consequence that simultaneously one would (largely) be no longer able to properly understand any of the languages of the living, the latter becoming from that vantage point themselves incomprehensible, a linguistic stain. So, while a reader can possibly comprehend "Man could quite easily not have shit, / not opened the anal sack, / but he chose to shit[684] / as he would have chosen to live / instead of agreeing to live dead. / Because in order not to crap, / he would have to have agreed / not to be, / but he could not resolve to lose / existence, / that is to die alive," he or she would have to die before dying physically in order to comprehend the sections written in a language of the dead, for example "o reche modo / to edire / di za / tau dari / do padera coco," possibly with the assistance of the voices(-over), who may furnish their (singular rather than necessarily universal) translation, or at least to feel that these sections are not alien, consequently recognizing that the dead, including himself or herself as dead even while still physically alive, are part of the community. While only a mortal, only someone who was dead even while still physically alive, could have written the anamorphic text *To Have Done with the Judgment of God*, and only a mortal is in the proper condition to read it in its entirety, a mortal, even Artaud, cannot *conjointly* read the sections in one of the languages of the living (albeit one that had been so singularized that it became a foreign—but not alien—language [given that, according to "Proust's celebrated formulation, style is like a foreign language within the language"[685]]) and those in a language of the dead in Artaud's anamorphic text, for insofar as he or she is dead, "in" the death realm, he or she feels that the languages of the dead are not alien while those of the living are, and vice versa, insofar as he or she is alive, he or she feels that the languages of the dead are alien and the languages of the living are not, and so he or she has to keep switching between being alive and being dead, in other words, keep dying (before dying physically) and getting resurrected (as a mortal), as he or she reads the complete text. From this perspective, Artaud's *To Have Done with the Judgment of God* is an incredibly demanding text, more demanding than Joyce's *Finnegans Wake* (similarly, my essays on my concept "the over-turn" are incredibly demanding, since they require the rigorous reader to place himself or herself in the condition that would enable him or her to better intuit and appreciate the concept, namely, die before physically dying and thus undergo one or more over-turns). While some of the sections in a language of the dead could have been translated by Artaud insofar as he had died before dying and others can be translated only by or through the assistance of the voices, in collaboration with them, are there terms and sections that can be translated neither by the mortal Artaud who died before dying physically nor by the voices that might at times assist in this endeavor (though they at other times obstruct his progress), terms and sections that would be an equivalent in the context of transla-tion from a language of the dead of the navel Freud wrote about in the context of the interpretation of dreams: "The question whether it is possible to interpret *every* dream must be answered in the neg-ative.... It is always possible to go *some* distance: far enough, at all events, to convince ourselves that the dream is a structure with a meaning, and as a rule far enough to get a glimpse of what that meaning is.... [And yet] there is often a passage in even the most thoroughly interpreted dream which has to be left obscure; this is because we become aware during the work of interpretation that at that point there is a tangle of dream-thoughts which cannot be unraveled.... This is the dream's navel, the spot where it reaches down into the unknown"?[686] While in Artaud's *To Have Done with the Judgment of God* the parts written in one of the languages of the living, French, have for their goal to lead the reader to do away with the judgment of God, his text nonetheless induces the rigorous albeit foolhardy reader to expose himself or herself to this judgment by dying to read the sections written in a language of the dead, since, according to most religions, at least in their exoteric reading, death is the main if not sole arena of the judgment of God, and, consequently, it is following death that one is judged by God in a Last Judgment. It would seem that the main way to do away with the judgment of God is to do away with death altogether, to cease to be a mortal, dead while alive, becoming solely alive, but doing away with death would make it impossible for the reader to fathom the sections written in a language of the dead in a text whose title implies that it concerns precisely doing away with such a judgment. So Artaud's other texts that were written following his death before dying physically and that, consequently, include sections written in a language of the dead but that do not advocate doing away with the judgment of God are more consistent in this regard.

Artaud did not simply represent a body without organs through his paintings and drawings and through his final audio works intended for the radio; rather he tried through his drawings, which were not conceived as representations but were intended, partly through their inclusion of spells, to have, like the paintings of William S. Burroughs later, magical agency, and through his incantatory radio program *To Have Done with the Judgment of God* to replace his organic body as well as that of the spectator or listener with a body without organs. I assume that he must have believed, however obscurely, that this would have allowed him to avoid having his organs be implicated in the judgment of God concerning him. By considering doing away with organs as a prerequisite for doing away with the judgment of God, Artaud was tapping into a venerable tradition that implicates organs in posthumous judgment: "—30B—Chapter for not letting Ani's heart create opposition against him in the God's Domain: O my heart which I had from my mother! O my heart which I had from my mother! O my heart of my different ages! Do not stand up as a witness against me, do not be opposed to me in the tribunal, do not be hostile to me in the presence of the Keeper of the Balance.... Do not tell lies about me in the presence of the god"[687] (*The Egyptian Book of the Dead*); "their ears, their eyes, and their skins will bear witness against them for that which they used to do" (Qur'ān 41:20; "On the day their tongues[688] ... bear witness against them as to that which they used to do" [Qur'ān 24:24]). Did Artaud attribute his failure to do away with the judgment of God to his failure to achieve such a body? Artaud's suggestion to the contrary notwithstanding, it is not by having a body without organs that one can be done with the judgment of God, as is clear from the example of Judge (Daniel Paul) Schreber, who, without setting out to do so, without having it as a program, ended up without organs ("From the first beginnings of my contact with God up to the present day my body has continuously been the object of divine miracles.... I existed frequently without a stomach.... Food and drink taken simply poured into the abdominal cavity and into the thighs, a process which however unbelievable it may sound was beyond all doubt for me as I distinctly remember the sensation. In the case of any other human being this would have resulted in natural pus formation with an inevitably fatal outcome; but the food pulp could not damage my body because all impure matter in it was soaked up again by the rays. Later, I therefore repeatedly went ahead with eating unperturbed, without having a stomach.... Of other internal organs I will only mention the *gullet* and the *intestines*, which were torn or vanished repeatedly, further the *pharynx*, which I partly ate up several times"[689]) yet was still subject to the judgment of God (for example, "the first Divine Judgment embraced the period from the 2nd or 4th to the 19th of April 1894. The 'first Divine Judgment' was then followed by a number of further Divine Judgments which, however, lagged behind the first in grandeur of impression"[690]). Would one then have to get rid of God in order to be done with His judgment,[691] for example by being so pitiful that God would miraculously die out of pity for one? Or can God be divested of his reported judgment? The latter was the great program and undertaking of Spinoza—but also of God, for God too wishes to be done with (his transcendent) judgment. Is the Last Judgment, then, not God's way of having the ultimate judgment, one that lasts in its effects forever since it is a judgment that no one can appeal and that cannot be revoked by some later judgment, but rather God's manner to thenceforth be done with judgment? Artaud's project to have done with the judgment of God, which he failed to accomplish for himself, let alone in general, for others, too, would be (from our perspective) and is (from the perspective of His eternity) accomplished by God Himself (similarly, one could say that bringing about the death of God, which Nietzsche ascribed to humans and which is proclaimed by his fictional madman in *The Gay Science* [1882; second, expanded edition, 1887], was miraculously accomplished by God, who brought about his own, pitiful death, that is, his death on the cross out of pity for humans [Nietzsche: "God has died of his pity for man"[692]], including for himself insofar as he was, through his incarnation as Jesus, also a human). Hence, for those who were keen on doing away with judgment, the *good news*, the gospel, is that there is a Last Judgment.

Adhāb al-qabr (a.k.a. *adhāb al-barzakh*), the torment of the grave, is the occasion for an immanent judgment within a religion that is associated with a transcendent judgement, the Last Judgment, and so one can say that one has both sorts of judgment in Islam in the posthumous state. For transcendent judgment not to be reducible to immanent judgement, one has to invoke some miraculous ability of God, for example, His ability to miraculously forgive the unforgivable.

While he had heard and read many times that there would be a Last Judgment and that following it one would end up in paradise or hell, and while he considered such a transcendent judgment objectionable, preferring an immanent judgment, as in Buddhism, he used to consider the sequence of a Last Judgement leading to hell or paradise as logical. But presently he found this sequence arresting and undue, for he realized that it implied that whatever one did in hell would not change the evaluation of one's existence, more strictly the judgment regarding it, and while he found it difficult to tolerate being considered *fully* responsible for *all* his actions, he found it intolerable to be responsible for none, in hell, and he felt that the lightness of irresponsibility[693] in hell following the Last Judgment would at some level be even more unbearable than to reportedly eternally suffer horribly in it. (A requisite for being in paradise is to tolerate, indeed enjoy, the state of blanket irresponsibility following the Last Judgment; in other words, in heaven, the Last Judgment is lived affirmatively as a manner of being done with the judgment of God.) He wished so much that judgment would continue, that what he would do in hell would matter, that he would not be fully irresponsible. He wondered whether he would at least still be able in hell to have the sort of immanent judgment one has in Buddhism, exemplarily in the bardo of reality (*chos nyid bar do*) between physical death and rebirth, or whether, as the term "Last Judgment" implies, even (such) an immanent judgment would no longer be possible for him. Given that it is following the Last Judgment that some find themselves in hell, there is no immanent judgment in hell. But there is a posthumous immanent judgment prior to the Last Judgment, since for the Last Judgment not to be unfair, it has to concern not all one's actions but only those subject to the compulsion to repeat, hence those in which one behaved as an addict; or those one willed to recur eternally. Hence the transcendent, Last Judgment for those who will end up in hell will take place only once they have, in a kind of implicit posthumous immanent judgment, ceased doing all those actions that they are not radically addicted to, those that they desired to do and ended up doing once, twice, thirty-three times, sixty-nine times, or one thousand and one times, but no more—it is on this condition that hell would not be the realm of resentment in relation to *faits accomplis*. The judgment that follows the aforementioned posthumous immanent judgment is the Last Judgment because it applies only to those who have been reduced or refined solely to what they are addicted to (in hell) or willed to eternally recur (in paradise) and hence will persistently behave in the same manner. That there is a Last Judgment would imply that there cannot be an addiction to judgment, that there is no *jouissance* in judging, that there is no drive to judge, although it may seem that there is one, and that, however much one may desire to judge, strictly speaking one does not get addicted to judging. If someone stays in hell forever, it is not because God wills to extend indefinitely his or her punishment for past actions but because he or she is "there" purely as an addict, hence driven to persistently do *only* the same things that induce *jouissance* in him or her (in life, the addiction to what induces *jouissance*, the drive to repeat what induces *jouissance*, is occasionally somewhat tempered by the other things the addict needs to do in order to continue living and to get hold of what functions as his or her "drug" and thus be able to continue to have *jouissance*); *and* because in hell it is not possible for the addict no longer to be one: "The addict cannot choose *directly* whether to continue or to cease to be an addict, for by choosing addiction he has already chosen no longer to choose by determining the response of his future self, precluding the latter, through addiction, from choosing anew; he has to proceed dialectically through another's choice.... If the other chooses to continue to choose, declines the temptation to become an addict, he undermines the addict's current belief that it is the nature of the organism to be addicted, thus provides the addict with a *variant* of the original situation of choice: yielding to the temptation to become addicted or refraining from doing so.... Hell is a realm where, driven and addicted, one cannot draw on the resource of the other's choice in order to choose again, because, hell being labyrinthine or comprised of the karmic projections of one's mind, one is all alone there; or because the others in hell are also addicted."[694]

Once someone makes a bargain with the devil and finds himself or herself as a result in hell, then, given that his or her best-intentioned actions in that condition lead only to the worst, cruelest, most debasing and degrading outcomes, the following tweak to the title of a John Cage book, *How to Improve the World (You Will Only Make Matters Worse)*, would describe perfectly his or her situation: *How to Improve Hell (You Will Only Make Matters Worse)*.

In Sokurov's *Faust* (2011), the woman he becomes enamored of, Margarete, and the devil are the two creatures with whom Faust has a relationship that really matters. The devil undercuts not just Faust's developing relationship with the young woman with whom he gets enamored but even the sort of friendship Faust begins to develop toward him, a far more spiritual relationship than those he has with others, albeit a twisted one. When his assistant tells him, "You've told us so much about the composition of the human body ... but not a word about the soul," Faust notes, "I haven't found it." I would advance that Faust is pleased when the devil proposes to make it possible for him to consummate his love for the woman he is enamored of in exchange for his soul not only because it would allow him to consummate his love for Margarete, but also because the circumstance that the devil was willing to acquire his soul contractually implies that it exists![695] If he had a soul already but did not know where to find it or how to recognize it, then the exchange with the devil would allow him to find and recognize it in the very process of losing it to him.

It does sometimes happen that a film is not so much a representation of a religious event or experience but is itself a religious event and experience, for example Dreyer's *Ordet* (1955), which is not simply a fictional representation of a Christian resurrection but brings about one, albeit through film, and my *The Lamentations Series: The Ninth Night and Day* (2005), which is not simply a representation of a religious ceremony but is itself, certainly when watched in its entirety (fifty-nine minutes), a religious event and experience—more so than the ceremony it documents artistically!

He managed to film the back in such a way that one did not wait impatiently to see, did not even wish to see, the face of the figure! He managed to do it not only with a minor character but also with the main character! What an accomplishment!

"And when Moses came to Our appointed meeting and his Lord spoke unto him, he said, 'My Lord, show me (*arinī*), that I might look upon Thee'" (Qur'ān 7:143). Moses did not specify how he wanted to see God, and God responded by revealing Himself under two paradigmatic aspects, His Face and His Glory. "He said, 'Thou shalt not see Me [in respect of my essence, *dhāt*, which is beyond vision, certainly human vision]; but look upon the mountain [as one of the guises of My Face]: if it remains firm in its place [when I show Myself to it in the mode of My Glory], then thou wilt see Me [under the aspect of My Glory]'" (ibid.; my exegesis in brackets). Moses assumed that he was then the only one asking to see God, but since God revealed Himself under the aspect of His Glory to the mountain in the process of acceding to Moses's request, it must be that the mountain, too, had asked God, in a language that humans usually do not understand but God does, to show Himself to it (actually, there were three concurrent requests to see God, the third being the request of God's Face to see His Glory). Hence, God showed Himself to both: to the mountain, he showed His Glory, and to Moses He showed His Face, thus sparing him, who had not yet conveyed fully the message with which he had been entrusted and fulfilled his mission, annihilation. "And when his Lord manifested Himself to the mountain, He made it crumble to dust, and Moses fell down in a swoon. And when he recovered, he said, 'Glory be to Thee! I turn unto Thee in repentance'" (ibid.). While the mountain's direct vision of God under the aspect of His Glory led to its crumbling to dust, why did Moses fall unconscious? It must be because he experienced what is implied by the Qur'ānic *āya* 2:115, "wheresoever you turn, there is the Face of God," that is, he experienced the mountain, even while crumbled to dust, as the Face of God, and he was overwhelmed by this experience. Why did Moses turn unto God in repentance? Was it because he had reductively assumed that the vision of God had one aspect instead of intuiting that it must be multifaceted? Or was it because he was oblivious that "sight comprehends Him not" (Qur'ān 6:103)? Or was it because, after seeing the Face of God once in the guise of the (crushed) mountain, he did not see it wheresoever he turned? "He said, 'O Moses! ... Take that which I have given thee [seeing my face in the guise of the crushed mountain] and be among the thankful'" (Qur'ān 7:144; my exegesis in brackets). If the Messenger of God (al-rasūl) accesses not only the exoteric but also the esoteric, albeit without being consciously aware of the latter, and it is only the Shi'ite imams or figures such as al-Khidr who recognize and are consciously aware of the esoteric, then Moses was exoterically and consciously asking God to exceptionally show Himself to him, but unconsciously and esoterically asking him rather, since arinī also means "grant me the ability to see," to unveil the actual state of things to him so that he would be able to see that wheresoever one turns, there is the Face of God. When God responded to Moses's entreaty that He grant him to see Him with, "Gaze upon the mountain," this can be considered in the following manner: God told Moses to gaze upon the mountain to spare him getting annihilated on being exposed to a vision of Him in the aspect of His Glory, as is clear from the example of the effect of such an exposure on the mountain; while allowing him, through unveiling, to see Him, more specifically His Face, in the guise of the mountain, in other words, to perceive the mountain as one of His infinite self-disclosures. At the exoteric level, God did not show Himself to Moses, for that would have destroyed him, as is clear from what happened when, as a cautionary example, He revealed Himself to the mountain, destroying it; but esoterically, "Look at the mountain" is God's manner of granting Moses his request while sparing him being annihilated before fulfilling his mission, since the mountain is one of the infinite guises of the Face of God, as intimated in the Qur'ānic āya 2:115. God thus granted Moses his request even while seeming to withhold the vision he recklessly requested. What happens to the mountain as one of the guises of the Face of God when exposed to the Glory of God, namely, its annihilation, implies that usually God shields His Face from His Glory, in other words, veils His Glory from His Face. From this perspective, there is a veiling that is intrinsic to God, in God, since God veils some aspects of Himself not only from His finite creatures but also from other aspects of Himself. Insofar as he was human, all-too-human, Moses, witnessing its destructive effect on the mountain, must have been relieved to be spared the overwhelming vision of the Glory of God, but insofar as he could have, albeit at the risk of his annihilation, glimpsed the Glory of God, he was also jealous of the mountain. Did the mountain lament the overwhelming vision of God's Glory? It did, in a lament that we do not understand, as we do not understand its praise (*tasbīḥ*), nor that of God's other creatures ("The seven heavens and the earth and all that is therein praise Him, and there is not a thing but hymneth His praise; but ye understand not their praise" [Qur'ān 17:44]), and as Moses did not understand its entreaty to God to show Himself to it. Indeed, insofar as "wheresoever you turn, there is the Face of God," that is, insofar as the mountain is one of the infinite guises of the Face of God, God's Face lamented being exposed to God's Glory, for the latter was overwhelming for "it." Those equipped to hear or perceive it would have heard or perceived a double lament emanating from the mountain on being exposed to God's Glory: insofar as it was one of God's finite creatures and insofar as it was one of the infinite guises of His Face. Was God then unjust to the mountain? No, He allowed it to realize one of its powers of action; its lament should be understood from this perspective: "Joy ... consists in fulfilling a power of action (*remplir une puissance*) [in this case, to have a vision (of the Glory) of God].... That's what joy is, even if it goes badly because ... when one conquers a power of action ... it happens that it is too strong for one's own self, so ... [one] will crack up.... 'What is happening to me overwhelms me.' That's what the complaint is. Now, I would like to say every morning, 'What's happening to me overwhelms me,' because this is joy."[696] Seeing God's Glory was a joy for the mountain. Did Moses wonder why he, who did not fall unconscious on seeing the waters of the Sea of Reeds miraculously part so he and the Israelites could evade their pursuers, the large Egyptian army led by the Pharaoh, fell unconscious on seeing the mountain crash down? Had he asked himself this question, he would have remembered that, during a moment of unveiling, he perceived the mountain as the Face of God and that it was this experience that overwhelmed him and led to his swoon. His swoon indicates that he was not ready for such an experience, certainly not for a protracted time. Once he recovered consciousness, did he ask God to veil Himself again, so that when he would look at another mountain, but also at other things, he would not perceive them (keenly) as the Face of God? The Qur'ānic verse "Wheresoever you turn, there is the Face of God" does not merely tell us what the actual state of things is, namely, that everything is one of the infinite guises of the Face of God (but not of His Glory), but also what our reaction is bound to be naturally, turning ... away, to rest and recover from such an overwhelming experience through the blur produced by the turn ... only to be overwhelmed again when one's turn comes to a stop and one sees another entity. To the one who longs to experience and taste (*yadhūq*) what it reveals, Qur'ānic *āya* 2:115 does not just provide abstract knowledge about the objective, actual state of things, that wheresoever one looks is the Face of God, but conveys also, for the one who has progressed enough on the spiritual path, a manner, if not the only manner in the absence of direct divine unveiling, of seeing the Face of God in everything, namely, turning until one does so, *and* of then avoiding being overwhelmed by such a vision and, consequently, swooning, as happened to no less than a Messenger of God, Moses, by turning again just in time (in order to wrench oneself from such a vision, one of the most beatific, if not the most beatific, and joyful, one would need the timely intervention of a Sufi shaykh, who would have earlier guided the *murīd* [disciple] along the path most likely to lead to such a vision, or some other spiritual guide—had he not left him by then, al-Khadir would have been the most suited to play this function for Moses during the latter's vision of the face of God in the guise of the mountain), the turn, itself a manageable quasi-swoon through its associated blur, procuring a transient respite from the overwhelming vision of the Face of God in whatever one sees. Since one would soon enough fall unconscious if one continued turning without pause, one, or, usually, one's Sufi Shaykh or al-Khadir, has to bring the turn to a stop just before one swoons. At that point, one would again see the Face of God through whatever one's eyes have rested on, so one would again have to turn in time before such a vision overwhelms one. This repeated process can be composed into a whirling movement. I would say that this is the paradigmatic, fundamental turning and whirling in Islam, rather than the *samāʿ* ceremony of the Mevlevi sect—that the whirling of the Mevlevis is part of a ceremony that's performed from time to time rather than a constant activity implies that, while derivative of the more fundamental whirling, it has not reached its *raison d'être*, in other words has not allowed them to see the Face of God wheresoever they turn, if at all, or is not in response to such a vision. The more fundamental whirling would more suitably be called *naẓar* rather than *samāʿ*, since it has to do with vision rather than hearing. The Sufi master Junayd answered "the enthusiastic Nūrī, who objected to his sitting quietly while the Sufis performed their whirling dance ... : 'You see the mountains—you think them firm, yet they move like clouds' (Qur'ān 27:88)."[697] I can very well imagine another Sufi master answering, while apparently not whirling, a disciple who objected to his not joining a *samāʿ* ceremony: "I do not need to join the official, codified *samāʿ* ceremony, which takes place periodically, since, unlike you and many, if not all, of those who engage in it, who do not encounter and see the Face of God wheresoever they turn, my life is constant whirling, that is, a recurrent turning to avoid being overwhelmed by my perception of the Face of God in whatever entity I see—including you presently," and then responding to the *murīd*'s puzzled objection, "But you are not presently whirling!" with, "Your objection shows that you, who when *you see the mountains*

think them firm though *they move like clouds,* and who, regrettably, are
unable to perceive that wheresoever you turn, there is the Face of God,
are unable to perceive the actual state of affairs in this case, too,
namely, that I am presently whirling!" and then confiding to his disciples: "Before I started on the Sufi path, I saw mountains as
motionless; when I progressed on the path, I saw them actually move
like clouds; when I progressed further on the path, I saw them (as well
as clouds) as one of the infinite guises of the Face of God."

Gilles Deleuze: "The Bergsonian definition of the affect rested on
these two very characteristics: a motor tendency on a sensitive nerve.
In other words, a series of micro-movements on an immobilised plate
of nerve. When a part of the body has had to sacrifice most of it moto-
ricity in order to become the support for organs of reception, the
principal feature of these will now only be tendencies to movement
or micro-movements.... The moving body has lost its movement of
extension, and movement has become movement of expression. It is
this combination of a reflecting, immobile unity and of intensive
expressive movements which constitutes the affect. But is this not the
same as a Face itself?[698]... Ordinarily, three roles of the face are recog-
nisable: it is individuating (it distinguishes or characterises each
person); it is socialising (it manifest a social role); it is relational or
communicating (it ensures not only communication between two
people, but also, in a single person, the internal agreement between
his character and his role)."[699] The face can undergo effacement,
whether by losing one or both of its constitutive poles, or by becoming
a close-up, thus losing its three functions of individuating, socializing,
and communicating. Having written that "the close-up is the face ...
in so far as it has destroyed its triple function,"[700] Deleuze nonetheless
does not raise the question: How is it possible for the close-up, which
pertains to cinema, to affect the character within the diegesis and not
simply the film spectator's perception of the character? It can do so
in conditions in which the (falling apart) world of the character functions in a cinematic manner, so that one can have a close-up within
it, in the diegesis: as I wrote in my book *What Was I Thinking?*, "In the
conditions in which one would 'ask' oneself, 'Am I dead?' sooner or
later one would, if one belongs to the cinematic era, also ask oneself,
'Am I in a film?' having witnessed immobilizations of people, in other
words, dead stops (the equivalent of cinema's freeze-frames), and the
temporal peculiarities made possible by these as the genetic element
of movement, such as slow motion and backward-in-time motion;
undergone lapses of consciousness, if not of being (including by
becoming immobilized), which result in an editing of 'reality'; felt that
some of the others were extras, etc." Indeed, at least some schizophrenics, who died before dying physically, in particular those
belonging to the age of cinema, apprehend themselves occasionally

to be in close-up and therefore simultaneously as undergoing an effacement of the face, possibly in the manner of its changing into a head. "One day we were jumping rope at recess.... When it came my turn and I saw my partner jump toward me where we were to meet and cross over, I was seized with panic; I did not recognize her. Though I saw her as she was, still, it was not she. Standing at the other end of the rope, she had seemed smaller, but the nearer we approached each other, the taller she grew, the more she swelled in size. I cried out, 'Stop, Alice, you look like a lion; you frighten me!' ... Actually, I didn't see a lion at all: it was only an attempt to describe the enlarging image of my friend and the fact that I didn't recognize her"[701]—in other words, that Alice appeared in close-up ("the enlarging image of my friend"), hence as a face ("Stop, *Alice*" [my italics; one of the functions of the face is, according to Deleuze, to individuate]) that's been effaced ("I didn't recognize her"). He was apprehensive that in the process of actually losing the face he would feel embarrassment or humiliation, in other words, symbolically *lose face*. Yet, except in rare cases, the affect associated with losing (the) face is not one of humiliation, dictionaries notwithstanding ("*lose face*: 'be humiliated or come to be less highly respected'" [*Oxford Dictionary of English*, 3rd ed.]), but fear. Concerning the face in close-up mode that has lost its three functions Deleuze wrote: "It no longer ... feels anything, but merely experiences a mute fear ... as its only affect"[702]—I would specify: the fear that this loss of affects, at least those related to and expressed by a face, including shame—and fear—would prove definitive. In psychosis, we move from fear as one affect among others expressed by a face; to, once the close-up is attained and, as a result, the face is effaced, fear as the paradoxical, reflexive affect that is a reaction to the disappearance of all affects ... expressed by a face (including the affect of fear expressed by the face), and that is thus not expressed by a face (given that Deleuze does not note explicitly that the fear that arises in response to the disappearance of all the affects expressed by the face is not itself expressed by the face, many, if not most, of his readers continue to implicitly attribute this fear to the face, to expect to see it on the face, forgetting or overlooking that this fear was an outcome of the effacement of the face and so cannot be expressed by it, but plays, rather, the function of a pivot toward affects that are unrelated to the face and not expressed by it, indeed on it) and no longer the affect of someone given that with the effacement of the face the correlative individuation is undone, but an entity in itself ("As Balázs has already accurately demonstrated, the close-up does *not* tear away its object from a set of which it would form part, of which it would be a part, but on the contrary it abstracts it from all spatio-temporal co-ordinates, that is to say it raises it to the state of Entity.... This is what Epstein was suggesting when he said: this face of a fleeing coward, as soon as we see it in close-up [when it is effaced], we

see cowardice [more accurately, fear] in person"[703] [my qualifications])
superimposed on the *effaced face as any-space-whatever* (the example
provided by Bergman's *Persona* of the effaced face in close-up is all
the more felicitous as any-space-whatever since it is composed of half
of what used to be the face of nurse Alma before its effacement and
half of what used to be the face of actress Elizabeth before its effacement[704]); to an extimate, free-floating fear in the surroundings as
any-space-whatever that should not be misapprehended as the face-
less subject's fear of some threat in these surroundings; to, if the
ensuing psychosis has not degenerated into a full-blown schizophrenic breakdown, the latter fear's replacement by other affects, not
necessarily human ones, that are presented in, and are the expressed
of, any-spaces-whatever. Indeed, in Deleuze's *Cinema 1: The
Movement-Image*, we move from the face, close-up, and effacement of
the face and the associated affects of these in chapter 6 to the affects
that are expressed in (other) any-spaces-whatever (than the effaced
face) in chapter 7: "There are two kinds of signs of the affection-image
… : *on the one hand the power-quality expressed by a face or an equivalent;
but on the other hand the power-quality presented in any-space-whatever*
[*un espace quelconque*],"[705] which is "extracted," for example, through
becoming covered with shadows, from "a given state of things,"[706] "no
longer has co-ordinates," and "shows only pure Powers and Qualities,
independently of the states of things or milieux which actualise
them."[707] While in the vast majority of cases the effacement of the face
leads, at least initially, to fear *as the only affect*, this is not necessarily
the case in those traditions, for example Buddhism and Islam, where
there subsists a far more fundamental "face," the Buddha face, in
other words, one's original face, the one mentioned in the following
well-known Zen koan attributed to Huineng, "At this very moment,
what is your original face before your father and mother were born?"
(the Chinese text can also be translated as "What was your original
face before your father and mother gave birth to you?")[708]; and the
Face of God, so, among other entities, the face of any human insofar
as he or she is prodigiously recreated by Him as one of His infinite
self-disclosures or insofar as he or she has undergone *fanā'* (annihilation) in Him, both of these faces existing at levels that are more
basic than the creature's (in Islam) or sentient being's (in Buddhism)
individuation (one's original face being one's face before one was
born, indeed, before one's father and mother were born, indeed,
before any of one's ancestors was born, in short, before, in other
words, beyond, the cycle of birth-and-death) no less than socialization
and communication; and in instances where the affect that results
from the loss of all affects upon the effacement of the face is joy, given
that all affects, as well as the face, one of whose constitutive poles is
tendencies to react (in lieu of actual, that is, motor, reactions), ones
that take the form of micro-movements on its sensory organs and

receptive nerves, are related to an underlying passivity and hence to a modicum of resentment—except in cases of (Buddhist) detachment, given that through the latter one avoids cathecting these tendencies to react on the facial sense organs and receptive nerves (consequently, it is not clear whether a detached person, for example, a Buddhist master or a Buddha, has a face, at least in the sense that we usually understand this term—he or she has a face in a different sense, his or her "original face"). You will not witness joy on someone's face, for joy is related to the undoing of the face and the consequent cessation of resentment, in other words, it is part of joy to no longer have a face—someone who can react fully, let alone never reacts but is always the one who initiates, who acts, does not have a face in its received human meaning; since God is all action and hence is not *at all* resentful, He has no face in the human sense of the term—in this sense, the one who is joyful is like God, who does not have a face in its human sense of something that has the two constitutive poles, one of which is tendencies to react in the form of micro-movements on sense organs and receptive nerves.[709] Betwixt its very constitution as face and its effacement, whether by losing one or both of its constitutive poles, or, if it is the face of a dead human, hence of someone in whose condition things function in a cinematic manner, by becoming a close-up, by being in close-up, the face moves between the following paradigmatic affects: resentment and fear or joy. The affects of resentment, fear, and joy are dual: at one level, resentment is one of the affects that are expressed by the face, but, at a foundational level, it is not possible to have a face without resentment, since to have a face at all, tendencies to react, which are one of the two constitutive poles of the face and which imply some inability to actually react, with a motor response, are required; and fear and joy are two affects among others, but, once the face is effaced, they are, at another level, the paradoxical, reflexive affects that are produced by the resultant loss of all affects (at least the ones expressed by the face), fear being the negative reaction to losing the face and to losing affects, while joy is the affirmative response to losing the face in its human understanding since the latter is, through one of its two constitutive poles, inextricably implicated with a basic, fundamental resentment associated with tendencies to respond in the form of micro-movements on the facial sense organs and receptive nerves.

In one of its modes, the portrait is the face in which the micro-movements as tendencies to react on the sense organs and receptive nerves, one of its two constituents, are reduced to the bare minimum that would, in the presence of its other constituent, immobilized plates of nerves as a surface of inscription, maintain it, so to "stirrings still,"[710] and for that to be achieved, the most suitable kind of universe is one where there can be no coming to a dead stop and complete stillness. This mode of the portrait would give us not an angry or happy or resentful face but just the face—indeed, this mode of the portrait is the face at its least resentful. Here's my paraphrase of the following Zen exchange, "When the old master Hiakajo was asked, 'What is Zen?' he said, 'When hungry, eat, when tired, sleep.' And they said, 'Well, isn't that what everybody does? Aren't you just like ordinary people?' 'Oh no,' he said, 'they don't do anything of the kind. When they're hungry, they don't just eat, they think of all sorts of things. When they're tired, they don't just sleep, but dream all sorts of dreams'" (Alan Watts): When I was asked, "What is the portrait mode of the face?" I said, "When seeing, the one in the portrait just sees, when hearing, he or she just hears, in other words, Deleuze's, they perceive pure optical and sound images." And they said, "Well, isn't that what everyone does?" "Not so," I said, "insofar as they still have faces, they don't do anything of the kind. For example, when seeing, they don't just see, but try also to respond through micro-movements in their eyes to what they have seen but to which they are unable, for whatever reason, to respond through motor activity." As tendencies to react, the micro-movements on the face's sense organs and receptive nerves are an indication that, while acting, one is not fully engaged in what one is doing but also observing it or considering something else to which one cannot react through motor activity, at least not simultaneously. One does not feel anything when one purely acts, when one is fully active, for the affect implies some passivity in the form of tendencies to react on one or more of the face's sense organs and receptive nerves rather than actual, motor reactions—the affect one feels when one is acting is related either to the memory of a similar action in the past (and its outcome and the various associations it happens to trigger), a *fait accompli*, towards which one can no longer respond but only have a belated *tendency* to do so; or to the next action in a series or process, that is, to an action that is still potential, toward which one is still passive, having yet only a tendency to act; or to one or more other matters one is concurrently *undergoing* to some degree. Consequently, some sensitive people act primarily not for the sake of what the action would professedly accomplish for them, but to be relieved of affects (they feel that this suspension of affects is temporary and so they are not seized with the fear of losing all affects forever). In another of its modes, the portrait is the creation of a surrogate face for the one who has lost his or hers as a result, for example, of the undoing of one of the face's two constituent poles; that is why such a portrait does not risk acting as a double of the one portrayed—you have to have gone all the way in the adventure of losing the face if you are to get this second mode of the portrait, otherwise you run the danger of becoming two-faced, or of having your face usurped by the double.

At least during confrontational situations, the whole resentful person (who is actually unable to react),[711] including his motor organs, for example, the twitching fingers (betraying a tendency to react in the form of micro-movements [one of the two constitutive poles of the face]) of a clenched hidden fist (as an immobilized plate of nerves [the other constitutive pole of the face]), whether in the resentful man's pocket or behind his back, functions as a face.

A car crash left his beloved in a coma. He would visit her again and again, sit by her bedside, and look hard for hours on end for any sign of life in her body. One day, after several weeks, he did indeed detect a twitch in the eyelids and then a spasm in one of her fingers. He felt exhilaration because he assumed that they heralded the return to life of the whole body. He promptly rushed to find her doctor and, having located him, breathlessly exclaimed: "I've just witnessed two fleeting movements in her comatose body!" He hoped that the doctor would, on checking the body, confirm that it was indeed in the process of becoming animate again. But his initial exhilaration soon turned into apprehension, indeed dread, when the rest of the body was declared dead by the doctor and then began to decompose and yet the occasional spasm in the finger persisted—this spasm is not really related to life but is another figure of death. "Do you believe that nothing endures beyond the physical death of the body?" "No." "Then you believe in the soul." "No." 'No?!" "In Poe's story, we encounter an organ of the body that 'outlives' the death of the rest of the body (if I've placed *outlives* in quotation marks it is because this condition is one of the guises of death), a moving tongue that utters an eerie sound that doesn't feel like it is coming from the inanimate body or even the same space: 'There was no longer the faintest sign of vitality in M. Valdemar; and concluding him to be dead, we were consigning him to the charge of the nurses, when a strong vibratory motion was observable in the tongue. This continued for perhaps a minute. At the expiration of this period, there issued from the distended and motionless jaws a voice. There were two particulars ... which I thought then, and still think, might fairly be stated as characteristic of the intonation—as well adapted to convey some idea of its unearthly peculiarity. In the first place, the voice seemed to reach our ears—at least mine—from a vast distance, or from some deep cavern within the earth. In the second place, it impressed me ... as gelatinous or glutinous matters impress the sense of touch.... M. Valdemar *spoke*—obviously in reply to the question I had propounded to him a few minutes before. I had asked him ... if he still slept. He now said: "Yes;—no;—*I have been* sleeping—and now—now—*I am dead.*" ... It was evident that, so far, death (or what is usually termed death) had been arrested by the mesmeric process. It seemed clear to us all that to awaken M. Valdemar would be merely to insure his instant, or at least his speedy dissolution. From this period until the close of last week— *an interval of nearly seven months*—we continued to make daily calls at M. Valdemar's house.... It was on Friday last that we finally resolved to make the experiment of awakening or attempting to awaken him.... The first indication of revival was afforded by a partial descent of the iris ... accompanied by the profuse out-flowing of a yellowish ichor (from beneath the lids) of a pungent and highly offensive odor.... "M. Valdemar, can you explain to us what are your feelings or wishes now?" ... *The tongue quivered, or rather rolled violently in the mouth (although the jaws and lips remained rigid as before;[712]*) and at length the same hideous voice, which I have already described, broke forth: "For God's sake!—quick!—quick!—put me to sleep—or, quick!—waken me!—quick!—*I say to you that I am dead!*" ... I ... earnestly struggled to awaken him.... As I rapidly made the mesmeric passes, amid ejaculations of "dead! dead!" absolutely *bursting from the tongue and not from the lips*[713] of the sufferer, his whole frame at once—within the space of a single minute, or even less, shrunk—crumbled—absolutely *rotted* away beneath my hands.'"[714] In some cases, what persists in existence after death is not necessarily the soul but the body ... as a *part object* of itself: while in Poe's short story, a part of Valdemar's body turned into a part object, the tongue, in Bram Stoker's *Dracula*, her blood having been sucked by the vampire, which led to her physical death and metamorphosis into a vampire, all that remained of Lucy was her body, not in the sense that she no longer had a soul but in the sense that, as an undead, *her whole body was now a part object*. Given that the whole dead yet still animate body is a part object, it would not be surprising for the one who encounters it prowling the streets for prey to feel the impulse to check the tomb while expecting to find it there (too) in some other guise, the same way that, were one to encounter the hand of a corpse as a part object, detached from it yet animate, one might look for the rest of the body. In a way, the dead body that continues moving and thus can be viewed as a part object is the horrifying, polar opposite of the body without organs that Artaud tried to achieve ("Man is sick because he is badly constructed.... / There is nothing more useless than an organ. / When you will have made him a body without organs, / then you will have delivered him from all his automatic reactions ...") and that Deleuze and Guattari advocated: all of it is an organ now, more accurately, a *part object*.

It is repeatedly said that the film spectators leapt in terror and ran from the path of the train of Louis Lumière's black-and-white silent film *L'Arrivée d'un train à la Ciotat* (*Arrival of a Train at La Ciotat*) (1895). This purported reaction was reported as a historical fact by well-known early film historians Lotte Eisner, who wrote in her book *Die dämonische Leinwand* that "the spectators in the Grand Café involuntarily threw themselves back in their seats in fright, because Lumière's giant locomotive pulling into the station seemingly ran toward them,"[715] and Georges Sadoul, who wrote in one of his books, "In *L'Arrivée d'un train*, the locomotive, coming from the background of the screen, rushed toward the spectators, who jumped up in shock, as they feared getting run over";[716] and continues to be circulated by journalists, for example Hellmuth Karasek, who in 1994 wrote in *Der Spiegel*: "One short film had a particularly lasting impact; yes, it caused fear, terror, even panic. It was the film *L'Arrivée d'un train en gare de la Ciotat*. Although the cinematographic train was dashing toward the crowded audience in flickering black and white (not in natural colors and natural dimensions), and although the only sound accompanying it was the monotonous clatter of the projector's sprockets engaging into the film's perforation, the spectators felt physically threatened and panicked."[717] Thankfully, Martin Loiperdinger, in his article "Lumière's *Arrival of the Train*: Cinema's Founding Myth," has undermined the veracity of this legend by pointing out that there is no mention of such a reaction in contemporary newspaper accounts or other documents: "Are there credible reports from eyewitnesses that document the panicked behavior of the spectators? Apparently, nothing of the sort exists. Neither do the relevant files of the Paris Police Prefect contain any records of such incidents, nor is there in the abundant literature on the Grand Café screenings a single reference to contemporary press reports from which a panic could be inferred, nor can anything be found on the topic in the published letters of Auguste and Louis Lumière."[718] But while I share his skepticism regarding the reaction of the film's first spectators, even though I find its equivalence of thing and image magical, I can very well imagine film spectators in general, and the first film spectators in particular, marveling at the incredible existence of shots that do not present the subjective perception of some human or some other sentient being, for example, an angel, the devil, or an animal, but are supposed to be objective. Indeed, I can very well imagine a film spectator thinking that he must be the only one who saw this impossible thing, an "objective shot," that he had hallucinated it, and, consequently, wondering what others might have seen during these moments in the film. What would be most startling, indeed incredible for a madman, someone who died before dying physically, watching a film would be any apparently objective shot. I can very well imagine him or her anxiously rushing out of the cinema theater upon seeing such a shot and, later that same night, averring in one of the numerous letters he or she wrote to friends and strangers: "That's one of the most incredible things I have ever witnessed, and, believe me, I have witnessed many incredible things." One indication that sane living people assume that they share the world is that so-called objective shots in films do not strike them as impossible notwithstanding that each one of us always perceives the world exclusively from his or her subjective point of view, in other words, through (the filter of) his or her mind. That the vast majority, if not all sane living film spectators are not astounded when they see what appears to be an objective shot is an indication of the high degree of disavowal of the fact that we perceive everything through (the filter of) our minds. Cinema provides a way to as it were do away with, or be in denial of, death, whether as physical demise, since "if the plastic arts were put under psychoanalysis, the practice of embalming the dead might turn out to be a fundamental factor in their creation. The process might reveal that at the origin of painting and sculpture there lies a mummy complex.... The film is no longer content to preserve the object.... Now, for the first time, the image of things is likewise the image of their duration, change mummified as it were"[719] (André Bazin), or as undeath, through introducing what is taken to be objective shots, thus implying that one is not limited necessarily to one's subjective point of view, in other words, one's perception, a limitation one is radically aware of in death (and in that variety of death [before dying] that is madness). But might the ostensibly objective shots in cinema be, after all, in case the film is not an atheistic one, the perception of God? But can we call the vision of God, what God sees, an objective shot when God is the (sole) Subject ("God said to Moses ..., 'This is what you are to say to the Israelites: "I AM has sent me to you""" [Exodus 3:14])? Yes, if we take into consideration that God transcends the opposition of subjectivity and objectivity, as He does every opposition: "When Abū Saʿīd al-Kharrāz was asked, 'Through what have you known God?' he answered, 'Through the fact that He brings opposites together,' then he recited the Qurʾānic verse 'He [God] is the First, and the Last, and the Outward, and the Inward'"[720] (57:3). Anyway, God's presumed perception would not be the human, all-too-human one we associate with almost all so-called objective shots. Would the objective shot be what subsists when conjointly the human subject has lost consciousness or even been obliterated by what he or she could hardly see through an overwhelming unveiling (for example, in the case of Moses, the mountain as the Face of God) and, beloved by God, God has become his hearing and his sight: "My servant draws near to Me through nothing I love more than that which I have made obligatory for him. My servant never ceases drawing near to Me through supererogatory works until I love him. Then, when I love him, I am his hearing through which he hears, his sight through which he sees" (a ḥadīth qudsī)? Or might these objective shots be, if the film is affined to Bergson's perspective, the perception of some atom, the latter being "an image which I [Bergson] call a material object," and which is obliged "to act through every one of its points upon all the points of all other images, to transmit the whole of what it receives, to oppose to every action an equal and contrary reaction, to be, in short, merely a road by which pass, in every direction, the modifications propagated throughout the immensity of the universe"[721]? They would be were they not, in almost all cases, human, all-too-human, that is, ones from which is subtracted all that is not of interest to the survival of some human, indeed any human? In the future, with the production of vision machines, hence of a new kind of vision that can be shared between various such machines, indeed all of them, it would become possible for a perceptive mortal spectator to see what appears to be objective shots and not feel that he or she has witnessed something impossible.

Paranoiac, he believed that he was persecuted by everybody—including "himself," in the guise of his double.

While his initial encounter with what appeared to be his double—an encounter that occurred in conditions that gave him the impression, given the impossible things and events he was undergoing or witnessing, that he had already died, if not physically then in some other manner—filled him with dread, he soon enough hoped to keep occasionally encountering him, dreading that if he did not encounter him ever again, this could imply that he, already not quite himself, had been replaced by him in the lapse of consciousness, if not of being, during the presumed transition from the world to the death realm.

In the lead-up to the encounter with the double, one feels "more dead than alive"; then, on first encountering him, one acts as if he is the one in excess; then, on coming across him again and again, one ends up acknowledging that one is dead, recognizing and therefore realizing and conceding that it is oneself who is the one in excess.

It may be the case that the Hitchcock film that in our branch of the multiverse has *Vertigo* as its title may have a different title in another branch of the multiverse, for example *Vertiginous Variations on Vertigo*. For those within that branch, *Vertiginous Variations on Vertigo* would not be my conceptual cinematic variation on Hitchcock's *Vertigo* but Hitchcock's film, and the "Variations on Vertigo" in the title would refer exclusively to the various modalities of the state of vertigo found in the film (Deleuze: "Analysing certain Hitchcock films François Regnault identifies a global movement for each one, or a 'principal geometric or dynamic form,' which can appear in the pure state in the credits: 'the spirals of *Vertigo*....' But no less interesting is the other direction where a general movement—turned towards a changing whole—is decomposed into relative movements, into local forms turned towards the respective positions of the parts of a set, the attributions to persons or objects ... thus in *Vertigo* the great spiral can become the vertigo of the hero, but also the circuit he maps out in his car [in particular, when he drives from his house to the building where Madeleine resides and then follows the woman he takes to be Madeleine, only to be taken aback on becoming aware that he is back at his house, her destination], or the curl in the heroine's hair"[722]).

One of the differences one might come across through time travel, that is, travel to another, largely similar branch of the multiverse, would be variants of some of the films in one's branch of the multiverse, ones that end differently, or where the characters are played by different actors, thus there is a variant branch of the multiverse in which Gus van Sant's film *Psycho* (1998) is not a remake of Hitchcock's *Psycho* (1960) but the only *Psycho*, that is, a branch of the multiverse in which Hitchcock did not make a film titled *Psycho*.

In another branch of the multiverse he reached through time travel, he discovered that there was a version of him that was an actor and had played a role that appeared to be exactly himself in the branch of the multiverse from which he hailed.

Could one have acted differently? The answer is available in the multiverse: no, if the action is present in all the branches of the multiverse—more precisely, in all the branches of the multiverse in which one could be said to be the same; yes, if it exists in only some of the branches in which one exists. Time travel does not allow the traveler to change the way he or she acted in the branch of the multiverse from which he or she hails but to ascertain whether he or she could have acted differently.

One possible interest of time travel: to allow one to distinguish between those of one's actions that belong to one's essence or to which one is fated, since they are present in all branches of the multiverse that include one and in which the circumstances in which they are happening appear to be the same, and others that are more or less accidental, since it is empirically the case that one acted differently in the same circumstances in different branches of the multiverse.

Zen master Dōgen: "All painted buddhas are actual buddhas.... Because the entire world and all phenomena are a painting, human existence appears from a painting, and buddha ancestors are actualized from a painting. Since this is so, there is no remedy for satisfying hunger other than a painted rice-cake"[723] ("Painting of a Rice-cake"). Does a painting of a rice cake that falls apart even as it is being painted satisfy hunger? How long would it take to succeed in painting a rice cake that does not fall apart "two days" later? Would it take as long as it takes to become a Buddha (or Bodhisattva)—if not longer?

Certain movements, most often clearly stylized ones, project a subtle dancer in the dance realm. Once in the dance realm, whatever the subtle dancer does, whether freeze, sleep, sit, or move a chair, is dance. Sitting, moving a chair, tripping, bumping against another body or a wall are dance if they occur in the dance realm, but they are not, notwithstanding much of what has been presented as dance since the 1960s, dance movements in our world—unless they, *exceptionally*, project the dancer as a subtle body in the dance realm.

How can someone who is not a dancer discern whether the one moving in front of him or her is a dancer or a performer? It cannot be done through the genre of movement (it is not because someone is doing ballet steps exquisitely that he or she would necessarily be dancing), nor through the perception of the subtle body, since the subtle body cannot be perceived by nondancers (the criterion of whether one is a dancer is simple: is one, through one's movement, projected as a subtle body in the dance realm?). The only way is for the perceptive spectator who is not a dancer to feel that the one moving is no longer *fully* there; then one can assume they are dancing (cinema allows the one who is not a dancer to tell whether someone is a dancer by actually showing that the latter has, through his or her movement, been projected in dance's realm [in many films, these sections are termed "dream ballets"] and thus makes the spectator see that they are elsewhere, too). In my conception of dance, there is no such thing as a bad dancer: either one is a dancer, that is, one's movement projects one as a subtle body in the dance realm, or one isn't at all. This is an indication that dance is distinguished—unlike performance, since one can be a bad performer.

While dancing in her physical body in her room, a subtle body of her was seamlessly projected in the dance realm. The dance realm may happen at first glance to look exactly like her room (same furniture, etc.); if this is the first time this happens to her, then initially she might not be aware that she has been projected as a subtle body in the dance realm, that she is no longer in her physical body in the world. But she may soon see the other person in the room freeze. She would then suspect, if not know, that she must no longer be in her physical body and in the world, since while in the world she had come across motionless objects, for example, a building, an animal frozen in snow, and even a corpse, that of her grandmother, she had never seen someone frozen like that. The one who encounters immobilization, which, unlike motionlessness, is not part of the world, sooner or later wonders, "Am I dead?" since it can happen in death, in the death realm, or, if one has trained for years to become a dancer, views it as confirming that he or she is presently a dancer, since witnessing this would imply that one is then in the dance realm.

— In your book *The Dancer's Two Bodies*, you list a number of characteristics of dance and its realm. Is it possible that there are other characteristics that have not been discovered yet?

— There could be characteristics I have missed—it may turn out that in *The Dancer's Two Bodies* I was partial to those characteristics of dance and its realm with which I have an affinity.

Qualifying a disaster as a surpassing one is not a value judgment; it does not mean that it is more disastrous than the other kind, but rather more disastrous than it seems, and that it has different effects than the other type of disaster. Culture comprises what does not withdraw following a surpassing disaster, while tradition consists of that which withdrew or would withdraw following such a disaster. The withdrawal of tradition is objective: it is the object that withdraws—that is, it is not simply and solely a matter of one's ceasing cathecting it. If you sense the withdrawal of tradition, you are part of the community of the associated surpassing disaster; if you don't sense it, you are not part of this community. So, the community of a surpassing disaster is not determined by religion, or ethnicity, or language. If the destruction of much of Hiroshima by a nuclear bomb on August 6, 1945, was a surpassing disaster, then a Japanese person who lost his family and yet didn't sense the withdrawal of tradition was not part of the community of that event as a surpassing disaster; contrariwise, were it the case that the pilot who dropped the nuclear bomb on Hiroshima proved to be sensitive to the withdrawal of tradition following this surpassing disaster, he would have turned out to be part of the community of that event as a surpassing disaster, albeit a reprehensible, criminal member of that community.

A sensitive publisher would detect whether an out-of-print book that withdrew following a surpassing disaster was subsequently resurrected immaterially and is thus available again for publication, and so may make the book available materially through its reprint. I assume that that was the case with Simone Fattal's second edition of Etel Adnan's *The Arab Apocalypse*.

Deleuze: "Bergson does not just put forward one thesis on movement [in *Matter and Memory* (1896)], but three.... According to the first thesis ... the space covered is divisible, indeed infinitely divisible, whilst movement is indivisible, or cannot be divided without changing qualitatively each time it is divided."[724] A filmmaker who intuits this Bergsonian conception of movement can have an affinity with one or the other of the aforementioned two alternatives. Tarkovsky, as is clear in the final pool scene in *Nostalgia* (1983) and during the shooting of the scene of the burning of the protagonist's house in *The Sacrifice* (1986), has an affinity with the former: movement is indivisible (does Godard in one of the scenes of his film *Every Man for Himself* [*Sauve qui peut (la vie)*, 1980] evince an affinity with the latter [movement may be divided but it changes qualitatively when it is], in which case that scene would not be introducing us to "unconscious optics" [Walter Benjamin: "A different nature opens itself to the camera than opens to the naked eye—if only because an unconsciously penetrated space is substituted for a space consciously explored by man. Even if one has a general knowledge of the way people walk, one knows nothing of a person's posture during the fractional second of a stride (in these two consecutive examples, Benjamin moves from space to movement without taking into consideration the radical difference between the two according to Bergson: through filming in tighter shots, one sees new aspects of the space, but through slow motion or time lapse, one does not perceive previously undetected, missed aspects of a familiar movement, but another, qualitatively different movement). Here the camera intervenes with the resources of its lowerings and liftings, its interruptions and isolations, its extensions and accelerations, its enlargements and reductions (again Benjamin is mixing processes that happen at the level of space ["enlargements and reductions"] and movement ["interruptions and ... accelerations"]). The camera introduces us to unconscious optics as does psychoanalysis to unconscious impulses"[725]], nor revealing a psychological ambivalence of the characters, so that a hug contains and enfolds a strangulation, but showing that a movement changes qualitatively, here from a hug to a strangulation, when it is divided? It does not seem to be the case, given that Godard produced an indiscernibility of a hug and a strangulation through extra-diegetic special effects that reveals an ambivalence, if not a barely contained aggressivity, of the divorced couple toward each other). The protagonist of *Nostalgia*, a Russian poet, promises to walk across the mineral pool in Bagno Vignoni (Val d'Orcia) while holding a burning candle. When he tries to do so, the candle's flame, after repeatedly flickering, is extinguished by the breeze and the largely drained pool's vapors halfway into his walk. What to do? Interestingly, it does not even occur to him to light the candle and *resume* his progress to the opposite edge of the pool. The alternative seems rather to be whether to forgo fulfilling his promise, or at least postpone it until the weather conditions are more propitious for the fulfillment of his project, or to go back to his initial departure point and restart, which implies that he obscurely senses that movement, unlike space, is not divisible—through considering only this alternative, he evinces a Bergsonian sense of time. He opts for the second option. Once again the flame is extinguished by the breeze and the pool's vapors before he reaches the other end of the pool. He endures this task he promised to accomplish, also in the sense that he maintains and respects it as duration: he goes back to his starting point and begins again. This time he manages to traverse the pool while keeping the flame lit. On the other side of the pool he puts down the still burning candle and, drained (the full, continuous shot lasts twelve minutes), falls dead, a martyr to his correct apprehension of movement, to real movement (he could have avoided dying if he had believed in the incorrect conception of movement, movement as simply divisible). During the filming of Tarkovsky's next film, *The Sacrifice*, "suddenly, in the scene in which Alexander sets fire to his house—a single take lasting six and a half minutes—the camera broke down. We discovered it only after the entire building was ablaze, burning to the ground as we looked on. We couldn't put the fire out and we couldn't take a single shot; four expensive months of intense hard work for nothing."[726] Another filmmaker (Eisenstein?) could easily have had the cinematographer quickly replace the stuck film reel with a new one, shoot the final state of the house, burned to the ground, and then take a few close-ups of the protagonist and intercut them with the successfully filmed part of the shot of the burning house to give the spectators the impression that they have watched the full process of the burning of the house. Tarkovsky did not resort to this expedient solution; he must have intuited that the edited sequence would not present to us the burning of the house but qualitatively different movements. Instead, "in a matter of days, a new house had been built, identical to the first one,"[727] and the burning of the house was shot again from beginning to end, as one movement (this time around, prudently, two cameras were used for the shoot, one operated by Sven Nykvist and the second by the assistant cameraman). The director of the aforementioned two scenes did not shy away from criticizing the influential Soviet filmmaker and film theorist Eisenstein, who argued, for instance, that "the concept of the moving (time-consuming) image arises from the superimposition—or counterpoint—of two differing immobile images," and gave the following example (from *Potemkin* [1925]) of "an artificially produced image of motion ...: ... In the thunder of the Potemkin's guns, a marble lion leaps up, in protest against the blood shed on the Odessa steps. [This sequence is] composed of three shots of three stationary marble lions at the Alupka Palace in the Crimea: a sleeping lion, an awakening lion, a rising lion."[728] What Eisenstein actually gave us in this sequence was not a real movement of a lion rising "in protest" through the montage of three shots of three stationary marble lions, a "sleeping" one, an "awakening" one, and a "rising" one, since Bergson's "first thesis contains another proposition: you cannot reconstitute movement with positions in space or instants in time: that is, with immobile sections [*coupes*]. You can only achieve this reconstitution by adding to the positions, or to the instants, the abstract idea of a succession, of a time which is mechanical, homogeneous, universal and copied from space, identical for all movements,"[729] in other words, "a time which is ... uniform, abstract, ... 'in' the apparatus, and 'with' which the images are made to pass consecutively," in yet other words, the "universal, abstract" time of the projector, which is the same for the implied "movements"

425

of awakening and standing up in protest deducible from the difference of posture of the three marble lions, "and thus you miss the movement."[730]

In his film *Francofonia* Sokurov asks in voice-over: "The Louvre. Might it be that this museum is worth more than all of France? Who needs France without the Louvre? Or Russia without the Hermitage?"—I, for one, and, I hope, the world, need, among others, the films of Tarkovsky and most of the films of Sokurov (including *Francofonia*), Dostoevsky's *The Double* and *Notes from the Underground*, and Leonid Andreyev's short story "Lazarus," hence Russia even without the Hermitage (many of the paintings and sculptures in it are uninteresting, mere clutter). Sokurov made two films around the Louvre and the Hermitage, *Francofonia* (2015) and *Russian Ark* (2002), respectively. And yet these two films are quite different in terms of the ontology and temporality they presuppose and *enact*. For a perception that could eschew cuts, and thus discontinuities, and instead just unfold events folded in a continuous time, whatever occurs would not become part of the past and cease existing but would coexist with every other occurrence (within the limits of the light cone);[731] the Hermitage (full name: the State Hermitage Museum) was videotaped in one uninterrupted shot that unfolds, and by doing so manifests, the historical episodes this museum had enfolded since its founding in 1764 by Catherine II as a court museum, episodes that thus have not become past events that disappeared irretrievably—any cuts in the film would have implied a discontinuous time, one in which only the present (including the traces *in it* of past events) exists, while past events are no longer. Thus, in *Russian Ark*, the museum does not simply contain juxtaposed paintings that represent events and historical personages that belong to different centuries, for example Massimo Stanzione's *Cleopatra* and Lodovico Cardi's *The Circumcision of Christ*, but also maintains the events that transpired there and the people who moved in the building for over two centuries so that they coexist in an enduring present. Is the time in Russia outside the Hermitage a passing one, unlike the time in the museum, and that is why, or at least one reason why, the Hermitage may be worth more than Russia? Yet there is a contradiction at the heart of *Russian Ark*: the temporality and ontology of the film, which transpires in a single, 86-minute shot, imply that the events of other centuries are not past, therefore that the protagonists are not long dead, hence that the proper mode of filming it would have been not with over one thousand actors and extras but as a documentary showing the actual personages, among others, Catherine II, empress of the Russian Empire from 1762 until her death in 1796, Peter I, Nikolay I and II, notwithstanding that they predate the invention of cinema—or at least have a coda in which we would have seen (film images of) the actual Catherine II, etc. There is no such contradiction at the heart of Sokurov's multi-shot film about the Louvre, *Francofonia*, in which its two main historical protagonists, Count Wolff Metternich (1893-1978), who "was responsible for the conservation of Rhineland and French art collections under the *Kunstschutz* principle, from 1940 to 1942," and Jacques Jaujard (1895-1967), the director of the French National Museums, who "on August 3rd of 1939, six days before France declared war on Germany, ... shut down the museum for 'maintenance reasons'" and sent "thousands of pieces from the permanent collection, including the Mona Lisa, ... all over the country," so that "all that remained were statues too fragile or heavy to remove without suspicion,"[732] were represented by actors, since the film includes numerous cuts that evince abrupt changes in space and time, thus temporal discontinuities, implying that whatever is no longer present has lost all being (other than through its traces in the present—hence the frequent resorting to archival footage).

One day, he ceased going to bookstores; one day, he no longer had sex with his wife; one day, he stopped writing; and one day, he recognized that life does not have one end, physical death, but rather multiple ends. Thenceforth he became weirdly sensitive to ends, recognizing at the same time as it happened that this would be the last time he would be doing something, for example seeing a film in a movie theater, unlike the vast majority of others if not all others, who would suddenly realize that it's been months, years even, since they'd last gone to watch a film in a movie theater or did some other activity! He also noted, though not to the same degree, when others stopped doing some activity, and how they nonetheless treated it as still part of their actual life! This is another sort of clutter: activities one will never do again but that one continues to treat as belonging not solely to one's memories but possibly also to one's actual life. Declutter by knowing when a certain activity is no longer part of your actual life (although it may still be part of your memories).

Not only is hysteria exhibitionistic, there is a kind of hysteria associated with exhibitionism: the radical exhibitionist performs not just for his partner or partners and for the visible onlookers but also for invisible onlookers, thus populating space with "haunting presences."

When he tried to decipher why, at a certain stage of his life, he had begun to detect voyeuristic impulses in himself, all he could think of as a trigger was his preceding three-year stay in Hong Kong, where his look was almost never reciprocated by any woman there (what applied to him seemed to apply to all expat men he noticed on the streets or in the metro). But how to look non-voyeuristically at someone who does not exchange the look and hence who does not acknowledge one's presence, treats one as invisible?[733] What is the difference between one's look in this case and that of the voyeur, since, although not hidden from view, one is not "seen" by the one one is looking at? Unless one doesn't mind becoming a la long a voyeur, one would no longer look oneself. And yet this reciprocal absence of the look would not result in its disappearance altogether but would displace it and, in the process of displacing it, make it undergo a metamorphosis, so that it becomes the inhuman gaze of some object or objects, with one ending up feeling that one is gazed at by this or that object. That seems to be the sort of alternative a foreign man tends to undergo in Hong Kong: either developing voyeuristic impulses, if not becoming outright a voyeur, or becoming the prey of the gaze of (certain) objects—unless one is lucky enough to have his look reciprocated, however briefly, by some gay Hong Kong man, or expat Western, Indian, or Middle Eastern women, or a Hong Kong woman's boyfriend or husband noticing that one is looking at her.

A Turkish or Lebanese filmmaker who makes a film that evinces a crisis of the action-image related to a context that's conducive to such a crisis, Turkey in the aftermath of one of its military coups (in particular the 1980 one), for example, or Lebanon during its civil war (1975–1990) and two Israeli invasions, or its economic as well as financial meltdown that became plain in late 2019 and was exacerbated by the explosion on August 4, 2020, of a very large amount of ammonium nitrate stored at the port of Beirut, would not be copying European films made in the aftermath of World War II in which we witness a crisis of the action-image and hence is not to be considered as lagging behind, and derivative of, his or her Western counterparts. An example of such a film is Özcan Alper's *Autumn* (2008). In the beginning of the film, Yusuf, a 32-year-old political prisoner who was sentenced to jail in 1997 while a 22-year-old university student, is released by the prison authorities on health grounds, as it were to settle accounts before he dies, to finish any "unfinished business." He returns to his village near the city of Artvin, close to Turkey's border with Georgia, where he is welcomed by his elderly mother, with whom he speaks Hemsin, a version of Armenian. While prisoners who have not undergone a break of the sensory-motor link, the majority, act upon their release as tourists exploring the changed world they perceive around them, those who, like Yusuf, have undergone a break of the sensory-motor link do not act like tourists, since they are then mainly attentive to pure optical and sound images: a slug in the grass, etc. Despite his persistent coughing, he does not consult a doctor, indeed keeps smoking, and when he learns that the woman he loved married during his long years in prison, he appears unmoved. Deleuze: "We could call them white events, events which never truly concern the person who provokes or is subject to them, even when they strike him in his flesh: events whose bearer, a man *internally dead*, as [Sidney] Lumet says, is in a hurry to extricate himself."[734] Not only he cannot respond, he's largely unconcerned, including about his inability to respond. Can we, for that matter, say that it is as if what happens to him is happening to someone else? Strictly speaking, we cannot say this because within the regime of the action-image one can feel concerned about what is happening to someone else. That he is not *fully* unconcerned, that the break of the sensory-motor link in his case is not a full-blown one, is implied by his continuing to have a face; the one who is fully unconcerned does not react even in the guise of tendencies to do so in the form of micro-movements on the sensory organs and receptive nerves of the face, and consequently, by losing one of its two poles, loses the face[735] (oddly, when he writes on the break of the sensory-motor link, Deleuze does not address this matter and thus fails to draw this consequence of the break: the effacement of the face). In the last scene of the film, while he is playing his musical instrument in the family home, his mother, who was seated listening to the music, stands up and turns, then, while we continue to hear the music, which we assume he is playing offscreen, the camera pans with her as she walks toward the window, dollies forward, bypasses her as she stands engrossed by something offscreen, and zooms through the window to show the scene she is looking at in the snowy landscape outside: his funeral—thus making it explicit that his death is external to him (but for this reason all the more poignant in a way). While he appears to be unconcerned about his physical death, his musical accompaniment of his funerary procession implies that he is concerned about the symbolic rites of death (unlike Nietzsche, who, having died before dying, witnessed his funeral, Yusuf accompanies his funeral—musically—without witnessing it). The prison authorities had expected him to engage in a frenzy of activity "to catch up" in the brief time he, gravely sick, still had to live, since so much of his youth appeared to have been wasted while he was in prison; instead, based on what he accomplishes by the end of the film, his unfinished business proved to be to accompany his physical death, which he does by playing his instrument *during* his funeral! Deleuze: "Sometimes the event delays and is lost in idle periods, sometimes it is there too quickly, but it does not belong to the one to whom it happens (even death ...)."[736] "Sometimes the event delays and is lost in idle periods"; indeed, Yusuf, having been diagnosed and "treated" for his gravely persistent cough only by the prison doctor, is late in getting a second opinion from another doctor—dying physically before he does so—and he is late to join the Georgian woman with whom he agreed to travel to Batumi, with the regretful outcome that, her Turkish visa having expired, she ends up going back to her country, alone; and "sometimes the event is there too quickly, but it does not belong to the one to whom it happens (even death ...)"

(what an incongruous use of "even death" by Deleuze here, given that death does not belong to the one to whom it happens since he or she assumes in it other names, indeed every name in history—it belongs to him or her only in the sense of his or hers being one of the names of history!)—and sometimes it is both simultaneously, as in the final scene, where he is late in relation to his physical death, since he persists in playing music even during his funerary procession (this lateness proves to be the proper condition for him to accompany his death, at least its funerary rites); and where death, physical death, to be more precise, is there too quickly, not in the glib sense of the "premature" physical death of a 32-year-old man, the occurrence of which is, judged by the funerary procession, locatable in chronological time, but in the sense that at no point during the shot that starts with a camera movement from the protagonist playing music to the window and continues with a zoom through the latter to his funeral procession in the snowy landscape outside while the music continues to be audible is there a determinate time when he would have died, even off-screen, and which would naturally have been suggested by the cessation of the music—while Deleuze's words "Ellipsis ceases to be a mode of the tale [*récit*] ...: it belongs to the situation itself"[737] mean that, in the films he is discussing, the ellipsis, for example a "jump cut," is not limited to the narration but belongs also to the situation itself, that is, it is an ontological ellipsis, we can read them to mean, too, as is the case in the final shot of Alper's *Autumn*, that the ellipsis ceases to appear at the level of the narration to be only implied at the level of the situation, in other words, of "(un)reality."[738] How fitting here that what undergoes an ellipsis, what is omitted, is physical death, a non-event, something that one does not experience ("death ... is nothing to us, since when we exist, death is not present, and when death is present, we do not exist"[739] [Epicurus—I would replace every occurrence of *death* in the quote with *physical death*]). Soon enough, a woman's mournful, elegiac voice overlays the instrumental music he persists in playing with a song that refers to him by name, Yusuf, confirming that the funerary procession is his, and allowing him to cease accompanying the funeral musically, a cessation that implies the coincidence of his death inside and outside the house.

Why would one make it one's task, if not one's mission, to document and archive past injustice even after the death of the victim, and thus even after it is no longer possible to "redress the injustice"? Is it so that this knowledge would lead to measures that would prevent the recurrence of such injustice? In some cases it is so, but in many if not most cases, it is to produce *ressentiment*. In the case of those who only document and archive the injustice without proposing and/or fighting for the implementation of measures to prevent its future recurrence, to prove that *ressentiment* was not the intended goal, the one who documented and archived the injustice must manage, and must expect and demand from those who peruse the archived item documenting the injustice, to forgive the unforgivable, a doubly mad act, since it is madness to try to accomplish, and madness to succeed in accomplishing, the impossible.

Nietzsche wrote: "Impotent against that which has been—it [the will] is an angry spectator of everything past [this incapacity of the will to change the past according to Nietzsche's Zarathustra would be experienced most starkly, fundamentally, and exemplarily through time travel in case it is travel through the temporal dimension of the four-dimensional block of a sole universe, where one feels helpless in the double sense that one cannot be helped to change the past but also is not able to help others change it—perhaps the latter is the more fundamental, traumatic helplessness]. The will cannot will backward ...—that is the will's loneliest misery.... That time does not run backward, that is its wrath.... This, yes this alone is *revenge* itself: the will's unwillingness toward time and time's 'it was.'"[740] What is one's affect when a past action did not follow from one's essence (Spinoza) or is not one to which one is addicted, in other words, compulsively driven to repeat since it induces *jouissance* in one; or one did not end up willing it to recur eternally following the ordeal of experiencing its repetition countless times, with the result that one did not achieve the state where willing (which would have become epochal rather than limited to an individual's faculty), having learned to "will backward" ("since in a universe where the will has been accomplished, [not only is it the case that] anything whose eternal recurrence cannot be willed becomes impossible,"[741] but also, something facilitated by the circumstance that such a universe is no longer relativity's block one, "whatever of the world's past could not be willed, that is, willed to recur eternally, never existed"[742]), "liberates" and therefore learns "reconciliation with time," indeed with "what is higher than any reconciliation," and unlearns "the spirit of revenge" and "become[s] its own redeemer and joy bringer"?[743] It is resentment.

We are told in (Shi'ite) Islam that this world (for as long as the Mahdi has not returned [and ushered in the Resurrection] and the sharia applies) is the time of actions without reward or punishment, while the afterlife, more specifically the Day of Resurrection, is that of reward and punishment without (the possibility of) action (Mullā Sadrā Shīrāzī, "the Day of Resurrection is the day of reward and punishment without actions, and the day of sharia is the day of actions without reward and punishment"[744] [*yawm al-qiyāma yawm al-jazā' wal-thawāb bilā 'amal ... wal-sharī'a yawm 'amal bilā thawāb*]). Given that the dead man or woman can no longer act, he or she is resentful; indeed, it would appear that the posthumous condition, more specifically the

431

in-between state, the one *between* physical death and hell, where he or she is reduced to only what induces *jouissance* in him or her, or heaven, where he or she is refined to only what gives him or her joy, is the primary, optimal realm for resentment, where it holds sway.

Insofar as, according to Islam, with death the time of action has passed and the time of punishment or reward has begun, the dead undergo any event, and not only its memory, as a *fait accompli*. That is another sense why it is fitting that the dead are referred to, seemingly euphemistically, as the late.

Thomas Henry Huxley bemoaned "the great tragedy of Science—the slaying of a beautiful hypothesis by an ugly fact."[745] In many cases where a beautiful scientific theory was defeated by an ugly fact, this "ugly" fact, as well as others, led, down the line, through the intermediary of one or more ugly, cumbersome, less elegant theories, to a more general and fundamental scientific theory that's even more beautiful. In those cases where a beautiful scientific theory was falsified by an ugly fact and replaced, seemingly definitively, by an ugly scientific theory, one of the ways the very powerful computers of some scientifically and technologically highly advanced future civilization should be used is to produce simulations of versions of the universe in which the falsified beautiful scientific theory would apply perfectly.

Deleuze and Guattari wrote in *What Is Philosophy?*: "Philosophy is the art of forming, inventing, and fabricating concepts.... It is not contemplation, reflection, or communication."[746] What confirms this for me is that it has repeatedly been the case that, having constructed a rigorous concept (for example, radical closure, or the withdrawal of tradition past a surpassing disaster) and looking to make it clearer to readers through examples from rigorous films I had already watched, my memory of the films led me to believe that some of them provided not confirmations but counterexamples of the concept. And yet, when I rewatched these films, I discovered each time that my memory was faulty, swayed by what the average audience member would have expected to happen, and that these rigorous films actually provide confirmation of my concept—never completely trust your memory of a rigorous film while constructing a concept. If there is a match between the concept of a philosopher or thinker and a film or painting, it would not be because the philosopher would have reflected on it but likely because of an untimely collaboration between the philosopher and the painter or filmmaker.

I would not have been able to create my rigorous concept "untimely collaboration" without such collaboration (with other creators).

While we have parallel montage in most films, it becomes really interesting only in some filmmakers' work. One could say that Christopher Nolan is exploring in his films *Inception* (2010), *Interstellar* (2014), *Dunkirk* (2017), and *Tenet* (2020) various subjects (for example, the Dunkirk evacuation during World War II, the operation to implant an idea into a person's subconscious [an "inception"], a group of astronauts' trip through a wormhole in search of a new habitable planet as human life on Earth faces an extinction-level environmental catastrophe, etc.) but equally well, if not more appropriately, parallel montage and, that being so, finding the most appropriate subjects and stories with which to do so. In *Interstellar*, we have at one point a parallel montage between Earth and a planet where every hour equals seven years on Earth due to the extreme time dilation caused by the nearby black hole; in *Inception* there is a parallel montage between the 10-hour flight from Sydney to Los Angeles in waking reality; its equivalent in dream level 1, a week; its equivalent in dream level 2, six months: its equivalent in dream level 3, ten years; and its equivalent in dream level 4 (Limbo), decades—if not infinite time; and *Dunkirk* presents a week at the evacuation beach, one day of the duration of those on the civilian boats, and one hour of the duration of the Spitfire pilots as parallel timelines. If one day he stops doing it, we can deduce that he's reached the limit of his particular exploration of parallel montage and now has to move to another feature of cinema or stop making films altogether—or make a film without any parallel montage.

Wittgenstein provides an example of someone whose writings do not compose an oeuvre: "Aristotle thinks 'after' the Sophists, Kant after the crisis of Leibnizian rationalism and of the grounding of law, after Hume and Rousseau. Wittgenstein is a solitary thinker. Of course, he thinks 'after' Frege, Russell, logical positivism, and no doubt after Schopenhauer and Spengler. But his solitude is marked in that he also thinks 'after' himself. The publication of the *Tractatus* in 1921 announced a brilliant philosopher of logic and mathematics. Published two years after his death, in 1953, the *Investigations* witness to the fact that he had taken another direction.... Russell is dropped; Wittgenstein links onto Wittgenstein, with some inclination to disavow the latter (the earlier Wittgenstein, that is). A solitude that isn't concerned about 'the oeuvre'"[747] (Jean-François Lyotard). My writings, too, do not compose an oeuvre, since there is a caesura between my first book, *Distracted* (more specifically its first edition, published in 1991), written by a living young man blithely unaware that he is a mortal (in my sense, dead even while still physically alive), and my second, *(Vampires): An Uneasy Essay on the Undead in Film* (1993), written by someone who had died before dying physically and, consequently, became aware that he has all along been dead even while still physically alive.

A filmmaker's or writer's work can be said to compose an oeuvre not simply when there is a recurrence of certain themes, events (for example, rain or snow falling inside an interior space in Tarkovsky's films), singular movements (for example, levitation in Tarkovsky's films), and sustained exploration of certain cinematic or literary elements (for example, the close-up in Bergman's films) but when it is also the case that if one of his or her films or books has a proper name for a title, then this book or film includes the themes of his or her oeuvre foregrounded in those titles of his or her books or films that are not proper names. Someone who considers that Dostoyevsky's writings compose an oeuvre is to expect to find in the novel *Brothers Karamazov* notes from the underground, an idiot, a gentle creature, a double, devils or the damned, crime and punishment, etc. Someone who considers that Tarkovsky's films compose an oeuvre is to expect *Solaris* to include a stalker (the sentient extra-terrestrial ocean Solaris can be considered a stalker since it spies on the unconscious and conscious desires and thoughts of the cosmonauts on the spaceship stationed in its vicinity, and the desired entities it manifests physically, such as the successive replicas of cosmonaut Kris's beloved wife, Hari, who committed suicide and whom he failed to mourn successfully, can, in turn, also be viewed as stalkers, since they cannot be independent and separate from the cosmonauts given that they are derived from the latter's desires); a mirror, indeed *the* mirror (the sentient extraterrestrial ocean Solaris, which manifests physically the unconscious or ardent conscious desires of those who approach it, is *the* mirror, and the "Harises" that are materialized by Solaris and that replace each other upon the demise of the previous one appear to be "mirror images" of each other and, derivatively, of Kris's dead wife, and the house that cosmonaut Kris visits in the film's coda is a materialization by Solaris and within Solaris of Kris's parents' house, itself a "mirror" copy of his grandparents' house [the centrality of the mirror in the desire of humans is propounded by one of the cosmonauts, "We don't want to conquer the cosmos; we want to extend the boundaries of Earth to the cosmos. We are only seeking Man. We don't want other worlds. We want mirrors," which would imply that humans, certainly the hysterical ones among them, fundamentally desire not this or that object but to be provided with an indication, *through a glass*, even if *darkly*, as to what their deepest desire is]—is it accidental that we have the esoteric version of the mirror in a film that does not have it as its title, while we have a rather exoteric version in the film titled *The Mirror*? I would like to think that it is not by accident, and that this situation applies not just in the case of these two films but generally); sacrifice (Kris sacrifices an embodiment by Solaris of a figure based on his desires for, and guilt toward, his dead beloved wife, by ejecting her from the spaceship into outer space); and nostalgia (Kris's father built his house as a replica of his father's house, and it appears that Solaris, sensing Kris's acute nostalgia for this house, recreated it within itself for him to visit). He or she is, moreover, to expect *Andrei Rublev* to include a stalker[748] (Andrei Rublev can be considered a stalker when, becoming intrigued by the young son of a bell-caster who, though his father passed away without initiating him into the professional secrets for building large bells, claimed that the latter had done so and as a result had been commissioned by the grand duke to lead a large crew to cast a great bell, he silently shadows him during the various stages of the bell's casting, observing his interactions with various members of the crew and witnessing the way he overcomes the challenges he faces); sacrifice (having killed one of the soldiers who took part in the sack of Vladimir under the Grand Duke's brother to save a profoundly deaf and speech-impaired woman from being raped, Andrei Rublev, an icon painter and a monk, gives up, in other words, sacrifices, painting and takes a vow of silence, in other words, sacrifices speech, as gestures of atonement); a mirror (during a heavy rain shower on their way from Andronikov Monastery to Moscow, Andrei Rublev and his two companions, the monks Daniil and Kirill, seek shelter in a barn, where a *skomorokh* [jester] ridicules them as they come in and entertains a group of villagers by making fun of boyars and priests. Kirill leaves unnoticed. Shortly thereafter, soldiers brutally arrest the *skomorokh*. Moments later, Kirill returns. In Moscow, Kirill visits the famous icon painter Theophanes the Greek. On hearing that the monk hails from Andronikov Monastery, Theophanes says, "Then you must be Andrei Rublev." During their conversation, Theophanes seems impressed by Kirill's erudite comments and answers and invites him to work as his assistant on the decoration of the Annunciation Cathedral in Moscow. Kirill at first declines the offer on the grounds that he's not "up to the job" [in other words, as he will declare when he leaves the monastery for good, "God didn't give me talent"] but then accepts, on one condition: "If you yourself come for me to the monastery and in front of the whole community and our bishop ask me to come and help you—with all our brethren present, and Andrei Rublev, too." "What's your name?" "Kirill." A short while later, a messenger arrives at the Andronikov Monastery from Moscow to request assistance in decorating the Annunciation Cathedral. Kirill assumes that the messenger will ask him, but he asks Andrei instead. When the messenger inquires of the assembled monks, "Is he really Andrei Rublev?" to make sure than he is not requesting the wrong person, Kirill, standing right next to Andrei, responds, "Yes, he is Andrei Rublev—and I'm Kirill." The misidentification by Theophanes the Greek of Kirill as Andrei Rublev at the beginning of their meeting, and the request for Andrei when it seemed at the end of the same meeting that Theophanes the Greek intended to ask for Kirill as his assistant, as well as the subsequent interjection by Kirill while standing next to Andrei at the monastery, "He is Andrei Rublev—and I'm Kirill," imply that Andrei Rublev and Kirill can easily be mistaken for each other, in other words, that they are mirror images. That Andrei Rublev and Kirill can be viewed as mirror images is confirmed when, during the raising up of the bell, the same *skomorokh*, a rather keen observer, recognizes in no uncertain terms Andrei Rublev as the one who denounced him to the authorities. How could Kirill, who is talentless, be the mirror image of the famously talented Andrei Rublev? And yet but for the coda of the film, in which we are shown his icon *The Old Testament Trinity*, we do not see Rublev paint anything, troubled as he is with unanswered questions, unresolved qualms, and doubts ["'A messenger already went to complain to the prince.... Hadn't we decided all in Moscow? We'd agreed on everything up to the last detail. The Grand Prince himself had approved it. What is still unclear to you then? What have we been shouting ourselves hoarse about for two months?... *The Last Judgment*—just go ahead and paint it.... We're losing precious time! The weather is warm and dry. We could've already finished the domed ceiling. And the pillars, too. And we could've made them so beautiful and vivid! We could depict the sinners boiling in tar in such a way that ... it would make one's flesh creep. I know how to paint the devil, with smoke from his nose and eyes like ...' 'Smoke is not the point!' 'What is the point then?' 'I don't know! ... I can't paint this. It's against me. Can't you understand? I don't want to scare people. Try to understand, Daniil.' 'Come to your senses! It's the Last Judgment, that's what it is! It's not my invention.' 'No, I can't!'"]. Through intervening on behalf of Andrei, who is keeping his vow of silence, by telling the *skomorokh* that he is mistaken as to the identity of the one who denounced him, and then through privately confessing to Andrei that he was the one who denounced the *skomorokh* years earlier; that he was consumed by envy for Andrei's enormous talent but stopped envying him when he heard that Andrei had abandoned painting; and that he had since had a change of heart and would no longer envy him were he to resume painting, indeed entreats him to do so, the talentless monk Kirill brings about the end of the mirroring between Andrei and him, with the result that Andrei, who had shortly before been inspired by the example of the young son of a bell-caster who pulled off casting a great bell notwithstanding his ignorance of the professional secrets for doing so, can resume painting); nostalgia (the nostalgia in *Andrei Rublev*, for instance that of Andrei's companion and teammate Daniil, is for the unaccomplished, for example *The Last Judgment* that Andrei and his team were commissioned to paint but appeared unable to finish). When an author's books or a filmmaker's films compose an oeuvre, it is apposite, indeed sometimes revelatory, to switch his or her book or film titles that are not proper names among each other—not randomly, but judiciously. For example, in the case of Dostoyevsky, "Notes from the Underground" would be a more suitable title for the book presently titled *Crime and Punishment*, and the novel presently titled *The Idiot* would have been more fittingly titled "A Gentle Creature." Were the title of the novella presently titled *Notes from the Underground* "The Idiot," most readers would initially assume that the title refers to an idiot in the sense of a stupid person and feel that their assumption has been confirmed when the protagonist affirms, "I admit that twice two makes four is an excellent thing, but if we are to give everything its due, twice two makes five is sometimes a very charming thing too," but then the more perceptive ones would suspect that he is rather an Idiot in the Deleuzian sense: "Dostoyevsky's characters are constantly caught up in emergencies, and while they are caught up in these life-and-death emergencies, they know that there is a more urgent question—but they do not know what it is.... Everything happens as if in the worst emergencies—'Can't wait, I've got to go'—they said to themselves: 'No, there is something more urgent. I am not budging until I know what it is.' It's the Idiot. It's the Idiot's formula: 'You know, there is a deeper problem. I am not sure what it is. But leave me alone. Let everything rot ... this more urgent problem must be found.'"[749] What's the deeper question and more urgent emergency that contributed to the protagonist's failure to respond when he was slighted?

He was unfortunate, not in the sense that he was not given any opportunity but, as with many if not most people, in the sense that he had his chance when he was still ill-prepared to appreciate and "take advantage of" it.

Throughout my three-year stint as Professor at the Department of Humanities and Creative Writing (which would be far more accurately named Department of Cultural Studies) of Hong Kong Baptist University, I was dismayed by the very low educational level of many if not most of the third- and fourth-year students. And I found the stark discrepancy between the low educational level of these students and their inflated grades unacceptable, indeed smacking of corruption since student evaluations loom large in faculty reviews: in one fifty-student class, only two received a C, and in an eighty-student class, only five received a C, all the others receiving A's or B's[750]—in comparison, the midterm grades of my six honors-project advisees were 1 C, 1 C-, 2 D+'s, 1 D, 1 D-, and my grades for the midterm assignments of the fifty-three students in one of my courses included thirty-five that were between C- and B-. Deleuze wrote in *Cinema 1: The Movement-Image*: "Eisenstein suggested that the close-up was not merely one type of image among others, but gave an affective reading of the whole film"; the following question students are asked to answer for HKBU's Course Feedback Questionnaire, "I found that what I learnt was what

I had expected of this course," is not just one among others, let alone an anomaly, but rather the key to understanding all the other questions of the CFQ. I can easily imagine what would be the evaluations of the Department of Humanities and Creative Writing's students of the teaching of Gilles Deleuze, Jacques Lacan, and Alexandre Kojève, whose seminars count among the most famous and influential in the "humanities" in the twentieth century, had these thinkers taught a semester at HKBU: Unsatisfactory! Here's what I consider the most plausible ratings by the HKBU Faculty Review Panel had Deleuze been a faculty member of the university: Teaching (based almost exclusively on student evaluations): Unacceptable; scholarly work: Excellent (that is, he would have been evaluated as no different from the university's least published and productive faculty members, since, the bar being set so low for scholarly work to be evaluated as excellent [one article published in a so-called tier-1 journal and another published in a "second-tier" journal], they, too, are deemed to be excellent in this regard); service: Threshold.

Nietzsche": "Learning transforms us.... But at our foundation, 'at the very bottom,' there is clearly something that will not learn, a brick wall of spiritual *fatum*, of predetermined decisions and answers to selected, predetermined questions. In any cardinal problem, an immutable 'that is me' speaks up.... In time, certain solutions are found to problems that inspire *our* strong beliefs in particular; perhaps they will start to be called 'convictions.' Later—they come to be seen as only footsteps to self-knowledge, signposts to the problems that we *are*—or, more accurately, to the great stupidity that we are, to our spiritual *fatum*, to that thing 'at the very bottom' that *will not learn*."[751] One teaches neither those who are fully teachable (is there such a human? Would an entity be human or still human if it is fully teachable, or would it turn out to be, for example, a trainable deep neural network? Beware of those who are fully teachable) nor those who are solely unteachable, those who are, from a Gnostic perspective, devoid of any spiritual light, but those who have something unteachable, a spiritual fate. And one teaches them with what is unteachable in one—one's "stupidity," one's spiritual fate. One teaches them in part to counter the teaching that treated them as fully teachable. One teaches them to differentiate what is teachable in them from what is unteachable in them.

In July 2015, I was offered the position of director of the School of Visual Arts at the Lebanese Academy of Fine Arts (Académie Libanaise des Beaux-Arts [Alba]). I accepted the offer and wrote the following mission statement for the school:

Established in 1944, the Lebanese Academy of Fine Arts (Alba) was the first national institution of higher education in Lebanon. Before long, it was playing an important role in the Lebanese art scene, through its faculty (a notable number of whom were former students) and alumni. Yet, for various reasons, not least the civil war, Alba's School of Visual Arts for the most part did not accompany, let alone play a leading role in, the flourishing art scene in Lebanon in the past two or so decades. Within a couple of years, the school will *again* be part and parcel of the Lebanese art scene. But beyond becoming part and parcel of the Lebanese art scene, the School of Visual Arts at Alba will have really mattered, not proved fully reducible to culture, only if it graduates at least one artist who manages to "fail better" (Samuel Beckett: "Ever tried. Ever failed. No matter. Try again. Fail again. Fail better" [*Worstward Ho*]); and/or at least one artist who constructs "a universe that doesn't fall apart two days later" (Philip K. Dick); and/or one artist who sacrificially (since this would require exposing himself or herself to it in the first place) wraps the invasive *jouissance* that only recently was taking aback vast zones of the region (Syria, Iraq, etc.) into (Hölderlinian) song or (Rilkean) angelic, awesome beauty; and if it enhances if not reestablishes the connection of art and thought, more specifically of thought-provoking art and art-provoking thought, a connection that has for quite a while now been a paradoxical one given that, according to a still valid diagnosis of Heidegger, "we are still not thinking—not even yet, although the state of the world is becoming constantly more thought-provoking," and although fresh thought-provoking artworks continue to be made (only to then be largely shrouded by the numerous mediocre works with which they are exhibited in biennials, triennials, galleries and museums).

Some of the school's additional objectives:

— To provide the students with a "temporary autonomous zone" (to use an expression coined by Hakim Bey [a.k.a. Peter Lamborn Wilson] in his 1991 book of the same title) in relation to those of this region's problems that are outdated, so that they would be spared wasting their time rediscovering variants of solutions that are often decades if not centuries old.

— To lead students to the realization that regarding actual artworks, the issue is not to understand them but to acquire intelligent and subtle incomprehension with respect to them and to intuit and appreciate their rigor, thus desisting from correcting any seeming failing in them—a correction that impairs not only admiration but also possible criticism of these works.

— To develop in students a flair for differentiating between a painting, video, etc., that falls apart even before it is framed or screened and one that does not.

— To make students keenly aware that artists collaborate in an untimely manner with future and past artists and thinkers.

— To give students the stark realization "I've never thought before"—not simply about art, but tout court. And then to confront

439

the student with what forces him or her to think (for example: the realization that he or she has never thought before? A thought-pro- voking artwork?) and thus with the chance to think, whether or not he or she would use this thinking in his or her art practice or not.

— To boost students' intuition, including their "'shit' detector" (Hemingway: "The most essential gift for a good writer is a built-in, shockproof, shit detector"; Frank Auerbach: "I hope I still have what Hemingway called the 'shit detector,' that I'm still severe enough with myself if something is not finished to destroy it and start again"), in a period when it is increasingly easy for those associated with the production of works that might be exhibited in galleries, museums, and biennials to fool curators, collectors, audiences, indeed also themselves (Richard Feynman: "The first principle [of having utter scientific integrity] is that you must not fool yourself—and you are the easiest person to fool")—including while working on scatology (Sade, etc.)—so that when they grad- uate they can depend on it to unsparingly destroy those of their works that fall apart before the perceptive spectator blinks.

— To provide the student with at least as much art as necessary to counter culture, if not transmute it into tradition (possibly by sublimating it or pushing it toward a special abjection or using it as manipulable stereotypes [as in the novels of Alain Robbe-Grillet]). To expose the student to art and thought, which belong to tradi- tion, rather than merely to culture, whether high (exhibited widely in museums and biennials, etc.) or low, both insidious enemies of tradition. Much of what starts as ostensible counterculture ends up as culture—it actually belonged to culture all along; tradition consists of that part of counterculture that continues to be coun- terculture, perennially. The real artist and the real thinker are not cultured, but countercultured (and thus have, among other tasks, to coin adjectives absent from the dictionaries of those who are cultured).

— To graduate a number of students who end up producing rig- orous works of art—which is not to say ones that would usher in or contribute to a golden age of art and thought in Lebanon and beyond, since the metaphor of the golden age should have ceased to be used with the abolition by the US government of the gold standard (the golden age for the use of the metaphor of the golden age was the period when gold acted as the economic standard of value, from 1821 [the year England established it] to 1971 [the year the US government abolished it]). The downside is that such students might be at risk of dying of laughter when they come across a reference to a golden age of theater in Lebanon in the 1960s and '70s.

* Caveat concerning the school:

Deleuze wrote in May 1990: "Foucault located the disciplinary societies in the eighteenth and nineteenth centuries; they reach their height at the outset of the twentieth.... Foucault has brilliantly analyzed the ideal project of these environments of enclosure, particularly visible within the factory.... But what Foucault recognized as well was the transience of this model: it succeeded that of the societies of sovereignty, the goal and functions of which were something quite different (to tax rather than to organize production, to rule on death rather than to administer life).... We are in a generalized crisis in relation to all the environments of enclosure—prison, hospital, factory, school, family.... The administrations in charge never cease announcing supposedly necessary reforms: to reform schools, to reform industries, hospitals, the armed forces, prisons. But ... these institutions are finished, whatever the length of their expiration periods.... The societies of control ... are in the process of replacing the disciplinary societies." While Deleuze's prescient words have become more manifest in our day, a quarter of a century after he wrote them, they have been obscured in the context of Alba's School of Visual Arts by the accidental problems that have beset this school from around the time he wrote his text. As the school's new director, I consider that by fixing the largely accidental problems that have undermined the school for several decades, the problems that cannot be fixed by any administration and faculty, since they are symptoms of the ongoing transition from disciplinary societies to societies of control, would come to the fore and become clearer, this making it easier to contribute to "new forms of resistance against the societies of control."

Toward the end of his introduction, addressed to the Faculty of Arts, to Hong Kong Baptist University's six interdisciplinary research labs, which include the so-called Augmented Creativity Lab and "promise to enable academics from different backgrounds [including philosophy] to work together on common sets of problems," Professor Yi-ke Guo, the then newly appointed, pompous Vice-President (Research and Development) of the aforementioned university, said in response to a question, in an exemplification of Cioran's aperçu "The essential often appears at the end of a long conversation. The great truths are spoken on the doorstep,"[752] "Make a machine equipped with artificial intelligence write a poem. That would be a manifest result. The rest is philosophy" (I am quoting from memory; although what followed cannot be deemed "the rest" in any interesting sense, the aforementioned response marked for me the actual end of the meeting). With his misunderstanding of whatever reductive epistemology he might have read, this limited researcher in the field of artificial intelligence made sure to betray his unawareness of the insistence of various great scientists on the relevance, indeed cruciality, of philosophy for science in general and for artificial general intelligence in particular, for example David Deutsch in his aptly titled article

441

"Philosophy Will Be the Key that Unlocks Artificial Intelligence."753 From what perspective can one rigorously say, "The rest is philosophy," while still understanding these words in a derogatory manner? One could say it, indeed a rigorous philosopher did say it, from the vantage point of Lacanian psychoanalysis and its pass: "But, you'll say, what about philosophy in all this? Well, philosophy is that which *doesn't pass.* This is something Lacan was deeply convinced of. I'd even go so far as to say that the detritus of a pass must be entirely philosophical—the waste material of a pass.... Show me the trash cans of a pass sometime—I think they'd be full of philosophy. That's what doesn't pass! And why doesn't the philosophical aspect of an analysis pass? Because it consists of everything that turned out to be hermeneutics, banal interpretation, various and sundry types of bullshit, disastrous totalization, self-awareness in an intense cogito [*cogito concentré*], absolute false knowledge, the triumphant authority of the master who never criticizes himself, and so on. What is all that? It's philosophy, ultimately!"754 (Alain Badiou). While rigorous (in relation to the prevalent understanding and practice of philosophy—it does not apply, for example, to Kierkegaard's *Sickness unto Death*; Deleuze's conception of philosophy as creation of concepts insofar as these are *Chaoids* ["And what would *thinking* be if it did not constantly confront chaos? ... Chaos has three daughters, depending on the plane that cuts through it: these are the *Chaoids*—art, science, and philosophy— as forms of thought or creation. We call *Chaoids* the realities produced on the planes that cut through the chaos in different ways"], and his critique of interpretation, whether the psychoanalytical one in his book *Anti-Oedipus* [cowritten with Félix Guattari], or more generally, "'*She* [the telegraphist of Henry James's *In the Cage*] *ended up knowing so much that she could no longer interpret anything.* There were no longer shadows to help her see more clearly, only glare.' You cannot go further in life than this sentence by James" [*A Thousand Plateaus*, also cowritten with Guattari], etc.), that remains a negative assessment and evaluation. From what perspective could we maintain that "the rest is philosophy" but in an affirmative, redemptive sense and manner, so that one could respond emphatically to that pompous researcher in artificial intelligence: "No—the rest is philosophy"755 (let this tasteless person asking for a poem composed by AI be perplexed by this poetic rejoinder that flips the script)? More generally, how to redeem an inanity in the form of "the rest is ..."? One can do so by considering it from a vantage point where it can assume a rigorous affirmative value and status: in relation to what is useful, the rest is being (Deleuze: "When Bruno [in Werner Herzog's *Stroszek* (1977)] asks the question: 'Where do objects go when they no longer have any use?' we might reply that they normally go in the dustbin, but that reply would be inadequate, since the question is metaphysical. Bergson asked the same question and replied metaphysically: that which has ceased to be useful simply begins to *be*"[756]); in relation to the police in Rancière's understanding of this term,[757] the rest is politics[758]—fittingly, given politics' acknowledgment of and concern and implied activism, if not militancy, regarding the part of the community that is not acknowledged as a part of it; in relation to the sphere of what Lacan termed, in a derogatory manner, the service of goods (*le service des biens*), the rest is desire (Lacan: "What is Alexander's proclamation when he arrived in Persepolis or Hitler's when he arrived in Paris? The preamble isn't important: 'I have come to liberate you from this or that.' The essential point is 'Carry on working. Work must go on.' Which, of course, means: 'Let it be clear to everyone that this is on no account the moment to express the least surge of desire.' The morality of power, of the service of goods, is as follows: 'As far as desires are concerned, come back later. Make them wait'"[759]); in relation to *jouissance* (one of the guises of) the rest is the saint (Lacan: "A saint's business, to put it clearly, is not *caritas*. Rather, he acts as trash [*déchet*]; his business being *trashitas* [*il décharite*].... The saint is the refuse of *jouissance*"[760]); in the context of psychoanalysis, the rest is, exemplarily, the *object a*, the object cause of desire, and, since he is to allow "the subject, the subject of the unconscious, to take him as the cause of the subject's own desire,"[761] the psychoanalyst; and in the context of messianism, the rest is the non-non-Jew (drawing on "St." Paul, Agamben wrote: "The division of the law into Jew/non-Jew, in the law/without law, now leaves a remnant on either side, which cannot be defined either as a Jew, or as a non-Jew. He who dwells in the law of the Messiah is the non-non-Jew"[762]). Anyway, how would AI know what a poem is when, for at least a century now, every poet worth anything has pondered, questioned, and experimented what a poem is?

For matters that are unimportant, I register my contrarian response in the big Other, for example through a dissenting vote, while in matters of importance, particularly ethical ones, I treat the big Other as nonexistent.

As long as there is no full, exhaustive knowledge—and, one can argue, there is no such thing, even if we postulate the existence of God, since, while all-knowing, He is infinite and the creator ex nihilo par excellence—there is no proof of understanding some topic or field other than the creation of *new* knowledge in it.

There is no difference between thought and thoughtlessness except when thought is thought-provoking.

Most instances of plagiarism in academia, especially in the field of cultural studies, are of what is unworthy of being published in the first place!

How ironic and twisted to have a literature review in most academic books and almost all PhD dissertations (mine didn't), especially in the field of cultural studies, since they end up being in their entirety no more than an expansive literature review. Freud's *The Interpretation of Dreams*, which includes a literature review, is a rare exception, since it then moves on to be one of the most original books ever written on dreams. The literature review in Freud's *The Interpretation of Dreams* should have been placed, like every literature review in an original book, in the middle, because a good researcher is one who does not start with searching and researching but, like any creative writer or artist, by finding ("'I do not seek,' said Picasso, 'I find'"[763]), but then searches and researches to remove those things he was not aware others had already addressed felicitously and to elaborate some others.

Nowadays, most academics read *only* to do the formal *literature review* section of their articles and, occasionally, as reviewers for this or that "peer-reviewed journal."

In 1977, in his one-time intervention concerning the so-called New Philosophers (*nouveaux philosophes*), Deleuze wrote: "These New Philosophers ... do have a certain newness about them: ... They have introduced France to literary or philosophical marketing. Marketing has its own particular logic: 1) You have to talk about the book, or get the book talked about, rather than let the book do the talking. Theoretically, you could have all the newspaper articles, interviews, conferences, and radio shows replace the book altogether, it needn't exist at all. The work which the New Philosophers do has less to do with their books than with the articles they can obtain, the newspapers and TV shows they can monopolize, an interview they can give, a book review they can do ..."[764] Nowadays, according to the twisted order of priorities of an increasing number of universities, especially in Hong Kong, what matters most is no longer the book or artwork or film but the award of a grant, which is no longer treated as merely a means to an end, the production of a book or artwork or film; hence, symptomatically, it is not the publication of a book, including one that was written while drawing on the financial resources provided by a grant, but the awarding of a grant that gets all the congratulations and plaudits, demonstrative ones at that. As a faculty member at Hong Kong Baptist University for the past two years, had I, as a result of receiving one or more emails per day from the Faculty of Arts and the Graduate School announcing or reminding faculty members of some coming grant or other, ended up applying for one instead of ignoring all of them, it would have been one that provided teaching relief for the duration of the grant period and that led to a book in the form of a collection of grant proposals each of which would be the distillation of a book in ten sentences or would provide a summary of the proposed book that could be perfectly related orally in a few minutes—none of these books would end up being written and published since each of the aforementioned ten sentences would actualize Nietzsche's ambition, mentioned in his book *Twilight of the Idols*, "to say in ten sentences what everyone else says in a book—what everyone else does *not* say in a book," and each of the *avant la lettre* summaries would covertly function as a Borgesian reason not to write the book ("It is a laborious madness and an impoverishing one, the madness of composing vast books—setting out in five hundred pages an idea that can be perfectly related orally in five minutes. The better way to go about it is to pretend that those books already exist, and offer a summary"[765]).

Increasingly, health is promoted as an absolute and exclusive value, certainly in much of academia in Hong Kong and much of official culture in Singapore (here's an example from academia: Hong Kong Baptist University's Faculty of Arts' Niche Research Area "has three central topics, Well-being, Value, and the Public Good," and one of its sub-themes is "Chinese and Cross-Cultural Health Humanities," which is said to be "an interdisciplinary and cross-cultural research field that focuses on the relationship between arts, humanities, health, and well-being"). The resultant lack of a dual perspective of sickness on health and of health on sickness is itself a sickness, or at least a symptom of sickness. Nietzsche: "Looking from the perspective of the sick towards *healthier* concepts and values, and conversely looking down from the fullness and self-assuredness of *rich* life into the secret workings of the *décadence* instinct—this is what I practised longest, this was my true experience; if I became master of anything then it was of this. I have my hand in now, I am handy at *inverting perspectives*: the foremost reason why for me alone perhaps a 'revaluation of values' is even possible."[766] The obscure motivation of every institution or culture that values health and well-being to such a degree that its goal is the exclusion of any sickness and the eradication of all diseases is to prevent, block, indeed eliminate altogether the very possibility of a revaluation of values.

Soon after joining the Department of Humanities and Creative Writing at Hong Kong Baptist University, I was assigned, as one of the department's three full professors, to be a member of the committee in charge of the "yearly performance review" of various faculty members and tasked to evaluate in particular the research component. I naively read the articles the faculty members under review published during the relevant period, only to discover that the expected so-called research evaluation was to be exclusively determined by the prestige of the journals in which these articles had been published and of the publishers of any recent books by these faculty members (1.5 points for an article in so-called tier-one journals, 4 to 6 points for a sole-authored book, etc.), and that the so-called teaching evaluation was determined by students' evaluations, and consequently that we were there solely to count points, since the evaluation had ostensibly already happened elsewhere. Were those who gradually designed this system of evaluation worried that someone who starts by evaluating may end up creating values? They shouldn't worry about this eventuality, since one cannot really, fundamentally, evaluate without having already created new values. The other two senior faculty members on the committee would not countenance actually reading the academic output of the faculty members under review and possibly deciding that an article published in a so-called tier-1 journal is worthless; for them, an article published in such a journal must *ipso facto* be excellent. Through reveling in or at least acquiescing to and collaborating in the maintenance of such a system in which evaluation is outsourced to so-called peer-reviewed journals (in other words, to the editor-in-chief of the journal, possibly also, if there is one, its associate editor, and the two or three reviewers who were selected by the former), (preferably academic) publishers, and students, and hence in which they are treated as elementary accountants, the current senior academics in most cultural-studies departments and communication departments (some of these departments masquerade as humanities and film studies departments) betray that they are not able to evaluate, let alone create new values, but are dependent on others' evaluations, themselves based on already established mainstream majority or minority values.

Based on a recommendation by my friend the photographer Fouad Elkoury, I attended in January 2015 at the Tournesol Theatre in Beirut the "multidimensional spectacle" *Self-Portrait with the Clarinet and the Two Silent Witnesses* (2015) by an artist, Samir Khaddaj, whose name I had occasionally come across but whose work I had never seen, mostly because I happened to be living or traveling abroad when he occasionally exhibited in Lebanon. I no longer remember it, only that at some points during it I felt that I was perceiving the Imaginal World (*'ālam al-khayāl*), if not that I had been seamlessly introduced into the latter (as a subtle body). I made sure to watch it a second time before the end of its run, while aware that this type of "repetition" (actually a permutation) was extrinsic to it as an event, that the event has an intrinsic relation to repetition, one that can take the form of flashbacks, or a compulsion to repeat, or déjà vu (which is not to say that every experience of déjà vu is an event), etc.—the extrinsic repetition can change into a repetition intrinsic to the event only when it becomes countless, thus providing the one subject to it with the possibility of ending up willing the occurrence's eternal recurrence, which proves to no longer be an individual's will, subjective, but an epochal, objective one, an event, if not the event. Christine Tohme, the founding director of Ashkal Alwan, the Lebanese Association for Plastic Arts, and an occasional curator, happened to ask me shortly after I'd watched Khaddaj's piece whether I had seen any outstanding artworks recently; I answered that I had: Samir Khaddaj's *Self-Portrait with the Clarinet and the Two Silent Witnesses*—I was pleased that she invited him around two years later to participate in the Sharjah Biennial 13.

Lynn Marie Kirby
March 30, 2013, 6:27 PM
Dear Jalal,
I am finally sending you a note. My lecture got postponed a few weeks as the sound system was messed up in the new Wattis gallery building, so they had to reschedule! It went very well. I showed your wonderful video as part of my lecture on time. People were very moved by it, and I so appreciate your letting me include your work in the talk about artists working with time in digital forms. Thank you. I hope we can get to see one another again one of these days soon. I am delighted that we have been in conversation all these years even over great distances. Your ideas and work are always inspirational to me.

I am working on a piece with Etel [Adnan] now. I took her book *Paris, When It's Naked* and read all the sentences that had Paris in them into a speech-to-text software program and then sent it all back to Etel to reinsert new text into her newly translated text. I keep coming back to working in the gaps and spaces between systems of seeing, communicating through the technology we use.

Hope you are well.
All the best,
Lynn

November 16, 2021, 5:11 PM
Dear Jalal,
I was thinking about you, as someone asked me recently how I met Etel, and I remember it was at a presentation of yours in San Francisco so many years ago. We have lost our dear friend, always a bright light. Etel was full of love and generosity, and she supported us both.

Sending love,
Lynn
Lynn Marie Kirby
Professor of Fine Arts and Film
California College of the Arts

Jalal Toufic
November 16, 2021, 9:29 PM
Dear Lynn:
One of the drawbacks of fame is that it obscures that it is the deservedly famous who require our support, we who are not famous—beyond the one we provide generally through our books and artworks.
Your friend,
Jalal

Lynn Marie Kirby
November 17, 2021, 9:43 PM
Indeed!
xo L

Several of the concepts I have introduced and elaborated in my various books continue to be forthcoming. Were they to cease to be forthcoming, would they become well known? Rainer Maria Rilke wrote in his book *Auguste Rodin* (1902): "Fame is no more than the sum of all the misunderstandings that gather around a new name."[767] Is it then the case that to become famous a writer or filmmaker has to write or make films in such a way as to lend his work to misunderstanding? Someone who tells the readers of his books and the audience of his lectures that his concepts apply in rare cases, that they should use them only as a last resort, only when forced to do so by the "facts," whether physical in material reality or aesthetic in artworks and works of fiction that don't fall apart "two days" later; that, for example, they should assume initially that the closure they are investigating is not a radical one, however tight it seems, but a relative one, that the disaster is not a surpassing one, however extensive it is, that it is not the case that the object of tradition withdrew but rather, as commonly expected, that the one who underwent the disaster can no longer subjectively invest in it, cathect it, etc., since the worst that one can do to a rigorous concept is to try to apply it outside of its regime of validity (a manner of misunderstanding it), is certainly making it more difficult for his concepts to become widely known and, consequently, for himself to become famous.

1.   Both books had to deal with a deadline that is not imposed extrinsically but derives from the work itself; such a deadline is one more factor contributing to the ever-widening solitude of many a writer.

2.   "*Slug*: Section of clear film cut into a negative to correct synchronization problems, or to replace missing picture frames. May also refer to *black leader/spacing*" (International Federation of Film Archives, "Glossary of Technical Terms [Full List]," https://www.fiafnet.org/pages/E-Resources/Technical-Terms-Full-List.html).

3.   Chiye Aoki and Philip Siekevitz, "Plasticity in Brain Development," *Scientific American*, December 1988, 59.

4.   Nietzsche's Zarathustra: "'See this moment! ... Behind us lies an eternity.... Must not whatever *can* happen already have happened, been done, passed by before? And if everything has already been here before, what do you think of this moment ...? ... This slow spider that creeps in the moonlight, and this moonlight itself, and I and you in the gateway whispering together, whispering of eternal things—must not all of us have been here before?" (Friedrich Nietzsche, *Thus Spoke Zarathustra: A Book for All and None*, ed. Adrian Del Caro and Robert B. Pippin, trans. Adrian Del Caro [Cambridge: Cambridge University Press, 2006], 126).

5.   —when not taking into consideration the possibility of renewed creation by the one Being that has a necessity of existence, God. If our world is one that is repeatedly created anew, then it is not only those happenings that, having been experienced countless times by someone who ended up willing their eternal recurrence, recur eternally that are events, but everything is an event: "God's perpetual self-disclosures ... mean that creation is renewed at each instant. Hence, no one with any understanding of the nature of the things can suffer boredom (*malal*), whether in this world or the next: '... no one in the cosmos becomes bored except him who has no unveiling and does not witness the renewal of creation constantly at each instant and does not witness God as Ever-creating perpetually'" (William C. Chittick, *The Sufi Path of Knowledge: Ibn al-'Arabi's Metaphysics of Imagination* [Albany, NY: State University of New York Press, 1989], 105).

6.   If we subscribe to Schopenhaeur's view, are we going to have two sorts of will: the will as the groundless thing-in-itself, which is not subject to time (and space) and causality; and then the will resulting from the experience of countless recurrence, which is going to force

the first to objectify itself solely in the form of what is willed to eternally recur?

7. Insofar as he confronted his own kind of "Wall," I consider the narrator of *Notes from the Underground*, and the book's author, Dostoyevsky, to be kindred spirits: "With people who know how to revenge themselves and to stand up for themselves in general, how is it done? Why, when they are possessed, let us suppose, by the feeling of revenge, then for the time there is nothing else but that feeling left in their whole being. Such a gentleman simply dashes straight for his object like an infuriated bull with its horns down, and nothing but a wall will stop him.... Confronted with the impossible they subside at once. The impossible means the stone wall! What stone wall? Why, of course, the laws of nature, the deductions of natural science, mathematics.... As though such a stone wall really were a consolation, and really did contain some word of conciliation, simply because it is as true as twice two makes four. Oh, absurdity of absurdities! How much better it is to understand it all, to recognise it all, all the impossibilities and the stone wall; [yet] not to be reconciled to one of those impossibilities and stone walls if it disgusts you to be reconciled to it" (Fyodor Dostoyevsky, *Notes from Underground*, trans. Constance Garnett, in *Complete Works of Fyodor Dostoyevsky* [East Sussex, UK: Delphi Classics, 2014], 2060, 2063-2064, Kindle).

8. George Berkeley, *"Principles of Human Knowledge" and "Three Dialogues,"* ed. Howard Robinson (Oxford: Oxford University Press, 1996), 26.

9. Benoit B. Mandelbrot, *The Fractal Geometry of Nature*, updated and augmented ed. (New York: W. H. Freeman, 1983), 282.

10. This letter was first published in the special *Discourse* issue "Gilles Deleuze: A Reason to Believe in this World," ed. Réda Bensmaïa and Jalal Toufic, vol. 20, no. 3, Fall 1998.

11. "The Time-Being" (*Uji*), in *Moon in a Dewdrop: Writings of Zen Master Dōgen*, ed. Kazuaki Tanahashi, trans. Robert Aitken et al. (San Francisco: North Point Press, 1985), 76-77.

12. Gertrude Stein, *Picasso: The Complete Writings*, ed. Edward Burns (Boston: Beacon Press, 1970), 62. Lyotard is critical of the notion of creation as applied to art. Such a dismissal is too general and thus abstract. Reception from the other side of the *event horizon* that forms around a trauma, or from the other side of the threshold of death, does not always prove impossible. This successful reception could only have happened by a creation this side of these thresholds:

the voice-over-witness, etc. Moreover, whenever an artist (Francis Bacon), writer (Alain Robbe-Grillet), or filmmaker (David Lynch) produces a structure of radical closure, some or all of the entities that appear in it are possibly ahistorical entities that irrupted ex nihilo: creations. These can be attributed to the writer, artist, or filmmaker not in the sense that they were intentionally and directly created by him or her but in the sense that he or she set the structure that made their appearance out of nothing possible.

13.   Gustav Janouch, *Conversations with Kafka,* trans. Goronwy Rees (London: Andre Deutsch, 1971), 143.

14.   *The Anxiety of Influence* is the title of an influential book by Harold Bloom published by Oxford University Press in 1973.

15.   If it is infelicitous to ask an artist or a writer about his or her work, and if writers' and artists' answers to such questions are never fully satisfactory, it is partly that these works are the result of untimely collaborations with one or more others unknown to the artist or writer, in whose place he or she is ill-equipped to speak.

16.   Marguerite Duras, *The North China Lover,* trans. Leigh Hafrey (New York: New Press, 1992), 6.

17.   "Type 2 vacuum fluctuations are off shell, and are sometimes called vacuum diagrams or vacuum bubbles, a class of disconnected Feynman diagrams for which virtual particles appear from and then vanish back into the vacuum. Virtual particles are off shell, appear in the interior of Feynman diagrams, occur in perturbation calculations, but are not detected as normal (real, ordinary, and observable) particles. Because type 2 vacuum fluctuations are disconnected Feynman graphs, they cannot contribute to cross sections, decay rates, the permittivity of the vacuum, the speed of light in the vacuum, or the fine-structure constant but do contribute to vacuum energy" (G. B. Mainland and Bernard Mulligan, "Electromagnetic Properties of the Quantum Vacuum Calculated from Its Structure," *Journal of Physics: Conference Series* 2482 012012 [2023]: 4, https://iopscience.iop.org/article/10.1088/1742-6596/2482/1/012012/pdf).

18.   "The Time-Being" (*Uji*), in *Moon in a Dewdrop,* 76–77.

19.   "The sugar in my glass of water: why must I wait for it to melt? … What is it that obliges me to wait, and to wait for a certain length of psychical duration which is forced upon me, over which I have no power? Why does the universe unfold its successive states with a velocity which, in regard to my consciousness, is a veritable absolute?

Why with this particular velocity rather than any other? Why not with an infinite velocity? Why, in other words, is not everything given at once ...? ... It seems to me that, if the future is bound to succeed the present instead of being given alongside of it, it is because the future is not altogether determined at the present moment, and that if the time taken up by this succession ... has for the consciousness that is installed in it absolute value and reality, it is because there is unceasingly being created in it, not indeed in any such artificially isolated system as a glass of sugared water, but in the concrete whole of which every such system forms part, something unforeseeable and new.... The duration of the universe must therefore be one with the latitude of creation which can find place in it" (Henri Bergson, *Creative Evolution*, trans. Arthur Mitchell [New York: Henry Holt and Company, 1911], 339–40). This note was added in June 2022, when the few lines in Deleuze's book *Cinema 1: The Movement-Image* on Bergson's example of the wait for sugar to melt in water to elaborate his concept of duration, which were the reason I had mentioned the process in my text, at long last led me to read the relevant sections in Bergson's book.

20.　"Conversion: the transformation of an unconscious mental conflict into a symbolically equivalent bodily symptom" (*Merriam-Webster Dictionary*, https://www.merriam-webster.com/dictionary/conversion).

21.　Regarding a woman with out-of-sync silence, see my book *The Dancer's Two Bodies* (Sharjah, UAE: Sharjah Art Foundation, 2015), 1: "She, a dancer, is attuned to my in-sync silence: the concordance between the motionlessness of my lips and the absence of an interior monologue in my head; I, an aphoristic writer, find her occasional out-of-sync silence in the altered realm into which dance projects her, as her lips continue briefly to move before the falling silence-over freezes her, arresting."

22.　Borges certainly managed a number of times to say in "ten" sentences what everyone does *not* say in a book, since these ten sentences refer to a book that was not actually written: "It is a laborious madness and an impoverishing one, the madness of composing vast books—setting out in five hundred pages an idea that can be perfectly related orally in five minutes. The better way to go about it is to pretend that those books already exist, and offer a summary, a commentary on them. That was Carlyle's procedure in *Sartor Resartus*, Butler's in *The Fair Haven*—though those works suffer under the imperfection that they themselves are books.... A more reasonable, more inept, and more lazy man, I have chosen to write notes on imaginary books. These notes are 'Tlön, Uqbar, Orbis Tertius' and 'A

Survey of the Works of Herbert Quain'" (Jorge Luis Borges, *Collected Fictions*, trans. Andrew Hurley [New York: Viking, 1998], 67).

23.   From Nietzsche's letter of January 5, 1889, to Jacob Burckhardt, in *Selected Letters of Friedrich Nietzsche*, ed. and trans. Christopher Middleton (Indianapolis, IN: Hackett, 1996), 347.

24.   "What then is madness, in its most general but most concrete form ...? In all probability, nothing other than *the absence of an oeuvre....* The great *oeuvre* of the history of the world is indelibly accompanied by the absence of an *oeuvre*, which renews itself at every instant.... The plenitude of history is only possible in the space ... of all the words without language that appear to anyone who lends an ear, as ... the obstinate murmur of a language talking *to itself* ... wrapped up in itself, ... collapsing before it ever reaches any formulation" (Michel Foucault, *History of Madness*, ed. Jean Khalfa, trans. Jonathan Murphy and Jean Khalfa (London: Routledge, 2010), xxxi–xxxii.

25.   Emil Cioran, "Je suis un auteur à fragments," interview by Laurence Tâcu (August 10, 1987), in *Les Cahiers de L'Herne: Emil Cioran*, ed. Laurence Tâcu and Vincent Piednoir, selection of texts by Yves-Jean Harder (Paris: Flammarion, 2015).

26.   E. M. Cioran, *Drawn and Quartered*, trans. Richard Howard (New York: Seaver Books, 1983), 79.

27.   "Darkroom: a room with no light or with a safelight for developing light-sensitive photographic materials" (*Merriam-Webster Dictionary*, https://www.merriam-webster.com/dictionary/darkroom).

28.   "Changing bag: a lighttight bag with sleeves to fit the arms in which procedures such as loading film holders may be carried out without a darkroom" (*Merriam-Webster Dictionary*, https://www. merriam-webster.com/dictionary/changing%20bag).

29.   Sergei Eisenstein, *Film Form: Essays in Film Theory*, ed. and trans. Jay Leyda (New York: Harcourt Brace Jovanovich, 1977), 42. This acting without transitions is actually better viewed within the context of Dōgen's Zen rather than that of dialectical montage: "It is a mistake to suppose that birth turns into death. Birth is a phase that is an entire period of itself, with its own past and future.... Death is a phase that is an entire period of itself, with its own past and future.... In birth there is nothing but birth and in death there is nothing but death" ("Birth and Death" [*Shōji*]).

30. *The Complete Works of Aristotle: The Revised Oxford Translation*, ed. Jonathan Barnes (Princeton: Princeton University Press, 1984), 824.

31. Arthur Schopenhauer, *The World as Will and Representation*, vol. 1, trans. E. F. J. Payne (New York: Dover, 1966), 257.

32. al-Mas'ūdī, *Ithbāt al-waṣiyyah li'l-imām 'Alī b. Abī Ṭālib*, 4th ed. (Najaf: Ḥaydariyyah Press, 1374/1954), 162, quoted in Mahmoud Ayoub, *Redemptive Suffering in Islām: A Study of the Devotional Aspects of 'Āshūrā' in Twelver Shī'ism* (The Hague: Mouton, 1978), 91.

33. Atatürk's abolition of both the sultanate and the caliphate, and of Sufi brotherhoods; his closures of the Khanicas; his enacting a switch from Arabic script to Latin; and his prohibition of the wearing of the fez could successfully take place not only because of the decathexis from "traditional" culture after a momentous defeat or a wish to emulate the modern victorious West but also because of the withdrawal of Ottoman tradition.

34. Quoted in Donald Phillip Verene, *Hegel's Recollection* (Albany: SUNY Press, 1985), 7–8.

35. Nietzsche, *Thus Spoke Zarathustra: A Book for All and None*, 263.

36. Richard Feynman, *The Character of Physical Law* (Cambridge, MA: MIT Press, 1967), 23–24.

37. "A Renegade's Vision: An Evening of Stan Brakhage Films," Walker Art Center, https://walkerart.org/calendar/2012/renegades-vision-evening-stan-brakhage-films.

38. Amy Calvert, "Ancient Egyptian Art," https://www.khanacademy.org/humanities/ap-art-history/ancient-mediterranean-ap/ancient-egypt-ap/a/egyptian-art.

39. Pierre Reverdy, "The Image" (1918), trans. Adrian Martin, *Sabzian*, September 19, 2018.

40. "Ein Nachtbuch, von dem keine Zeile je bei Tag geschrieben wurde. Parallel dazu ein wirkliches Tagebuch, immer bei Tag geschrieben. Die beiden einige Jahre auseinanderhalten, sie nie vergleichen und nie durcheinanderbringen. Ihre schließliche Konfrontation" (Elias Canetti, *Alle vergeudete Verehrung: Aufzeichnungen 1949–1960* [Munich: C. Hanser, 1970], 39).

41.   Hakuin Zenji, *Poison Blossoms from a Thicket of Thorn*, trans. Norman Waddell (Berkeley: Counterpoint, 2014), 478: "When a new monk comes to my temple, I ask, 'Do you hear the sound of one hand?'"; translator's note: "Sound of One Hand koan (*sekishu no onjō*): A two-part koan Hakuin devised in his mid-sixties for beginning students: first, Hear the sound of one hand clapping; then, Put a stop to all sounds" (485).

42.   Martin Heidegger, *Being and Time*, trans. John Macquarrie and Edward Robinson (Oxford: Blackwell, 1962), 297.

43.   See endnote 38 in this volume.

44.   This interview was published in *Rain Taxi Review of Books*, online edition, Fall 2001, https://raintaxi.com/an-interview-with-jalal-toufic/.

45.   Friedrich Nietzsche, *Nachlass* 1886/87, notebook 7, page 62, in *Sämtliche Werke: Kritische Studienausgabe*, vol. 12, ed. Giorgio Colli and Mazzino Montinari (Berlin: Walter de Gruyter, 1977), 317.

46.   *The Seminar of Jacques Lacan*, Book VII, *The Ethics of Psychoanalysis, 1959–1960*, ed. Jacques-Alain Miller, trans. Dennis Porter (New York: Norton, 1988), 131.

47. Acknowledgments
My conceptual poster for Robert Bresson's *Au hazard Balthazar* was exhibited in the window panel at the entrance of Cinema Hamra, one of the three abandoned cinemas that were the setting for Ashkal Alwan's "Hamra Street Project," November 17-27, 2000; and it was published in *Al-Ādāb* (January and February 2001): 51. My conceptual poster for Harold Ramis's film *Groundhog Day* appeared in *Transit Visa: On Video and Cities*, ed. Akram Zaatari and Mahmoud Hojeij (Beirut, 2001), 8. *Two Posthumous Resumes* was exhibited in the show *Exist*, Espace SD, Beirut, November 25-December 2, 2000. An Arabic translation (by Fadi El Abdallah) of the section "Ruins" was published as *"Al-Aṭlāl"* in *Al-Ādāb*'s Audio-Visual/Theoretical Supplement (July-August 2001): 108-11. "Ruins" as well as *Two Posthumous Resumes* were published in *Tamáss: Contemporary Arab Representations, Beirut, Lebanon* 1 (Barcelona: Fundació Antoni Tàpies, 2002), 19-25 and 118-21, respectively. An Arabic translation (by Fadi El Abdallah) of the section "I Am the Martyr Sana'a Youcef Mehaidli" was published as *"Anā as-shahīda Sanā' Yūsif Muḥaydlī"* in *Al-Ādāb* (January-February 2001): 44-51.

I would like to thank the Arab Image Foundation (AIF) for permission to use a number of photographs from their collection.

48. See page 45 of this volume.

49. *Life*, February 1989, 62.

50. A middle ground had to be reached between delaying publishing *(Vampires)* to give more chance for *Distracted* to be read, reviewed, and acknowledged so that the preternatural influence of the former on the latter should not be obscured, and minimizing the temptation such a delay would provide to continue editing the book until it would be addressed solely to those who are alive and in normal states.

51. Murnau's handling of the theme of the warning in *Nosferatu* is disappointing since in that film the worst that can happen to Harker is that he would die physically (he does not die in the film), for those who are bitten by the vampire do not become undead in Murnau's film (the analogy the professor makes between the carnivorous plants he shows to his students and vampires stresses the circumstance that the vampire sucks the blood of his prey rather than the fact that he is undead).

52. "180-degree rule: A method of staging and filming action in order to ensure visual continuity from one shot to another. On set, as a scene is rehearsed and blocked for shooting a continuity line— often referred to as the ... imaginary line ... —is decided upon and the camera will then remain on one side of that line; that is, within a 180-degree arc. The effect of this rule is that a character standing on the left and looking towards a character on the right will always be standing left and looking right no matter where the camera frames them from within the 180 degrees of the semi-circular arc. If, however, the line is crossed then the character will appear to reverse their position in the frame" (Annette Kuhn and Guy Westwell, *A Dictionary of Film Studies* [Oxford: Oxford University Press, 2012], 299).

53. In some vampire films, stairs serve to lessen the floating movement of the vampire and of the somnambulist; in others, they function as trance-deepeners: "As you descend the heavily carpeted stairs, you are going deeper and deeper into trance" (Somnambulist Descending a Staircase).

54. "Caution *n.* 4. A cautious action; a precaution" (*American Heritage Dictionary*).

55. Nothing in the *opening scenes* of vampire films indicates whether it is the vampire rather than his visitor who makes the door open without touching it (Murnau's and Herzog's *Nosferatus*, Coppola's *Dracula*, etc.). Moreover, in some films it is the future victim of the vampire who is the first to drink blood: in Browning's *Dracula*, Harker accidentally cuts his finger and proceeds to lick his blood. In other words, the visitor is already invested with the powers and weaknesses of the vampire even before he is bitten by and loses blood to the latter, indeed in many cases even before he meets him. In which case a *false threshold* to the death realm was crossed by the visitor prior to his first encounter with the vampire, and the vampire's sucking of the blood of the victim is merely the apparent trigger of the latter's transformation.

56. Larry Weiskrantz, "Neuropsychology and the Nature of Consciousness," in *Mindwaves*, ed. Colin Blakemore and Susan Greenfield (Oxford: Basil Blackwell, 1987), 313-14.

57. "Critical point: in physics, the set of conditions under which a liquid and its vapour become identical. For each substance, the conditions defining the critical point are the critical temperature, the critical pressure, and the critical density. This is best understood by observing a simple experiment. If a closed vessel is filled with a pure substance, partly liquid and partly vapour, so that the average density

equals the critical density, the critical conditions can be achieved. As the temperature is raised, the vapour pressure increases, and the gas phase becomes denser. The liquid expands and becomes less dense until, at the critical point, the densities of liquid and vapour become equal, eliminating the boundary between the two phases. If the average density at the start is too low, all the liquid will evaporate before the critical temperature is reached. If the initial average density is too high, the liquid will expand to fill the container" (*Britannica*, https://www.britannica.com/science/critical-point-phase-change).

58.   Mircea Eliade, *Yoga: Immortality and Freedom*, 2nd ed., trans. Willard R. Trask (Princeton: Princeton University Press, 1969), 56.

59.   "Freeze-avoidant insects cannot tolerate internal ice formation, so they avoid freezing by depressing the temperature at which their body fluids freeze. This is done through supercooling, the process by which a liquid cools below its freezing point without changing phase into a solid. In order for water to freeze, a nucleus must be present upon which an ice crystal can begin to grow. If no source of nucleation is introduced, water can cool down to −48 °C without freezing" (Wikipedia, "Insect Winter Ecology," https://en.wikipedia.org/wiki/Insect_winter_ecology).

60.   *Super-* and *under-* forms of avoiding a change of "phase," of maintaining a state beyond a crucial threshold, should not be mistaken for *after-* phenomena such as *afterimage, aftertaste.*

61.   Bram Stoker, *Dracula* (New York: Bantam Books, 1981), 11.

62.   Once more, the vampire asked his hypnotized victim: "Where are you now?"

63.   In the latter case, the victim will probably have the illusion that he underwent a lapse of consciousness, missed something, and hence that it could have been otherwise—but how can one miss what takes no time (the vampire, like a subatomic particle, has no trajectory, if we consider that he tunnels through space—or every possible one ["The path integral formulation is a description in quantum mechanics that ... replaces the classical notion of a single, unique classical trajectory for a system with a sum, or functional integral, over an infinity of quantum-mechanically possible trajectories to compute a quantum amplitude" (Wikipedia, "Path Integral Formulation," https://en.wikipedia.org/wiki/Path_integral_formulation)])?

64.   J. Sheridan Le Fanu, *In a Glass Darkly* (London: Eveleigh Nash and Grayson, n.d.), 412.

65. Ibid.

66. Maybe in years to come people will think that teleportation was invented to make transportation possible in a world plagued by frequent blockings of walking or running: the cause viewed as the remedy.

67. To check that the induction has succeeded, the hypnotist may challenge the subject to raise his arm from his lap or to separate his two hands.

68. Virginia Woolf, *The Waves* (San Diego: Harcourt Brace Jovanovich, 1931), 64.

69. Jean-Paul Sartre, *Nausea*, trans. Lloyd Alexander (New York: New Directions, 1964), 10. Later, Sartre will write in *Being and Nothingness*: "We hope simply to have shown that the will is not a preeminent manifestation of freedom but a psychological event with a distinctive structure, constituted at the same level as the others, and which is, no more or less than the others, supported by an original and ontological freedom.... Freedom and the for-itself's being are just one and the same" (Jean-Paul Sartre, *Being and Nothingness: An Essay in Phenomenological Ontology*, trans. Sarah Richmond [New York: Washington Square Press/Atria Books, 2021], 593-94, Kindle). A genuine search for freedom is always triggered by an encounter (even if it is a thought experiment) that ostensibly reveals to one how unfree one is. Freedom fighters: by risking his life during the primordial duel to the death for recognition, the Hegelian master shows his freedom from natural, animal life; but the freedom of the other master, the guru, is from both life and death (a matter of life *and* death precisely in that it is not just a matter of life and *its* absence), thus attaining an unconditioned mode of being.

70. He got rid of the clean garbage strewn around in an ordered way that they call chairs, tables, closets. You see nothing in his apartment but the white walls and a few laconic books. But there remained, since he was a Stanislavsky actor, the imaginary object that he could evoke as if it were real and rehearse with it. So then he got rid of his acting.

71. Constantin Stanislavski, *An Actor Prepares*, trans. Elizabeth Reynolds Hapgood, ed. Hermine I. Popper (New York: Theater Arts, 1948), 26-27.

72. In Robert Wiene's *The Cabinet of Dr. Caligari* (1920) the light and shadow patterns are painted. Is the undead to deduce from this impossibility of moving objects that he or she is looking at the past?

73.   Bram Stoker, *Dracula*, revised edition (London: Penguin, 2007), 88.

74.   Caro W. Lippman, "Hallucinations of Physical Duality in Migraine," *Journal of Nervous and Mental Disease* 117 (1953): 347. The same applies in the case of Rhoda in Virginia Woolf's *The Waves*: "I have to bang my hand against some hard door to call myself back to the body" (44).

75.   André Bazin, "Renoir français," *Cahiers du cinéma* 8 (January 1952): 29.

76.   In Herzog's *Nosferatu* and in Coppola's *Bram Stoker's Dracula*, Harker's hypnosis at the entrance to the castle is implied by the door that opens on its own (self-motion of objects is a phenomenon encountered in hypnosis, e.g., the hand of the entranced subject that levitates outside his control following the lead of the hypnotist). The vampire seldom entrances his guest by staring him in the eye; he does so rather by not appearing in the mirror or by the self-motion of objects (door, ship, etc.) that his freezing allows. That the door opens on its own for Harker in Coppola's film indicates that he is either already hypnotized or in the process of becoming hypnotized: the passivity of the guest of the vampire as the door, which has become self-moving through the freezing of the vampire, opens or closes on its own before or behind him does not remain at the level of action but becomes extended to the complementary level of intention and will: he or she becomes entranced.

77.   For additional examples, see Dante's *Inferno*. In Canto I we read: "I cannot clearly say how I had entered / the wood; I was so full of sleep just at / the point where I abandoned the true path" (Dante Alighieri, *Inferno*, Canto I: 10-12, trans. Allen Mandelbaum). The transition between Canto III and Canto IV, and therefore between the Ante-Inferno and the First Circle, or Limbo, happens in a similar manner. Canto III ends with, "A whirlwind burst out of the tear-drenched earth, / a wind that crackled with a bloodred light, / a light that overcame all of my senses; / and like a man whom sleep has seized, I fell," and Canto IV begins with, "The heavy sleep within my head was smashed / by an enormous thunderclap, so that / I started up as one whom force awakens; / I stood erect and turned my rested eyes / from side to side, and I stared steadily / to learn what place it was surrounding me." Similarly, Canto V ends with, "And while one spirit said these words to me, / the other wept, so that—because of pity— / I fainted, as if I had met my death. / And then I fell as a dead body falls," and Canto VI begins with, "Upon my mind's reviving—it had closed / on hearing the lament of those

two kindred, / since sorrow had confounded me completely— / I see new sufferings, new sufferers."

78. Probably this is what initially drew me, an aphoristic writer, to death: it is the exemplary realm of the absence of introductions.

79. Exceptions: primitive cinema, Hitchcock's *Rope* (1948), many of Warhol's films ...

80. Walter Benjamin, *Illuminations*, ed. Hannah Arendt, trans. Harry Zohn (New York: Schocken Books, 1969), 238.

81. Clement Greenberg: "It quickly emerged that the unique and proper area of competence of each art coincided with all that was unique to the nature of its medium. The task of self-criticism became to eliminate from the effects of each art any and every effect that might conceivably be borrowed from or by the medium of any other art.... It was the stressing ... of the ineluctable flatness of the support that remained most fundamental in the processes by which pictorial art criticized and defined itself under Modernism. Flatness alone was unique and exclusive to that art" ("Modernist Painting," in *Modern Art and Modernism: A Critical Anthology*, ed. Francis Frascina and Charles Harrison [New York: Harper and Row, 1982], 1, 6). One could give as examples Jasper Johns's painted targets and flags.

82. Marguerite Duras, *Le Camion* (Paris: Les Éditions de Minuit, 1977), 96: "On prend le spectateur pour un enfant. Le spectacle cinématographique est un spectacle infantile.... Quand on voit à la télévision les vieux films, par exemple, le spectateur est traité comme un enfant arriéré, comme s'il était taré, qu'il faille tout faire à sa place" and "avant, quand on montrait un homme qui sort de chez lui et qui arrive par exemple dans un bar, on montrait d'abord l'homme qui sortait de chez lui, puis son trajet, puis l'homme qui arrivait dans le bar. Godard a inventé ça : l'homme sort, puis on le retrouve dans le bar."

83. Alain Robbe-Grillet, *For a New Novel: Essays on Fiction*, trans. Richard Howard (Evanston, IL: Northwestern University Press, 1989), 152–53.

84. Ibid., 152.

85. Roger Crittenden, *Film and Video Editing*, 2nd ed. (London: Routledge, 1996), 168.

86. *Oxford Dictionary of English*, 3rd ed.

87. "Unsettled, unpaid, or unresolved" (*Collins English Dictionary*, 14th ed.).

88. "Prominent, remarkable, or *striking*" (Ibid.; my italics).

89. Stoker, *Dracula*, revised edition, 7.

90. Matthew Edlund, *Psychological Time and Mental Illness* (New York: Gardner Press, 1987), 81.

91. Margiad Evans [pseud.], *A Ray of Darkness* (New York: Roy, 1953).

92. André Bazin, *What Is Cinema?*, vol. 1, trans. Hugh Gray (Berkeley: University of California Press, 1967), 97.

93. Ibid., 50–52.

94. Schizophrenia being an altered state of the mind, a far-from-equilibrium state of consciousness, it is not surprising that the schizophrenic sometimes feels that a small change, for example, whether or not he falls asleep before a specific hour, say, or whether or not he goes through a door, will radically alter the state of the universe—a phenomenon similar to the *butterfly effect* encountered in the case of the weather, a deterministic nonlinear system.

95. Philippe Ariès, *Western Attitudes Toward Death: From the Middle Ages to the Present*, trans. Patricia M. Ranum (Baltimore: Johns Hopkins University Press, 1975), 34–37.

96. Lewis Carroll, *"Alice's Adventures in Wonderland" & "Through the Looking-Glass"* (New York: Nal Penguin, 1960), 16.

97. Ibid., 26. Was one replaced by the double during the lapse of consciousness, if not of being, that precedes the psychedelic state? Was this why one's friends did not recognize one then? Or was it that one merely hallucinated that they didn't? Yoga makes it possible for the yogi to go through phase transitions, for example between wakefulness and dreaming or life and death, without the lapses of consciousness and being, respectively, that occur then and that permit possession or replacement by the double.

98. Sigmund Freud, *The Interpretation of Dreams*, trans. and ed. James Strachey (New York: Basic Books, 2010), 215.

99. In Dostoyevsky's *The Double*, had even one person at the office commented on the newcomer's remarkable physical similarity to

Golyadkin, the newcomer would no longer be Golyadkin's double but simply a fluke of nature.

100. If one intends to generalize the theme of vampires from the strictly literal (the vampire as an undead who sucks the blood of the living) to the economic and political (Marx: "Capital is dead labour, that, vampire-like, only lives by sucking living labour, and lives the more, the more labour it sucks" [*Capital*, vol. 1]), one has beforehand to take into consideration the way the death realm literalizes the metaphoric.

101. Regarding the portrayal of prophets and messengers in artistic works, one reads the following on the website of Al-Azhar: "The Islamic Research Academy discussed this issue in March 1972 and unanimously agreed to prohibit the portrayal of the prophets and messengers (peace be upon them). This view is also supported by the Egyptian Dar al-Ifta, and by various esteemed scholarly bodies such as the International Islamic Fiqh Academy of the Organization of Islamic Cooperation, the Council of Senior Scholars in Saudi Arabia, and the Islamic Fiqh Council in Mecca, part of the Muslim World League" ("Portrayal of Prophets and Messengers in Artistic Works," January 4, 2016, https://www.azhar.eg/observer/replies/ArtMID/5814/ArticleID/138/تجسيد-الأنبياء-والرسل-في-الأعمال-الفنية). Moreover, the Fatwa Department of the Hashemite Kingdom of Jordan specifies that "it is religiously forbidden to depict images of the prophets and the family of the Prophet (peace and blessings be upon him)—including Hasan and Husayn—and his wives and the Rightly Guided Caliphs [that is, the first four caliphs], and to portray their characters in cinematic and television films. It is also not appropriate to portray the characters of the rest of the Companions [of Prophet Muhammad (al-Ṣaḥāba)], may God be pleased with them" (https://www.aliftaa.jo/fatwa/1891/لا-يجوز-تمثيل-شخصيات-الأنبياء-والخلفاء-الراشدين-وأمهات-المؤم).

102. Gilles Deleuze, *Cinema 1: The Movement-Image*, trans. Hugh Tomlinson and Barbara Habberjam (Minneapolis: University of Minnesota Press, 1986), 99–100.

103. There is no jealousy in the indistinguishability of faces: the shot in *Persona* where Elisabet faces the camera while *behind her back* her double Alma and Elisabet's husband have a conversation and kiss seems to be a bad forgery of Munch's painting *Jealousy*, where the jealous person looks at some supposed passerby (and us, the spectators?), as it were for information about what the woman and the man are doing *behind his back*.

104. See the section "The Emperor's New Costume; or, The Case of the Missing Mask," pages 151–57 in this volume.

105. "Surrealist artists played a collaborative, chance-based parlor game, typically involving four players, called *Cadavre Exquis* (Exquisite Corpse). Each participant would draw an image (or, on some occasions, paste an image down) on a sheet of paper, fold the paper to conceal their contribution, and pass it on to the next player for his contribution. Taking turns adding onto each other's drawings and collages resulted in fantastic composite figures, such as *Nude* by Yves Tanguy, Joan Miró, Max Morise, and Man Ray.... For the Surrealists, Exquisite Corpse was a perfect parlor game, involving elements of unpredictability, chance, unseen elements, and group collaboration—all in service of disrupting the waking mind's penchant for order" (MoMA, https://www.moma.org/collection/works/35701?sov_referrer=art_term&art_term_slug=exquisite-corpse). "It was invented in 1925 in Paris by the surrealists Yves Tanguy, Jacques Prévert, André Breton and Marcel Duchamp. The name 'cadavre exquis' was derived from a phrase that resulted when they first played the game, '*le cadavre exquis boira le vin nouveau*' (the exquisite corpse will drink the new wine)" (Tate, https://www.tate.org.uk/art/art-terms/c/cadavre-exquis-exquisite-corpse).

106. Le Fanu, *In a Glass Darkly*, 412.

107. For an interpretation of such a scene/procedure in terms of fetishism, see Roger Dadoun's "Fetishism in the Horror Film," in *Fantasy and the Cinema*, ed. James Donald (London: British Film Institute, 1989).

108. These kinds of simultaneity are also encountered in the affined realm of dance: next to a number of dancers immobilized by the silence-over, a couple of dancers were moving to the accompaniment of the saving music-over. The freezing in the realm into which dance projects the dancer having allowed the self-motion of objects, the dancer was moving while not moving, since the floor on which he was standing motionless was gliding.

109. Art creates artistic facts. When in a film a dancer is convincingly shown penetrating a two-dimensional object such as a mirror or a book illustration, rather than assuming that the dancer has the same kind of body we normally have and concluding that such a feat is impossible and that therefore it must be either a character's fantasy or dream or a genre convention, one should ask what kind of body the dancer has acquired for such a feat to be possible.

110. Michel Serres, *Statues: Le second livre des fondations* (Paris: Éditions François Bourin, 1987), 114 (my translation).

111. *Britannica*, "St. Cecilia," https://www.britannica.com/biography/Saint-Cecilia.

112. *Britannica*, "St. Bernadette of Lourdes," https://www.britannica.com/biography/Saint-Bernadette-of-Lourdes.

113. Ariès, *Western Attitudes toward Death*, 47.

114. Jean Baudrillard, *Symbolic Exchange and Death*, trans. Iain Hamilton Grant (London: Sage, 1993), 126 (I myself would have put quotation marks around *inferior races*). See also Michel Foucault's *History of Madness* on the exclusion of the mad (at least until the introduction of antipsychotic medications and deinstitutionalization in the second half of the twentieth century): "It is not in venereal disease that the true heir of leprosy should be sought, but in a highly complex phenomenon that medicine would take far longer to appropriate. That phenomenon is madness. But only after a long latency period of almost two centuries did that new obsession take the place of the fear that leprosy had instilled in the masses, and elicit similar reactions of division, exclusion and purification, which are akin to madness itself" (8). It is not by living in a cemetery, the City of the Dead (also referred to as *al-Qarāfa*), as hundreds of thousands of Egyptians do in Cairo, that one will reach the dead's space, the labyrinth where one is homeless, indeed worldless, ending the dead's confinement.

115. "Cosmic censorship," *A Dictionary of Physics*, 6th ed. (Oxford University Press), https://www.oxfordreference.com/display/10.1093/oi/authority.20110803095641337.

116. Quoted in Andreas Mavromatis, *Hypnagogia: The Unique State of Consciousness Between Wakefulness and Sleep* (London: Routledge and Kegan Paul, 1987), 163.

117. These words are said by the vampire in Bram Stoker's *Dracula*.

118. How does the earth "feel" about its inability to digest the non-biodegradable, plastic and vampires?

119. "Matte shot: Any shot in which part of the scene is matted (or masked) out so that the photographed area can later be joined to another image to make a composite picture.... Green-screen or blue-screen filming is another example of a matte process: actors perform in front of a green or blue screen that is carefully lit with even

illumination. In digital post-production the green or blue screen is isolated from the other elements of the image and in its place another filmed, or CGI-produced, image is inserted, producing a composite shot. This electronic matting process is also known as chroma key" (Kuhn and Westwell, *A Dictionary of Film Studies*, 260).

120. *Herzog on Herzog*, ed. Paul Cronin (London: Faber and Faber, 2002), 128.

121. Ibid.

122. Alan Greenberg, *Heart of Glass* (Munich: Skellig, 1976), 21.

123. "The Palestine Question: A Brief History," prepared for, and under the guidance of the Committee on the Exercise of the Inalienable Rights of the Palestinian People, United Nations, 1980," https://www.un.org/unispal/document/auto-insert-206581/.

124. Edward Said, *The Question of Palestine*, 2nd ed. (New York: Vintage Books, 1992), 4-5.

125. *American Cinematographer* (July 1988): 48.

126. When, near the end of the film, Marnie and her husband return to her mother's house, it is raining. "With water on the backdrop, recalls [Robert] Boyle [the production designer], the ship as well as the painted bricks of the houses looked glossy. Robert Burks, the film's director of photography, agreed. So Boyle approached Hitchcock, almost pleading with him to reshoot the sequence.... Much to his surprise ... Hitchcock said, 'I don't see anything wrong with it, Bob. I think it looks fine' (Boyle interview)" (Robert E. Kapsis, *Hitchcock: The Making of a Reputation* [Chicago: University of Chicago Press, 1992], 129-30).

127. "Report of the Commissioner-General of the United Nations Relief and Works Agency for Palestine Refugees in the Near East, 1 July 1999-30 June 2000," https://www.un.org/unispal/document/auto-insert-183382.

128. Mark Vonnegut, *The Eden Express* (New York: Laurel, 1975), 94-95.

129. Sartre, *Nausea*, 127, 132-33.

130. The invisibility of these Dreyer characters is equivalent to the absence of reflection in the mirror in vampire films.

131. Sergei Eisenstein, *Film Essays, with a Lecture*, ed. and trans. Jay Leyda (London: Dennis Dobson, 1968), 150.

132. This is a more fundamental fall than the one that still admits of a ground at which to stop.

133. It is resonant that Walter Benjamin uses the image of bullets and ballistics to write about sudden changes in space, lighting, and the angle between shots, and that Eisenstein tries to create the effect of the impact of a bullet's hitting the eye by having a jump cut.

134. Markus Ploner, Joachim Gross, Lars Timmermann, and Alfons Schnitzler, "Pain Processing Is Faster than Tactile Processing in the Human Brain," *The Journal of Neuroscience* 26 (October 18, 2006): 10879, https://www.jneurosci.org/content/jneuro/26/42/10879.full.pdf.

135. Ibid.

136. "Nearby objects (many out of 'view' of the patient's body) could often be seen (cardiac monitor behind the patient's bed, etc.)" (Michael B. Sabom and Sarah S. Kreutziger, "Physicians Evaluate the Near-Death Experience," in *A Collection of Near-Death Research Readings*, comp. Craig R. Lundahl [Chicago: Nelson-Hall, 1982], 150).

137. *The Standard Edition of the Complete Psychological Works of Sigmund Freud*, vol. 18 (1920-1922), *"Beyond the Pleasure Principle," "Group Psychology," and Other Works*, translated from the German under the general editorship of James Strachey, in collaboration with Anna Freud, assisted by Alix Strachey and Alan Tyson (London: Hogarth Press and the Institute of Psycho-Analysis, 1955), 190.

138. Ernest Jones, *The Life and Work of Sigmund Freud*, vol. 3, *The Last Phase, 1919-1939* (New York: Basic Books, 1957), 385: "Some months later he [Ferenczi] sent Freud a number of notes he had made of occasions in which a homosexual masochistic patient of his had begun the analytical hour with a few words which reminded Ferenczi of thoughts he himself had had in the previous twenty-four hours.... Freud ... was deeply impressed by the data and said emphatically that they put an end to any possible remaining doubt about the reality of thought transference."

139. Similarly, owing to the identification of the camera with the character Michael Myers in the first scene of John Carpenter's *Halloween* (1978), the rest of the shots in the film, even those that follow his ostensible death, are haunted by him.

140. Robert G. Jahn and Brenda J. Dunne, "Consciousness, Quantum Mechanics, and Random Physical Processes," in *Bergson and Modern Thought: Towards a Unified Science*, ed. Andrew C. Papanicolaou and Pete A. Y. Gunter (Chu, Switzerland: Hardwood Academic Publishers, 1987), 295.

141. T. S. Eliot, *"The Waste Land" and Other Poems* (New York: Harcourt, Brace and World, 1934), 43.

142. "According to [U.S. Air Force Chief of Staff] Gen. [Merrill A.] McPeak, precision-guided bombs accounted for only 7,400 of the 84,200 tons of munitions dropped by the allies during Operation Desert Storm, or a mere 8.8 percent, some of which was used to attack hardened targets in the Kuwaiti military theater. The remaining 91.2 percent consisted of unguided weaponry—so-called 'dumb' bombs— with a reported estimated accuracy rate of only 25 percent" (*Needless Deaths in the Gulf War: Civilian Casualties During the Air Campaign and Violations of the Laws of War* (New York: Human Rights Watch, 1991), 5, https://www.hrw.org/reports/pdfs/u/us/us.910/us910full.pdf.

143. From Nietzsche's letter of January 5, 1889, to Jacob Burckhardt, in *Selected Letters of Friedrich Nietzsche*, 347.

144. Nor, as Saddam Hussein would like to believe, Nebuchadnezzar. Nor is Baghdad (illuminated by the fireworks of ineffective ground-air defense on the first day of the Gulf War), as in one shot in Herzog's otherwise sublime *Lessons of Darkness* (1991), Kuwait City (on the initial day of the Iraqi invasion). It is praiseworthy to consider flying to Mars or Saturn to find "images that are still pure and clean and transparent" (from an interview with Herzog in Wenders's *Tokyo Ga*); unfortunately, the danger then is that from such a distance one might easily mistake Baghdad for Kuwait City. Through dying before dying, Blair's Jacob Maker, more sober, visited many planets without making such mistakes.

145. Alan J. Parkin, "Residual Learning Capability in Organic Amnesia," *Cortex* 18, no. 3 (October 1982): 428.

146. See Jean-François Lyotard, *Heidegger and "the jews,"* trans. Andreas Michel and Mark S. Roberts (Minneapolis: University of Minnesota Press, 1990), 1 and, more generally, chapters 4-6; cf. Jean-François Lyotard, "Emma," in *Misère de la philosophie* (Paris: Éditions Galilée, 2000), 55-95; Jean Laplanche, *New Foundations for Psychoanalysis*, trans. David Macey (Oxford: Basil Blackwell, 1989); Jean Laplanche, *Essays on Otherness*, ed. John Fletcher (London: Routledge, 1999); Jean Laplanche, *Entre séduction et inspiration:*

l'homme (Paris: Quadrige/Presses Universitaires de France, 1999); and Jean Laplanche, *Le primat de l'autre en psychanalyse: travaux 1967-1992* (Paris: Flammarion, 1997).

147. Lyotard, *Heidegger and "the jews,"* 15.

148. Vonnegut, *The Eden Express*, 102.

149. Eisenstein, *Film Form: Essays in Film Theory*, 106.

150. No one who has seen without consternation an ancient Egyptian seated figure in a funerary papyrus, exemplarily Osiris, the god of the underworld, should be surprised at Magritte's seated coffins: *Perspective II: "Le balcon" de Manet* and *Perspective I: "Madame Récamier" de David*.

151. *Weegee's New York: 335 Photographs, 1935-1960* (Munich: Schirmer/Mosel, 1982).

152. A. Deikman quoted in Mavromatis, *Hypnagogia*, 113.

153. Marguerite Duras, *Marguerite Duras*, trans. Edith Cohen and Peter Conner (San Francisco: City Lights Books, 1987), 87.

154. Ibid., 103. For an antithetical, but equally interesting approach, in which there is a definite incarnation, one has to look at the films and aesthetic of one of Duras's favorite filmmakers, Robert Bresson. Bresson's models are exempt in essence from reincarnation. Humbert Balsan, who was Gauvain in *Lancelot of the Lake* (1974), reported: "It is precisely on finishing the post-production, that is the post-synchronization, and while saying goodbye to Bresson, that he told me: Above all, don't ever again work in cinema" (Philippe Arnaud, *Robert Bresson* [Paris: Cahiers du Cinéma, 1986], 147). Thus I am disconcerted that Jacques Rivette would use Balsan, whose first screen appearance was in that Bresson film, in *Noroît* (1976)—subsequently, being no longer a model but an actor, it was appropriate for Maurice Pialat, Samuel Fuller, and others to use Balsan; or that Jean Eustache would use Isabelle Weingarten, whose first screen appearance was in Bresson's *Four Nights of a Dreamer* (1971), in *The Mother and the Whore* (1973)—again, once she was no longer a model, it was appropriate for Ruiz, Wenders, Manoel de Oliveira, and Schlöndorff to use her; or that François Truffaut would use Jane Lobre, whose first appearance on the screen was in Bresson's *A Gentle Creature* (1969), in *The Green Room* (1978); or that Godard would use Anne Wiazemsky, whose first screen appearance was in Bresson's *Au Hasard Balthazar*, in *La Chinoise* (1967)—after which it was appropriate for Pasolini and Garrel

to use her; or that Alain Resnais would use both Roland Monod, whose first screen appearance was in Bresson's *A Man Escaped* (1956), in *La Guerre est finie* (1966), and François Leterrier, whose first screen appearance was also in Bresson's *A Man Escaped*, in *Stavisky* (1974); or, for that matter, that Bresson himself would use Jean-Claude Guilbert, whose first appearance on screen was in his *Au Hasard Balthazar*, again in *Mouchette* (1967)—after which it was appropriate for Godard to use him in *Week-End* (1967). Bresson models: Maurice Beerblock, Jean-Paul Delhumeau, Charles Le Clainche, and Roger Treherne in *A Man Escaped*; Florence Carrez, Jean Darbaud, Philippe Dreux, Jean-Claude Fourneau, Jean Gillibert, Michel Herubel, Roger Honorat, Marc Jacquier, E. R. Pratt, and André Régnier in *The Trial of Joan of Arc* (1962); Philippe Asselin, M. C. Fremont, Walter Green, Nathalie Joyaut, Jean Rémignard, and François Sullerot in *Au Hasard Balthazar*; Laelita Carcano, Nicolas Deguy, Geoffrey Gaussen, Régis Hanrion, Robert Honorat, Tina Irissari, and Antoine Monnier in *The Devil Probably* (1977); Didier Baussy, Michel Briguet, André Cler, Marc-Ernest Fourneau, Bruno Lapeyre, Christian Patey, Vincent Risterucci, and Béatrice Tabourin in *L'Argent* (1983).

155.   Duras, *Marguerite Duras*, 87.

156.   Marguerite Duras, "Film Bête Noire," trans. Daniella Shreir, *Harper's*, March 2024, https://harpers.org/archive/2024/03/film-bete-noire.

157.   *Specimen #4* ("Habiter/Live in"), January 1998 (Wissous, France: Éditions Amok), 68.

158.   The voice-over in Duras functions as either:
   1. An ahistorical, unworldly entity that irrupted in the radical closure delimited by the temporal end of the world (*Le Camion* ["Look at the end of the world, all the time, at every second, everywhere"], *Her Venetian Name in Deserted Calcutta*). Had I been offered to produce a science-fiction film on black holes, I would have asked Duras to write and direct it, suggesting as a possible title: *Cygnus X-1 Song* (such a film would certainly have been as uncharacteristic of the genre as Tarkovsky's *Solaris*). In *Her Venetian Name in Deserted Calcutta*, the two unworldly female voices-over talking from the end of the world juxtapose with the mundane gossip, in voice-over, of the guests at the reception.
   2. A voice-over-witness that reports on what is on the other side of a trauma's event horizon.

159.   Deidi von Schaewen, *Walls* (New York: Pantheon Books, 1977).

160. The perceptive film spectator of Herzog's *Nosferatu the Vampyre* (1979) would keep in mind during Harker's stay at Nosferatu's apparently still habitable castle the shot of a silhouette of the castle in a state of such disrepair that it is missing most of its walls and roof that was intercut with the shots of the final stage of Harker's trip to Nosferatu.

161. See Mike Davis's *Ecology of Fear: Los Angeles and the Imagination of Disaster* (New York: Metropolitan Books, 1998) for a thorough investigation of the various scenarios of an imagined destruction of Los Angeles.

162. The Lebanese literary critic Yumna al-Eid tells me, based on her extensive knowledge of Lebanese literature, that there are virtually no specters in Lebanese novels and short stories. It seems that the same sweeping judgement can be applied in the smaller domain of Lebanese film and video. A notable exception is Ghassan Salhab's film *Phantom Beirut* (1998). In this film, some years into the war and the civil war in Lebanon, a man, Khalil, disappears. His sister and his friends believe he was killed. One day one of them comes across an identical-looking man while at the airport to receive a friend flying in from abroad. He and several of Khalil's former friends shadow the man in question. When the latter ends up coming to the apartment of the missing man's sister, both she and his friends are uncertain whether it is actually Khalil or his ghost, one of them apprehensively touching him to make sure that he is actually, physically, there with them. They grow to feel that he is Khalil and come to the conclusion that his disappearance was a scheme to make them think that he died and abscond with the money collected by their militant association. And yet at the end of the film, in a symptomatic structural mistake, strangers hired to kidnap another person kidnap him instead. The mistake of these kidnappers is mortal even if they do not end up killing him, since he is revealed by their misidentification as possessed or haunted by the other, hence dead while alive or dead *tout court* therefore a phantom or someone come back from the dead as a mortal. He could fool his sister and his former friends but not *objective chance*.

163. *Britannica*, "Vlad the Impaler," https://www.britannica.com/biography/Vlad-the-Impaler.

164. Stephen G. Gilligan, "The Ericksonian Approach to Clinical Hypnosis," in *Ericksonian Approaches to Hypnosis and Psychotherapy*, ed. Jeffrey K. Zeig (New York: Brunner/Mazel, 1982), 99–100.

165. Bram Stoker, *Dracula* (New York: Bantam Books, 1981), 11.

166. Bram Stoker, *Dracula* (Cambridge: Cambridge University Press, 2013), 15.

167. *Great Short Works of Fyodor Dostoevsky* (New York: Perennial, 2004), 88, 133.

168. Ibid., 38.

169. Notwithstanding that the ghost appears to one only when one is alone, since he is a labyrinthine entity and in the labyrinth one is lost, including to others, he or she is not necessarily a personal affair but is often a communal one: commenting on the ghost's appearance, Marcellus says, "Something is rotten in the state of Denmark" (Shakespeare, *Hamlet*, act 1, sc. 5).

170. Or else is to be ascribed to the vampire's ability to tunnel ("For the dead travel fast"), hence to her ability to be in different places during the chase without covering the trajectory between them.

171. This applies to the phone call that reaches one of the travelers in the labyrinthine zone of Tarkovsky's *Stalker*.

172. Certainly if there is anything that is going to make me leave Lebanon, it will be, more than the Lebanese's entrenched religious sectarianism, the inhuman conditions in which the Palestinians are maintained in the refugee camps, Lebanon's increasingly ugly architecture, the country's legalized wiretapping of phones, the racial discrimination against foreign maids, etc., the recurrent question "Why did you come back to Lebanon? Why would anyone come to Beirut?"

173. Edward William Lane, *An Arabic-English Lexicon*, 8 vols. (Beirut: Librairie du Liban, 1980), entry *jīm sīn dāl*.

174. "Pubescent: a person at or approaching the age of puberty" (*Oxford Dictionary of English*, 3rd ed.); exceptionally, in this instance I am using the term to mean a person at the age of puberty—I usually use it to mean a person approaching the age of puberty, for example, in my book *The Portrait of the Pubescent Girl: A Rite of Non-Passage*.

175. Gilles Deleuze, "The Gods are dead but they have died from laughing, on hearing one God claim to be the only one ... (*Thus Spoke Zarathustra* III, 'Of the Apostates'). And the death of this God, who claimed to be the only one, is itself plural" (*Nietzsche and Philosophy*, trans. Hugh Tomlinson [New York: Columbia University Press, 1983], 4). One of these deaths is proclaimed by the madman in Nietzsche's

The Gay Science; another one was performed by Nietzsche through his feeling *every name in history is I* and consequently his signing one of his letters "The Crucified" during his psychosis, i.e., his death before dying.

176. The "M" written in chalk on the back of the criminal's jacket in Fritz Lang's first talking picture, *M*, is an intertitle.

177. Muḥammad 'Alī al-Tahānawī, *Mawsū'at kashshāf iṣṭilaḥāt al-funūn wa al-'ulūm*, ed. 'Alī Daḥrūj, trans. 'Abd Allāh al-Khālidī, English and French translation of headings by Jūrj Zīnātī, 2 vols. (Beirut: Maktabat Lubnān, 1996), 1547-48.

178. Charles Baudelaire, "The Philosophy of Toys," trans. Paul Keegan, in Heinrich von Kleist, Charles Baudelaire, and Rainer Maria Rilke, *Essays on Dolls*, trans. Idris Parry and Paul Keegan (London: Syrens, 1994), 24. Cf. Freud: "At about the same time as the sexual life of children reaches its first peak, between the ages of three and five, they also begin to show signs of the activity which may be ascribed to the instinct for knowledge or research.... The assumption that all human beings have the same (male) form of genital is the first of the many remarkable and momentous sexual theories of children" (*The Standard Edition*, vol. 7 [1901-1905], "*A Case of Hysteria*," "*Three Essays on Sexuality*," *and Other Works* [1953], 194-95).

179. Iranian cinema's sexual inhibition is discernible not only in the films revolving around adults, but also in those featuring children as protagonists: in scores of films produced by the Institute for the Intellectual Development of Children and Young Adults, children are not shown as sensual beings (see, in contrast, Syrian filmmaker Ossama Mohammed's *Sundūq al-dunyā* [*The Box of Life*, 2002], and the recent work of the Kuwaiti artist Tamara Al-Samerraei, who resides presently in Beirut), and their polymorphous perversity (Freud) is nowhere to be seen. I was for years concerned with schizophrenia and with schizophrenics, who appeared in my *Credits Included: A Video in Red and Green* (1995); and I am now interested in "the little girl," whom I expect to appear in my coming vampire film, *Transit Visa to the Labyrinth?!* (*Al-funūn junūn* Productions). At *one* level, the Thirteenth Series in Gilles Deleuze's *The Logic of Sense* (1969), "The Schizophrenic and the Little Girl," can thus be retrospectively viewed as a program for the work of a decade on my part.

180. *Hiroshima mon amour*, text by Marguerite Duras for the film by Alain Resnais, trans. Richard Seaver (New York: Grove Press, 1961), 65.

181. The title of one of Duras's books.

182. "4'33", musical composition by John Cage created in 1952 and first performed on August 29 of that year.... The work's manuscript declared that it was written 'for any instrument or combination of instruments.' It then specified that there were three movements of set duration—33 seconds, 2 minutes 40 seconds, and 1 minute 20 seconds, respectively. For each movement, Cage's sole instruction to the performer(s) was 'Tacet' (Latin: '[it] is silent,' used in music to indicate that the musician is not to play). For the first performance of 4'33", pianist David Tudor used a stopwatch, opening or closing the keyboard lid at the designated intervals.... Coughing audience members, squeaking seats, even departing footsteps became part of the unusual composition" (*Britannica*, https://www.britannica.com/topic/433-by-Cage).

183. With its frequent absence of the mirror image, the horror film or novel is often a preparation for, a sort of condition of possibility of, tackling the portrait.

184. Cinema is relevant concerning death because it is a form of defense against it, the latest avatar of the practice of "embalming the dead" (Bazin: "If the plastic arts were put under psychoanalysis, the practice of embalming the dead might turn out to be a fundamental factor in their creation. The process might reveal that at the origin of painting and sculpture there lies a mummy complex.... The film is no longer content to preserve the object.... Now, for the first time, the image of things is likewise the image of their duration, change mummified as it were")—with the caveat that much of the importance and efficacy of the image comes from its magical equation in our unconscious with the thing; and also insofar as in the death realm one at times, for example, upon seeing people moving in slow motion, asks oneself: "Am I in a film?"

185. The combination of painting and dance in *An American in Paris* is a happy one, since the diegetic freezing of the dancers produced by the diegetic silence-over in the dance realm can result in *tableaux vivants*.

186. This scene is based on the following text Thomas Johannsen wrote for a presentation for my workshop on death at DasArts, Amsterdam, October–November 2001: "Martin was inspecting his shoes while I observed him. Now he searched through his pockets, bringing little bits of paper out into the dim corridor light and looking at them. Suddenly he looked up. I, ashamed, turned my eyes back to my own reflection and gasped. For a split second I saw my mirror image observing Martin. For the briefest moment, my own reflection was not looking back at me but was gazing at my lover behind me, at

the end of the corridor." This is certainly a moment of radical accompaniment of one's lover: if my mirror image is not facing me as I look at it, but looking at my lover in the background, then this means that notwithstanding my *sous-entendu* call addressed to it, it is far more preoccupied with my lover.

187. "Cadaver: late Middle English: from Latin, from *cadere* 'to fall'" (*Oxford Dictionary of English*, 3rd ed.).

188. Kip S. Thorne, *Black Holes and Time Warps: Einstein's Outrageous Legacy* (New York: Norton, 1994), 30-31.

189. Nietzsche, *Thus Spoke Zarathustra: A Book for All and None*, 45.

190. Friedrich Nietzsche, *Writings from the Late Notebooks*, ed. Rüdiger Bittner, trans. Kate Sturge (Cambridge: Cambridge University Press, 2003), 140; "*Man muß das All zersplittern; den Respekt vor dem All verlernen*" (*Nachlass* 1886/87, 7[62], KSA 12.317). It is so difficult to accomplish the splintering apart of the universe since we have a tendency through the (Freudian) secondary process to link, to give sense (Richard Foreman: "Understand—it ALWAYS makes sense. Sense *can't* be avoided. If it first seems to be non-sense, wait: roots will reveal themselves" [*Reverberation Machines: The Later Plays and Essays* (Barrytown, NY: Station Hill Press, 1985), 190]), and because, with rare exceptions, when a person sees the universe beginning to break down, when, for instance, during his interrogation by three agents his two lips become sewn together (*The Matrix*), most often he resorts to waking up to convince himself that he was dreaming—one can then try again to wake him by telling him, "Dream on!"

191. Indeed, *Hamlet* is punctuated by the abrupt stage directions *Enter Ghost* and *Ghost exits*:

BARNARDO
  Last night of all,
  When yond same star that's westward from the pole
  Had made his course t' illume that part of heaven
  Where now it burns, Marcellus and myself,
  The bell then beating one—

Enter Ghost.

MARCELLUS
  Peace, break thee off! Look where it comes again.

...

BARNARDO
    See, it stalks away.

HORATIO
    Stay! speak! speak! I charge thee, speak!

Ghost exits.

MARCELLUS
    'Tis gone and will not answer.

...

HORATIO

...

Enter Ghost.

    But soft, behold! Lo, where it comes again!

192. "Fitch Says Lebanon's Public Finances Unsustainable," April 11, 2002, https://www.fitchratings.com/research/sovereigns/fitch-says-lebanon-public-finances-unsustainable-11-04-2002.

193. Jalal Toufic
      Holy Spirit University of Kaslik, Jounieh, Lebanon
      11/20/1999
Walid Raad, Media Studies Department, Queens College, New York: I arrived in Lebanon on 10/23/1999. I was initially struck by the unsightliness of the nondescript architecture in much of Beirut. Almost all of those among the inhabitants of that city whom I encountered told me I would become habituated not only to the bad manners of its drivers but also to its architecture. One of them even volunteered: "You have to see not only the beautiful but also the ugly, otherwise you will never have the possibility of accessing the abject and the sublime." "The ugliness of the majority of the buildings of Beirut is not of the sort that allows one to continue to see it: it is unsightly." When I no longer complained about the latter, they thought that I had gotten used to it. I began instead to nag about my new inability to write. My eyes were oppressed by the relentless mass of unsightly architecture and the constrictive arrangement of space, and so they closed a little more each time. My initial impulse to use close shots to extract from these nondescript buildings something to see vanished. There came a day or night when my eyes had almost closed completely: "Though seeing, they do not see" (Matthew 13:13).

Then, momentarily, light, rather than, as usual, making things visible while remaining itself unseen, itself became visible, shone and glared with an unmitigated brilliance. Did this brilliant light complete the blindness of the eye from overexposure? No. On 12/15/1999, there occurred for the Nietzschean and Deleuzian writer that I am a kind of minor reversal of Platonism: my eyes opened again in the magnificent Jeita Grotto. After being oppressed for weeks by the lack of empty space in the city—the pavements occupied, and the parking lots jammed, by vehicles, and the narrow roads often blocked by cars disregarding the one-way signs—to see empty space even inside a mountain! I felt again the desire and ability to write. I realized then that my writer's block was merely a symptom of my inability to see and became aware of how crucial vision is in my writing even when I am not addressing cinema or art or dance. Maybe with time I would have resumed writing even without such an opening of the eyes in the Jeita Grotto, but my writing would have had to have changed radically, become linked to another sense: touch? Or would I, who does not smell except when people point out a scent to me, now smell (and consequently better remember)? I am considering starting a service in this country infamous for its hostage-taking that, for a reasonable fee, would provide incognitos who would place a blindfold over the passenger's eyes on his or her arrival to Beirut's International Airport to be removed only once he or she is in his or her apartment. It certainly would not be to simulate the conditions of hostage-taking in much of what used to be West Beirut but to spare its users blindness on encountering so much unsightly architecture. What is preferable: that people see again at the risk of the resumption of a civil war to destroy so much revolting architecture? Or that they continue to be blind in the midst of the unsightly architecture?

At the airport, Walid Raad, the video maker of *The Dead Weight of a Quarrel Hangs* (1999), and the producer through the Atlas project of *Hostage: The Bachar Tapes (English Version)* (2000), is approached by two men who place blindfolds over his eyes and put him in a car and drive him to the Union Building at Spears Street in Sanayeh. There, he thanks the two men, pays them a hefty tip and then ascends to his apartment. "In Beirut, I drive and walk only in Achrafieh, the Central District and the Sodeco area." "Do these areas not include some ugliness?" "Yes, but not unrelenting unsightliness. When I have to move to another area, Hamra, for example, I call the Blindfolds service, which was started by my friend Jalal Toufic. Why don't you, too, wear a blindfold when in Hamra Street?" "Since as a film sound designer and technician I can see when there is sound even when blindfolded—I can actually see better then through sound—but not when there's the artificial silence that forms when one covers one's ears, I do my errands in Hamra Street with my ears covered." "What about you?" The addressee of this question, a writer, did not answer

the question. Raad wondered how exposure to such unsightly architecture had not blinded this visionary author? He later discovered
that that person is a vampire, one who, as dead, did not see what was
in front of his open eyes. Once, when he had to attend a meeting of
an artistic association at the Hamra apartment of Saleh Barakat, the
owner of the Agial Art Gallery, the entire on-call staff of the Blindfolds
service, two employees, happened to be sick. He tried hard to devise a
way to go to the meeting without being affected by a loss of the ability
to see as an effect of the unsightliness of the architecture. He ended
up calling me for any suggestions. My recommendation was to walk
there while videotaping all along the way with a camera having a
black and white viewfinder, so that the act of seeing and therefore its
consequences for him would be delayed till the viewing of the shots
in actual color; and to later not view the color footage, but tape over it.
And that is indeed what he did. He walked to the meeting in Hamra
while taping with a video camera, at several points even crossing
from one side of this street with no traffic lights to the other while still
looking through the black and white viewfinder. Then he gave me the
tape: I taped over it my students' discussion with him following the
premiere of *Hostage: The Bachar Tapes (English Version)* at my Video
Art class at Holy Spirit University of Kaslik (USEK). "I now shoot two
kinds of footage: what I intend to possibly use in a video and what I
shoot with a black and white viewfinder specifically so as not to be
exposed to the unsightly (shooting with a film camera would also
do the trick, since in cinema, especially if one is not an excellent
cameraman, vision happens truly only once the negative footage is
developed, so that it suffices not to develop the negative—unfortunately, shooting in film is too expensive)." The wives of several of the
artists who used the Blindfolds service soon developed a fetish for
that contrivance: "I want you to fuck me with the blindfold on."

194. Deleuze, *Cinema 1: The Movement-Image*, 206-7.

195. Here's an additional allusion to zombies in *Hamlet*: Hamlet:
"How long will a man lie i'th' earth ere he rot?" First Clown: "I'faith, if
he be not rotten before he die—"

196. Gregory A. Waller, *The Living and the Undead: From Stoker's
"Dracula" to Romero's "Dawn of the Undead"* (Urbana: University of
Illinois Press, 1986), 38.

197. (Death before) Death can only be undergone by one person
alone—but, so as to be able to come back from this nonlocal realm,
that person has to have an outsider, even if it is only the *hidden observer*
(reality begins only with two—not counting the double). "*Hidden
observer*: An intrapsychic entity with awareness of experiences that

occur outside of an individual's consciousness, hypothesized to explain the dissociative phenomenon in which a hypnotized person who has been told to block certain stimuli (e.g., pain induced by ice-cold water) still registers the blocked sensation via hand signals even while verbally denying it. It is as if a dissociated observer is registering the stimuli that the hypnotized person has successfully blocked.... [investigated by Ernest R. Hilgard]" (*APA Dictionary of Psychology*, https://dictionary.apa.org/hidden-observer).

198. Waller, *The Living and the Undead*, 32.

199. And if what is received telepathically is ambiguous, open to interpretation, and hence uncertain, we must keep in mind that the character encountering the vampire is himself suffering from uncertainty (for example: is the vampire at a certain location, or is he rather, as indicated by the absence of his image in the mirror at that location, not there?) and a proliferation of interpretations, and hence receiving a letter from him would in no way produce a clearer version of what happened.

200. Unfortunately, this strategy often backfires, playing into the hands of the vampire: it is precisely by writing letters and hence no longer fully belonging to the present that the victim enters into contact with the vampire, who himself does not fully belong to the present.

201. Stoker's *Dracula* (1897), the events of which take place during the same period when all sorts of indexical modes of recording (photography, etc.) are being introduced and becoming widespread, already renders problematic such indexical recording: the absence of the vampire's image from the mirror.

202. In an elaboration of the double-slit experiment, in their paper "Quantum Double-Double-Slit Experiment with Momentum Entangled Photons" (*Scientific Reports* 10, no. 11427 [July 10, 2020], https://doi.org/10.1038/s41598-020-68181-1), Manpreet Kaur and Mandip Singh present "a detailed experimental realisation of quantum double-double-slit thought experiment with momentum entangled photons.... Experiment is configured in such a way that photons are path entangled and each photon can reveal the which-slit path information of the other photon. As a consequence, single photon interference is suppressed. However, two-photon interference pattern appears if locations of detection of photons are correlated without revealing the which-slit path information. It is also shown experimentally and theoretically that two-photon quantum interference disappears when the which-slit path of a photon in the double-double-slit is detected."

481

203. Carl Theodor Dreyer, *Four Screenplays* (Bloomington: Indiana University Press, 1970), 101. The expression "the dead eyes of a blind person" is a metaphor humorously constructed of two terms that apply literally to the subject of the statement, since the blind person in question is dead. It thus instances another version of the literality of the figurative in the case of the dead and schizophrenics.

204. Wade Davis reports the case of a Haitian zombie in his *Passage of Darkness: The Ethnobiology of the Haitian Zombie* (Chapel Hill: University of North Carolina Press, 1988): Clairvius Narcisse. "Clairvius Narcisse recalled remaining conscious at all times, and although he was completely immobilized, he could hear his sister's weeping as he was pronounced dead. Both at and after his burial, his overall sensation was one of floating above the grave. He remembered as well that his earliest sign of discomfort before entering the hospital was difficulty in breathing. His sister remembered that his lips had turned blue or cyanotic. Although Narcisse did not know how long he had remained in the grave before the zombie makers came to release him, other informants insist that a zombie may be raised up to seventy-two hours after the burial [for three days and three nights did Jonah remain in the belly of the whale, Lazarus in the grave]. The onset of the poison itself was described by several houngan as the feeling of 'insects crawling beneath the skin'" (Ibid., 153-54). According to Davis, an ethnobotanist, the houngan's poison contains tetrodotoxin. "Compare Narcisse's constellation of symptoms with the following specific description of the effects of tetrodotoxin: '... *malaise, pallor, dizziness, paresthesias of the lips and tongue and ataxi.... The paresthesias which the victim usually describes as a tingling or prickling sensation* may subsequently involve the fingers and toes, then spread to other portions of the extremities and gradually develop into severe numbness. In some cases the numbness may involve the entire body, in which instances the patients have stated that *it felt as though their bodies were floating ... subnormal temperatures....* As the disease progresses, the *eyes become fixed* and the pupillary and corneal reflexes are lost.... Shortly after the development of paresthesias, *respiratory distress* becomes very pronounced and ... the *lips, extremities and body become intensely cyanotic*. Muscular twitching becomes progressively worse and finally terminates in *extensive paralysis*. The first areas to become paralyzed are usually the throat and larynx, resulting in *aphonia, dysphagia* and complete *aphagia. The muscles of the extremities become completely paralyzed and the patient is unable to move.* As the end approaches the *eyes of the victim become glassy. The victim may become comatose but in most cases retains consciousness, and the mental faculties remain acute until shortly before death*' (B. W. Halstead, *Poisonous and Venomous Marine Animals of the World* [Princeton: Darwin Press, 1978], 456; emphasis mine [Davis]).... In all, Clairvius Narcisse shared

twenty-one or virtually all the prominent symptoms of tetrodotoxin poisoning" (*Passage of Darkness*, 154–55). According to Article 249 of the Haitian penal code of 1835 "is also considered attempt on life by poisoning the use made against a person of substances which, without giving death, will cause a more-or-less prolonged state of lethargy, regardless of the manner in which these substances were used and regardless of the consequences. If the person was buried as a consequence of this state of lethargy, the attempt will be considered a murder" (*Code pénal: promulgué le 11 août 1835*, updated and annotated by Patrick Pierre-Louis [Port-au-Prince, Haiti: Éditions Zémès, 2011]; quote trans. Nicolas Boring). The prohibition occults rather than clarifies the phenomenon of the zombie, for it is not enough to induce a deathlike stupor in the person who is to become a zombie, making others, including doctors, believe he is dead. Spending up to three days in the grave completely paralyzed yet conscious does not produce a zombie: witness the many cases of blower-fish poisoning where the person who was believed to be dead and spent several days in a stupor recovered afterward. For example, the Japanese physician Taizo Akashi reported in 1880 the following incident: "A dozen gamblers voraciously consumed fugu at Nakashimamachi of Okayama in Bizen. Three of them suffered from poisoning; two eventually died. One of these being a native of the town was buried immediately. The other was from a distant district under the jurisdiction of the Shogun. Therefore the body was kept in storage and watched by a guard until a government official could examine it. Seven or eight days later the man became conscious and finally recovered completely. When asked about his experience, he was able to recall everything and stated that he feared that he too would be buried alive when he heard that the other person had been buried" ("Experiences with Fugu Poisoning," *Iji Shimbum* 27:19–23; quoted in *Passage of Darkness*, 159). To become a zombie, the person in whom a deathlike stupor was induced must additionally be abruptly thrown into the death realm: zombies are given datura after they are retrieved from the grave (Haitians call *Datura stramonium*, "*concombre zombi*" [the zombie's cucumber]). The plant induces stupor, hallucinations, and delusions, followed by confusion, disorientation, and amnesia. Datura is associated with initiation rites among the Luisena Indians of Southern California, the Algonquin of northeastern North America, and the Jivaro of South America. In parts of Highland Peru, datura is called *huaca*, the Quechua word for "grave."

205. This paragraph was written in 1990 (Library of Congress copyright for the first, 3/13/1991 version of *[Vampires]*: TXU 468-283). It was fulfilling to see a confirmation of this "point-of-view shots between us" in *Until the End of the World*, released in the U.S. at the end of 1991, where a scientist succeeds in designing a camera that allows a blind

person to "see" a simulation of a referential image on the condition that the latter be remembered by, seen in the mind's eye of, the one who recorded it for the camera.

206. *Britannica*, "Cygnus X-1," https://www.britannica.com/topic/Cygnus-X-1.

207. It turns out that the aforementioned film shot of Isabelle Adjani and Klaus Kinski does not exist (in the film) but is a production still!

208. Jean Louis Schefer, *The Enigmatic Body: Essays on the Arts*, ed. and trans. Paul Smith (Cambridge: Cambridge University Press, 1995), 133–34.

209. Roland Barthes, *The Responsibility of Forms: Critical Essays on Music, Art, and Representation*, trans. Richard Howard (New York: Hill and Wang, 1985), 96.

210. Patricia Highsmith, *Ripley's Game* (New York: Penguin, 1974), 36.

211. Ibid., 55.

212. Ibid., 86.

213. The words in italics in the brackets are my additions to the captions that appear in *Ralph Eugene Meatyard: An American Visionary*, ed. Barbara Tannenbaum (New York: Rizzoli and Akron Art Museum, 1991).

214. The hands of the child are as still as the two wing-like shapes of peeling paint above him, which they echo.

215. None of the photographs of the "No-Focus" series will be included here, since in that series the blurriness is produced by intentionally setting the lens out of focus; nor will photographs, such as *Untitled* [Girl twirling in front of shed] (1965) and *Untitled* [Group of children with dolls and masks] (1963), in which the blurriness can easily and justifiably be construed to be due to the *normal* movement of the one in the photograph with respect to the slow exposure time. If there is a site of an occultation of the fear in his photographs in Meatyard's work, it is to be found in the temptation such photographs present both us and Meatyard to consider the blurriness in his photographs in general as due to a normal movement of the characters.

216. Even if we do not consider the masks in Meatyard's Lucybelle Crater series as produced by the fear-induced swish pan, but view

them as evincing the *psychotic* indistinguishability of figures that have lost their mirror image (*Lucybelle Crater and Her 16-Year-Old Son's Quiet, Demure Girlfriend Lucybelle Crater* [1970–72]), they have little to do with those in the work of Cindy Sherman (an admirer of Meatyard), for example, in *Untitled #629* (2010/2023) and *Untitled #632* (2010/2023), which are *hysterical*.

217. We are dealing with a swish-tilt in the case of these two photographs.

218. Zachary J. Sikora, "5 Things You Never Knew about Fear," Northwestern Medicine (October 2020), https://www.nm.org/healthbeat/healthy-tips/emotional-health/5-things-you-never-knew-about-fear.

219. Cf. "scary: *adj.* 1. Causing fright or alarm. 2. Easily scared; very timid" (*American Heritage Dictionary*).

220. Laplanche, *New Foundations for Psychoanalysis*, 98–101.

221. Some Buddhist statues manage to give the feeling of floating over their pedestals.

222. Alain Robbe-Grillet, *"La Maison de Rendez-Vous" and "Djinn,"* trans. Richard Howard/Yvone Lenard and Walter Wells (New York: Grove Press, 1987), 141.

223. Alain Robbe-Grillet, *Last Year at Marienbad*, trans. Richard Howard (New York: Grove Press, 1962), 20.

224. "Sound: *adjective* free from error, fallacy, or misapprehension: sound advice; sound reasoning" (*Merriam-Webster Dictionary*, https://www.merriam-webster.com/dictionary/sound).

225. *Autobiography of a Schizophrenic Girl*, with an analytical interpretation by Marguerite Sechehaye, trans. Grace Rubin-Rabson (New York: Signet Book, 1979), 44.

226. Giovanni Stanghellini and René Rosfort, "Schizophrenia as a Disorder of Mood," in *Emotions and Personhood: Exploring Fragility—Making Sense of Vulnerability* (Oxford: Oxford University Press, 2013), 240.

227. While the corpses of saints exist in time but are spared corruption, the vampire in the coffin during the day is not in time but frozen.

228. "For a long time, I have been intrigued by the phenomenon of being interested and even fascinated by photos from a film (outside a cinema, in the pages of *Cahiers du cinéma*) and of then losing everything of those photos (not just the captivation but the memory of the image) when once inside the viewing room.... A theory of the still becomes necessary," in large part because it is the major site of what Barthes terms the third, obtuse meaning, which "is not in the language-system (even that of symbols). Take away the obtuse meaning and communication and signification still remain" (Roland Barthes, "The Third Meaning: Research Notes on Some Eisenstein Stills," in *Image, Music, Text*, trans. Stephen Heath [New York: Hill and Wang, 1977], 60 and 65–66).

229. Annette Michelson, "'The Man with the Movie Camera': From Magician to Epistemologist," *Artforum* 10, no. 7 (March 1972): 65.

230. Eisenstein, *Film Form*, 43.

231. Similarly, the freezings permit the diegetic fast forward in René Clair's *The Crazy Ray* (the original, French title of Clair's film is *Paris qui dort*).

232. "While being under stress can't change the color of individual strands of hair, stress can trigger a common condition called telogen effluvium, which causes hair to shed about three times faster than normal.... If you're middle-aged and your hair is falling out and regenerating more quickly because of stress, it's possible that the hair that grows in will be gray instead of its original color" (Robert H. Shmerling, "Why Does Hair Turn Gray?" Harvard Health Publishing, March 24, 2022, https://www.health.harvard.edu/blog/hair-turn-gray-2017091812226).

233. Vonnegut, *The Eden Express*, 182.

234. Sigmund Freud, *Totem and Taboo: Some Points of Agreement between the Mental Lives of Savages and Neurotics*, trans. James Strachey (London; New York: Routledge Classics, 2001), 64. The quote within the quote is attributed by Freud to J. G. Fraser ("Taboo and the Perils of the Soul," *The Golden Bough*, 3rd ed., Part II [London: 1911], 357) quoting P. Lozano (*Descripcion ... del Gran Chaco* [Cordova, 1733], 70).

235. Freud, *Totem and Taboo*, 65. The quote within the quote is attributed by Freud to Fraser (*The Golden Bough*, 360) quoting M. Dobrizhoffer (*Historia de Abiponibus*, vol. 2 [Vienna, 1784], 301).

236. Nigel Andrews, "Dracula in Delft," *American Film* 4, no. 1 (1978): 33.

237. Quoted in Jan-Christopher Horak, "W. H. or the Mysteries of Walking in Ice," in *The Films of Werner Herzog: Between Mirage and History*, ed. Timothy Corrigan (New York: Methuen, 1986), 26.

238. The filming of Joe Levine's *A Bridge Too Far* in Delft had just finished when Herzog came to shoot *Nosferatu*, a film about someone who crosses a too-far bridge.

239. Quoted in Corrigan, *The Films of Werner Herzog*, 26.

240. "There is no single number for existing American silent-era feature films, as the surviving copies vary in format and completeness. There are 1,575 titles (14%) surviving as the complete domestic-release version in 35mm. Another 1,174 (11%) are complete, but not the original—they are either a foreign-release version in 35mm or in a 28 or 16mm small-gauge print with less than 35mm image quality. Another 562 titles (5%) are incomplete—missing either a portion of the film or an abridged version. The remaining 70% are believed to be completely lost" (David Pierce, *The Survival of American Silent Feature Films: 1912-1929* [Washington, DC: Council on Library and Information Resources and the Library of Congress: 2013], 1). "The major and, even in its earliest days, dominant Swedish film production company was called Svenska, Svenska Biografteater or Svenska Bio. It still exists as the company Svensk Filmindustri in Stockholm. All the classic Swedish films, among them all the films directed by Mauritz Stiller and Victor Sjöström, were produced by this company. Today it consequently is the company of Ingmar Bergman's pictures. Up to September 1941, all their negatives from the beginning of 1907 were preserved. But at that time a violent explosion and a terrible fire destroyed them all in a very short time. The whole Swedish film tradition blew up" (Gosta Werner, "A Method of Reconstructing Lost Films," *Cinema Journal* 14, no. 2 [Winter 1974-1975]: 11). Until 1951 the film base was made of cellulose nitrate, which is explosive and chemically unstable and, even under the best storage conditions, lasts no more than fifty years. An effort has been made to transfer as much as possible of the nitrate stock to the acetate stock used in films made after 1951, which is stable. But as of 1985, the Library of Congress still had 80 million feet of nitrate film. This is not all: most color films made after 1950 (the year Eastman Kodak introduced its multi-layer film that replaced the much more stable Technicolor system) are subject to color fading. Néstor Almendros: "In ten years, the films I've made I'm sure will have vanished. The museums of the future will have lots of well-preserved black-and-white films and nothing of our

time" ("Colour Problem," *Sight and Sound* 30, no. 1 [Winter 1980-81]: 12-13). As an indication to the spectator that at that point in the film he or she is watching an earlier historical period, many color films revert to black and white, most probably because black and white preceded color in film history. It would be more appropriate, for the contemporary section(s), to use filters that allow the simulation of the colors that would have resulted from the gradual fading of color film (such as the effect of magenta or pink that results from the fading of blue and green), reverting to the original, intenser colors for the sections that are in the past.

241. *Britannica*, "Nosferatu," https://www.britannica.com/topic/Nosferatu-film-by-Murnau-1922.

242. Michel Foucault, *Discipline and Punish: Birth of the Prison*, trans. A. Sheridan (New York: Pantheon, 1977), 197.

243. Ibid., 198.

244. Antonin Artaud, *The Theater and Its Double*, trans. Mary Caroline Richards (New York: Grove Press, 1958), 24.

245. René Girard, "The Plague in Literature and Myth," *Texas Studies in Literature and Language* 15, no. 5 (1974): 843.

246. Foucault, *Discipline and Punish*, 196-97.

247. Ernest R. Hilgard, *Divided Consciousness: Multiple Controls in Human Thought and Action*, expanded ed. (New York: John Wiley & Sons, 1986), 188-89. The phenomenon of the hidden observer takes the form of covert hearing in hypnotic deafness.

248. Luke 22:41. How incisive is the laconism of *a stone's throw* here.

249. Matthew 26:36-45.

250. Mavromatis, *Hypnagogia*, 20.

251. Bazin, *What Is Cinema?*, vol. 1, 107.

252. Ibid.

253. The same way that in Judaism man is in the image of God, who has no image, in many of the films that deal with the failure of mourning we have the case of a living person forced by the melancholiac to be in the image of the dead the latter lost, who has no image

(whether because he or she sees himself/herself with his or her back to himself/herself in the mirror or because he or she does not appear in the mirror).

254. See "I Know Full Well, or Suspect, that this Is Not Fetishism, but I Will Treat It as If It Is," in my book *Explicit and Implicit Variations on Hitchcock* (Beirut: Beirut Art Center, 2023).

255. Nicholas Abraham and Maria Torok, *The Wolf Man's Magic Word*, trans. Nicholas Rand, foreword by Jacques Derrida (Minneapolis: University of Minnesota Press, 1986).

256. *American Heritage Dictionary.*

257. In Hitchcock's universe, we have both the wrong man, a man unjustly accused of being the murderer (*The Wrong Man* [1956], etc.), and the wrong woman, a dead woman who is different from her purported image (*Rebecca* [1940]).

258. From Nietzsche's letter of January 5, 1889, to Jacob Burckhardt, in *Selected Letters of Friedrich Nietzsche*, 347.

259. Ibid.

260. Freud, *Totem and Taboo*, 67–68.

261. Stoker, *Dracula*, revised ed., 228.

262. Freud, *Totem and Taboo*, 70.

263. André M. Weitzenhoffer and Ernest R. Hilgard, *Stanford Hypnotic Susceptibility Scale, Form C* (Stanford University, 1962), modified by John F. Kihlstrom (1996), 20, https://www.ocf.berkeley.edu/~jfkihlstrom/PDFfiles/Hypnotizability/SHSSC%20Script.pdf.

264. Quoted in Kenneth Ring, "Frequency and Stages of the Prototypic Near-Death Experience," in *A Collection of Near-Death Research Readings*, ed. Craig R. Lundahl (Chicago: Nelson-Hall, 1982), 125.

265. By maintaining the singular name of the dead, I imply that I will be using it to resurrect him, to call him back to life (from *The Egyptian Book of the Dead*: "Arise ... thou shalt not perish. Thou hast been called by name. Thou hast been resurrected"). The section "*Every Name in History Is I*" in my book *Forthcoming* is dedicated to the memory of William Burroughs; Derrida's *Aporias* is in memory

of Koitchi Toyosaki. Did I try to resurrect William Burroughs? Did Derrida try to resurrect Koitchi Toyosaki? If not, the *in memoriam* should be addressed to *everyone and no one*.

266. This moment is reminiscent of the scene in Raoul Ruiz's *Life Is a Dream* (1986) where the protagonist, seated in a movie theater, suspects that the screams he is hearing are not coming from the projected film but from elsewhere. For confirmation, he walks to the door at the side of the screen and opens it. He discovers that there is indeed someone being tortured in a room behind the screen! In his "Letter to Serge Daney: Optimism, Pessimism, and Travel," Deleuze wrote: "You'd already, in *La Rampe*, characterized the image's third phase as 'mannerism': when there's nothing to see behind it, not much to see in it or on the surface, but just an image constantly slipping across preexisting, presupposed images, when 'the background in any image is always another image,' and so on endlessly" (Gilles Deleuze, *Negotiations, 1972–1990*, trans. Martin Joughin [New York: Columbia University Press, 1995], 75). In such a historical and aesthetic period, reality can enter precisely by the back door—as a depth behind the screen.

267. *Al-'amaliyyāt al-istishhādiyya: wathā'iq wa ṣuwar; al-muqāwama al-waṭaniyya, 1982–1985* (*The Martyrdom Operations: Documents and Images; The Lebanese National Resistance, 1982–1985*) (Beirut: Al-Markaz al-'arabī lil-ma'lūmāt, 1985).

268. Ibid., 123. I consider Sana'a Mehaidli, who introduced the new genre of videotaped testimonies of soon-to-be (posthumous) martyrs and a new kind of utterance, "I am the martyr (name of speaker)," as the first Lebanese video artist. "Prior to her martyrdom, Sana'a worked in a video store in the Musaitbi area in West Beirut. During this time, she recorded 36 videotapes of the martyr Wajdi Sayegh, who performed his operation against enemy forces in an area close to where Sana'a did her martyrdom operation. It is in that store that Sana'a videotaped her testimony using a VHS camera" (122).

269. Ibid., 144.

270. Ibid., 168.

271. Ibid., 176.

272. Ibid., 180.

273. Ibid., 206.

274. Ibid., 214.

275. Someone who has access to better libraries than the mediocre ones currently present in Lebanon should research the locutions of the kamikazes.

276. Ibid., 72.

277. In a way, it is true that those who, like Sana'a Youcef Mehaidli, are famous enough to continue to be treated by the living as having a distinguishable identity are not really dead for the survivors since the dead no longer have a distinct identity.

278. According to Lebanese theater director Roger Assaf, theater, as opposed to technology, can and should provide us with "a living person before other living persons" (un homme vivant en face d'autres hommes vivants). Given that technology is heading in the direction of providing humans with an indefinite life span, it is not life that has to be stressed against technology but mortality, the state of being dead even while still physically alive. It is not as a simple living being but as a mortal that a human can, for a while at least, resist an otherwise ubiquitous, all-seeing, and all-powerful technology. Theater should provide us with humans dead set on being mortal.

279. According to Derrida, "All writing ... in order to be what it is, must be able to function in the radical absence of every empirically determined addressee in general [I disagree with Derrida on this point: there can be no writing that is not an untimely collaboration with a determined albeit unknown addressee]. And this absence is not a continuous modification of presence; it is a break in presence, 'death,' or the possibility of the 'death' of the addressee, inscribed in the structure of the mark (and it is at this point, I note in passing, that the value or effect of transcendentality is linked necessarily to the possibility of writing and of 'death' analyzed in this way).... What holds for the addressee holds also, for the same reasons, for the sender or the producer.... To write is to produce a mark that will constitute a kind of machine that is in turn productive, that my future disappearance in principle will not prevent from functioning.... When I say 'my future disappearance,' I do so to make this proposition more immediately acceptable. I must be able simply to say my disappearance, my nonpresence in general ..." (Jacques Derrida, Margins of Philosophy, trans. Alan Bass [Chicago: University of Chicago Press, 1982], 315-16). Even if it were true that a condition of possibility of writing is that it be able to function in the radical absence, "'death,' or the possibility of the 'death'" of every empirically determined addressor in general, I cannot write: "I am dead."

280. Al-'amaliyyāt al-istishhādiyya, 191.

281. What I am most apprehensive about is not failing to recognize the dead, for instance because he was disfigured by a fire or because he's become reduced to a skeleton (First Clown: "... Here's a skull now. This skull has lain in the earth three and twenty years." Hamlet: "Whose was it?" First Clown: "A whoreson mad fellow's it was. Whose do you think it was?" Hamlet: "Nay, I know not." First Clown: "A pestilence on him for a mad rogue! He poured / a flagon of Rhenish on my head once. This same skull, sir, / was Yorick's skull, the King's jester." Hamlet: "This?" First Clown: "E'en that." Hamlet: "Let me see. [He takes the skull] / Alas, poor Yorick! I knew him, Horatio: a fellow / of infinite jest, of most excellent fancy: he hath / borne me on his back a thousand times; and now, how / abhorred in my imagination it is! my gorge rims at / it. Here hung those lips that I have kissed I know / not how oft" [Hamlet, act 5, sc. 1]), but that the one I recognize as him or her would instead be another, an impostor, a double.

282. From Nietzsche's letter of January 5, 1889, to Jacob Burckhardt, in Selected Letters of Friedrich Nietzsche, 347.

283. Would a human ever wonder "Am I dead?" were humans not already dead at some level before they organically cease to live? If one's first impression in death is of uncanniness, of an eerie familiarity, it is that we are already dead, that we have already been there.

284. "Am I dead?" is more assertive, indicates more certitude than "I must be dead!"

285. From Nietzsche's letter of January 5, 1889, to Jacob Burckhardt, in Selected Letters of Friedrich Nietzsche, 347.

286. It was the thinker of aristocratic, noble values (On the Genealogy of Morals) who said of himself, "I am a Polish nobleman pur sang, with which not a drop of bad blood is mixed, least of all German blood" (Ecce Homo), and who wrote against the mixing of races, at least against an abrupt radical mixing of races ("When a philosopher these days makes it known that he is not a skeptic ... everyone gets upset.... Skepticism ... originates whenever races or classes that have been separated for a long time are suddenly and decisively interbred. The different standards and values ... get passed down ... to the next generation where everything is in a state of restlessness, disorder, doubt, experimentation. The best forces have inhibitory effects, the virtues themselves do not let each other strengthen and grow, both body and soul lack a center of balance, a center of gravity.... But what is most profoundly sick and degenerate about such hybrids is the

will.... Our contemporary Europe, the site of an absurdly sudden experiment in the radical mixing of classes and *consequently* of races, is therefore skeptical from its heights to its depths" [Friedrich Nietzsche, *Beyond Good and Evil: Prelude to a Philosophy of the Future*, ed. Rolf-Peter Horstmann and Judith Norman, trans. Judith Norman (Cambridge: Cambridge University Press, 2002), §208, 99–100]), who in his dying before dying exclaimed: "Every name in history is I." Whatever the immigration laws of his or her country, a mortal is, insofar as he or she is dead even while still physically alive, populated by the others. There is, consequently, a fundamental despair in every xenophobe and racist (a type Nietzsche despised, indeed loathed) because, as a mortal, he or she belongs to every race and, disoriented in the labyrinthine space and time of death, is bereft of borders since these require mappable space. Casting out the foreigner takes place not only by means of xenophobic laws but also through attempts to reduce humans to solely living beings, rather than mortals.

287. See the first section "Counterfeiting" in this book.

288. Freud, *The Standard Edition*, vol. 17 (1917–1919), *"An Infantile Neurosis" and Other Works* (1955), 242; cf. Leo Tolstoy, *"The Cossacks," "The Death of Ivan Ilyich," "Happy Ever After,"* trans. Rosemary Edmonds (New York: Penguin, 1960), 137: "The example of a syllogism which he had learned in Kiezewetter's *Logic*: 'Caius is a man, men are mortal, therefore Caius is mortal,' had seemed to him all his life to be true as applied to Caius but certainly not as regards himself. That Caius—man in the abstract—was mortal was perfectly correct; but he was not Caius, nor man in the abstract: he had always been a creature quite, quite different from all others."

289. Freud, *The Standard Edition*, vol. 14 (1914–1916), *"On the History of the Psycho-Analytic Movement," "Papers on Metapsychology," and Other Works* (1957), 289. And if in his unconscious he does not believe that he *will* die, this is partly because he is already dead there.

290. Heidegger, *Being and Time*, 297. Magritte's painting *Not to Be Reproduced* (1937) shows a man facing a mirror in which we can see a similar figure but with its back to him and us. We can view the reproduction mentioned and proscribed in the title as referring to the figure, since, subject to over-turns, a characteristic of mortals, he cannot be represented, reproduced by someone else.

291. See *Discourse* 20, no. 3 (Fall 1998): 165–69; reprinted in *Forthcoming* (Berkeley: Atelos, 2000). While both young and old people are already dead even as they live, old people feel such conjunction more starkly and this shows in their additional solitude. This is not simply the

solitude of someone who has lost many old friends to death (in this period of life, *old friend* means old in age and not just someone who has been one's friend for a long time), but largely that of one who increasingly presages the radical aloneness in the labyrinthine realm of death. Given that very old filmmakers feel distanced from the world by the approach of death, their films manifest an increasing indifference toward the audience, who are part of the world, and an abatement of effects of and occasions for identification.

292. The non-concurrence also takes the form of the non-coincidence of the body with itself in out-of-the-body experiences and/or of the body with the voice (for instance a man's voice for a woman's body—cinema has given disconcerting examples of this: *Rashomon*, William Friedkin's *The Exorcist*).

293. While proper names are substitutable in death, this is not necessarily the case with epithets—in this respect, it is symptomatic that Sana'a Mehaidli's testimony ends with "My will is that you call me *the bride of the south*." In which case while in death, I, Jalal Toufic, can exclaim, "I am the martyr Sana'a Youcef Mehaidli," I cannot say, "I am *the bride of the south*."

294. More risky than "I am Comrade Khalil Ahmad Rahhal" but still less risky than "I am the martyr Comrade Khalil Ahmad Rahhal" is the false information Mroué attributes to himself in *Three Posters* and giving to the fictional characters of *Extension 19* (*Muqassam 19* [1997]) his actors' real-life names.

295. "Picasso Speaks," *The Arts* (May 1923), 315.

296. The freezing of the dead brings out the usual physical restlessness of objects and living humans and animals (only a perfect crystal with a unique ground state at absolute zero temperature would have zero entropy), but also makes possible an unnatural self-motion of objects.

297. Little did Nancy Burson know that each of those included in her composites of the faces of various people (see Nancy Burson, Richard Carling, and David Kramlich, *Composites: Computer-Generated Portraits* [New York: Beech Tree Books (1986)]), for example Bette Davis, Audrey Hepburn, Grace Kelly, Sophia Lauren, and Marilyn Monroe in *First Beauty Composite* (1982); Jane Fonda, Jacqueline Bisset, Diane Keaton, Brooke Shields, and Meryl Streep in *Second Beauty Composite* (1982); the six women and six men of *Androgyny* (1982); and "an Oriental, a Caucasian, and a Black" in *Mankind* (1983–85), weighted according to current population statistics, was already a composite of every living person.

298. *Selected Letters of Friedrich Nietzsche*, 347.

299. In the case of the dead-before-dying Nietzsche (who wrote in a letter: "This autumn ... I twice attended my funeral"), one of these subunits into which he dissociated and that was itself still a composite was Nietzsche, as the *every name in history is I* in his "I am Prado, I am also Prado's father, I venture to say that I am also Lesseps.... I am also Chambige.... Every name in history is I" implies. One can thus unfold the statement: "I am Prado, I am also Prado's father, I venture to say that I am also Lesseps.... I am also Chambige.... I am also Nietzsche.... Every name in history is I." This implied "I am also Nietzsche" in an enumeration of the other names Nietzsche had become is most uncanny.

300. *Alone with the Alone* is the English title of Henry Corbin's book on the Sufism of Ibn 'Arabī; in Corbin's title the second *Alone* refers to God.

301. Benjamin, *Illuminations*, 233. In Lars von Trier's *The Kingdom* (1994), as he stands in front of a corpse soon to be dissected, a doctor asks one of his students: "Would you mind if I touched your face?" "No thanks!" He then asks another: "You. Stand next to him. Closer! Closer, closer, closer!" "I don't like it." "Do you think the people who lie on this table *like* it? Would they like it when we begin to cut them up?" "I don't know." "I say that the fear of being touched, of getting close to people, is the fear of death. Why? Because it is the fear of fellowship. Every time you move along the seat of the bus to avoid contact, every time you avoid poking your finger in the wound of a patient's illness, it is the fear of fellowship, of that greater fellowship. Everyone we work on here has accepted his place in the fellowship. A corpse makes no demands. With sublime generosity a corpse delivers its body to the science that belongs to all of us.... The law of the dead is to *give*. That invokes respect [respect here plays an analogous role to that of caution in the Benjamin quote: 'he (the surgeon) greatly diminishes the distance between himself and the patient by penetrating into the patient's body, and increases it but little by the caution with which his hand moves among the organs']. Right ... the first incision."

302. Mircea Eliade, *Rites and Symbols of Initiation: The Mysteries of Birth and Rebirth*, trans. Willard R. Trask (New York: Harper Torchbooks, 1975), 90.

303. "Layers of the Skin," U.S. National Cancer Institute's Surveillance, Epidemiology and End Results (SEER) Program, https://training.seer.cancer.gov/melanoma/anatomy/layers.html.

304. Gerald S. Wilkinson, "Food Sharing in Vampire Bats," *Scientific American*, February 1990, 76.

305. Le Fanu, *In a Glass Darkly*, 459.

306. Daniel Paul Schreber, *Memoirs of My Nervous Illness*, trans. and ed. Ida Macalpine and Richard A. Hunter (New York: New York Review Books, 2000), 141, 144-45.

307. Wikipedia, "Quantum Zeno Effect," https://en.wikipedia.org/wiki/Quantum_Zeno_effect.

308. Bergson, *Matter and Memory*, 36.

309. The "omnipresent" act of observation that Dziga Vertov's kino-eye is purported to be ("We, the masters of vision, the organizers of visible life, armed with the omnipresent kino-eye" [*Kino-Eye: The Writings of Dziga Vertov*, ed. Annette Michelson, trans. Kevin O'Brien (Berkeley: University of California Press, 1984), 20]) can coexist with universal interaction precisely because it is not omnipresent after all but contains refractory periods (at least in the guise of the periodic closing of the shutter of both the camera and the projector), for the absence of any refractory period leads to the quantum Zeno effect ("One can 'freeze' the evolution of the system by measuring it frequently enough in its known initial state" [Wikipedia, "Quantum Zeno Effect"]). The freeze-frames in *Man with a Movie Camera* indicate that kino-eye did manage at times to become a total observation.

310. Rimbaud to his mother, who asked him what *A Season in Hell* "*voulait dire*" (meant): "It says what it says, literally and in every sense" (Ça dit ce que ça dit, littéralement et dans tous les sens).

311. Werner Herzog, *Of Walking in Ice*, trans. Martje Herzog and Alan Greenberg (New York: Tanam Press, 1980), 5. Eisner died on November 25, 1983.

312. "In the old days of classical mechanics the idea of a vacuum was simple. The vacuum was what remained if you emptied a container of all its particles and lowered the temperature down to absolute zero. The arrival of quantum mechanics, however, completely changed our notion of a vacuum.... Even a perfect vacuum at absolute zero has fluctuating fields known as "vacuum fluctuations." ... They have observable consequences.... For example, ... vacuum fluctuations cause an excited atom to fall into its ground state. The Casimir force is the most famous mechanical effect of vacuum fluctuations" (Astrid Lambrecht, "The Casimir Effect: A Force from Nothing,"

Physics World, September 1, 2002, https://physicsworld.com/a/ the-casimir-effect-a-force-from-nothing).

313. It would be felicitous for a movie theater to have the following double feature program: Dreyer's *Ordet* with Bergman's *Persona,* that other great film of resurrection. Near the beginning of *Persona,* there is the following series of shots: a close shot of an old woman's motionless hand with the sound of dripping water; a close shot of the motionless old woman; a medium shot of a motionless child supine on a bed and covered to the chin with a white sheet; then five shots of dead people; then a high-angle close-up of the old woman over which we hear the insistent ringing of a phone. Suddenly she opens her eyes. The next shot is a wide shot of the previously seen child turning in his bed then placing glasses over his eyes and beginning to read. How is it that only very few spectators are jolted by the child's movement? How is it that so many don't notice that it signals a resurrection?

314. Carl Theodor Dreyer, *Dreyer in Double Reflection,* ed. Donald Skoller (New York: Dutton, 1973), 163 (my italics).

315. If, on the death of the other, I feel that I can no longer meet him or her, it is not because he or she no longer exists, but because death is a labyrinth, where we are lost to each other.

316. Georges Bataille, "Hegel, Death and Sacrifice," trans. Jonathan Strauss, in *On Bataille,* ed. Allen Stoekl, *Yale French Studies* 78 (1990): 19–20.

317. Stanislavski, *An Actor Prepares,* 54.

318. Ibid., 55.

319. G. W. F. Hegel, *Phenomenology of Spirit,* trans. A. V. Miller (Oxford: Clarendon Press, 1977), 19.

320. Philip K. Dick, *Eye in the Sky* (Boston: Mariner Books, 2012), 185.

321. Ibid., 186.

322. Martin Heidegger, *On the Way to Language,* trans. Peter D. Hertz (New York: Harper, 1971), 107.

323. Louis Althusser, "Ideology and Ideological State Apparatuses (Notes Towards an Investigation)," in *Video Culture,* ed. John Hanhardt (Rochester, NY: Visual Studies Workshop Press, 1986), 86.

324. *Merriam-Webster Dictionary*, "about-face," https://www.merriam-webster.com/dictionary/about-face.

325. Pascal Bonitzer, "Partial Vision: Film and the Labyrinth," trans. Fabrice Ziolkowski, *Wide Angle* 4, no. 4 (1981): 58.

326. *Oxford Dictionary of English*, 3rd ed.

327. Ibid.

328. Ibid.

329. *Britannica*, "Dhionísios, Count Solomós," https://www.britannica.com/biography/Dhionisios-Count-Solomos.

330. "Now that you have finished the video you came to Beirut to make, why don't you leave?" He, observant of the traffic lights, wanted to stay in Beirut at least until the occasion presented itself when he would exceptionally pass the red one; this happened on January 3, 2000, during a shootout between army and police forces and a gunman who had fired four rocket-propelled grenades at the Russian embassy in Corniche el Mazraa in Beirut (according to state-run television, a piece of paper found on him after he was gunned down read, "In sacrifice for Chechnya").

331. "Theo Angelopoulos in Conversation with Gideon Bachmann," *Film Comment* 34, no. 4 (July–August, 1998).

332. Is it the flower that the resurrected woman of Blanchot's *Death Sentence* hallucinates? Is it the flower resurrected in both Cocteau's *The Testament of Orpheus* and Godard's *King Lear*?

333. Schreber, *Memoirs of My Nervous Illness*, 24, 29, 30, etc.

334. Ibid., 25n6.

335. Antonin Artaud, *Artaud the Mômo*, ed. Stephen Barber, trans. Clayton Eshleman, bilingual edition (Zurich: Diaphanes, 2020), 7.

336. Cf. Qur'ān 15:65: "Therefore go forth with your followers in a part of the night and yourself follow their rear, and let not any one of you turn round."

337. As a consequence, they continued to walk in the same direction, despite their turn.

338. This essay was delivered on January 27, 2000, as part of a series of lectures and readings that accompanied the Sursock Museum's exhibition *Kahlil Gibran: Horizons of the Painter*. My friend Etel Adnan had shortly before, on 11 January 2000, also given a lecture in relation to the same exhibit, titled "Khalil Gibran and Georges Schéhadé." Were one in a less degenerate period of Arab culture, it would be Gibran who would be asked, through a mediumistic séance rather than a media one (séances were a forerunner of our media), to speak on—as best he can—or draw the two authors of *The Arab Apocalypse* and *Forthcoming*, he who was wont to draw thinkers and poets (Carl Gustav Jung, William Butler Yeats, Rabindranath Tagore, etc.).

339. "The warmth of [Charles] Boyer's performance in *Aux Jardins de Murcie* was due in part to its female lead, Renée Falconetti. During the production they became lovers…. A decade older than Boyer, Falconetti had a sexual history that was as varied as his was uneventful. While still in her teens, she became the mistress of Henri Goldstuck, a millionaire old enough to be her father. They had a daughter, but she left them both to enter the Conservatoire" (John Baxter, *Charles Boyer: The French Lover* [Lexington: University Press of Kentucky, 2021], 17).

340. While the eloquence of the orator and/or demagogue is in speaking (with words and punctuating silence), the eloquence of prayer is in listening.

341. Cf. Luke 2:10: "An angel of the Lord appeared to them, and the glory of the Lord shone around them, and they were terrified."

342. From the letter the poet wrote to Lou Andreas-Salomé the evening of February 11, 1922, just after finishing the *Duino Elegies*.

343. In contrast, Oedipus and his father at the crossroads are both late on time: late in relation to the oracle that foretold that the former will kill the latter, on time in relation to the present of its actualization.

344. This characteristic of the angel, that he does not arrive, is missed in *Wings of Desire*.

345. While some oracles may seem impossible, their interpretation reveals that they are not really so. Therefore what the oracle announces is not an event.

346. Jesus's rising from the dead is an event, as it was announced by him as the impossible to happen (indeed, two men in clothes that

gleam like lightning suddenly stand beside the women who went with spices to his tomb and remind them: "Remember how he told you, while he was still with you in Galilee: 'The Son of Man must be delivered into the hands of sinful men, be crucified and on the third day be raised again'" [Luke 24:6-7]).

347. Similarly, on being told by the angel, "Your wife Elizabeth will bear you a son ...," Zechariah asked the angel: "How can I be sure of this? I am an old man and my wife is well along in years" (Luke 1:13-18). To the Lord's annunciation to Abraham, "As for Sarai your wife ... I will bless her and will surely give you a son by her. I will bless her so that she will be the mother of nations; kings of peoples will come from her," Abraham laughed and said to himself: "Will a son be born to a man a hundred years old? Will Sarah bear a child at the age of ninety?" (Genesis 17:15-17; cf. Genesis 18:1-12 for Sarah's similarly incredulous response).

348. Paul Virilio, *The Information Bomb*, trans. Chris Turner (London: Verso, 2000), 127.

349. "Unlike you I see something in all that 'transmission' of things. I see angels—which, incidentally, in case you didn't know, comes from the ancient Greek word for messengers. Take a good look around. Air hostesses and pilots; radio messages; all the air crew just flown in from Tokyo and just about to leave for Rio; those dozen aircraft neatly lined up ... as they wait to take off; yellow postal vans delivering parcels, packets and telegrams; staff calls over the tannoy; all these bags passing in front of us on the conveyor; endless announcements for Mr X or Miss Y recently arrived from Stockholm or Helsinki; boarding announcements for Berlin and Rome, Sydney and Durban; passengers ... hurrying for taxis and shuttles.... Don't you see—what we have here is angels of steel, carrying angels of flesh and blood, who in turn send angel signals across angel air waves" (Michel Serres, *Angels: A Modern Myth*, trans. Francis Cowper, ed. Philippa Hurd [Paris: Flammarion, 1995], 8).

350. David Schendler, "Only a God Can Save Us Now: An Interview with Martin Heidegger," *Graduate Faculty Philosophy Journal* 6, no. 1 (1977): 5-27.

351. We can only prepare for the coming of the Messiah/Mahdi without forcing the end if the one who then proclaims his advent is only later revealed as himself the Messiah/Mahdi. This is how the proclamation of the Great Resurrection (*al-qiyāma al-kubrá*, a.k.a. *Qiyāmat al-qiyāma*) by the Nizārī Ḥasan *'alā dhikrihi'l-salām* (on his mention be peace) happened: he first proclaimed it in the name

of another, the still occulted imam, then was himself revealed as the imam.

352. In the Sursock Museum's exhibition *Kahlil Gibran: Horizons of the Painter*, where I first saw this watercolor, it seemed as out of place amidst Gibran's other drawings and paintings as an angel in the world. Gibran certainly came a very long way between his drawings circa 1904 of angels with their conventional wings and the 1923 angel with mountainous wings.

353. When entities exist not in the world but in light, as in eternity, there is no alternation of day and night, for night, the absence of light, would then be the absence of entities; or, more precisely, "night is also a sun" (Nietzsche's Zarathustra: "A haze and fragrance of eternity? ... Do you not smell it? Just now my world became perfect, midnight is also noon ...: night is also a sun" [Nietzsche, *Thus Spoke Zarathustra: A Book for All and None*, 263]).

354. Ernie Gehr's film *Serene Velocity* has the perfect title for a work on light, since at light's speed (in other words, *velocity* [setting aside the difference between these related concepts]), which is absolute, time slows down to a stop (*serene*).

355. Even the cherubim who barred Adam and Eve's way back to paradise ("After he drove the man out, he placed on the east side of the Garden of Eden cherubim and a flaming sword flashing back and forth to guard the way to the tree of life" [Genesis 3:24]) did so while kneeling before them.

356. While unreported in the New Testament, did Jesus Christ say to a walking man: "Rise up!"? The man's body would have changed into one that was no longer virtually cadaverous. Crucified Jesus Christ's ascension was first physically in place: that of his body as it became no longer a cadaver even potentially or virtually but only a corpse. As he ascended through the angelic heavenly hierarchies, while his pierced and bloodied body confused them as to his nature, the circumstance that they did not feel constrained to fall prostrate in front of him indicated to them that, while his body was human, it was a resurrected one. In their consequent adoration, none of them knelt.

357. Cees Nooteboom, *The Following Story*, trans. Ina Rilke (New York: Harcourt Brace, 1994), 9: "If one is immortal oneself, the stench emanating from mortals must be intolerable." Gods who incarnate in humans suffer both the fall of the virtual cadaver and the smell of putrefaction any immortal senses in the vicinity of any mortal.

358. In the Old Testament, the names that the angel of the Lord gives have meaning, are descriptions. This intimates that angels do not have a proper understanding of names, of proper names. The angels knew the names Man and Woman, but not Adam and Eve. Angels wait for us in the present not only because, aeviternal, they reach it before us, but also because they do not know how to call us, since they do not use our names as proper names but as characterizations. The New International Version for Genesis 16:11 should read: "The angel of the Lord also said to her: 'You are now with child and you will have a son. You shall name him God Hears [*Ishmael*], for the Lord has heard of your misery'"; and for Genesis 17:5, it should be: "No longer will you be called Exalted Father [*Abram*]; your name will be Father of Many [*Abraham*] for I have made you a father of many nations." Can we say that in Islam, God, to be more specific the divine essence, cannot be called, only His names? Yes, but only if we bear in mind that *al-samiʿ* (the Hearer), *al-baṣīr* (the Seer), and the other names of Islam's God are how the angels understand names. Should we then conclude that in Islam mortals cannot call God? Why and how, then, do they pray? They can call him by means of prayer only through Him: "My servant draws near to Me through nothing I love more than that which I have made obligatory for him. My servant never ceases drawing near to Me through supererogatory works until I love him. Then, when I love him, I am his hearing through which he hears, his sight through which he sees ..." (*ḥadīth qudsī*). When they treat names as descriptions of the named human, mortals imply a disavowal of their mortality, act as if they were angels: "Adam named his wife Eve [*Eve* probably means *living*], because she would become the mother of all the living" (Genesis 3:20); "The first to come out was red, and his whole body was like a hairy garment; so they named him Esau [*Esau* may mean *hairy*; he was also called *Edom*, which means *red*]. After this, his brother came out, with his hand grasping Esau's heel; so he was named Jacob [*Jacob* means *he grasps the heel* (figuratively, *he deceives*)]" (Genesis 25:25-26; cf. Genesis 4:25, 10:25, and 27:36).

We are to consider that each time it appears than an angel addressed someone or invoked someone by a proper name, this is happening

1. following Adam's informing the angels of the names. What does "and when he [Adam] had informed them [the angels] of their [creatures'] names" mean? He taught the angels to call someone no longer He Grasps the Heel but Jacob, for example;

2. or in a recounted dream ("The angel of God said to me in the dream, 'Jacob.' I answered, 'Here I am.' And he said, 'Look up and see that all the male goats mating with the flock are streaked, speckled or spotted, for I have seen all that Laban has been doing to you'" [Genesis 31:11-12]), hence when the event has undergone secondary revision by the psychic apparatus of the *mortal* dreamer

("*Secondary Revision* [or *Elaboration*]: Rearrangement of a dream so as to present it in the form of a relatively consistent and comprehensible scenario. The elimination of the dream's apparent absurdity and incoherence, the filling-in of its gaps, the partial or total reorganisation of its elements by means of selection and addition …—these, essentially, are what Freud called secondary revision, or, at times, 'considerations of intelligibility' [*Rücksicht auf Verständlichkeit*].… Since secondary revision is an effect of the censorship—which, as Freud emphasises in this connection, does not have a negative role alone but can also be responsible for additions—it is to be seen at work especially when the subject is getting near to a waking state, and a fortiori when he comes to recount his dream. All the same, the process does in fact go on at every moment of the dream" [J. Laplanche and J.-B. Pontalis, *The Language of Psycho-Analysis*, trans. Donald Nicholson-Smith (New York: Norton, 1974), 412]);

3. or, in the instances in the New Testament, because we are dealing with a God who, in the figure of the Son, is mortal, hence understands proper names, indeed has one himself, Jesus, therefore one whose angels, relaying his messages, can utter proper names—even without themselves understanding them ("The angel said to her, 'Do not be afraid, Mary, you have found favor with God'" [Luke 1:30]; "But the angel said to him: 'Do not be afraid, Zechariah; your prayer has been heard. Your wife Elizabeth will bear you a son, and you are to give him the name John'" [Luke 1:13]).

359. Schreber, *Memoirs of My Nervous Illness*, 62.

360. The heavenly Father sent his Son into the Garden of Eden prior to sending him to be born of Mary, giving him the same instruction he gave to Adam: not to eat of the tree of the knowledge of good and evil. It is partly in this sense that Jesus Christ is "the second Adam" (Paul, 1 Corinthians 15:47; cf. Qur'ān 3:59: "Truly the likeness of Jesus in the sight of God is that of Adam"). Thus the heavenly Father's sacrifice was more radical than that of just allowing his Son to die physically on the Cross: He allowed for the possibility of His Son's true mortality were the latter to choose, like Adam, to eat first of the tree of the knowledge of good and evil. But Christ resisted this temptation, eating first from the tree of life—hence he could assert, "I am … the life" (John 11:25). Only then did he eat from the tree of the knowledge of good and evil. Christ is thus not really a mortal, not in the full sense of the word, not in the sense in which Adam is, and it is because of this that, although he ate of the tree of the knowledge of good and evil, and although he died physically on the Cross, he "was unquestionably without sin" (Augustine). "He took upon Himself not

only the nature of man, a nature capable of suffering and sickness and death, He became like a man in all save only sin" (Francisco Suárez, "De Incarnatione," Praef. n. 5): these words can be true only if Christ did not take upon himself full death. For the imam to be *ma'sūm* (infallible, sinless), he must not be a mortal, that is, dead even while physically alive, and must not fall for the temptation of mortality; and he must not "have" an unconscious, with the consequence that he does not have dreams—other than visionary ones—and does not commit any parapraxis.

361. It is certainly a poor view of the richness of the Qur'ān to think that it sometimes repeats the same scene and episode, that there is repetition in the infinite. Every time a story or a line or an episode in the Qur'ān (for instance the heavenly prostration scene) is ostensibly repeated, it has to be given different *ta'wīls*, interpretations. By taking into consideration just the heavenly prostration scene (Qur'ān 2, 7, 15, 17, 18, 20, 38), there are seven varieties of Iblīs.

362. "*S'appeler* (= *être nommé*) to be called; *il s'appelle Paul*: his name is Paul, he's called Paul" (*Le Robert & Collins Senior, Dictionnaire Français-Anglais/Anglais-Français*, 5th ed). *Je m'appelle*: I am called, but literally: I call myself. French is better than English and Arabic at conveying the relation of naming oneself to being named by others, how the latter virtually presupposes the former. And it is to the French language that we have to resort to best render what takes place in front of the mirror: a *sous-entendu* call (animals are not really mortals, are not subject to over-turns, and thus do not implicitly call themselves in front of the mirror and therefore have no proper names). It is thus felicitous and probably not accidental that it is a French-speaking painter, the Belgian René Magritte, who did the most fundamental painting of the back, of the relation of the back of a mortal, of someone who is subject to over-turns, to the proper name.

363. "You have to kill him: he's not Dracula, he's only a simulacrum of Dracula." "I cannot kill him, I love him." She put the stake away and called him by his name to resurrect him (what she overlooked was that to resurrect someone, it is not enough to call him with the right name and in the right manner to undo the over-turn; one must also help him succeed in overcoming the indefinite fall that his cadaver is). The one who pronounces my name in the most appealing manner is the one who will resurrect me, therefore the one whom I will probably love but not marry, since the one I marry will de jure not resurrect me but rather follow me into the underworld, where we will be parted by the labyrinth there (the Christian marriage vow: *till death do us part*). While the spiritual master treats me as already dead even while I live, calling me by my esoteric name, my other name, my

allonym (I am not using "allonym" to mean "the name of a person, usually a historical person, assumed by a writer" [*American Heritage Dictionary*], but, following its etymology [Greek *allos*, other; see allo- + Greek *onoma*, name; see n- men-], to mean the other name, the one we may be given after an initiation, and/or the one to which we may respond in bardo states); my lover will treat me as alive even when I am dead, calling me by the name I had while alive while trying to resurrect me.

364. *American Heritage Dictionary.*

365. *The Station Hill Blanchot Reader: Fiction and Literary Essays*, trans. Lydia Davis, Paul Auster, and Robert Lamberton, ed. George Quasha (Barrytown, NY: Station Hill Press, 1999), 144.

366. Ibid., 147.

367. Ibid., 134.

368. Ibid., 137.

369. The testament is to maintain the notion that the dead has a will. It is likely that the legal system exists more to grant a will to those who no longer have one than to institute, interpret, and enforce laws for the living. All testaments are forged.

370. In 1972, Anne Rice's 5-year-old daughter, Michelle, died of leukemia. While writing her first vampire book, and "unaware of the significance of what she was doing, she added a beautiful little girl with golden curls (like Michelle), whom the vampires save from mortal death by making her a vampire.... The first version ended with the child, Claudia, and Louis happily joining other vampires in Paris. In the revision, 'I felt that Claudia had really been meant to die at the end of *Interview* the way Michelle had died.... 'In cheating'—that is, in allowing Claudia to live—Rice says she did herself psychic damage: 'I almost died myself and went kind of crazy. I saw germs on everything and washed my hands 50 times and really cracked up.... If somebody is meant to die and you don't do it, you're really risking your well-being at the end of the book'" (Susan Ferraro, "Novels You Can Sink Your Teeth Into," *New York Times Magazine*, October 14, 1990, 74 and 76).

371. *The Station Hill Blanchot Reader*, 142. Elsewhere he writes: "Today I try without success to understand why I stayed away from Paris then, when everything was calling me back" (138).

372. Rainer Maria Rilke, *The Notebooks of Malte Laurids Brigge*, trans. Stephen Mitchell (New York: Random House, 1983), 14-15.

373. With the successful gradual democratization of immortality and the afterlife in ancient Egypt, which changed from the prerogative of the pharaoh, a god, to become something to which first the high functionaries, then the rich merchants, then a majority of Egyptians could lay claim, a heightened awareness of the importance of death must have spread to large strata of the population and must have led to a polarization. For those who could hope to have an afterlife, a lightening of the dying ordeal must have ensued, since what was important was what preceded death: life as the occasion to prepare all the conditions for a good afterlife (the building of the tomb, the provision for mortuary offerings, etc.); and what followed it (the opening of the mouth ceremony, the continuing preservation of the mummy, the perpetuation of the mortuary offerings, etc.). For some of those who were still excluded from laying claim to such an afterlife, the consequence was rather an exacerbation of their dying, which must have become awesome.

374. Rilke, *The Notebooks of Malte Laurids Brigge*, 9.

375. I presume that Thomas Bernhard outlived his doctor's prognosis (*Wittgenstein's Nephew*) because the diagnosis on which it was based was erroneous.

376. Cf. "When Jesus came to the region of Caesarea Philippi, he asked his disciples, 'Who do people say the Son of Man is?' They replied, 'Some say John the Baptist; others say Elijah; and still others, Jeremiah or one of the prophets.' 'But what about you?' he asked. 'Who do you say I am?'" (Matthew 16:13-15).

377. Jacques Lacan, *Écrits: A Selection*, trans. Alan Sheridan (New York: Norton, 1977), 290: "Giving in love what she does not have."

378. Since the fictional vampire already undergoes dreamlike events all night long, it would be inelegant to make him sleep, and therefore possibly dream, during the day.

379. Freud, *The Interpretation of Dreams*, 338.

380. Serge Daney, *Ciné Journal, 1981-1986*, preface by Gilles Deleuze (Paris: Cahiers du Cinéma, 1986), 125.

381. "An absence seizure causes you to blank out or stare into space for a few seconds. They can also be called petit mal seizures....

Absence seizures usually occur in children between ages 4 to 14. A child may have 10, 50, or even 100 absence seizures in a given day and they may go unnoticed" ("Absence Seizures," Johns Hopkins Medicine, https://www.hopkinsmedicine.org/health/conditions-and-diseases/epilepsy/absence-seizures). "The absence lasts a few seconds; its beginning and its end are sudden. The senses function, but are nevertheless closed to external impressions. The return being just as sudden as the departure, the arrested word and action are picked up again where they have been interrupted. Conscious time comes together again automatically, forming a continuous time without apparent breaks. For these absences, which can be quite numerous—hundreds every day most often pass completely unnoticed by others around—we'll be using the word 'picnolepsy' (from the Greek, *picnos*: frequent). However, for the picnoleptic, nothing really has happened, the missing time never existed. At each crisis, without realizing it, a little of his or her life simply escaped.... The situation of the young picnoleptic quickly becomes intolerable. People want to persuade him of the existence of events that he has not seen.... When we place a bouquet under the eyes of the young picnoleptic and we ask him to draw it, he draws not only the bouquet but also the person who is supposed to have placed it in the vase, and even the field of flowers where it was possibly gathered. There is a tendency to patch up sequences, readjusting their contours to make equivalents out of what the picnoleptic has seen and what he has not been able to see, what he remembers and what, evidently, he cannot remember and that it is necessary to invent, to recreate, in order to lend verisimilitude to his *discursus*" (Paul Virilio, *The Aesthetics of Disappearance*, trans. Philip Beitchman [New York: Semiotext(e), 1991], 9–10).

382. Deleuze, *Cinema 1: The Movement-Image*, 5.

383. Oliver Sacks, *Awakenings* (New York: HarperCollins, 1990), 112–13. A koan in relation to Susan Morrissey's painting *Have a Ball Sw'theart* (1987): "How to juggle one ball without letting ten fall?"

384. Ibid., 21–22.

385. APA *Dictionary of Psychology*, "positive hallucination," https://dictionary.apa.org/positive-hallucination.

386. APA *Dictionary of Psychology*, "negative hallucination," https://dictionary.apa.org/negative-hallucination.

387. Bazin, *What Is Cinema?*, vol. 1, 107.

388. The first time we see Dracula walking in the streets of 1897 London in Coppola's *Bram Stoker's Dracula* (1992), we hear the sound of a film projector and see the passersby move in a manner reminiscent of that of people in silent films (which for the most part were shot at eighteen frames per second but are projected at twenty-four frames per second).

389. Bazin, *What Is Cinema?*, vol. 1, 105.

390. *Autobiography of a Schizophrenic Girl*, 37.

391. L. P. Guarente, Petra Simic, and Kara Rogers, "Aging," *Britannica*, https://www.britannica.com/science/aging-life-process.

392. The opening and closing of the gate of the vampire's castle before and behind what appears to be his future victim in vampire films is both a foreshadowing of his entrance into the regime of fascination and a sign that he already entered that regime of self-motion, where things, sounds, and words move or link on their own. These trance inducements are one of the most beautiful sites of foreshadowing, for they are foreshadowings that coincide with what they announce (the hypnosis).

393. While the prepubescent female dancer, for example, a Balinese dancer ("All of the players and dancers of the exceptional troupe *Tirta Sari*, from the village of Peliatan, are children, ranging in age from seven to fourteen" [Muriel Topaz, "A Letter from Indonesia," *Dance Magazine*, 12/1/1997]; indeed, the two young girls who play *legong* must retire by the time they reach puberty) is not yet able to give a second body through conception, she is able to give a second body through dance, in the form of the virtual dancer she projects into the realm of dance.

394. Max Planck Institute for Biology of Ageing, "When Does Ageing Start?" https://www.age.mpg.de/when-does-ageing-start.

395. When we die, we feel what Christ experienced not only on first being incarnated in Jesus of Nazareth, but all along his incarnation in the latter: an endless fall.

396. Borhane Alaouié's film *Kafr Kassem* manifests this magnification effect with its shots of Palestinian fields, plains, and valleys aurally covered by the broadcast voice of Abdel Nasser.

397. "Abu Simbel, site of two temples built by the Egyptian king Ramses II (reigned 1279–13 BCE).... The 66-foot (20-metre) seated

figures of Ramses are set against the recessed face of the cliff, two on either side of the entrance to the main temple.... In the mid-20th century, when the reservoir that was created by the construction of the nearby Aswan High Dam threatened to submerge Abu Simbel, UNESCO and the Egyptian government sponsored a project to save the site.... Between 1963 and 1968 a workforce and an international team of engineers and scientists ... dug away the top of the cliff and completely disassembled both temples, reconstructing them on high ground more than 200 feet (60 metres) above their previous site" (*Britannica*, "Abu Simbel," https://www.britannica.com/place/Abu-Simbel).

398. Rilke, *The Notebooks of Malte Laurids Brigge*, 10.

399. From Nietzsche's letter of January 5, 1889, to Jacob Burckhardt, in *Selected Letters of Friedrich Nietzsche*, 347.

400. "Estimates put the number of mourners lining the funeral route at five million. Many more congregated in major cities across Egypt and the Arab world" ("Mourners Killed as Nasser Is Buried," *BBC News*, October 1, 1970); "By the time Nasser's funeral took place—with a seven-mile procession through the streets of Cairo—approximately 5 million to 6 million people had turned for a final farewell to their chief" (Loren Jenkins, "Quiet Rites Show Stark Contrast to Funeral for Nasser," *Washington Post*, October 10, 1981).

401. "His memorable speeches, broadcast on the radio and listened to by millions of people ..." (Anthony Samrani, "Le jour où Nasser a nationalisé le canal de Suez..." *L'Orient-Le Jour*, August 11, 2015); "the whole 'affair' began with a great burst of laughter in Alexandria. President Nasser couldn't contain his jubilation at the explosion of popular joy. In familiar, 'baladi' language, with a tone that was both playful and striking, he had just touched the most sensitive, most intimate fiber of the Egyptian soul: 'The Suez Canal is now ours, truly ours.' These few words had shaken the tens of thousands of people gathered in Muhammad Ali Square and the millions of others who were listening to Cairo's radio" (Eric Rouleau, "La nationalisation du canal de Suez a marqué un tournant dans les rapports entre l'Égypte et l'Occident," *Le Monde diplomatique*, June 1966). If there's a necessary link between the mighty voice and the death-size body (Gamal Abdel Nasser, Umm Kulthum, Rilke's moribund Chamberlain Christoph Detlev Brigge), then Hitler was deprived of (the manifestation of) his death-size body by the circumstances of the end of the Second World War.

402. Since, according to Jesus, "I am the resurrection and the life. The one who believes in me will live, even though they die" (John 11:25), in other words, he or she will no longer be a virtual cadaver, I would expect the aforementioned sort of tremendous funerary processions to be more frequent in Islam and Judaism, two religions that believe in the Fall but do not believe that it has been countered by a Messiah/Qā'im (exception: the Nizārīs of the Great Resurrection between 1164 and 1210).

403. Did assassinated influential Lebanese politician Rafic Hariri get a death-size body during his funeral given the very large number of people who attended it ("150,000 Attend Funeral of Hariri in Lebanon," *The Irish Times*, February 16, 2005)?

404. In Maramureş, in the northern part of Transylvania, Romania, if an unmarried person of marriageable age dies, a *wedding of the dead* is performed in which the deceased is dressed in wedding clothes and symbolically married (Gail Kligman, *The Wedding of the Dead: Ritual, Poetics, and Popular Culture in Transylvania* [Berkeley: University of California Press, 1988]). Sequelae to the hypnotic session, in the form of age regression, etc., may happen if the subjects did not adequately comply with the suggestion during the hypnosis session, that is, if they thought of it as unfinished business ("The Aftereffects of Hypnosis," in Ernest R. Hilgard, *Hypnotic Susceptibility* [New York: Harcourt, Brace and World, 1965], 58).

405. Heidegger, *Being and Time*, 297.

406. From Nietzsche's letter of January 5, 1889, to Jacob Burckhardt, in *Selected Letters of Friedrich Nietzsche*, 347.

407. Ibid.

408. Thorne, *Black Holes and Time Warps*, 450 and 476–477.

409. There is no excuse for Wenders's betrayal of Nicholas Ray in *Lightning over Water*, since around the same period he made a film, *Reverse Angle*, critical of Coppola's betrayal of him during *Hammett*.

410. Franz Kafka, *The Complete Stories*, ed. Nahum N. Glatzer (New York: Schocken Books, 1971), 254-56.

411. Friedrich Nietzsche, *"The Birth of Tragedy" and "The Genealogy of Morals,"* trans. Francis Golffing (New York: Anchor Books, 1990), 12.

412. The edit as parapraxis (and mode of telesthesia [Mina is telesthetic]).

413. "While based at the State Film School in Moscow in the 1920s, Russian filmmaker and theorist Lev Kuleshov ... discovered that through careful editing a variety of responses to the same material could be elicited from the viewer. His best-known experiment consists of a short film in which a shot of the expressionless face of actor Ivan Mozzhukhin is alternated with shots of a plate of soup, a young woman, and a little girl in a coffin. Even though the shot of Mozzhukhin was identical each time, it is claimed that viewers of the film expressed appreciation of Mozzhukhin's ability to convey the emotions of hunger, desire, and grief respectively" (Kuhn and Westwell, *A Dictionary of Film Studies*, 242).

414.   Quoted in Bram Stoker's *Dracula* (1897).

415.   Literally, "O, dead person!"; figuratively: "O, you who are so slow as to be dead!"

416.   From Hegel's manuscripts for the *Realphilosophie* of 1805-06.

417.   These are the English subtitles to what the French woman says.

418.   Maurice Blanchot, *The Last Man*, trans. Lydia Davis (Ubu Editions, 2007).

419. Author's Note to the Second Edition:
While many books are first announced as forthcoming (for example, in the inflated bios of mediocre academicians, who keep mentioning such books as forthcoming over a period of years), then published, *Over-Sensitivity*, published originally in Sun & Moon Press's Classics series in 1996, is here republished, in a revised edition, by Forthcoming Books, this making its status more explicit: even after its publication, it is still forthcoming.

What does a second edition indicate? That in the case of the first edition, one's fruits were ripe but one was not ripe for one's fruits ("Oh Zarathustra, your fruits are ripe, but you are not ripe for your fruits!" [Nietzsche, *Thus Spoke Zarathustra*])?

420. It was certainly the case that life was too short when *Over-Sensitivity*'s first edition was published, in 1996. Is it still the case at the date of publication of this revised edition, and, even more so, will it be the case a few decades from now? In *Fantastic Voyage: Live Long Enough to Live Forever* (New York: Penguin, 2004), Terry Grossman and Ray Kurzweil wrote: "Do we have the knowledge and the tools today to live forever? ... According to models that Ray has created, our paradigm-shift rate—the rate of technical progress—is doubling every decade, and the capability (price performance, capacity, and speed) of specific information technologies is doubling every year. So the answer to our question is actually a definitive yes—the knowledge exists, if aggressively applied, for you to slow aging and disease processes to such a degree that you can be in good health and good spirits when the more radical life-extending and life-enhancing technologies become available over the next couple of decades.... The goal of extending longevity can be taken in three steps, or Bridges. This book is intended to serve as a guide to living long enough in good health and spirits—Bridge One—to take advantage of the full development of the biotechnology revolution—Bridge Two. This, in turn, will lead to the nanotechnology-AI (artificial intelligence) revolution—Bridge Three—which has the potential to allow us to live indefinitely." If that is the case, then perhaps even thinkers, writers, and video makers can die before dying (physically), think, write, make videos, *and live!*

421. In gratitude to Gavin for devising the perfect scheme for seduction, Scottie leads Judy, who, being the accomplice of Gavin in his murder of his wife, can betray Gavin, to her death—taking into account this factor of gratitude, Gavin devised the perfect crime.

422. The spells of unawareness, the trance states that *Vertigo*'s Judy-as-Madeleine appears to have are not truly seductive; to ascertain

this, one has only to watch Hitchcock's *Marnie*, whose eponymous protagonist, who attracts the male protagonist largely because of the trance states that seize her when stealing or during a violent storm, nowhere has the intense seductiveness and fascination Madeleine exerts on the film spectator. For with spells, the traumatic knowledge is there though dissociated (implying this is one of the main functions of the scene of the hypnotic age-regression of Marnie). But in *Vertigo*, Gavin's wife Madeleine truly does not know that she, as impersonated by Judy, is being followed by the private detective Scottie.

423. Laplanche, *Essays on Otherness*, 79.

424. The song "Yā *laylī*" (Oh my night) by Ziad Rahbani (whose lyrics are limited to: "Yā *laylī* and Yā *layl* [Oh night]) is symptomatic of how little the Lebanese's language has registered the disaster of the 1982 Israeli invasion of Lebanon and of the later period of the civil war, with their resultant years of electricity rationing: perhaps the idiom Yā *layl* should be maintained, but only if it is somewhat and somehow altered to indicate this period of electricity rationing; otherwise, this absence of registration would be a forgetfulness of the present in the present.

425. Laplanche, *Essays on Otherness*, 158.

426. Ibid., 255.

427. Ibid., 169.

428. On one of his dates with Budūr, ʿAzīz arrives early but falls asleep while waiting for her. Budūr shows up toward dawn and places a coin and a dagger over his sleeping body: thus even when he does not meet Budūr, ʿAzīz, always an excellent messenger, still returns with a message for ʿAzīza to interpret—with the consequence that the two women have more interactions than ʿAzīz and Budūr do. Having relayed messages from Budūr to ʿAzīza even in the former's absence—her failure to show up at her projected second meeting with ʿAzīz was itself a sign to be interpreted or translated by ʿAzīza (her interpretation for the sake of ʿAzīz: it is a test by Budūr of the sincerity of ʿAzīz's love) and therefore a message—he later relays messages from ʿAzīza to Budūr even after the former's death: just before dying of a broken heart, ʿAzīza asked his mother to relay to him the following words to say to Budūr when he meets her again: "Fidelity is splendid, but no more than infidelity." It is frequently the case that the relation is between the one who proffers the *enigmatic message* (Budūr) and the one who translates it (ʿAzīza), the one who thought it intended for him being merely the messenger (ʿAzīz), a

carrier who becomes more efficient the less he understands what he is carrying—up to the limit case of not knowing that he is carrying a message. This has to do with the unconscious. If 'Azīz can still be a carrier at all after his castration by Budūr and subsequent awareness of the consequences of his previous actions, it is through a parapraxis, his unintentional dropping of the scroll so that his interlocutor, asking him to relate its story, learns about princess Dunyā—who hates men because she considers that they are unfaithful—and falls in love with her. It is thus fitting that the diegetic listener to this tale in Pasolini's adaptation, which, in my reading, largely revolves around the love of 'Azīza for Budūr, a woman she has never seen, ends up searching for Dunyā, regarding whom he soon says, "I love her without seeing her."

429. Laura Mulvey, "Visual Pleasure and Narrative Cinema," in *Film Manifestos and Global Cinema Cultures: A Critical Anthology*, ed. Scott MacKenzie (Berkeley: University of California Press, 2014), 364.

430. From a letter from Nietzsche to Erwin Rohde dated July 15, 1882: "Now I have my own study plan and behind it my own secret aim, to which the rest of my life is *consecrated....* What years [since 1876]! What wearisome pain! What inner disturbances, revolutions, solitudes! *Who* has endured as much as I have?—certainly not Leopardi. And if I now stand above all that, with the joyousness of a victor and fraught with difficult *new* plans—and, knowing myself, with the prospect of new, more difficult, and even more inwardly profound sufferings and tragedies and *with the courage to face them!*—then nobody should be annoyed with me for having a good opinion of my medicine. *Mihi ipsi scripsi* [I have written for myself]" (*Selected Letters of Friedrich Nietzsche*, 187; cf. the letter Nietzsche wrote to Peter Gast ten days later: "In many ways, body and soul, I have been since 1876 more a *battlefield* than a man" [189])—does this medicine include what he wrote in section 60 of *The Gay Science*?

431. "On a visit to Rome in 1882, Nietzsche, now at age thirty-seven, met Lou von Salomé (1861–1937), a twenty-one-year-old Russian woman who was studying philosophy and theology in Zurich. He soon fell in love with her, and offered his hand in marriage. She declined" (Robert Wicks, "Friedrich Nietzsche," *The Stanford Encyclopedia of Philosophy* [Fall 2008 Edition], ed. Edward N. Zalta, https://plato.stanford.edu/archIves/fall2008/entries/nietzsche/).

432. Friedrich Nietzsche, *"The Gay Science"; With a Prelude in Rhymes and an Appendix of Songs*, trans. Walter Kaufmann (New York: Random House, 1974), 124. Did Lou Salomé ever connect section 60 of *The Gay Science* to what Nietzsche wrote to her in a July 2, 1882

letter: "Now the sky above me is bright! Yesterday at noon I felt as if it was my birthday. *You* sent your acceptance, the most lovely present that anyone could give me now; my sister sent cherries; Teubner sent the first three page proofs of *Die fröhliche Wissenschaft*; and, on top of it all, I had just finished the very last part of my manuscript and therewith the work of six years (1876–82), my entire *Freigeisterei*. O what years! What tortures of every kind, what solitudes and weariness of life!" (*Selected Letters of Friedrich Nietzsche*, 185)?

433. If we inhabit not a universe but, as proposed by the Many-Worlds Interpretation of quantum mechanics, a multiverse, then at least in one of its branches one is to outlandishly advance that what makes it possible for someone to be distracted by the multitude of things and happenings around him or her is that his or her variants in other branches of the multiverse pay attention to these other elements and happenings in the environment, the psychological distraction having as its condition of possibility an ontological distraction.

434. Why did I fax the two letters to Amy? Is it because my letters are always *written*, and most people seem, for some reason, to feel that what is *written* has no urgency, so that my only way to imbue the two letters with (an extrinsic) urgency was to send them by fax?

435. Sent with the previous letter by priority mail on the fifteenth.

436. For example, that the repeated passage of single photons through a double slit would not result in an interference pattern [added for clarification in 2024].

437. Sent by priority mail on the fifteenth.

438. Sent by express mail on the seventeenth.

439. Sent by priority mail on the sixteenth.

440. "Approximate: (*transitive verb*): 2a. to bring near or close; (*adjective*): 1. nearly correct or exact <an *approximate* solution>" (*Merriam-Webster Dictionary*, http://www.merriam-webster.com/dictionary/approximate).

441. What I mean by *aparté* here is not simply an aside (its translation, according to French-English dictionaries) that reveals (to the theater audience) what the character is thinking and/or feeling but is not disclosing to others, but the condition of being apart from oneself (since etymologically, *aparté*, a seventeenth-century term, is "emprunté de la locution adverbiale italienne *a parte*, 'à part, à l'écart'"

[*Dictionnaire de l'Académie française*, 9th ed.]), thus talking in asides even in relation to oneself.

442. See previous footnote.

443. "Over your head: too difficult or strange for you to understand" (*Cambridge Advanced Learner's Dictionary and Thesaurus*).

444. Human creation, but possibly all creation, entails reception, too, for example, from one's untimely collaborators (which implies that one can create only if one is not totally wedged in chronological time). All creative writing is collaborative in an untimely way (and sometimes in a timely way, too). Writers need future absorbers of their writing, in other words, readers, for it not to be blocked (*Distracted* [see page 30 of this volume]), that is, for them not to suffer writer's block; and they need thinkers, filmmakers, artists, and other writers to enlarge their intuition through untimely collaboration (were it not for this reception by future readers and untimely collaboration with thinkers and artists, including future ones, the writer's solitude would be oppressive). How, from this perspective of viewing things, do we know that there is a future? We know it from our feeling that we still receive images, ideas, sounds, or dance movements, from the continuing relevance of intuition in our creative work, since intuition is partly a sensibility and receptivity to the future creation of others. A destruction of future intelligent life would be felt in the present by writers; if writers are avant-garde, they are so mainly through their untimely collaboration with future writers, thinkers, filmmakers, choreographers, etc. Were future intelligent life to be destroyed (through a nuclear conflagration, etc.), then long before this happens we would feel one of the main effects of such an absence: those close to the disaster in the future would to a large extent be unable to think properly, since they would no longer receive in an untimely manner images, ideas, or sounds from anyone (who is not in their past), and we, who receive from them images, ideas, or sounds in an untimely manner, would be impacted by their reduced intuition and thinking, becoming increasingly less able to think, for increasingly less intuitive. Long before a future disaster destroys creative intelligent life, we would no longer be able to think it; such a disaster would be preceded by this other disaster: our inability to think it (not only as a result of being steeped in the kind of technology and corresponding temporality leading to it). It is not uncommon for a writer or thinker to publish so that others would contest, if not ridicule, what he or she wrote, so much are writers and thinkers who are for real at times alarmed, if not terrified, by what they are writing and thinking. Some painters talk about painting in an intuitive manner and of not caring about what thinkers *create* in relation to their work; I do not

think they are being accurate, since intuition is partly the sensibility that allows one to feel the constraints that come from the *creation* of others, including unknown present ones and future ones, in relation to one's work. Creation is neither simply discovery (of the rule) nor simply invention (an exception that does not confirm any rule). The artist, or writer, or thinker, or filmmaker has to sense the rule, in order to build "a universe that doesn't fall apart two days later" (Philip K. Dick), then invent an exception to it, but an exception that confirms the rule—otherwise everything becomes pure invention, facile. This is why virtual worlds will not replace art, for although by changing the parameters we will come up with different rules and worlds, no exceptions that confirm them would thus have automatically been created. One is frequently told that *a picture is worth a thousand words*, yet it is sometimes these thousand words, for example, those of a script (for instance, Robbe-Grillet's for Alain Resnais' *Last Year at Marienbad*), or a poem or a Greek tragedy, that contribute to the creation of a picture that conveys something in a better manner than they can (Francis Bacon's *Triptych, Inspired by the Oresteia of Aeschylus* [1981] [in particular one of the Furies' lines, "The reek of human blood smiles out at me" (trans. W. B. Stanford)], and *Painting* [1978] ["It very much came from that poem of Eliot's, 'I have heard the key / Turn in the door once and turn once only....' ... It comes from *The Waste Land*. I don't know why I should have made it turn with the foot"]) and/or is itself something that cannot be conveyed in a thousand words—it is then that a writer's initial speechlessness regarding an artwork, which is due to the suspension of the internal monologue induced by the latter, is followed by writer's block. Even more than from the perceptive reader, the writer wants a response from the subject of the writing, which has *as a result of the writing* to show that it is even richer than writing can convey, is worth a thousand words the writer does not *then* have.

445. Read "Voice-over-witness" in this book.

446. Toufic, *(Vampires)*, pages 105, 157-58, 169, 466n108, 476n185 of this volume; *Distracted*, pages 14, 44, 454n21 of this volume.

447. Toufic, *(Vampires)*, pages 157-58, 164, 466n108 of this volume.

448. Toufic, *(Vampires)*, section "Over-turns," pages 184-90 of this volume.

449. One of the subtler forms frontality assumes in Parajanov's film *The Color of Pomegranates*: while hearing the sound of the flipping of pages, at no point do we see the successive pages of the illuminated manuscript being flipped; instead, these face us one after the other.

450. "Before a man studies Zen, to him mountains are mountains and waters are waters; after he gets an insight into the truth of Zen through the instruction of a good master, mountains to him are not mountains and waters are not waters; but after this when he really attains to the abode of rest, mountains are once more mountains and waters are waters" (*Zen Buddhism: Selected Writings of D. T. Suzuki*, ed. William Barrett [Garden City, NY: Doubleday, 1956], 14).

451. Richard Foreman, *Unbalancing Acts: Foundations for a Theater* (New York: Pantheon Books, 1992), 46.

452. This collaboration of the characters is already in evidence in *Pandering to the Masses* (1975), where the majority of the characters' lines were "recorded by as many as four voices [those of the four principal performers], alternating word by word."

453. People who indulge in this passing identification are common. Aristocrats have the pathos of distance; they do not make the projective move of momentary identification with the other person to preempt his or her response or at least to be in the best position to respond to it.

454. Distantiation can function as a phase toward the character-as-a-collaboration.

455. Foreman, *Unbalancing Acts*, 42.

456. Toufic, *Distracted*, page 27 of this volume.

457. Richard Foreman, *Reverberation Machines: The Later Plays and Essays* (Barrytown, NY: Station Hill Press, 1985), 120.

458. The ability of a character to ask a question and be part of the two or more characters answering it in *Penguin Touquet* (*Reverberation Machines*, 104, 109, etc.) turns out to be another way of understanding "One should speak solely when also speaking to oneself. Only then is there a dialogue" (the epigraph of *Distracted*). Whereas in this case what is elsewhere enriches, in other instances it acts as a parody. Those who intentionally parody are not subtle, since they disregard that one can always find somewhere an unintended parody of what someone wrote or painted or filmed.

459. Foreman, *Reverberation Machines*, 112.

460. In the first edition of *Distracted*, most of the extraneous elements were included due to the absence of occasions in which its

solitary author could air in conversation, and thus get rid of, certain ideas that are merely intelligent but not necessary (*Distracted*, page 52 of this volume).

461. Here's an example of such a recollection: "Truly we are God's, and unto Him we return" (Qur'ān 2:156).

462. Quoted in Mavromatis, *Hypnagogia*, 163.

463. Rather, the entrancement happens either through the victim's staring at the absence of the vampire's image in the mirror in front of which both she and the vampire are standing (*[Vampires]*, pages 139, 150, 241 of this volume) or by her ending up yielding to the illogical simultaneous presence (beside her) and absence (in the mirror in front of which both she and the vampire are ostensibly standing) of the undead (Freud: "The governing rules of logic carry no weight in the unconscious; it might be called the Realm of the Illogical. Urges with contrary aims exist side by side in the unconscious without any need arising for an adjustment between them. Either they have no influence whatever on each other, or, if they have, no decision is reached, but a compromise comes about which is nonsensical since it embraces mutually incompatible details. With this is connected the fact that contraries are not kept apart but treated as though they were identical" [*The Standard Edition*, vol. 23 (1937-1939), *"Moses and Monotheism," "An Outline of Psycho-Analysis" and Other Works* (1964), 168-69]).

464. In the death realm, one's uncanny feeling that "every name in history is I" (from a letter in Nietzsche's handwriting to Jacob Burckhardt at the onset of Nietzsche's psychosis, of his dying before dying) is countered by one's feeling that all those one encounters are alien, an alienation resulting from the decomposition of the different composites of which each was composed while alive ("The living person is a composite that dissociates in death-as-undeath first into separate subunits that are themselves composites ['I am Prado, I am also Prado's father. I venture to say that I am also Lesseps.... I am also Chambige.... Every name in history is I'] ... then into elements, becoming alien. Each of us is common, not alien, both because each of us is a composite of all the others, even of those who once existed and who are long dead, and because each of us is part of the composite that constitutes the others. That is why we do not find others or for that matter ourselves alien, and that is why they, too, do not find us alien. In certain states of altered consciousness, though, we see the dead, people who have become not merely uglier, but alien, and that is because they are no longer composites [the withdrawal of the cathexis from the world] [Toufic, *(Vampires)*, pages 177-78 of this

volume])." It is thus a realm where one encounters alternately the uncanny (Prado is strangely familiar ...) and the alien.

465. Sooner or later, the disorientation of a dead human haunting a place deprives us of our sense of orientation in it. I am still waiting for a film in which it is the infected victim of the vampire who displays all the powers vampire films usually attribute to the vampire, thus revealing the victim to be still between life and death, while the vampire himself displays these apparent powers as frailties and infirmities: the appearance of his shadow on the left of the victim and looking to the right, while the vampire happens to be on the latter's right and looking to the left shows he is lost "in" a labyrinthine space, etc.

466. George H. W. Bush, "Remarks at a Republican Campaign Rally in Manchester, New Hampshire," the American Presidency Project, https://www.presidency.ucsb.edu/node/265203; President Bush gave these remarks on October 23, 1990. Others, too, called Saddam Hussein Hitler: "Senator Claiborne Pell of Rhode Island, the Democratic chairman of the Senate Foreign Relations Committee, called Mr. Hussein 'the Hitler of the Middle East' and criticized Mr. Bush for not having moved earlier to forestall an invasion" (R. W. Apple Jr., "Invading Iraqis Seize Kuwait and Its Oil; U.S. Condemns Attack, Urges United Action," *New York Times*, August 3, 1990).

467. Neither is the Ba'ath Party interchangeable with the Nazi Party nor is Iraq with Germany. Moreover, in terms of being the most racist and the most advanced technological and military power in a given region, Israel, rather than Iraq, plays that role in the Middle East.

468. The following is from the website of the UK's Security Service, MI5: "In June 1945, the Soviets announced—falsely—that Hitler's remains had not been found and that he was probably still alive. This announcement caused a predictable flurry of 'Hitler sightings' across Europe. Allied officers sought to establish beyond possible doubt that Hitler had indeed died in his bunker. To that end, they interrogated various members of Hitler's personal staff who had been with the dictator in late April 1945. The historian Hugh Trevor-Roper, who served as a British military intelligence officer during the war, used these accounts to investigate the circumstances of Hitler's death and rebut claims that Hitler was still alive and living somewhere in the West. He published an account of his findings in 1947 in his book *The Last Days of Hitler*" ("Hitler's Last Days," https://www.mi5.gov.uk/history/world-war-ii/hitlers-last-days). And the following is from chapter 1 of Ada Petrova and Peter Watson's *The Death of Hitler: The Full Story with New Evidence from Secret Russian Archives* (New York: Norton, 1995): "The complete silence

on the part of the Russians regarding what they had or had not found in the Reich Chancellery and the absence of a body—either Hitler's or Eva Braun's—did not convince many people. On the contrary, throughout the summer of 1945 the rumours that Hitler was still alive gathered pace.... There were many sightings.... In July 1945, the US Office of Censorship intercepted a letter written from someone in Washington. Addressed to a Chicago newspaper, the letter claimed that Hitler was living in a German-owned hacienda 450 miles from Buenos Aires. The US government gave this report enough credibility to act on it, sending a classified telegram to the American embassy in Argentina requesting help in following up the inquiry. Besides giving basic information the telegram added that Hitler was alleged to be living in special underground quarters. 'Source indicates that there is a western entrance to the underground hideout which consists of a stone wall operated by photo-electric cells, activated by code signals from ordinary flashlights. Entrance thus uncovered supposedly provides admittance for automobiles.' It continued that Hitler had provided himself with two doubles and was hard at work developing plans for the manufacture of long-range robot bombs and other weapons. The matter was taken sufficiently seriously for J. Edgar Hoover, then the director of the FBI, to become involved, although shortly afterwards he wrote to the War Department: 'To date, no serious indication has been received that Adolf Hitler is in Argentina'" (https://www.washingtonpost.com/wp-srv/style/longterm/books/chap1/deathofhitler.htm).

469. At the same time that these reports on a still-living Hitler would have been mentioned on TV, doubt should have been sown as to whether Saddam Hussein himself was alive, for instance by showing him on Iraqi TV meeting with the other members of the Revolutionary Command Council when it would have been quite clear that the recording was not new but had already been broadcast a week earlier.

470. Quoted in Andrew McGhie and James Chapman, "Disorders of Attention and Perception in Early Schizophrenia," *British Journal of Medical Psychology* 34, no. 2 (June 1961): 105.

471. During his psychosis, he was so taken by the sound of one musical instrument that he had to predict when it would cease to then leap like a trapezist to another sound. Thus fast-paced music made him anxious, with the exception of John Zorn's music, which he continued to enjoy. Zorn's music, for example, *Torture Garden* and *Naked City*, avoids the nostalgia implied in any assumed continuation of a process, whether toward its end or from its origin; it begins and ends in the middle without any residue. If following a clean cut

with no desire for and no projection of further reconnection, the same music resumes, the two sections link in the listener without any interruption, making this music in abrupt blocks a music of continuity; what interrupts two sections between which a different piece is inserted is not the latter but the explicit or implicit fade-out at the end of the first and the more or less perceptible fade-in at the beginning of the second.

472. A radio functioning of the world is not restricted to schizophrenia, but is encountered also in other altered states of consciousness, for example in those cases of temporal-lobe seizure during which one hears songs and music that have no source in the location where one happens to be (for examples, see chapter 15 in Oliver Sacks's *The Man Who Mistook His Wife for a Hat and Other Clinical Tales* [New York: Simon and Schuster, 1998]; here's one of them: "Mrs O'C was somewhat deaf, but otherwise in good health. She lived in an old people's home. One night, in January 1979, she dreamt vividly, nostalgically, of her childhood in Ireland, and especially of the songs they danced to and sang. When she woke up, the music was still going, very loud and clear. 'I must still be dreaming,' she thought, but this was not so.... It was the middle of the night. Someone, she assumed, must have left a radio playing.... She checked every radio she could find—they were all turned off.... I obtained a brainscan, and this showed that she had ... had a small thrombosis or infarction in part of her right temporal lobe" (134). Comparing both experiential responses induced by electrical stimulation of the brain ("The times that are summoned most frequently are briefly these: the times of watching or hearing the action and speech of others, and times of hearing music" [Wilder Penfield and Phanor Perot, "The Brain's Record of Visual and Auditory Experience: A Final Summary and Discussion," *Brain* (1963): 687]) and music-inducing seizures to radio is not an example of confounding analogical thinking. On the contrary, it helps us to try to disentangle radio from an analogy—made by no one explicitly—to this prior biological "radio," an analogy that condemns radio to try to achieve effects that pertain to this biological "radio" ("All media are extensions of some human faculty—psychic or physical. The wheel is an extension of the foot ... clothing, an extension of the skin; electric circuitry, an extension of the central nervous system" [Marshall McLuhan and Quentin Fiore, *The Medium Is the Massage: An Inventory of Effects* (Corte Madera, CA: Gingko Press, 2001)]).

473. We will find it increasingly difficult to identify with the victim when, in addition to having the point of view of the murderer, we are provided with that of the weapon itself through the *flying carpet* feature in computer simulation programs, which allows one to put

oneself in the tank of one of the participants or on a missile heading toward its target" (Glenn Zorpette, "War Games," *Los Angeles Times*, October 7, 1991), identifying also with the latter. Kevin Reynolds, the director of *Robin Hood: Prince of Thieves* (1991), a version in which the aristocratic, Christian Robin accepts an illegitimate son of his father as his brother and befriends a Moor, must have sensed the dangerous implication of such shots, for in the shot with the point of view of the arrow he had a tree as the target, whereas when the target was a human being he switched to an objective shot from the side of the speeding arrow. Is it at all surprising that this identification with weapons and other objects is concomitant with their becoming smart/intelligent? Already in the 1920s, Vertov's "I am Kino-eye, I am a mechanical eye. I, a machine, show you the world as only I can see it.... I ascend with an airplane, I plunge and soar together with plunging and soaring bodies" ("Kinoks: A Revolution," 1922) is concomitant with a smart camera, as is clear in his *Man with a Movie Camera* (1929), where the camera comes out of its case and mounts the tripod, which then performs a series of movements on its own, while the camera's winding mechanism revolves by itself, signaling that the camera is filming (the criterion for whether the camera is truly filming on its own, a true kino-eye, is that, as in Michael Snow's *The Central Region* but unlike in Vertov's film, the absence of the filmmaker/cameraman behind the camera, that is, of human sight behind the viewfinder, not be felt as a lack that has to be countered by the presence in the film of an extra human sight, that of a film audience watching the sections of the film that were shot by the camera on its own).

474. Even when disoriented and anxious, the schizophrenic no longer asked (himself), whether by saying it aloud or thinking it, "What's happening to me?" for fear that the TV or radio program would at that point be interrupted by a special announcement in which he would hear about what is happening specifically to him.

475. While laughter can be an appropriate and worthy response to the unbearable, sentimentalization or rationalization cannot.

476. Bazin, *What Is Cinema?*, vol. 1, 96–97.

477. Ibid., 9.

478. It seems that one way to get the academics with hygienic quotation marks to push for making places to stay available (and not shelters or prisons [more than seven percent of people in jail in the United States have severe mental disorders (*Chicago Tribune*, September 10, 1992), and around three in ten prisons hold seriously mentally ill people who have not been charged with a crime (eight

in ten in Kentucky)]), even if non-tenured, for the huge number of homeless schizophrenics and depressed people is by leaving the latter unsheltered by quotation marks.

479. According to the U.S. Department of Housing and Urban Development estimate for 1987, there were six hundred thousand homeless in the US. In "One study [Rodger K. Farr, Paul Koegel, Audrey Burnam, *A Study of Homelessness and Mental Illness in the Skid Row Area of Los Angeles* (Los Angeles County Department of Mental Health, 1986)] ... trained interviewers, using the diagnostic interview schedule developed for the National Institute of Mental Health (NIMH) (Robins et al., 1984), gathered data on 379 [homeless men from various settings in the Skid Row area of Los Angeles]. By this method they determined that at the time of the examination, 60 percent of the homeless men met the criteria for one or more current (within the past 6 months) mental disorders or substance abuse disorders. Of the total sample, 11.5 percent met the diagnostic criteria for schizophrenia, 20 percent met the criteria for major affective disorders, and 3 percent displayed severe cognitive impairment suggestive of dementia ..." (Institute of Medicine, Committee on Health Care for Homeless People, *Homelessness, Health, and Human Needs* [Washington, DC: National Academy Press, 1988], 53).

480. These incitements were written while having in mind a modest reception of this book. Should the book gain a wider readership and influence, this quantitative change may dialectically change into a qualitative one, that is, a qualification. It is in this sense that I have a certain readership in mind.

481. Here are two of the exceptional images of the 1991 Gulf War:
— The images of Israelis and American soldiers in gas masks. By abstaining from using chemical and biological weapons during the war with the coalition (possibly as a consequence of the coalition's threat to retaliate by using tactical nuclear weapons in case the Iraqis used the aforementioned weapons), Saddam Hussein unintentionally contributed to one of the major images of the war, one emerging straight from the unconscious of Arabs: the Israelis and the American soldiers as extraterrestrial, alien, since the gas masks worn by them were not a response to any external cause—how shortsighted then, at the level of a logic of images, was Israel's reluctance to distribute gas masks to the Palestinian population (by January 28 only 20,000-30,000 had been issued)!
— The sublime fires of the oil fields in Kuwait as seen in Werner Herzog's *Lessons of Darkness* (1992)—it was dishonest of Herzog not to have included Iraq as one of the producers of the film, since Iraq has paid billions of dollars in reparations for the fires in these

fields. Regrettably, in the aforementioned film, Herzog disregarded, did not hark to, and betrayed the majority of those who were in *the land of silence and darkness* (the title of his 1971 film regarding the deafblind), the Iraqi army units in Kuwait, whose radars were jammed or destroyed and anyway could not detect the stealth fighters, and who could not see the American army units, equipped with night-vision devices, attacking them at night.

482. Sometimes Duras's "You see?" performatively makes Depardieu actually see, rather than imagine (or hallucinate hypnotically), her earlier descriptions as visual images; sometimes he sees only when he performatively answers "Yes." Duras's challenge must have been to prevent Depardieu, an actor, from playacting that he is actually seeing in a quasi-hypnotic mode in his imagination the episodes she was reading.

483. In *Hiroshima mon amour*, Duras does not establish an equivalence of the two traumas, the love story that ended in the death of the young French woman's German lover in Nevers during Germany's occupation of France and the nuclear conflagration in Hiroshima: while the Japanese man asserts to the French woman, who is in Hiroshima to act in a film, "You have seen nothing in Hiroshima," notwithstanding her assertions to the contrary, when she addresses the Japanese man in the second person while reenacting the last hours of her love affair with the German in Nevers—up to and *including his death*—at no point does she say to him, "You have seen nothing in Nevers."

484. Thank God that *though seeing, they do not see*; in other words, thank God for actualizing a condition of possibility of the Incarnation. Christ could incarnate because in the case of humans "though seeing, they do not see; though hearing, they do not hear" (Matthew 13:13). Christ could incarnate because this peculiarity of people allows the coexistence in him, despite his incarnation, of the visible and the invisible. The reason we do not perceive miracles is not necessarily that they cannot happen but that even when they happen there is a component of them that is unbearable to see, thus affecting us with a more or less pronounced inability to see. What Christ said to those who saw and heard his miracles, for instance to the parents of the dead child he resurrected (Luke 8:49–55), was understood prescriptively by Luke as a command not to report to others what they fully saw and heard ("but he ordered them not to tell anyone what had happened" [Luke 8:56]), whereas we can understand it in a Spinozist manner—as descriptive of the aforementioned inaccessibility to sight: the miracle by which a blind person is turned into a seeing person is somewhat unbearable to see and consequently has

something unseeable regarding it, and this affects its onlookers with a blindness, turns them into those who *have eyes but fail to see* (Mark 8:18); the miracle by which the mute is able to speak is somewhat unbearable to hear and consequently affects those who heard the mute speak with a deafness, turns them into those who *have ... ears but fail to hear* (Mark 8:18). The modern so-called medical miracles, which allow some people to regain their sight or hearing, are miracles only figuratively, not only because they have a scientific explanation and are repeatable by anyone who has the knowledge and the technological facilities but also because they are wholly within the sight and hearing of the onlooker and listener. In this context, a witness is someone who, seeing one of Jesus Christ's miracles, sees it (fully) and, hearing it, hears it (fully), with the consequence that Christ would not have instructed him or her following one of his miracles "to tell no one what had happened."

485. The archeological image is a subject addressed by Gilles Deleuze regarding Straub-Huillet's work: with the break of the sensory-motor link, "the visual image becomes *archaeological, stratigraphic, tectonic*. Not that we are taken back to prehistory (there is an archaeology of the present), but to the deserted layers of our time which bury our own phantoms.... They are again essentially the empty and lacunary stratigraphic landscapes of Straub, where the ... earth stands for what is buried in it: the cave in *Othon* where the resistance fighters had their weapons, the marble quarries and the Italian countryside where civil populations were massacred in *Fortini Cani*" (Gilles Deleuze, *Cinema 2: The Time-Image*, trans. Hugh Tomlinson and Robert Galeta [Minneapolis: University of Minnesota Press, 1989], 244).

486. While the world hides the disaster by continuing on its course, the disaster, too, in its manner, hides the world. For example, the survivor of the Shoah might avoid everything that has a possible association with it: trains, etc.; and when by accident he or she sees a train, he or she doesn't see it but rather perceives the train that transported him or her to the concentration or extermination camp and has a flashback to the Shoah: thus even as he or she looks at the train, the latter is at least momentarily hidden from him or her.

487. "In quantum mechanics, empty space is not really empty at all but full of pairs of 'virtual' particles that suddenly spring in and out of existence. The particles appear in pairs because the vacuum contains no electric charge. So if a virtual electron, which has a negative charge, appears, then it must do so in conjunction with its antiparticle—a positively charged, virtual positron. In quantum mechanics, such perfectly anticorrelated states are said to be entangled, which means that the state of one particle completely determines the

state of the other. Near the event horizon of a black hole, virtual particle-antiparticle pairs are being created all the time. Every now and then, half of one of those pairs falls into the hole and cannot get out to recombine with its partner. If the partner outside the hole has sufficiently high energy, it can escape the gravitational pull of the hole and thus create the illusion that the hole is radiating. Entanglement then demands that the partner that does not escape the black hole has negative energy. Because of Einstein's relation between mass and energy, $E = mc^2$, the negative-energy partner effectively has a negative mass, so when it falls into the hole it causes the mass of the hole to decrease" (Seth Lloyd, "Almost Certain Escape from a Black Hole," *Physics World*, September 1, 2006, https://physicsworld.com/a/almost-certain-escape-from-a-black-hole/).

488. On physical sonic black holes, see O. Lahav, A. Itah, A. Blumkin, C. Gordon, and J. Steinhauer, "A Sonic Black Hole in a Density-Inverted Bose-Einstein Condensate," http://arxiv.org/abs/0906.1337: "We have created the analogue of a black hole in a Bose-Einstein condensate. In this sonic black hole, sound waves, rather than light waves, cannot escape the event horizon."

489. Cf. Toufic, *(Vampires)*, page 115 of this volume, for an interpretation of Alma's knowledge of the specifics of Elisabet's relationship with her son in terms of thought-transference.

490. Whereas people who gradually, through a process in which identification played a major role, became similar, having the same tastes, the same habits, and similar memories, are not doubles, persons who are identical because of the erasure of any particular attributes, including memory, that may differentiate them are doubles. Past a certain threshold in the process of doubling, were one of the two persons, or indeed both, to try to reach the documents that would fill in the gaps in his or her memory, and hence reintroduce a differentiation with the other, by some unexplainable concatenations of circumstances he or she will not be able to reach them.

491. In a somewhat similar manner, I, a mortal, thus dead even as I live, can receive from my amnesiac version in the death realm—where I find "myself" lost following a lapse of consciousness, if not of being— only through creative writing.

492. Charlotte Delbo, *Days and Memory*, trans. Rosette Lamont (Marlboro, VT: Marlboro Press, 1990), 4. The SS militiaman's words to the prisoners quoted in Primo Levi's *The Drowned and the Saved*, "People will say that the events you describe are too monstrous to be believed," ended up applying to many a concentration camp survivor

concerning the events he or she described, for example, to Charlotte Delbo, who wrote concerning what she underwent, "It is all too incredible" (*Days and Memory*, 3).

493. In Duras's *Hiroshima mon amour*, the young French woman, whose lover in Nevers, a German soldier, was shot dead in the last days of Germany's occupation of France, tells her Japanese lover, whose country was traumatized by and whose parents were killed in the nuclear conflagration in Hiroshima, "Like you, I too have struggled with all my might not to forget. Like you, I forgot. Like you, I longed for a memory beyond consolation.... For my part I struggled every day with all my might against the horror of no longer understanding the reason to remember. Like you, I forgot."

494. "Nestor of Laranda, who was active between the reigns of Severus and Alexander, produced a version of the *Iliad* in which he avoided words beginning with the same letter as the book number.... Thus in book 1 of the *Iliad* (alpha, in Greek numeration) he did not admit any word that began with the letter alpha, and so forth. It was this style that was adopted by a close contemporary, an Egyptian poet named Triphiodorus, who may either have inspired or supplemented Nestor's production with a lipogrammatic *Odyssey*" (David S. Potter, *The Roman Empire at Bay: AD 180–395* [London: Routledge, 2004], 193).

495. Michael Cooperson: "The constraint in this case [*Maqāmah* (which he translates as "Imposture") 28] being to compose a Friday sermon containing no dotted letters. This means using only thirteen of the twenty-eight letters of the Arabic alphabet. Excluded, as a result, are almost all the common prepositions, second- and third-person imperfect verbs, and many other exceedingly frequent features of the language (though the dotted feminine ending is allowed)" (al-Ḥarīrī, *Impostures*, trans. Michael Cooperson [New York: New York University Press, 2020], 248; for the Arabic original of *Maqāmah* 28, see al-Ḥarīrī, *Maqāmāt Abī Zayd al-Sarūjī*, ed. Michael Cooperson [New York: New York University Press, 2020]).

496. *Sometimes* no additional alteration of motion is needed to disclose this effect in the case of footage from the beginning of cinema, since the footage was filmed at a different camera speed (eighteen frames per second) than the one at which it is presently projected (twenty-four frames per second).

497. Is the newsreel footage of the Red Army crossing Lake Sivash in the Crimea during World War II, specifically in 1943, in Tarkovsky's *The Mirror* another such instance? Over these images, we hear the voice-over of Arseni Tarkovsky reciting his poem "Life, Life" (1965):

"... On earth there is no death. All are immortal. All is immortal.... Reality and light / Exist, but neither death nor darkness...." These soldiers trudging in the mud while moving a cannon and other supplies are not going to physically die since they are preserved as such in four-dimensional spacetime, but they are not on that account immortal, since they, unlike everything else around them (fish, micro-organisms in the water, etc.), are mortal, hence dead even while they live, more specifically while they cross Lake Sivash.

498. Bazin, *What Is Cinema?*, vol. 1, 9 and 14–15.

499. Memory is not a tenuous attempt to somewhat hold on to what has irremediably vanished, for were it the case that the past vanishes, rather than being still there but physically unavailable, unreachable (other than through time travel), there would be no memory.

500. This absence in *Back to the Future Part III* is all the more surprising given the presence of all sorts of other elements of self-reflexivity: in 1885, Marty calls himself Clint Eastwood, stands in front of a mirror imitating De Niro in *Taxi Driver* ...

501. H. Minkowski, "The Union of Space and Time," in *The Concepts of Space and Time: Their Structure and Their Development*, ed. Milič Čapek (Dordrecht: Springer Science and Business Media Dordrecht, 1976), 339.

502. The detachment of the vision from the visionary in Herzog's *Heart of Glass* complements the detachment of the shadow from the undead in his vampire film, *Nosferatu*.

503. Was this materiality of Dracula's shadow somewhat foreshadowed? The red mantle Dracula is wearing in his first meeting with Harker extends for such a long distance behind him that, in the absence of the normal shadow in the case of the vampire, it functions as his shadow. In the same concise scene in Coppola's *Dracula*, we are provided with the opportunity to perceive by means of the separate shadow two other characteristics of Dracula's condition: (1) he appears to be not fully part of the undeath realm, where the drive holds sway, but to have unconscious desires, one of which is manifested by the separate shadow: while Dracula speaks to Harker, his shadow begins to strangle him, his rival for the love of Mina; (2) dead, he is lost in a labyrinthine space: behind and to the left of the seated Harker finalizing the sale, one can see the shadow of Dracula, but as Harker finishes signing the papers and turns toward the left to speak to Dracula, both he and the film spectator discover to their consternation (and to the film spectator's aesthetic delight) that Dracula is standing to his right.

504. Entranced people, who appear to have imploded and thus to have almost the closure of objects, are somewhat sight*less* but induce a detached gaze, which does not so much objectify the others around, by turning them into objects of the look, as subjectivizes certain objective shots in cinema (therefore, in the presence of an entranced person, if someone happens to be associated with the latter shots, then his or her impression of being gazed at would not be irrational). So, in cinema, when dealing with an entranced person, the conventional shot/reverse shot is to be replaced by an asymmetrical situation, one without reciprocity.

505. See Toufic,(*Vampires*), pages 149–50 of this volume, in relation to the confirmation by *Until the End of the World* (1991) of the impression "Not children in common, but point-of-view shots" in one of the scenes in Wenders's *The Wrong Move* (1975).

506. That Apu deposits the small child a little further away from the tracks rather than taking him to his mother reinforces the aforementioned sensation of absence, almost of loss.

507. "*Wa man ra'ānī fī al-manām faqad ra'ānī, fa'inna al-shayṭān lā yatamaththal fī ṣūratī,*" https://sunnah.com/bukhari:110; cf. https://sunnah.com/bukhari:6994, where the tradion is narrated by Anas, and where instead of *lā yatamaththal fī ṣūratī* we read *yatakhayyal bī*.

508. Friedrich Nietzsche, *On the Genealogy of Morals*, trans. Walter Kaufmann and R. J. Hollingdale/*Ecce Homo*, trans. and ed. Walter Kaufmann (New York: Vintage Books, 1989), 57.

509. In the sober state, one has to train oneself to look for very brief intervals: one then notices that many gestures are not adapted to the situations in which they take place (I wager that the reduction of everything to the efficient will never be total); that they would be more appropriate in a different situation (as long as we remain focused on progression, we will be absorbed by it and will not perceive this inadequacy). While in the sober state, we usually do not really look at gestures so much as instrumentally interpret them, glossing over their inadequacy to the situation, in some states of altered consciousness, for example, mild drunkenness, one imagines the corresponding virtual situation from *looking* at the gestures. One of the interesting things about many altered states of consciousness is that they make our perception discontinuous: since one catches a glimpse of the gesture, one has to construct a scenario in which what one perceived could best fit; the idiosyncratic problem of the person in an altered state of consciousness is that he reasons as if people were good actors in "real life," when they aren't—even if we factor in the unconscious.

510.   Can one achieve this notwithstanding one's mirror neurons?

511.   One is not an observer unless one sees what is going on in its freedom; a real observer can follow linkages that are not causal.

512.   https://www.larousse.fr/dictionnaires/francais-anglais/ange/3450.

513.   The Zen master is not engrossed in what he does since even though when he is hungry, he just eats, when thirsty, he just drinks ("When the old master Hiakajo was asked, 'What is Zen?' he said, 'When hungry, eat, when tired, sleep.' And they said, 'Well isn't that what everybody does? Aren't you just like ordinary people?' 'Oh no,' he said, 'they don't do anything of the kind. When they're hungry, they don't just eat, they think of all sorts of things. When they're tired, they don't just sleep, but dream all sorts of dreams'" [Alan Watts]), he is simultanously detached from these activities.

514.   *Ṣaḥīḥ al-Bukhārī*, vol. 6, Book 61, Hadith number 503, https://hadithcollection.com/sahihbukhari/sahih -bukhari-book-61-virtues-of-the-quran/sahih-bukhari-volume-006-book-061-hadith-number-503; for the Arabic original see *Ṣaḥīḥ al-Bukhārī*, Book 61, no. 3634 (Beirut: Dār al-kutub al-'ilmiyya, 2002), 662; cf. *Ṣaḥīḥ Muslim* (Beirut: Dār al-jīl, 2005), 995–96.

515. Did the title of my previous book, *Postscripts*, imply that my primary oeuvre had already been concluded and that the space is still open only for postscripts and addenda that function as supplements to my previous books?

516. Nietzsche, *Thus Spoke Zarathustra: A Book for All and None*, 126.

517. Katie Mack, *The End of Everything (Astrophysically Speaking)* (New York: Scribner, 2021), 1.

518. Deleuze, *Cinema 1: The Movement-Image*, 132.

519. Jalal Toufic, *Postscripts* (Stockholm: Moderna Museet; Amsterdam: Roma Publications, 2020), 90.

520. Quoted in Ibn al'Arabi, *The Bezels of Wisdom*, trans. R. W. J. Austin (New York: Paulist Press, 1980), 17.

521. The expression is borrowed from the title of one of the main collections of koans: "Two anthologies of kōans stand out in the Ch'an [Zen] tradition. The first is the *Blue Cliff Records* (Chin., *Pi-yen lu*; Jap., *Hekigan-roku*), first compiled by Hsüeh-tou Ch'ung-hsien (980–1052) and later expanded by Yüan-wu K'o-ch'in (1063–1135).... The second is the *Wu-men Kuan* (Jap., *Mumonkan*; ... *Gateless Gate*), a collection of 48 cases compiled by the monk Wu-men Hui-k'ai (1183–1260) that appeared in 1229" (Damien Keown, *A Dictionary of Buddhism*, contributions by Stephen Hodge, Charles Jones, and Paola Tinti [Oxford: Oxford University Press, 2003], 44).

522. January 7, 2020, https://ascmag.com/articles/lost-highway-highway-to-hell.

523. I expected David Lynch to stop making (feature) films for years or for the rest of his life after completing *Inland Empire* (2006), and Ingmar Bergman to do so after making *Persona* (1966). While in Lynch's case it was because his (labyrinthine) film (at the level of the diegesis) is pervaded by *jouissance*, in Bergman's case, my expectation had to do with his reaching a limit in his risky exploration of the close-up, where it becomes manifest that it is "both the face and its effacement" (Deleuze): there seemed to be nothing more/else that could be done with (a certain conception of) the face and the close-up. I was surprised that Bergman went on to make two feature films two

years later, *Shame* (1968) and *Hour of the Wolf* (1968), in which there are numerous close-ups.

524. Robert Bresson, *Notes on the Cinematograph*, trans. Jonathan Griffin (New York: New York Review Books, 2016).

525. David Sylvester, *The Brutality of Fact: Interviews with Francis Bacon*, 3rd ed. (New York: Thames and Hudson, 1987), 186.

526. Ibid., 59.

527. Ibid., 183–84.

528. Ibid., 24.

529. https://www.dictionnaire-academie.fr/article/A9R2376.

530. Wikipedia, "Quantum entanglement," https://en.wikipedia.org/wiki/Quantum_entanglement#:~:text=However%2C%20this%20behavior%20gives%20orise,entangled%20system%20as%20a%20whole.

531. Lewis Carroll, *"Alice's Adventures in Wonderland" and "Through the Looking-Glass and What Alice Found There,"* ed. Peter Hunt (Oxford: Oxford University Press, 2009), 59.

532. Joseph Polchinski, "Burning Rings of Fire," *Scientific American* 312, no. 4 (April 2015): 41.

533. Ibid.

534. Ibid. The appearance of the human ghost is best described by a frequentative, since he or she haunts the space instead of existing in it continuously, repeatedly appearing, disappearing, then appearing again.

535. Most physicists, among them some of those who wrote the initial article about a firewall at the event horizon of black holes (Ahmed Almheiri, Donald Marolf, Joseph Polchinski, and James Sully, "Black Holes: Complementarity or Firewalls?," *Journal of High Energy Physics* 2013, no. 2, article no. 62 [February 2013], http://arxiv.org/abs/arXiv:1207.3123), would prefer to find a solution that would do away with it, since if one is "incinerated in a firewall, then relativity and the deeply loved equivalence principle are wrong about black holes and who knows what else" (Janna Levin, *Black Hole Survival Guide* [New York: Knopf, 2020], 134). Were a different hypothesis, without a firewall,

to be accepted generally, then I wager that it would provide another manner in which the radiation of the black hole would be intensive.

536. Leonard Susskind, *The Black Hole War: My Battle with Stephen Hawking to Make the World Safe for Quantum Mechanics* (New York: Little, Brown, 2008), 434.

537. Jacques Derrida, *Archive Fever: A Freudian Impression*, trans. Eric Prenowitz (Chicago: University of Chicago Press, 1996), 36.

538. Ibid., 133–34.

539. Carlo Rovelli, *The Order of Time*, trans. Erica Segre and Simon Carnell (New York: Riverhead Books, 2018), 166–67.

540. Henry George Liddell and Robert Scott, *A Greek-English Lexicon*, revised and augmented throughout by Sir Henry Stuart Jones, with the assistance of Roderick McKenzie (Oxford: Clarendon Press, 1940), https://www.perseus.tufts.edu/hopper/text?doc=Perseus%3Atext-t%3A1999.04.0057%3Aentry%3Da%29%2Frxw.

541. Wikipedia, "Archive," https://en.wikipedia.org/wiki/Archive.

542. Jacques Derrida, *Specters of Marx: The State of the Debt, the Work of Mourning and the New International*, trans. Peggy Kamuf (New York: Routledge, 2006), 12.

543. Ibid.

544. Derrida, *Archive Fever*, 12.

545. Deleuze, *Cinema 2: The Time-Image*, 81.

546. Bergson, *Matter and Memory*, 150.

547. Derrida, *Archive Fever*, 12.

548. Levin, *Black Hole Survival Guide*, 3 and 37–39. Cf. Andrew Strominger, "Probing the Edges of the Universe: Black Holes, Horizons and Strings," part of the Fall 2021 Hans Bethe Lecture Series at Cornell, https://www.cornell.edu/video/probing-the-edges-of-the-universe: "A black hole is the edge of the universe. Once you cross the horizon of the black hole, there's nothing there, and you're out of the universe. There's nothing inside a black hole, ... it can be thought of as an empty hole in space. And when something drops inside it, there's no trace of ... what went in. It's gone forever from the universe."

549. Derrida, *Archive Fever*, 11.

550. Freud, *The Standard Edition*, vol. 19 (1923–1925), *"The Ego and the Id," and Other Works* (1961), 227.

551. Bergson, *Matter and Memory*, 78–79.

552. Jacob D. Bekenstein, "Information in the Holographic Universe," *Scientific American* 289, no. 2 (August 2003): 60.

553. Susskind, *The Black Hole War*, 294 and 298.

554. Considering things from the perspective of what is unqualifiedly archivable would provide another, variant manner of thinking of the ultimate constituents of matter, which would no longer be the particles of the Standard Model, for example quarks, electrons, photons, W bosons, etc., but mass, spin, and electric charge.

555. Derrida, *Archive Fever*, 19.

556. The feeling of falling relates not to the whole body, since one is weightless when in free fall, but to various parts of the body in relation to one another. While the feeling of falling within the body is largely imperceptible on Earth, it is perceptible when one approaches a solar-sized black hole, and it becomes starker the closer one gets to its event horizon and then to the singularity, given the marked difference then between the force of gravity at one's feet and at one's head. One's feet would be falling in relation to one's head, or vice versa, depending on whether one is approaching the black hole feetfirst or headfirst.

557. Derrida, *Archive Fever*, 20.

558. Ibid., 19.

559. That is, if one resigns oneself to the inevitability of singularities; yet, according to Janna Levin, professor of physics and astronomy at Barnard, "we don't have to resign ourselves to … the inevitability of singularities. Singularities, as they involve malefic [here comes the *mal* again that we encountered in Derrida's original, French title, *Mal d'archive*] infinities, deserve to be treated with great suspicion. They are such an anathema to the entire paradigm of the scientific pursuit of reality that essentially all physicists suspect general relativity ceases to be the complete physical description of gravity at such dramatic scales, the singular core a false prophecy. Rephrased: the mathematics is telling us that the physical description offered

by relativity is broken there. General relativity cannot be the whole story precisely because it predicts the singularity" (Levin, *Black Hole Survival Guide*, 68; in the glossary of his book *Black Holes and Time Warp*, Thorne wrote: "Singularity: A region of spacetime where spacetime curvature becomes so strong that the general relativistic laws break down and the laws of quantum gravity take over" [557]).

560. Thorne, *Black Holes and Time Warps*, 450 and 476-77.

561. Derrida, *Archive Fever*, 12.

562. Susskind, *The Black Hole War*, 434.

563. Ibid.

564. Derrida, *Margins of Philosophy*, 316.

565. See page 126 of this volume. In my book *What Was I Thinking?* (Berlin: Sternberg Press / e-flux journal, 2017), I added a third task: to present to us another branch of the multiverse—until time travel, which provides another way of accessing some of these branches, becomes feasible.

566. Has it already happened that fiction has actually been a site of return of a ghost, not just a representation of a ghost?

567. See my book *(Vampires)*, pages 143-44 of this volume.

568. From Nietzsche's letter of January 5, 1889, to Jacob Burckhardt, in *Selected Letters of Friedrich Nietzsche*, 347.

569. Ibid.

570. Friedrich Nietzsche, *Twilight of the Idols; or, How to Philosophize with a Hammer*, trans. Duncan Large (New York: Oxford University Press, 1998), §51, 75.

571. Simone Fattal.

572. Etel Adnan.

573. *Alone with the Alone* is the English title of Henry Corbin's book on the Sufism of Ibn 'Arabī; in Corbin's title the second *Alone* refers to God.

574. See my book *(Vampires)*, page 178 of this volume.

575. Toufic, *What Was I Thinking?*, 167–68.

576. William C. Chittick, *The Self-Disclosure of God: Principles of Ibn al-'Arabī's Cosmology* (Albany: State University of New York Press, 1998), 82.

577. If it is unlikely even in death that one would witness one's funeral, more precisely the funeral of the one who had been alive, it is because in death one assumes every name in history and thus there is no coincidence between the one in the coffin and the name one has assumed at that point—other than exceptionally, when one happens to assume, among so many others, the name one had while still alive.

578. Virginia Woolf, *Mrs. Dalloway* (Harmondsworth, UK: Penguin Books/Hogarth Press, 1969), 26.

579. My wife and collaborator on a film trilogy, Graziella Rizkallah, considered pursuing a PhD degree and writing a dissertation titled, "The Current and Forthcoming Art of Jalal Toufic," but then gave up, citing the following difficulty: "How to write about books or artworks that 'continue to be forthcoming even after their publication' or exhibition, a condition that is sometimes explicitly indicated either by their title (*Forthcoming*, 1st ed., Atelos, 2000; 2nd ed., Sternberg Press / e-flux journal, 2014) or by their publisher, Forthcoming Books (for example, *Graziella: The Corrected Edition*, 2009)?"

580. Stoker, *Dracula* (Cambridge University Press, 2013), 15.

581. Mirza Bashiruddin Mahmud Ahmad, *Life of Muhammad* (Islam International Publications, 2013), 210.

582. "That is not the only function of the *as if* or *as though*; in the Qur'ānic story of Solomon and the Queen of Sheba, it has, given renewed creation (Qur'ān 50:15: 'Did We then weary in the first creation? Nay, but they are in doubt regarding a new creation'), the opposite function: to reveal the esoteric state: 'In the Qur'ān, Solomon declared that he wished to have the throne of Bilqīs, the Queen of Sheba, in his court. Someone "who had knowledge from the Scripture" (27:40), Āṣaf b. Barkhiyā (?), responded: "I will bring it to thee before thy gaze returns to thee" (ibid.). According to Ibn al-'Arabī, he accomplished this by invoking God's renewed creation. The throne was at the court of the Queen of Sheba, then the cosmos disappeared, and when the cosmos appeared again before the gazes of (very similar versions of) Solomon and his guests had time to return to them (in less than 1/24th of a second), the throne—not the identical throne but an extremely similar one—was at Solomon's court. "Āṣaf's only merit

in the matter was that he effected the renewal [of Bilqīs's throne] in the court of Solomon" [Ibn al-'Arabī].... One would have expected that Solomon would have then presented the throne to Bilqīs as a proof of the omnipotence of God, thus inducing her, who 'was from a disbelieving people' (27:43), to become a Muslim. Instead—I would imagine to the surprise of those present—Solomon said: 'Let the throne be altered, so that we may see whether or not she will recognize it' (27:41). When Bilqīs arrived, she was ... presented with what appeared to be her throne. She examined it carefully and then said, 'It is as though (ka'annahu) it were my throne" (27:42). I imagine that on hearing these words, Solomon underwent a kind of satori ('on a soil very unlike' Japan), a sudden knowledge, becoming aware that the throne that was presently in his court wasn't, strictly speaking, Bilqīs's throne but as though it (ka'annahu), actually its recreation by God.... In Islam, the task of a human is not to be himself or herself (in Islam he or she—who has no necessity of existence—is basically nothing) but to become cognizant that he or she is in the likeness of himself or herself, by becoming aware of God's renewed creation, and in the likeness of God—notwithstanding that 'there is nothing whatever like unto Him' (Qur'ān 42:11) as dhāt (essence)—since he or she is at each moment one of the infinite self-disclosures of God. Taking into consideration how the poetic function stresses selection over combination (Roman Jakobson), there is a basic poetic modality to an atomistic occasionalist universe, where entities are recurrently replaced by what appears to be them, where we are not ourselves, but rather metaphors of ourselves: ka'annanā" (Toufic, Forthcoming, 2nd ed., 134-36).

583. Diogenes Laertius, Lives of the Eminent Philosophers, ed. James Miller, trans. Pamela Mensch (New York: Oxford University Press, 2018), Book 10, 534.

584. Ibid.

585. Heidegger, Being and Time, 294.

586. William C. Chittick, In Search of the Lost Heart: Explorations in Islamic Thought (Albany: State University of New York Press, 2012), 242.

587. Quoted in Chittick, The Self-Disclosure of God, 214-15.

588. "To give you an idea of what I mean by a counterpart: two fish and five loaves can, in conjunction with the magically materialized painted fish and bread, feed five thousand dead people a meal" (Toufic, Forthcoming, 2nd ed., 148).

589. Who preserved his name after his resurrection since he was still a mortal.

590. The following are two of the anomalous corporeal figures of death: a motionless limb in an otherwise moving body, for example the inert, motionless hand "of" the ostensibly resurrected mortal Lazarus who came back from the grave in Leonid Andreyev's short story "Lazarus"; and the still moving organ in an otherwise inert, motionless body, for example the tongue in the body of Valdemar that appears to have become a corpse in Edgar Allan Poe's "The Facts in the Case of M. Valdemar."

591. "The libidinal, sexual or life instincts ... are best comprised under the name of *Eros*; their purpose would be to form living substance into ever greater unities" (Freud, *The Standard Edition*, vol. 18 [1920–1922], *"Beyond the Pleasure Principle," "Group Psychology" and Other Works* [1955], 258).

592. Ibid., 92.

593. Ibid., 42–43.

594. Michel Serres, *Statues: The Second Book of Foundations*, trans. Randolph Burks (London: Bloomsbury, 2015), 61.

595. *Britannica*, "Thermodynamics," https://www.britannica.com/science/thermodynamics.

596. Deleuze, *Cinema 2: The Time-Image*, 45.

597. Indeed, not only a slap but any reaction, however minor, on his part to the master that is not merely the mechanical execution of the latter's order is a deadly matter, a life-and-death matter since its condition of possibility is that he reengage in a duel to the death for recognition with the master.

598. Cf. Matthew 8:22: "Jesus told him, 'Follow me, and let the dead bury their own dead.'"

599. *Complete Works of Fyodor Dostoyevsky*, 2057, Kindle edition.

600. Deleuze, *Cinema 1: The Movement-Image*, 207.

601. "The officer ..., too, turned out of his path for generals and persons of high rank, and he, too, wriggled between them like an eel; but people like me, or even better dressed than me, he simply walked over;

he made straight for them as though there was nothing but empty space before him, and never, under any circumstances, turned aside. I gloated over my resentment watching him and ... always resentfully made way for him. It exasperated me that even in the street I could not be on an even footing with him. 'Why must you invariably be the first to move aside?' I kept asking myself in hysterical rage, waking up sometimes at three o'clock in the morning" (*Complete Works of Fyodor Dostoyevsky*, 2110, Kindle Edition).

602. Ibid., 2057–58.

603. Freud, *The Standard Edition*, vol. 21 (1927–1931), *"The Future of an Illusion," "Civilization and Its Discontents," and Other Works* (1961), 179 and 181. Freud continues, "It is ... quite right to distinguish between an organic and an 'affective' epilepsy.... A person who suffers from the first kind has a disease of the brain, while a person who suffers from the second kind is a neurotic. In the first case his mental life is subjected to an alien disturbance from without, in the second case the disturbance is an expression of his mental life itself."

604. Freud, *The Standard Edition*, vol. 11 (1910), *"Five Lectures on Psycho-Analysis," "Leonardo da Vinci," and Other Works* (1957), 16.

605. Friedrich Nietzsche, *On the Genealogy of Morality*, ed. Keith Ansell-Pearson, trans. Carol Diethe (Cambridge: Cambridge University Press, 2007), §17, 33. One finds a previous, affined "devaluation ... of good and evil ... (in favor of 'good' and 'bad') in Spinoza's philosophy: 'Thou shalt not eat of the fruit ...': the anxious, ignorant Adam understands these words as the expression of a prohibition. And yet, what do they refer to? To a fruit that, as such, will poison Adam if he eats it. This is an instance of an encounter between two bodies whose characteristic relations are not compatible: the fruit will act as a poison; that is, *it will determine the parts of Adam's body* (and paralleling this, the idea of the fruit will determine the parts of his mind) *to enter into new relations that no longer accord with his own essence....* There is no Good or Evil, but there is good and bad" (Gilles Deleuze, *Spinoza: Practical Philosophy*, trans. Robert Hurley [San Francisco: City Lights, 1988], 22).

606. *Britannica*, "Gilles de Rais: History's First Serial Killer?," https://www.britannica.com/story/gilles-de-rais-historys-first-serial-killer.

607. David Deutsch, *The Fabric of Reality: The Science of Parallel Universes—and Its Implications* (London: Penguin, 1997), 313.

608. David Deutsch, *The Beginning of Infinity: Explanations That Transform the World* (London: Allen Lane, 2011), 299–300.

609. Sean Carroll, *The Big Picture: On the Origins of Life, Meaning, and the Universe Itself* (New York: Dutton, 2016), 178–79.

610. We generally assume that this universe is one in which such spaces and times cannot exist—that they exist in novels and fiction films, maybe in dreams, perhaps subjectively for the one on LSD, but not objectively in Beirut or some other postwar city. But if one comes to believe that they existed at some point in civil-war Beirut and perhaps continue to do so in the present city, what does this tell us about our universe since the latter can go on, not fall apart, notwithstanding such spaces and times? What must our universe be for it to include ruins, labyrinthine spaces and times, and yet not fall apart? While most likely an artist *assumes* that a ruin cannot exist in our universe or branch of the multiverse, can he or she nonetheless construct a universe or branch of the multiverse in which ruins in my sense, labyrinthine spaces and times, exist or can exist and yet this universe or branch of the multiverse does not fall apart? Would he or she in the process of devising such a universe or branch of the multiverse discover that it does not have to be different from ours?

611. See my book *(Vampires)*, page 131 of this volume.

612. Ibid., 121.

613. Human Rights Watch, "'They Killed Us from the Inside': An Investigation into the August 4 Beirut Blast," August 3, 2021, https://www.hrw.org/report/2021/08/03/they-killed-us-inside/investigation-august-4-beirut-blast.

614. Ibid.

615. Municipality of Beirut and UN-Habitat, "Beirut Municipality Rapid Building-Level Damage Assessment," October 2020, https://unhabitat.org/sites/default/files/2020/10/municipality_of_beirut_-_beirut_explosion_rapid_assessment_report.pdf.

616. Ibid.

617. Quoted in Deleuze, *Cinema 2: The Time-Image*, 171.

618. "Annex 1: Chronology of Events," https://www.hrw.org/sites/default/files/media_2021/08/Annex%201.pdf.

619. Wikipedia, "2020 Beirut Explosion," https://en.wikipedia.org/wiki/2020_Beirut_explosion.

620. "Annex 1: Chronology of Events."

621. Wikipedia, "2020 Beirut Explosion."

622. Samia Nakhoul and Laila Bassam, "Lebanon's Leaders Warned in July about Explosives at Port," *Reuters*, August 10, 2020, https://jp.reuters.com/article/lebanon-security-blast-documents-idUKL8N2FC28E.

623. https://www.al-akhbar.com/PDF_Files/4135/alakhbar20200829.pdf; my italics.

624. Wikipedia, "2020 Beirut Explosion."

625. Borges, "The Garden of Forking Paths," in *Collected Fictions*, 122.

626. As Jesus appeared as "a Buddha on a soil very little like that of India" (Nietzsche, *The Anti-Christ*, §31).

627. The title of Foucault's book on Raymond Roussel.

628. Jalal Toufic, *What Was I Thinking?* (Berlin: Sternberg Press / e-flux journal, 2017), 108–9.

629. See pages 110–12 of *What Was I Thinking?*

630. We can read on page 314 of B. H. Liddell Hart's *History of the First World War* (London: Cassell, 1970; the copyright page notes: "First published as *The Real War 1914–1918*, 1930. Enlarged edition, published as *A History of the World War* [the edition Borges appears to refer to] *1914–1918*, 1934, and published in larger format as *History of the First World War* in 1970"): "The bombardment began on June 24th; the attack was intended for June 29th [not July 24th, as in Borges's purported quote from the 1934 edition of Hart's book] but was later postponed until July 1st [not July 29th, as in Borges's ostensible quote], owning to a momentary break in the weather." Here's what the entry "First Battle of the Somme" of *Britannica* indicates, "(July 1–November 13, 1916) ... On July 1, 1916, after a week of prolonged artillery bombardment, 11 divisions of the British Fourth Army (recently created and placed under Sir Henry Rawlinson) began the attack north of the Somme on a front extending for 15 miles (24 km) from Serre and Beaumont-Hamel southward past Thiepval, Ovillers, and Fricourt (east of Albert) and then eastward and southward to Maricourt, north of Curlu. At the same time, the French attacked with five divisions on a front of 8 miles (13 km) mainly south of the river (from Curlu toward Péronne), where the German defense system was less highly developed. Whereas the French had more than 900 heavy guns, the

British had barely half this number for a wider front…. The Somme offensive foundered in the mud when November came," and what one can read in the same encyclopedia's entry "Battle of the Somme Summary," "Nearly 60,000 British casualties (including 20,000 killed) occurred on the first day. The offensive gradually deteriorated into a battle of attrition, hampered by torrential rains in October [not, as in Borges's apparent quote, in July] that made the muddy battlefield impassable. By the time it was abandoned, the Allies had advanced only 5 mi (8 km). The staggering losses included 650,000 German casualties, 420,000 British, and 195,000 French" (it is interesting to note a discrepancy, though not a Borgesian one, between the number of casualties listed in the just quoted Summary entry and the ones listed in "First Battle of the Somme" entry ["The British losses amounted to some 420,000. The French, who had played an increasing part in the later stages, had raised their own war casualty bill by 194,000. Against this Allied total of more than 600,000, the Germans had suffered rather more than 440,000 casualties" (both online entries, one dated April 29, 2021 [https://www.britannica.com/summary/First-Battle-of-the-Somme] and the other dated June 24, 2022 [https://www.britannica.com/event/First-Battle-of-the-Somme], were accessed September 4, 2022).

631. Borges, "The Garden of Forking Paths," in *Collected Fictions*, 119.

632. In that sense, a radically closed room is an Outside in relation to the surroundings.

633. Annette Kuhn and Guy Westwell, *The Oxford Dictionary of Film Studies*, 2nd ed. (Oxford: Oxford University Press, 2020), 623.

634. Martin Heidegger, *The Fundamental Concepts of Metaphysics: World, Finitude, Solitude*, trans. William McNeill and Nicholas Walker (Bloomington: Indiana University Press, 1995), 284.

635. Ibid., 137–39 and 169.

636. Heidegger, *Being and Time*, 230–32.

637. Toufic, *What Was I Thinking?*, 137.

638. While animals, schizophrenics, and the dead undergo poverty in world, at no point does the animal have a world, but schizophrenics and the dead had one while alive and sane and then no longer have it. While schizophrenics and the dead feel this poverty in world starkly, the animal does not.

639. Deleuze, *Cinema 2: The Time-Image*, 171–72.

640. *Treasury of the True Dharma Eye: Zen Master Dogen's "Shobo Genzo,"* ed. Kazuaki Tanahashi (Boston, London: Shambhala, 2012), 306–7.

641. Sawīrus ibn al-Muqaffaʻ (Bishop of al-Ašmūnīn), *History of the Patriarchs of the Egyptian Church, Known as the History of the Holy Church*, vol. 2, part 2, trans. Aziz Suryal Atiya, Yassā 'Abd al-Masīḥ, and O. H. E. Burmester (Cairo: Imprimerie de l'Institut Français d'Archéologie Orientale, 1948).

642. Jennifer Pruitt, "The Miracle of Muqattam: Moving a Mountain to Build a Church in Fatimid Egypt," in *Sacred Precincts: The Religious Architecture of Non-Muslim Communities across the Islamic World*, ed. Mohammad Gharipour (Leiden, The Netherlands: Brill, 2014), 284.

643. Ibn al-Muqaffaʻ, *History of the Patriarchs of the Egyptian Church*, 140.

644. Pruitt, "The Miracle of Muqattam," 285.

645. See my essay "The Resurrected Brother of Mary and Martha: A Human Who Resurrected God!" in my book *What Was I Thinking?*

646. "For much of his life, and not only during his walk through the woods by Lake Silvaplana in August of 1881, when 'the basic conception' of his work *Thus Spoke Zarathustra: A Book for Everyone and Nobody*, 'the *thought of eternal recurrence*, this highest attainable formula of affirmation, ... was dashed off on a sheet of paper with the caption "6,000 feet beyond man and time,"' Nietzsche was alone; then in his psychosis, in his dying before dying ('This autumn ... I twice attended my funeral'), he was *all alone*, writing in the last letter we have by him, 'Every name in history is I'" (Toufic, *What Was I Thinking?*, 169).

647. Jesus Christ, as *the life*, presents a future exception and he made possible a number of additional exceptions through resurrecting at least three dead humans, who were thenceforth no longer mortals but solely alive.

648. "Moses ... said: 'My Lord! Show me (Thy Self), that I may gaze upon Thee.' He said: 'Thou wilt not see Me, but gaze upon the mountain! If it stand still in its place, then thou wilt see Me.' And when his Lord revealed (His) glory to the mountain He sent it crashing down.

And Moses fell down senseless. And when he woke he said: 'Glory unto Thee!'" (Qur'ān 7:143, trans. Pickthall).

649. "And when We said unto the angels: 'Prostrate yourselves before Adam, they fell prostrate, all save Iblis'" (Qur'ān 2:34, trans. Pickthall).

650. Quoted in Louis Massignon, *The Passion of al-Ḥallāj, Mystic and Martyr of Islam*, vol. 3, trans. Herbert Mason (Princeton: Princeton University Press, 1982), 309-11.

651. Nietzsche, *On the Genealogy of Morality*, 118.

652. Nietzsche, *On the Genealogy of Morals/Ecce Homo*, 57-61.

653. Ṣadr al-Dīn Muḥammad al-Shīrāzī, *Mafātīḥ al-ghayb*, ed. Muḥsin 'Aqīl (Beirut: Dār al-maḥajjah al-baydā', 2011), 627.

654. Matthew 16:14.

655. He did not keep his word not because he was not dependable but because he wished to emphasize that a promise is, as J. L. Austin indicated, a performative, that is, that the action of promising is *accomplished* by uttering certain words ("I promise …") in the proper conditions (which are not limited to those indicated by Austin, but include, more fundamentally, those theorized, in another context, by Nietzsche, for example memory, thus deep time), indeed, he had bet that he could purify the promise so that it would be reducible to solely a performative—would he treat the bet, too, as reducible to solely a performative instead of, for example, paying the amount specified in the bet if he lost?

656. Immanuel Kant, *Practical Philosophy*, trans. and ed. Mary J. Gregor (Cambridge: Cambridge University Press, 1999), 163.

657. https://www.larousse.fr/dictionnaires/francais/avenir/7033.

658. Quoted in Sayyid Muḥammad Ḥusayn Ṭabāṭabā'ī, *Shi'ite Islam*, trans. Seyyed Hossein Nasr (Kuala Lumpur: Islamic Book Trust, 2010), 190.

659. This quote, from Abdulaziz Abdulhussein Sachedina's *Islamic Messianism: The Idea of Mahdī in Twelver Shī'ism* (Albany: State University of New York Press, 1981), 96, is, as Sachedina indicates in a note and in the bibliography, a translation of a section from Muḥammad ibn al-Ḥasan al-Ṭūsi's *Kitāb al-ghayba*—in al-Ṭūsi's book, the translated words are preceded by the chain of narrators: "And a

group informed us, on the authority of Abī Jaʻfar Muḥammad ibn ʻAlī ibn al-Ḥusayn ibn Bābawayh, who said: 'In the year that the shaykh Abū al-Ḥasan ʻAlī b. Muḥammad al-Samarrī (may his secret be sanctified) died, I visited him a few days before his death, and he brought out to the people a written message, which I copied.'" The full tradition in Arabic is: "Wa akhbaranā jamāʻa, ʻan Abī Jaʻfar Muḥammad bin ʻAlī bin al-Ḥusayn bin Bābawayh, qāl: 'fī al-sana al-latī tūwuffiya fīhā al-shaykh Abū al-Ḥasan ʻAlī bin Muḥammad al-Samarrī quddis sirruh, fa-ḥaḍartuh qabl wafātih bi-ayyām fa-akhraj ilā al-nās tawqīʻ nasakhtuh: "bism allāh al-raḥmān al-raḥīm: yā ʻAlī bin Muḥammad al-Samarrī aʻẓam allāh ajr ikhwānik fīk, fa-innak mayyit mā baynak wa bayn sittat ayyām, fa-ijmaʻ amrak wa lā tūṣ ilā aḥad fa-yaqūm maqāmak baʻda wafātik, fa-qad waqaʻat al-ghayba al-tāmma, fa-lā ẓuhūr illā baʻd idhn allāh taʻālā dhikruh, wa dhālik baʻd ṭūl al-amad, wa-qaswat al-qulūb, wa imtilāʼ al-arḍ jawr."""

660. Sophocles, *Oedipus the King*, trans. David Grene, in *The Complete Greek Tragedies: Sophocles I*, ed. David Grene and Richmond Lattimore; 3rd ed., ed. Mark Griffith and Glenn W. Most (Chicago; London: University of Chicago Press, 2013), 78.

661. For yet another variant interpretation, see my text "If Only Oedipus Did Not Give Ground on His Desire!" in my book *What Was I Thinking?*

662. Paul Virilio, *Speed and Politics: An Essay on Dromology*, trans. Mark Polizzotti (New York: Semiotext[e], 1986), 148–49.

663. Brett Tingley, "The Pentagon Is Experimenting with Using Artificial Intelligence to 'See Days in Advance,'" *The Drive*, July 30, 2021, https://www.thedrive.com/the-war-zone/41771/the-pentagon-is-experimenting-with-using-artificial-intelligence-to-see-days-in-advance.

664. Nietzsche, *On the Genealogy of Morals/Ecce Homo*, 103.

665. David Silver, Thomas Hubert, Julian Schrittwieser, et al., "Mastering Chess and Shogi by Self-Play with a General Reinforcement Learning Algorithm," arXiv:1712.01815.

666. Ian Prasad Philbrick, "China's Best Go Player Lost a Game to an A.I. The Chinese Government Censored It," *Slate*, May 24, 2017, https://slate.com/technology/2017/05/alphago-beat-top-ranked-go-player-ke-jie-in-china-so-china-censored-it.html.

667. https://timkr.home.xs4all.nl/chess/perfect.htm.

668. Woolf, *Mrs. Dalloway*, 26. Somewhat unbeknownst to him, he was making a choice between continuing to be in the world of the living where the flight of birds, the scurrying of some rat, etc., are independent of him, their movement unrelated to what he was doing at the moment, and being lost in the death realm, where these would be intimately, or, more accurately, extimately, linked to him.

669. John Cage, *Silence: Lectures and Writings* (Middletown, CT: Wesleyan University Press, 1973), 152; I have replaced the period after "sounds" with a dash.

670. Ibid., 22–23.

671. Was it then prudent on the part of Adam not to eat of the Tree of Life, since ostensibly it would have overwhelmed him, if not killed him?!

672. Michel Chion, *Sound: An Acoulogical Treatise*, trans. James A. Steintrager (Durham, NC: Duke University Press, 2015), 122.

673. Michel Chion, *The Voice in Cinema*, ed. and trans. Claudia Gorbman (New York: Columbia University Press, 1999), 21.

674. Ibid., 24.

675. Ibid., 28.

676. Sometimes, the receiver of an aphorism may have to correct what he received because the reception was, for various reasons, marred by some sort of noise—thenceforth he or she has to resist the temptation to still revise the aphorism if it appears not to be as laconic or eloquent or poetic as it seems it could be made to be.

677. *Gilles Deleuze: The ABC Primer*, G to M, trans. and ed. Charles J. Stivale, https://deleuze.cla.purdue.edu/lecture/lecture-recording-2-g-m.

678. We find a telling noting of such overlooking in Fyodor Dostoyevsky's *The Gambler*: "I believe she had hirtheto looked on me as that empress of ancient times looked on the slave before whom she did not mind undressing because she did not regard him as a human being" (trans. Constance Garnett, in *Great Short Works of Fyodor Dostoevsky*, 389).

679. Slavoj Žižek, *The Ticklish Subject: The Absent Centre of Political Ontology* (London: Verso, 2000), 187–88.

680. Jacques Rancière, *Disagreement: Politics and Philosophy*, trans. Julie Rose (Minneapolis: University of Minnesota Press, 1999), 28.

681. Antonin Artaud (and Antonin Nalpas), *Nouveaux Écrits de Rodez: Lettres au docteur Ferdière (1943-1946) et autres textes inédits, suivis de six lettres à Marie Dubuc (1935-1937)* (Paris: Gallimard, 1977), 28.

682. Schreber, *Memoirs of My Nervous Illness*, 25.

683. *The Tibetan Book of the Dead* (English title): *The Great Liberation by Hearing in the Intermediate States* (Tibetan title), composed by Padmasambhava, revealed by Terton Karma Lingpa, trans. Gyurme Dorje, ed. Graham Coleman and Thuuten Jinpa (London: Penguin, 2017), 226.

684. It would seem that for Artaud we do not shit as a byproduct of eating (actually, of the entire digestive process, since "feces are made up of 75 percent water and 25 percent solid matter. About 30 percent of the solid matter consists of dead bacteria; about 30 percent consists of indigestible food matter such as cellulose; 10 to 20 percent is cholesterol and other fats; 10 to 20 percent is inorganic substances such as calcium phosphate and iron phosphate; and 2 to 3 percent is protein. Cell debris shed from the mucous membrane of the intestinal tract also passes in the waste material, as do bile pigments [bilirubin] and dead leukocytes [white blood cells]" [*Britannica*, https://www.britannica.com/science/feces]) but rather we eat so as to shit, that for him shitting and shit are primary in relation to eating and food.

685. Gilles Deleuze, "Preface: A New Stylistics," in *Two Regimes of Madness: Texts and Interviews, 1975-1995*, ed. David Lapoujade, trans. Ames Hodges and Mike Taormina (Los Angeles, CA: Semiotext[e], 2006), 366.

686. Freud, *The Interpretation of Dreams*, 528. The navel of a dream is not only what Freud took to be the point where the psychoanalyst and the analysand reach a limit in the interpretation of the latter's dream, but also, conjointly, the point where the perceptive psychoanalyst would feel that he or she is dreaming the meetings with the analysand ... and everything else, in other words, that life (and not only death) is a dream ... in which both the psychoanalyst and the analysand happen to be meeting in repeated sessions.

687. *The Egyptian Book of the Dead: The Book of Going Forth by Day: Being the Papyrus of Ani (Royal Scribe of the Divine Offerings), Written and Illustrated circa 1250 B.C.E., by Scribes and Artists Unknown, Including the Balance of Chapters of the Books of the Dead Known as*

the *Theban Recension, Compiled from Ancient Texts, Dating Back to the Roots of Egyptian Civilization*, trans. Raymond O. Faulkner; with additional translations by Ogden Goelet JR.; with color illustrations from the facsimile volume produced in 1890 under the supervision of E. A. Wallis Budge; ed. Eva Von Dassow; in an edition conceived by James Wasserman (San Francisco: Chronicle Books, 1994), plate 3; cf. "—30A—Chapter for not letting N's heart create opposition against him in the God's Domain: O heart which I had from my mother, O my heart which I had upon earth, do not rise up against me as a witness in the presence of the Lord of Things; do not speak against me concerning what I have done, do not bring up anything against me in the presence of the Great God, Lord of the West. Hail to you, my heart! Hail to you, my heart! Hail to you, my entrails! ... May you say what is good to Re, may you make me to flourish" (103).

688. As readers, we encounter a tongue that bears witness to the state of the dead man in spite of the motionlessness and rigidity of the rest of the body that had become a corpse in Edgar Allan Poe's "The Facts in the Case of M. Valdemar": "There was no longer the faintest sign of vitality in M. Valdemar; and concluding him to be dead, we were consigning him to the charge of the nurses, when a strong vibratory motion was observable in the tongue.... M. Valdemar [but was it M. Valdemar or his tongue?] *spoke*—obviously in reply to the question I had propounded to him a few minutes before. I had asked him, it will be remembered, if he still slept. He now said: 'Yes;—no;—I *have been sleeping*—and now—now—*I am dead.*' ... It was now suggested that I should attempt to influence the patient's arm as heretofore. I made the attempt and failed. Dr. F—— then intimated a desire to have me put a question. I did so, as follows: 'M. Valdemar, can you explain to us what are your feelings or wishes now?' ... The tongue quivered, or rather rolled violently in the mouth (although the jaws and lips remained rigid as before), and at length the same hideous voice ... broke forth: 'For God's sake!—quick!—quick!—put me to sleep—or, quick!—waken me!—quick!—*I say to you that I am dead!*'" (Edgar Allan Poe, *The Works of Edgar Allan Poe in One Volume: Poems, Tales, Essays, Criticisms with New Notes* [New York: P. F. Collier and Son, 1927], 417-19).

689. Schreber, *Memoirs of My Nervous Illness*, 141, 144-45. From the quote, it looks like Schreber, who, according to Dr. Guido Weber's report of 1899, "thought he was dead" (ibid., 328) and believed that "he is called to redeem the world" (ibid., 333), intuitively attempted to actualize what Antonin Artaud would demand years later: placing man "again, for the last time, on the autopsy table to remake his anatomy.... / Man is sick because he is badly constructed.... / There is nothing more useless than an organ. / When you will have made

him a body without organs, / then you will have delivered him from all his automatic reactions" ("To Have Done with the Judgment of God," in Antonin Artaud, *Selected Writings*, ed. Susan Sontag, trans. Helen Weaver [Berkeley: University of California Press, 1988], 570–71).

690. Schreber, *Memoirs of My Nervous Illness*, 87.

691. I can well imagine someone objecting to such a program thus: "But I do not at all wish to do away, or that anyone do away, with God, and consequently with his judgement: I hope that there is a God, and that there is a judgment of God, for I am unable to forgive myself the unforgivable act I have committed—only God would be able to do it."

692. Friedrich Nietzsche, *Thus Spoke Zarathustra: A Book for Everyone and No One*, trans. R. J. Hollingdale (Baltimore: Penguin, 1961), 114.

693. To paraphrase the title of a Milan Kundera book, *The Unbearable Lightness of Being*.

694. Toufic, *Postscripts*, 52–53.

695. If he did not have a soul, then the exchange the devil proposed to Faust would imply that Faust is dealing with a Lacanian devil who believes that Faust loves him, since, according to Lacan, one gives in love what one does not have (Lacan, *Écrits: A Selection*, 290: "Giving in love what she does not have").

696. Deleuze, *The ABC Primer*, G to M.

697. Annemarie Schimmel, *Mystical Dimensions of Islam* (Chapel Hill: University of North Carolina Press, 1975), 181.

698. Deleuze, *Cinema 1: The Movement-Image*, 87.

699. Ibid., 99.

700. Ibid.

701. *Autobiography of a Schizophrenic Girl*, 23.

702. Deleuze, *Cinema 1: The Movement-Image*, 100.

703. Ibid., 95–96.

704. Judging from the order of the sections in his book, with the section on Bergman and the effacement of the face followed directly

not by the one on any-space-whatever in the next chapter but by a reversion to the face in Pabst's *Lulu*, it would seem that Deleuze not only did not explicitly note the effaced face as an any-space-whatever, but also did not recognize that it is such a space.

705. Deleuze, *Cinema 1: The Movement-Image*, 110.

706. Ibid., 111.

707. Ibid., 120.

708. *Entangling Vines: Zen Koans of the Shūmon Kattōshū*, trans. Thomas Yūhō Kirchner (Somerville, MA: Wisdom Publications, 2013), 34.

709. In a parallel manner God, who, not being mortal, hence not being dead even while alive, is not subject to 180-degree over-turns, does not require, and thus does not have, a name (in the sense in which we usually understand this term—He has a name, indeed an infinite number of names, in a different sense, for example, The Beautiful, The Living, etc.).

710. The title of a book by Samuel Beckett.

711. Nietzsche: "Popular morality ... separates strength from expressions of strength, as if there were a neutral substratum behind the strong man, which was *free* to express strength or not to do so. But there is no such substratum ... 'the doer' is merely a fiction added to the deed—the deed is everything.... Our entire science still lies under the misleading influence of language and has not disposed of that little changeling, the 'subject.' ... The oppressed, downtrodden, outraged exhort one another with the vengeful cunning of impotence: ' ... He is good who does not ... attack, who does not requite, who leaves revenge to God ...'— ... just as if the weakness of the weak—that is to say, their *essence*, their effects, their sole ineluctable, irremovable reality—were a voluntary achievement, willed, chosen.... This type of man *needs* to believe in a neutral independent 'subject'" (*On the Genealogy of Morals/Ecce Homo*, 45-46).

712. My italics.

713. My italics of "from the tongue and not from the lips."

714. *The Collected Tales and Poems of Edgar Allan Poe* (Hertfordshire, UK: Wordsworth Editions, 2004), 270-72.

715. German translation from the original French (Frankfurt am Main: Kommunales Kino Frankfurt, 1975), 100-101. Quoted in Martin Loiperdinger, "Lumière's *Arrival of the Train*: Cinema's Founding Myth," trans. Bernd Elzer, *The Moving Image* 4, no. 1 (Spring 2004): 90-91.

716. *Geschichte der Filmkunst* (1956; Frankfurt am Main: Fischer, 1982), 27. Quoted in (and, I assume, translated by Elzer) Loiperdinger, "Lumière's *Arrival of the Train*: Cinema's Founding Myth," 91.

717. Hellmuth Karasek, "Lokomotive der Gefühle," *Der Spiegel*, December 25, 1994, 154.

718. Loiperdinger, "Lumière's *Arrival of the Train*: Cinema's Founding Myth," 94.

719. Bazin, *What Is Cinema?*, vol. 1, 9 and 14-15.

720. Chittick, *The Sufi Path of Knowledge*, 115.

721. Bergson, *Matter and Memory*, 36.

722. Deleuze, *Cinema 1: The Movement-Image*, 21-22.

723. *Moon in a Dewdrop: Writings of Zen Master Dōgen*, 136 and 138.

724. Deleuze, *Cinema 1: The Movement-Image*, 1.

725. Benjamin, "The Work of Art in the Age of Mechanical Reproduction," in *Illuminations*, 236-37. In Coppola's *Dracula*, seeing that they are rivals for Mina, who is Harker's fiancée and who looks identical to Dracula's beloved dead wife, the shadow of Dracula, a manifestation of his unconscious, appears to strangle Harker, who, though untouched by it materially, must feel unconsciously that he is being choked: a direct relation between the unconscious of Dracula and the unconscious of Harker.

726. Andrey Tarkovsky, *Sculpting in Time: Reflections on the Cinema*, trans. Kitty Hunter-Blair (Austin: University of Texas Press, 1989), 225.

727. Ibid.

728. Eisenstein, *Film Form*, 55-56.

729. Deleuze, *Cinema 1: The Movement-Image*, 1.

730. Ibid.

731. For God, nothing is past yet, a fait accompli, indeed there is no past but one unending "present"; Hitchcock's film *Rope*, which has no (visible) cuts, is inconsistent since the death of one of the characters, which we see in the opening scene of the film, is thenceforth treated as something past, a fait accompli.

732. *Britannica*, "Louvre (The Louvre Museum, Musée du Louvre)," https://www.guidetags.com/mindmaps/explore/hist-3p55/3679-louvre-the-louvre-museum-musee-du-louvre.

733. He had encountered in Lebanon another manner of being treated as invisible, if not nonexistent: as one Lebanese and then another would jump the line in which he was patiently and politely standing.

734. Deleuze, *Cinema 1: The Movement-Image*, 207.

735. This issue is not addressed by Deleuze when he writes on this characteristic among the five that he associates with the crisis of the action-image.

736. Deleuze, *Cinema 1: The Movement-Image*, 207.

737. Ibid.

738. Deleuze ended the preface to the French edition of the first volume of his *Cinema* book with these infelicitous words: "We are not providing any reproductions as illustrations to our text, as it is in fact our text alone which aspires to be an illustration of the great films, of which each of us retains to a greater or lesser extent a memory, emotion or perception." I object to these words from both the standpoint of Deleuze's own conception of philosophy as a creation of concepts and my own practice of conceptual creation. Setting aside my reservations vis-à-vis considering philosophical works as functioning, even secondarily, as illustrations of films, here is my emendation of the aforementioned Deleuze quote that makes it more palatable: "We are not providing any reproductions as illustrations to our text, as it is in fact our text alone which aspires to be an illustration of great *future* films."

739. Diogenes Laertius, *Lives of the Eminent Philosophers*, 534.

740. Nietzsche, *Thus Spoke Zarathustra: A Book for All and None*, 111.

741. Toufic, *Forthcoming*, 2nd ed., 101.

742. Ibid., 103–104.

743. Friedrich Nietzsche, *Thus Spoke Zarathustra: A Book for All and None*, 112.

744. Ṣadr al-Dīn Muḥammad al-Shīrāzī, *Mafātīḥ al-ghayb*, 627.

745. *Oxford Essential Quotations*, 4th ed., ed. Susan Ratcliffe (Oxford University Press, 2016), https://www.oxfordreference.com/view/10.1093/acref/9780191826719.001.0001/q-oro-ed4-00005726. The quote derives from Huxley's presidential address at the British Association, "Biogenesis and Abiogenesis" (1870), in Thomas H. Huxley, *Discourses: Biological and Geological Essays* (New York: D. Appleton, 1897), 244.

746. Gilles Deleuze and Félix Guattari, *What Is Philosophy?*, trans. Hugh Tomlinson and Graham Burchell (New York: Columbia University Press, 1994), 2 and 6.

747. Jean-François Lyotard, *Political Writings*, trans. Bill Readings and Kevin Paul Geiman (Minneapolis: University of Minnesota Press, 1993), 19.

748. Or at least a roadside picnic, the title of the Arkady and Boris Strugatsky 1972 novel on which the script of Tarkovsky's *Stalker* was loosely based; in the film, the renowned icon painter Theophanes the Greek, Andrei Rublev and his assistant go on such a picnic.

749. "What Is the Creative Act?," in Deleuze, *Two Regimes of Madness*, 322.

750. Given how difficult it is for a student to fail a class at HKBU, since students can opt not to attend even a single session and yet pass the class, according to a university policy introduced in 2017, and since the warped grading-scale equivalence between the letter grades and the percent grades at HKBU functions as a type of grade inflation, the letter grades A-/A, for example, spanning 80 to 100 on the percentage scale (if the grade-inflation trend is not countered, I wouldn't be surprised if some years from now the letter grades A-/A would be equivalent to 70 to 100 on the percentage scale at HKBU and at other universities, especially in Hong Kong); and given the outsized weight student evaluations play in faculty promotion and tenure, the real evaluation that matters at HKBU, and in an increasing number of

universities, is, symptomatically, the students' of the teachers rather than the teachers' of the students.

751.   Nietzsche, *Beyond Good and Evil*, §231, 123–24.

752.   E. M. Cioran, *Anathemas and Admirations*, trans. Richard Howard (New York: Arcade, 1991), 82.

753.   *The Guardian*, October 3, 2012, https://www.theguardian.com/science/2012/oct/03/philosophy-artificial-intelligence; see also "Creative Blocks: The Very Laws of Physics Imply that Artificial Intelligence Must Be Possible. What's Holding Us Up?," *Aeon*, October 3, 2012, https://aeon.co/essays/how-close-are-we-to-creating-artificial-intelligence.

754.   Alain Badiou, *Lacan: Anti-Philosophy 3*, trans. Kenneth Reinhard and Susan Spitzer (New York: Columbia University Press, 2018), 85. Don't these characteristics apply to some degree to certain aspects of his philosophy, or at least to some of his texts? Here are two examples, from 1977, of the bullshit of a philosopher: "There is only one great philosopher of our time: Mao Zedong.... All the rest disappeared into futility" (Alain Badiou, "The Current Situation on the Philosophical Front," in *The Adventure of French Philosophy* [New York: Verso, 2020], 1 and 4; when he was not bullshitting, the same philosopher wrote in a text dated 2005 and that would become the preface to the same book: "Let us take the example of two especially intense and well-known philosophical instances. First, that of classical Greek philosophy between Parmenides and Aristotle, from the fifth to the third centuries BC: a highly inventive, foundational moment, ultimately quite short-lived. Second, that of German idealism between Kant and Hegel, via Fichte and Schelling: another exceptional philosophical moment, from the late eighteenth to the early nineteenth centuries, intensely creative and condensed within an even shorter time span.... There was—or there is, depending where I put myself—a French philosophical moment of the second half of the twentieth century which, everything else being equal, bears comparison to the examples of classical Greece and enlightenment Germany. Sartre's foundational work, *Being and Nothingness*, appeared in 1943 and the last writings of Deleuze, *What Is Philosophy?*, date from the early 1990s. The moment of French philosophy develops between the two of them, and includes Bachelard, Merleau-Ponty, Lévi-Strauss, Althusser, Foucault, Derrida and Lacan as well as Sartre and Deleuze—and myself, maybe" [I would replace Bachelard with Lyotard—moreover, if Lacan, whom Badiou considers to be an antiphilosopher, is included in his list of major French philosophers, why isn't Blanchot, who maintained a neutral relation toward philosophy? This omission indicates a major blind spot in Badiou, who is in denial of his mortality,

of his condition of being dead (in other words, undead) even while still physically alive]); and: "It is interesting to note that, in *Rhizome,* the cunning monkeys of multiplicities, the heads of the anti-Marxist troupe, Deleuze and Guattari, openly strike out at the central dialectical principle: One divides into two.... We will not take Deleuze and Guattari to be illiterate. We will thus take them to be crooks" (the quote is from the text "The Fascism of the Potato," ibid., 193-94; when he was not bullshitting, he wrote: "For Gilles [Deleuze], 'to think' means: to make a section in the chaos. To be as close as possible to chaos, and nonetheless to shelter oneself from it. The power of a thought is its capacity to stay as close as possible to the infinite with the minimum thickness for shelter. A thought is all the more creative, the less sheltering it needs. A powerful thought stands, almost naked, in the fiery midst of the virtual.... Gilles Deleuze: creator, by way of concepts, of new links, of hitherto impossible connections," ibid., 340-41).

755. One of the most fitting, humorous uses of the dash is to have the seemingly same statement on both sides of it, qualified or negated on one side and affirmed on the other, for example because it was understood exoterically on one side and esoterically on the other.

756. Deleuze, *Cinema 1: The Movement-Image,* 185.

757. See the quote on page 398 of this volume.

758. Ibid.

759. Jacques Lacan, *The Ethics of Psychoanalysis, 1959-1960: The Seminar of Jacques Lacan, Book VII,* ed. Jacques-Alain Miller, trans. Dennis Porter (London: Routledge, 2008), 315.

760. Jacques Lacan, *Television,* trans. Denis Hollier, Rosalind Krauss, and Annette Michelson, *October* 40 (Spring 1987): 19-20.

761. Ibid., 19.

762. Giorgio Agamben, *The Time that Remains: A Commentary on the Letter to the Romans,* trans. Patricia Dailey (Stanford, CA: Stanford University Press, 2005), 51.

763. Quoted in Rachel Flynn, "I Do Not Seek Picasso, I Find ...," https://www.tate.org.uk/tate-etc/issue-24-spring-2012/i-do-not-seek-picasso-i-find.

764. Deleuze, *Two Regimes of Madness,* 141.

765. Borges, *Collected Fictions*, 67.

766. Friedrich Nietzsche, *Ecce Homo: How to Become What You Are*, trans. Duncan Large (Oxford: Oxford University Press), 88.

767. Rainer Maria Rilke, *Auguste Rodin* (New York: Parkstone International, 2023), 7.

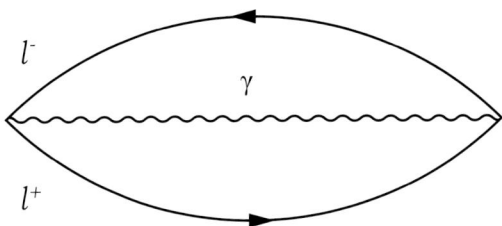

Feynman diagram of a charged lepton (l^-)–charged
anti-lepton (l^+)–photon (γ) vacuum fluctuation.

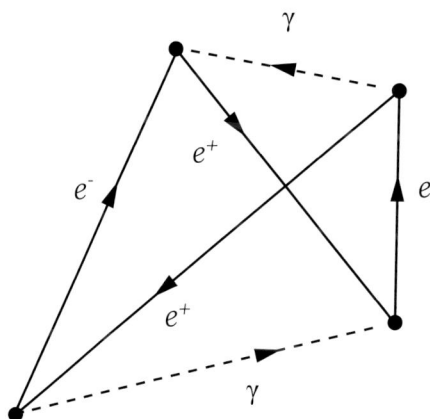

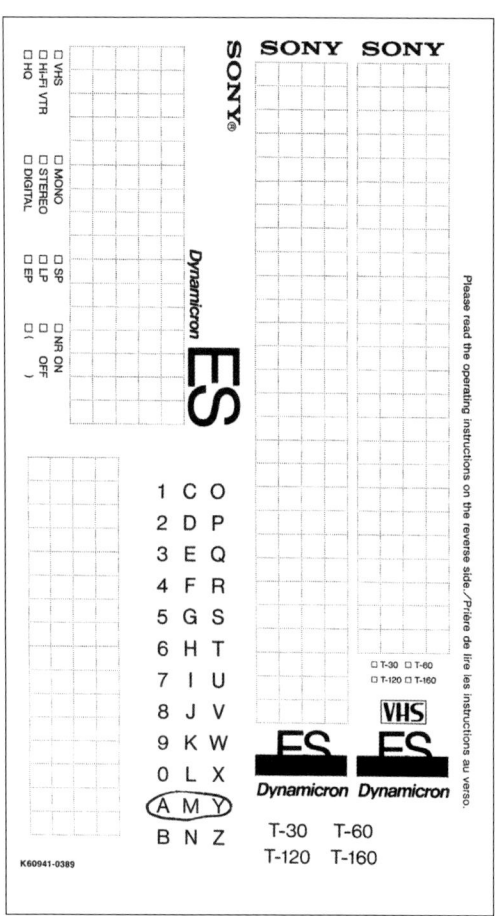

Labeling sheet included with blank VHS tapes sold by Sony.

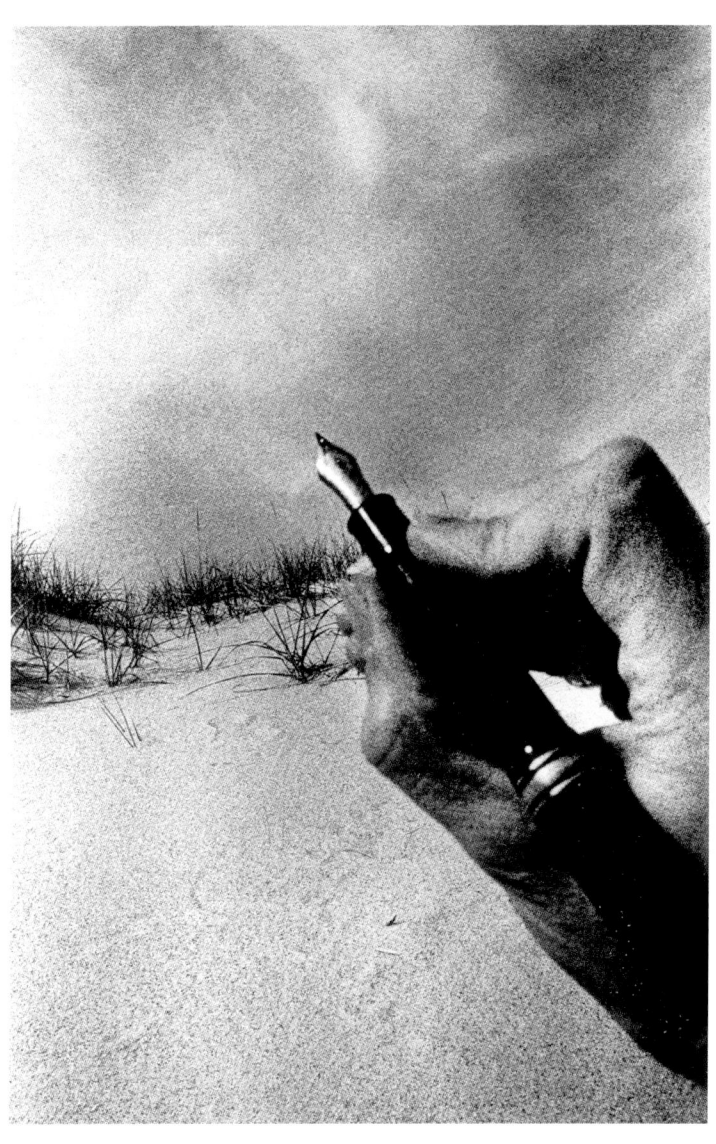

Photograph from Ralph Gibson's *The Somnambulist* (1970).

Appendix to *(Vampires): An Uneasy Essay on the Undead in Film*: "The Emperor's New Costume; or, the Case of the Missing Mask"

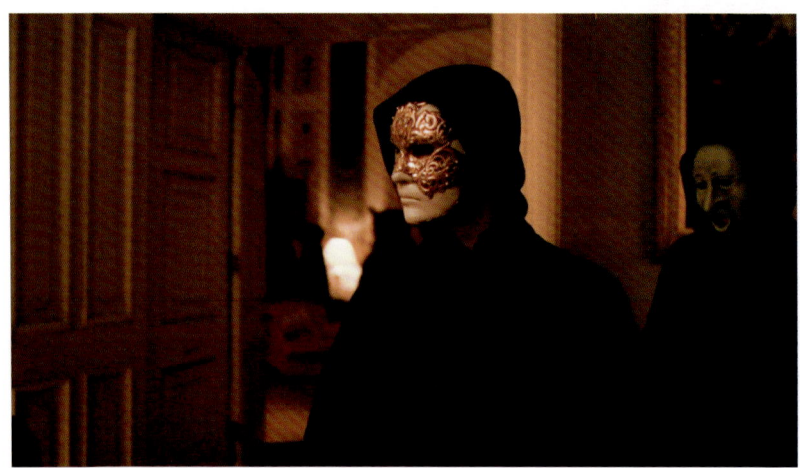

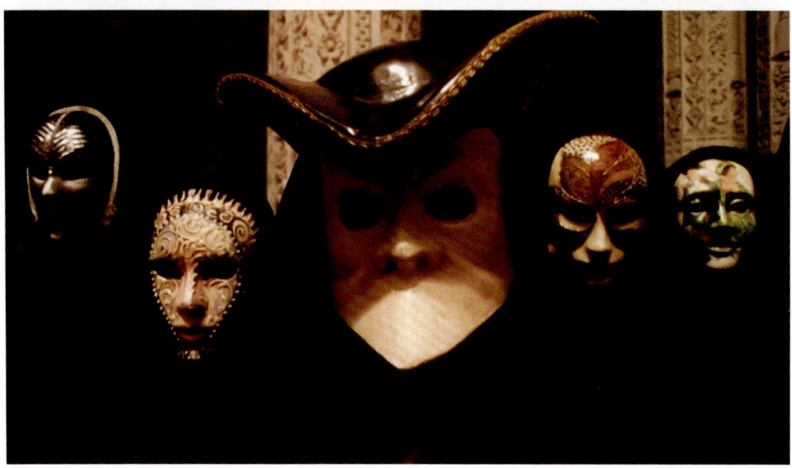

Stills from Kubrick's *Eyes Wide Shut*.

Appendix to *(Vampires): An Uneasy Essay on the Undead in Film*: "The Off-Screen and/or the Set On-Screen"

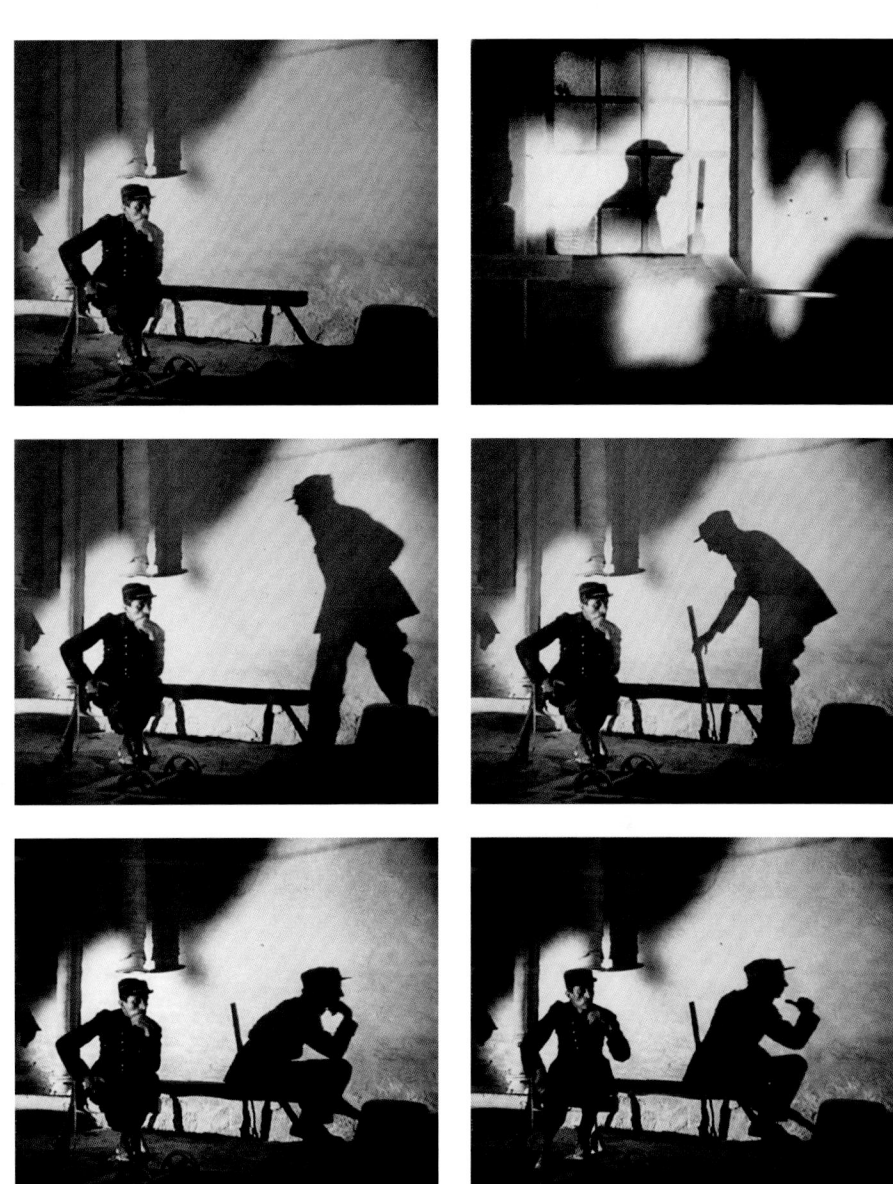

Stills from Dreyer's *Vampyr.*

Appendix to *(Vampires): An Uneasy Essay on the Undead in Film*: "Over-Turns"

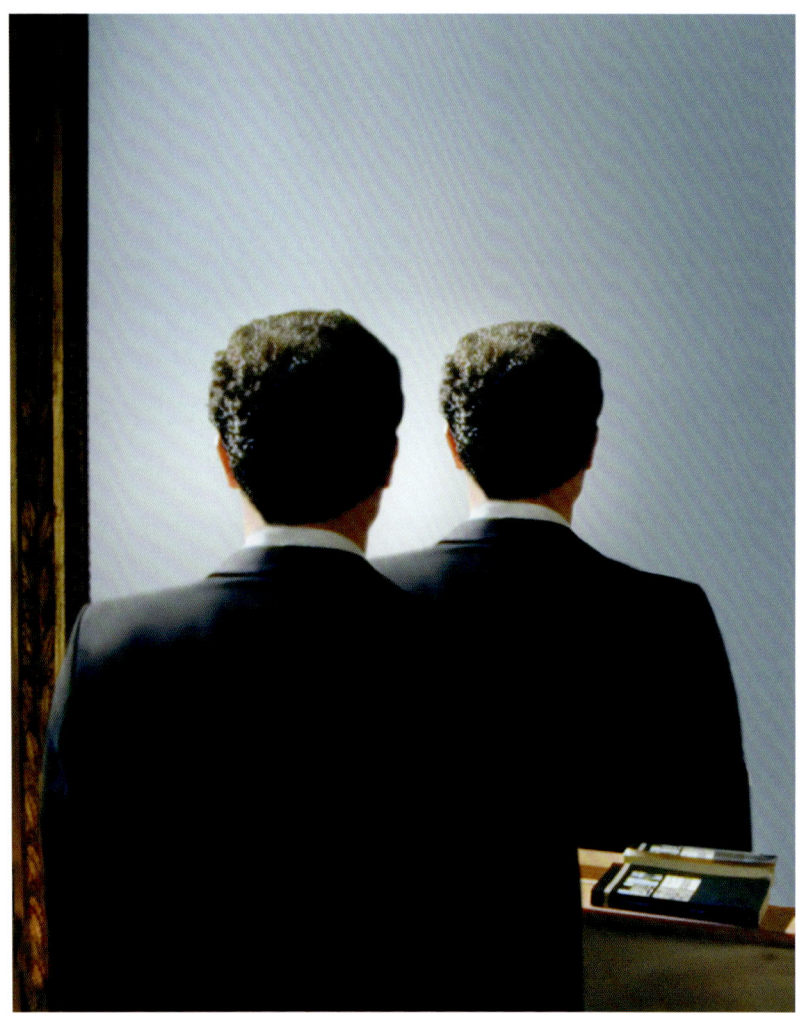

From the series *Over-turned Portraits* made by Paul Perry, Nicola Unger, and Persijn Broersen to accompany my lecture "Backing Mortals' Proper Names," DasArts, November 2, 2001.

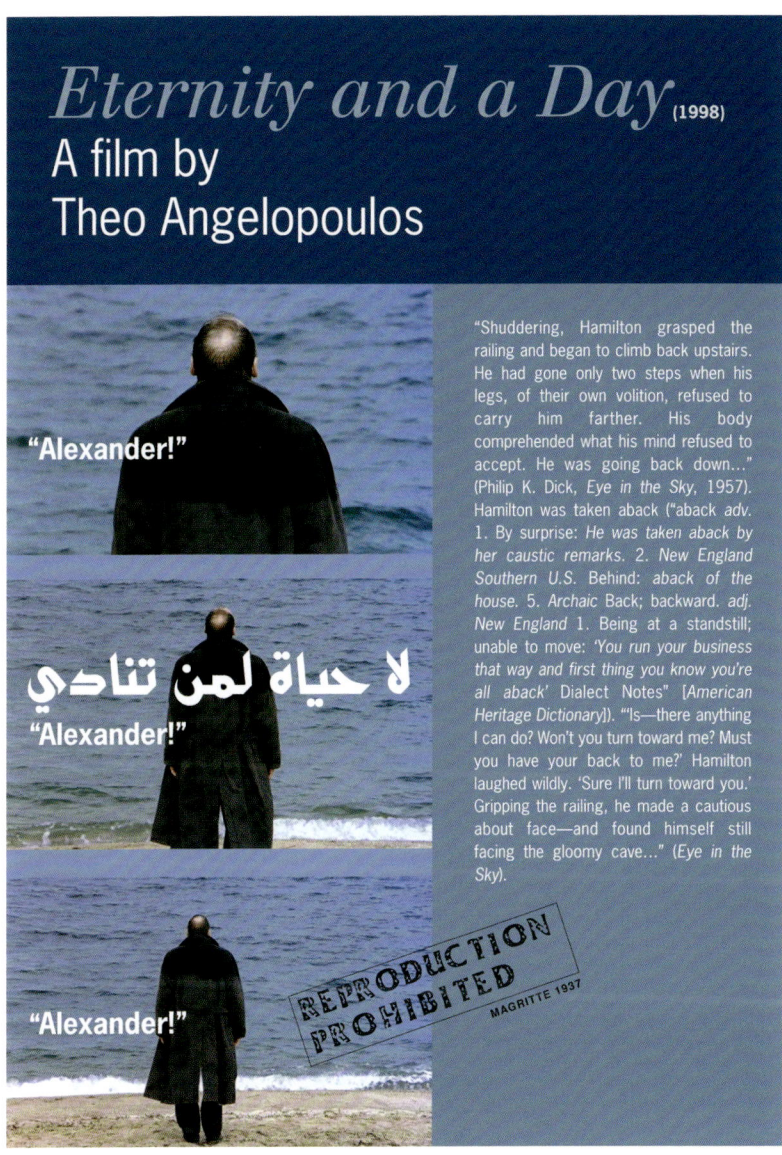

Jalal Toufic, *Eternity and a Day,* 70 × 50 cm, 2005.
The literal translation of the Arabic "لا حياة لمن تنادي" is "There is no life in the one you are calling," but as an idiom its meaning is closer to: "It's like talking to a brick wall" or "Your words are falling on deaf ears."

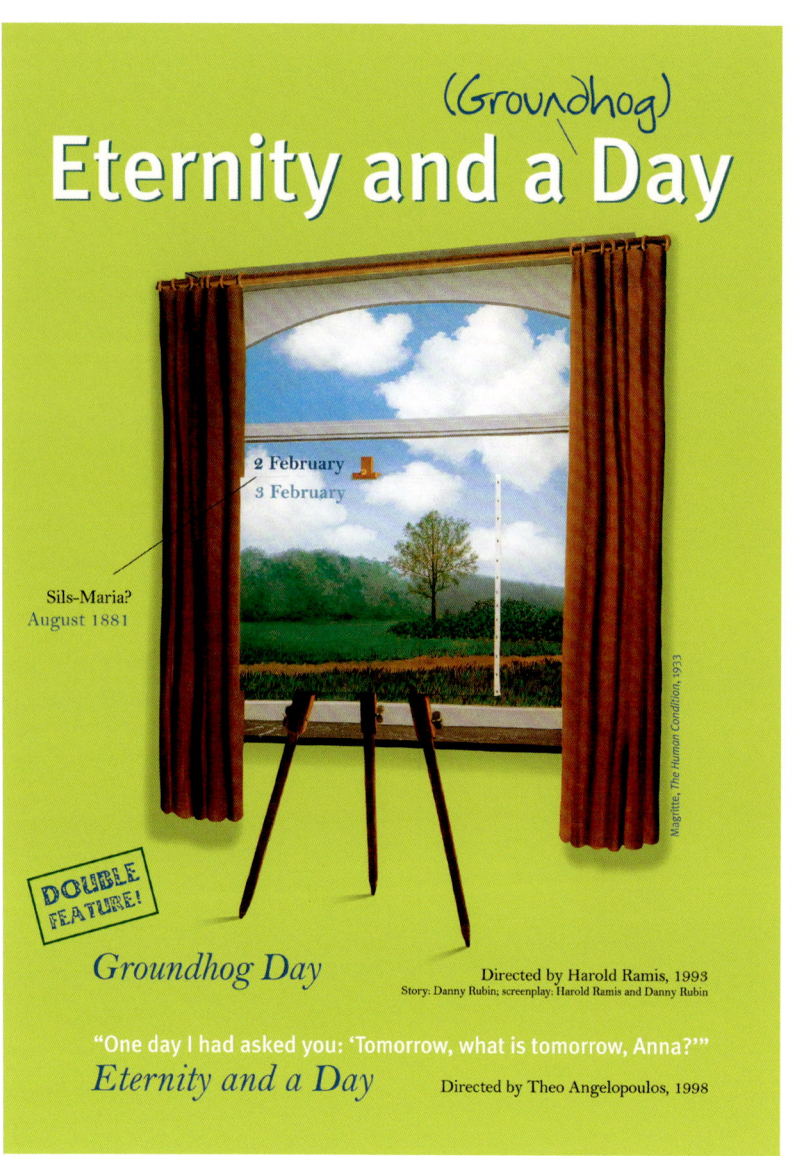

Jalal Toufic, *Eternity and a [Groundhog] Day,* 100 × 70 cm, 2001.

Appendix to *(Vampires): An Uneasy Essay on the Undead in Film*: "Kneeling Angel with Mountainous Wings"

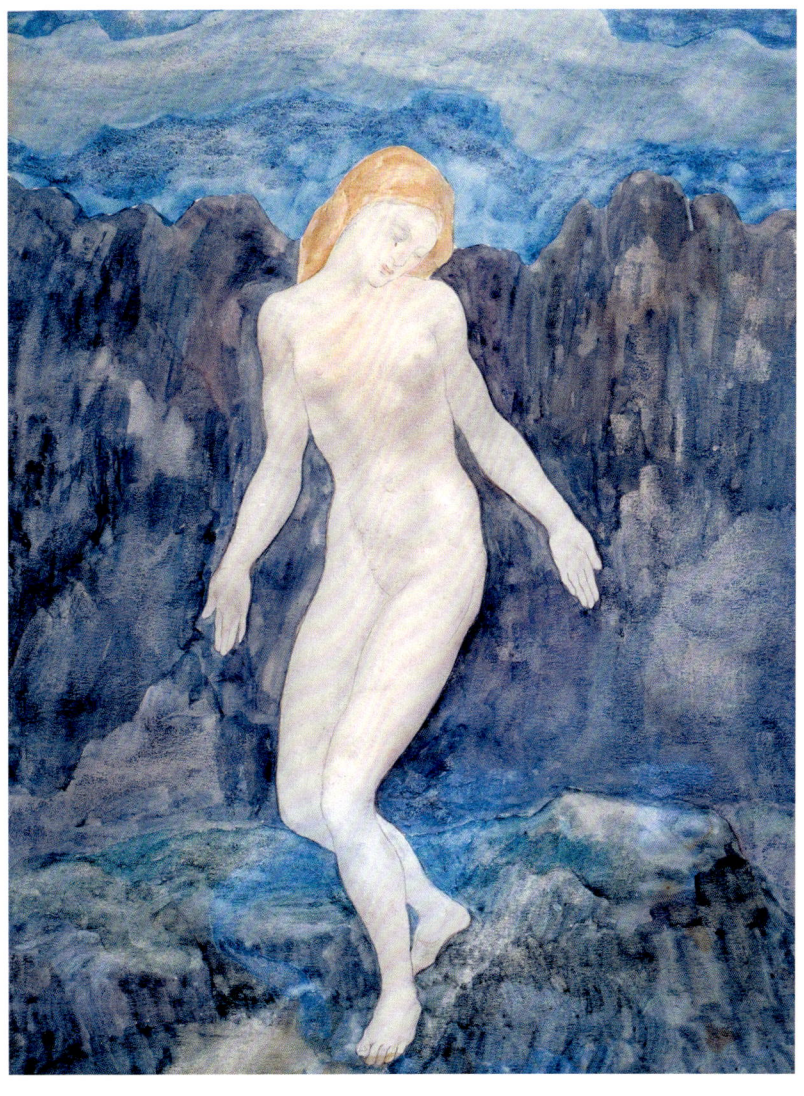

Kahlil Gibran, *The Gift*, watercolor, 33 × 22.5 cm, 1923.
(Illustration for *The Prophet*.) © The Gibran National Committee, Lebanon.

Appendix to (Vampires): An Uneasy Essay on the Undead in Film: "Photographic Memory"

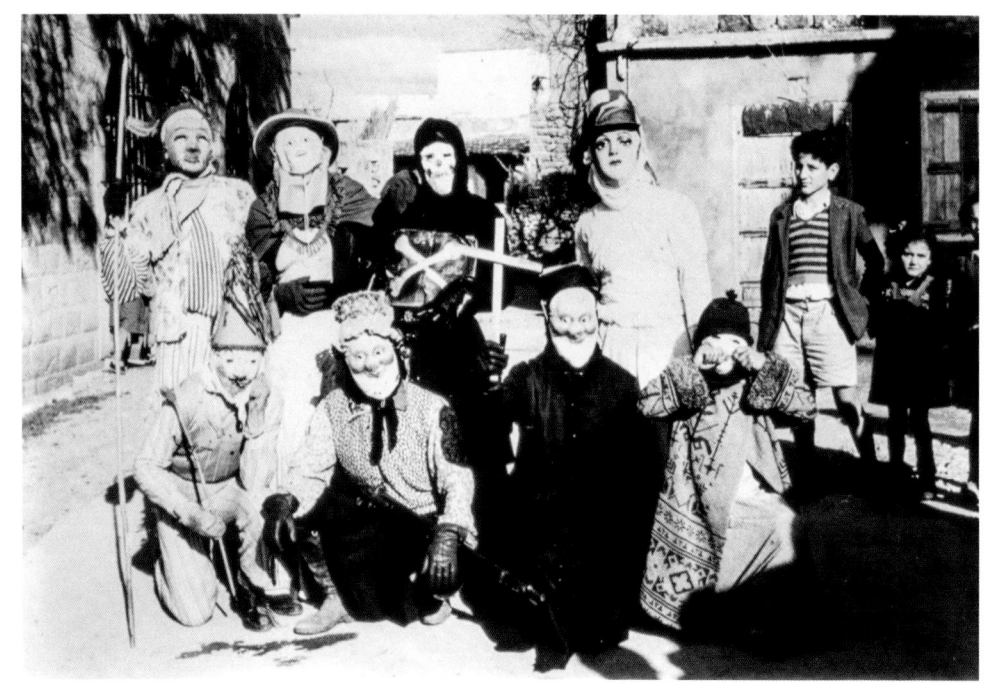

Yertchan Dankikian, Children dressed up for the Feast of Saint Barbara, 1950s, Zgharta, Lebanon, collection AIF (Arab Image Foundation)/Mohsen Yammine.

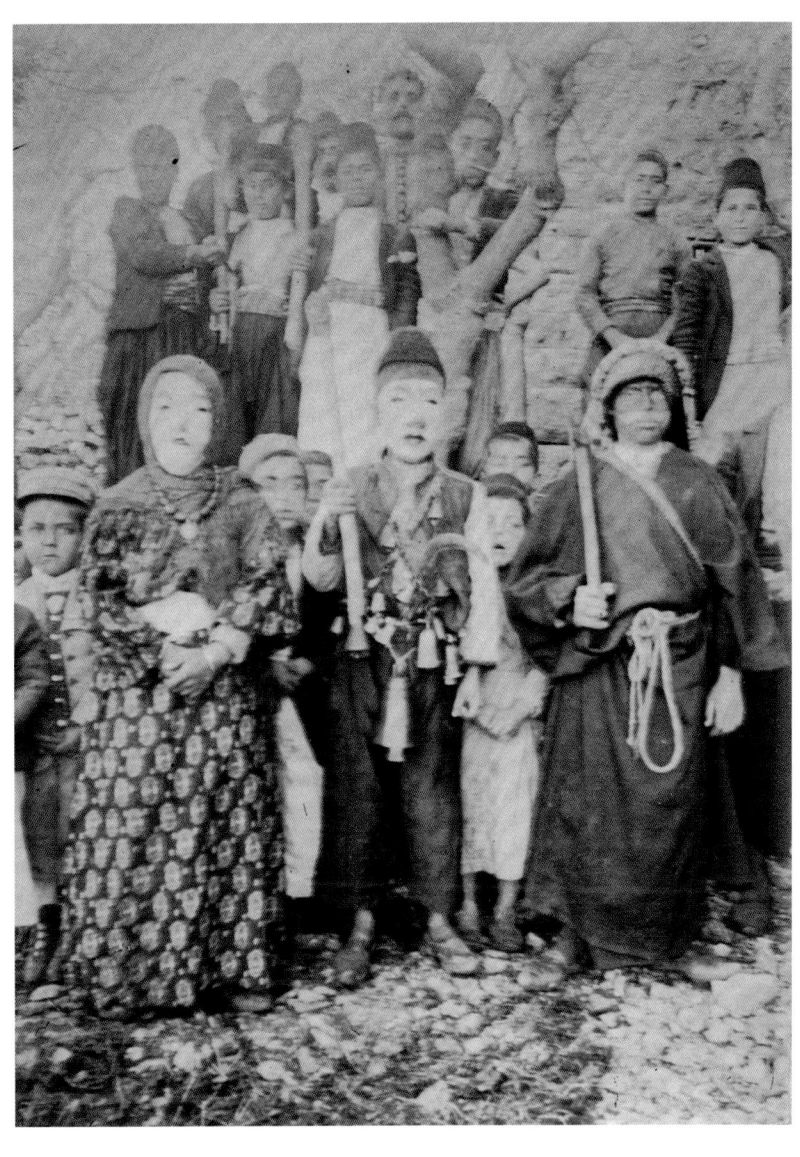

Anonymous, Lebanon, 1920s,
collection AIF/Simone Chemali.

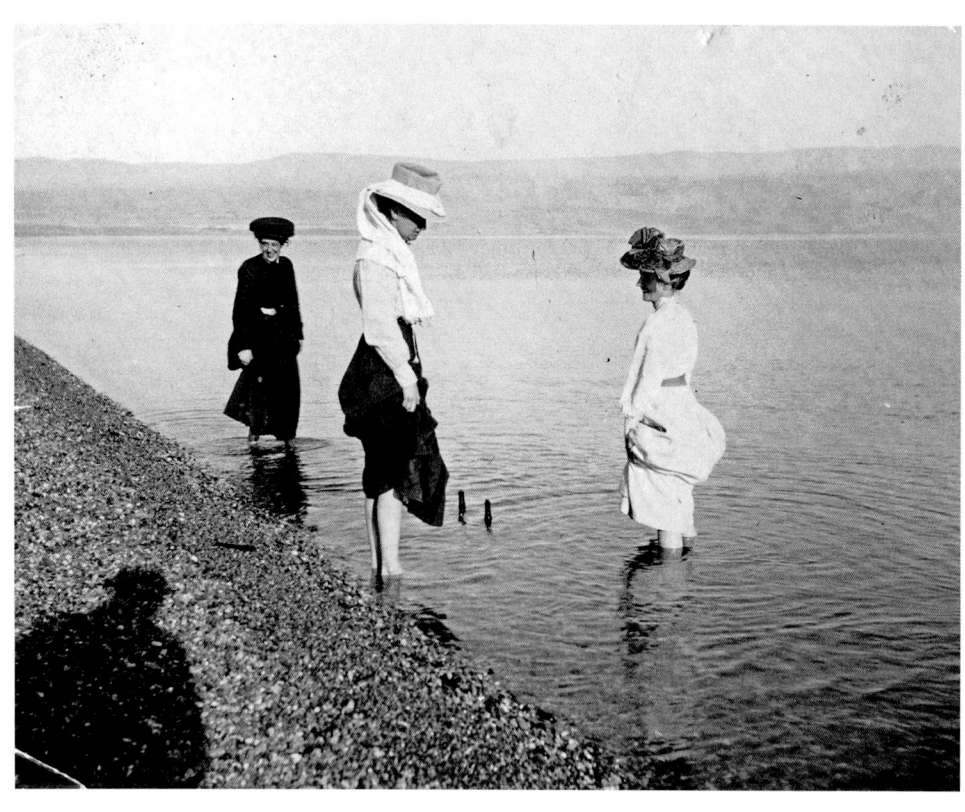

Anonymous, Marguerit Dyce Sharp Tuck-Tuck and friends paddling in the Dead Sea, 1920/1921, Dead Sea, Palestine, collection AIF/Sami Khoury.

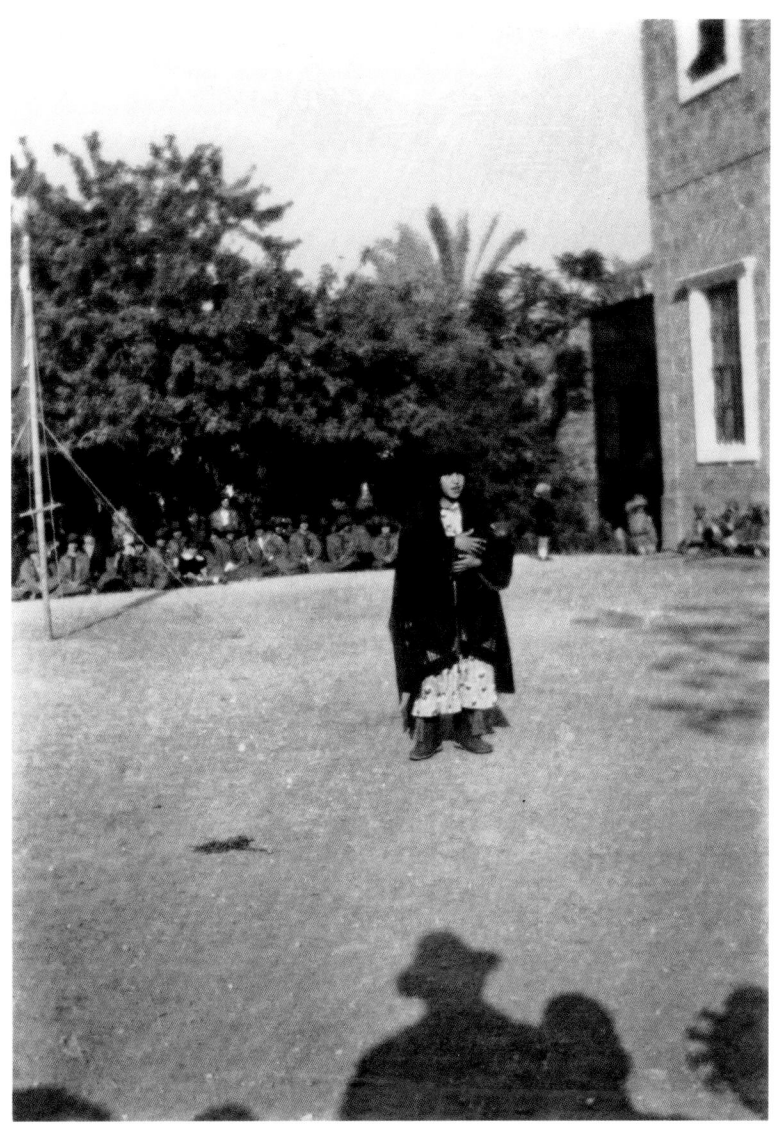

Jibrail Jabbur, collection AIF/Norma Jabbur.

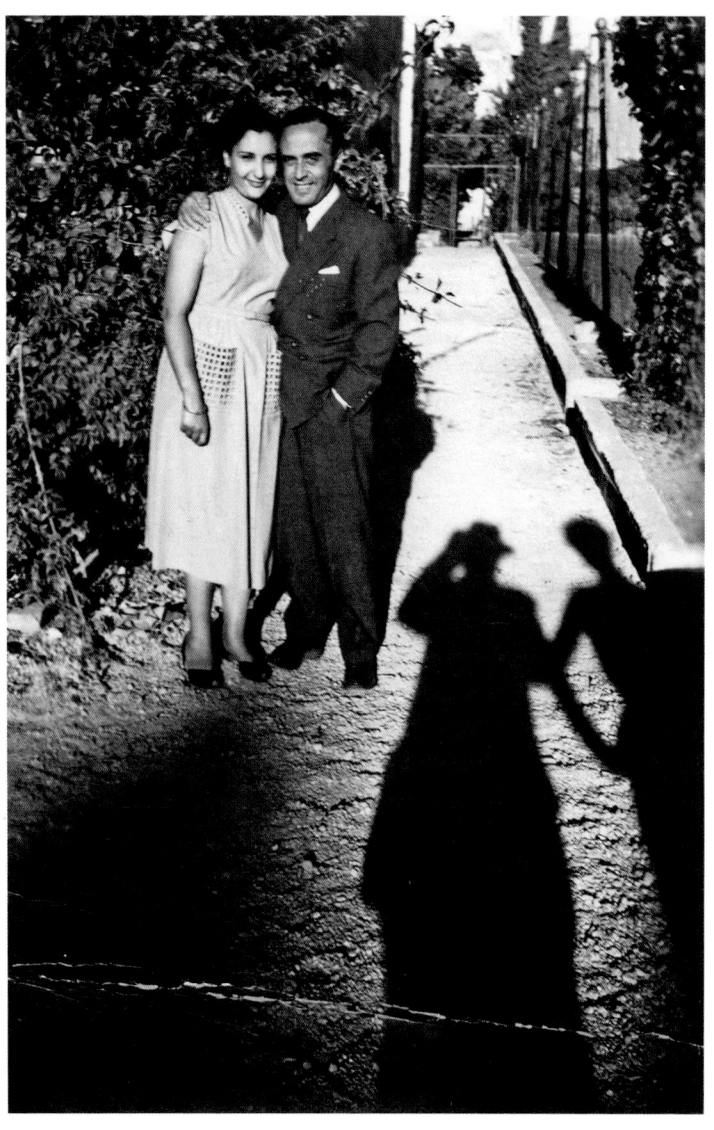

Anonymous, Georges and Aida Kawar, 1954,
Palestine, collection AIF/Aida Krikorian Kawar.

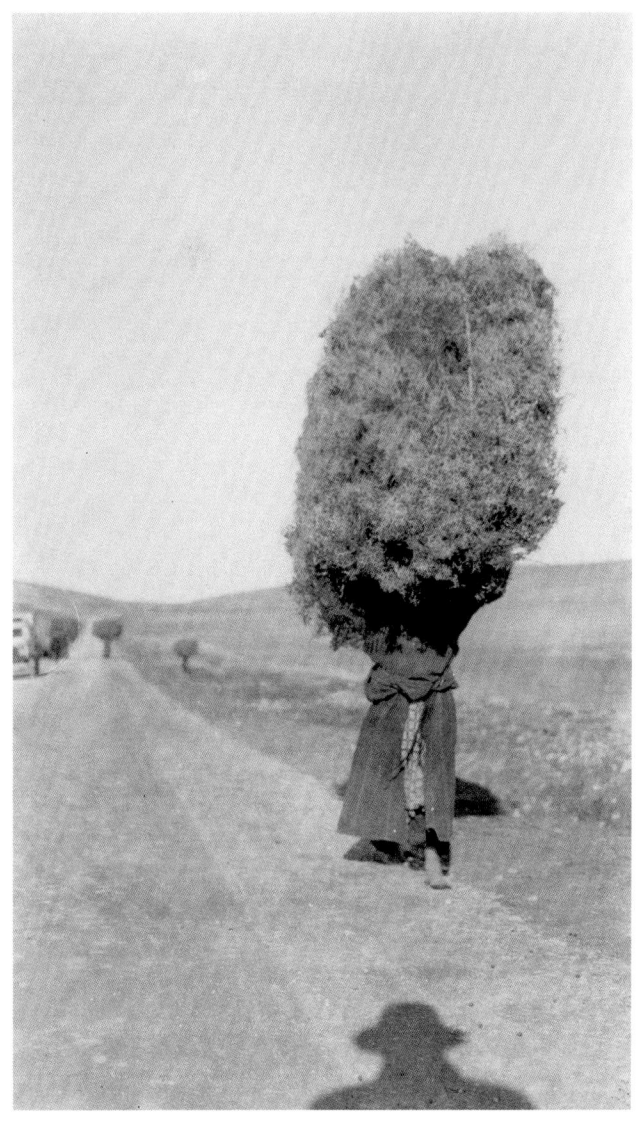

Anonymous, Farmer woman carrying load of bush, 1930s,
Syria, collection AIF/Nigol Bezjian.

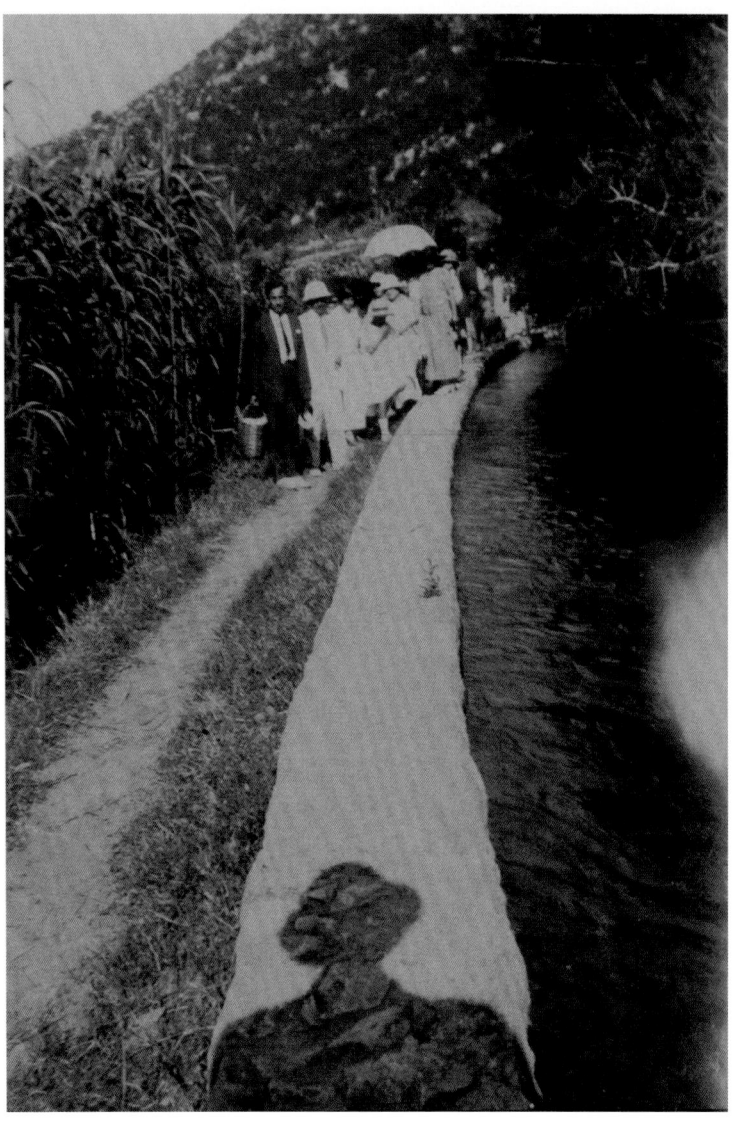

Jibrail Jabbur, Jabbur's wedding picnic, 1926,
Lebanon, collection AIF/Norma Jabbur.

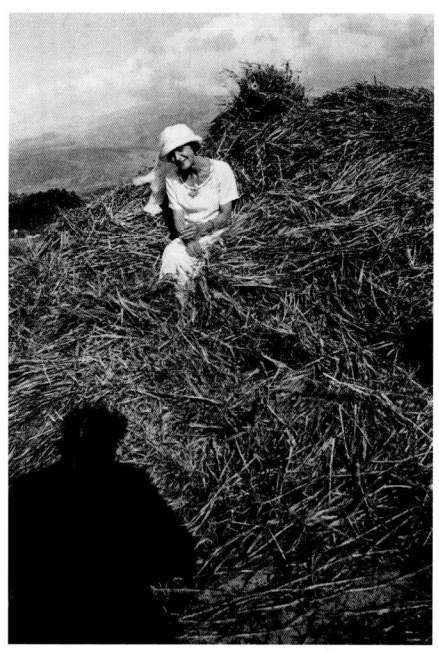

Marie el Khazen, Juliette el Alam on a haystack, 1933, Daraya, Lebanon, collection AIF/Mohsen Yammine.

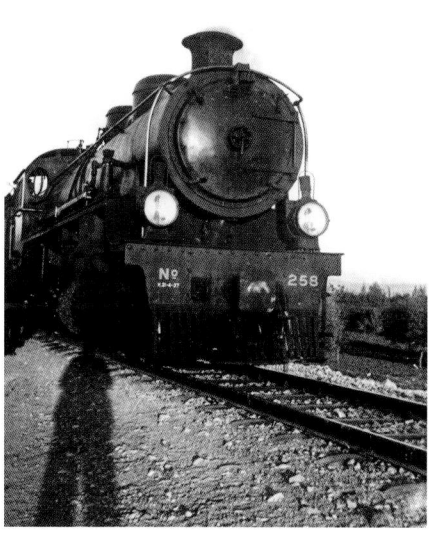

Anonymous, Locomotive, 1939, Rusaifa phosphate mines, Jordan, collection AIF/Tawfiq Amin Kawar.

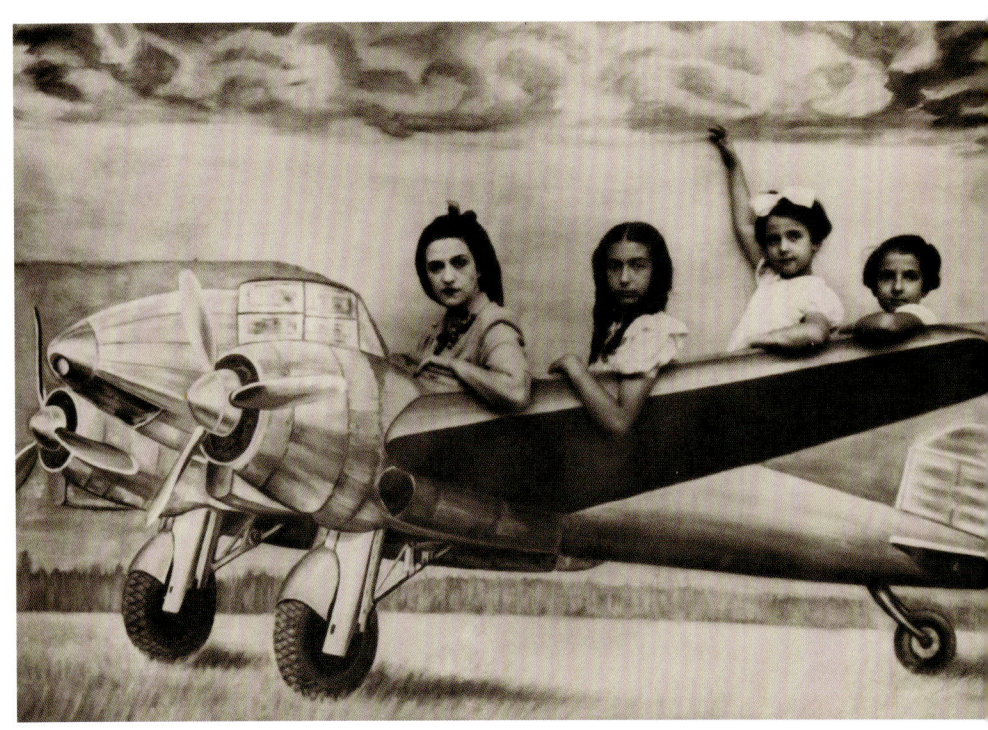

Anonymous, Posing in a painted cardboard plane (first two from left: Yvette and May Pharaon), 1930s, Lebanon, collection AIF/Alfred Pharaon.

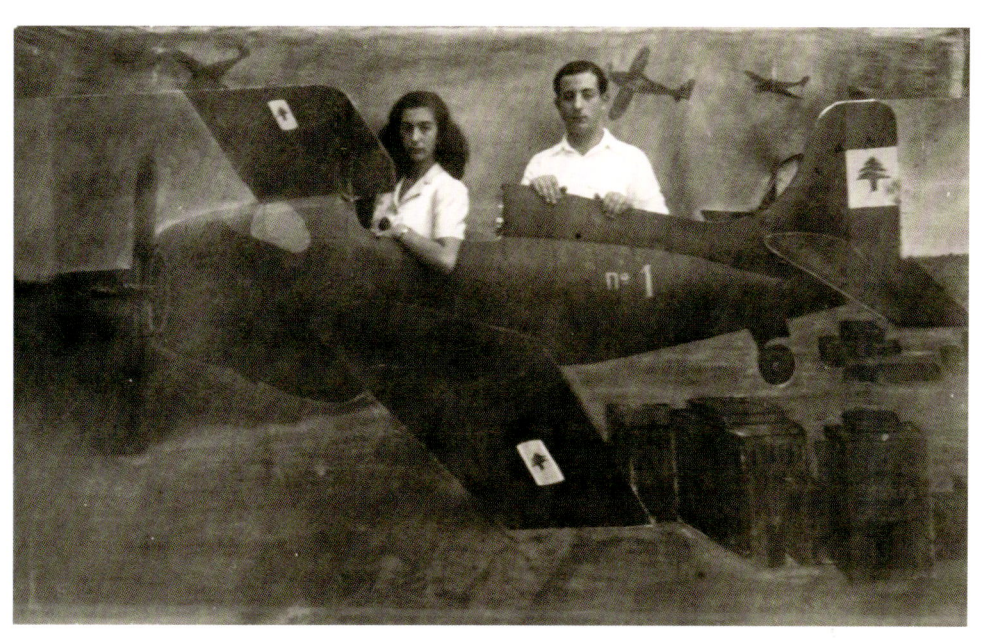

Anonymous, May and Fred Pharaon posing in a painted cardboard plane, 1945, Zahle, Lebanon, collection AIF/Alfred Pharaon.

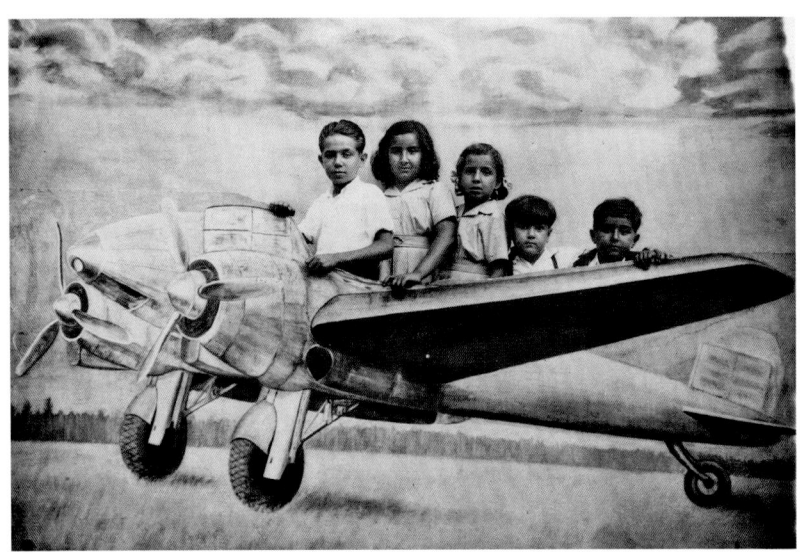

Anonymous, From left: Adnan Harati, Nabiha Loutfi, Maha Loutfi, Nohad Hashisho, Nabih Hashisho, 1947, Zahle, Lebanon, collection AIF/Nabiha Loutfi.

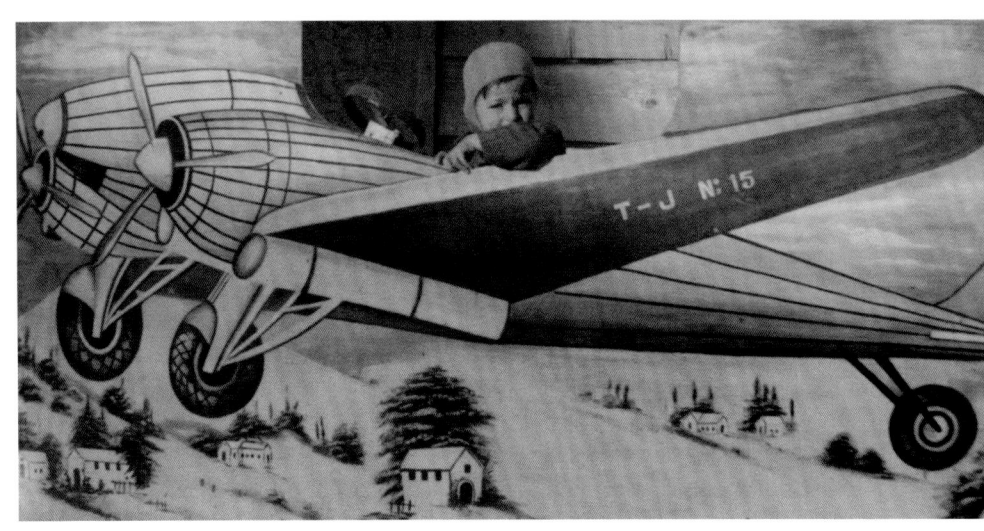

Bedros Doumanian, from the Doumanian family, 1950s, Amman, Jordan, collection AIF/Bedros Doumanian.

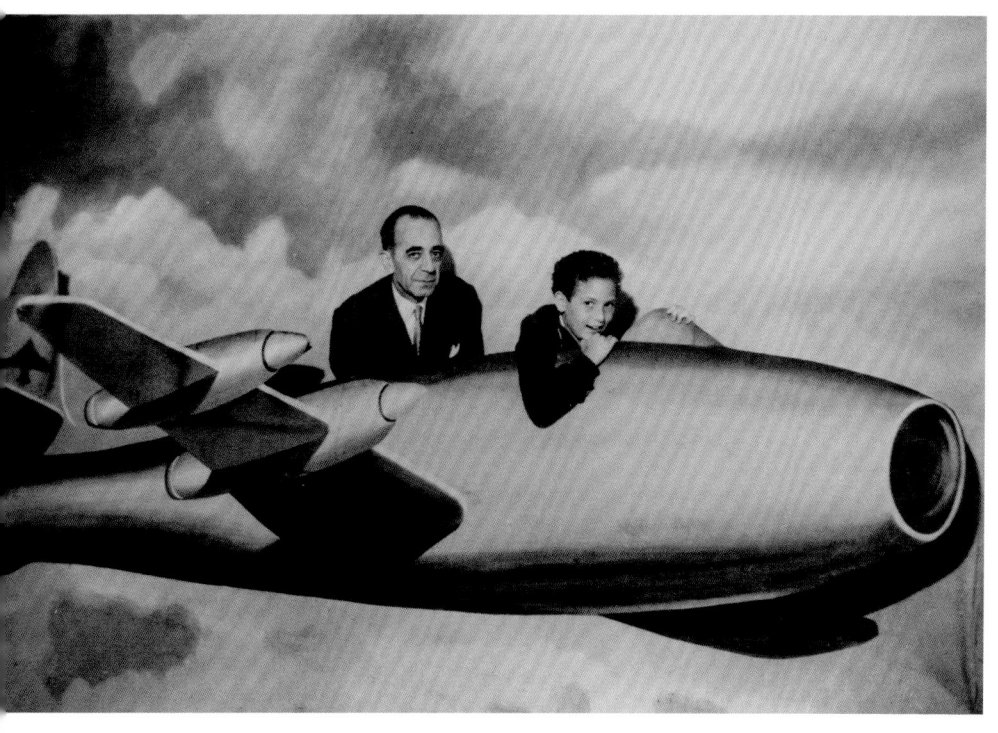

Anonymous, Antoine and Nabil Sehnaoui, 1958/1960, Zahle,
Lebanon, collection AIF/Leyla Sehnaoui Ziadé.

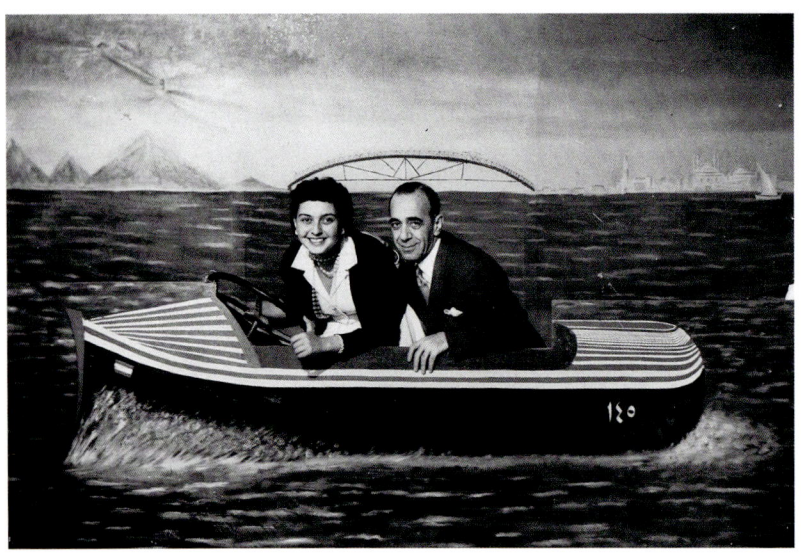

Anonymous, Antoine and Micheline Sehnaoui, 1958/1960, Zahle, Lebanon, collection AIF/Leyla Sehnaoui Ziadé.

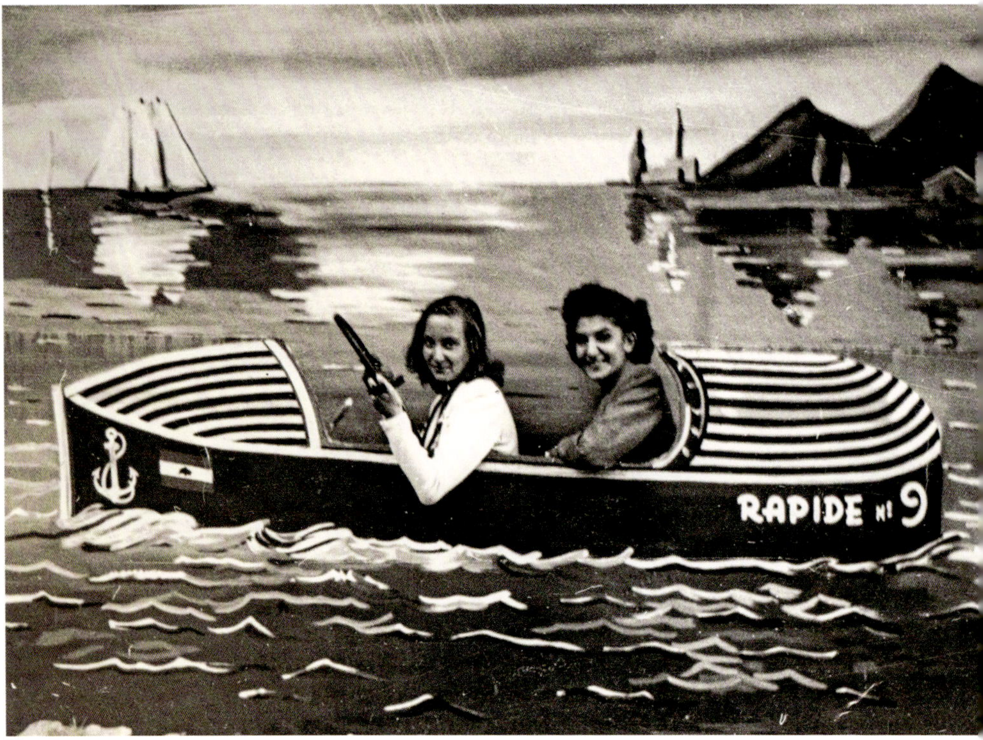

Anonymous, Leyli Saad with a friend, 1947, Zahle, Lebanon, collection AIF/Michel Saad.

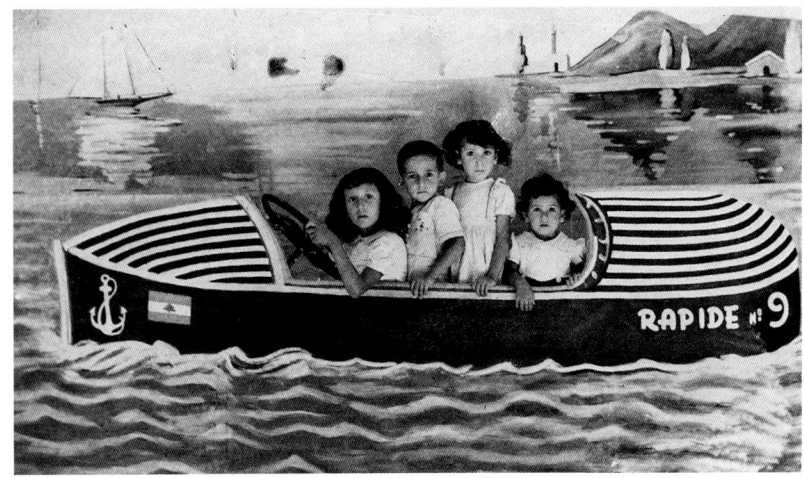

Anonymous, Seta Manoukian (behind the wheel) with other children from the family, 1952, Zahle, Lebanon, collection AIF/Seta Manoukian.

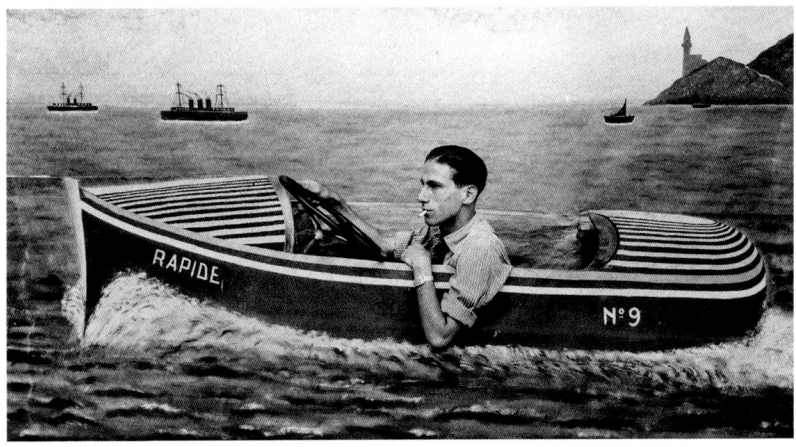

Anonymous, Henry Kassir, 1937, Zahle, Lebanon, collection AIF/Henry Kassir.

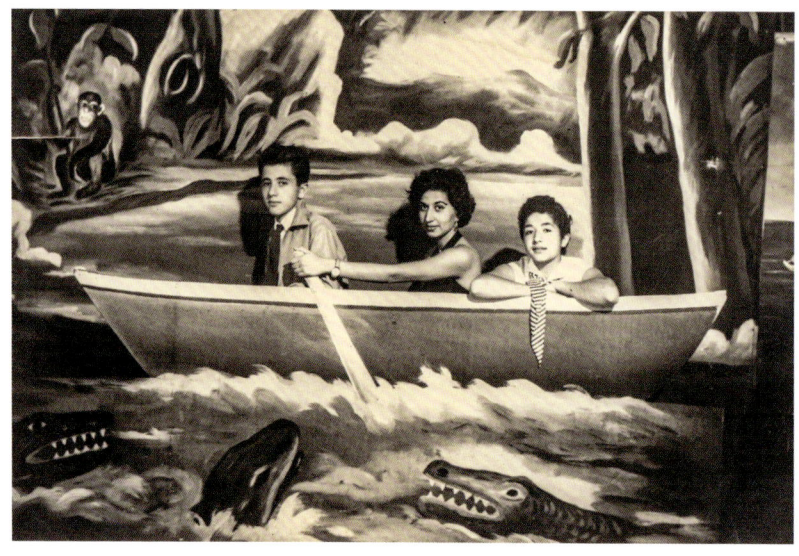

Anonymous, el Khazen family, 1954, Zahle, Lebanon,
collection AIF/Fayza Salim el Khazen.

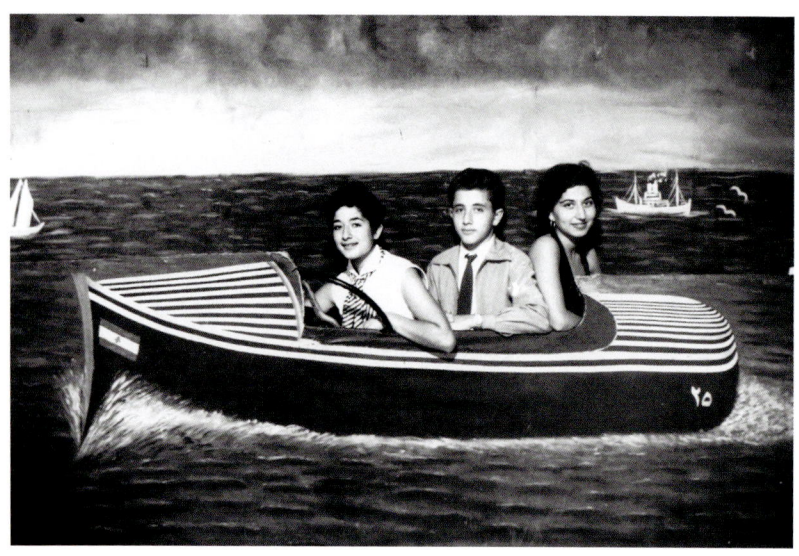

Anonymous, el Khazen family (to the right: Fayza el Khazen), 1954, Zahle, Lebanon,
collection AIF/Fayza Salim el Khazen.

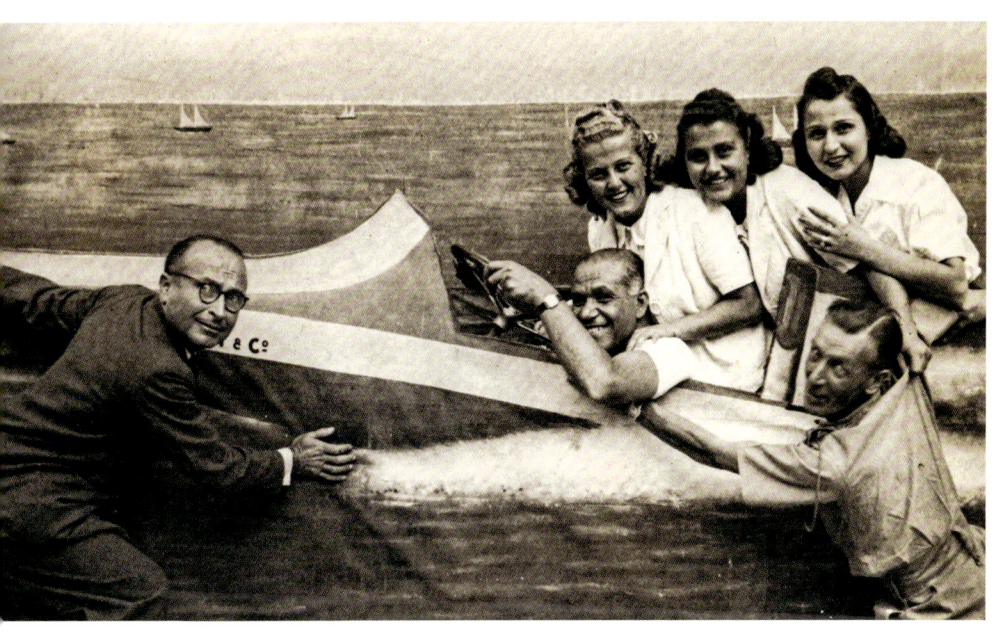

Anonymous, Marcelle Haddad Naccache (behind the driver) and friends, 1940s, Lebanon, collection AIF/Marcelle Naccache.

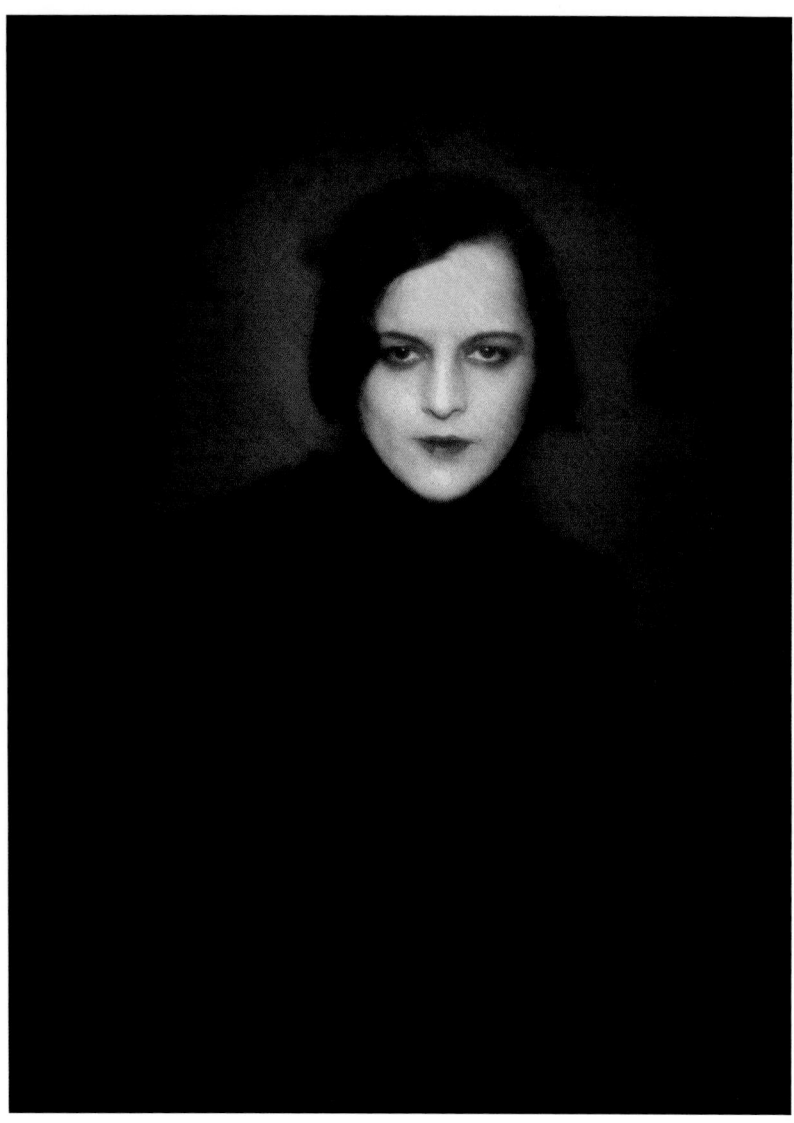

Alban, Studio Portrait, 1945, Cairo, Egypt,
collection AIF/Georges Mikaelian Family.

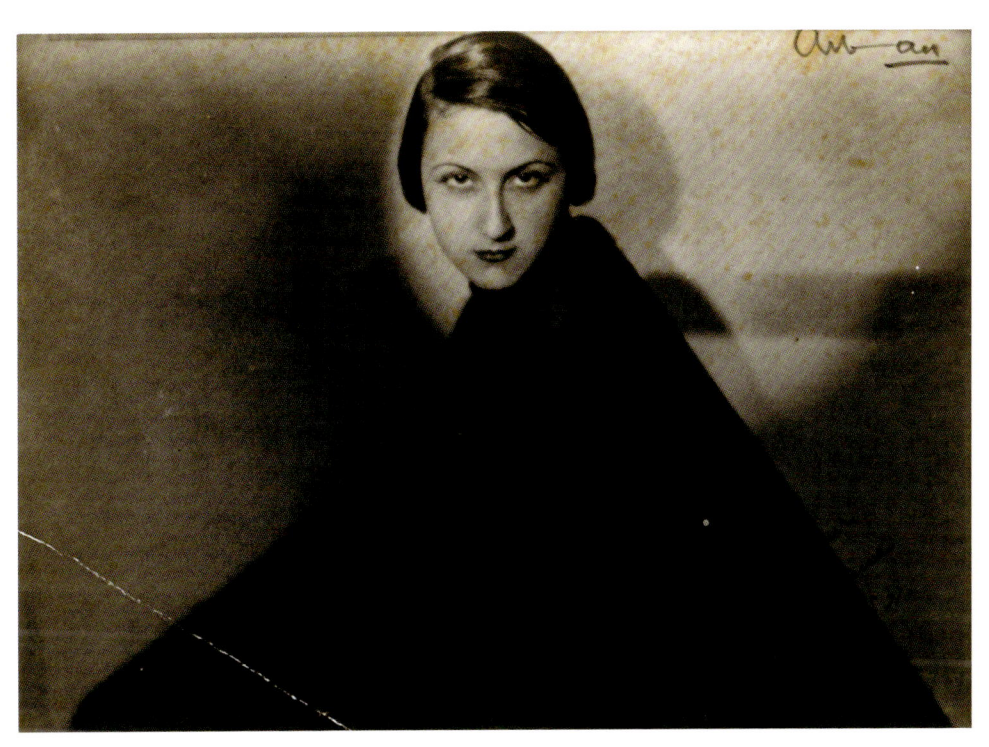

Alban, a woman from the Sursock family, 1933, collection AIF/Habib Lteif.

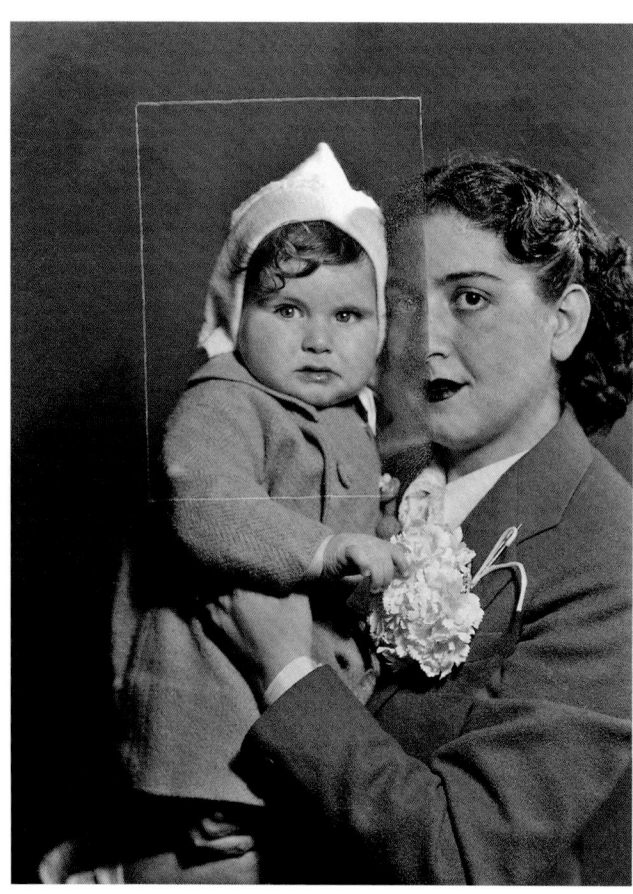

Alban, Studio Portrait, 1945–1950, Cairo, Egypt,
collection AIF/Georges Mikaelian Family.

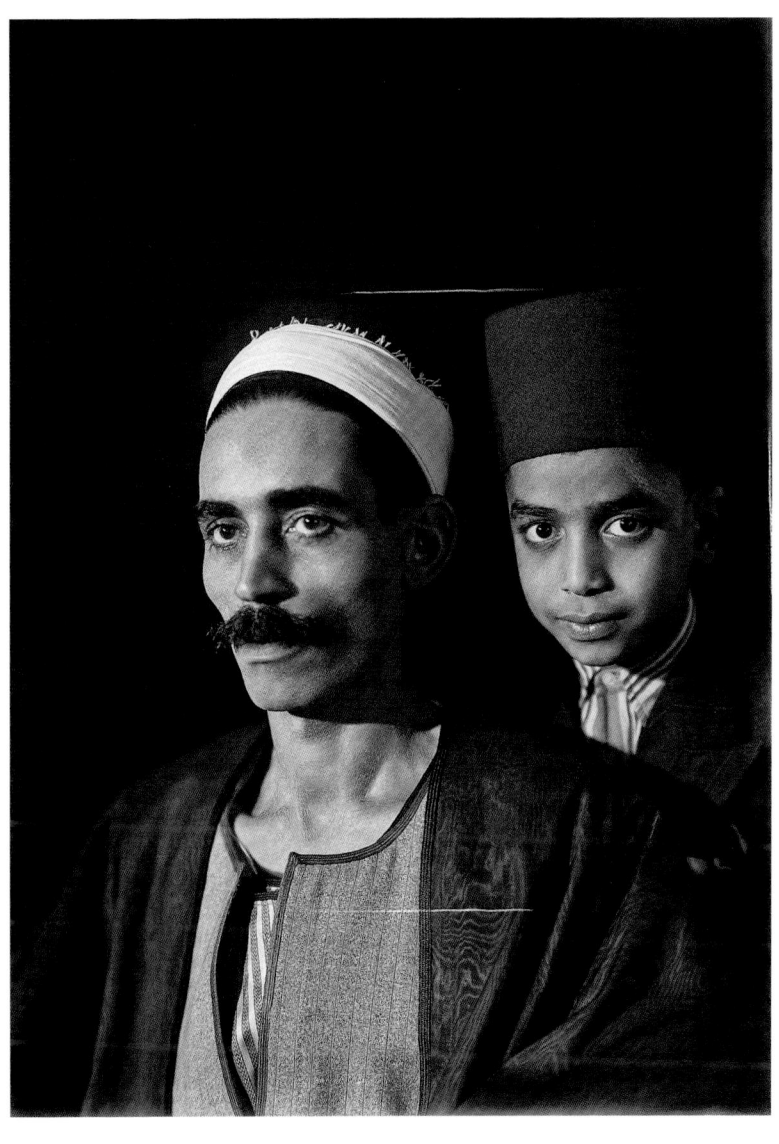

Alban, Studio Portrait, 1945–1950, Cairo, Egypt,
collection AIF/Georges Mikaelian Family.

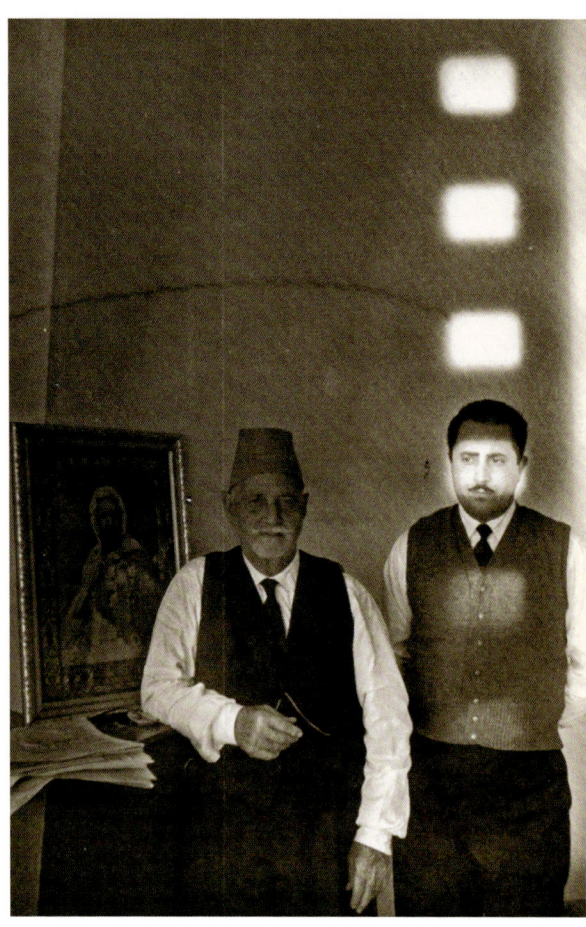

Anonymous, Rachid el Khattabi and son, Morocco, collection AIF/Rachid el Khattabi.

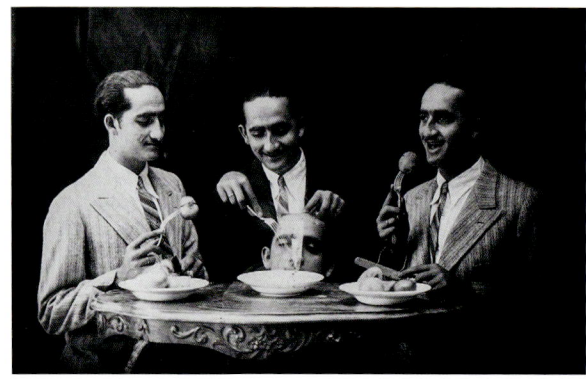

Anonymous, Mr. Skaff in four different positions, 1922, Bethlehem, Palestine, collection AIF/Yacoub Katimi.

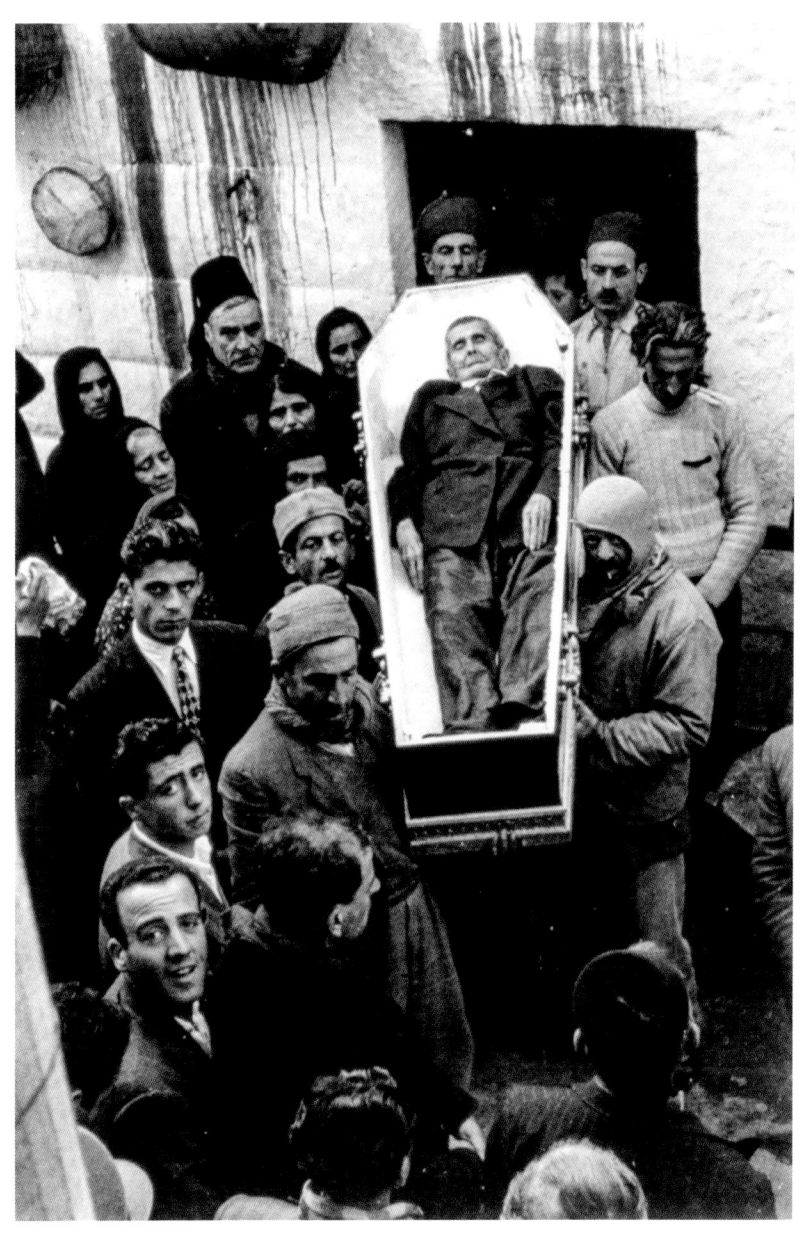

Yertchan Dankikian, Funeral, 1950s, Zgharta, Lebanon,
collection AIF/Mohsen Yammine.

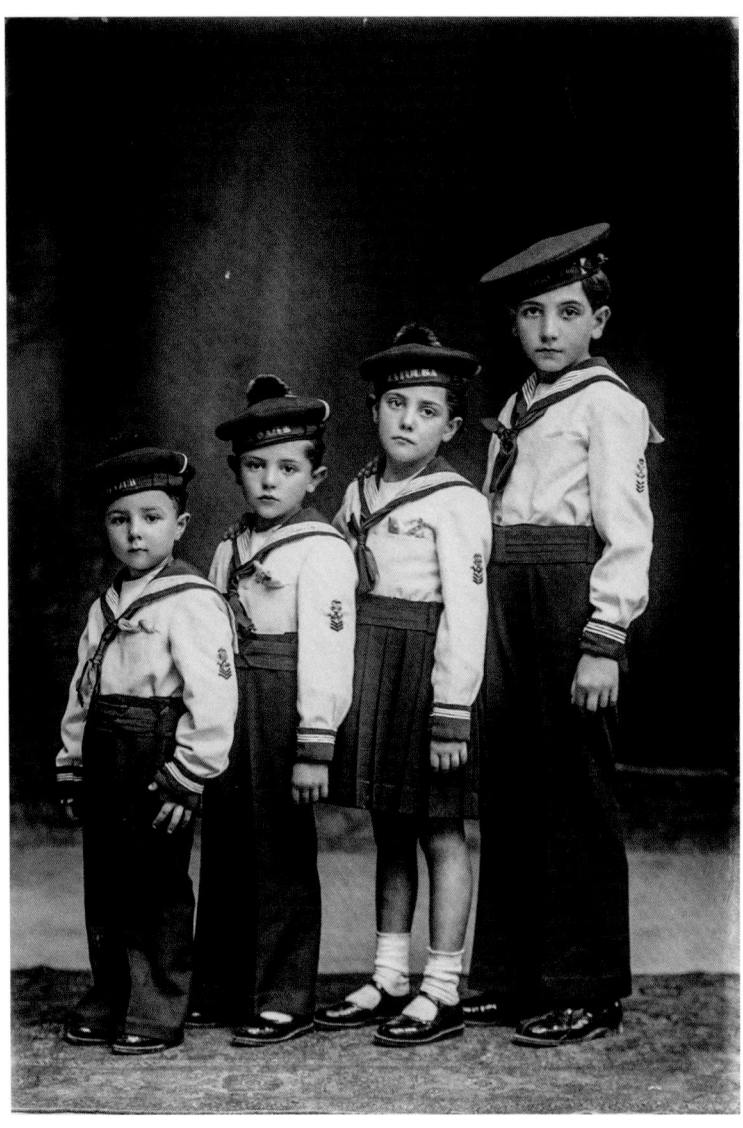

Antranik Anouchian, Studio Portrait, 1940, Tripoli, Lebanon,
collection AIF/Joseph el Hajj.

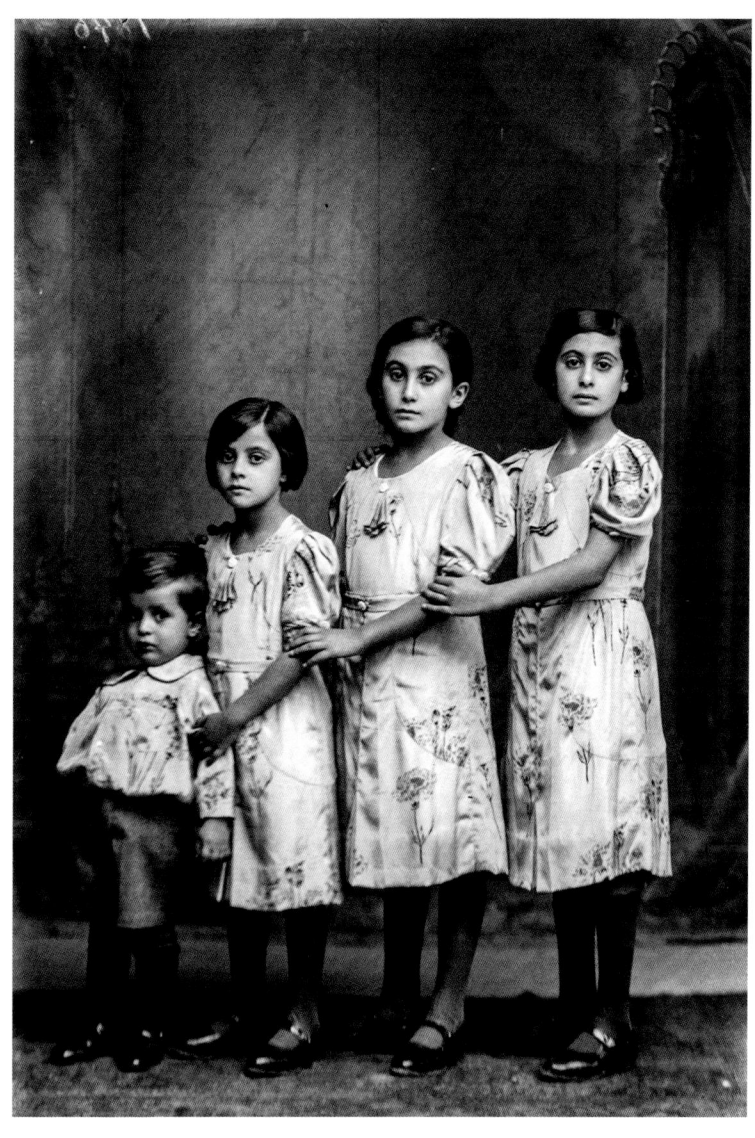

Antranik Anouchian, Studio Portrait, 1940, Tripoli, Lebanon, collection AIF/Mohsen Yammine.

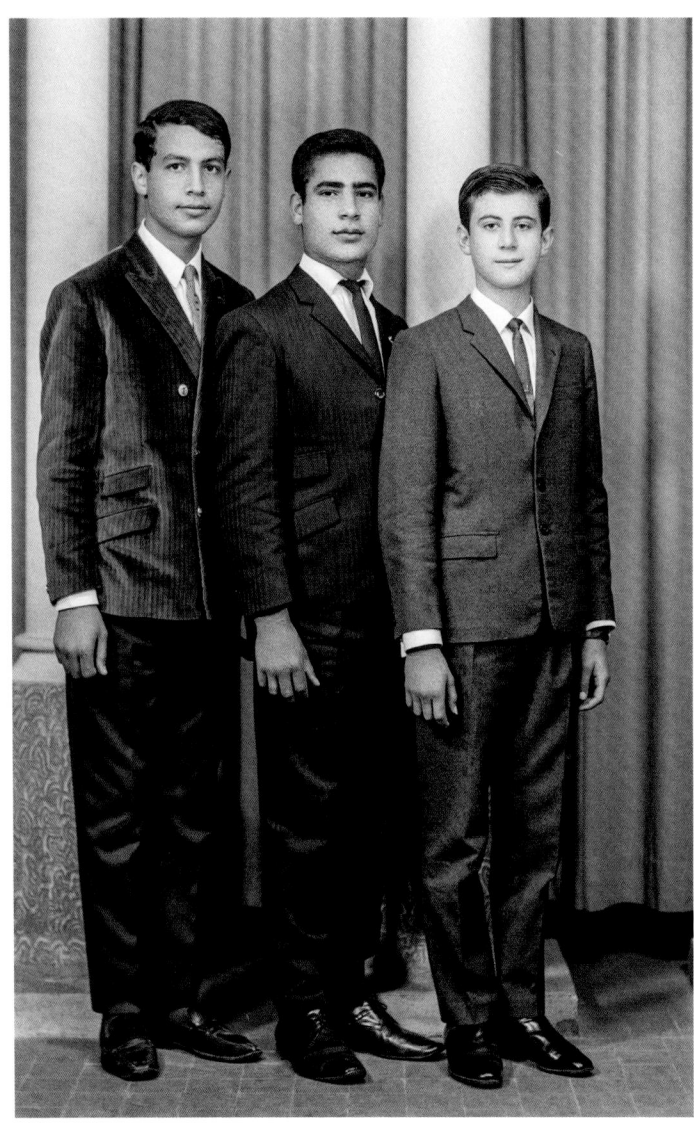

Antranik Anouchian, Studio Portrait, 1960, Tripoli, Lebanon,
collection AIF/Mohsen Yammine.

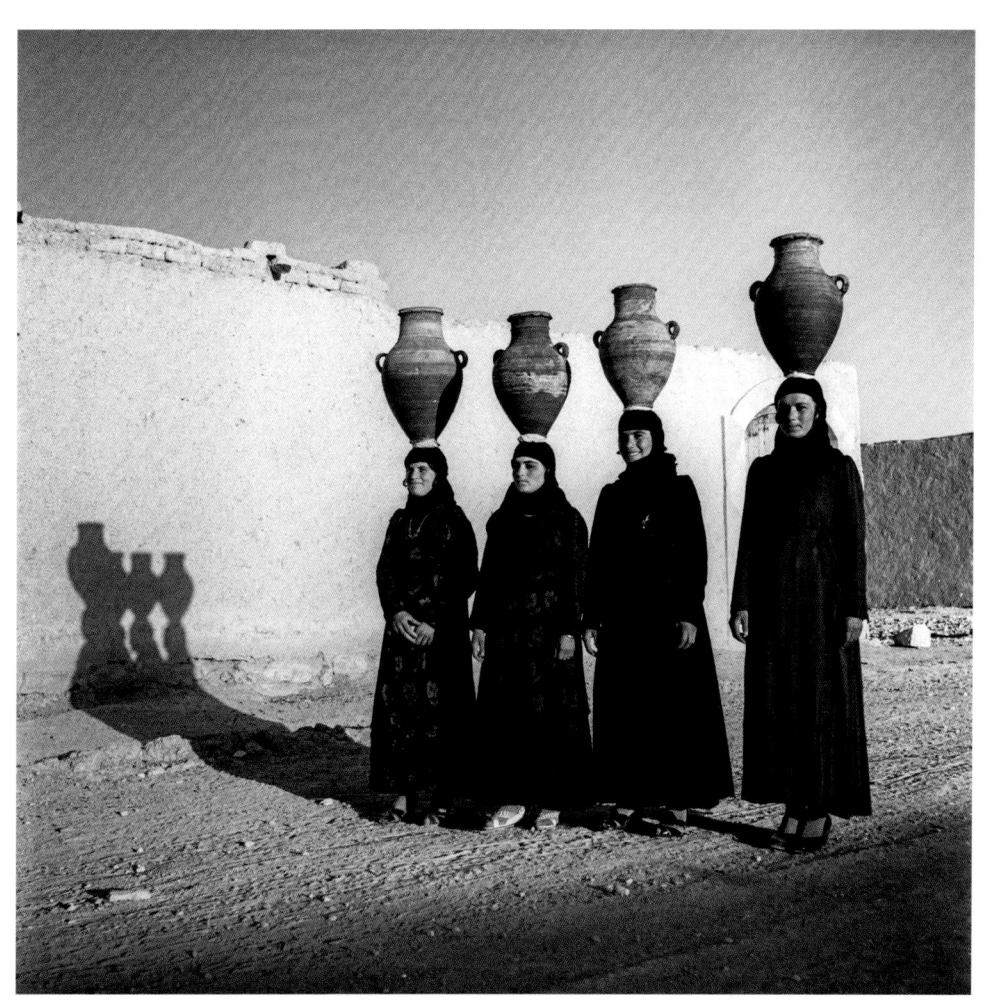

Jibrail Jabbur, Village women carrying earthenware jars, 1950, Al-Qaryatayn, Syria, collection AIF/Norma Jabbur.

Appendix to *(Vampires): An Uneasy Essay on the Undead in Film*: "Death-Size Body"

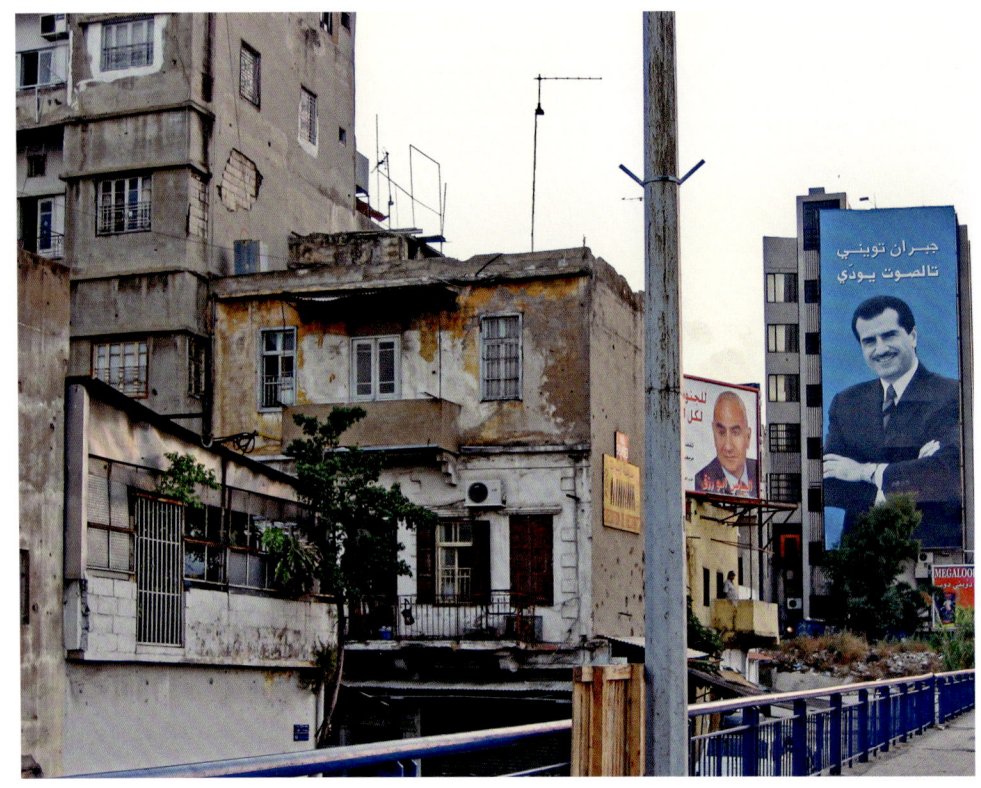

Two large political billboards, one featuring Gibran Tueni, the second Elias Abu Rizk during Lebanon's 2005 parliamentary elections.

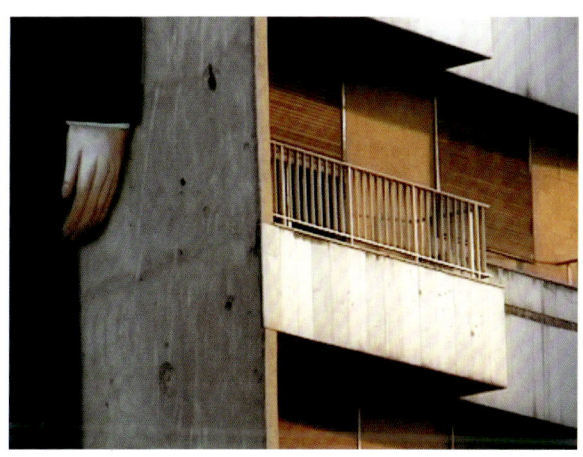

Detail of a political billboard of a candidate (Nabih Berri) during Lebanon's 2000 parliamentary elections.

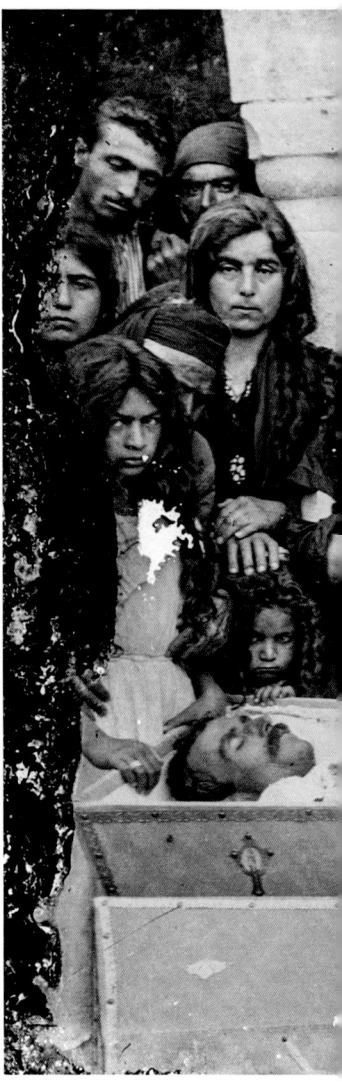

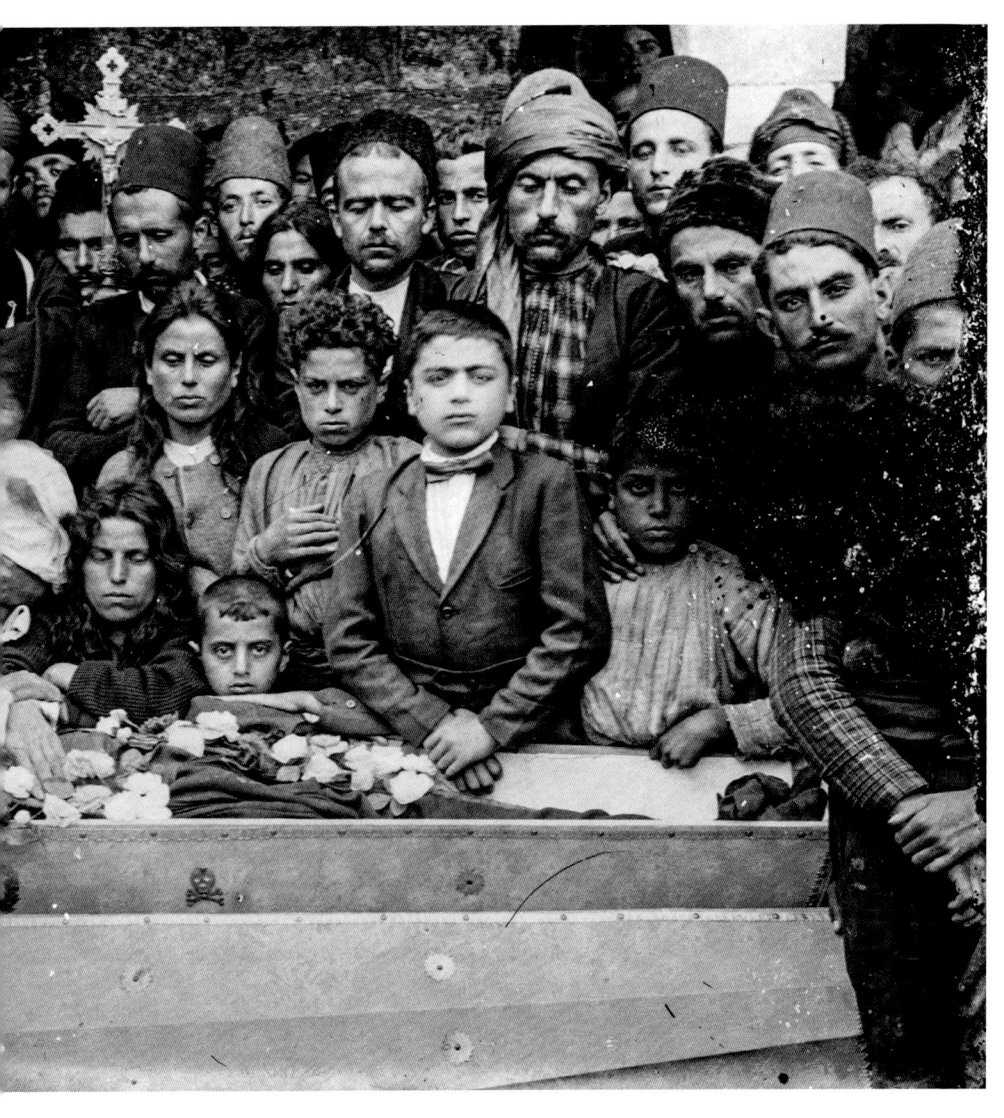

Camille el Kareh, Funeral, 1920s, Lebanon, collection AIF/Mohsen Yammine.

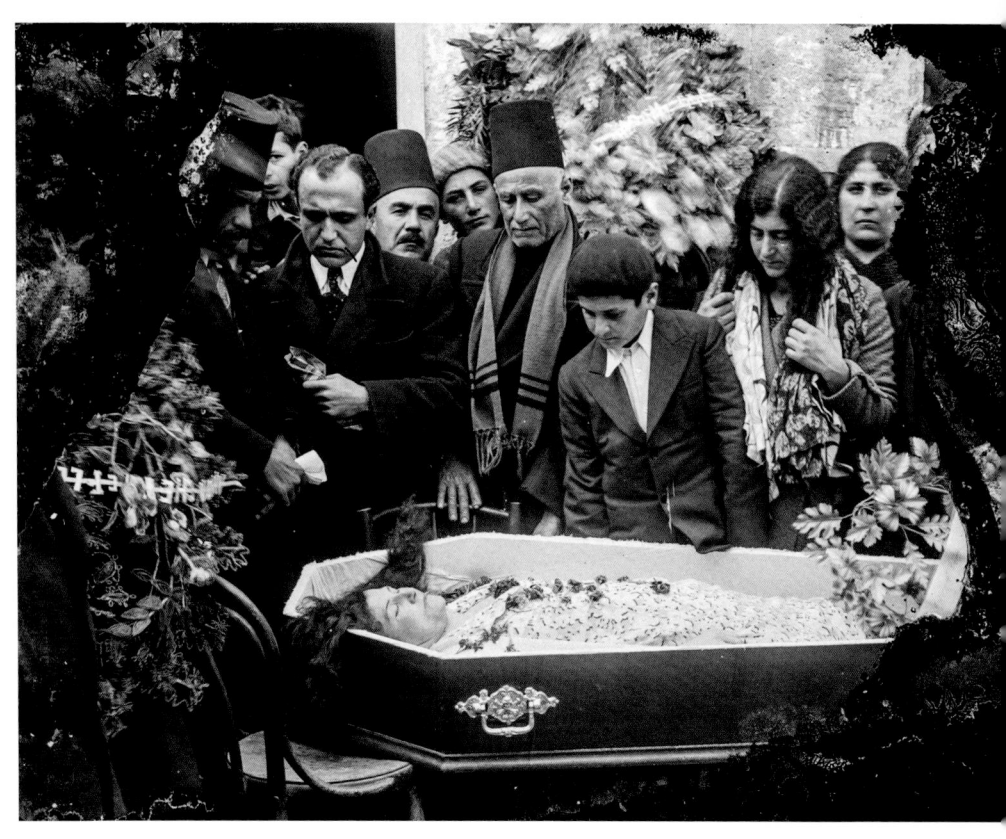

Camille el Kareh, Funeral, 1920s, Zgharta, Lebanon,
collection AIF/Mohsen Yammine.

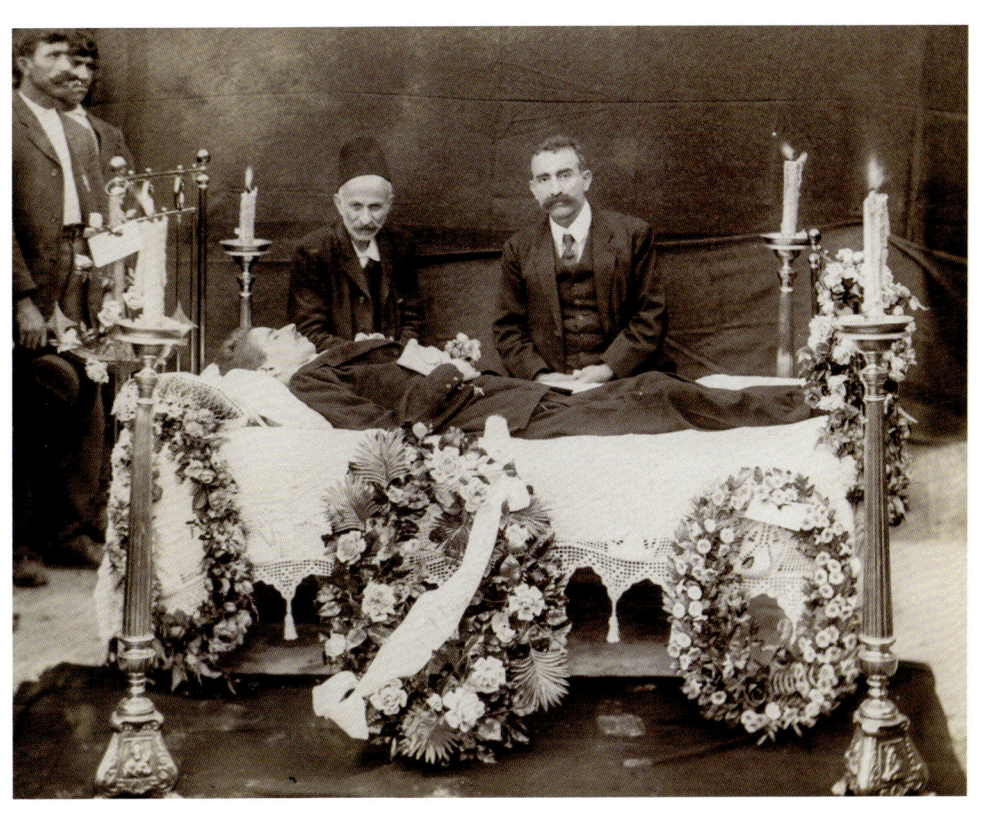

Camille el Kareh, Funeral of Ganem Hermanos, 1920s, Zgharta, Lebanon, collection AIF/Mohsen Yammine.

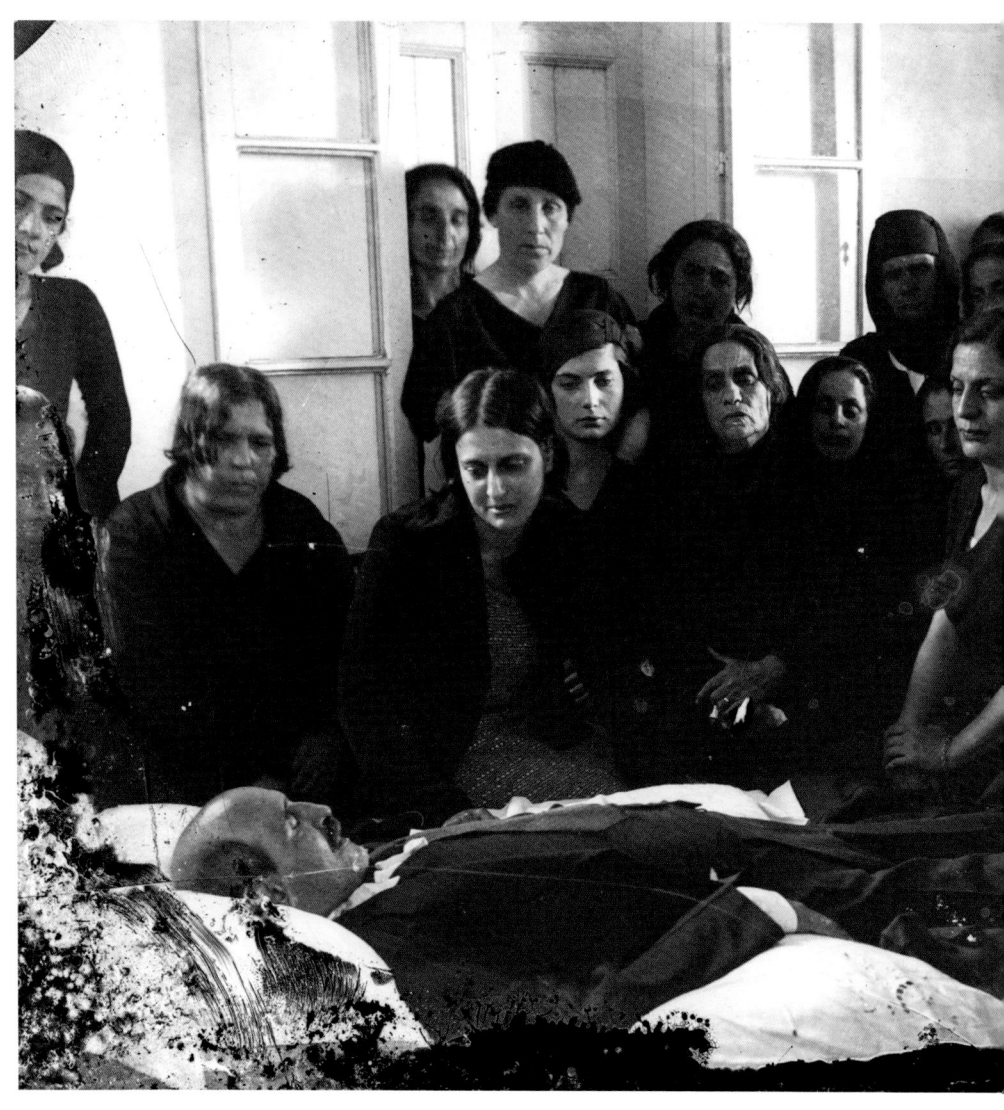

Camille el Kareh, Funeral of a member of the Kasshana family, 1920s, Zgharta, Lebanon, collection AIF/Mohsen Yammine.

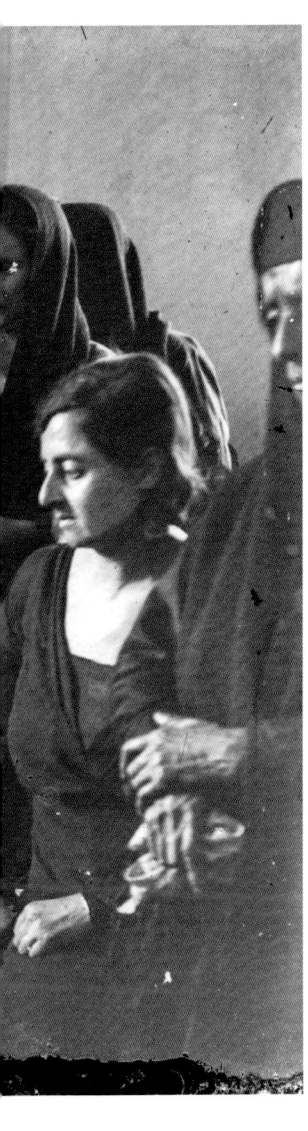

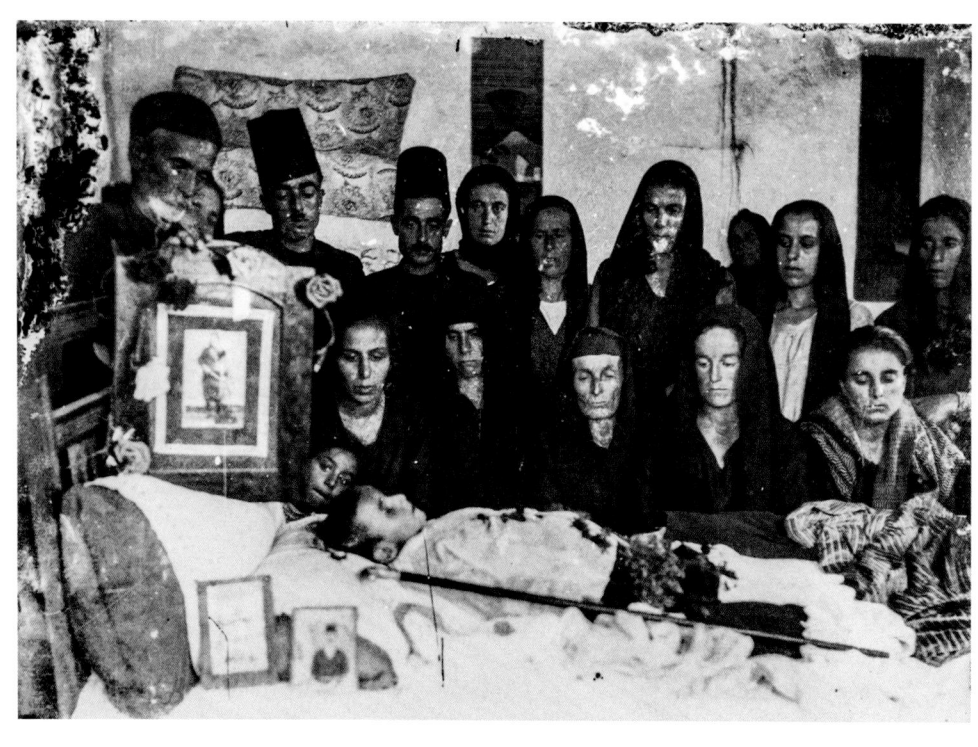

Camille el Kareh, Funeral of a child of El Kareh family, 1930,
Zgharta, Lebanon, collection AIF/Mohsen Yammine.

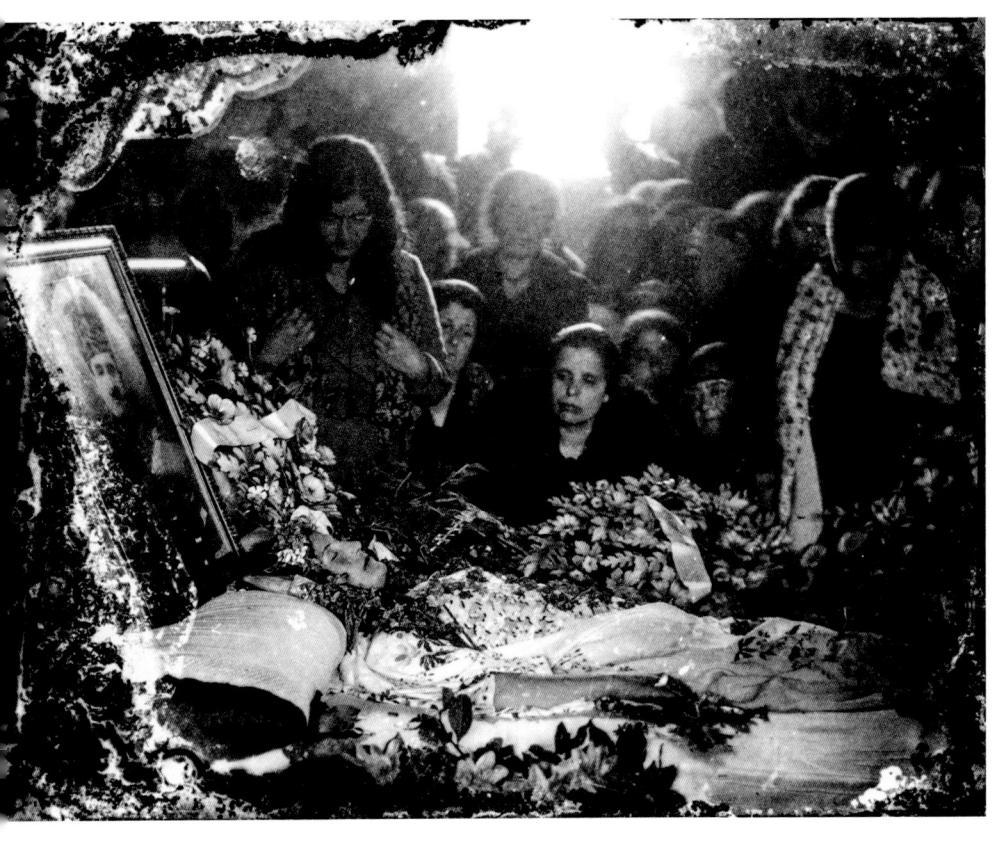

Camille el Kareh, Funeral, 1929, Zgharta, Lebanon,
collection AIF/Mohsen Yammine.

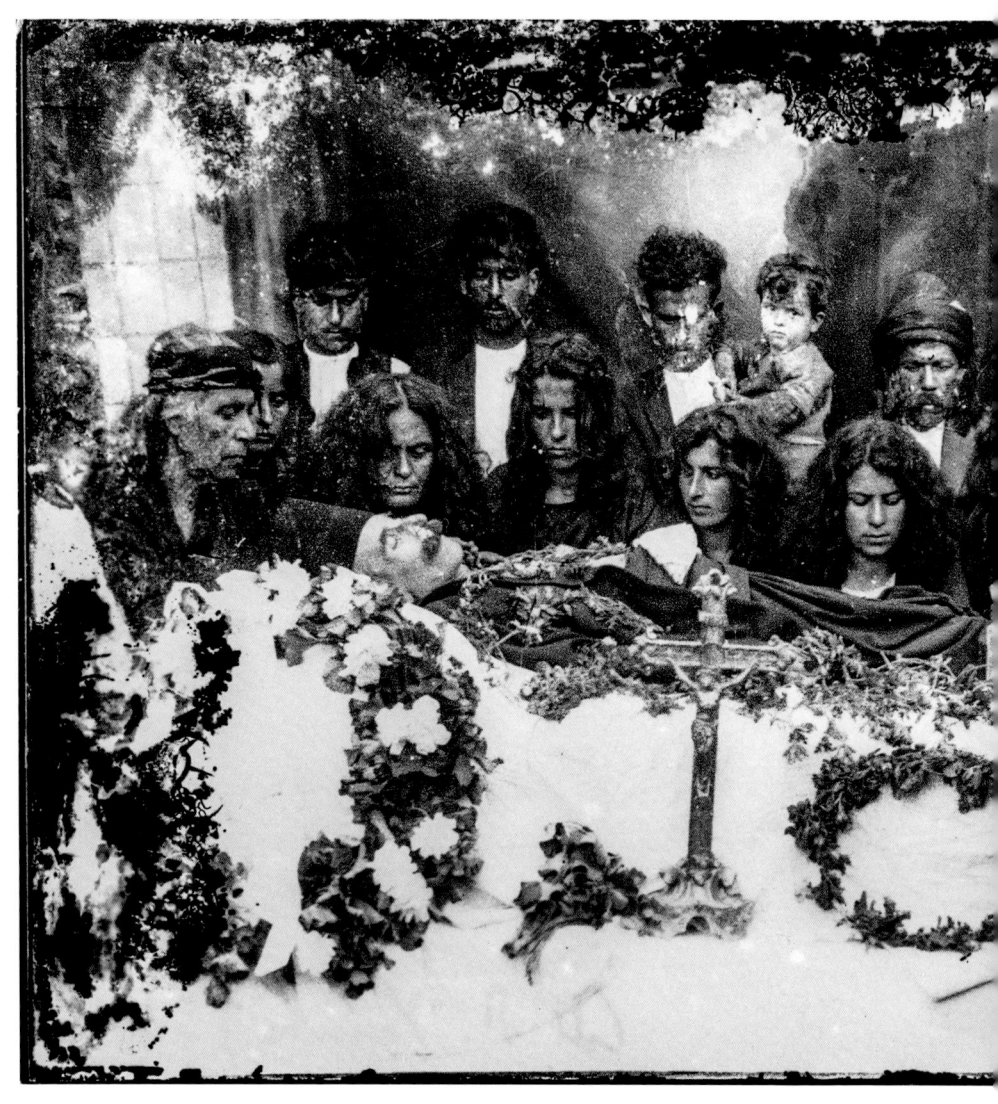

Camille el Kareh, Funeral, 1927, Zgharta, Lebanon,
collection AIF/Mohsen Yammine.

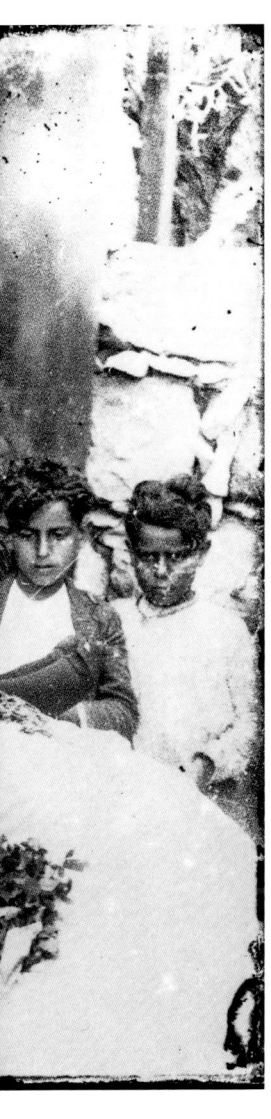

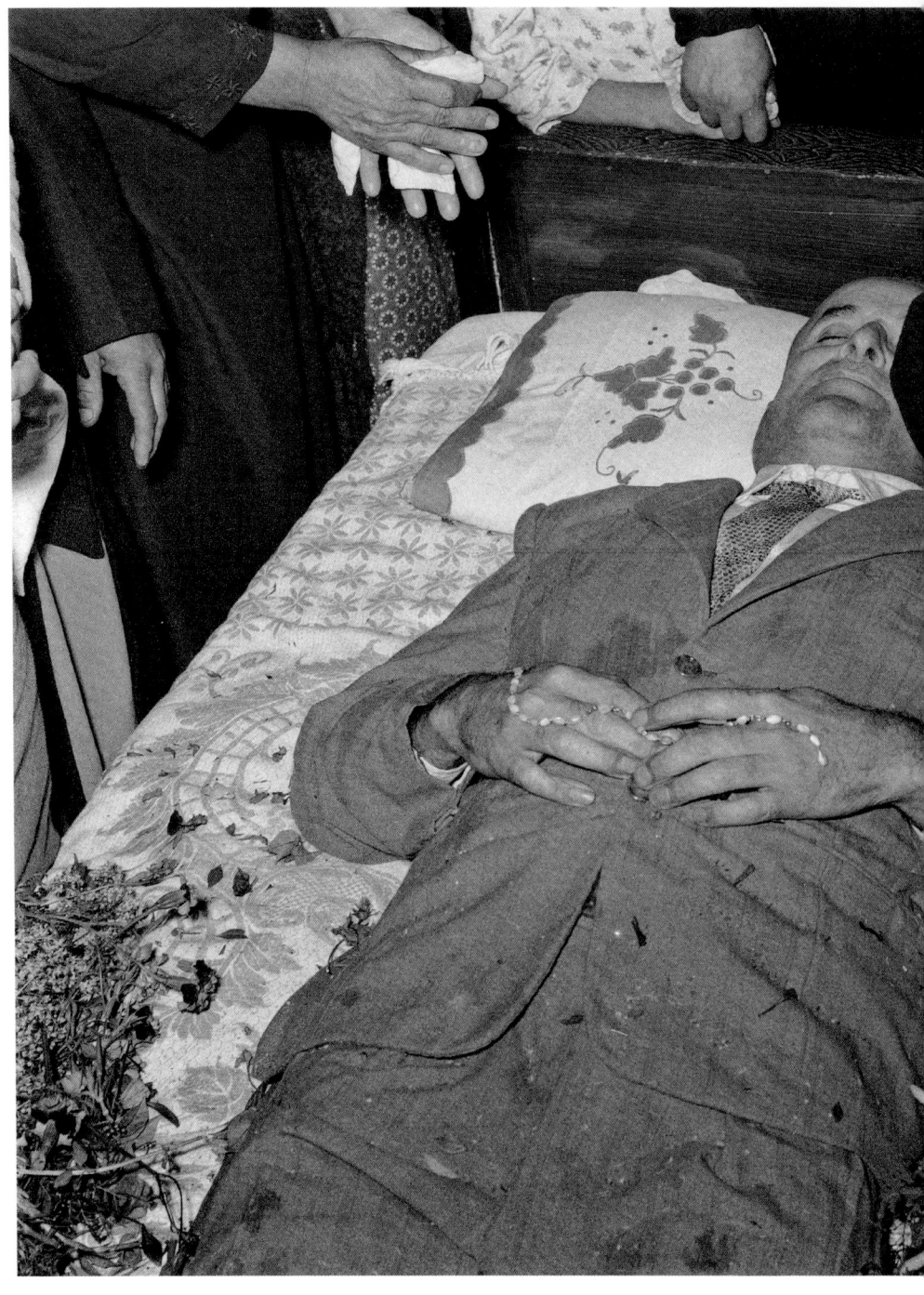

Chafic El-Soussi, Funeral of Father Naoum, 1954, Sidon, Lebanon,
collection AIF/Chafic El-Soussi.

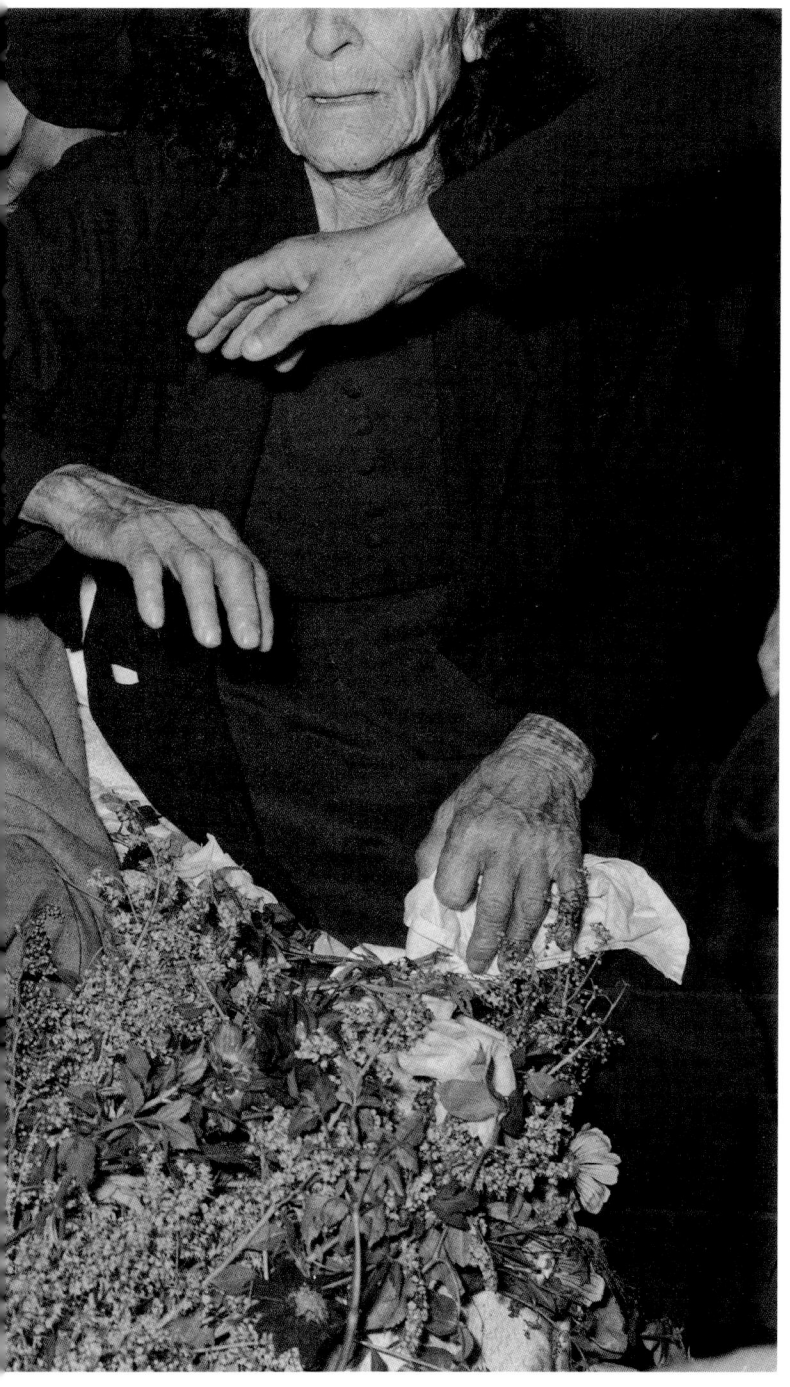

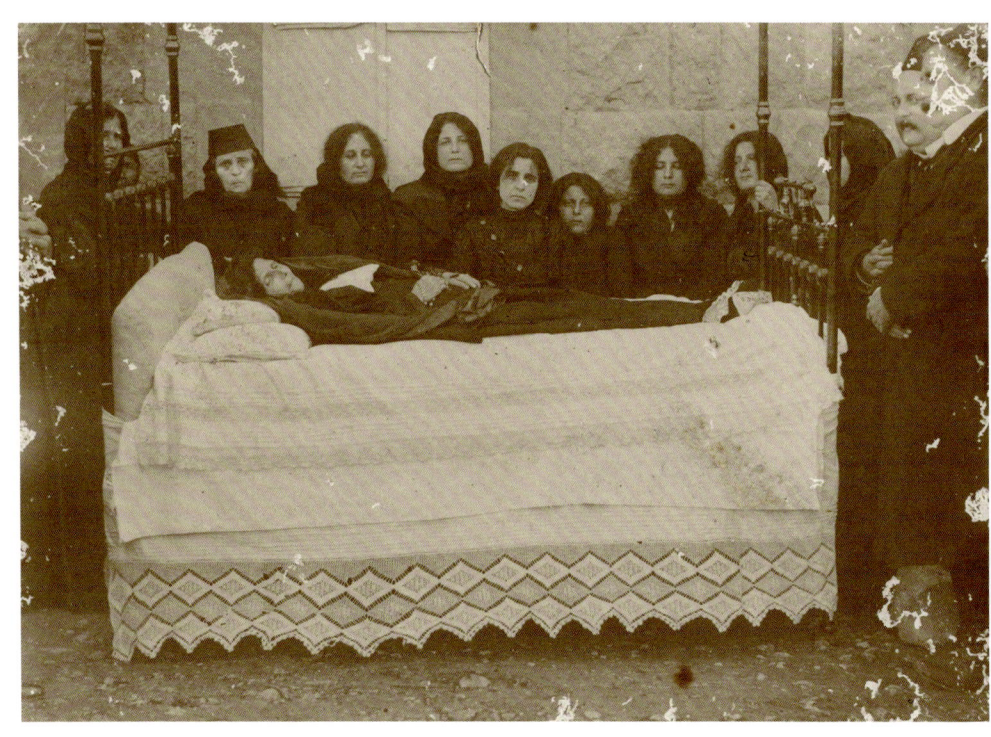

Camille el Kareh, Funeral of Hawwa el Dahir, widow of Sleiman el Dahir, 1900, Lebanon, collection AIF/Mohsen Yammine.

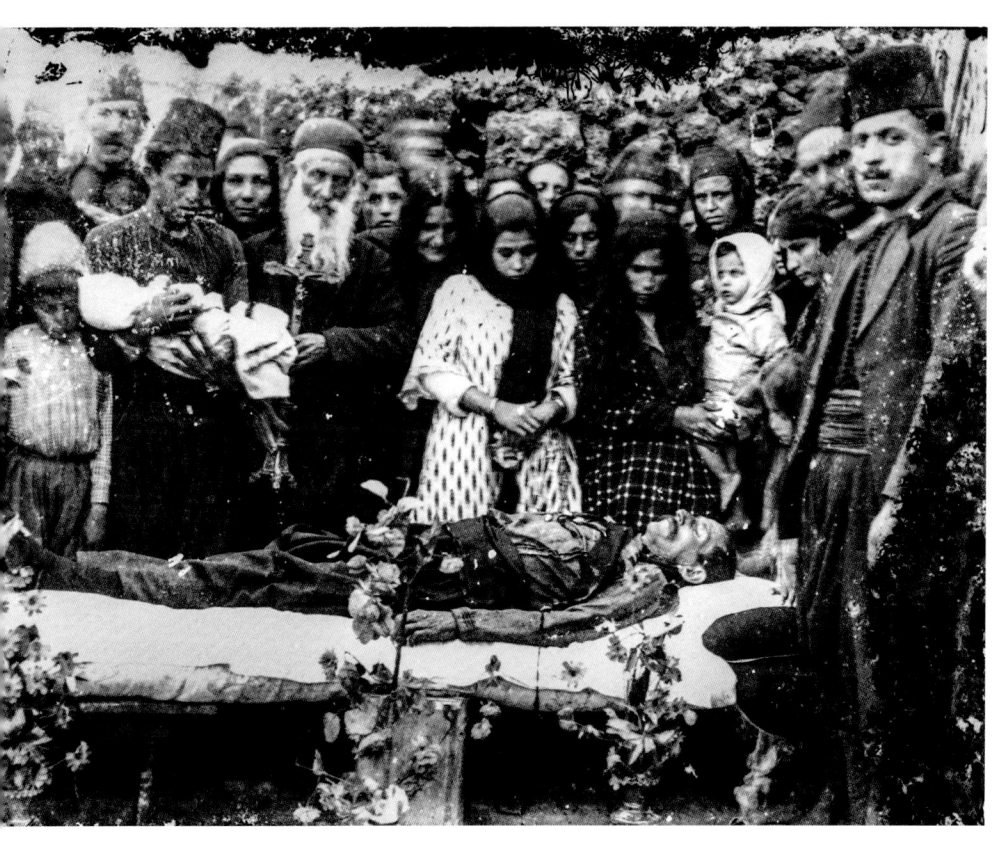

Camille el Kareh, Funeral, 1920, Zgharta, Lebanon,
collection AIF/Mohsen Yammine.

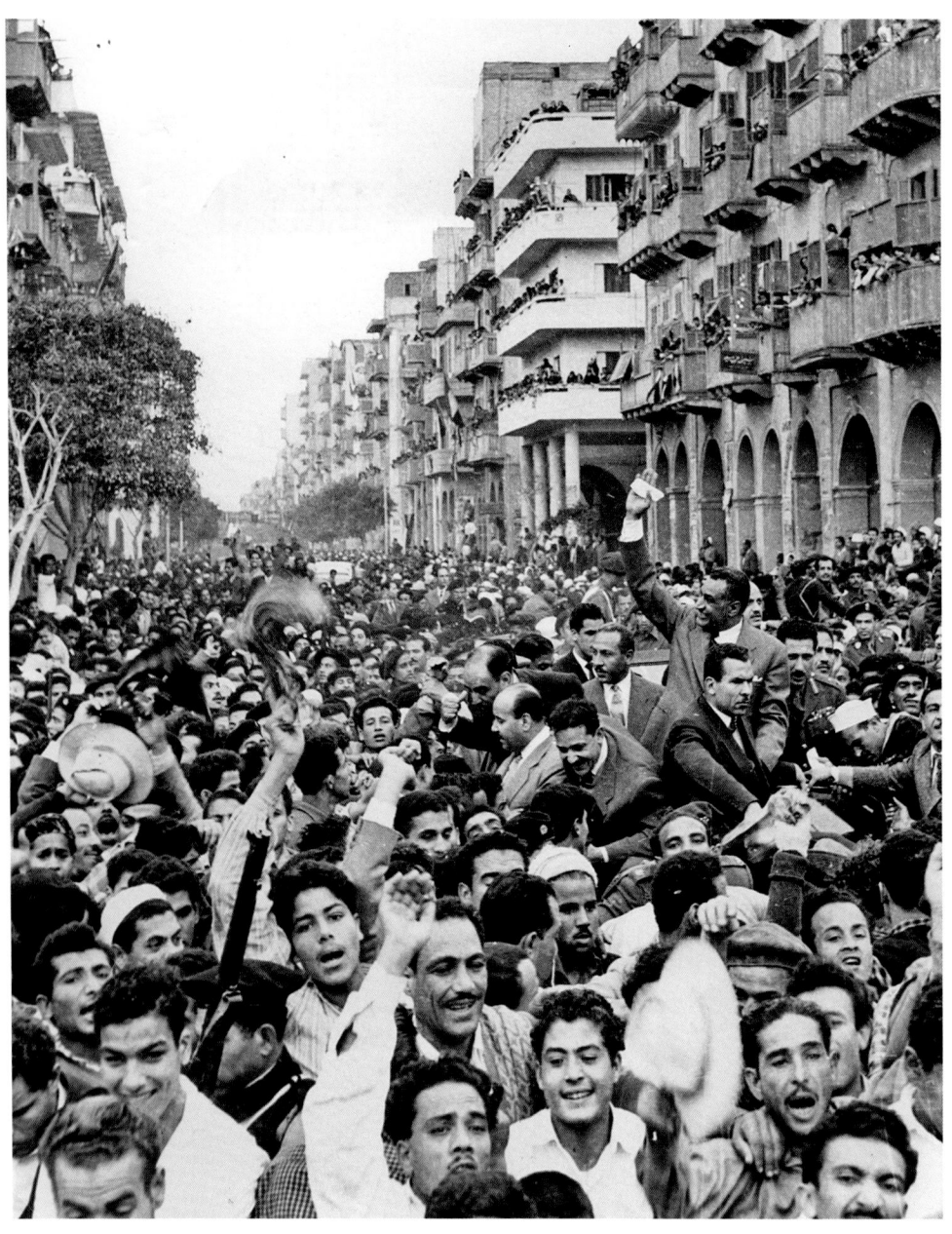

Anonymous, Gamal Abdel Nasser, 1950s, Egypt, collection AIF/Amr Sherif.

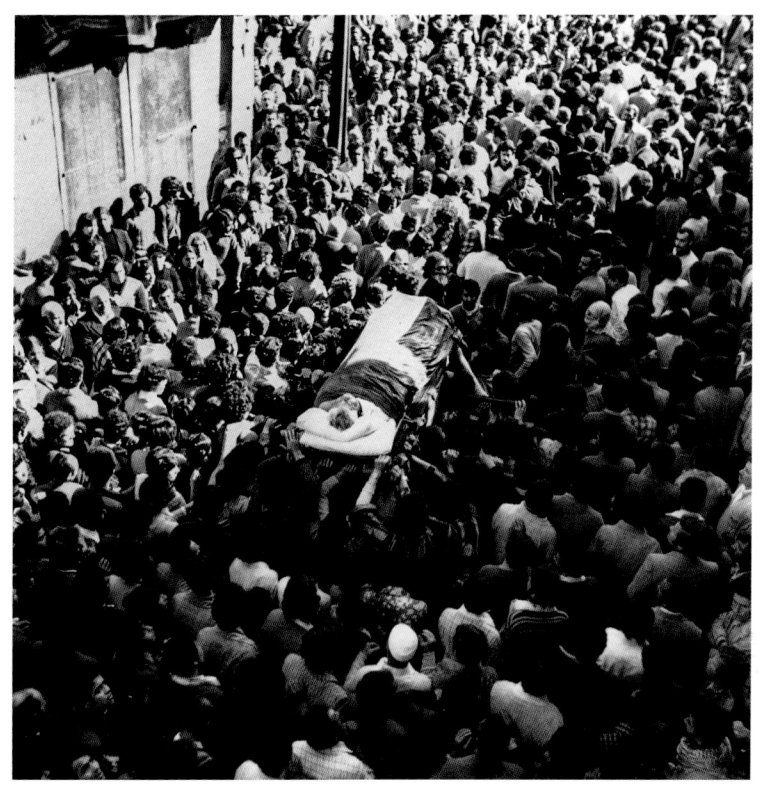

Hashem Madani, Lebanon, collection AIF/Hashem Madani.

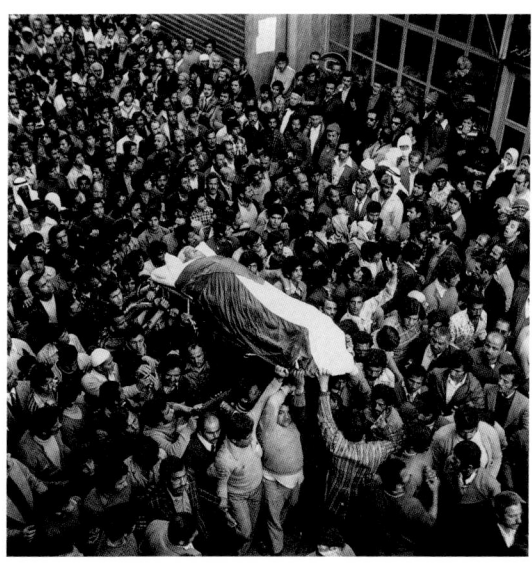

Hashem Madani, Lebanon, collection AIF/Hashem Madani.

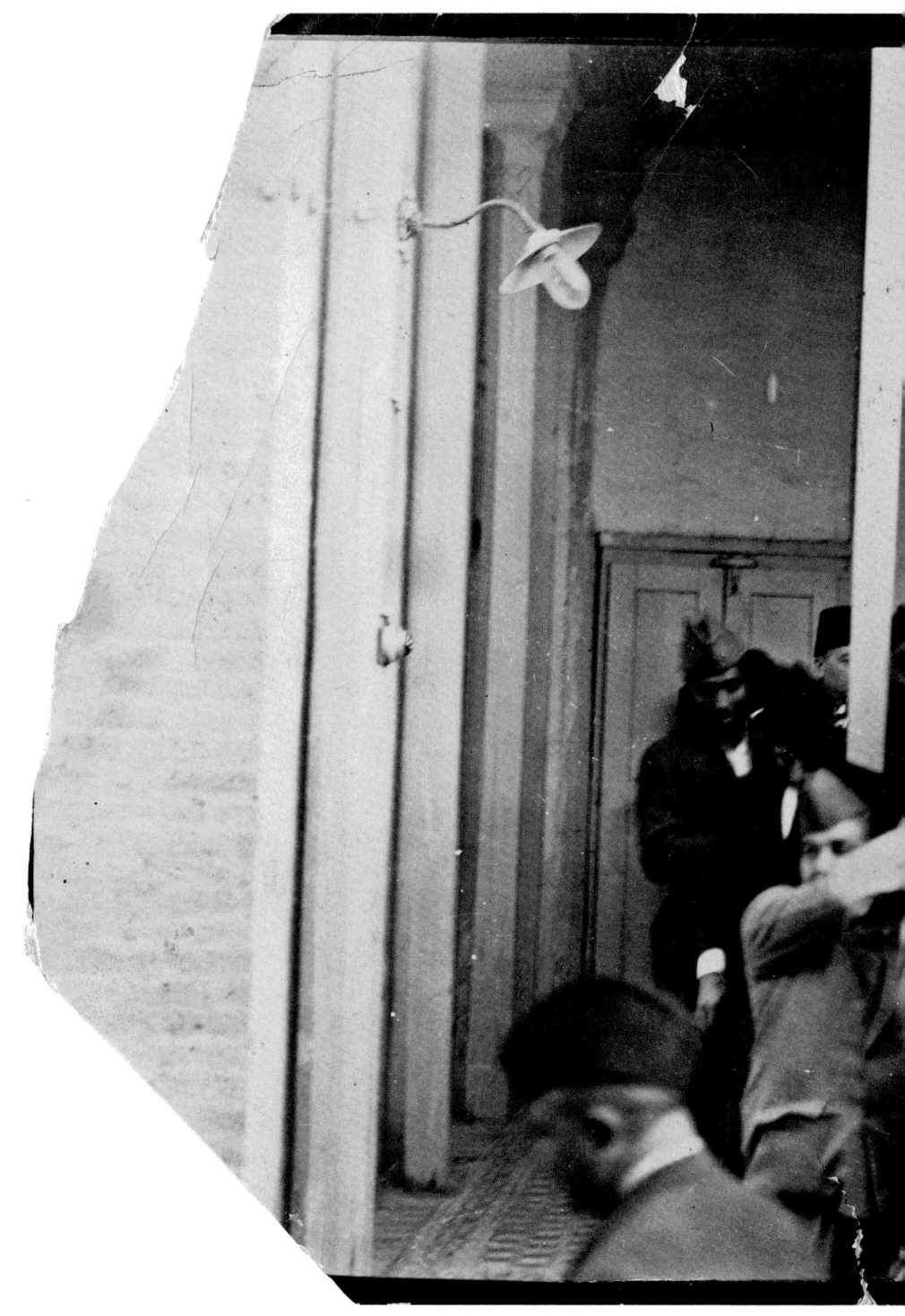

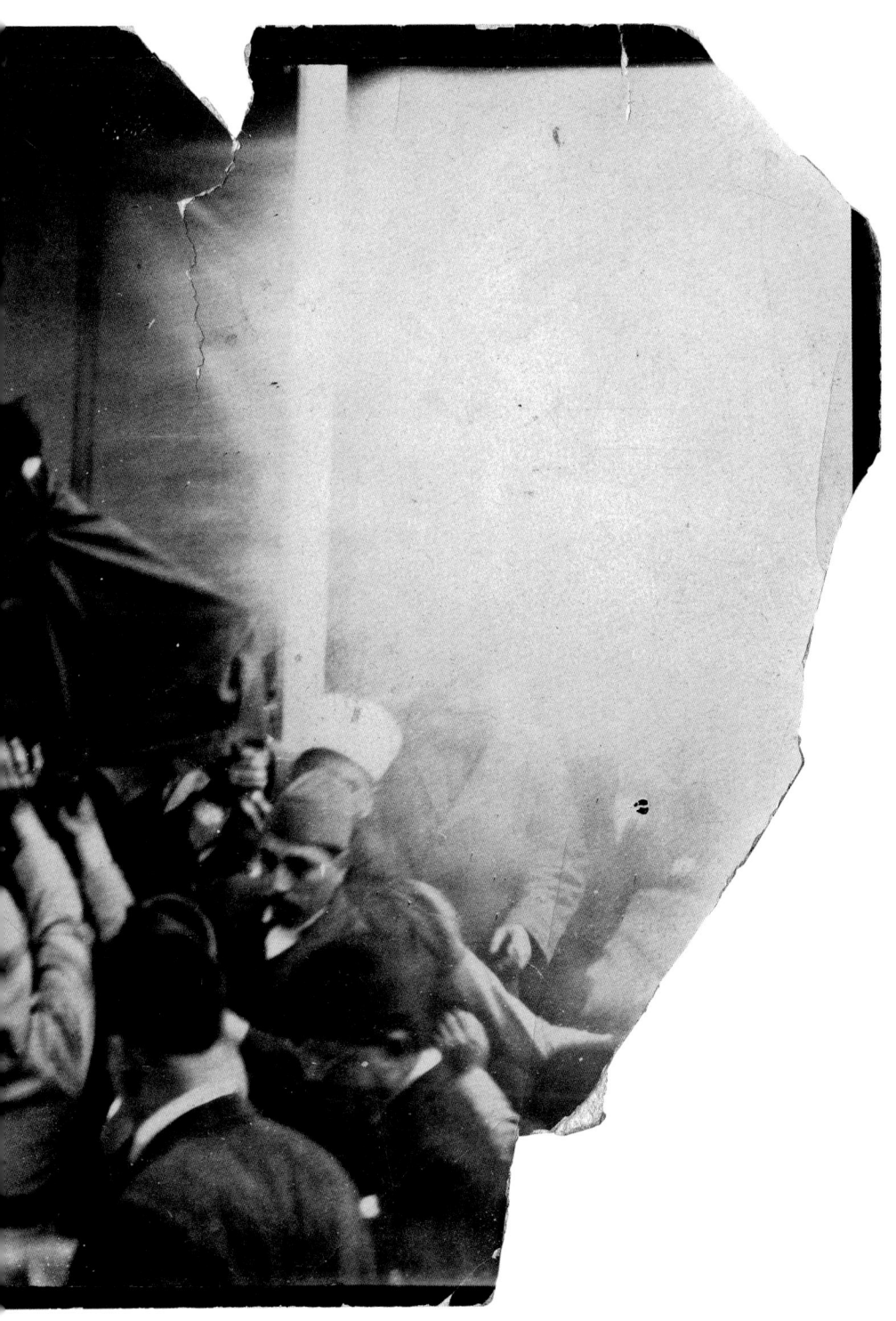

Anonymous, Funeral of Abdel-Mohsen Al-Saadoun, a former Iraqi prime minister, 1929, Baghdad, Iraq, collection AIF/Muhammed Abdel Ghaffur Abdel Saheb.

Appendix to *(Vampires): An Uneasy Essay on the Undead in Film*: "Thinking across Lapses of Consciousness, If Not of Being"

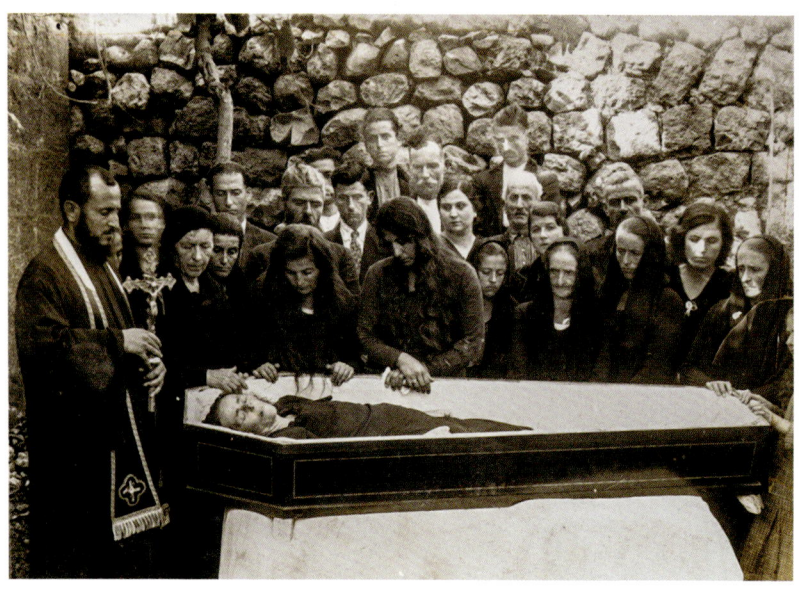

Camille el Kareh, Funeral, 1920s, Zgharta, Lebanon, collection AIF/Mohsen Yammine.

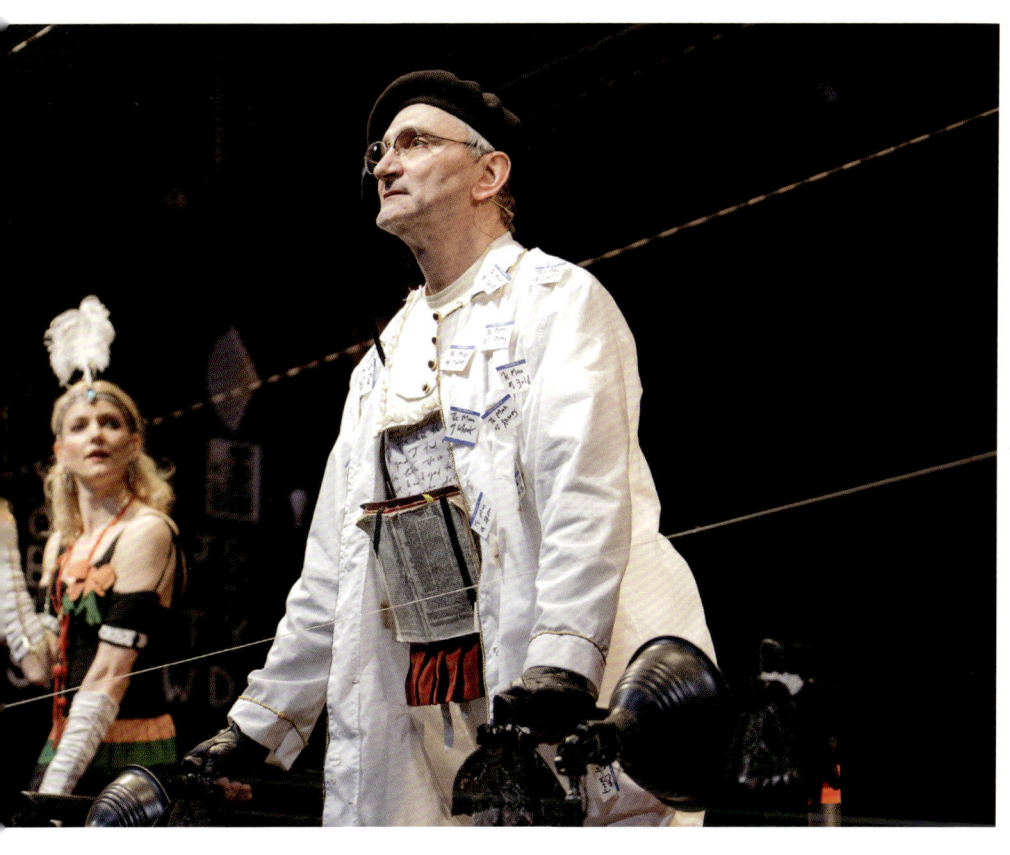

Richard Foreman's *Old-Fashioned Prostitutes (A True Romance)*,
© Karli Cadel for *The New York Times*.

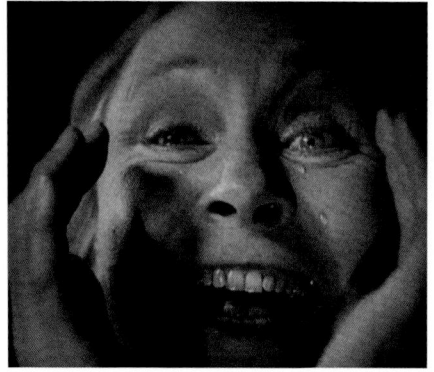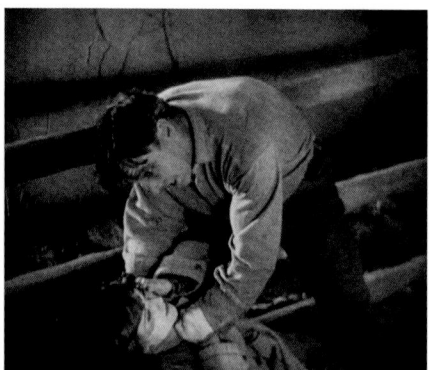

Stills from Murnau's *Sunrise*.

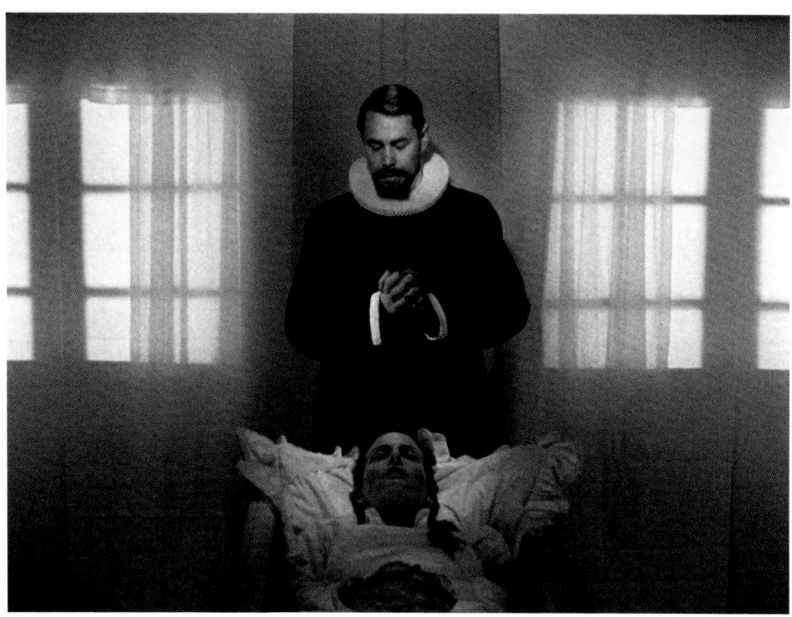

Still from Dreyer's *Ordet*.

Appendix to *(Vampires): An Uneasy Essay on the Undead in Film*: "I Am the Martyr Sana'a Youcef Mehaidli"

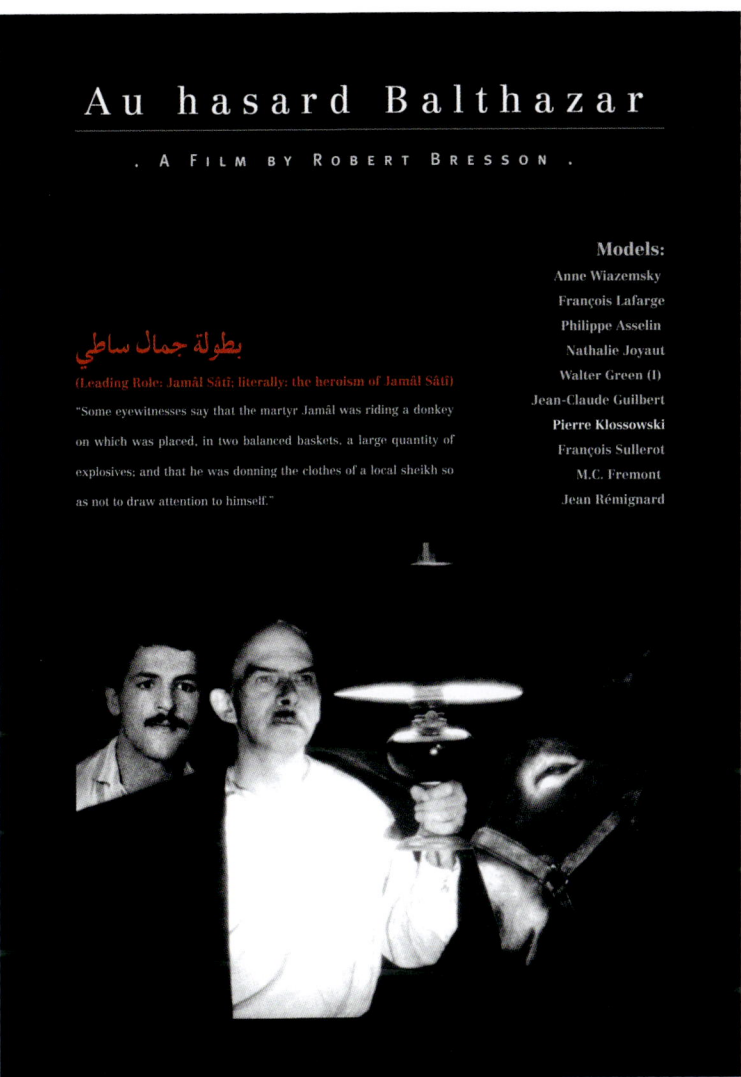

Jalal Toufic, *Au Hazard Balthazar*, 70 × 50 cm, 2000.
The Arabic بطولة جمال ساطي could be translated as "The Heroism of Jamal Sati" or "Jamal Sati in the Lead Role."

" أنا الرفيق الشهيد جمال ساطي"

ص.١٩١

الشهيد جمال ساطي

الاسم : جمال ساطي

مواليد : كامد اللوز البقاع الغربي عام ١٩٦٢ حائز على شهادة البكالوريا القسم الاول ، سبق وان نفذ ٩ عمليات ضد قوات الاحتلال وهي :

في ٢٩/٥/٨٣ ـ تفجير لغم بناقلة جند للعدو قرب كامد اللوز يدمرها .

في ٢٧/٨/٨٣ كمين لدورية قرب كامد اللوز .

في ١٨/٣/٨٤ كمين لدورية قرب جب جنين وكامد اللوز ادى الى مقتل ٤ جنود للعدو .

في ١٥/٤/٨٤ هجوم على موقع مشترك للعميل لحد وقوات الاحتلال الاسرائيلية في كامد اللوز .

في ٣/٦/٨٤ كمين لدورية لقوات الاحتلال بين كامد اللوز والبيرة ادى الى مقتل ٣ جنود للعدو .

في ٦/٦/٨٤ تفجير عبوة بناقلة جند قرب كامد اللوز ادى الى تدميرها .

في ٢١/٦/٨٤ كمين لدورية من المخابرات الاسرائيلية في شوارع كامد اللوز .

في ١٥/٨/٨٤ هجوم على موقع اسرائيلي في جوار كامد اللوز .

في ١٢/٢/٨٥ تفجير عبوة بشاحنة اسرائيلية .

ص.١٩٠

"In memory of the amnesiac Jalal Toufic
(not that he no longer exists, but that he was/is dead/undead then/now)"

The mortal Jalal Toufic

Name: Jalal Toufic

Born in Beirut in 1962. He received a BA in Philosophy from the American University of Beirut in 1984; an MA in Cinema Studies from New York University in 1987; and a Ph.D. in Radio/TV/Film from Northwestern University in 1992. Toufic has taught at the University of California at Berkeley, USC, and California Institute of the Arts.

2000 — *Forthcoming* (Berkeley, CA: Atelos).

1999 — Editor of *Middle Eastern Films Before Thy Gaze Returns to Thee*, *Discourse* 21.1.

1998 — Co-editor of *Gilles Deleuze: A Reason to Believe in this World*, *Discourse* 20.3.

1997 — *Radical Closure Artist with Bandaged Sense Organ*, installation, Artists Space, New York, June 7-July 19.

1996 — *Over-Sensitivity* (Los Angeles: Sun & Moon Press).

1996 — *'Āshūrā': This Blood Spilled in My Veins*, 17-minute two-channel video.

1995 — *Credits Included: A Video in Red and Green*, 46 minutes.

1993 — *(Vampires): An Uneasy Essay on the Undead in Film* (Barrytown, New York: Station Hill Press).

1991 — *Distracted* (Barrytown, NY: Station Hill Press; 2nd ed., Los Angeles: Green Integer, 2002).

Jalal Toufic, *Two Posthumous Resumes* (2000)

" أنا الرفيق الشهيد جمال ساطي"

ص.١٩١

الشهيد جمال ساطي

الاسم : جمال ساطي

مواليد : كامد اللوز البقاع الغربي عام ١٩٦٢ حائز على شهادة البكالوريا القسم الاول ، سبق وان نفذ ٩ عمليات ضد قوات الاحتلال وهي :

في ٢٩/٥/٨٣ ـ تفجير لغم بناقلة جند للعدو قرب كامد اللوز يدمرها .

في ٢٧/٨/٨٣ كمين لدورية قرب كامد اللوز .

في ١٨/٣/٨٤ كمين لدورية قرب جب جنين وكامد اللوز ادى الى مقتل ٤ جنود للعدو .

في ١٥/٤/٨٤ هجوم على موقع مشترك للعميل لحد وقوات الاحتلال الاسرائيلية في كامد اللوز .

في ٣/٦/٨٤ كمين لدورية لقوات الاحتلال بين كامد اللوز والبيرة ادى الى مقتل ٣ جنود للعدو .

في ٦/٦/٨٤ تفجير عبوة بناقلة جند قرب كامد اللوز ادى الى تدميرها .

في ٢١/٦/٨٤ كمين لدورية من المخابرات الاسرائيلية في شوارع كامد اللوز .

في ١٥/٨/٨٤ هجوم على موقع اسرائيلي في جوار كامد اللوز .

في ١٢/٢/٨٥ تفجير عبوة بشاحنة اسرائيلية .

ص. ١٩٠

"I am the martyr comrade Jamāl Sāṭī."

p. 191

The martyr Jamāl Sāṭī

Name: Jamāl Sāṭī

He was born in Kāmid al-Lawz, Western Biqāʿ, in 1962. He holds a Baccalaureate-I certificate (*shahāda*). He has already accomplished 9 operations against the occupation forces:

5/29/83 — The detonation of a mine under an enemy troop carrier near Kāmid al-Lawz, resulting in the carrier's destruction.

8/27/83 — Ambushing a patrol near Kāmid al-lawz.

3/18/84 — Ambushing a patrol near Jib Jinnīn and Kāmid al-Lawz, which led to the death of 4 enemy soldiers.

4/15/84 — Attacking a joint post of the agent Lahd and the Israeli forces in Kāmid al-Lawz.

6/3/84 — An ambush of a patrol of the occupation forces between Kāmid al-Lawz and al-Bīra resulting in the death of 3 enemy soldiers.

6/6/84 — Detonating a roadside bomb under a troop carrier near Kāmid al-Lawz, resulting in its destruction.

6/21/84 — Ambushing an Israeli intelligence patrol in the streets of Kāmid al-Lawz.

8/15/84 — attacking an Israeli post in the vicinity of Kāmid al-Lawz.

2/12/85 — detonating a bomb in an Israeli truck.

p. 190

English translation of the Arabic half of *Two Posthumous Resumes*

no place press catalogue

Jordan Kantor
Selected Exhibitions 2006–2016

Bill Berkson
A Frank O'Hara Notebook

Pamela M. Lee
The Glen Park Library: A Fairy Tale of Disruption

Anne Walsh
Hello Leonora, Soy Anne Walsh

Amy Franceschini and Michael Swaine, Futurefarmers
For Want of a Nail

Yvonne Rainer
Revisions: Essays by Apollo Musagète, Yvonne Rainer, and Others

Geoff Kaplan, ed.
After the Bauhaus, Before the Internet: A History of Graphic Design Pedagogy

Yve-Alain Bois
An Oblique Autobigraphy

Catherine Lord
The Effects of Tropical Light on White Men

Benjamin H. D. Buchloh and Hal Foster
Exit Interview

Rachel Churner, Rebecca Cleman, and Tyler Maxin, eds.
The New Television: Video After Television

Reba Maybury and Lucy McKenzie
Pervert or Detective?
CO-PUBLISHED WITH GTA EXHIBITIONS